Aging
IN THE
Right Place

by

Stephen M. Golant, Ph.D.

HPP
Health Professions Press

Baltimore • London • Sydney

Health Professions Press, Inc.
Post Office Box 10624
Baltimore, Maryland 21285-0624

www.healthpropress.com

Interior and cover designs by Mindy Dunn.
Typeset by Barton Matheson Willse & Worthington, Baltimore, Maryland.
Manufactured in the United States of America by Versa Press, East Peoria, Illinois.

Library of Congress Cataloging-in-Publication Data

Golant, Stephen M., author.
  Aging in the right place / by Stephen M. Golant.
      p. ; cm.
  Includes bibliographical references and index.
  ISBN 978-1-938870-33-0 (pbk.)
  I. Title.
  [DNLM: 1. Aged. 2. Homes for the Aged. 3. Housing for the Elderly.
4. Quality of Life. 5. Social Environment. WT 30]
  RA564.8
  362.16—dc23
                                                    2014045378

British Library Cataloguing in Publication data are available from the British Library.

E-book edition: ISBN 978-1-938870-36-1

I dedicate this book to my granddaughter, Ella

CONTENTS

About the Author

Stephen M. Golant, Ph.D., is professor at the University of Florida (Gainesville) and previously was associate professor at the University of Chicago. He has been conducting research on the housing, mobility, transportation, and long-term care needs of older adult populations for most of his academic career.

Dr. Golant is a Fellow of the Gerontological Society of America and a Fulbright Senior Scholar award recipient. In 2012, he received the Richard M. Kalish award from the Gerontological Society of America in recognition of his insightful and innovative publications on aging and life development in the behavioral and social sciences. Print and Web-based media have often featured his research and ideas and he has appeared on numerous television and radio programs, including ABC's national news program *20/20*.

Dr. Golant has written or edited more than 140 papers and books, including *Location and Environment of Elderly Populations* (Wiley, 1979); *A Place to Grow Old: The Meaning of Environment in Old Age* (Columbia University Press, 1984); *Housing America's Elderly: Many Possibilities, Few Choices* (Sage Publications, 1992); *The Columbia Retirement Handbook* (Columbia University Press, 1994); *Encyclopedia of Financial Gerontology* (Greenwood Press, 1996); the *CASERA Report* (Creating Affordable and Supportive Elder Renter Alternatives) (Margaret Lynn Duggar & Associates, Inc., 1999); and *The Assisted Living Residence: A Vision for the Future* (The Johns Hopkins University Press, 2008).

Dr. Golant serves on the editorial boards of *The Gerontologist*, *Journal of Aging Studies*, *CSA Journal* (Society of Certified Senior Advisors), *Journal of Housing for the Elderly*, *Research on Aging*, and *Seniors Housing & Care Journal*.

Dr. Golant is frequently called on by corporations, universities, state government agencies, and national organizations as a lecturer or an adviser. He also served as a consultant to the Congressionally appointed Commission on Affordable Housing and Health Facility Needs for Seniors in the 21st Century (Seniors Commission), a bipartisan 14-member panel created by an act of Congress to study the housing and healthcare needs for the next generation of elderly Americans and to offer specific policy and legislative recommendations to the U.S. House of Representatives and the U.S. Senate.

ACKNOWLEDGMENTS

It took me longer to write this book than I had originally planned, undoubtedly because it incorporated many years of material from my research and writing on the housing and care arrangements of older Americans—especially as seen through their idiosyncratic eyes. I was also slowed by my quest to convince readers that there is no one prescription for aging successfully—despite what the experts claim—and that whatever the life course pathways of aging adults, the places they occupy during their old age do matter.

I am grateful to the many individuals who helped make this effort possible. Most importantly, my wife, Dora, steadfastly supported me as I labored over the manuscript. My daughter, Alexandra, reminded me that the meaning of life rested on far more than just another published book. My sister, Annette, continually cheered me on through my writing efforts. My good friend and colleague, Jay Gubrium, has been an invaluable academic sounding board throughout my career and has always offered good counsel with humor and honesty over many a glass of wine.

This book would not have reached fruition, however, if not for the persistence and support of Mary Magnus, Director of Publications for Health Professions Press, and her confidence in this effort. I also benefitted greatly from working with her highly professional staff, who helped move this book from an overly long manuscript to a succinctly written book. Special thanks to Teresa Ingraham Iafolla, who contributed mightily to the effort of shortening my original manuscript. Kudos to Cecilia González, who skillfully and cheerfully managed the copyediting, typesetting, proofreading, and indexing of my manuscript and tolerated my countless queries. Only authors will appreciate how important a publisher's production manager is to the final book product. I am also much appreciative of the marketing and promotional efforts of Kaitlin Konecke.

It is unquestionably a humbling exercise to conduct one's own life review and remember the mentors and colleagues who played critical roles in your own intellectual growth. The most important of these valued individuals to whom I owe a debt of gratitude, and the universities where our lives originally crossed, include Larry Bourne, Jim Simmons, Alan Baker, and Ian Burton at the University of Toronto; Dick Morrill and Arthur Farber at the University of Washington; and Brian Berry, Bernice Neugarten, Morton Lieberman, Bert Cohler, Mike Czikszentmihalyi, and Sheldon Tobin at the University of Chicago.

PREFACE

What makes us happy in old age? Throughout my academic career, I believed that studying the personalities or demographics of older people (e.g., their financial means, race, ethnicity, marital status, gender) offered only an incomplete explanation. It was also insufficient just to focus on the declines in their physical and mental prowess. Although important factors, there was another body of knowledge to tap. I had to know how the residential and care settings occupied and used by older people impacted their physical and mental well-being. Did their homes, neighborhoods, and communities or their tailor-made senior housing alternatives and long-term care services and supports offer them opportunities to more fully enjoy their lives, feel better about themselves, and enable them to access quality assistance to cope with their aging bodies? What were the upsides and downsides of these options? How did where they live matter for their happiness?

I also recognized that although academics and professionals must assess the quality of older people's residential and care environments, their detached and scientific judgments were not enough. We had to get into the heads of older people to fully appreciate whether their places of residence influenced their well-being. This was the impetus for my theoretical model showing that when older people find their right places to live, they have achieved *residential normalcy*. This happens in,

> *Places where they experience overall pleasurable, hassle-free, and memorable feelings that have relevance to them; and where they feel both competent and in control—that is, they do not have to behave in personally objectionable ways or to unduly surrender mastery of their lives or environments to others.*

However, arguing that aging successfully depends on where older people live is not an easy sell. Older Americans devote an incredible amount of time and money to become prettier, stronger, and healthier. They spend far less energy adjusting their housing and care arrangements, actions that would often make for a happier old age.

In earlier stages in life, it is different. In response to changes in their circumstances, younger Americans usually move to other places. Not so for older people, who despite some potentially tumultuous events, such as retirement, widowhood, poor health, mobility declines, and changes in their financial status, usually stay put or age in place in their currently occupied residences. Even significant changes in the social and physical fabric of their dwellings, neighborhoods, and communities do not necessarily prompt them to change addresses. Rather, strong magnetic forces keep them in their familiar environs, even as a paucity of destination alternatives offers them few moving incentives.

An unfortunate consequence is that older people often occupy incongruous living situations. Dwellings seem frustratingly and even dangerously too large, poorly designed, difficult to maintain, out of date, or too expensive to occupy; once attractive neighborhoods change for the worse as valued friends move away or, sadly, die; familiar stores and restaurants close; leisure opportunities seem to target the young; grocery stores and doctors' offices become difficult to reach; and help is not available to perform once taken-for-granted self-care tasks, such as bathing, dressing, or just getting around.

Residential normalcy is again possible, however. When older people experience discord in their lives, they do not have to fold their cards. Rather, they can take proactive steps to alleviate or eliminate the unpleasant or offensive aspects of their residential or care arrangements—they become agents of change. The human development literature repeatedly tells us that constructive responses to adversity are the hallmark of aging successfully.

Much of this book focuses on how stakeholders from all sectors of American society influence whether older people successfully cope with their housing and care deficiencies. Indeed, they stand to benefit the most from reading this book, because their fortunes depend on knowing their consumers. These stakeholders include a diverse array of healthcare and long-term care providers—professionals such as case managers, nurses, and occupational therapists, but also in-the-trenches home care workers. They also encompass a fast-growing group of vendors who are responsible for the home modifications, repairs, assistive devices, and smart home technologies that older people introduce into their dwellings to make them safer, more accessible, and easier to monitor. On this list are also for-profit and nonprofit groups responsible for funding, creating, marketing, and managing an increasingly diverse array of senior housing options and age-friendly community initiatives. And it includes administrators in the public sector charged with the critical role of providing these housing and service solutions to those elders who cannot afford the private sector options. Most importantly, this book will be appreciated by the pre-eminent caregivers of our older population, namely the families responsible for enabling their loved ones to stay in their homes and who advocate for their well-being when they occupy other residence options, such as assisted living developments.

Benefiting from this book will also be senior undergraduate and graduate students who seek a comprehensive overview of the residential and long-term care challenges faced by older adults and why they seek out some solutions over others. If we can put this topic on our university and professional school curriculums, perhaps our future generation of stakeholders will be better prepared to offer older Americans a selection of options that they find more appealing and effective.

For in the end, it is older people who must take charge of their lives to maximize their happiness, and the places they live and receive care can make their quest easier.

Part I

GROWING OLD

Place Matters

1

GROWING OLD SUCCESSFULLY

Place, the Missing Ingredient

AGING BECOMES REAL

American society offers older adults and aging baby boomers a comforting message to assuage their fears about their golden years: Avoid aging altogether. It is a strong and persistent message that seems to come from everywhere: celebrities, academics, government, business, and medical professionals. It is hard to ignore and has become the basis by which most Americans judge whether they are aging successfully.

There is no need to get old and become sick and disabled, the message tells us. If you do the right things and take personal responsibility for your well-being, you can fend off forever the assaults of old age. Not aging well is your fault. So eat right, get exercise, avoid stress, get regular checkups, keep your brain active, and you will be fine. And to keep up your appearance, go ahead and get a facelift, use Botox, dye your hair, and take the newest youth-enhancing vitamins and hormones.

This message did not happen by chance. In 1987, the John D. and Catherine T. MacArthur Foundation initiated funding of a large multidisciplinary research effort designed to gather knowledge that would shed light on *"what determines how well we age."* Hundreds of scientific studies were reviewed to understand *"the genetic, biomedical, behavioral, and social factors"*[1] influencing the effective physical and mental functioning of older adults. The findings were widely disseminated, both nationally and internationally, and were popularly assembled in a 1998 book titled *Successful Aging* by its two prominent researchers, John W. Rowe and Robert L. Kahn.[2]

This ambitious effort claimed to show the American public that they could control the quality of their lives in old age and had real choices. The most widely used definition of successful aging is now based on its conclusions.[3] It required older adults to follow three principles:

- Avoid disease and disability.
- Maintain high mental and physical functioning.
- Keep actively engaged in life.

Furthermore, the authors emphasized that it is never too late to embrace their brand of successful aging:

> The frailty of old age is largely reversible. Most older people, even the very old and weak, have the capacity to remarkably increase their muscle strength, balance, walking ability, and overall aerobic power.[4]

Moreover,

> Older people can significantly improve their short-term memory by making lists and training their memory with practice games.

These pronouncements communicated a powerful message that questioned what was "usual" or "normal" aging. Americans were told that they were in charge of how well they aged. They could mitigate or even prevent chronic health problems and disabilities if they changed their lifestyles and practiced good dietary, exercise, mental, and personal habits. And to be sure, Americans liked this "healthy aging" message. Why wouldn't they want to bathe forever in the fountain of youth? It was an especially hopeful message to those who had not exercised, ate badly, or had abused their bodies during their younger years, for they were given a way to thrive in their old age, if only they corrected their former bad behaviors.

NOT JUST HEALTHY AGING BUT ACTIVE AGING

The scientists could have limited their focus to the physical and cognitive functioning of older people, but they did not. Rather, aging successfully meant taking proactive steps not only to keep healthy, but also to keep active; they equated successful aging with being *"actively engaged with life."*

The authors of what is now known as the New Gerontology[5] paradigm were critical of a conception of old age that presumes people slow down and, even worse, avoid any deviation from earlier practiced ways of living. On the contrary, New Gerontology advocates believed,

> Older people, after retiring from employment, must find appropriate substitute activities and must either find ways to maintain friendships that grew out of work, or replace them. . . . After child-rearing and employment . . . almost nothing is expected of the elderly. The spoken advice from youth to age is "take it easy," which means do nothing, or amuse yourself. The unspoken message is "find your own way and keep out of theirs." Many older men and women do

better than that . . . they find new friends, partially replace paid employment with useful voluntary activity, maintain some form of regular exercise, and enjoy a measure of increased leisure. Our purpose [is to] increase the numbers of those who age successfully.[6]

Moreover, their research showed that there is

a strong link between physical activity and physical and mental illness, disability, and survival . . . [and] a positive relationship between certain activities and cognitive status among older people; [and that] older people who are more engaged in a variety of leisure, cognitive, and physical activities have been found to score higher on cognitive batteries compared to individuals who reported to be less engaged; [and that] the total number of productive activities (employment, formal and informal volunteering, and caregiving) has been found to be associated with both self-reported health and functional status.[7]

In fact, these arguments were not new. In the first half of the 1960s, three prominent professors from the University of Chicago presented what they called the activity theory of aging, which offered remarkably similar arguments.[8] At the time, however, their interpretation radically departed from the prevailing wisdom of what it meant to age successfully, a position known as disengagement theory. Researchers at the University of Chicago in the 1950s had consistently documented that older people were different from middle-aged people. That is, they were less physically rigorous or active, experienced decrements in their mental abilities, and had reduced the breadth of their social relationships, implying smaller social circles, contacts with only the closest family members or friends, less frequent social gatherings, and fewer social responsibilities (e.g., retiring from work).

These disengagement theorists further argued that as aging people reduced their roles in society, engaged in fewer activities, did not keep up with new knowledge and skills, and became less interested in the world around them, they became more introspective, withdrawn, and introverted (i.e., preoccupied with their inner lives).[9]

The most controversial part of their theory, however, was their explanation for why this disengagement occurred. The theorists argued that this social withdrawal was a voluntary response by older people who were preparing for their own impending death and recognized their declining usefulness and participation in a rapidly changing and modernizing society. Most significantly, they argued that this pattern of aging was biologically natural and inevitable, a normal and healthy response to growing old rather than an imposed process that was pathological or deviant. This was both a statement as to what constituted normal aging and an argument that the most successfully aging older adults were those who psychologically disengaged from society.[10]

Today, it is hard to believe that we once endorsed the ideas of the disengagement theorists, given the strong empirical evidence for the New Gerontology paradigm. The new message was clear: There are no predetermined biological or prewired human developmental influences that determine how you age. Aging people can be fully engaged throughout their later lives and control their own destinies.

NOT ON THE SAME PAGE

Given its upbeat message, one might have expected unanimous support for the New Gerontology paradigm. Not so—there were many critics. They viewed the pronouncements of the New Gerontology paradigm as a 21st-century brand of American ageism that was no less deplorable than racism and sexism. From their perspective, the anti-aging message of the New Gerontology paradigm introduced gross and unrealistically positive stereotypes about how we should expect older people to look and behave. These critics rejected the proposition that *"whole social groups and areas of life should become marginalized"*[11] and discriminated against, if only because they had arthritic knees, diabetes, memory lapses, wrinkles, or congestive heart failure; used hearing aids; or practiced different—often less active—lifestyles than in their middle years.[12]

They pointed to a frequently cited statistic that after people reach age 65, about 70% eventually need long-term care later in their lives.[13] For some adults, aging becomes a burden. Even the most proactive older adults experience declines and losses that assault their physical and mental health, mobility, and cognitive functioning. They wrestle with complicated health problems and cannot take care of themselves without help. They deplete their retirement savings and do not achieve long-sought goals. They lose people who were important to them and become depressed. Often, the bad things that happen in life are outside the control of aging people and are simply the price they pay for living longer. It was irresponsible to view these older adults as losers who were not aging successfully.

Critics of the New Gerontology paradigm also argued that its formulation discriminated against less fortunate people who, when they were young, had fewer opportunities and resources to practice so-called healthy habits: the poor, the working class, the developmentally disabled, ethnic and racial minorities, and so on. It also failed to acknowledge those who had fallen on hard financial times in their old age and did not have the same access to high-quality medical or long-term care as their more prosperous peers. The views of the New Gerontology paradigm were also considered sexist because women, who usually live longer than men, are disproportionately and irreversibly afflicted by the vagaries of old age.[14]

It is because of these declines and losses that gerontologists have long recognized that older people often do not experience an active and healthy quality of life right up to the time of death. This observation led them to partition old age into two broad segments: the number of years older people can expect to behave competently (i.e., able to perform most of their everyday activities, disability free) and the number of years during which they are seriously limited, physically or cognitively, by their declines and losses.[15] Scholars have assigned different labels to these two stages in older people's lives: the young-old versus the old-old, active versus dependent life expectancy, and Third Age versus Fourth Age seniors. As of 2006, people turning age 65 were on average expected to have another 12.2 years of active life and 6.3 years of dependent life.[16]

Some experts had especially strident reactions. William Thomas, internationally renowned innovator of nursing homes, argued that equating healthy and successful aging was "pathetic."[17] He argued that the term *anti-aging* is nothing less than a *"euphemism for youth perpetuation"* and that the proponents of this position do not simply want to avoid the *"ravages of aging,"* but rather *"seek the divine gifts of perpetual strength, energy, and health so that they may remain in full possession of the pleasures and prerogatives of adulthood."*[18] Because they do not view old age as a distinctive period in life that is qualitatively different from youth, they devalue old age.[19] Erlene Rosowsky, a Harvard psychotherapist, similarly argued,

> Antiaging is less about achieving the best possible old age than about extend-
> ing youth until it meets death, thereby avoiding old age all together.[20]

The depiction of successful aging as the maintenance of activity at all costs was a major concern to another group of vocal critics. They took issue with the message that con-tinually being active and busy—actively engaged in life, as in middle age—is neces-sarily an appropriate model for all aging adults.[21] They attacked the assumption that physically healthy and active older people were all necessarily satisfied with their lives and pointed to the many examples of "youthful" seniors leading unhappy and unful-filled lives.[22] They argued that there are alternative ways to age successfully and that there is nothing abnormal or deviant about older people wanting to be less active and spend their time differently than in their middle years. Older people can enjoy their lives without being out-and-about, attending parties, or volunteering in their commu-nity. They can practice sedentary lifestyles, spend their time with just their spouses, pass their days reading, hang around the house, dabble in their gardens or workshops, and surf the Internet. This view was consistent with that of psychoanalytical theorist Carl Jung, the father of the modern study of adult development. He also saw old age as a period that was very distinctive from midlife, a time for greater contemplation, self-reflection, and introspection—what is often wrapped together as reminiscing or life review—as a way the person prepares for dying.[23]

THE NEW GERONTOLOGY PARADIGM:
ONLY THE INDIVIDUAL MATTERS

The New Gerontology paradigm and comparable successful aging formulations were open to another source of criticism because they focused predominantly on individual indicators or variables as antecedents of physical and mental well-being. Their toolbox of predictive indicators included the demographics (e.g., income, race, ethnicity, and age), physical health, functional abilities, cognitive functioning, and sensory skills of older adults. They focused on studies that attributed the successful aging of older Americans to their good health, being married, working for pay, higher levels of edu-cation, and the consumption of moderate amounts of alcohol.[24] This individual bias had important applied or practical implications. When older people received advice on how they could age successfully, they were counseled on getting the appropriate drugs for their ailments, taking vitamin supplements, eating right, exercising regu-larly, keeping their brain healthy, protecting their skin, strengthening their immune system, checking their colon, and improving their digestion.

THE MISSING PART OF THE PUZZLE: WHERE OLDER PEOPLE LIVE

The premise of this book is not that these messages are wrong, but that focusing predominantly on individual-based remedies is an incomplete recipe for aging successfully. It is necessary to incorporate the ideas of a branch of gerontology known as environmental gerontology and its multidisciplinary cadre of academics, professionals, and practitioners.[25] Their theoretical focus is to understand and predict how the residential and care environments occupied and used by older adults influence their physical and psychological well-being, and their mission is to find solutions that will optimize the fit or congruence between aging people and the places they live.[26]

Environmental gerontologists argue that the prescription for successful aging offered by the New Gerontology paradigm erroneously assumes that older people grow old in some situational, contextual, or environmental vacuum. It is as if the dwellings, buildings, neighborhoods, communities, and regions in which they live and their built, natural, social, organizational, and political environments make little difference in whether they enjoy their lives, feel good about themselves, live independently, and achieve healthy lifestyles. Absent from its discourse is the recognition that in some places more than others, older people will be better able to fend off disease and disability, remain independent despite their physical and mental declines or chronic health problems, and keep actively engaged in life—whether this means keeping forever busy or merely feeling emotionally fulfilled and intellectually stimulated.

Many other academic and professional specialties besides environmental gerontology have these concerns. For example, healthcare providers emphasize how older people's residential arrangements crucially influence their lives.[27] A Robert Wood Johnson Foundation 2011 national survey of primary care providers reported that *"85 percent believe that unmet social needs—things like access to nutritious food, reliable transportation and adequate housing—are leading directly to worse health for all Americans."* Their solution: *"If they had the power to write prescriptions to address social needs, such prescriptions would represent approximately 1 out of every 7 prescriptions they write."*[28]

The views of environmental gerontologists and the authors of the New Gerontology paradigm differ in another important way. Unlike the latter's single prescription for successful aging, the scientific and case studies of environmental gerontologists emphasize that there are many environmental pathways for older people to achieve the good life and to receive competent and compassionate care. If we put older people, academics, professionals, and practitioners in the same room, we find that they do not agree on what constitutes the right place to live and age successfully. Above all, it quickly becomes clear that there is no one-size-fits-all utopian residential or care setting.

WHY ENVIRONMENT MATTERS

This book offers a more complex formula for aging successfully that emphasizes the key roles played by the residential and care environments of older adults. Its conclusions are also based on a wealth of evidence produced by academics and professionals.[29] Consider that by the time they have reached their mid-60s and certainly their 70s, most older Americans have retired, stopped looking for work, or have switched to part-time work. Consequently, they spend a disproportionate share of their time and activities in and around their dwellings, neighborhoods, and circumscribed areas of their community. The totality of their ways of living—how and where they have fun, enjoy their friendships, keep stimulated, feel wanted and supported, attend religious services, shop, bank, obtain medical care, volunteer, and pursue new encore careers—becomes far more tightly synchronized with their physical addresses. Their immediate environment becomes a prominent space around which they organize and perform their everyday activities.[30]

With their propensity to age in place or stay in their current abodes, their environs take on special significance if they have chronic health problems or physical limitations. Their homes or apartments become important not just as places to enjoy a comfortable lifestyle, but as settings that can compensate for their declines and losses. Once-sacred boundaries between residential and care environments become blurred. Now their ability to enjoy an independent lifestyle depends on their ability to find in-home care and whether they easily and safely use and access their dwelling and all its contents—even though they were not designed with older people in mind. Confronted with their age-related limitations, older people view their residential environs as something to get around or overcome—as an external constraint on their actions rather than as a source of incentives, opportunities, or resources.[31] Reaching what were once accessible destinations becomes a crucial concern. Older people cannot assume that they can easily accomplish their most essential activities, such as getting to a grocery store or doctor or attending their religious services.[32]

Because older Americans tend to remain in their residences a long time, they are particularly susceptible to any changes that occur in their surroundings. Sometimes the changes are favorable: A family member may move closer, or a new retail strip mall and health clinic may open up just minutes away. More often, however, their neighborhoods or communities change for the worse. Compatible neighbors leave, friends move elsewhere, favorite doctors retire, the house across the street remains vacant and poorly maintained, and the nearby convenience store goes out of business. Along with the obvious negatives produced by these events, older people often feel more anxious or fearful because these changes assault the status quo, a highly valued aspect of where they live.[33] The absence of environmental change may be just as significant. A community's once favorable leisure opportunities become inconsistent with a newly chosen lifestyle or avocation, once highly rated medical facilities turn out to be inadequate to treat a new chronic health problem, once attractive suburbs become isolated islands for older people who lose their driver's licenses, and the stairs to a third-floor apartment become a major hindrance for the older widow with arthritic knees.

When older people do decide to move, the new environment often constitutes a major part of the solution to their individual problems. By vacating their current places of residence, they hope to introduce new surroundings, activities, and people into their lives; eliminate their currently unpleasant and stressful housing situations; or find dwellings, neighborhoods, and communities that allow them to embark on new ways of living and to cope with their declines and losses.

However, proposing that the residential and care environments of older people influence their ability to age successfully is not an easy sell. Few studies have established unequivocal causal linkages, and many methodological pitfalls await the researcher daring to conclude that where older people live matters.[34] Moreover, the analysts who recognize the significance of place cannot agree on how we should portray and measure the residential and care contexts occupied and used by older people. Their multiple analytical perspectives can be broken down into two broad worldviews. The first encompasses the objectively defined perspectives of a diverse cadre of experts, and the second encompasses the voices of older people and their idiosyncratic, subjective experiences.

AN OBJECTIVE ANATOMY OF PLACES

> AVAILABLE NOW—Very affordable dream house to enjoy in your old age. Accommodates unmarried and even grossly mismatched husband–wife households. Neighborhood and community have every imaginable amenity and convenience. Social networks are unsurpassed. No need to move again, ever—your new abode will automatically adapt to all changes in your life. CEMETERY PLOTS AND CREMATORIUMS LOCATED NEARBY. CRYOGENIC SITES WITHIN DRIVING DISTANCE.

The first worldview focuses on the *objective anatomy* of places. Experts rely on a plethora of objective indicators to conceptualize and measure the quality of the residential environments of older people. They derive their measures using scientific and emotion-free methods, but as the above advertisement emphasizes, this does not prevent them from imposing their own value judgments and priorities when they assess the best and worst places for older people to live.

Family members often rely on such indicators to judge the appropriateness of their loved ones' housing arrangements. Long-term care professionals join them: geriatric physicians, case managers, care coordinators, nurses, occupational and physical therapists, and social workers who claim to know what residential and care qualities best serve their aging clientele. Other self-appointed experts include university-based academics, senior housing and residential care developers, federal agency professionals responsible for funding healthcare and long-term care, state social service and healthcare funding agencies, marketing firms, financial institutions, and consumer-based nonprofit organizations, such as the American Association for Retired Persons (AARP).

Then there are magazines, popular books, and Internet sites churning out their collective wisdom on the best places for older people to live and receive care. They continually offer quality-of-life rankings of states and communities distinguished by their size; population density; remoteness; economic health (e.g., unemployment rate, foreclosure rates, level of poverty); tax rates (e.g., state income and property tax burdens, inheritance and estate taxes); cost of living; housing and social opportunities; climate, cultural, and recreational resources; natural amenities; spiritual life; healthcare and long-term care resources; crime rates; and prevalence of natural disasters.[35] For example, one magazine reported on the most affordable communities for aging adults that had the best year-round weather, water views, recreation pursuits, college-related activities, and second-career opportunities.[36] What is particularly notable about all of these rating exercises is their lack of consensus. Even more troubling for older people seeking to plan their retirement futures, the place rankings continually change from one year to the next.

Given all of this expertise in the air, it is not surprising that there is no shortage of self-help and how-to guides. Older adults can choose from a large cache of information sources that offer them encyclopedic descriptions and assessments of the "right place to live." These so-called objective assessments allow older people to become instant experts on the pros and cons of living in any type of housing or care arrangement in the United States and even in places as diverse as Italy, Mexico, Israel, South America, Spain, Ecuador, and India.[37]

We will probably never agree on how we should describe or depict the residential environments occupied by older Americans. Consider the very different environmental portrayals by academics and professionals. The economist focuses on financial and fiscal indicators when judging older people's housing or communities, the sociologist is interested in the status of family or social networks, the focus of the political scientist is on changes in a state's regulatory environment and subsidized government programs, the architect and occupational therapist are preoccupied with the interior design of the dwellings, the planner emphasizes the role played by zoning and land use regulations and alternative transportation modes, and the environmental engineers emphasize the technological capacities of older people's dwellings.

Any catalog of the hundreds of possible objective indicators portraying the quality of older people's residential environments is likely to be incomplete. However, Figures 1.1 and 1.2 offer a framework that incorporates the most frequently identified environmental components and attributes. This typology distinguishes a hierarchically arranged set of settlement contexts (from nations to rooms) occupied by older

Figure 1.1. Objective anatomy of residential and care environments

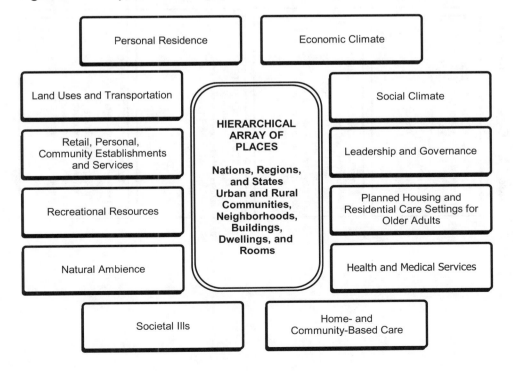

Figure 1.2. Objective quality-of-life indicators of residential settlements

PERSONAL RESIDENCE
Tenure (owner, renter, coop, condo)
Emergency shelter
Size, physical design, and condition
Equity, affordability
Possessions (e.g., photos, books, antiques)

LAND USES AND TRANSPORTATION
Land use patterns, density, sprawl
Compactness, walkability
Building and street design features
Zoning regulations
Driver education and licensing rules
Auto, public transit accessibility
Paratransit availability

RETAIL, PERSONAL, COMMUNITY ESTABLISHMENTS AND SERVICES
Shopping, restaurants, beauty shops
Religious clubs, places of worship
Banks, accountants, brokers
Police and fire protection

RECREATIONAL RESOURCES
Spas, exercise, and fitness
Hiking, bicycle trails, camping
Parks, nature preserves
Libraries, museums, dancing
Movies, plays, cultural activities
Computer, card clubs
Arts and crafts, gardening

NATURAL AMBIENCE
Climate, weather
Open space
Topography
Scenic features (e.g., lakes, rivers)

SOCIETAL ILLS
Crime
Traffic congestion
Natural disasters
Pollutants
Environmental toxins

ECONOMIC CLIMATE
Cost of living, housing affordability
Economic vitality, unemployment rate
State and local property taxes
Property tax relief
Estate taxes

SOCIAL CLIMATE
Socioeconomic, ethnic status, and gender orientation of population
Family, friend, neighbor availability
Staff and employee behaviors
Civic engagement (volunteerism) opportunities
Resiliency of older population

LEADERSHIP AND GOVERNANCE
Public sector affordable housing and long-term care programs
Age-friendly community programs
Regulatory environments
Motivated, innovative, and capable private and public leaders

PLANNED SENIOR HOUSING
Active adult and cohousing communities
Elder villages
NORC-supportive service programs (SSPs)
Independent living properties
Assisted living properties, board and care
Continuing care retirement communities

HEALTH AND MEDICAL SERVICES
Hospitals, subacute care, clinics
Nursing homes, rehabilitative care
Primary care, specialist doctors
Emergency room services
Wellness centers
Pharmacies

HOME- AND COMMUNITY-BASED CARE
Assistive devices
Home repair and modification services
Smart Home technologies, security
Geriatric care managers
Licensed or certified professionals
Direct care workers
Senior centers
Adult day care

12

adults in the United States[38] and outlines 12 broad categories of features and qualities by which we typically distinguish these places.

Notable about this *residential* typology is the inclusion of indicators that depict the availability of supportive services in healthcare and long-term care. As they chronologically age, older people often have to cope with a variety of chronic health ailments and physical and cognitive limitations. Most are living in conventional apartments and homes, and their dwellings, neighborhoods, and communities become focal points for the delivery of all forms of healthcare and long-term care. Consequently, objective conceptualizations of where older people live must also include indicators describing their personal assistance and healthcare arrangements.

But even the detailed classifications offered in Figures 1.1 and 1.2 fall short. We often need a distinctive set of objective quality-of-life indicators to assess the desirability of planned housing and care alternatives for older consumers. These include active adult communities for younger and more active seniors (see Chapter 10) and housing care settings, such as independent living communities, assisted living residences, board and care settings, and continuing care retirement communities for older people who have difficulty maintaining their independent households and who seek a protective and supportive environment to accommodate their chronic health problems and physical or cognitive limitations (Chapters 11 and 12). Figure 1.3 presents a typology of the planned senior housing options constructed by the major housing-focused professional organizations in the United States.

To describe the environmental qualities of these planned housing and care options, we also need more specialized indicators than are outlined in Figure 1.3. Useful in this regard are the detailed typologies of Rudolf Moos and Sonne Lemke. Figures 1.4a and 1.4b offer two of their five residential (sheltered) care classifications.[39] Experts can rate these specialized settings by their physical attractiveness, their barrier-free and safety designs, their leisure and recreational resources, the availability and skills of their staff, the availability of their services, the clarity and fairness of their rules and regulations, and the degree of privacy and autonomy they offer residents.

AN EMOTIONAL ANATOMY OF PLACES: THE VIEWS OF OLDER PEOPLE

The second worldview focuses on the *emotional anatomy of places.* It requires that we listen to the voices of older people, communicating both their favorable and unfavorable thoughts and feelings about what matters most in their residential and care arrangements.

Importantly, the recognition of older people's subjective worlds does not imply that we ignore or deny the objective judgments of the experts. We acknowledge that older people live in *"an empirical reality, independent of thinking and perceiving human beings, that is capable of being described in rational and detached terms."*[40] However, we also recognize that older people do not similarly attend, perceive, interpret, and respond to this empirical reality.[41] Consequently, the objectively defined environments portrayed by the experts do not necessarily have the same functional relevance for older people. That is, they will not evoke, reinforce, or modify the same feelings, experiences, and

Figure 1.3. Planned housing and residential care settings for older people in the United States (National Investment Center for the Seniors Housing & Care Industry and American Seniors Housing Association, 2014)

Active Adult Communities: For sale single-family homes, townhomes, cluster homes, mobile homes, and condominiums with no specialized services, restricted to adults 55 years of age or older. Rental housing is not included in this category. Residents generally lead an independent lifestyle. Projects are not equipped to provide increased care as the person ages. May include amenities such as clubhouses, golf courses, and recreational spaces. Outdoor maintenance is normally included in the monthly homeowner's association or condominium fee.

Senior Apartments: Multifamily residential rental properties restricted to adults 55 years of age or older. These properties do not have central kitchen facilities and generally do not provide meals to residents, but may offer community rooms, social activities, and other amenities.

Independent Living Communities: Age-restricted multifamily rental properties with central dining facilities that provide residents as part of their monthly fee access to meals and other services, such as housekeeping, linen service, transportation, and social and recreational activities. In a majority of the units, such properties do not provide assistance with activities of daily living (ADLs), such as supervision of medication, bathing, dressing, and toileting. There are no licensed skilled nursing beds in such properties.

Assisted Living Residences: State-regulated rental properties that provide the same services as independent living communities as well as, in a majority of the units, supportive care from trained employees to residents who are unable to live independently and need assistance with ADLs, including management of medications, bathing, dressing, toileting, ambulating, and eating. These properties may have some nursing beds, but the majority of units are licensed for assisted living. Many of these properties include wings or floors dedicated to residents with Alzheimer's or other forms of dementia. A property that specializes in the care of residents with Alzheimer's or other forms of dementia that is not a licensed nursing facility should be considered an assisted living property.

Nursing Homes: Licensed daily rate or rental properties that are technically called skilled nursing facilities (SNFs) or nursing facilities (NFs), where the majority of residents need 24-hour nursing or medical care. In most cases, these properties are licensed for Medicaid or Medicare reimbursement. These properties may include a minority of assisted living or Alzheimer's and dementia units.

Continuing Care Retirement Communities (CCRCs): Age-restricted properties that include a combination of independent living, assisted living, and skilled nursing services (or independent living and skilled nursing) all on one campus. Resident payment plans vary and include entrance fee, condo or coop, and rental programs. The majority of the units are not licensed skilled nursing beds.

Figure 1.4a. Physical and architectural features checklist (PAF) (Moos & Lemke, 1980)

Physical amenities	Measures the presence of physical features that add convenience, attractiveness, and special comfort.	Is the main entrance sheltered from sun or rain? Are the halls decorated?
Social recreational aids	Assesses the presence of features that foster social behavior and recreational activities.	Is the lounge by the entry furnished for resting and casual conversation? Is there a pool or billiard table?
Prosthetic aids	Assesses the extent to which the facility provides a barrier-free environment as well as aids to physical independence and mobility.	Can one enter the building without having to use stairs? Are there handrails in the halls?
Orientational aids	Measures the extent to which the setting provides visual cues to orient the resident.	Is each floor color-coded or numbered? Is a map with local resources marked on it available in a convenient public location?
Safety features	Assesses the extent to which the facility provides features for monitoring communal areas and for preventing accidents.	Is the outside walk and entrance visible from the office or station of an employee? Are there call buttons in the bathrooms?
Architectural choice	Reflects the flexibility of the physical environment and the extent to which it allows residents options in performing necessary functions.	Does each resident have access to both a bathtub and a shower? Are there individual heating controls?
Space availability	Measures the number and size of communal areas in relation to the number of residents, as well as size allowances for personal space.	How many special activity areas are there? How large are these areas altogether? What size is the smallest per person closet area?
Staff facilities	Assesses the presence of facilities that aid the staff and make it pleasant to maintain and manage the setting.	Are the offices free of distractions from adjacent activities? Is there a staff lounge?
Community accessibility	Measures the extent to which the community and its services are convenient and accessible to the facility.	Is there a grocery store within easy walking distance? Is there a public transportation stop within walking distance?

Figure 1.4b. Policy and program information form (POLIF) (Lemke & Moos, 1980)

Selectivity	Reflects the extent to which there are financial and entrance requirements for prospective residents.	Is there an initial entrance fee? Must a prospective resident be ambulatory?
Expectations for functioning	Measures the minimum capacity to perform daily living functions that is acceptable in the facility.	Is the inability to clean one's own room tolerated? Is incontinence tolerated?
Tolerance for deviance	Measures the extent to which aggressive, defiant, destructive, or eccentric behavior is tolerated.	Is refusing to bathe tolerated? Is pilfering or stealing tolerated?
Policy clarity	Measures the extent of formal institutional mechanisms that contribute to clear definition of expected behavior and open communication of ideas.	Is there a handbook for residents? Is there a newsletter?
Policy choice	Reflects the extent to which the facility provides options from which residents can select individual patterns of daily living.	Is there a curfew? Are residents allowed to drink a glass of wine or beer at meals?
Resident control	Assesses the extent of formal institutional structures that provide residents with a voice in running the facility and the amount of influence that residents have over policy.	Is there a residents' council? Are residents involved in deciding what kinds of new activities or programs will occur?
Provision for privacy	Measures the degree of privacy that is given residents.	How many private rooms are there? Are residents allowed to lock the door to their rooms?
Availability of health services	Measures the availability of health-related services in the facility.	Is there an on-site medical clinic? Is there physical therapy?
Availability of daily living assistance	Measures the availability of services provided by the facility that assist residents in tasks of daily living.	Is there assistance with personal grooming? Is dinner served each day?
Availability of social–recreational activities	Assesses the availability of activities within the facility.	How often is there outside entertainment? How often are there classes or lectures? How often are there parties?

activities.[42] Older occupants will not be aware of or perceive the same opportunities or resources in the places they live or the same barriers or constraints accessing them.

These varied experiences of older people reflect not just the different objective realities (functionally relevant environments) of their external worlds, but also the complex blended effects of their different personal histories; personalities; ethnic, racial, and religious backgrounds; chronological age; marital status; gender; education; employment status; financial circumstances; and health and impairment status. Consequently, older people do not tune their sensory antennas to the same features, activities, or events. They evaluate differently—both correctly and incorrectly—what they see, touch, smell, and hear, and they hold more intense or stronger positive or negative feelings about some aspects than others. They do not value or care about the same things; some residential and care features or activities simply have greater relevance or salience and are more meaningful or engaging than others.[43]

How they subjectively experience their residential and care arrangements are highly personal affairs. When they communicate their feelings about where they live

> They are telling us a great deal about themselves, how happy their lives are, what's important about their life-styles, what their housing expectations and aspirations are, how physically and mentally competent they are, how willing they are to overlook or minimize the undesirable aspects of their environment, what their dwellings say about their status and position in the community, how significant their housing is for their emotional well-being and how they are able to cope with diversity and adversity.[44]

RESOLVING DIVERGENT WORLDVIEWS

Even the most carefully constructed and detached assessment of the objectively defined qualities of residential and care environments may be at odds with how their older occupants subjectively experience these places. When an 80-year-old woman dismisses the recommendations of her occupational therapist, who has judged her dwelling as unsafe and difficult to use, she risks falling and a costly emergency room visit. The older man who has relocated from his long-occupied and unquestionably rundown house may be miserable in his spanking new and well-equipped rental apartment, for he yearns for the warm memories that permeated his previous abode and the good humor of his earlier neighbors. And the older mother may be saddened by her adult daughter's "expert" caregiving because she acts like an impersonally hired staff person rather than a comforting and warm confidant.

The potentially very different quality-of-life conclusions that emerge from these two worldviews complicate generalizations about how the residences of older people influence their ability to age successfully. Ideally, we should distinguish and be open to both perspectives. We should not casually discard either the scientifically based findings and solutions of the experts or the impassioned views of older people. There are often no simple answers as to who should be the final arbiters of the best places to live. It will always be difficult to achieve the right balance of viewpoints.

Currently, most studies rely on objective environmental classifications to gauge the quality of where older people live.[45] In contrast, there are few guiding frameworks for assessing the appropriateness of older people's subjective place experiences. To fill this gap, Chapter 2 outlines an emotion-based theoretical model to judge whether older people feel that their residential arrangements are satisfying their needs and goals. When they occupy such congruent or fitting environments, the model deems them as being in their *residential comfort* and *residential mastery* zones and achieving *residential normalcy*.

AGING IN PLACE: BANE OR BLESSING?

The schism between these objective and subjective environmental perspectives is especially apparent when we scrutinize the arguments given for why older people are better off aging in place in their current homes than moving to another residential or care setting. It is not difficult to find objective indicators that dismally portray the broken and failing residential environments occupied by a significant share of older people who stay put. Their dwellings may be physically hazardous places and financially stressful to maintain, they may be located in unsafe neighborhoods with limited public transportation access to their basic shopping needs, and they may be socially isolated and not receiving adequate healthcare or personal assistance.

However, these signs of residential disarray are not always apparent to their older occupants. They may not notice the downsides cited by professionals, academics, and family members, or if they do acknowledge them, they judge them as largely insignificant. They cannot fathom living in any other place that could be as emotionally fulfilling.

It is not just older residents who seem oblivious to the countless objective indicators that point to their incongruous living arrangements. A diverse array of stakeholders representing the media, the long-term care industry, the financial sector, and government legislators—unfortunately, many with self-serving motives—strongly endorse their residential inertia. Later chapters of this book look at both sides of the question of aging in place versus moving.

THE COPING BEHAVIORS OF OLDER AMERICANS

If we followed the lives of people after they turned age 65, we would find that most eventually end up—if only temporarily—in residential or care settings that are incongruous with their lifestyles and capabilities. However, these experiences do not mark the end of their individual or place biographies. Rather, the majority of older people look for ways to remedy their incompatible environments. Numerous adult development and life course theories agree that older adults who age optimally are able to cope well with adversity. Chapter 5 proposes that older people adapting the most successfully have more *enriched coping repertories*. These persons are more resilient, make their decisions more autonomously, and live in or relocate to neighborhoods and communities that offer them more opportunities and resources to address their problems.

Consequently, when they feel their lives are unfulfilled after retirement, they are motivated and capable enough to find churches, mosques, temples, or synagogues that welcome their volunteering efforts. If their current communities offer inadequate recreational opportunities, they relocate to an active adult community or to a university community to enjoy a more enriched lifestyle. Unhappy with the institutional ambience of their assisted living accommodations, they may cajole the management to reduce restrictions on alcohol consumption or on bringing personal furnishings or memorabilia into their rooms. When they can no longer perform their most basic self-care tasks (e.g., bathing or grooming), they hire a home aide, move closer to a family member, or relocate to the protected environment of an assisted living development.

Later chapters of this book examine the strengths and weaknesses of such coping solutions and whether they are feasible choices for older Americans. Chapter 6 looks first at a variety of low- and high-tech ways that older people seeking to age in place can physically and technologically transform their current dwellings to help them compensate for their physical limitations, make their physically inhospitable environments safer and more livable, alert others about their health-related problems, get help quickly, and enlarge their social networks.

Chapter 7 argues that although these physical and technological fixes have obvious benefits, the ability of physically and cognitively impaired older people to age in place depends on the availability of immediate family members, the preeminent long-term care providers. The chapter also examines the complex duties expected of today's caregivers and emphasizes both the benefits and costs of their contributions to the old.

Chapters 8 and 9 consider the options older Americans must rely on when even the herculean caregiving assistance of their families falls short. Here we evaluate the preventive health and long-term services and supports that are available in their neighborhoods and communities, offered by both the private and public sectors. Older people are increasingly relying on these resources to prolong their ability to remain competent, independent, and in better control of their lives. When successful, they are able to avoid hospital stays, emergency rooms, and prematurely entering the most dreaded alternative, the nursing home. Faith-based charitable organizations offer some of these long-term care solutions, but others result from the grassroots initiatives of older people who shun the help of any government assistance. Federal government programs, such as Medicaid and the Older Americans Act, fund other programs, and these specifically target lower-income and other vulnerable older groups. Other government programs offer older adults affordable rental accommodations, and some of the sponsors or owners of these publicly funded properties offer their older tenants supportive and health-related services, enabling them to maintain their independent households.

When aging in place is no longer desirable or feasible, a small number of older people look to housing and care options created by private developers. Chapter 10 focuses on the age-segregated residential options selected by younger, healthier, and active older people seeking to feel more actively engaged in their lives. They move to active adult communities and, to a much lesser extent, to cohousing communities tailored to those seeking hedonistic or communal lifestyles. Chapters 11 and 12 focus on options that attract older people for very different reasons. To cope with their physical impairments, cognitive declines, and chronic health problems, they need the physical settings and personal assistance found in residential care alternatives, such as independent living communities, assisted living developments, board and care settings, and continuing care retirement communities.

NOTHING IS PERFECT

The New Gerontology paradigm has been criticized for its failure to recognize the diversity of aging adults and its limited focus on individual determinants of their well-being. In contrast, this book emphasizes how the very different residential and care environments of heterogeneous older individuals influence their ability to age successfully, the importance of their aging in place and moving decisions, and the need for multiple solutions to address the inadequacies of where they live. Like New Gerontology proponents, however, we agree that it is never too late for older people to be proactive and take steps to cope effectively with the discordant aspects of their lives or environments.

Nonetheless, this book is realistic. It seeks to be as critical as possible of the residential and long-term solutions adopted by older people. Despite the many advantages and benefits of the places older people live and receive care, they often fall short in various ways. Some deviate too dramatically from their life experiences or their personal conceptions of the good life. Others are incompatible with their ethnic or racial backgrounds. Older adults construe other remedies as ageist and demeaning, communicating to others that they are "officially" old. Other solutions are not a good fit because they only offer partial fixes and fail to recognize the multiple and complex residential or care needs of impaired older people with chronic health problems. The coping responses of other older people are limited because they occupy places where private or public sector solutions are unavailable, poorly developed, unaffordable, or simply too difficult or complicated to access.

Consequently, neither aging in place nor moving strategies are perfect pathways to aging successfully, and despite enthusiastic endorsements, both approaches have downsides and limitations. Many older adults simply have limited coping repertoires. They have difficulty finding their optimum residential and care settings because they do not square with their personalities, demographics, lifestyles, health status, and functional capabilities or because they live in places with limited opportunities. Because *"older Americans are now asking more of their residential environments than at any time in history,"*[46] they will often be frustrated in their quest to find the right place.

NOTES

1. (Rowe & Kahn, 1998, p. xii)
2. (Rowe & Kahn, 1998)
3. (Jeste et al., 2013)
4. (Rowe & Kahn, 1998, p. 102)
5. (Holstein & Minkler, 2003); Gerontology is defined as the multidisciplinary study of the biological, psychological, and social aspects and processes of aging and the problems of older adults. (Achenbaum & Levin, 1989)
6. (Rowe & Kahn, 1998, pp. 51–52)
7. (Caro, Caspi, Burr, & Mutchler, 2009, p. 116)
8. (Havighurst, Neugarten, & Tobin, 1968); the first author is most associated with the activity theory.
9. (Cumming & Henry, 1961)
10. (Cumming & Henry, 1961)
11. (Blaikie, 1999, p. 109)

12. (Strawbridge, Wallhagen, & Cohen, 2002)
13. (Kemper, Komisar, & Alecxih, 2005)
14. (Holstein & Minkler, 2003)
15. (Molla & Madans, 2010)
16. (Katz et al., 1983; Molla & Madans, 2010; Neugarten, 1974)
17. (Thomas, 2004, p. 149)
18. (Thomas, 2004. p. 150)
19. (Holstein & Minkler, 2003)
20. (Rosowsky, 2005, p. 55)
21. (Scheidt, Humpherys, & Yorgason, 1999)
22. (George, 2006)
23. (Jung, 1969)
24. (Pruchno, Wilson-Genderson, Rose, & Cartwright, 2010)
25. (Golant, 2003a, 2011a; Iwarsson et al., 2007; Lawton, 1983; Scheidt & Windley, 2006; Wahl & Oswald, 2009)
26. (Golant, 2012)
27. (Diez Roux, 2002; Kawachi & Berkman, 2003)
28. (Fenton, 2011, p. 6)
29. (Gitlin, 2000; Glass & Balfour, 2003; Golant, 1984; Lawton & Nahemow, 1973; Scheidt & Schwarz, 2009)
30. (Burns, Lavoie, & Rose, 2011)
31. (Gubrium, 1973)
32. (Krause, 2003)
33. (Hormuth, 1990)
34. (Diez Roux, 2002; Golant, 2005)
35. http://www.topretirements.com/Home.html; (Bankers Life and Casualty Company, 2011; Brandon, 2011; The Washington Economics Group, 2012)
36. (Brandon, 2011)
37. The AARP website typically contains an extensive list of these alternative retirement destinations.
38. (Doxiad's, 1968)
39. (Lemke & Moos, 1980; Moos & Lemke, 1980; Moos & Lemke, 1996)
40. (Golant, 1998a, p. 35)
41. (Magnusson, 1985)
42. (Golant, 1984, 1998a, 2003a)
43. (Berridge & Kringelbach, 2011)
44. (Golant, 1986, p. 123)
45. (Golant, 1984; Wachs, 1999)
46. (Golant, 2011a, p. 207)

2

ACHIEVING RESIDENTIAL NORMALCY

Balancing on an Emotional Tightrope

Settings elicit emotions, which, in turn, systematically influence other behaviors. Pleasure–displeasure is a continuum ranging from extreme pain or unhappiness to extreme pleasure or ecstasy at the other end. Dominance–submissiveness refers to the extent a person feels powerful vis-à-vis the environment that surrounds him. A person feels dominant when he is able to influence or control the situation he is in; he feels submissive when the environment influences him.[1]

AN EMOTIONAL ANATOMY OF PLACE

We have emphasized that older people living in the same place often do not share the same feelings about the quality of their residential environments. However, the studies that report these findings fail to offer a conceptual language, a set of organizational principles, by which to group these individuals according to why they feel as they do. We are unable to generalize about whether these older adults are occupying residential and care settings congruent with their needs and goals and, thereby, aging more successfully.

To that end, this chapter presents a theoretical model that introduces the construct of *residential normalcy* to identify those older people who feel they are living in very desirable or congruent places. These individuals report having two categories of positive emotional experiences in their residential or care arrangements:

[Here,] they experience overall pleasurable, hassle free, and memorable feelings that have relevance to them; and they feel both competent and in control—that is, they do not have to behave in personally objectionable ways or to
unduly surrender mastery of their lives or environments to others.[2]

Focusing on the emotional experiences of older people to judge the qualities of where
they live has long been of interest to many academic and clinical disciplines, including the neurosciences, gerontology, architecture, psychology, and anthropology.[3] Early
on, Bernice Neugarten and colleagues,[4] focusing on the antecedents of life satisfaction,
recognized the importance of older people deriving pleasure from their activities. More
recently, the socioemotional selectivity theory of aging by Carstensen[5] emphasized that
as older adults recognize the finitude of their lives, they attach even greater importance
to their emotionally significant and rewarding activities and goals.

Psychologists have long argued that the emotional experiences of individuals
represent *"the common core of human response to all types of environments."*[6] One expert reporting on the emotions people experience over their life spans expressed their significance in this way:

They [are] integral to our sense of well-being or lack of well-being. . . . They
are what make individuals care about outcomes, and care in particular ways,
with fear, revulsion, joy, shame, excitement, guilt, indignation, and so forth.[7]

Consequently, by ascertaining the emotional experiences of older people, we can assess
the appropriateness or individual–environment fit of a wide range of settings, whether
ordinary homes or planned senior housing, residential care settings, or even nursing
homes.

WHY THE VIEWS OF OLDER PEOPLE AND THE EXPERTS DIFFER

If the experts and older adults could agree as to what constituted great places to live,
then we would have a much weaker rationale for studying these emotional experiences.
Often, however, the objective indicators relied on by academics and professionals do
not yield the same quality-of-life conclusions as the subjective experiences reported by
older people. There are six specific reasons for this discordance.

First, older adults do not have the same encyclopedic awareness and knowledge
of the contents and features of their residential settings and their strengths and weaknesses. Except possibly when they live in very small communities, their perceived
residential worlds are less complete, accurate and coherent. Consequently, their place
descriptions or evaluations often deviate from the computer-generated outputs of professionals or scientists. Older adults do not necessarily conduct their activities in places
that these experts recommend or take advantage of their so-called opportunities or
resources. When asked, they cannot recite the names of the same banks, grocery stores,
restaurants, services, counseling centers, health clinics, senior centers, recreational opportunities, and affordable housing developments. They often are unaware of the extensive long-term care supports offered by government programs or the benefits of
hiring a geriatric case manager or physician.

Older people do not identify the same dangers or hazards in their residential arrangements as the experts. Whereas they appraise their dwellings and neighborhoods as rewarding and beneficial places to live, professionals see their surroundings as harmful or threatening.[8] They may be oblivious to the physical design deficiencies in their bathrooms that experts believe increase their risk of falling. They do not know that some retail stores are overpriced. They are naive about how the poorly trained staff working in their assisted living residence are providing inadequate care.

Second, older adults do not have the same motivations, capabilities, or confidence to take advantage of what they do agree is available. Despite the nutritional benefits of hot lunches offered by a nearby community senior center, older people may not patronize these centers if they believe that their participation will be a demeaning experience. Foreign-born older people who speak English poorly and are easily intimidated by government bureaucracies do not consider many public assistance and care options as helpful ways to address their vulnerabilities. For older people who cannot drive, the most familiar and highly rated establishments in their community may just as well not exist because of their geographic remoteness. Older people who do not feel in good health—despite their excellent physicals and lab reports—will not participate in vigorous exercise programs offered by their local senior center. Nearby and high-quality assisted living residences are of no use to low-income people who cannot afford them.

Third, older adults today have their own highly personalized views of what constitutes a great place to live, which may clash with the assessments of professionals. Because of their different demographics, personalities, and life experiences, they enter old age with very different residential preferences and expectations that profoundly shape how they think and feel about their surroundings and activities.

Such individual differences help explain what would otherwise be illogical findings. A 1970s study reporting on the residential satisfaction of Americans found that higher-income older residents were less satisfied with their communities, neighborhoods, and homes than lower-income occupants.[9] Yet by most objective criteria, the financially better-off residents were living in settings with far superior features and amenities. The researchers explained this apparent inconsistency by theorizing that higher-income people had much higher expectations or aspirations—and held them more strongly—about how their residential arrangements should look. But this increased the odds that they would have unfulfilled aspirations. The result for many was a large gap between their goals or aspirations and where they ended up living, which translated into higher levels of dissatisfaction. In contrast, the lower expectations and aspirations of the lower-income group—perhaps because of their past disappointments and unmet goals—were more closely matched in their objectively less-desirable residential worlds. Consequently, they experienced higher satisfaction levels.[10] The simple lesson: Older people with more ambitious residential dreams were more likely to end up in places that disappointed them.

Personality differences especially explain why some older people appear happy even as calamities surround them. Some people have very positive dispositions and seem happy and optimistic about everything. Theorists argue that older people who think more positively about themselves—as indicated by their levels of happiness, optimism, morale, satisfaction with their lives, and self-esteem—are also those who are more likely to feel better about everything in their lives. They are more likely to report better physical and mental health, fewer mobility limitations, less physical frailty, and emphasize the upsides of getting old.[11] They are also more likely to feel positively about where they live.[12] Conversely, chronically unhappy people complain about everything in their residences, even as others find them blissful places to live.[13]

This relationship was illustrated by the finding of a prominent Harvard psychiatrist who showed how the moods of older people can accentuate the usual hassles of homeownership:

> The perception of home maintenance as a burden is influenced not only by the physical and mental demands of housekeeping but also by the mood state of the resident. Depression, that most common mental disorder of late life, tends to diminish the capacity for effort as well as the pleasure to be derived from the home; at the same time, depressive irritability intensifies the hassles involved in caring for the home, and depressive pessimism promotes the conclusion that things will only get worse in the future.[14]

Fourth, as people get older, their views of what constitutes an ideal place to enjoy their lives and to live independently evolve in ways unanticipated by the experts. They expect their residential environments to satisfy very different retirement or leisure-related lifestyles and help compensate for a variety of newly experienced, age-related declines or losses.[15]

As I tell my young undergraduate students, old age often extends over a period that is much longer than the age at which they will graduate—typically in their early 20s. It is absurd to believe that an 80-year-old man will feel the same about his residential situation as he did in his 60s. That is why it is inappropriate to generalize about the residential and care needs of older people based on opinion polls targeting 50- or 60-year-olds. One study found that among older people who had moved in the past 2 years, only 20% had anticipated their adjustments.[16]

Fifth, the feelings older people report about their dwellings, neighborhoods, and communities may less reflect their own deliberations than the opinions and communications of others—spouses, children, friends, neighbors, professionals, or the media.[17] When some older people repeatedly hear that their valued friends or family enjoy a particular housing choice, they also feel more positively about it; conversely, they think less positively about residential situations that elicit cynical and critical comments from people whose opinions they trust.[18] Sometimes, there is a "lemming" effect. Older people are so impressed with the residential choices of their friends that they mimic their moves. For example, many new arrivals to the large active adult community in Sun City, Arizona, previously had years of favorable communications with earlier settled residents.[19]

A sixth reason for the disconnect between objectively defined environmental assessments and the subjective experiences of older people is that experts typically view the residential environments of older adults through contemporary lenses, as momentary or cross-sectional depictions. However, when we ask older people what they like or dislike about where they live, they inevitably reference events or activities in their pasts. Their subjective experiences are not static snapshots of their current residential contexts, but rather longitudinal frames of an environmental movie.[20] Older people have often lived at the same address for decades and they typically have occupied several earlier residences. Consequently, they have several temporal reference points when judging the quality of their current dwellings, neighborhoods, and communities.[21] Listen to the words of an 83-year-old woman when asked how she felt about the abandoned and boarded-up houses across the street:

> I have news for you. I don't see those houses across the street, In my mind's eye those are the houses that I've seen for 40 years, and that's the way I look at them. I remember the people that used to live there. I remember how it used to be in the summer time, and all like that.[22]

Consequently, when professionals conduct point-in-time environmental evaluations, their conclusions may differ dramatically from these remembered feelings.[23]

TWO CATEGORIES OF RESIDENTIAL EMOTIONAL EXPERIENCES

To comprehensively judge whether older people occupy congruent places to live, the model distinguishes two broad categories of subjective assessments: *residential comfort emotional experiences* and *residential mastery emotional experiences*. Together, these two independent sets of experiences holistically portray how older people feel about their residential settings and if they have achieved residential normalcy (Figure 2.1).

RESIDENTIAL COMFORT EMOTIONAL EXPERIENCES

The first category of emotional experiences captures whether older people feel that their residential settings are pleasurable, comfortable, enjoyable, and memorable places as well as free of hassles. Using the terminology of the New Gerontology paradigm of successful aging, these reported feelings inform us whether older people are experiencing the good life and are actively engaged in life (see Chapter 1).

Figure 2.1. Two categories of residential emotional experiences

RESIDENTIAL COMFORT EMOTIONAL EXPERIENCES

Pleasurable/Unpleasurable Feelings About Residential Environment and Activities

Hassle-Free/Hassled Feelings About Residential Environment and Activities

Good/Bad Memorable Feelings About Past Residential Environment and Activities

RESIDENTIAL MASTERY EMOTIONAL EXPERIENCES

Feeling Competent/Incompetent in Residential Environment

Feeling In/Out of Control of Residential Environment

When older people have such favorable residential comfort experiences, they variously report feeling pleasure (vs. displeasure), comfortable (vs. uncomfortable), contented (vs. discontented), happy (vs. sad), joyful (vs. sorrowful), elated (vs. heartsick), stimulated (vs. bored), cheerful (vs. glum), delighted (vs. disappointed), relaxed (vs. unrelaxed), accepted (vs. rejected), and admired (vs. despised).[24]

Some feelings are aligned along a negative continuum (e.g., disagreeable vs. very disagreeable as opposed to pleasurable vs. unpleasurable) because they vary as to how distasteful they are. Others refer to these more stressful experiences as the hassles of life, calling attention to *"the irritating, frustrating, distressing demands that to some degree characterize everyday transactions with the environment."*[25] Examples include snow to shovel, grass to mow, an annoying neighbor, and an irritating staff person in an assisted living residence.

Some aspects of a place of residence will elicit feelings that their occupants uniformly share.[26] Reliable and compassionate companions consistently generate pleasurable feelings. Older people typically do not enjoy occupying physically dilapidated buildings, communities with high crime rates, or nursing homes with sterile and hospital-like qualities.

However, it is easy to find examples of how objectively similar places generate very different feelings. Older people disagree among themselves about what it means to experience the good life or to be fully engaged in life. What makes a place of residence pleasurable, comfortable, enjoyable, or hassle-free is very much an individual affair. My own idiosyncrasies remind me of the dangers of simple generalizations. I have always enjoyed the kitchen in my house—not just as a place to cook or eat in, but also as a homey space to gather, mingle, and socialize. I have felt that a warm and welcoming dwelling would have a great kitchen. However, this is not how my cosmopolitan friend in New York City views the world. She convincingly argues that most urban professionals—who apparently eat out 7 times a week—do not care about the quality of their kitchens.[27]

Evidence for these diverse individual appraisals abounds. Living in a warm climate and playing golf and tennis year-round attracts some older people, but turns off those who like seasonal changes. Some older people enjoy taking care of their gardens; others feel it is a boring chore, even a hassle. Some older people feel invigorated by the natural beauty of sandy beaches and snow-capped mountains; however, others are energized by places with lots of stores, busy streets, a performing arts theater, and universities where they can hear lectures on the human condition. Whereas some are enthralled with the architecture of a historical building, others cynically suggest that it should be torn down. The social scene matters most for other older people. They feel most comfortable with neighbors who are friendly and compatible and who share their same values. Others feel that the most desirable neighbors keep to themselves. Some older people judge their culturally diverse neighbors as hostile; others see them as potential friends. And whereas some older people view a subdivision steadily filling with younger people as invigorating, others are depressed by their neighbors' youth.

Some older people enjoy sedentary or passive activities, such as watching TV, relaxing, listening to the radio, and doing crossword puzzles.[28] Their paradise is to hole up in their abodes and be alone to read the hundred greatest books. They do not feel the need to be physically active, continually attend fitness classes, or be surrounded by people. These home dwellers may be less judgmental about the downsides of their communities because they do not spend a lot of time outside their neighborhoods. In contrast, for other older people an enjoyable lifestyle means keeping active, socializing with neighbors and friends,[29] and volunteering in their community—or as the experts call it, being civically engaged.

For some older people, a place's emotional appeal is its offerings of new activities. They get pleasure when they confront novel events, activities, and people; otherwise, they get easily bored with too much of a good thing.[30] Thus, they thrive in communities that offer opportunities for different dance classes, new hiking trails, and new inspirational speakers. Some older people thrive in places that offer them adventure and excitement; they are risk takers.[31] If we are to believe the experts,

> Epidemiological investigations have indicated that as humans get older, continued interest in novel aspects of their environment and exposure to intellectually stimulating activities may sustain cognitive functioning, produce a buffer against mental decline, and foster longevity.[32]

RESIDENTIAL MASTERY EMOTIONAL EXPERIENCES

A second category of emotional experiences captures whether older people occupy residential settings in which they feel *competent* and *in control*. When older people have such favorable residential mastery experiences, they variously report feeling influential (vs. influenced), dominant (vs. submissive), autonomous (vs. dependent), secure (vs. anxious), powerful (vs. overpowered), strong (vs. helpless), encouraged (vs. frustrated), confident (vs. uncertain), and unafraid (vs. afraid).

OUTCOMES, NOT ANTECEDENTS

Gerontologists often distinguish older people by their capabilities, usually because they want to *explain* differences in their behavior. In contrast, the residential normalcy model treats these efficacy constructs as *outcomes* or *end states,* as indicators of whether older people are aging successfully. A vast literature has argued that older people who feel competent and in control of their lives and environments are happier, are more satisfied with their lives, and have a greater sense of self-worth or self-esteem.[33]

Life span theorists emphasize that older people are more likely to have these feelings of mastery when they live in places where they feel capable of doing things, can make things happen, and can shape their environments to fit their needs and capabilities.[34] Here they do not feel pushed around by others, do not have to accept unsolicited advice, and do not have to act in ways that they never behaved throughout most of their adult lives. In short, they do not have to be under somebody's thumb; they are in charge. And for better or worse, older people have this sense of confidence even if they have only the illusion of control—that is, if they perceive it to be true.[35]

WHEN OLDER PEOPLE FEEL COMPETENT OR INCOMPETENT

We can distinguish three sets of transactions older people have with their residential or care arrangements that influence their feelings of competence and four sets of transactions associated with their feelings of being in control.

Feeling Competent: Physical and Cognitive Declines

Older people feel more competent when they also feel in good health and functionally capable. Unfortunately, as they become older, they are at greater risk of experiencing a variety of chronic illnesses that make it impossible for them to perform even the most basic motor activities without some assistance (e.g., getting around, bending, getting up from a chair, taking a shower). They also experience declines in their cognitive functioning (e.g., remembering, reacting, processing, thinking) or their sensory abilities (e.g., hearing, seeing, tasting, smelling).

But feelings of competence depend on more than just physiological or physical health indicators. The design and contents of their dwellings may worsen or improve these feelings of vulnerability.[36] Older people are continually reminded of their frailties when they cannot perform once-mundane tasks, such as opening windows, turning on faucets or stove dials, changing the furnace filters, doing housekeeping chores, and simple dwelling repairs.[37] They also have a heightened awareness of their limitations when they confront inaccessible or unusable parts of their dwelling, such as a second floor or high closet shelves.

Neighborhoods also can magnify their feelings of incompetence. Older people feel insecure walking on sidewalks with uneven or hilly surfaces and negotiating car-heavy busy intersections. They feel fatigued when they must negotiate long walking distances, especially if they must carry heavy packages in inclement weather. Older drivers are reminded that they are losing their skills when they have difficulty negotiating even familiar places at night or feel frightened about the prospects of driving in rush hour traffic.

Feeling Competent: Lost Interpersonal Relationships

Older people often first feel vulnerable when the people they depended on for their physical assistance or financial stability die, move away, or experience physical or mental declines themselves.[38] Particularly strong feelings of incompetence arise when physically frail husbands or wives lose spouses who have been caring for them. With the loss or incapacitation of this significant other, taken-for-granted tasks become insurmountable chores. The older woman who depended on her husband to drive her around finds it difficult to access even the nearest community destinations. Small household repairs are no longer just hassles, but rather uncompleted tasks that reinforce her feelings of vulnerability. And older people are further reminded of their vulnerabilities when they must reassign these tasks or responsibilities to others.[39]

The loss of a significant other may produce feelings of incompetence for a very different reason. Older people no longer have someone to reinforce their positive self-concepts—that is, affirm their beliefs that they led successful or productive lives—as provider, loving spouse, reliable friend or neighbor, or indispensable confidant.[40] Absent are persons who can allay their insecurities and feelings of uselessness.

Feeling Competent: Pride in Residence

The residential environments occupied by older people may assuage feelings of incompetence by offering them material evidence that they have lived successful, worthy, or accomplished lives. Living in a well-appointed house in a reputable neighborhood affirms that they have achieved their personal goals. The residential setting becomes a major source of pride. Just the opposite occurs, of course, when older people feel embarrassed by their addresses.

Feeling in Control: Choosing Activities and Spending Time as They Want

Whether or not older people feel in control in their residential or care arrangements often depends on their ability to practice desired lifestyles—to do their own thing. Older people with decreases in cognitive abilities and body strength are particularly at risk of having their activities and routines disrupted.[41] They feel especially out of control when others start dictating how they should deal with their vulnerabilities. This occurs when family members urge them to introduce home modifications, take away their car keys, or demand that they hire a home aide to take care of their housekeeping needs. Moving "recommendations" may be the worst affront. Even the most loved adult daughter has felt the wrath of an older parent when she recommends a move to a senior housing arrangement.[42]

Paradoxically, older people who are under the constant care of their loved ones feel this sense of helplessness because they are now told how to conduct their lives—when to get up, eat, bathe, and take their medications. As one expert explains,

> Dependence on a spouse . . . may threaten self-esteem and lead to feeling loss of control over important life outcomes, arousing anxiety and, eventually, depression.[43]

Older people particularly feel a deep sense of lost control when they cannot enjoy activities that they view as rituals,[44] such as Sunday brunch with close friends, the daily exercise walk in the nearby shopping mall, the daily outing with a pet in the neighborhood, Friday dinner with family members, and Sunday religious services.[45]

Being able to perform their preferred activities may even compensate for the challenges older people confront when they occupy deteriorated or rundown neighborhoods. Consider the findings from an early pioneering study of low-income older people living in a depressed inner-city neighborhood in New York City. The residents were surprisingly optimistic about the other advantages of city life.

> They talk about the ease and availability of desired facilities and services, the opportunities for work. . . . City life means having at one's fingertips most of the services needed and wanted, including both the necessities of life and the special cultural and recreational facilities found in a large cosmopolitan city.[46]

Older people are also less able to initiate new activities when they feel continuously assaulted by the uncontrollable circumstances of where they live—store closings, abandoned dwellings, abusive remarks, fear of strangers, insensitive neighbors. As two experts put it,

> When people feel a chronic loss of control, they don't take risks and they retreat into an all too familiar world. When people feel they can exercise some control of their environment, they seek out new information, plan, strategize, and so on.[47]

Fear of losing control over how they conduct their lives also deters older adults from considering different residential options. Many older people are averse to occupying planned senior housing because of the restrictive rules in these places that would prevent them from coming and going when they please.

Feeling in Control: Achieving Environmental Privacy

Scholars have often examined privacy as an environmental control issue—namely, the ability of people to influence who intrudes on the real or perceived spatial boundaries they have established between themselves and others.[48] Having privacy means that older people can influence who sees and hears them, who speaks to them, and to whom they are physically close. It includes their ability to selectively disengage from the intrusions of others[49] and opt for solitude and anonymity rather than group participation. It means that they can control who administratively or technologically monitors their activities, behaviors, and movements.[50]

Older people reasonably worry that they will lose control over who enters their personal spaces if they occupy congregate settings, such as assisted living communities that accommodate more physically or cognitively frail seniors. Here they can face formidable challenges controlling the actions of other occupants. We hear complaints about residents entering the apartments of others without invitation and about *"residents who napped in the public sitting areas."*[51] The seating arrangements in their common dining rooms often become a battlefield in which residents impose their preferences about who sits at a particular table.[52] In contrast, older people sometimes feel that active adult gated communities are appealing because they keep out "undesirable" people, ranging from solicitors to children, who they feel are offensive or threatening.[53]

Even the older occupants of ordinary homes may feel that others are violating their territories, such as when a wife must share household space all day with her recently retired husband or when a daughter "takes over" her home in the course of performing caregiving activities.[54]

Feeling in Control: Trusting Human Relationships

Older people feel more in control when they trust their friends, family, staff, or professionals. They have confidence that these relationships will yield predictable and certain outcomes, that they will be treated honestly, compassionately, and with dignity, and that they will not be abused. Trusting relationships may be contractual, such as the terms of the services offered by management or staff of an assisted living development or home care agency; alternatively, they may depend on moral consensus, such as informal handshake understandings with friends who come through on their promises and can be relied on in times of need.[55]

Feeling in Control: Financial Environment Certainty

Older people feel less in control when they can no longer manage or afford their residential, care, or medical expenditures. They consider their failure to meet these obligations as much more than just a hassle because their inability to cover these taken-for-granted costs broadcasts their poor financial health. Older homeowners may especially feel this lost sense of control if they can no longer count on the equity in their dwellings as a source of wealth, perhaps because of falling home values or an inflated mortgage or because they received earlier cash payments from reverse mortgages. Many view their dwelling's equity as a last-resort emergency fund to pay for end-of-life long-term care or catastrophic out-of-pocket medical expenses. Absent this security blanket, they feel particularly vulnerable, especially when they contemplate a future in which they must rely on their adult children or the government to pay for their housing or care expenses.[56]

LINKING RESIDENTIAL COMFORT AND MASTERY EXPERIENCES

Residential comfort and residential mastery emotional experiences are theorized as being independent of each other (i.e., uncorrelated).[57] In practice, this may not always be true. That is, older people who feel more (or less) competent and in control will have more pleasant (or unpleasant) experiences; conversely, older people who feel less competent or more vulnerable will sometimes have more pleasurable residential experiences.

This latter relationship may appear unlikely, but studies show that when people become older and experience declines in their physical and cognitive functioning, they actually can report higher levels of happiness, higher self-ratings of successful aging, and lower feelings of stress, worry, and anger.[58] The message is that even as aging people feel increasingly less competent and in control, they may find compensating new sources of pleasure and enjoyment.

It is easier to understand why older people who live in places where they feel less competent and in control have more negative residential comfort experiences.[59] M. Powell Lawton, a pioneer in the field of environmental gerontology, frequently argued that older people's feelings toward their residential settings depended on whether they could competently perform their activities. His environmental docility hypothesis argues that older people with more serious physical or cognitive limitations have a greater share of their behaviors unfavorably explained by the attributes of their place of residence.[60] For example, older people who have difficulties walking are more afraid to go out on an icy day and thus feel miserable because they must remain in their houses until the hazard clears, and older people who feel insecure on their feet are more afraid to use public transit and thus miss going to an enjoyable card game at a friend's house.

We can also point to various examples whereby older people alter their sources of pleasurable residential experiences after they have experienced a decline in their capabilities. Consider the person who most of her life played singles tennis games but who now substitutes doubles tennis games because she cannot move around the court as easily. Alternatively, consider the older man who has jogged regularly for exercise and fun who finds that his painful knees require him instead to walk briskly to obtain the same pleasurable benefits.

Fewer studies have examined the reciprocal relationship; that is, older adults feel more competent and in control when they have more comfortable, hassle-free, and memorable residential experiences. The experiences of lower-income older people occupying affordable rent-assisted housing that is staffed by social workers offers one example. When these residents feel more positively about these staff, they are more open to receiving information about available services and felt more secure.[61] More generally, when older people enjoy living in their residential care settings—because they interact with staff members who have warm and friendly dispositions—they are more open to receiving help and adhering to health practices, and have reported fewer mobility limitations.[62]

TAKING STOCK OF A PLACE'S EMOTIONAL EXPERIENCES AND SETTING PRIORITIES

Older people experience a wide array of both positive and negative feelings as a result of where they live.[63] The theoretical model assumes that older people can sort through and categorize these disparate feelings according to their directions (good vs. bad) and their intensities or arousal levels (how pleasurable or how stressful).[64]

The model also assumes that older people can appraise the salience or relevance of their emotional experiences.[65] Not all of their feelings about their residential or care arrangements will have the same significance in their lives. No matter how intensely favorable or unfavorable they are, some simply have greater psychological importance than others. That is, they speak more to the needs, expectations, hopes, sensitivities, and preferences of older people and weigh more heavily in their overall place assessments.[66] Consequently, older people may report having a large number of positive but insignificant residential experiences that are trumped by a few unpleasant but extremely salient ones. By the same reasoning, a large number of negative but insignificant residential experiences may be more than offset by a few highly salient positive ones. In the lingo of theoreticians, we are assuming that older people can *"form complex, multivalenced representations of situations."*[67] That is, older adults can appraise the net consequences of each of their sets of residential comfort and residential mastery experiences, taking into account their directions, intensity, and relevance (Figure 2.2).

Consider the physically frail older woman who despises almost everything about where she lives, save one. She savors being close to her loving and very helpful daughter. The salience of this favorable mother–daughter relationship trumps all of her other negative place experiences and is her single most important reason for remaining in her current abode.

Figure 2.2. Achieving overall favorable residential experiences

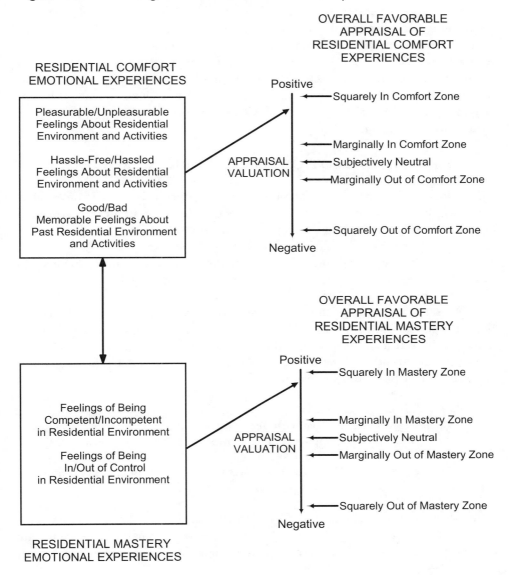

As another example, my racially intolerant aunt in Chicago hates how her neighborhood is filling up with residents from foreign countries, but these negative feelings influence little her overall residential assessments. Rather, her most salient experiences are positive: She finds her house extraordinarily comfortable, loves the nearness of stores for her everyday shopping needs, and has a small and highly valued group of close friends living nearby.

Understanding these priorities is critical when interpreting the results of national surveys and opinion polls. We spend millions of dollars annually interviewing older adults on nearly every aspect of their lives and environments. For example, AARP regularly polls older people on dozens of residential issues potentially of interest to them. But when interviewed, Americans answer everything asked of them, whether or not they have thought very hard about the questions or whether or not they have relevance in their lives. Furthermore, they tend to offer socially correct answers that are at odds with their actual feelings.[68] This is the challenge faced by researchers attempting to measure the quality of older people's residential environments. It is time consuming but essential to identify the unequal importance older people assign to their many residential experiences.

OLDER PEOPLE IN EMOTIONALLY CONGRUENT PLACES

When older people appraise the places they live as pleasurable, enjoyable, comfortable, appealing, hassle free, and memorable, we theorize that they are in their *residential comfort zones*. When they occupy places in which they feel competent and in control, we theorize that they are in their *residential mastery zones* (Figure 2.2). In the best of all worlds, older people find themselves in both their residential comfort and mastery zones. They have found their sweet or congruent spots to live and, thus, have achieved *residential normalcy* (Figure 2.3).[69]

We often immediately think about healthy, active, upper-income older people living the good life in their pristine dwellings and neighborhoods as examples of those falling in this category. But we can find less obvious examples of physically frail older people who are in both their residential comfort and mastery zones. Listen to the words of this older (age 86) stroke survivor:

> Rather difficult . . . since I had a stroke and live alone. . . . I'm happy with my life in spite of it. . . . I can write and I can eat and . . . I couldn't do either at first. . . . I think I've improved quite a lot. I can get up on my own, too. I have handles on the wall, I can roll myself out onto the balcony, I can go to the bathroom on my own also and I can wash myself. . . . I think I have come a long way, actually. One must be pleased, you know.[70]

In worst-case scenarios, older people find themselves out of both their residential comfort and mastery zones (Figure 2.4). Those who end up in nursing homes often are out of their comfort zones because of their very unpleasant hospital-like, institutional

Figure 2.3. Residential normalcy: the sweet spot to live

Figure 2.4. Alternative residential normalcy outcomes

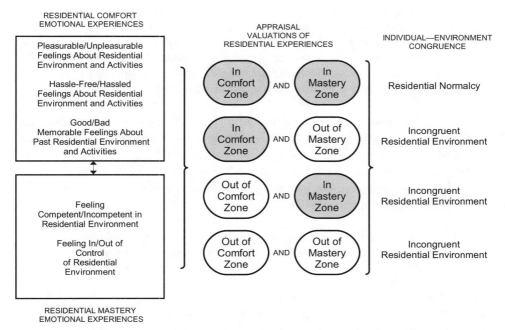

ambience, which diverges from their past homes. They are out of their mastery zones because staff and an omnipresent physical environment (e.g., nursing stations, medication carts) continually remind them of their vulnerabilities, and they have little control over their everyday activities or care.

In practice, the emotional outcomes experienced by older Americans are more equivocal. Many older people find themselves occupying places—whether ordinary dwellings or specially designed senior housing or residential care properties—with split environmental personalities. In some ways, they are wonderful places to live, but in other ways, they diverge spectacularly from their needs and goals. Consequently, they find themselves in their residential comfort zones but out of their residential mastery zones, or out of their residential comfort zones but in their residential mastery zones (Figure 2.4).

The following two residential scenarios show why older people can be so emotionally conflicted.[71]

In his residential comfort zone and out of his residential mastery zone:

An older man thoroughly enjoys living in his two-story house overlooking a river in a rural county. He loves being close to nature and the activities of the boaters and anglers. He has a cadre of close friends who frequently meet for drinks and conversation. However, he is also very anxious that his arthritic knees are making it difficult for him to negotiate the stairs in his dwelling, and he is nervous because of how far away he is from his doctors. He is beginning to admit that taking care of his house is a source of frequent worries.

In her residential mastery zone and out of her residential comfort zone:

> An older woman having difficulty walking and transferring (getting out her bed by herself) feels more secure and protected in her assisted living residence and feels confident about the prospects of getting help when needed. Although she no longer worries about her ability to live independently, she is sad about living in a place that is so different from her past home. She especially misses her regular book club meetings and conversations with her closest friends.

Older people also live in both congruous and incongruous residential situations that might not be immediately apparent. One study described the experiences of an older woman who enjoyed living in her own home (in her comfort zone) but felt her autonomy was slipping away (out of her mastery zone) because her children decided to hire a nurse to help her. Her words clearly communicate the frustration she feels about not being in charge in her own home:

> I have a nurse who comes and puts pills in my little boxes, and I feel like I have decreased in stature as a person. It hurts me. It's an insult to my dignity. . . . I feel like I'm delegated to the old and helpless regime more than I was.[72]

Figure 2.5 relates a story of how difficult it is for some older people to achieve residential normalcy even when those helping them have the best intentions. It describes how a concerned daughter was trying to help her father, Joe, cope with the early stages of Alzheimer's disease. Yet even as Joe was in his mastery zone, his perceived enjoyment of life was on the decline.

THE DILEMMA

Such accounts point to the dilemma faced by older people and their concerned families, especially as they deal with the declines and losses in their lives. Older people want it all: a comfortable and autonomous way of living, both at the same time. In practice, they find that achieving residential normalcy becomes an emotional balancing act or, less kindly, an emotional battlefield.

They recognize that environmental congruence is not an all-or-nothing affair. Older people often feel very comfortable living in their dwellings, even as they are having great difficulties performing the simplest household tasks, such as maintaining their homes, showering, or getting groceries. Inevitably, older people find they must make difficult emotional tradeoffs. To remain in their comfortable and familiar dwelling filled with satisfying memories, older people must tolerate others serving as their caregivers and introducing physical modifications to their dwellings. Alternatively, so as not to feel anxious about taking care of themselves, they must tolerate a place that offers care and supportive services but that lacks their ideal home-like qualities (Chapter 4).

In the next chapter, we focus on older people who truly feel that they are in both their residential comfort and residential mastery zones. These older adults who are aging in place have achieved their residential normalcy.

Figure 2.5. Out of his comfort zone, despite the best intentions of a caring daughter

Joe lived alone in a high-rise condominium apartment in Miami Beach, Florida. A people person, he was always surrounded by friends; parties and card games were his life and the basis for his happiness. He outlived his wife and three subsequent girlfriends. He gave many friends car rides, and he always was available to take them to their doctor appointments or help them get their groceries.

When Joe was in his mid-80s, he started having memory and hearing problems. He started writing some very large checks to charities that his daughter had never heard of and forgetting he wrote them.

His very concerned daughter, living in another part of Florida, hired a round-the-clock caregiver to live in his condominium and provide for all of his needs, so he would feel safe and secure. And she was successful: Joe liked his caregiver.

Joe's daughter thought everything was under control, and she was partly right. Joe was aging in place successfully—as the textbooks say—and he did not have to worry about taking care of himself or his apartment. He was unquestionably in his *residential mastery zone*. He felt as competent and in control as his limitations allowed. One might also have guessed that he was also in his residential comfort zone. After all, he was in his familiar and long-occupied condominium that he loved so much, surrounded by all manner of personal possessions that brought all manner of good memories.

However, Joe's many friends began dropping off like flies. They were frustrated being with someone who forgot how to play poker, and was no longer fun to be with. They did not want to deal with Joe's faulty memory and hearing problems.

To be fair, as we get older and begin counting not our birthdays but how many years we have left, we get picky, more demanding, and more selfish about how we spend our days. Joe's friends didn't want him to cramp their happy lifestyles.

Joe's view of his world was very different from his daughter's. With all of his self-sustaining needs being met, he was in his residential mastery zone, but he was rapidly slipping out of his *residential comfort zone*. Joe became very lonely and subsequently depressed. His social world was unquestionably central to how he judged the quality of his life.

NOTES

1. (Russell & Mehrabian, 1976, pp. 6, 17)
2. (Golant, 2011b, p. 193)
3. (Lewis, Haviland-Jones, & Barrett, 2008)
4. (Neugarten, Havighurst, & Tobin, 1961)
5. (Carstensen, 2006)
6. (Mehrabian, 1980, p. 7)
7. (Magai, 2001, p. 399)
8. (Barrett, Mesquita, Ochsner, & Gross, 2007)
9. (Campbell, Converse, & Rodgers, 1976; Turner, 2007)
10. (Campbell, et al., 1976; Turner, 2007)
11. (Collins, Goldman, & Rodriguez, 2008; Fredrickson, 2001)
12. (Golant, 1984; Maguire, Arthur, Boustead, Dwyer, & Currie, 1996)
13. (James, 1902)
14. (Fogel, 1992, p. 17)
15. (Barrett, 2006)
16. (Sergeant, Ekerdt, & Chapin, 2010)
17. (Golant, 1986; Pressman & Cohen, 2005)
18. (Turner, 2007, p. 87)
19. (Gober & Zonn, 1983)
20. (Golant, 2003a; Lewin, 1936)
21. Environmental psychologists studying the everyday environments of people have often criticized the laboratory assessments of their peers for this very reason. Lab settings requiring point-in-time assessments do not mimic the real-world experiences of most people.
22. (Rubinstein, 1998, p. 99)
23. (Tuan, 1975)
24. (Csikszentmihalyi & Rochberg-Halton, 1981)
25. (Kanne, Coyne, & Schaefer, 1981, p. 3)
26. (Berridge & Kringelbach, 2011; Magnusson & Torestad, 1992)
27. Lorraine Hiatt, personal communication (February 2010)
28. (Caro, et al., 2009)
29. (Pruchno & Rose, 2002)
30. (Klapp, 1986)
31. (Kahana, Liang, & Felton, 1980; Nehrke et al., 1984)
32. (Daffner et al., 2007, p. 297)
33. (Filipe, 1996; Schulz & Heckhausen, 1996)
34. (Gecas, 1989; Gurin & Brim, 1984; Schulz & Heckhausen, 1998)
35. (Langer & Abelson, 1983)
36. (Diehl & Willis, 2003)
37. (Ormond, Black, Tilly, & Thomas, 2004; Sabia, 2008)
38. (Hays, 2002)
39. (Klumb & Maier, 2007)
40. (Cumming & Cumming, 1963; Hays, 2002; Hormuth, 1990)
41. (Wolinsky, Callahan, Fitzgerald, & Johnson, 1993)
42. (Golant, 2011b)
43. (Muramatsu, Yin, & Hedeker, 2010, p. 8)
44. (Perin, 1970, pp. 77–78)
45. (Golant, 2003a)
46. (Cantor, 1975, p. 27)
47. (Langer & Abelson, 1983, pp. 207–208)
48. (Margulis, 2003)
49. (Carstensen, Isaacowitz, & Charles, 1999)

50. (Margulis, 2003)
51. (Eckert, Morgan, Carder, Frankowski, & Roth, 2009, p. 157)
52. (Eckert, et al., 2009)
53. (Diehl & Willis, 2003)
54. (Rowles, Oswald, & Hunter, 2004)
55. (Walker, Smith, & Adam, 2009)
56. (Munnell, Soto, & Aubry, 2007)
57. (Mehrabian, 1980; Osgood, Suci, & Tannenbaum, 1957)
58. (Jeste et al., 2013; Stone, Schwartz, Broderick, & Deaton, 2010)
59. (Magai, 2001; Schulz & Heckhausen, 1996, 1998)
60. (Lawton, 1983)
61. (Sheehan & Guzzardo, 2008)
62. (Collins, Goldman, & Rodriguez, 2007)
63. (Zautra, Potter, & Reich, 1998)
64. (Mehrabian, 1980)
65. (Lazarus, 1991)
66. (Russell, 2003)
67. (Labouvie-Vief & Medler, 2002, p. 582)
68. (Golant, 1986)
69. (Golant, 2011b)
70. (Hammarström & Torres, 2012)
71. Earlier reported in (Golant, 2011b, p. 8)
72. (Porter, 2008, p. 174)

Part II

Aging in Place

Bane or Blessing?

3

THE POWERFUL INFLUENCES
FOR AGING IN PLACE

Older people overwhelmingly prefer to age in place—to stay in their homes or apartments as they age, rather than move to new settings. . . . A long-time {occupied} residence is more than just a building; it is the site of memories and a place to welcome friends and family. It represents familiarity—with people and community resources, the location of the light switches, and the local shortcuts—as well as privacy, control, and stability amid life changes, such as widowhood or declining health.[1]

Aging in place has become the *residential normalcy* of the masses.[2] Most older Americans now live in dwellings they purchased or began renting much earlier in their lives and then opted not to move. Like buy-and-hold investors in stock markets, they believe that they will achieve the greatest returns and claim their "sweet spot to live" by staying put. Of course, as in the stock market, there will be rough patches that change the fundamentals and values of their holdings. Disrupted lifestyles, undesirable changes in their dwellings, neighborhoods, and communities, and debilitating personal declines and losses are the hallmarks of aging. But despite these unsettling life events, older Americans are usually reluctant to move. They have strong emotional ties with their places of residence.

AGING IN PLACE AND RESIDENTIAL PATTERNS

Americans aging in place are predominantly homeowners[3] who are especially reticent about selling their properties.[4] As one group of experts explains,

45

The current cohorts of older people have benefited greatly from the housing opportunities made available over the post–Second World War era by increasing real incomes, declining real costs of housing, readily available housing finance, and tax concessions and direct subsidies for home-buying.[5]

Even as the homeownership rate of Americans overall decreased sharply between 2005 and 2013 (from 69% to 65%) because of the economic recession and housing market crash that began in 2007, the homeownership rate of older people was relatively stable. As of 2011, 82% of householders aged 65–74 and 79.5% of householders 75 years and older owned their dwellings (81% of householders aged 65 and older).[6] After age 85, however, homeownership rates decline more rapidly. Couples are more likely to be homeowners than single people, and White older adults are more likely to be owners than those in minority groups.[7]

About 55% of older homeowners have lived at the same address for 20 or more years.[8] Even when they do relocate from their dwellings, the majority still plant themselves in nearby destinations, usually in the same or adjacent county. Moreover, they typically purchase another home.[9] Consequently, they often end up aging in place even longer in their same communities. These staying-put behaviors are especially characteristic of older homeowners living in rural counties and smaller metropolitan areas (less than 250,000 people).[10]

Older renters, on the other hand, occupy their dwellings for a much shorter time, and only 15% have lived 20 or more years in their current buildings.[11] However, renting is increasingly likely after age 75,[12] when own-to-rent transitions become more common.[13]

THE SUBURBAN AGE BOOM

In 2011, U.S. householders age 65 and older were predominantly metropolitan or urban dwellers, with only 26% of homeowners and 18% of renters living in rural counties. Additionally, about two-thirds of older metropolitan dwellers (71% of homeowners and 50% of renters) were living in suburban neighborhoods.[14] Most moved to these locales earlier in their lives and when advancing careers, higher incomes, and larger families spurred them to move again, it was usually not back to city or rural locations but to other suburbs.

Consequently, two generations of adults age 65 and older predominantly occupy suburban areas. In 2011, these 12.5 million households included the G.I. Generation, born in 1924 or earlier (also called the Greatest Generation), and the Silent Generation (sometimes called the Great Depression and War Baby generations), born from 1925 to 1945. Altogether, almost half of the suburban older population (47%) is aged 75 or older, and they are especially likely to be homeowners (about 82%).

Their demographic imprint is particularly apparent in the oldest or first-tier inner U.S. metropolitan suburbs, those built before World War II and during the rapid suburban growth of the 1950s and early 1960s. Here we find countless building and neighborhood enclaves of older people. However, unlike the clusters of older people found in options such as planned active adult communities or assisted living communities, which are the deliberate inventions of elder housing and care developers, these residential concentrations have demographic origins. They are a result of the residential inertia of the old, the selective departures of the young, and the attraction of these places to newer populations of older people.[15] In recognition of these distinctive population dynamics, experts have labeled these residential settlements *naturally occurring retirement communities* (NORCs).[16]

But these residential patterns are just the leading edge of a suburban age wave. Beginning in 2011, our suburbs became the home of yet another generation of older adults as our oldest baby boomers (born from 1946 through 1964) began celebrating their 65th birthdays. They constitute the first "truly suburban generation"[17] of older Americans, because they did not arrive from our city centers or rural areas; rather, they have lived their entire lives in the suburbs.

Based on the most current U.S. Census growth projections,[18] from 2010 to 2020 our suburbs will witness a massive increase—close to 50%—of boomers aged 65 to 74. As they age over the next two decades (2020 to 2040), the number of those in their mid-70s and older will double, and by 2040 almost one in five of our older suburban occupants will be age 85 or older.

Moreover, if history is a guide, most of these aging baby boomers will never leave suburbia.[19] Only a small share will return to the cities. Over the period 2012–2013, for example, the residential moves by older people within the United States resulted in net losses of 81,000 people age 65 and older in our principal cities (i.e., the largest core cities of metropolitan statistical areas) and net gains of 115,000 in this age group in our suburbs (the remainder area of metropolitan statistical areas).[20]

OLDER PEOPLE FEEL SATISFIED WITH WHERE THEY LIVE

AARP regularly carries out consumer surveys that show how older Americans are happy with where they live, want to stay put,[21] and have high levels of residential satisfaction—especially homeowners.[22] Those who most feel this way tend to live in aesthetically pleasing, larger, and better-maintained dwellings.[23] They also feel that their neighborhoods are attractively landscaped, safe, crime free, well maintained, and architecturally attractive, and they report good relationships with nearby residents. They can easily access their everyday needs, particularly shopping, healthcare, and places of worship. These places are affordable and have lower taxes and an overall lower cost of living.[24]

But not all studies agree. One national investigation showed that apartment dwellers age 70 and older were actually more satisfied than homeowners because they enjoyed the reduced upkeep demands of their accommodations, such as home maintenance and yard work.[25]

Predictably, different residential features satisfy rural and urban older adults. Rural residents emphasize their favorable community life and their natural amenities: weather, scenery, and closeness to nature. However, they complain more than urban dwellers about the lack of job opportunities and less access to shops and restaurants.[26] Urban residents, on the other hand, enjoy the accessibility of shops and restaurants and the proximity of educational and cultural facilities. However, they complain more about their high cost of living and their divisive community politics.

Despite their insights, these telephone-based national surveys have inherent limitations. They include only the responses of older people who are willing and able to participate in polls. Consequently, they often fail to adequately capture the extent to which the very old, ethnic or minority groups, the physically frail, and the very poor feel differently about their places of residence. Moreover, their conclusions are only as complete and thoughtful as the interviewer's questions.

Unfortunately, it is prohibitively expensive to conduct surveys that ask the range of questions necessary to assess fully the reasons for why older people stay put. And although open-ended qualitative[27] interviews would better inform us about the reasons for older people's strong emotional connections to their residential settings, they would rely on smaller samples and thus have less scientific validity. Still, these inquiries reveal that the aging-in-place behaviors of older Americans are a consequence of the powerful influences of their places of residence.

THE STRONG APPEAL OF THE FAMILIAR

A good knowledge of where they live is a strong incentive for older people to stay put in their dwellings, neighborhoods, and communities because they can more easily achieve their material and social needs. If they move, they give up all of the advantages of living in known physical surroundings, with favorite shops and services, reliable friends and neighbors, and affiliations with religious or fraternal groups.[28]

In these familiar environs, older adults can usually accomplish their everyday tasks more quickly and effectively and with minimal mental and physical energy. When they have to make home repairs, they are far more likely to know whom to call. They do not have to think very hard about where to shop and eat, where to get medical care, and where to have fun. They have developed well-honed mental maps of their community's transportation routes and the shortcuts to reach their destinations. This knowledge can help blunt many of the driving difficulties that will accompany their physical or cognitive declines, perhaps adding many years to how long they can drive their cars. Altogether, living in a familiar place increases their feelings of efficacy and competence—and thus their residential mastery.[29]

Older people feel especially secure in their long-occupied dwellings. When they lose electricity and must negotiate their surroundings in the dark, they do not panic. They know where everything is and how to negotiate the turns, steps, and hallways. Older people cannot easily acquire this spatial competence in a new house or apartment; it takes time.

Older people especially dislike the prospects of occupying a place where they do not know anyone. They have palpable fears of having to make friends anew. They fret over the prospects of eating alone in a restaurant or sitting by themselves in a theater. They worry about being sick or anxious without a reliable shoulder to cry on. The prospects of not knowing anyone weigh especially heavily on the alone and unmarried.

Consequently, even the most confident older adults question why they should risk living in a different community where they feel like permanent visitors. Fear of estrangement often trumps any benefits they might realize by moving to a new dwelling and neighborhood because they would feel like a fish out of water.[30]

Older people want to enjoy trusting relationships. They want to feel confident that their transactions and relationships are fair, honest, and predictable. This is true whether they are receiving affection or love from another person, purchasing or contracting for products, or obtaining the supportive services of a home care agency.[31] It often takes years to establish such trusting networks, and it is more difficult in a new community where older people feel like out-of-towners.[32]

Older people also find it enabling to know that they can return to a familiar destination. This means they can enjoy vacations away, second homes, and snowbird and sunbird escapes, because they are confident that after these temporary sojourns, they have return tickets to their own reliable piece of geography.[33] This fear of losing a familiar residential anchor and experiencing feelings of placelessness deters them from moving. As philosopher and architect Norberg-Schulz aptly expressed,

> The word "home" simply tells us that any man's personal world has a centre. . . .
> The centre represents to man what is known in contrast to the unknown and
> somewhat frightening world around.[34]

Becoming homeless is the ultimate placeless experience. Although this is outside the experience of most of America's older adults, it is rare for a week to go by without reports of people losing their homes to fire, floods, or financial scams. This once unfathomable nightmare became the reality for thousands of older people who lost their homes because of the 2007–2010 foreclosure epidemic. It was a sad outcome for Louisiana and New Jersey residents after natural disasters such as Hurricane Katrina and Superstorm Sandy. On any given night, thousands of older people cannot claim a permanent mailbox and are living on the street, in temporary shelters, drop-in centers, emergency accommodations, and public shelters.[35]

ATTACHMENT FEELINGS TOWARD PERSONAL BELONGINGS

Older people feel strongly attached to the material possessions in their dwellings.[36] These feelings are often no less powerful than those that connect them to their closest family members and friends. Despite our throwaway society, most Americans, by the time they are in their 60s, have accumulated an incredible amount of books, clothing, childhood toys, furniture, dishes, artwork, religious items, photos, and memorabilia.[37]

So why do older people have such potent attachments to their material possessions? Research suggests a litany of reasons (Figure 3.1).[38] Older boomers construe their dwellings and everything in them as treasured archeological evidence of their pasts. These artifacts constitute reliable material signposts that document the history of their dwelling occupancy and the repository of their remembered life events, including their family and friendship relationships, events, and activities.[39] This explains why, in one study, a chair generated such strong emotional connections for its widowed owner. It conjured up very pleasurable memories of her recently deceased husband, who had built it.[40] These attachments extend not just to material environments but also to pets. Older people often emphasize how sad they would be if they had to give up their pets, a possible scenario if they move to another address, especially to many planned senior housing options that disallow pets.[41]

Figure 3.1. Why people acquire possessions (Ekerdt, et al., 2004)

Things Seem Useful: "People maintain some belongings because they satisfy a need or help manage everyday life—if not today, then on some probable occasion."

Things Are Worth Money: "Objects might be kept for no other reason but that they could be converted into cash."

Things Give Pleasure: "People judged some belongings to be beautiful or delightful in their own right . . . and also served as prompts to the imagination."

Things Represent Us: "Belongings, singly but also composed into sets or ensembles, express our meanings or feelings . . . reinforce our conformity or uniqueness . . . and remind us who we are and tell our story to others. Things can also be retained as material biography, memorializing personal occasions, relationships, achievements, ways of engagement in the world, and past selves."

Things Conjure the Future: "People keep things that they have not explored, used, or incorporated."

Social Reciprocity to Gift Lovers: "Things received as gifts remind their keepers of past occasions or emotions, but some gifts can carry an obligation to conserve the gift and so perpetuate a bond with the giver. Keeping things is keeping ties."

Responsibility to Forebears: "Heirlooms are legacies, literally 'emissaries' sent from the past into the present. The conservation of heirlooms immortalizes forebears and ensures the continuity of family history."

Conservation Is a Virtue: "Some people 'never throw things away' [and have] a strong moral compulsion to retain things that might be useful, if not to the saver, then to someone else."

Because They Can: "Americans dwell in ever larger containers wherein the convenience of storage exceeds the inconvenience of decision making about one's goods. For example, the average size of new homes sold in the United States grew from 983 square feet in 1950 to 1,500 square feet in 1970 to 2,265 square feet in 2000."

The construction of their autobiographies from their possessions[42] is especially valuable for those older residents who have forgotten not just the minutiae of their pasts but also the major events.[43] Moreover, older people can have these experiences on their terms.[44] They can decide what and why to remember. Consequently, if only for fleeting moments, older people have control over what they experience, and they feel masters of their environments.

Older women in particular may have stronger attachment emotions than men, because in their traditional gender roles of homemaker, wife, and mother, they invested a large amount of their past lives in their dwellings and feel special connections to their personal belongings—especially if they are now living alone.[45] For those with strong religious or ethnic affiliations, possessions are also reminders of their highly valued cultural roots, even if their influences have weakened over time.[46]

These material artifacts are more than just a way to channel memories about their past lives. They also allow older people to refamiliarize themselves with their successful achievements and perhaps also their failed hopes and goals.[47] They trigger the remembering and assessment of the successes and failures that have defined their lives. Their possessions become catalysts for their introspection, contemplation, and reminiscence, what some gerontologists call life reviews, which they consider psychologically healthy and conducive to aging successfully. In the words of the humanist Tuan, *"Our fragile sense of self needs support, and this we get by having and possessing things because, to a large degree, we are what we have and possess."*[48]

The attitudes and behaviors of their adult children may further fuel the attachments older people have to their material worlds. Even as they have left their family homes and established their own independent households, their children may harbor strong emotional bonds to the places where they were raised. Their connections then motivate their parents to age in place. One study reported the story of a young woman who expressed apprehension that her parents were selling their house. *"She feared that, if all of the old objects, furnishings, and rooms were gone, her memories would disappear as well."*[49]

These strong attachments help explain why many people in late life fear a serious breach in their emotional comfort and mastery zones if they break these autobiographical connections with their pasts and relocate elsewhere.[50] They fear losing their ability to conjure up those sources of pleasure from their remembered pasts—memories that now frame their self-perceptions. One might argue that older people can take their possessions and move them to another dwelling, but separating these possessions from their original contexts (i.e., their current dwellings and rooms) would irreparably weaken their past connections and in turn their most appealing qualities.

PRIDE IN WHERE THEY NOW LIVE

I still remember when a high school teacher asked my class to explain the difference between a house and a home. Most of us stammered out unsatisfactory answers, emphasizing the importance of the physical appearance and artifacts of our dwellings, neighborhoods, and communities. We lacked the intellectual sophistication to argue that a person's home is not merely physical shelter, a street address, a way to protect oneself from the elements, or a place where we could be near friends or family; rather, our dwellings become our identity bracelets that communicate to others who we are.

Studies continually remind us that how older people judge their lives depends on the opinions of others: family, friends, work associates, and so on. However much we dislike our society's indicators of success, a person's material possessions are one important basis for these opinions.[51] This explains why older people are concerned about what others think about their residential environments. If by their 60s they are not occupying dwellings and neighborhoods that mirror their achievements or accomplishments, then they reasonably fear that others, whose opinions they value, will consider them failures. [52]

Consequently, when older people exhibit pride in where they live, these are not merely feelings that express their residential satisfaction or pleasure.[53] Rather, they are

Figure 3.2. The proud widow aging in place

An older woman in her late 80s, Mrs. Jones now lives alone because her husband, a very famous cardiac surgeon, died a year ago. She lives in a beautiful house of more than 5,000 square feet in an attractive, upper-class neighborhood. Yet by most objective indicators, this house is no longer appropriate for her. Diagnosed with congestive heart failure, she almost never climbs to the second floor. In fact, she uses only the kitchen, living room, bedroom, and bathroom, an area of less than 1,000 square feet—the size of a modest one-bedroom apartment. Given the actual amount of space she uses, heating and cooling the house are needlessly expensive. Property taxes are also high. Her home maintenance expenses are eating into her savings. Fortunately, she can still rely on a trustworthy fix-it guy who is indebted to her husband for saving his life. However, he has recently informed her that he's thinking of retiring, and she will have to find a replacement. Mrs. Jones never learned how to drive, and because her gated suburb is miles away from the closest transit stop, even getting groceries is difficult.

Most of Mrs. Jones's social life revolved around her husband's professional friends, and their relationships have waned. Additionally, she has outlived most of her own friends, and few acquaintances live close by. One might have expected Mrs. Jones to move after her husband's death. She could find more affordable quarters that are better suited to her needs. Rather, she stays. How does she rationalize staying put, given all the reasons she has to move?

Mrs. Jones admits that she still very much regards herself as the doctor's wife, with all the status that goes with that past relationship. Thus, she is loath to abandon this dwelling because her material world reminds her and others that she is still a surviving spouse of a doctor. This strong emotion—pride in her house and neighborhood—is what powers her inertia. Leaving, she would lose the one piece of tangible evidence of her successful life and risk a major hit to her personal status and self-esteem.

emotional declarations that their abodes are showcasing their competent, worthy, and successful lives and in turn helping them to feel positive and approving about themselves. When older people occupy residential settings that affirm their self-worth, they can be very reluctant to move elsewhere, as the story in Figure 3.2 illustrates.

THE JOY OF THE STATUS QUO

How older people view novelty or variation in their lives can powerfully influence how much pleasure they get from their place of residence. Some older people have personalities that predispose them to favoring the status quo. They feel better when they live in a place where the events and physical surroundings remain largely the same, predictable, and uneventful. They enjoy their ritualistic everyday activities (see Chapter 2) and are loath to move and risk ending them. For these older people, redundancy is good.[54] The threat of losing these predictable and foreseeable things and relationships is what prevents them from moving elsewhere, however dysfunctional their current residential environments may be. Constancy, not change, is the hallmark of an enjoyable place because under these circumstances older adults feel most in control.

At the other extreme are older people who feel invigorated and happy when novel, unexpected, and challenging experiences and activities continually flood their senses. For them, aging in place in their current residence, especially after they no longer need to live near a workplace, is a prescription for boredom.[55] They flourish when their surroundings are continually changing.

Still, we must be careful about equating boredom with staying put. Older people who enjoy variation and change can still feel tightly bound to their current place of residence even as their dwellings and neighborhoods change little. They may feed their thirst for the new and stimulating by participating in new activities in their communities. Consider the residents of large, population-dense, bustling, culturally-rich, and population-diverse urban metropolises—such as New York, San Francisco, Boston, or Chicago—who can easily enjoy a continual stream of novel and stimulating leisure and recreational experiences.

Similarly, older adults with stimulus-seeking personalities who live in rural areas may be revitalized by their changing seasonal landscapes, the ebb and flow of tourist activities, or the complexities of nature itself. Even older recluses may vicariously experience variation in their lives by reading new plots, historical analyses, and freshly portrayed characters in books.

Others with more adventuresome personalities are comfortable staying put because they satisfy their need for variation by frequently taking vacations to get away from their uneventful turf.[56] These seasonal movers include the snowbirds who escape their winters by spending several months in states such as Florida, Arizona, and Texas, where they often have vacation homes. One such group are known as cruisers because they enjoy navigating by boat for several months of the year on waterways such as the Atlantic Intracoastal Waterway (e.g., from Key Largo, Florida, to Gloucester, Massachusetts).[57]

MOVING AND THE FEAR OF LOSING SELF-IDENTITY

Older people are reluctant to move from their current homes because they fear that they will find themselves in a place where "nobody knows their name,"[58] as a stranger with no history. This is a powerful deterrent because older people dread having to confront people who know nothing about them. In a different community, they risk finding themselves in the same social bind as single people trying to impress on their first dates. They especially worry that no one will acknowledge that they have had successful, productive, meaningful, and valuable lives. Because their concept of themselves *"no longer receives automatic reinforcement,"*[59] older people worry that they will have to establish new personal identities to gain recognition and acceptance. But this also means they must critically re-examine their accomplishments and the value of their lives. They worry that this self-scrutiny may be painful or unpleasant and leave them with their own doubts about their worthiness.[60]

This explains why psychologists[61] speak of a prospective change in residential settings as potentially destabilizing to an individual's sense of self. Having to prove yourself again and to question whether you led a successful life is a strong deterrent to relocating, even to what otherwise might be a more appealing place to live. Any pleasurable experiences older people might have in a new location take a back seat to assaults on their sense of their self-worth that will push them out of their residential mastery zones.[62]

Those holding on to their current abodes enjoy a different reality. They typically have a network of friends who know them quite well—their strengths and weaknesses, their habits and quirks. They accept them for who they are, whatever their physical traits, unorthodox lifestyles, past screw-ups, annoying behaviors, or personality flaws. They appreciate them as valuable members of their religious congregations. Not having to always impress others or demonstrate that they are really good and reliable friends or valuable members of their community saves these older adults time and energy and removes a great deal of anxiety from their everyday lives.

A POWERFUL NEED FOR PRIVACY AND TERRITORIAL CONTROL

Older Americans value their privacy. They want to occupy places where they choose their contacts and interactions and determine who watches and monitors them. We have many expressions for such territorial control: "my turf," "my place," "a man's home is his castle," "defensible space," "mine versus yours," and "insiders versus outsiders." Reminiscent of the castle-moats of Medieval times, we use various strategies to control who can gain access to our dwellings, neighborhoods, and communities.[63] These include door peepholes, dwelling alarm and visual surveillance systems, doormen, fences, landscaping and land use barriers, no-trespassing signs, and gated communities staffed by round-the-clock security personnel.

Many older Americans fear that if they relocate elsewhere, they will lose this privacy and find themselves in a place where others will continually infringe on their personal spaces. This is particularly true of older people who are considering moving to a family's dwelling or to a planned senior housing option, such as an independent living or assisted living community, but also an active adult community (Chapter 10).

The oldest adults may put a higher premium on protecting their privacy because they feel physically or mentally less able to defend themselves from unwelcome intrusions.[64] Such defensive postures are more salient if they have previously experienced a home robbery or have had demeaning contacts with dishonest, unfriendly, irritating, or abusive people. And to the chagrin of many experts—who laud the virtues of intergenerational relations—many older adults seek boundaries between themselves and younger people, whom they sometimes view as unsympathetic or even hostile to their lifestyles (Chapter 10).[65]

Our understanding of human development may help explain the exclusionary responses of the old. The aforementioned socioemotional selectivity theory (Chapter 2) argues that aging adults selectively interact with a much smaller but salient group of familiar friends, family members, and confidants, whom they feel particularly close to and trust, while discarding their more peripheral and less-reliable social contacts and disengaging from the physical or mental intrusions of others.[66]

Older people especially want to regulate the social interactions in their dwellings. The dwelling is the one physical arena where they have the best chances of enjoying their solitude,[67] avoiding conflicts or miscommunications, being their unpretentious selves, and escaping from the *"tensions of social life."*[68] As one scholar put it, the dwelling is the one place where

> one is free to withdraw into the cocoon of one's private home and yard and exclude unwelcome aspects of today's hectic world. One is free to dream in peace.[69]

ECONOMIC WELL-BEING AS A PREDICTOR OF RESIDENTIAL INERTIA

CONFOUNDING EXPLANATIONS

The residential inertia behaviors of older adults may reflect less the attractions of their current residences than the lack of favorably appraised and affordable housing alternatives (Chapter 9).[70] Despite the many unsuitable features of their dwellings or neighborhoods, older people do not move because they are *"stuck in place."*[71] Absent solutions from both the public and the private sectors, these more vulnerable older individuals are left with no relocation options.

Perhaps surprisingly, it is often difficult to disentangle these influences because of the less predictable and straightforward roles played by economic factors in the aging-in-place decisions of older adults. For example, studies have found that destinations with a lower cost of living may not offer a sufficient incentive for older people to move. Similarly, the prospect of paying lower inheritance and estate taxes or lower sales tax rates in another state or county is not a strong motive for moving.[72] And older people will even reject rent-free living in an adult child's dwelling because they do not want to give up their privacy and independence.[73] Other research argues that homeowners with low incomes will still stay put because they *"are protected from potential rapid increases in rents that they might face if they sold and entered the rental market."*[74]

It is also difficult to predict whether older people with burdensome dwelling costs will move (see Chapter 4).[75] Experts explain that Social Security recipients can weather increases in their housing costs because they receive a reliable source of monthly income that annually adjusts upward to account for higher costs of living in the United States.[76] This was particularly true between 1982 and 2003, when their benefits increased on average by 23%.[77]

Others explain that they cope not by moving, but by cutting back on other expenses, such as delaying house repairs, reducing their utility costs, or delaying other personal expenses. Alternatively, they return to work, often part-time. Still others increase their credit card debt burdens. Bankruptcy filings of older people have risen since 2000, often because of their unsustainably large credit card loan balances.[78]

The steadily increasing property values starting in the mid-1990s and through the mid-2000s also contributed to older homeowners' residential inertia. The single most important source of wealth for older Americans is the equity in their owned homes. Home equity is the appraised or selling value of the owned dwelling minus what the owner still owes on any mortgage. Older homeowners feared that if they sold their dwellings in a rapidly appreciating housing market—and at the time there seemed to be no upper limit—they would miss out on a significant increase in their dwelling equity, or what economists call an opportunity cost. And if they did sell in a heated market and wanted to downsize into a smaller dwelling, they worried about paying an inflated price for their new property. But higher house prices influenced them in another way. They were more likely to remodel their dwellings, confident that they could recoup their expenses when they later sold their homes.

ECONOMIC THEORY

Economists theorized that at older ages, homeowners would sell their dwellings to start "consuming" or using their equity to fund their living costs.[79] This seemed a reasonable prediction because older homeowners were usually mortgage free, and the major source of their wealth was tied up in their dwellings. In practice, however, older homeowners do not usually use the equity in their homes to finance their retirements, and higher proportions are entering old age with substantial mortgage obligations (Chapter 4). Rather, the evidence shows that *"nearly all homeowners have held on to most of the equity accumulated in their homes through their old age and only a few tap into it before they die."*[80] Confirming these patterns, a 2007 national poll asked 50- to 65-year-olds about their likelihood of using their home equity to pay for ordinary living expenses. Only 6% of homeowners in their early 60s said they were likely to do so. Of this small group, only 25% planned to age in place and take out a home equity or reverse mortgage loan (Figure 3.3).[81] A 2013 survey offers somewhat more support for the link between aging in place and home equity. In a national sample of people age 60 and older, 38% said they *"would consider using their home equity as a means to stay in their home."*[82]

National statistics confirm that the majority of older people are reluctant to use their home equity to address their financial needs. According to data from the 2011 American Housing Survey, only 7% of homeowners age 65 and older had home equity loans. Another 2% had reverse mortgages.[83] These are predominantly federally insured loans offered by the Federal Housing Administration (FHA) through the Home Equity Conversion Mortgage (HECM) program. These loans have made it possible for homeowners age 62 and older to *"consume their housing wealth"* and retain title to their dwelling.[84] They can receive a substantial amount of their home's equity in the form of monthly cash advances, line of credit advances, or an initial lump sum (Figure 3.3).

However, the small percentage of homeowners who have relied on their home's equity to help them age in place have had multiple motives for obtaining them. The original purpose of reverse mortgages was to offer financial relief to cash-poor and house-rich older homeowners (i.e., those who owned higher-valued homes, defined in one study as $125,000 or more).[85] These people were typically on low fixed incomes and were having difficulties paying their housing and other expenses, but they occupied dwellings—usually with mortgages that were paid up or almost paid up—of significant market value. The cash advances from these reverse mortgages made it financially easier for these homeowners to age in place.

Figure 3.3. The appeal of reverse mortgages (MetLife Mature Market Institute, 2009c; Munnell, 2014; and Stucki, 2013)

Background

In traditional or forward mortgages, homeowners take on debt to purchase their dwellings and then make monthly payments to reduce their loans. These payments usually include both a principal and an interest amount, so as homeowners pay back their loan they are rebuilding or adding to their equity. These forward mortgages are called falling loan balance, rising dwelling equity loans.

Reverse mortgages are just the opposite: They are rising loan balance, falling dwelling equity loans. Older homeowners are tapping or accessing funds from their homes' equity. Because they do not immediately pay back these loans (i.e., make monthly mortgage payments), interest accrues on their loan balances each month at a compounded rate. Consequently, over time the home equity of these borrowers decreases, and their loan balances increase.

Older homeowners do not have to pay back their loans until they die, sell their homes, or fail to live in the home for more than 12 consecutive months (e.g., as a result of an extended stay in a nursing home). Lenders can also demand repayment if homeowners fail to pay property taxes or property insurance or do not keep their dwellings in good repair.

Two obvious factors influence the size of these homeowner loans. Homeowners can draw more equity when they occupy higher-valued dwellings and when their lenders charge them lower interest rates. A third factor influencing loan size is less intuitive. Other things being equal, younger borrowers will receive lower loan proceeds than older borrowers. The latter group is closer to death, and so the interest on the loan balance is compounding for a shorter period and is "consuming" less equity then is the case for younger borrowers with many more years to live. Along with these fundamentals, the loan amount depends on the particular reverse mortgage loan. Over time, the rising loan balance can exceed the value of the home, especially if house values decline or borrowers live in the house for an unexpectedly long time. However, because of the nonrecourse feature of reverse mortgages, the occupants (or heirs) are generally not required to pay any additional loan balance in excess of 95% of the selling value of the home.

The Home Equity Conversion Mortgage Program

Almost all reverse mortgages are offered by the Federal Housing Administration (FHA), through its Home Equity Conversion Mortgage (HECM) program. FHA insures all mortgages and guarantees that lenders will have their loans repaid regardless of the home equity remaining at repayment or the unpaid (consumer) loan balance. The program started in 1990, and during its first decade it originated fewer than 40,000 HECM loans. Loan volume increased steadily over time, especially in the early 2000s, and between 2007 and 2009 more than 300,000 loans were made. Loan volume started to decline in 2010, probably linked to the decline in home prices, less promising price appreciation prospects, and a more uncertain secondary market purchasing these securities. In 2013, only just more than 60,000 loans were made

Figure continued next page

Figure 3.3. *Continued*

(statistics from the National Reverse Mortgage Lenders Association, accessed at https://www.nrmlaonline.org/).

Older people eligible for these HECM products must be age 62 or older, their home must be their principal residence (i.e., not a vacation home or investment rented property), and the property must meet minimum property standards. Before receiving loans, homeowners must receive counseling from an FHA-approved agency to discuss program eligibility requirements, borrower obligations, financial implications, and alternatives. Consumers have no restrictions on how they use the money withdrawn from their home's equity. However, before closing on a reverse mortgage, homeowners must pay off all existing mortgage debt they have on their property (including home equity loans). Older homeowners may use the loan advances of their reverse mortgage to pay off this debt. This assumes, of course, that the values of their homes are significantly larger than their current mortgage loan balances (i.e., they are not underwater).

Except for occupants of dwellings with insufficient equity, all homeowners generally qualify for these loans irrespective of their incomes or credit scores, but the maximum amount of the loan is currently set at $625,500 in most locales. Because homeowners retain title to their properties, they are still responsible for paying their property taxes and property insurance as well as for keeping their homes in good repair.

Loans can be received in several ways:

- A *lump sum* payment at closing, immediately making cash available to the homeowner. Since 2008, older people could also use a HECM reverse mortgage to purchase their homes (HECM for Purchase). A substantial down payment is usually required, and the lender disburses a lump sum loan amount to finance the remaining selling price.

- Equal monthly payments for as long as at least one of the borrowers (e.g., a surviving spouse) lives in the home (*tenure payment plan*)

- Fixed or equal monthly payments for a fixed number of months (*term payment plan*)

- A *line of credit* that allows the homeowner to draw funds on an as-needed basis

- A combination of these options

The number and types of HECM products have varied historically. Typically, they differ because of the size of their upfront and ongoing loan and service charges, the maximum size of their loan amounts, whether older people were charged fixed or variable interest rates on their loan balances, and whether they could receive their loans as a lump sum or as monthly payments.

Downsides of Reverse Mortgages

- *"Reverse mortgages are complex products and difficult for consumers to understand"* (Consumer Financial Protection Bureau, 2012, p. 7). In particular, they fail to recognize that they are rising loan balance, falling equity instruments.

- Homeowners do not have a clear idea of what their loans are costing them because of the variable sizes of their loan advances and compounded interest charges as well as their accruing servicing, insurance, and closing costs.

- Counseling procedures have not always fully informed consumers of the intricacies and downsides of this loan.

- Homeowners still assume the usual financial and maintenance costs of homeownership: If they do not keep their homes in good repair or do not pay their property taxes and insurance, they risk losing their homes to foreclosure.

- When the loan comes due, older people are often ignorant of their obligation to pay off the mortgage with their own funds or through the sale of the home, leaving them (or their heirs) with little or no equity to pay for moving expenses and future medical or long-term care expenses.

- Some homeowners use their reverse mortgage cash payments for investing in financial products (including bank savings accounts), but are earning returns at a lower interest rate than they are paying for their reverse mortgage.

- If only one spouse is named as a borrower and then dies or needs to move, the surviving and nonborrowing spouse must immediately pay back the loan, which usually means selling the home. Some spouses are unaware of the importance of applying for reverse mortgages as co-borrowers. FHA-backed reverse mortgages issued on or after August 4, 2014 will allow the nonborrowing spouse to remain in the home after the borrower dies, if certain conditions are met (Bennett et al. v. Donovan, 2013 WL 5442154 [D.D.C. Sept. 30, 2013]).

- Older homeowners fail to consider moving alternatives where they will incur lower dwelling expense burdens and realize higher financial returns on their home equity after they sell their current dwelling and invest the proceeds (Golant, 2008b).

- Proceeds from a reverse mortgage may negatively affect the older person's eligibility for Supplemental Security Income or Medicaid benefits.

Over time, however, older homeowners changed how they used the funds drawn from their home equity. During most of the 1990s and 2000s, the dwellings owned by older people (and other age groups) enjoyed historically unprecedented increases in value. This incentivized banks and mortgage companies to offer late-middle-aged and older people low-interest home equity loans, including reverse mortgages (especially between 2006 and 2010).[86] They salivated over the home equity owned by Americans age 62 and older, which peaked at $4 trillion in the fourth quarter of 2006.[87] However, older homeowners became *more interested in using the equity in their homes to increase their future well-being* and to improve the quality of their lives.[88] This sometimes translated into their using reverse mortgage cash advances to purchase a second home nearby, which they enjoyed as vacation abodes and at the same time did not require them to move elsewhere to enjoy a retirement lifestyle. Other homeowners used these funds to plan ahead for future *unexpected expenses and emergencies.*[89] When home prices collapsed after 2007, most older homeowners again changed how they used their reverse mortgage proceeds. Many were coping with high household expenses and an increased amount of debt, and so they used reverse mortgages as a *"crisis management tool."*[90] They focused again on their immediate cash needs, and their loans were a way to reduce their credit card or mortgage debt.[91] Between 2010 and 2012, about 70% of reverse mortgage borrowers received all or most of their loan advances upfront at closing.[92]

How older people plan to use their housing wealth offers further insights. They view the equity in their dwellings as a last-resort emergency fund—a large piggy bank—to pay for end-of-life long-term care or catastrophic out-of-pocket medical expenses, especially if they outlive their savings and other assets. Thus, by holding on to their homes, they feel more confident they can depend on this future financial cushion. Others plan to leave their dwellings to their children as inheritance or to a favorite charity.[93] In effect, aging in place becomes an estate planning tool to ensure the transference of the older person's major source of wealth.

However, two studies offer counter-findings that support economists' theories that homeowners would sell their dwellings to start "consuming" or using their equity to fund their living costs. When older homeowners have wealthy adult children, they are more likely to sell their homes and become renters. Because they do not have to bequeath their wealth, they can use their dwelling's equity to finance their *own* retirements. Similarly, when they live in states with more lenient Medicaid eligibility rules, implying lower future long-term care expenses (Chapter 8), they consume more of their current assets.[94]

Looking to the future, some financial experts argue that four factors will account for why older people stay put in their homes, rather than move to smaller owned dwellings or rented apartments[95]:

- Selling their current houses will not yield an acceptable financial return.
- There will not be enough buyers for their current homes.
- Mortgage borrowing rates will be unacceptably high, thereby discouraging potential buyers of their houses.
- Affordable housing alternatives will become scarce.

THE NATIONAL ECONOMY: FURTHER INCENTIVES TO AGE IN PLACE

The great economic recession of 2007–2010 produced a confluence of historically unique factors that forced many older homeowners to age in place. After rising for a decade and a half, home values sharply declined, and older homeowners experienced a substantial reduction in the size of their home equity positions.[96] They had to confront an uncomfortable reality. If they sold their houses and condominiums during a depressed "undervalued" housing market, they would get unrealistically low prices. This would severely jeopardize their future retirement nest egg. Even when older people were willing to sell their homes, potential buyers were scarce. Dwelling financing became more difficult and was limited to buyers with the best credit ratings. Potential buyers legitimately worried that if they bought during this period, the values of their new purchases would continue to decline.[97]

Older people who could not sell their homes were especially disadvantaged if they were interested in relocating to senior housing and care options such as independent living communities, assisted living residences, and continuing care retirement communities. Realizing the equity from their homes was often the only way lower-income older adults could afford these alternatives (Chapter 11). The recession made this impossible.

The recession also interrupted the usual life course transitions of older Americans. They incurred large declines in their stock market holdings, smaller private pension benefits, and lower interest rate and dividend returns on their investment portfolios, savings accounts, and certificates of deposit.[98] They could also not easily refinance their mortgages or obtain traditional home equity lines of credit as sources of income. Feeling financially stressed and not willing to give up their steady employment income, they postponed their retirements. Between 2000 and 2010, the labor force participation rate of men aged 65 to 69 increased from 30.2% to 35.8%; more dramatically, for women aged 65 to 69, the rate increased from 19.9% to 26.4%.[99] When these older people held on to their jobs, it also meant that they were still shackled to residential locations accessible to their places of employment. Job location is a major reason for why people (of all ages) choose where to live. Thus, even if they could sell their houses, they were reluctant to quit their jobs and move to another location with its uncertain employment opportunities.

The higher age requirement (age 66) to qualify for full Social Security benefits also helped delay their departure from the workforce and again motivated them to stay put. More generally, they could work longer because their service-oriented jobs did not require the physical prowess of past generations of blue-collar workers.[100] Younger people, also casualties of the recession, offered yet another reason for older adults to stay put. Because of their high unemployment and dwelling foreclosure rates, they looked to their older parents for free temporary accommodations.

All told, the economic recession increased the likelihood that late-middle-aged and older people would stay in their current dwellings. Between 2005 and 2009, the mobility rate of U.S. homeowners age 55 and older decreased by almost 38%.[101] After the recession ended, however, the overall migration rate of this group increased.[102]

Future events may present yet another basis for the residential inertia of older people. As the current housing market recovers, experts fear that large numbers of retiring age 60 and older baby boomers will try to sell their houses, flooding the market.[103] This will produce a historically high ratio of older sellers to younger buyers, a housing market imbalance that will suppress home prices. In such a scenario, many older homeowners will again be reluctant to sell their dwellings because of the intolerably low prices offered by potential buyers.[104]

Two other economic scenarios would also contribute to older people's residential inertia. First, a desire to move to rental accommodations by downsizing baby boomers and by younger populations shunning homeownership would result in a historically high demand for multifamily rental accommodations that would exceed the supply in most metropolitan housing markets. The resulting rise in apartment rents would deter large numbers of older homeowners from making own-to-rent transitions. Only a substantial increase in the supply of publicly subsidized rental units might mitigate these consequences (Chapter 9). Second, a recovering housing market may not produce sufficient dwellings to meet homeownership demand by middle-aged and older people, thereby driving up selling prices. In this scenario, the prospects of enjoying a larger home equity position would deter older people from moving, as would the higher prices they would have to pay for downsized accommodations.

HOLDING ON DESPITE LOSSES AND DECLINES

THE DECISION TO AGE IN PLACE

When older people experience age-related declines in their health and functioning, they still strongly favor their current dwelling environments.[105] They argue that they will have more control over who delivers their care and the frequency of this assistance. They also expect to get more personalized treatment than if they relocated to an assisted living community or nursing home facility. Receiving care in their own home also gives them hope that their health and mobility will improve enough, or at least not decline further, so that they can still enjoy their later years. But even when their health deteriorates, older people prefer to die in the comfort of their homes than in an unfamiliar hospital or nursing home. Later chapters explain why the physical and cognitive limitations experienced by older people are not necessarily deterrents to their aging in place. We show that those with the best chances to remain in their current dwellings will have the following four advantages going for them:

- They will live in a dwelling that can be physically retrofitted and redesigned (e.g., grab bars, improved lighting, accessibility modifications) and equipped with smart home technologies (Chapter 6).
- They will have at least one devoted and compassionate family member to assist them full time, ideally around the clock (Chapter 7). This person either will live with them or will live close by (in the same neighborhood or county).[106] Members of ethnic (or foreign-born) groups (e.g., Hispanics, Asians) are more likely to have family members who are willing to fulfill these caregiving roles.[107] All family caregivers will be able to find respite care to relieve them temporarily of their burdensome caregiving duties (Chapter 8).
- They occupy places where they can afford a growing array of home- and community-based care services offered by the private sector that can help them to better manage their chronic health problems or compensate for their mobility limitations. Alternatively, if they have very low incomes and a paucity of assets, they will be eligible for publicly funded and community-based long-term services and supports (Chapter 8). They may also be able to occupy a very small share of government-subsidized affordable rental buildings with supportive services that enable their older tenants to age in place (Chapter 9).
- They will occupy "age-friendly" or "healthy aging" buildings, neighborhoods, or communities that offer their older residents a variety of infrastructure and service responses designed to make it easier for them to age in place (Chapter 9).

THE GROUPTHINK FACTOR

Older adults are now bombarded with a singular and unrelenting message: They should cope with their age-related health problems and impairments in their familiar dwellings.[108] The stakeholders who are communicating this groupthink mantra of aging in place[109] include professionals, government bureaucrats, the courts, academics, practitioners, the media, and the families of older people. They believe they know what residential and care decisions are best for America's older adults and readily stereotype alternative courses of action as inferior, uninformed, or ill-advised.

A nationally known columnist who writes frequently on issues of old age observes,

> But by now, aging in place, unrealistic for some, scary or unsafe for others and potentially very isolating, has become so entrenched as the right way to live out one's life that not being able to pull it off seems a failure, yet another defeat at a time when defeats are all too plentiful.[110]

Older people cannot turn on a TV, search on the Internet, read books about old age, or pick up a newspaper without getting this persistent stay-at-home message. AARP continuously broadcasts that its older members prefer to deal with their vulnerabilities in the comfort of their current dwellings. Unending TV commercials cajole older people to buy products to assist them. Well-known media stars—such as Gail Sheehy, Robert Wagner, Henry Winkler, and Fred Thompson—enthusiastically endorse home-based solutions and offer advice to struggling caregivers and those with financial difficulties.

Family members are criticized for allowing their loved ones to enter anything that smacks of a planned senior housing or care option (not just nursing homes). Hundreds of page hits on the Internet highlight family members who feel incompetent, irresponsible, and guilty because their mothers or fathers live in group residential care settings.

The private sector has greatly increased its offerings of home-based care and assistance—at least to older people who can afford them. One of the fastest-growing occupational groups in the United States—with the future holding even greater promise—is home care and custodial care workers.[111] So lucrative are these activities that several senior housing properties now operate supportive service programs not only for their in-house paying residents but also for older residents in nearby neighborhoods. We are also witnessing a strong demand for dwelling-installed technological devices, from home security equipment to devices that monitor older people's health status (Chapter 6). Older people, particularly the more wealthy, can now benefit from a very small but growing share of physicians who are willing to make house calls. Private long-term care insurance, once covering only the care offered in nursing homes, now underwrites the costs of services and care offered in ordinary homes and apartments.

Poor and vulnerable seniors are also targeted. Rather than subsidizing the costs of their nursing homes, many government programs now deliver affordable products, services, and assistance into their homes. The U.S. Department of Health and Human Services (particularly the Administration on Aging and the Centers for Medicare & Medicaid Services[112]) now fund a vast array of home- and community-based services: information, counseling, referral assistance, case management, and assessment services;

homemaker services; assistance with performing everyday activities; and medication management (Chapter 8). Several national charitable service organizations fund programs that deliver custodial and nursing services into the homes of lower-income seniors or make them available in adult day centers (Chapter 8). Programs target the family caregivers of older people, offering them information about the resources in their communities, counseling them on how to evaluate their loved one's needs, and providing financial assistance to make their tasks easier.[113] Federal court decisions have reinforced these policies. The 1999 Supreme Court decision *Olmstead v. L.C.* called on states to serve disabled people in the least restrictive and most integrated setting—that is, in home and community settings as opposed to institutions.

Various public policies also reduce the financial burdens of homeownership. The aforementioned FHA reverse mortgage program has enabled homeowners age 62 and older to obtain financial assistance by drawing down the equity from their dwellings. Most states also have property tax relief programs targeting low-income, disabled, or older homeowners. These either reduce the amount of property assessment that is subject to taxation or put a cap on the amount of owed property tax.[114] Some state and local governments and several federal programs offer loans or grants to defray the costs of home repair and modification initiatives of older homeowners,[115] and federal programs offer financial assistance to older homeowners to reduce their heating and cooling bills.[116]

Of course, those offering these solutions may not have unselfish motives. The private sector hopes to capture a financially lucrative elder consumer market that can afford their services and products. And state governments drowning in their long-term care expenditures believe it is cheaper for them to spend their dollars helping older people age in place than to pay for the same care in Medicaid-subsidized nursing home beds.[117] Even municipal governments have conflicting interests when they offer property tax relief to older homeowners to defray their dwelling costs and reduce the likelihood that they will move because of high taxes. By keeping these older people in their communities, local governments help to ensure that their dwellings are not purchased by younger families, who are far more likely to have school-aged children. Consequently, even though municipalities initially lose revenue because of this tax relief, they save a lot more money because they do not have to fund the public education of these additional students[118] and thus they *"avoid a school-funding crisis."*[119]

THE BOTTOM LINE

A confluence of strong psychological, social, economic, and political factors now accounts for the powerful attractions of older people's current abodes. At the same time, alternative residential choices do not present them with sufficient counteracting incentives to move. Consequently, even older people with chronic health problems and functional impairments want to stay put. Older Americans now believe that aging in place is their path to being in their comfort and mastery zones and achieving residential normalcy. Just in case they have any doubts, unrelenting and single-minded groupthink responses by stakeholders from all segments of American society are continually reassuring them. The next chapter argues that the residential inertia behaviors of many older Americans may be seriously flawed and not in their best interests.

NOTES

1. Susan Lanspery (*Encyclopedia of Aging,* 2002).
2. In its original usage, aging in place was simply a demographic indicator referring to older occupants staying put in one's ordinary rented or owned dwelling. The 1980s witnessed the most popularized and widespread interpretation of aging in place. It referred to older persons staying put in their ordinary homes and apartments, even in the face of major life-changing events—such as retirement, widowhood, and impairments. Beginning in the 1990s, aging in place started to encompass older persons staying put in any kind of housing arrangement, including independent living communities, active adult communities, and assisted living facilities. It was no longer just a demographic or household characterization that referred to older persons remaining for a sustained duration in the same place. Rather, it became a catch-all term to communicate the strong desire of aging boomers to avoid nursing homes.
3. (Golant, 2008d)
4. Most also live in single-family detached or attached dwellings (86%), about 8% in manufactured (mobile) homes, and the remainder in multifamily buildings. In this latter group, only 2% lived in larger (50 plus units) buildings
5. (Kendig, Clemson, & Mackenzie, 2012, p. 151)
6. (U.S. Department of Housing and Urban Development, 2013)
7. (Banerjee, 2012; Engelhardt, Eriksen, & Greenhalgh-Stanley, 2013)
8. 2011 U.S. Census American Housing Survey Data, accessed at http://www.census.gov/housing/ahs/
9. (Venti & Wise, 2001)
10. (Megbolugbe, Sa-Aadu, & Shilling, 1997)
11. 2011 U.S. Census American Housing Survey Data, accessed at http://www.census.gov/housing/ahs/
12. (Banerjee, 2012)
13. (Banerjee, 2012)
14. (U.S. Department of Housing and Urban Development, 2013)
15. (Golant, 1975)
16. (Hunt & Gunter-Hunt, 1985). NORCs should not be confused with NORC-SSPs, which integrate services into these residential settings (see Chapter 9).
17. (Frey, 2007)
18. Available at http://www.census.gov/population/www/projections/usinterimproj
19. (Engelhardt, 2006)
20. (U.S. Census Bureau, 2013)
21. (Saloman, 2010)
22. (MetLife Mature Market Institute, 2011a)
23. (Sabia, 2008)
24. (Pinquart & Burmedi, 2003; Prisuta, Barrett, & Evans, 2006)
25. (James, 2008)
26. (Prisuta, et al., 2006)
27. That is, where the respondents are not required to structure their answers according to the preconceived categories of researchers.
28. (Sabia, 2008; UnitedHealthcare, 2014)
29. (Golant, 1984)
30. (Netherland, Finkelstein, & Gardner, 2011, p. 277)
31. (Walker, et al., 2009)
32. (Fisher, Johnson, Marchand, Smeeding, & Torrey, 2007)
33. (Smith & House, 2006)
34. (Norberg-Schulz, 1971, p. 19)
35. (Shelter Partnership, 2008)
36. (Rubinstein, 1998)
37. This is far from an exhaustive list, of course. More categories can be found in (Csikszentmihalyi & Rochberg-Halton, 1981; Kamptner, 1989)

38. (Ekerdt, Sergeant, Dingel, & Bowen, 2004)
39. (Golant, 1984)
40. (Shenk, Kuwahara, & Zablotsky, 2004)
41. (National Consumer Voice for Quality Long-Term Care, 2012)
42. (Rowles & Ravdal, 2002)
43. (Krause, 2003)
44. (Klapp, 1986)
45. (Shenk, et al., 2004)
46. (Fried, 2000)
47. (Klapp, 1986, p. 75)
48. (Tuan, 1980, p. 472)
49. (Kamptner, 1989, p. 176)
50. (Kalish & Knudtson, 1976; Lieberman, 1975; Rowles & Ravdal, 2002)
51. (Kemper, 1978; Turner, 2007)
52. (Kemper, 1978)
53. (Sweaney, Mimura, Vanderford, & Reeves, 2006)
54. (Klapp, 1986)
55. (Klapp, 1986)
56. (Wolf & Longino, 2005)
57. (Hughes, 2007)
58. To crib a lyric from a once popular song.
59. (Cumming & Cumming, 1963, p. 48)
60. (Rodin, 1986)
61. (Hormuth, 1990)
62. (Magnusson, 1981)
63. (Altman, 1975)
64. (Diehl & Willis, 2003)
65. (Rosow, 1967)
66. (Carstensen, et al., 1999)
67. (Altman, 1975; Margulis, 2003)
68. (Margulis, 2003, p. 412)
69. (Stefanonovic, 1998, p. 42)
70. (Fisher, et al., 2007)
71. (Torres-Gil & Hofland, 2012, p. 222)
72. (Bakija & Slemrod, 2004; Duncombe, Robbins, & Wolf, 2003)
73. (Golant & Salmon, 2004)
74. (Munnell, et al., 2007, p. 2)
75. (Lehning, Smith, & Dunkle, 2013; Walker, 2004)
76. (Goda, Golberstein, & Grabowski, 2011)
77. (Goda, et al., 2011)
78. (Pottow, 2011)
79. (Venti & Wise, 2001)
80. (Masnick, Di, & Belsky, 2006, p. 492)
81. (Munnell, et al., 2007)
82. (UnitedHealthcare, 2013, p. 27)
83. (U.S. Department of Housing and Urban Development, 2013)
84. Some estimates of the number of older homeowners holding reverse mortgages are higher—in 2012, about 578,000 senior households, or more than 3% of homeowners age 65 and older. Testimony of Peter Bell, president of National Reverse Mortgage Lenders Association before the Subcommittee on Insurance, Housing & Community Opportunity, May 9 (2012).
85. (MetLife Mature Market Institute, 2009c)
86. (Masnick, et al., 2006)
87. (National Mortgage Professional Magazine, 2013)

88. (MetLife Mature Market Institute, 2012, p. 14)
89. (MetLife Mature Market Institute, 2012, p. 14)
90. (Stucki, 2013)
91. (MetLife Mature Market Institute, 2012)
92. (Munnell, 2014)
93. (Fisher, et al., 2007; Munnell, et., 2007)
94. (De Nardi, French, & Jones, 2014; Painter & Lee, 2009)
95. (Masnick, et al., 2006)
96. (Joint Center for Housing Studies of Harvard University, 2008)
97. (Masnick, et al., 2006)
98. (Golant, 2008d; Louie, Belsky, & McArdle, 1998)
99. (Kromer & Howard, 2013)
100. (Masnick, et al., 2006)
101. (Masnick, Will, & Baker, 2011)
102. (Frey, 2013)
103. (Myers & Ryu, 2008)
104. Selling a dwelling is usually possible even when sellers exceed buyers if the price is set low enough.
105. (National Consumer Voice for Quality Long-Term Care, 2012)
106. (Painter & Lee, 2009)
107. (Federal Interagency Forum on Aging-Related Statistics, 2012; Strohschein, 2011)
108. (Golant, 2009a)
109. (Janis, 1982).
110. (Gross, 2013)
111. (Smith & Baughman, 2007)
112. (Shirk, 2007)
113. These have included the Family and Medical Leave Act of 1993 (12 weeks of unpaid leave for those caring for a spouse, child or parent with serious health condition) and the National Family Caregiver Support Program (support services such as information, counseling, caregiver training, respite care, and supplemental services, such as assistive technologies), enacted under the Older Americans Act Amendments of 2000.
114. (Meyer, 2004)
115. For example, HUD's Community Development Block Grants and HOME block grants; Department of Agriculture, Rural Development Section 504 loan/grant program; Title III, Older Americans Act; and the Medicaid Waiver program (Joint Center for Housing Studies of Harvard University, 2014).
116. The LIHEAP program (Low Income Energy Assistance Program) administered by the Department of Health and Human Services/HHS as a state block grant
117. (Mollica & Morris, 2005)
118. (Meyer, 2004)
119. (Christopherson, 2005, p. 213)

4

Aging in Place

When Things Go Wrong

I'd rather rot in my own home.[1]

That's the bad part of longevity: everybody goes away.[2]

I wish my mom would leave her home and go some place. It would be so much better than her laying there worrying about whether the insurance bill gets paid, or if she should paint the house, or when the guy is coming to pull weeds in the back yard (although I've been doing that). Just seems like too much bull for mom to go through. She needs peace, not a bunch of worry.[3]

There sat this little lady, in the dark, in the corner, dried-up food plates in the kitchen. She hadn't eaten in a long time. She was just going to sit there and die.[4]

ALL IS NOT WELL

Chapter 3 offered a strong case for why older Americans aging in place feel they have found their sweet spots to live—their residential normalcy. However, counterevidence warns about overzealously celebrating these positive portrayals. Diverse sources of information, including academic studies, testimonials from professionals and staff working with older people as well as from families, and a growing catalog of journalistic accounts, tell very different, often tragic stories.

Failing to question these aging in place behaviors also unrealistically argues for a portrayal of human development that is unchanging or static, not unlike that espoused by the New Gerontology paradigm (Chapter 1). The erroneous assumption is that residential environments, once congruent with the lifestyles, capabilities, or self-concepts of older people during their younger years, will forever be compatible with aging lives. This preconceived viewpoint risks overlooking many of the older adults who occupy places that have become deleterious to their physical or psychological health.[5]

The families and friends of older people are usually the first to document the lives of older residents falling apart, sometimes joined by the accounts of in-the-trenches care workers. Less obvious informers may be their neighbors, who are alerted by an unmowed lawn, overflowing mailbox, or damaged roof. Sometimes the signs are more dramatic, as when an ambulance or police car shows up, an indication that the older occupant has fallen or a caregiver has abused her.

Journalists are unquestionably the most vocal messengers. They have often drawn our attention to those isolated older people who are undernourished, depressed, and living alone without help in inadequately heated or cooled dwellings. We might dismiss these accounts as exceptional, given that newspaper stories tend to report on the sensational and most egregious situations. However, it is not as easy to ignore the growing number of more rigorous studies by academics and other researchers.[6] They find that increasingly large numbers and higher percentages of older people have difficulty paying for their current housing costs, report feeling lonely and socially isolated, have difficulty getting to places in their community, feel unsafe walking in their own neighborhoods, and have trouble safely and effectively performing even their most routine activities of daily living.

These studies warn us that older Americans who stay put in their long-occupied dwellings often do not live in residential utopias. In the early 2000s, a landmark congressionally mandated commission[7] produced a comprehensive report of the unmet housing and care needs of older Americans and the inadequate responses of federal government policies. It recognized what was not widely appreciated at the time, which was that we could not neatly analyze elder housing and long-term care issues as if they were separate concerns. Rather, older people often have housing and care difficulties that together create far more intractable problems than if they had to cope with each alone. The report relayed the plight of older adults who were doubly jeopardized: They not only had difficulties paying for their housing costs and were uncomfortable in their oversized and physically substandard dwellings and inhospitable neighborhoods, but also were afflicted with cognitive and physical limitations, making it difficult for them to live independently.[8] The report was titled, aptly, the *Quiet Crisis in America*.[9] As members of the Greatest and Silent generations, these older people had stoically lived through an economic depression and the traumas of a major world war, and they chose not to broadcast their housing and care challenges.

Such findings force us to rethink conventional wisdom regarding the virtues of aging in place. Although many researchers laud the emotional rewards of strong residential attachments,[10] others argue that it is sometimes not psychologically or physically healthy for older adults to hold tightly to their material pasts.[11] So strong is their preoccupation with their material possessions and dwelling-related biographies that they deprive themselves of the possibilities of encountering new and more rewarding future experiences to improve their well-being, whether this includes better quality dwellings and neighborhoods, more care, or more enjoyable lifestyles.[12]

The inevitable conclusion is that proponents of aging in place groupthink are doing a great disservice to millions of older Americans now occupying inappropriate residential environments. This chapter seeks to correct this imbalanced view by reviewing what has gone wrong in the dwellings, neighborhoods, and communities of these aging-in-place residents.

Six categories of problems contribute to older people being out of their residential comfort or mastery zones:

- Unaffordable housing
- Aging and physically inadequate dwellings
- Unmet needs for long-term services, supports, and care for chronic health conditions
- Social isolation and loneliness
- Unsafe or inhospitable neighborhoods and communities
- Limited or unsafe transportation options

Unfortunately, some older people will find themselves simultaneously in several of these problem categories.

UNAFFORDABLE HOUSING

The dwelling expenses of older people are their single largest spending category and put them at the greatest risk of feeling financially vulnerable and out of their residential mastery zones. The Bureau of Labor Statistics used 2010 data[13] to estimate that the average home-related expenses of people age 65 and older[14] represented about 35% of their total household spending; however, they represented 43% of the household expenditures of those in the lowest income quartile (annual income under $16,208). In comparison, food, out-of-pocket healthcare, and transportation costs average, respectively, 12%, 13%, and 14% of their total expenditures.[15]

These dwelling expenditures often consume a very large share of their monthly household incomes, especially for renters, who are exposed to regular cost increases and who have generally lower incomes. Consequently, they often must cut back on their other household expenditures, including food, transportation, and healthcare.[16,17] In 2011, 61% of renters age 65 and older and 35% of homeowners age 65 and older paid more than 30% of their household incomes on housing (referred to as *moderate cost burdens*).[18] Some older people face higher dwelling expense burdens. About 36% of renters and 18% of owners pay monthly dwelling costs that amount to more than 50% of their incomes (referred to as *severe cost burdens*).[19]

Treating older adults as a homogeneous group understates affordability difficulties faced by certain subgroups. Fourth Age elders (mid-70s and older) are far more likely than Third Age elders (65–74 years old) to suffer both moderate and severe dwelling cost burdens.[20] To show how lower-income households are more at risk, a study by AARP Public Policy Institute categorized older households into income quartile subgroups: $0–$17,991, $17,991–$33,782, $33,782–$61,268, and $61,268 and higher. They also distinguished renters, owners without a mortgage, and owners still paying off a mortgage. The most financially burdened by their housing costs were the lowest income quartile of older adults (Figure 4.1). Particularly large shares of African-American and Hispanic older adults were in this category.[21] The other at-risk low-income subgroups included women, especially those who were unmarried (divorced, widowed, or never married) and older than age 85, and those who did not graduate from high school.[22] Dwelling tenure and mortgage status of this lowest-income group also were key predictors. About 72% of renters, 98% of mortgage holders, and 58% of people without mortgage obligations paid 30% or more of their incomes on their dwelling costs. In contrast, the respective percentages for the highest income quartile were 13%, 18%, and 0%.[23]

As large as these numbers are, they still underestimate the dwelling expenses of older homeowners because most national tabulations do not measure dwelling repair, upkeep, or upgrades, home modification, or remodeling costs, typically incurred in older dwellings. This means they do not capture the higher repair costs confronting a widow after the death of her husband, who had performed most home maintenance.[24] They do not include the costs of replacing an air and cooling system or a roof. They would also not include the one-time financial assessments levied by condominium associations on their owners, because of unexpected physical upgrades of their building's common areas.

Older people still living in the large and expensive-to-maintain dwellings they purchased in their younger years, when their households were larger, are also at greater risk of having intolerable dwelling costs. Yet older homeowners often do not share

Figure 4.1. Percentage of U.S. owners and renters age 65 and older with dwelling cost burdens, by income quartile, 2009 (AARP Public Policy Institute, 2011)

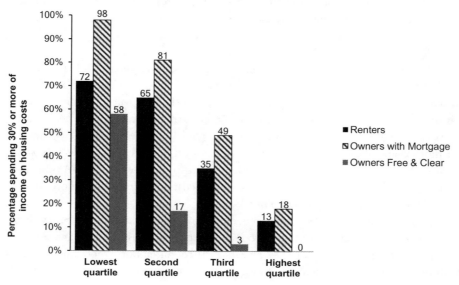

the view of experts who characterize them as overhoused.[25] They retort that they accommodate their unemployed children as houseguests and need their closet space for their possessions. Moreover, when they become physically impaired, they will be able to accommodate live-in caregivers to help them, thereby keeping them out of nursing homes.[26]

These national measures also tend to understate the shares of lower-income older people with both moderate and severe dwelling expense burdens who live in higher-cost housing markets throughout the United States, such as Boston, Los Angeles, San Francisco, and New York. A recovering U.S. economy also means rising rents and property taxes, especially for those occupying gentrifying neighborhoods.[27] By the same token, national indicators overstate the dwelling cost burdens of older rural residents, who are more likely to have paid off their mortgage loans and who typically benefit from a lower cost of living.[28]

Older people may be stressed paying for their monthly housing costs not because of high dwelling costs but because of declines in their income streams—a result of a job layoff, retirement, the loss of a spouse's income, reduced pension income, or declines in the interest rate returns on their bank savings accounts or CDs. Other times their financial pain results from their out-of-pocket medical, dental, prescription drug, and long-term care expenditures. About 20% of a 2013 national sample of people age 60 and older reported that it was very or somewhat difficult for them to pay for these monthly living expenses.[29]

THE "NEW" COST BURDEN OF OLDER HOMEOWNERS

Today's late-middle-aged and older homeowners are especially burdened because a historically high share have still not paid off their mortgages.[30] Consequently, they are entering old age having very stressful monthly expense obligations.[31] In 2010, 54% of homeowners age 55–64, 41% of age 65–74, and 24% of age 75 and older were still paying off their homes.[32] Compared with 10 years earlier, the percentage of homeowners age 75 and older holding mortgage debt quadrupled. In 2011, 14% of borrowers age 65–74 and 11% of borrowers age 75 and older also had underwater loans; that is, the amounts owed on their mortgage loans were greater than the current values of their properties.[33]

Far too many of these older homeowners were enticed by the easy mortgage lending standards of financial institutions that offered historically low interest rates and were willing to tolerate high loan-to-value ratios (i.e., someone buying a house with a large loan and little cash down) and longer payback periods. Some of these older homeowners were especially hard hit because they obtained adjustable-rate mortgages (ARMs). Consequently, the monthly interest on their loans became larger and more of a burden over time. Altogether, these lax lending practices contributed to a large increase in foreclosure and 90-day delinquency rates among the older population. In 2011, these bad loans represented almost 6% of the mortgage loans held by homeowners age 65 and older.[34] Consider the following situation:

> Edward Jordan is a typical homeowner with an ARM now in foreclosure. A
> 78-year-old retired post-office worker, Jordan has lived in his home in Bed-

ford-Stuyvesant, Brooklyn, since 1975. He was induced into refinancing his 6% fixed-rate mortgage with a "teaser rate" ARM, which started at 1% but jumped to 8% in just 2 months. From the outset, the loan was just a few dollars less than his Social Security income. But when the loan's interest rate reset, the monthly payments were double his fixed income.[35]

CASH-POOR AND HOUSE-POOR OLDER HOMEOWNERS

Some experts remain unconvinced. They contend that advocates inflate the number of older homeowners with dwelling expense burdens because they measure their economic status only by their income levels. Rather, a true measure of financial well-being should acknowledge the equity that older owners have in their dwellings, which is often substantial. The median home equity of homeowners age 65 and older in 2010 was $125,000, and they had a somewhat higher median net worth of $273,000.[36] Therefore, these experts argue that we should count older homeowners as dwelling expense burdened *only* when they are both income-poor *and* dwelling (equity) poor. They would exclude income-poor older households with high dwelling expense burdens occupying higher-valued and mortgage-free dwellings. To ease their financial stresses, these people should draw additional monthly income from their dwelling's equity through a reverse mortgage or home equity loan. Based on this argument, we would particularly focus on the dwelling expense burdens of subgroups such as low-income African-Americans who have a median equity of only $90,000 and manufactured home occupants with a median dwelling value of under $45,000. More generally, we should be most concerned about less-educated, unmarried, and Hispanic older adults who have a low median home equity. Their property values were especially hard hit as a result of the 2007–2010 economic recession and housing downturn.[37]

However, as emphasized in Chapter 3, whatever their home equity values, the majority of older people do not want to rely on this source of their net worth to pay for their everyday expenses, but rather as a last-resort fund to pay for their large future long-term care and medical costs or to leave as an inheritance. Consequently, older homeowners are more likely to cut back on other regularly incurring expenses than to tap into their home equity to pay for their dwelling costs.

AGING AND PHYSICALLY INADEQUATE DWELLINGS

Older homeowners aging in place occupy some of the earliest-built dwellings in the United States. In 2011, more than a third of their dwellings were at least 50 years old (built before 1960), and almost three quarters were at least 25 years old (built before 1984).[38]

We typically find these older dwellings in our early-established rural communities, particularly in the South, and in the older central cores of our metropolitan areas, particularly in the Northeast and Midwest.[39] We also find them in our oldest metropolitan suburbs, often called first-tier or inner-ring suburbs, which were built before World War II and during the rapid suburban growth of the 1950s and early 1960s.[40]

Many of these older suburbs are economically thriving and attractive, but others have the same social and economic problems as our urban core neighborhoods, including an aging housing stock, high poverty, slower (or negative) population growth, an aging infrastructure of roads and schools, and vacant commercial corridors.[41] Their older occupants are typically in their late 70s or older, have lower incomes, are less educated, live alone, and are overrepresented by African-Americans and Hispanics. Because of their higher ages, they are also more likely to have chronic health problems, mobility limitations, memory deficits, and vision and hearing problems.[42]

Older buildings are especially at risk of having three categories of physical deficiencies: physical disrepair requiring equipment or infrastructure upgrades; outmoded physical design features; and physical features incompatible with the mobility or sensory declines of their occupants. Altogether, these inadequacies make these dwellings not just less comfortable or less pleasurable places to live but also less safe and accessible, thereby reminding their older occupants of their age-related vulnerabilities and keeping them out of their residential mastery zones.[43]

PHYSICAL REPAIR AND UPGRADE NEEDS

Anything in older buildings can break down and need repairs. Many of these maintenance problems are predictable; others catch the older occupants unaware, such as when a strong thunderstorm causes property damage to an already vulnerable structure.[44] Some need drastic fixes, such as replacing the whole roof, rewiring part of the house, or buying a new air conditioning or heating system.

We find various types of hazards in these older dwellings, especially when their occupants maintain them poorly or have deficient hygiene habits. Poor ventilation, water leaks, and peeling paint increase the risks of exposure to dust, mold, dampness, lead, and air pollutants.[45] Poorly functioning furnaces may emit carbon monoxide. Deficient air and heating equipment put occupants at risk for hyperthermia or hypothermia.[46] Deteriorating and unsanitary sinks increase the risk of bacterial infections. And when they are not chemically treated, these dwellings are at greater risk of invasions by termites, rodents, roaches, and other pests, which in turn increase the risk of exposure to biological threats (e.g., toxins, vermin, bacteria, allergens, and viruses).[47] Minority, unmarried, and low-income older adults are more at risk.[48]

Older houses are typically far less energy efficient or well insulated than new houses, and their older occupants pay higher monthly bills for heating and cooling.[49] When they compare homes built before and after 1970, experts find that the newer homes in the Northeast, Midwest, and South use about 20%–30% less energy per square foot on average, and in the West they use 10% less.[50]

When compared with younger occupants, older homeowners—despite their older dwellings—spend less money to make routine home maintenance repairs, to replace or add major equipment or infrastructure to their houses (e.g., a furnace, roof, siding, plumbing or pipes, electrical wiring, insulation), and to perform major physical alterations (e.g., remodeling a kitchen).[51] These numbers probably understate the disparities. We would expect older people to spend more than younger people, if only because they rely less on their own sweat labor and must hire paid help.

OUT-OF-DATE PHYSICAL DESIGN AMENITIES

Whereas the first category of problems pose threats to the health, safety, and security of older people and pushes them out of their residential mastery zones, this second category of physical inadequacies pushes them out of their residential comfort zones: Their owned or rented dwellings have become unpleasant or unappealing places to live because of their physical or interior design. Their dwellings are uncomfortably large, and their room layouts, flooring, lighting, cabinetry, closet space, and decor are out of sync with their ideal retirement-oriented dwelling arrangement or their newly adopted way of life. When these occupants are higher income older homeowners, they are highly desirable consumers for the remodeling industry. According to the National Association of Home Builders, homeowners age 65 and older accounted for 20% of the money spent by U.S. homeowners (of all ages) on professional remodeling jobs.

PHYSICAL FEATURES INCOMPATIBLE WITH MOBILITY OR SENSORY DECLINES

Even when older people occupy dwellings with up-to-date infrastructure, free of repair problems, and with state-of-the-art interior designs, their accommodations may be physically inadequate for a third reason: Their architects never imagined aging occupants who would find their dwelling designs unsafe, inaccessible, or difficult to use.

These problems arise because older people suffer from mobility declines in their upper bodies (e.g., arms, shoulders) and lower bodies (e.g., knees, legs), as well as sensory declines (e.g., vision reduction and hearing impairments).[52] They become aware for the first time about how much they lack the muscle strength, stamina, speed, and flexibility to conduct their lives and accomplish chores that they once took for granted. They can no longer easily climb stairs to a second floor or access a long elevated pathway to the front door of a building. If they use a walker or wheelchair, they cannot easily use the bathrooms or laundry facilities because of narrow doorways or tight spaces.[53] They have difficulty reaching electrical outlets, high shelves, and cupboards or negotiating the uneven floor surfaces between rooms. Even the most common tasks around a dwelling—opening windows, turning on faucets, or changing the furnace filters—become difficult.[54] Older adults who are hard of hearing are at high risk of not being alerted by their doorbells, alarm systems, and smoke and carbon monoxide detectors. Those with vision loss find that their rooms have inadequate lighting for reading or dimly lit closets where it is impossible to find things. It is estimated that one in four older adults (age 65 and older) with at least one mobility limitation[55] would benefit from home modifications to address these types of problems.[56]

Older people have a greater risk of falling because of the hazards found inside or around their homes. About one-third of adults age 65 and older fall each year,[57] and the accident rates are higher for those in their late 70s or older who are unmarried.[58] Certain areas in the dwelling pose greater risks, such as slippery bathroom floors and shower areas, slick kitchen linoleum floors, or the leading edge of the stairs if it is not marked by contrasting materials.[59] Poorly arranged furniture and clutter also precipitate falls.[60]

The injuries of older people are often more serious because their bones are weaker and thus vulnerable to fractures. Consequently, many are serious enough to warrant treatment at an emergency department and often have long-run consequences. Nearly one-third of seniors with a fall injury later have difficulties performing their everyday activities, and they are more likely to need long-term care services.[61] Moreover, even minor injuries can be psychologically devastating because older people fear falling again and become reluctant to leave their homes. They then reduce their social, recreational, and religious activities, in turn increasing their risk of feeling lonely and socially isolated.

UNMET NEEDS FOR LONG-TERM SERVICES, SUPPORTS, AND CARE FOR CHRONIC HEALTH CONDITIONS

DISRUPTED WAYS OF LIVING

When older people express their strong preferences for aging in place to pollsters, they have not contemplated spending almost all of their time in the confines of their dwelling.[62] They do not envision scenarios in which they lack the energy or motivation to perform their most basic subsistence or homemaking tasks. They do not foresee a day when they cannot accomplish their everyday shopping activities or imagine they will be sick, alone, and with no one to call. Unfortunately, these experiences become very real for millions of older adults with chronic medical conditions or illnesses, cognitive or physical disabilities, debilitating injuries from an accident, or mood disorders. They are often out of their residential mastery zones; they feel incompetent and out of control.[63]

Older people whose ideas of a fulfilling and satisfying way of life depend on their being active, being involved in their community, and maintaining an extensive network of social relationships are likely to feel the most oppressed.[64] In contrast, older people may feel less demoralized if they are more content with solitude and conducting their leisure and recreational activities inside their homes.

About 89% of people age 65 and older in the United States now have at least one chronic health condition.[65] The most common in order of prevalence are hypertension (56%), arthritis (51%), heart disease (30%), any type of cancer (24%), diabetes (21%), asthma (11%), chronic bronchitis or emphysema (10%), and stroke (9%).[66] Millions of seniors are also confronting another health threat: The majority of both men (75%) and women (71%) age 65 and older are overweight or obese,[67] a risk factor strongly linked with heart disease and diabetes.[68] How older people feel about their health may not necessarily correlate well with these objective indicators, but almost a quarter of people age 65 and older rate their own health as fair or poor.[69]

Older people with these chronic health problems are more likely to suffer from various functional or mobility limitations. We rely heavily on two indicators to identify those at risk (Figure 4.2). The first, *activities of daily living* (ADLs), focuses on their ability to perform personal or self-care tasks, such as bathing, dressing, using the toilet

Figure 4.2. Indicators of the need for long-term care (Hayutin, Dietz, & Mitchell, 2010)

NEED FOR LONG-TERM CARE

Activities of Daily Living (ADLs)	Instrumental Activities of Daily Living (IADLs)
Getting out of bed Bathing or showering Dressing Eating Walking Using the toilet	Shopping for groceries Preparing meals Doing housework Using a telephone Managing money Taking medications

and maintaining continence, getting in and out of chairs or beds, indoor mobility, and eating.[70] The second, *instrumental activities of daily living* (IADLs), focuses on their ability to handle routine tasks, such as using the telephone, doing housework, preparing meals, shopping for groceries, using the telephone, managing money, and taking medications.

Estimates of the prevalence of these functional limitations vary because studies define and measure the performance of ADL and IADL indicators differently.[71] Moreover, generalizing about the impairments of the overall community-based older population obfuscates the greater prevalence of limitations experienced by both women and the oldest groups, especially those older than age 85.[72] Impairment rates are also higher for older people who are more socioeconomically disadvantaged, such as African-Americans and Hispanics.[73] Older people also have more difficulty performing certain activities than others (Figure 4.3).

The most conservative estimates identify about 10% of the community-based population (i.e., not in institutions) age 65 to 74 as having difficulties performing at least one IADL, but this increases to 18% among the age 75 to 84 group and to 38% among the age 85 and older group. Similarly, whereas just over 14% of the age 65 to 74 group has difficulty performing one or more ADLs, this increases to 23% among the age 75 to 84 group and to about 42% among the age 85 and older group.[74]

Other experts focus on indicators that assess the ability of older people to perform the following physical tasks: stooping or kneeling, reaching overhead, writing or grasping small objects, walking outside for two to three blocks, and lifting up to 10 pounds (Figure 4.4).[75] Findings show that 13% of men and 19% of women age 65 to 74 were unable to perform at least one of these five activities.[76] The comparable gender differences among the age 75 to 84 group were 22% versus 34%, and among those age 85 and older, 40% versus 53%.[77]

Figure 4.3. Percentages of young-old and old-old people with limitations in ADLs, 2009 (U.S. Department of Health and Human Services, 2012b)

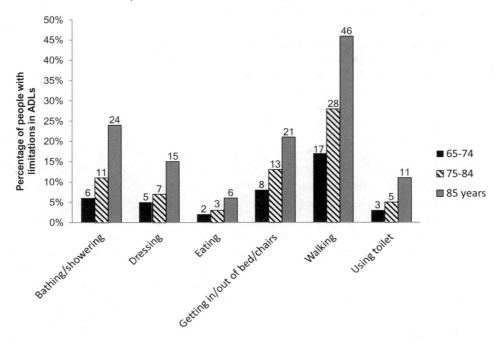

Figure 4.4. Percentage of Medicare enrollees age 65 or older who are unable to perform certain physical activities, 2009 (Federal Interagency Forum on Aging-Related Statistics, 2012)

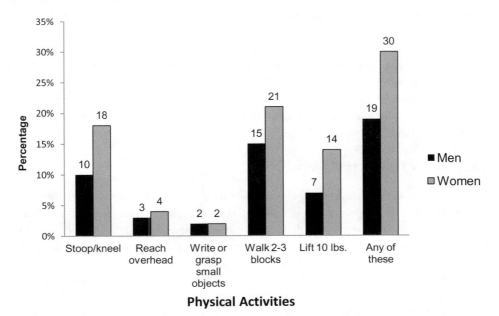

Depressive symptoms become more likely among older people with these physical and cognitive limitations, especially when they cannot easily leave their dwellings,[78] and suicide rates are higher.[79] As one expert explains,

> Depression is a major health issue for elders, yet late-life depression often goes undiagnosed. . . . Depressed elders do not typically report "sadness," as younger people do. Instead, they describe feelings of irritability, decreased pleasure, social withdrawal, physical symptoms (e.g., lack of appetite, decreased energy, insomnia), and hypochondriasis. . . . Depressed older adults report decreased independence, poor health, and increased chronic medical problems.[80]

As of 2008, about 14% of community-residing people age 65 and older reported clinically relevant depressive symptoms. Depression afflicts about 11% of men age 65 and older and 16% of women and increases to 19% and 18%, respectively, among men and women age 85 and older.

Vulnerability has many faces, but the onset of dementia is the most devastating. Alzheimer's disease is the most common category, but experts distinguish seven other types, such as vascular dementia caused by decreased blood flow to parts of the brain (because of stroke) and dementia with Lewy bodies, linked with abnormal aggregations of the protein alpha-synuclein.[81] Practically speaking, the specific diagnosis is usually important only for the medical profession. Most dementias produce similar symptoms that include memory loss, apathy, depression, withdrawal, confusion, impaired judgment, spatial disorientation, combative behaviors, and difficulty speaking, swallowing, and walking. Yet there are no cures, and despite some optimistic claims to the contrary, the debilitating symptoms of dementia increase over time.

The financial impact of this disease is horrendous. Experts estimate the yearly out-of-pocket healthcare costs per person with dementia at about $12,000 and the overall cost of home care purchased in the marketplace and the cost of family care at more than $56,000.[82]

In 2014, about 5 million people age 65 and older (about 11% of this group) had dementia. The rate increased to 32% among the 85 and older population, with women living longer being at greater risk.[83] Again, the disease was more prevalent among the less educated, African-Americans, Hispanics, and those with lower incomes.[84] By 2025, experts project a 40% increase in the number of people age 65 and older diagnosed with dementia.

No Longer Doing It Alone

It is not just their disrupted activities or their inability to take care of their dwellings that push older people out of their residential comfort and mastery zones. Additionally, to maintain their independent living arrangements, cope with their physical and cognitive declines, and manage their chronic health conditions, they must introduce long-term services and supports into their homes.

They need help performing their ADLs and IADLs, as well as managing their chronic health problems, particularly the administration of medications.[85] They may have to start using assistive devices (e.g., cane, walker, wheelchair) or smart home technologies (Chapter 6). Experts offer a concise overview of the scope of this assistance,

Long-term care services could entail cooking, cleaning, driving, shopping, bathing, dressing, assistance in using the toilet, mobility assistance, and even spoon-feeding or other help with eating and drinking. They could also entail assessment, rehabilitation, and treatments to reduce disability and functional impairment as much as possible. Finally, long-term care services include environmental assessment and modification, and provision of equipment and devices; these strategies improve functional abilities by rendering the environment easier for the consumer to manage.[86]

It is important to distinguish *long-term services and supports* from *medical care,* a category more familiar to Americans. Medical care consists of services, products, and surgical treatments for preventing, diagnosing, and treating health problems—often acute—typically delivered or directed by physicians or other medical personnel in a hospital or outpatient clinical setting. It also includes short-term nursing services and rehabilitation treatments (e.g., speech, physical, and occupational therapy) to help the healing and recovery process and to minimize further health complications.

Although medical problems often can be linked to long-term care needs, the correlation is far from perfect. Older people with a diagnosis of heart disease, asthma, or even arthritis do not always experience difficulties performing their ADLs or IADLs.

THE LIKELIHOOD OF NEEDING LONG-TERM CARE

It is important to note that the earlier-cited percentages of older people in the United States with physical and cognitive impairments and depressive symptoms that make it difficult for them to live independently were cross-sectional or single point-in-time measures. A lifetime perspective can be more meaningful. After people reach age 65, about 70% eventually will need long-term care *during their remaining lives* to address their ADL or IADL limitations. Almost two-thirds receive some of this help in their own homes (from either unpaid family care or paid home care workers), and the remainder will receive care in assisted living or nursing home facilities (see Chapter 9).[87] On average, older people receive long-term care for about 3 years. However, the duration depends on the seriousness of their health conditions and limitations and their remaining life span. About 17% need long-term care for 1 year or less, 12% for 1–2 years, 20% for 2–5 years, and 20% for more than 5 years.[88]

Women have a higher risk than men of needing long-term care.[89] Almost 80% of women but less than 60% of men eventually need assistance after they turn 65. Furthermore, women face the prospects of needing care longer—almost 4 years, compared with more than 2 years for men—and they are almost three times more likely than men to receive care for more than 5 years.[90] People in their late 50s and early 60s also sometimes need such assistance, and the unexpectedness of their dependency status is devastating to both them and their loved ones.[91]

WHO CARES FOR THEM?

Family members, and to a much lesser extent friends, provide most of older people's long-term care services and supports without financial compensation, referred to as *informal care.* Paid workers—referred to as *formal care*—supplement these family efforts or, less often, constitute the primary source of care. We can divide these providers into two broad groups:[92] *long-term care professionals,* including administrators, physicians, nurses, therapists (physical, occupational, and speech), case management workers, and social workers; and *direct care workers,* who provide hands-on care assisting older people with their ADLs and IADLs and some supervised healthcare services. These paid workers may be hired directly by older people and their families and serve them in their own dwellings, or they may staff long-term care facilities, such as home care agencies, healthcare clinics, hospitals, and community-based service centers (e.g., senior centers and adult day centers).[93] This formal care is referred to by the catch-all phrase *home- and community-based services* (HCBSs).[94] Chapter 8 explores older people's options for obtaining this assistance.

Unmet Healthcare and Long-Term Care Needs

Disturbingly high numbers of older people living in the community are not receiving appropriate long-term care assistance for the scope and seriousness of their physical and cognitive vulnerabilities.[95] Prevalence rates of unmet long-term care needs vary widely, from 3% to 35%, with one respected research group putting the number at 25%.[96] Some people are more at risk, specifically those older than age of 85, unmarried and living alone, with low incomes, having difficulty performing more than four ADLs, with dementia symptoms, without adult children to assist as caregivers, and living in locales deficient in home- and community-based services and supports.[97]

Consequently, there are millions of older people who could be living more independent, safer, and happier lives as well as better managing their health problems.[98] Many would be better off not aging in place but relocating to the homes of family members or to specialized senior housing care options, such as independent living communities or assisted living developments. A 2013 national survey of people age 60 and older found that 20% rated their community's healthcare services as fair or poor or could not rate them, and 43% rated their community-based support services as either fair or poor or could not rate them. About 29% felt that their communities were not responsive to their needs or simply could not rate them, and 51% felt that their communities were not doing enough to prepare for the needs of their growing senior population or simply had no idea.[99]

Vulnerable older people with unmet needs have a distinctive cluster of problems:

> [They] may display poor personal care and nutrition, have difficulty managing basic medications and personal finances, or live in unsafe environments regardless of physical appearance or behavior. Furthermore, vulnerable older adults are at risk for neglect, exploitation, and numerous safety hazards, as well as functional impairment, medical morbidity, and death.[100]

Dementia complicates the ability of older people to live independently because their caregivers often cannot leave them alone. Sadly, even those with minimal physical mobility limitations often need full-time supervision and hands-on assistance. They may need cueing for everything—dressing or undressing, grooming, getting to the bathroom, and eating. Even in a familiar dwelling, they need directions. Those with dementia are also prone to wandering—out of their dwellings and into their neigh-borhoods—at any time of day and night. They may also display uncontrollable and very difficult-to-manage behaviors that range from urinating or defecating indiscrimi-nately to physical aggression.

Additional factors exacerbate the plights of those needing assistance. Some older people have no families to call on for help. The families of others fall short as care-giving solutions (Chapter 7) because even though well intentioned, they improperly execute their caregiving tasks, which are physically and psychologically demanding and exhausting. Relying on formal care may be no panacea (Chapters 8 and 9). Neither affordable professionals nor direct care workers may be available when most needed; those hired may have inadequate backgrounds or training to perform their duties; and, even when qualified, they may simply make errors. Consequently, older people may receive inferior care if they cannot count on the assistance of family members.

Minority status may be key. Foreign-born older people may have limited knowl-edge about the paid or public services available in their communities, may be intimi-dated by their bureaucracy, or may lack the financial resources to use them. Language barriers and distrust may restrict their access to correct information or their willing-ness or ability to apply for potentially eligible services. Cultural beliefs requiring them to care for their older relatives may also make it difficult for them to approach paid service providers.[101]

Location also matters. Some older people find their home- and community-based service options extremely limited because they live in more service-deficient or iso-lated communities. Older adults in rural areas—where 25% of the U.S. population age 65 and older live—have higher rates of chronic conditions and functional declines that increase their risk of needing assistance.[102] Compared with older urban dwellers, they often live more years with impairments and have more service needs. Yet most studies conclude they have more limited resources and confront more barriers accessing care than urban dwellers. Rural minorities are particularly at risk, and they tend to cluster in places with historically persistent poverty conditions, such as the Mississippi Delta, the rural Southeast, Native American lands, including Alaska Native villages, and the Colonias along the U.S.–Mexico border.[103]

Money is obviously an important factor, except for those with high incomes. However, a large segment of those with modest incomes find themselves in a financial quagmire because although they cannot afford the services or housing options offered by the private sector, their incomes are not low enough to qualify for public programs that sometimes cover these solutions (Chapter 8). When help from their family mem-bers is not enough, in-home paid assistance or the care offered in group residential facilities such as independent living communities, assisted living, or nursing homes is costly and their expenses quickly drain their savings (Chapter 11). Long-term care is not covered by Medicare and only a small percentage of older people have long-term care insurance to cover these expenses. Renters are more at risk than homeowners be-cause they have saved less and cannot draw on the equity in their dwellings.

In contrast, low-income and asset-poor Medicaid beneficiaries or those who re-ceive priority to participate in programs funded through the Older Americans Act are often eligible for publicly funded community-based supportive services programs. It is now easier to find such programs because state governments have substantially shifted their Medicaid funding from nursing homes to community care (Chapter 8). The bad news is that the governments of many states underfund these affordable long-term care community-based options, resulting in long waiting lists. When their older occupants need assistance to cope with their severe mobility and cognitive limitations, they may have little choice but to enter a nursing home accepting Medicaid beneficiaries.[104]

SOCIAL ISOLATION AND LONELINESS

Consider the following newspaper story:

> As the population ages, police report a rise in the number of people found dead after days, even weeks. The 85-year-old World War II army veteran had lain lifeless on his living room floor for weeks, his death unnoticed by friends, family or neighbors, his home invaded by vermin. . . . Once we know that people are aging in their homes, there is also the possibility that they will die there.[105]

Although older people typically do not experience such devastating consequences, those who stay put in their buildings or neighborhoods often lose friends, neighbors, or family members because they died or moved to other locations.[106] Consequently, they are at risk of having inadequate social supports and contacts. Consider this story:

> Ms. Goldberg, 98, lives in a 19-story apartment house in Flushing, Queens, one of two neighboring buildings that were erected for survivors of the Holocaust. When she moved there in 1978, she said, her neighbors formed a tight community of predominantly Jewish refugees like her who had fled to the United States from Austria or Germany. "We had parties." . . . "We had card games. It was our people." Now, she said, "It's completely changed—I have no neighbors here."
>
> For Ms. Goldberg, the transformation has been steady and overwhelming. Of the 326 residents in her building, now only 31 are Holocaust survivors, and only 7 of them are German or Austrian. The new neighbors are friendly enough. But she said: "We do not talk. We say hello, goodbye. But that's it."[107]

Loneliness is more likely defined as *"an unpleasant subjective state of sensing a discrepancy between the desired amount of companionship or emotional support and that which is available in the person's environment."*[108] When we consider the pros and cons of older people aging in place, we often downplay the absence of personal connections. In one expert's opinion, *"We may think too little about the pain of isolation in old age."*[109]

Those who have lost spouses are at greater risk of feeling alone,[110] and gender and minority status are influential. In 2012, 37% of women age 65 and older and 12% of men were widowed, and White widows were more likely to live alone than African-American widows. Hispanic widows were the least likely to live alone.[111] All of these rates were higher among the oldest groups.[112]

It is especially traumatic when older people lose their spouses[113] because they can no longer count on a trusted and indispensable confidant, a warm, loving soul mate, a reliable companion, or a steadfast friend.[114] Now they must alone confront both the minor and major problems of life. Their spouses may have helped them to define who they were: a successful provider, a faithful wife, or a valued worker. Studies show that older people are less able to mitigate their anxieties and distresses when they lack the support and stability of a reliable and emotionally close marital partner.[115]

Sometimes losing a loving spouse is also a catalyst for other lost personal relationships. Early researchers recorded this effect:

> Every widow discovers that people who were previously friendly and approachable become embarrassed and estranged in their presence. Expressions of sympathy often have a hollow ring and offers of help are not followed up. It often happens that only those who share the grief or have themselves suffered a major loss remain at hand. It is as if the widow has become tainted with death in much the same way as the funeral director.[116]

Isolation and loneliness are also risk factors for other bad outcomes. The deficient social worlds of older people contribute to various adverse physical and mental health outcomes, including infection, cardiovascular disease, diminished immune function, depression, sleep dysfunction, and physical and cognitive decline.[117] These effects occur for three reasons. First, there are the practical consequences of lacking reliable family, friends, or associates to help them cope with threatening health conditions or functional declines by providing transportation, counsel, financial assistance, and so on. Second, they lack emotional supports, such as people to confide in and receive reassurance from in difficult times. And third, they lose those who affirmed their self-identities—their successes, achievements, and self-worth.[118]

Living Alone—Not the Only Risk Factor for Loneliness

In 2010, about 19% of men and 37% of women age 65 and older lived alone (Table 4.1). In their mid-70s and older, however, 23% of men and more than 47% of women lived alone.[119] Compared with older White men, older African-American men were more likely to live alone. Older Asians were the least likely to live alone. Compared with older Whites, older Asians and Hispanics are more likely to live with other relatives (that is, in extended family households).[120] The foreign-born living in such households were also more likely to be unmarried, had less education and income, lacked English-language proficiency, recently immigrated to the United States, or had disabilities. However, since 1900, the share of older people living in extended-family households has sharply declined.[121]

The number of people in a household is certainly an important explanation for loneliness but not the only one. Those living alone often compensate by having a more extensive outside network of reliable relationships. These socially adept people are more open to having new or more frequent social relationships with friends and family or becoming involved in community activities.[122] If the socioemotional selectivity theory of aging is valid, some aging adults intentionally reduce the size of their social networks and invest more energy in a selective set of people with whom they have more intimate and emotionally rewarding relationships.[123]

Living alone may also not be a product of old age. Some older people never married, or they previously divorced and never remarried (about 16% of the population

Table 4.1. Living arrangements of the population age 65 and older, by sex, race, and Hispanic origin, 2010

Age 65 and older subgroup	% Living with spouse	% Living with other relatives	% Living with nonrelatives	% Living alone	Total
Men					
Total	71.7	5.9	3.4	19.0	100.0
Non-Hispanic Whites	74.0	4.2	3.1	18.7	100.0
African-Americans	54.8	11.5	5.3	28.4	100.0
Asians	78.7	7.5	2.0	11.9	100.0
Hispanics (of any race)	61.9	17.4	5.3	15.4	100.0
Women					
Total	42.4	17.9	2.4	37.3	100.0
Non-Hispanic Whites	44.9	13.3	2.6	39.1	100.0
African-Americans	23.5	35.2	2.0	39.3	100.0
Asians	44.4	33.0	1.5	21.1	100.0
Hispanics (of any race)	38.7	35.8	2.0	23.4	100.0

Federal Interagency Forum on Aging-Related Statistics, 2012, p. 89.

age 65 and older).[124] Others always had shy or introverted personalities. These people have long since adjusted to the downsides of living alone. They compensate for their thin social networks by engaging in rewarding solitary activities, such as gardening, reading, playing computer games, or simply reminiscing about good times past. Paradoxically, because they have had so much practice living alone, they may deal with the vagaries of a solitary old age more effectively than those new to this situation.[125]

Other older people find that living alone for the first time is a liberating experience. They enjoy their lives more and feel more competent and in control. Some spouses never get along. Becoming a widow or widower can be a positive event for them and a catalyst for pursuing new interests and friendships.

MOBILITY DECLINES CONTRIBUTE TO PHYSICAL ISOLATION AND LONELINESS

Feelings of loneliness often follow from mobility declines that limit older people's participation in enjoyable activities and events that once nurtured their social relationships. Visiting friends at social gatherings becomes too exhausting. Alternatively, because of their physical limitations, they feel embarrassed communicating with others. Significant others could reduce these barriers if they visited the homes of their older friends or helped them participate in their social activities, but often this does not occur.

This is partly because the onset of vulnerability has an unspoken dark side. Friends, neighbors, and family members—even those living in the same household—often abandon older people because of their ailments. They no longer feel comfortable—indeed, they often feel frustrated or depressed—relating to someone who is no longer fun to be with or who cannot keep up or participate competently in their usual activities. They feel anxious and upset relating to someone who is hard of hearing, forgetful, and easily confused.

As cruel and heartless as this may sound, healthy older people often do not want to be reminded of their vulnerable futures, that their memories may fail or their legs may not transport them where they want to go. They deal with the prospects of their own old age through denial and the avoidance of their less-able friends. Sadly, they themselves become the reasons for the loneliness of older people affected by declines in mobility.

Similarly, even the most loving and devoted sons and daughters do not want to think of their mothers or fathers as anything but independent and competent. Throughout their lives, their parents were pillars of strength and reliability. They become distressed and curtail their visits when these former powerhouses in their lives become dependent and weak.

UNSAFE OR INHOSPITABLE NEIGHBORHOODS AND COMMUNITIES

Some neighborhoods or communities occupied by older people are in economic decline and become undesirable places to live. They are variously plagued with social disorders, such as crime, drug and alcohol use, vandalism, and squatters. They have an oversupply of vacant, abandoned, and physically rundown buildings, and trash and litter are visibly present.[126] Earlier I described the challenges planners face in these places:

> These communities offer especially difficult challenges to the planner and policymaker. They are often distinguished by a problem-laden housing stock, shrinking tax base, higher incidence of social ills, reduced public services and an elderly population in greater need of a range of medical, social, and personal services.[127]

We often find these depressed places in the older urban cores and earlier-built suburbs of our metropolitan areas, but they also include small towns and rural counties that lost their once viable agricultural, manufacturing, or energy economic bases.[128] Some experts have dubbed these the "aged left behind" localities,[129] because they have been vacated by younger people who seek better job opportunities and living conditions elsewhere and by younger, healthier, and higher-income retirees who have moved to localities more conducive to their active retirement lifestyles. Left behind are low-income and less-educated older persons who opted to age in place, either because they saw few other affordable options or they had strong historical or lifetime connections to their communities.

Older people who live in these economically depressed areas are sicker. They have a higher prevalence of chronic health problems, disabilities, and depression, poorer cognitive functioning, and lower self-assessments of health.[130] They have had a hospital stay during the past year or needed home care. Because they are very poor and have few economic assets, except possibly for their low-value dwellings, these residents usually depend on Medicaid assistance to pay for their long-term care.[131]

Researchers have shown how deficient neighborhoods and communities contribute to the poor physical and mental health of older residents.[132] They reason that these places offer older people limited preventive primary healthcare, in-home supportive services, responsive neighborhood organizations, and amenities, such as parks, public squares, gyms, bookstores, and libraries.[133] Their inadequate local government finances also result in poorer municipal services (e.g., fire, police, and sanitation).[134] Other researchers argue that these neighborhoods have higher levels of air pollution and other environmental toxins.[135] They have also linked the mobility limitations of older residents to the greater presence of unsafe and hazardous streets and sidewalks.[136]

Making matters worse, the older occupants sadly recognize that there is a gap between what they need and what is readily available. Consequently, they become even more psychologically distressed.[137] Because researchers document these relationships at a single point in time (i.e., cross-sectionally), their studies may understate the impact of these poor-quality neighborhoods. Some older people have lived in these disadvantaged environments throughout most of their adult lives, and their cumulative long-term exposure helps explain their current poor health and functional declines.[138]

A culture of poverty pervades these residential enclaves. Here the residents accept smoking and eating junk food, because everyone around them practices these unhealthy behaviors.[139] Others speculate that *"cigarette use becomes a form of self-medication . . . pursued in an effort to regulate mood and cope with hassles and strains arising from their material deprivation."*[140]

The more hostile environments of these places also contribute to the social isolation of their older residents.[141] They venture out infrequently because they lack a protective or trusting social network of close-knit, friendly, and supportive neighbors and acquaintances—referred to as *collective efficacy*—who can offer physical assistance, alleviate their feelings of anxiety or stress, or contribute to their emotional well-being.[142] When a disaster strikes these places, their older occupants are especially vulnerable. This was the case in Chicago during its summer 1995 heat wave, which resulted in a death toll of at least 750 residents over a 5-day period, most of whom were elderly poor seniors, and left 49,000 households without electricity and air conditioning.[143]

LIMITED OR UNSAFE TRANSPORTATION OPTIONS

Inadequate transportation options have devastating consequences for older people who seek to be fully engaged in life and live independently. Discretionary activities, such as participating in recreational or intellectually stimulating events or community volunteering efforts, are often the first to go when transportation access becomes difficult. One national transportation assessment found that,

> Among older adults 65 [and older] who report not having taken a trip outside their home in the past week, a little more than half reported that they would like to get out more often.[144]

But even nondiscretionary trips may be impossible. Amazingly, almost 15% of poor older households (below the 100% poverty level) are food insecure, meaning they are not eating properly and lack nutritious diets.[145] To be sure, transportation barriers are not totally responsible. Food insecurity is greater among people with low education and incomes. These people cannot afford to purchase enough food or have bad eating habits (e.g., consuming too much salt, fat, or sugar). However, poor transportation access is also an important part of the equation. A significant share of these older people occupy what policy makers call food deserts.[146] They are just too far away from stores that sell affordable and nutritious food items, lack public transit to reach them, or are unable to reach senior centers that offer low-cost nutritious meals to older adults or counsel them on how to eat better (Chapter 8).[147]

Safe access by automobile is key. When older people can no longer reliably count on driving to reach their destinations, they curtail activities outside their dwellings or drive only to locations close to their homes during the daylight hours.[148] One national study found that older nondrivers make 15% fewer trips to the doctor, 59% fewer shopping trips and visits to restaurants, and 65% fewer trips for social, family, and religious activities.[149]

Older nondrivers are especially disadvantaged when they live in auto-dependent, sprawling, low-density suburbs with no public transit. Moreover, those living in more remote rural locations face some unique challenges.[150] The higher rates of illness among these older nondrivers are explained partly by their difficulties accessing doctors, medical centers, and hospitals to help them manage their chronic health conditions.[151] They have an even harder time reaching physicians who practice various medical specialties, such as internal medicine and endocrinology.[152] Moreover, even when rural hospitals are physically accessible, they may be equipped to treat only more routine medical disorders, and, therefore, older people must access urban hospitals when they need more specialized surgical procedures and care.[153] Home care agencies, which often deliver nursing and rehabilitative care after a hospital stay, also tend to be less available in more sparsely located areas, if only because it is less profitable for them to operate in those locations.[154]

Older people in less-accessible places also have difficulty reaching social service agencies funded by charitable organizations or government programs that might help them remain independent in their homes. Moreover, even when accessible they have minimal staff because of their smaller budgets and fewer available volunteers. These transportation challenges help explain why older people living in these places rely more heavily on the institutional care found in nursing homes, which tend to be more available in rural than in urban areas.[155]

Lower-income older people who can drive confront another barrier when gas prices are high. These higher costs also make it difficult for government agencies, which are also operating under tighter budgets, to deliver social services to the homes of their older clients. In response, they curtail the frequency of their visits or charge higher service rates to compensate for their own higher transportation costs.

Some older people attempt to compensate for limited transportation by sharing auto rides with others. Almost 20% of people age 75–79 and 40% of those older than age 80 use ride sharing as their primary way of getting around.[156] This mobility comes at a cost. Their trips—both going and coming—must be convenient for their drivers. Moreover, the older people must have no qualms about asking others for help. Seeking this assistance inevitably reminds them of their permanent limitations and their dependency on others.[157]

DIFFICULTIES WITH DRIVING

About 88% of the everyday trips older people make to reach destinations in their communities are by car, with much smaller percentages by walking (9%), public transportation (2.2%), and taxis (0.2%).[158] Because they depend so heavily on automobiles, their worldview changes dramatically when they feel stressed while driving, continually get lost, become accident prone, or cannot drive at all. These are often the first signs that they are getting old and forebode their difficulties living independently.[159]

Even the young undergraduates I teach at the University of Florida can appreciate the impact of this mobility loss. They depend on their cars to get almost everywhere, and imagining a time without a car throws them into a panic. In an automobile-oriented state such as Florida, not being able to drive is almost equivalent to losing an arm or a leg. Although some 88% of people age 65–74 and 69% of people age 75 and older are currently drivers (80% of people age 65 and older), some subgroups lack this mobility. These include ethnic and racial minorities—African-Americans and Hispanics—and much older women who live alone, have low incomes, or live with a spouse. After age 75, for example, just over 60% of women still drive, compared with 83% of men.[160]

Three factors are crucial: A large proportion of these women never learned to drive earlier in their lives; age-related disabilities make driving unsafe or impossible, a scenario older women are more likely to confront because they live longer than men; and a high share of foreign-born women are not licensed to drive. For example, Hispanic and Asian women age 50 and older have the lowest driver's license rates. Older adults who are aging in place and seeking to maintain their comfortable and independent lifestyles keep their driver's licenses longer and travel more miles. However, a license does not guarantee safe driving. Older people often suffer from a confluence of physical and cognitive limitations (Figure 4.5) that make it more dangerous for them to be on the road.

The statistics are not comforting. After the number of miles they drive is controlled for, older people are more likely than younger age groups to get into crashes and—especially after age 80—they have higher injury and death rates.[161] They are particularly at risk of accidents at intersections.[162] After the severity of their crashes is controlled for, older drivers are three times more likely to die.[163] In 2012, almost 5,600 people age 65 and older were killed in traffic crashes, and almost 214,000 were injured. These older people represented 17% of all traffic casualties and 9% of all drivers injured in traffic crashes.[164] However, other experts argue that these higher death rates are due less to their unsafe driving than their greater physical fragility. Stats show that older people drive more cautiously and at lower speeds than younger people and are less likely to be involved in traffic accidents attributed to irresponsible or reckless driving.[165]

DIFFICULTIES WITH USING PUBLIC TRANSIT

About 31% of renters age 65 and older and 55% of homeowners report that public transportation is simply unavailable.[166] Many do not live within walking distance of public transportation services.[167] Others may be near transit stops but complain that

Figure 4.5. How physical and mental declines limit the ability of older people to drive safely[181]

Type of decline	How loss makes driving a car more difficult
Vision	
Reduced visual acuity	Difficulty reading or recognizing letters or symbols on road signs or avoiding road hazards (e.g., bad road surfaces)
Reduced visual contrast sensitivity	Difficulty distinguishing road surface area from road shoulder (when color or texture of road shoulder is similar to the paved surface or when the edge of the road is poorly defined relative to road shoulder)
Increased susceptibility to glare	Roadway objects (signs, signals, pedestrians) cannot be seen as well after exposure to glare (at night, caused by car headlights; during day caused by sun glare)
Poorer visual pattern perception	Difficulty extrapolating from only partial information and constructing the whole image from a scene, such as when a pedestrian or another vehicle is about to enter driver's path from behind some obstruction
Less-efficient visual search	Reduced ability of driver to find and identify safety threats or other important information (e.g., sign, landmark, or other directional information)
Reduced area of visual attention	A shrinking visual field, reflected by poor peripheral vision, increases likelihood of collisions with vehicles, pedestrians, and cyclists entering from side of road or at intersection
Cognition	
Impaired selective attention ability	Reduced ability to anticipate and respond quickly and appropriately to roadway objects, conditions, and hazards most critical to safety when operating and controlling vehicles
Less-efficient divided attention and slower attention switching	Reduced ability to monitor and respond effectively to more complex driving environments requiring the processing of multiple sources of information quickly and at the same time. For example, a driver entering a freeway must track the curvature of the ramp and steer appropriately, keep a safe distance behind the car ahead, and check for gaps in traffic on the highway while accelerating just enough to permit a smooth entry into the traffic stream.

Table continued next page

Figure 4.5. *Continued*

Type of decline	How loss makes driving a car more difficult
Less-efficient working memory processes	Reduced ability to think about and recall recently learned information while driving, without any lapses in safely controlling vehicle (e.g., while driving in heavy traffic being able to remember and apply a simple set of navigational instructions memorized before a journey)
Psychomotor and Physical Function	
Loss of limb strength, flexibility, sensitivity, or range of motion	Reduced ability to quickly shift the right foot from accelerator to brake when the situation demands, to apply correct pressure for appropriate speed control, and to safely maneuver the car through turns and around obstacles
Reduced ability to rotate the head and neck	Reduced ability to redirect gaze in many different directions to check for potential conflicts, such as the familiar "left–right–left" check before crossing an intersection and looking over one's shoulder before merging with traffic or changing lanes

Adapted from: Potts, I., Stutts, J., Pfefer, R., Neuman, T. R., Slack, K. L., & Hardy, K. K. (2004). Guidance for implementation of the ASSHTO strategic highway safety plan: Volume 9, A guide for reducing collision involving older drivers, NCHRP Report 500. Washington, DC: Transportation Research Board.

the existing public transit route schedules do not take them where they need to go, and they operate too infrequently, especially during off-peak hours and on weekends. A study investigating the availability of public transit lines and stops (bus routes and rail and ferry stations) in 242 U.S. metropolitan areas with a population of 65,000 or more reached the following conclusion:

> More than 11.5 million Americans 65 and older lived with "poor" transit access in 2000. If most seniors get their wish to "age in place," by 2015, our analysis shows that this figure will increase to more than 15.5 million older Americans, meaning a substantial majority of that population will be faced with declining mobility options.[168]

The unavailability of public transit is but one of five major barriers confronted by potential older users of this mode of transportation. This option is also of limited use when it is not accessible, acceptable, affordable, and adaptable (Figure 4.6).[169] Chapter 9 considers how some communities have responded to the host of barriers that make public transit stressful or difficult to use.

Figure 4.6. The five A's of senior-friendly transportation (Kerschner, 2003)

Availability: Transportation exists and is available when needed (e.g., evenings, weekdays, weekends)

Accessibility: Transportation can be reached and used (e.g., bus stairs can be negotiated; bus seats are high enough; vehicle comes to the door; transit stops are reachable)

Acceptability: Deals with standards including cleanliness and safety (e.g., bus stops are located in safe areas) and user-friendliness (e.g., transit operators are courteous and helpful)

Affordability: Deals with costs (e.g., fees are affordable; fees are comparable to or less than driving a car; vouchers or coupons help defray out-of-pocket expenses)

Adaptability: Transportation can be modified or adjusted to meet special needs (e.g., the vehicle can accommodate a wheelchair; trip chaining—several stops in one trip—is possible; escorts can be provided)

DIFFICULTIES WITH WALKING

Ideally, nondrivers could walk to their destinations, including bus stops or subway stations, but for most adults these distances are too far. One survey reported that less than one in five older people lived within walking distance of a grocery store.[170] Planners tell us that on average healthy people living in cities want to walk only about 1,500 feet before they must rely on other ways to reach their destinations.[171] By this measure, older people are disadvantaged not just when they live in rural locations but also in most American suburbs. Moreover, what might be tolerable distances to younger and healthier people are out of reach for those with mobility limitations, especially if they must carry parcels in inclement weather.[172] Even shorter walking trips may be challenging when older people must negotiate hilly routes, busy intersections, or pathways without sidewalks. Fear of crime may be another obstacle.[173] In the United States in 2012, 20% of pedestrian fatalities were incurred by people age 65 or older. Additionally, when older pedestrians are injured, their medical problems are more severe because of their greater fragility.[174]

Difficult walking conditions also have health consequences. Epidemiological studies emphasize the benefits of regular walking as part of an exercise regimen for older people. They link higher levels of walking with the reduced prevalence of various chronic health problems, greater body strength and flexibility, and even prolonging their ability to live independently.[175] Chapter 9 reviews how communities have attempted to reduce these barriers and to incentivize walking by older people.

GOING FORWARD

Unfortunately, it is only after a string of bad residential or care experiences that many older people begin to reassess the appropriateness of their home settings. Sometimes, the last straw comes only after a stressful episode dramatically pushes them out of their residential comfort or mastery zone. The likely candidates: a fall, a traffic accident, a bad check, no one to call, a complaint from a collection agency, an emergency room visit or hospital admission, an episode of abuse, severe depressive symptoms, unexpected wandering behavior, or a forgotten check made out to an unknown charity. Only then do older people, often cajoled by their family members, begin to question the aging in place groupthink.

If they can initiate effective coping behaviors, older people will no longer feel uncomfortable, incompetent, and out of control. This is the focus of Chapter 5: the range of coping strategies available to older Americans who are seeking residential and care settings that are more consistent with their needs and goals as they strive to achieve residential normalcy.

NOTES

1. Line from the movie *All Together* (*Et si on vivait tous ensemble?*, 2011)
2. (Netherland, Finkelstein, & Gardner, 2011, p. 278)
3. Reader's opinion as to whether an unhappy older person should stay in her assisted living development rather than age in place in her home, in column by author, columnist and speaker, Carol Bradley Bursack.: http://www.agingcare.com/Questions/time-pass-if-elder-hates-assisted-living-facility-138827.htm
4. Elaine Jarvik and Lois Collins, "Gray area: Home alone—Elderly face huge challenges in seeing that needs are met" Deseret News, November, 10, 2008.
5. (Strohschein, 2012)
6. (Lipman, Lubbell, & Salomon, 2010)
7. (Commission on Affordable Housing and Health Facility Needs for Seniors in the 21st Century, 2002)
8. (Golant & Lagreca, 1994a, 1994b)
9. (Commission on Affordable Housing and Health Facility Needs for Seniors in the 21st Century, 2002)
10. (Rubinstein, 1998)
11. (Fried, 2000)
12. (Fried, 2000)
13. (Social Security Administration, 2013)
14. This very comprehensive definition of home-related expenses included rent, mortgage interest, property taxes, maintenance, utilities, furnishings, renters' or homeowners' insurance, home appliances, cleaning supplies, textiles, and luggage. (Social Security Administration, 2013)
15. (Social Security Administration, 2013)
16. (Kendig, Clemson, and Mackenzie, 2012; Joint Center for Housing Studies of Harvard University, 2014)
17. For these statistics, the expenditures of older homeowners include mortgage payments, utilities and fuels, property taxes, insurance premiums, and condominium fees; those of renters include rent and utilities (assuming not included in their rent). The items usually included to measure dwelling expense burdens differ somewhat from the aforementioned items identified in note 14 (Social Security Administration, 2013).
18. This is the most frequently used cost/income ratio to identify the dwelling expense burdens in the United States today.
19. (U.S. Department of Housing and Urban Development, 2013)
20. (Lipman, et al., 2010)

21. In 2011, 21% of Americans age 65 and older were members of racial or ethnic minority populations: 9% were African American, 4% were Asian, 1% were American Indian or Native Alaskan, and 7% were Hispanic (U.S. Department of Health and Human Services, 2012b).
22. (O'Brien, Wu, & Baer, 2010)
23. (AARP Public Policy Institute, 2011)
24. (Sabia, 2008)
25. (Kneale, Bamford, & Sinclair, 2012)
26. (Golant, 2003b)
27. (Netherland, et al., 2011)
28. (Housing Assistance Council, 2003)
29. (UnitedHealthcare, 2013)
30. (Munnell, Soto, & Aubry, 2007)
31. (Masnick, Di, & Belsky, 2006)
32. (Trawinski, 2012)
33. (Trawinski, 2012)
34. (Trawinski, 2012)
35. (Ludwig, 2007, p. 6)
36. (Joint Center for Housing Studies of Harvard University, 2013a)
37. (Engelhardt, Eriksen, & Greenhalgh-Stanley, 2013; Joint Center for Housing Studies of Harvard University, 2014)
38. 2011 U.S. Census American Housing Survey Data. Accessed at http://www.census.gov/housing/ahs/ (U.S. Department of Housing and Urban Development, 2011)
39. (Golant, 2009b)
40. (Puentes & Orfield, 2002; Puentes & Warren, 2006)
41. (Hudnut, 2003)
42. (Freedman & Agree, 2008)
43. We do not have reliable estimates of the number of older households afflicted by these deficiencies (Joint Center for Housing Studies of Harvard University, 2014).
44. (Fausset, Kelly, Rogers, & Fisk, 2011)
45. (Cornwell, 2014)
46. Hyperthermia refers to abnormally high body temperature (106 degrees Fahrenheit or higher). Hypothermia refers to abnormally low body temperature (below 90 degrees Fahrenheit).
47. (Gershon et al., 2008)
48. (Cornwell, 2013)
49. (Joint Center for Housing Studies of Harvard University, 2007)
50. (Joint Center for Housing Studies of Harvard University, 2007)
51. (Davidoff, 2004; Ginzler, 2012; Joint Center for Housing Studies of Harvard University, 2003)
52. In 2010, about 38% of people age 65 and over have trouble hearing, and 14% have trouble seeing (Federal Interagency Forum on Aging-Related Statistics, 2012)
53. (Ormond, Black, Tilly, & Thomas, 2004)
54. (Sabia, 2008)
55. Older people with mobility limitations are those who have one or more of the following characteristics: fear of falling; holding onto walls when walking across the room; has difficulty or needs help with bathing, toileting, or walking; or uses a mobility device, such as a cane or walker. The barriers include stairs to get into dwelling or building with no ramp or handrails; no grab bars or bath seat; no grab bars in toilet area; or no raised toilet seat.
56. This is a very conservative estimate because it is based on a very narrow definition of dwelling barriers and safety hazards. (Freedman & Agree, 2008)
57. (Centers for Disease Control and Prevention, 2008)
58. (Engelhardt, et al., 2013; Schiller, Kramarow, & Dey, 2007)
59. (Unwin, Andrews, Andrews, & Hanson, 2009)
60. (Cornwell, 2013)

61. (Owens, Russo, Spector, & Mutter, 2009; Pynoos, Rose, Rubenstein, Choi, & Sabata, 2006; Schiller, et al., 2007)

62. (Hong, Hasche, & Bowland, 2009)

63. (National Investment Center for the Seniors Housing & Care Industry, 2007)

64. (Cornwell, Laumann, & Schumm, 2008)

65. (The Lewin Group, 2010a), based on 2006 data.

66. (Federal Interagency Forum on Aging-Related Statistics, 2012)

67. (Federal Interagency Forum on Aging-Related Statistics, 2012)

68. Overweight and obese people have a BMI of 25.0 or greater. Body mass index (BMI) is calculated as weight in kilograms divided by height in meters squared.

69. (Federal Interagency Forum on Aging-Related Statistics, 2012)

70. The specific ADL indicators vary in minor ways from study to study.

71. (Freedman et al., 2013)

72. (Federal Interagency Forum on Aging-Related Statistics, 2012)

73. (Federal Interagency Forum on Aging-Related Statistics, 2012; Population Reference Bureau, 2013; Scommengna, 2013)

74. (Freedman, et al., 2013)

75. (Federal Interagency Forum on Aging-Related Statistics, 2012)

76. These rates will are higher overall because they include Medicare enrollees in nursing homes.

77. (Federal Interagency Forum on Aging-Related Statistics, 2012)

78. (Hong, et al., 2009; Muramatsu, Yin, & Hedcker, 2010)

79. (Mann et al., 2008)

80. (Mann, et al., 2008, pp. 9-10)

81. (Alzheimer's Association, 2012)

82. (Hurd, Martorell, Delavande, Mullen, & Langa, 2013)

83. (Alzheimer's Association, 2014)

84. (Alzheimer's Association, 2012)

85. (Stone, 2011)

86. (Kane, Kane, & Ladd, 1998, p. 4)

87. (Kemper, Komisar, & Alecxih, 2005)

88. (Kemper, et al., 2005)

89. (Kemper, et al., 2005).

90. (Kemper, et al., 2005)

91. (Neugarten & Hagestad, 1976)

92. (Stone, 2011)

93. (Kaye, Harrington, & LaPlante, 2010)

94. We also hear references to long-term supportive services (LTSS)

95. (Lehning & Austin, 2010)

96. (Newcomer, Kang, Laplante, & Kaye, 2005)

97. (Roth, Haley, Wadley, Clay, & Howard, 2007; Weissert & Frederick, 2013)

98. (Harrington, Ng, Kaye, & Newcomer, 2009)

99. (UnitedHealthcare, 2013)

100. (Naik, Kunik, Cassidy, Nair, & Coverdale, 2010, p. 615)

101. (Li, 2004)

102. Eric Oberdorfer, "Keeping Rural Seniors in Their Homes," posted on Rooflines, The Shelterforce blog, February 28,, 2014.

103. (Melnick, Ferrer, Shanks-McElroy, & Dunay, 2013); Eric Oberdorfer, "How Will We Care for This Overlooked Population?" posted on Rooflines, The Shelterforce blog, April 4, 2014

104. (Reinhard, Kassner, Houser, Ujvari, Mollica, & Hendrickson, 2014)

105. (McGinty, 2004)

106. (Gardner, 2011)

107. (Leland, 2011)

108. (Golden et al., 2009, p. 694)

109. Howard Gleckman, blog on September 7, 2011, http://blog.howardgleckman.com/
110. (Golden, et al., 2009)
111. (Seltzer & Yahirun, 2013)
112. (U.S. Department of Health and Human Services, 2012b)
113. Cornwell & Waite, 2009)
114. (Shaw, Krause, Liang, & Bennett, 2007)
115. (Bierman, 2009)
116. (Parkes, 1972, p. 9)
117. (Cornwell & Waite, 2009; Greenfield & Russell, 2011; Perissinotto, Stijacic Cenzer, & Covinsky, 2012; Tang & Lee, 2011)
118. (Cornwell & Waite, 2009)
119. (Federal Interagency Forum on Aging-Related Statistics, 2012). The universe is the noninstitutionalized population of old (e.g., outside of nursing homes).
120. (Federal Interagency Forum on Aging-Related Statistics, 2010; Scommengna, 2013)
121. (Scommengna, 2013)
122. (Dishman, 2012)
123. (Carstensen, Isaacowitz, & Charles, 1999)
124. (U.S. Department of Health and Human Services, 2012b)
125. (Wolf & Wilmoth, 2010)
126. (Mendes de Leon et al., 2009)
127. (Golant, 1992, p. 54)
128. To this traditional list of risky places, we should also add economically distressed localities that were hit by the 2007–2010 collapse of the U.S. housing market, which resulted in high concentrations of vacant and foreclosed properties, comprised paradoxically of more recently built dwellings.
129. (Golant, 1992)
130. (Yao & Robert, 2008)
131. (Aaronson, Zinn, & Rosko, 1995)
132. (Kerr, Rosenberg, & Frank, 2012; Shih et al., 2011)
133. (Clarke et al., 2014)
134. (Beard, Cerda, et al., 2009; Krause, 2003)
135. (Krause, 2003)
136. (Clarke, Ailshire, Bader, Morenoff, & House, 2008)
137. (Wight, Ko, & Aneshensel, 2011, p. 31)
138. (Clarke, et al., 2014)
139. (Krause, 2003)
140. (Krause, 2003, p. 234)
141. (Krause, 2003)
142. (Beard, Cerda, et al., 2009; Bowling & Stafford, 2007; Cagney, Browning, & Wen, 2005; Ostir, Eschbach, Markides, & Goodwin, 2003)
143. "Dying Alone," an interview with Eric Klinenberg author of Heat Wave: A Social Autopsy of Disaster in Chicago http://www.press.uchicago.edu/Misc/Chicago/443213in.html
144. (Lynott & Figueiredo, 2011, p. 5)
145. (Durazo, Jones, Wallace, Arsdale, & Aydin, 2011; U.S. Government Accountability Office, 2011a)
146. (Farber & Shinkle, 2011)
147. (Grafova, Freedman, Kumar, & Rogowski, 2008; Yamashita & Kunkel, 2012)
148. (Connell, Harmon, Janevic, & Kostyniuk, 2013; Mezuk & Rebok, 2008)
149. (Baily, 2004)
150. (Golant, 2009b; Rosenbloom, 2009)
151. (Durazo, et al., 2011)
152. (Golant, 2003d)
153. (Medicare Payment Advisory Commission, 2001)
154. (Nelson & Gingerich, 2010)
155. (McAuley, Spector, & Van Nostrand, 2009)

156. (Ritter, Straight, & Evans, 2002)
157. (Baily, 2004)
158. (Lynott & Figueiredo, 2011)
159. (Golant, 1976)
160. (Lynott & Figueiredo, 2011; Pisarski, 2006)
161. (Insurance Institute for Highway Safety, 2011)
162. (Dumbaugh, 2008)
163. (Foley, Heimovitz, Guralnic, & Brock, 2002)
164. (U.S. Department of Transportation, 2014)
165. (McKnight, 2003, p. 26)
166. (Lipman, et al., 2010)
167. (Dumbaugh, 2008)
168. (Transportation for America, 2011, p. 4)
169. (Kerschner, 2003)
170. (Kerr, et al., 2012)
171. (Leinberger, 2005)
172. (Beard, Blaney, et al., 2009; Berke et al., 2006; Clarke, et al., 2008; Clarke & George, 2005; King, 2008; Li, Fisher, & Brownson, 2005; Michael, Green, & Farquhar, 2006; Yeom, Fleury, & Keller, 2008)
173. (Harrell, Lynott, Guzman, & Lampkin, 2014; Mendes de Leon, et al., 2009)
174. (National Highway Traffic Safety Administration, 2013)
175. (Kerr, et al., 2012)

Part III

COPING TO ACHIEVE RESIDENTIAL NORMALCY

Adapting Buildings and Families

5

COPING—OR NOT GIVING UP

The measure of success is how we cope with disappointment, as we must. . . . It doesn't matter if we feel that we're too old, too scared and disappointed. We get up in the morning. We do our best. Nothing else matters.

It will be all right in the end. If it's not all right now, it must not be the end.[1]

OUT OF THEIR ZONES: HOW OLDER PEOPLE COPE

Whether because of bad luck, poor judgment, uninformed decisions, apathy, or uncontrollable events, older people find themselves out of their residential comfort or mastery zones. Despite their *"good planning and sensible living,"*[2] their dwellings, neighborhoods, or communities become unsuitable places to live. As psychotherapist Erlene Rosowsky realistically informs us, there is no way *"to completely avoid these vicissitudes, challenges, and losses . . . they're part of life's tapestry."*[3] However, what ultimately influences whether older adults achieve residential normalcy is not whether they confront events, activities, or surroundings that they feel are unfavorable, whether preventable or not. Rather, what most matters is how effectively and skillfully they blunt or eliminate their stresses, discomforts, and losses.[4]

Recall that the authors of the New Gerontology paradigm (Chapter 1) argued that in order for older Americans to avoid disease, maintain their high physical and mental functioning, and keep active, they had to take responsibility for their futures and adopt proactive and preventive lifestyles. Even though many academics and professionals do not share their vision of successful aging, they do agree that older people should strive to be agents of change and *"control their own life course destinies."*[5]

101

Experts studying the course of human development have long argued that people who age the most successfully are those who adapt or cope effectively with the adversity in their lives and environments.[6] When these older adults feel out of their residential comfort or mastery zones, they do not passively sit back and accept their gloomy fates.[7] Rather, they take proactive steps to change their undesirable housing or care circumstances, and they aggressively make things happen by engaging and influencing the environments around them.[8]

DIFFERENT WAYS OF COPING

Human development theorists distinguish two different categories of coping strategies by which older adults address their unfavorable experiences. Jochen Brandstädter and his colleagues[9] referred to these as *accommodative* and *assimilative* coping patterns (Figure 5.1).

ACCOMMODATIVE COPING PATTERNS

When people rely on accommodative coping strategies, they respond to the obstacles, constraints, and discordant features in their residential settings by using a variety of mind strategies that allow them to *"maintain and regain a positive view of self."*[10] Other theorists have called these individual responses "emotion-focused coping,"[11] "secondary control adaptation strategies,"[12] and "defensive reappraisals."[13] Older people

Figure 5.1. Coping strategies available to older people out of their residential mastery zones

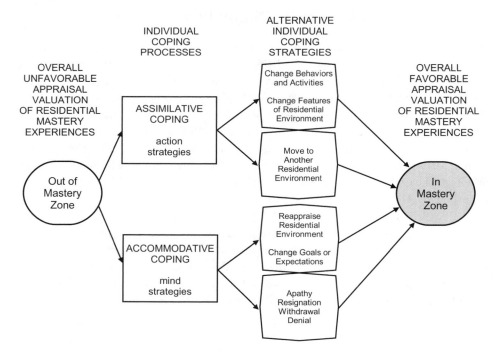

attempt to solve their residential problems by convincing themselves that they have been too critical of their surroundings and that, in any case, their housing problems should not be the focus in their lives. They rationalize that their unpleasant residential experiences or feelings of powerlessness are not so bad in comparison with other problems in their lives. Altogether, they put a positive spin on their difficulties and de-emphasize their salience.

Researchers investigating determinants of the residential satisfaction of older people drew on this interpretation to explain why their negative feelings about where they lived dissipated over time.[14] They found that those living longer in their current residences were more satisfied because they lowered their evaluation standards to conform to their less-than-ideal living conditions.[15] Their path of least resistance to "eliminating" their problems was to loosen their grip on their unattainable goals.[16] There are a host of mind strategies that older people might draw on:

- They give up on, reformulate, or change their goals, aspirations, expectations, or commitments by making them less ambitious or more doable.
  - They come to grips with the reality that their house will never appear in Architectural Digest, but it is still comfortable and secure.
- They immunize themselves against their current residential deficiencies by reappraising them as less consequential to their happiness—small potatoes in the scheme of things—or as having marginal effects on their self-esteem or self-identity; that is, the extent to which they see themselves as successful or self-fulfilled people.[17]
  - They rationalize that their neighborhoods are not as important for their happiness as their good health, or they will be okay even though a best friend has left the community.
- They minimize the severity of their problems by comparing themselves with others.
  - They favorably compare where they live with the abodes occupied by close friends or relatives, who they conclude are in worse shape than themselves.
- To "forget" their current residential deficiencies, they refocus their mental energies on the emotionally satisfying memories of past things, events, or people.[18]
  - They rationalize their current dwelling's downsides by remembering all their good past experiences as occupants.
- They look to their religious or spiritual beliefs to justify their losses.
  - They view their plight as an expression of God's will that they should not challenge.

Many housing and long-term care experts view these mind-coping strategies as irrational, ineffectual, and downright dangerous. They argue that when older people simply manipulate their thoughts and perceptions to achieve positive housing or care outcomes, they do not solve real problems that threaten their physical or psychological well-being. De-emphasizing the importance of their poorly heated houses does not eliminate the possibility that they will experience hypothermia. Minimizing the importance of clutter in their houses does not eliminate their risks of falling. Glossing over the deep emotional loss of a significant other does not reduce the painful consequences of loneliness. In short, mind strategies do little to reduce the real risk of harmful consequences.

Some psychologists go further. They argue that an overreliance on mind strategies may be pathological, as evidence of escapism or depression,[19] and counter to aging successfully.[20] They are most concerned with older people who cope with their "painful reality"[21] not just by changing or modifying their goals, preferences, or expectations or reassessing their salience, but also by consciously denying their plight. These people simply make their unpleasant or stressful feelings disappear by ignoring or forgetting them.[22] When interviewed, they report feeling fine about their personal or residential situations. It is as if they are quarantining a computer virus and hiding it in some inaccessible region of their brain. They become chronically apathetic, or as Seligman expressed it, they enter a state of "learned helplessness."[23]

There are, however, upsides to these accommodation strategies. Denial may be an especially adaptive strategy for older people wanting to age in place. By hiding their vulnerabilities and portraying themselves as healthy, competent, and problem-free, they hope to communicate to the outside world that they are not a burden and do not need extensive assistance in a more supportive environment—whether in the home of their family, an assisted living residence, or a nursing home.[24]

Moreover, they enable older people who are confronted with undesirable circumstances to exhibit an *"astounding stability of {their} self-esteem and subjective quality of life in later adulthood."*[25] In such ways, they avoid *problems of "self-esteem, identity deficits, and depression."*[26] As one psychologist aptly summed up,

> Under conditions where it seems impossible to maintain desired levels of functioning and performance, the gradual rescaling of self-evaluative standards may be the most effective way to manage gaps between aspirations and achievements and to retain a positive balance of gains and losses.[27]

Assimilative Coping Patterns

In contrast to the passivity of accommodation coping strategies, older people who rely on assimilative coping patterns engage in action strategies. Other theorists have referred to these coping strategies as "problem-focused" coping,[28] "selective optimization with compensation,"[29] and "primary control strategies."[30]

These older people make their problems go away by eliminating, changing, or modifying their activities, lifestyles, capabilities, or residential and care surroundings to make them better align with their needs or goals.[31] For example, older adults with physical or sensory impairments take proactive steps to maintain their autonomy by equipping their homes with emergency response systems, installing grab bars in their bathrooms, or putting in burglar alarm systems.[32] M. Powell Lawton, a distinguished environmental gerontologist, identified how older people with limited mobility often established a "control center" in their dwellings that contributed to their feelings of empowerment.[33] This typically consisted of comfortable seating, a telephone, an emergency communication device, grooming items, a TV remote, a cane, and a note-pad clustered in one spot of a room. Here, the older people spent a good deal of their time because they felt in control of their everyday surroundings.

Moving from their current residences is probably the most studied assimila-tive coping strategy, but it is only one of a host of adaptations by which older people achieve residential normalcy:

- They avoid the offensive confrontations.
  - They build a fence around their house to keep out annoying children.
- They attempt to better empower themselves to deal with their sources of dis-comfort or anxiety.
  - They learn new skills, such as how to avoid home accidents.[34]
- They eliminate or weaken the offensive aspects of their residential settings.
  - When a neighbor has noisy kids, they complain to the landlord or call the police.
- They compensate for their declines by using less energy and pursuing only selected activities.
  - They rely more on the familiar, the well-oiled routines that worked in the past. For example, when they cannot drive to a favorite Chinese restaurant, they rely on home delivery.

ACCOMMODATIVE VERSUS ASSIMILATIVE STRATEGIES

Human development theorists do not offer any clear-cut guidance about when older people are more likely to initiate accommodative as opposed to assimilative coping strategies. However, most believe that aging successfully requires older people to initi-ate action rather than mind-coping responses.[35]

Some theorists also argue that older people rely more on mind-coping strategies when they are overwhelmed with their housing and care problems and have experi-enced an *"accumulation of irreversible events."*[36] Their resolve may have been *"eroded by repeated unsuccessful attempts to alter the situation."*[37] These aging adults judge that they have a low probability of successfully eradicating the stressful aspects of their cur-rent residential or care arrangements, that their practical solutions are unfeasible, or that their *"losses and aversive events are . . . inevitable and uncontrollable."*[38] Alternatively, they judge possible solutions as too costly to initiate, materially or emotionally,[39] and decide that the time and energy it takes to eliminate a problem is more trying than experiencing the problem itself.[40] In the words of these vulnerable seniors, "I'm not strong enough," "I'm too weak," or "I feel broken."[41]

MOVING AS A COPING SOLUTION

Most older people do not agree with national aging expert Ken Dychtwald's prognosis that moving is the best way to cope with their incongruent residential settings:

> The reality is that, throughout your life, you have chosen different types of homes to meet your evolving lifestyle. From your parents' home, to college dormitories, to smaller apartments during your singlehood, to larger homes when raising your family, you have repeatedly moved to new homes that provide the best communities, living space, lifestyle, and amenities for each stage of your life. Your current stage in life is no different.[42]

Rather, older people's desire to age in place acts as a powerful deterrent to moving (Chapter 3), even when major stressful life events such as the death of a spouse, a divorce, or health declines radically change their residential needs.[43] Typically, older people choose to move only after they have met four conditions.

First, they have failed in their *in situ* coping efforts to resolve their housing problems and care deficiencies. Despite their accommodative and assimilative (other than moving) adaptive efforts, they have been unable to achieve residential normalcy.

Second, moving must be feasible. Older people must be able to sell their homes at acceptable prices or afford to live in an assisted living residence. However emotionally incongruent older people find their current residential arrangements, they must have credible alternatives if they are to move.

Third, older people must not only believe that they have feasible relocation alternatives but must also be convinced that these places will substantially increase their residential comfort or residential mastery appraisal valuations. So-called push (repelling) and pull (attracting) moving determinants are not independent; they must reinforce each other. However uncomfortable (out of their comfort zones) older people are in their current abodes, they move only if they expect to receive more enjoyment or pleasure in another residential arrangement.[44] The recent widow may feel her house is too big (the push factor), but she will not move to the cramped living quarters of a small rented apartment (the pull factor).[45] Their moves must be healing or therapeutic, with more rewarding lifestyles and an overall improved quality of life in their new locations. They must feel more fully engaged. In other words, they must feel they can rejuvenate the magnetic forces elsewhere that for so long nurtured their current residential inertia and their comfort zone experiences. This push–pull synergy means that moving to a new place must also be empowering and increase feelings of residential mastery. Older people must be able to compensate for their declines or losses and find new ways to conduct their lives more effectively and competently.[46] If an older woman recognizes she needs more assistance to perform her activities of daily living (ADLs), she must also be convinced that she can get the necessary help in her daughter's home and feel more autonomous.

There is corollary to this third moving condition. Older people must be convinced that they have credible information about their potential destinations, and they must trust the motives and abilities of their communicators. They must believe that the assisted living provider, the marketing agent for an active adult community, or the home care provider is a reliable source of information and has their best interests at heart. It matters who is dishing up all the positive indicators about a "wonderful" place to move. They also move only when they have thoroughly vetted their destinations and feel confident about their choices. This explains why many relocate to places they are already very familiar with, where they have had multiple past holidays or earlier purchased vacation homes.[47]

Fourth, older people must not appraise the act of moving itself as overwhelming. Taking up residence in a new place, however attractive, requires physical exertion and substantial psychological adjustments, not to mention money.[48] Moving entails various kinds of costs. Older people are less likely to consider moving as a coping strategy if they view the act itself as prohibitively stressful, threatening, exhausting, or expensive.

Given the challenges they face to satisfy all four of these conditions, it is hardly surprising that older people are reticent to move. They often muster up the courage to leave their current dwellings and communities only after many months or years. Just getting rid of a lifetime accumulation of cherished possessions can be overwhelmingly time-consuming and emotionally stressful.[49] One national survey reported that 45% of their older respondents spent a year or longer planning their moves.[50]

We generally stop scrutinizing the moving decisions of older people once they have selected their destinations. However, even after they move to their so-called utopia, an undocumented number of older adults become disillusioned with its downsides and quietly move back to their former locations.[51]

MULTIPLE DECISION MAKERS

Making generalizations about the conditions underlying the moving decisions of older people becomes more complicated when they are married or cohabitating with others who disagree about the suitability of their current residence and how they want to spend the rest of their lives. These households reveal *"an awkward mix of clashing ideas, sudden revelations, and silent standoffs."*[52]

This is not surprising. First, the two people may be differently suffering from the vagaries of old age. Consequently, one may be *"robust and energetic"* whereas the other is battling some *"longstanding chronic health problem."*[53] Members of these households juggle very different decision-making factors.

Second, the two people may not be at the same points in their life. For example, men may retire earlier than their younger wives and will not be constrained by their job locations when they consider their residential futures. Women, for their part, may be less able or wanting to move because they are reluctant to relinquish the professional accomplishments or financial rewards of their jobs or have stronger emotional attachments to their dwellings because they were primarily homemakers. Consider the following example reported in *The Fiscal Times*:

> Lois Arthur, a 61-year-old psychologist living in Boston, found herself at odds with her husband, Gene, a 66-year-old social worker. He wanted to retire and move to their country home in Vermont; she wanted to continue working and remain in the city to be close to family.[54]

And third, even when both spouses have stopped working and are open to making changes in their residential situation, they may not share the same visions for retirement. Consider this example:

Jackie Fishman, a 59-year-old media relations executive, always thought she and her husband would spend their retirement years in their Washington, D.C., condo, near their children, while taking frequent trips around the world. She wants to keep working so they can be financially secure and more easily pay their $1,200 monthly health insurance costs until they're eligible for Medicare. But her husband, also 59, is working as a fundraiser for a nonprofit, a job that will end within two years. He dreams of buying a house on a North Carolina mountain, getting a few pets, and gardening. They never discussed retirement plans until now. "We are totally at an impasse," she says.[55]

When discord rather than unanimity rules, neither partner is completely satisfied. Most experts agree that *"dragging an unwilling spouse to a new location, hoping she or he will have a change in heart"* is a losing proposition.[56] Consequently, reaching a compromise position may save a marriage but still produce a result in which neither spouse lands squarely in his or her residential comfort and mastery zones.

RESIDENTIAL MOVING BEHAVIORS OF OLDER AMERICANS

ODDS OF MOVING

One way of illustrating the low likelihood of older people moving is to show how their stats differ from those of the young. Between 2011 and 2012, almost 25% of Americans in their 20s moved from their dwellings at least once in the previous year.[57] Those in their middle years were much less likely to move: About 14% of those in the 30- to 44-year age group moved, and only about 7% of those age 45–64 moved. Thereafter, moving rates drop further. Only 3.7% of Americans age 65–74 moved, and only 3.1% of those 75 years or older did so.[58] When older people reach their mid-80s and older, there is a slight upward blip in their moving propensity as they give up aging in place in their homes and apartments because of their more severe chronic health conditions and mobility limitations.[59]

Dwelling tenure is an important predictor. Between 2011 and 2012, homeowners age 65 and older were especially unlikely to move (1.8%) compared with renters (12.2%).[60] Homeowners are more likely to transition to rented accommodations first in their 60s, usually in response to amenity and lifestyle changes, and then again in their 70s and later, usually in response to changes in their health and capabilities.[61]

MOVING DESTINATIONS

One might expect that when older people change residences they relocate to a different region of the country, or at least to a different state. Florida is one of the premier Sunbelt destinations for new retirees from the Northeast and Midwest seeking to escape cold, brutal winters and enjoy a warm and snow-free year-round climate.

The reality is different. Almost 60% of older people who moved between 2011 and 2012 chose to live in the same county, and another 25% moved to a different county but remained in the same state. Just over 15% of moving older adults crossed state lines, and just over half of these relocations were to an entirely different region, such as from New York to Florida.[62] These destination selections varied according to their dwelling tenure status. More than 64% of relocating renters age 65 and older who moved in the past year remained in the same county, in contrast to only 49% of homeowners of the same age who moved to more distant communities.[63]

The motivations for longer-distance moves may be very different and partly explained by age differences. Young-old (age 65–74) people are more likely to make these longer moves than their old-old (age 75 and up) counterparts.[64] These more healthy, often married older adults seek amenity-rich residential settings where they can enjoy leisure and recreational activities to ensure a more fully engaged and active lifestyle and to be more squarely in their residential comfort zones.[65] In contrast, the old-old move across the country because they want to live closer to family members who can help them cope with their declines in health and mobility—that is, to be more squarely in their residential mastery zones.

Whatever their motivations, most interstate moves by older adults are highly channelized. That is, older people depart from many scattered state locations, but they end up in a few *"relatively focused state destinations."*[66] These states include Arizona, Arkansas, California, Colorado, Florida, Missouri (specifically the Ozarks), Nevada, North Carolina, Oregon, Texas, and Washington.[67] These migration streams help explain the small number of important traditional and new "retirement magnet metropolitan areas" (Figure 5.2).[68]

Although urban places attract the most retirees, a small but significant share gravitate to rural and small-town America.[69] More than 270 rural counties (out of a possible 2,052) have consistently received above-average influxes of older people.[70] Often the rural and small-town destinations are within driving distance of an urban center.[71] Among the favored destinations are the *"mountain and coastal regions of the West, in the upper Great Lakes, in coastal and scenic areas of New England and upstate New York, in the foothills of the Appalachians and Ozarks, and in coastal regions from Virginia to Florida."*[72] Some experts predict that the attractions of rural and small-town America will be greater for older baby boomers, and they will increasingly move to *"counties with desirable physical attributes—pleasant climates, mountains, beaches, lakes."*[73]

SELECTING DESTINATIONS

A 2009 national survey offered insights into why older movers (in a previous 2-year period) favored certain communities.[74] It distinguished older people who moved into single-family detached units as opposed to multifamily units.[75] Those moving into multifamily units tended to be living alone and female. They favored communities with better public transportation and public services. The most often cited reason for choosing a community for both groups, but especially for the new occupants of multifamily units, was being close to relatives and friends. The attractiveness of the housing unit was the third most common reason for choosing a community.

Another national survey offered further insights. In late 2009, the Del Webb corporation polled 64-year-olds about whether they expected to move to a new home during their retirement years. About a third of these boomers said they were, with more than 50% of this group planning to relocate to another state. The top states they

Figure 5.2. Largest average net migration gains of people age 55 and older in 51 U.S. metropolitan areas with more than 1,000,000 in population, 2009–2012 (average annual net migration for periods 2009–2010, 2010–2011, and 2011–2012; [Frey, 2013])

1. Phoenix–Mesa–Scottsdale, Arizona, metro area: 18,401

2. Riverside–San Bernardino–Ontario, California, metro area: 11,125

3. Tampa–St. Petersburg–Clearwater, Florida, metro area: 8,028

4. Atlanta–Sandy Springs–Marietta, Georgia, metro area: 5,713

5. Denver–Aurora–Broomfield, Colorado, metro area: 3,966

6. Austin–Round Rock, Texas, metro area: 3,500

7. Orlando–Kissimmee, Florida, metro area: 3,495

8. Jacksonville, Florida, metro area: 3,334

9. Charlotte–Gastonia–Concord, North Carolina–South Carolina, metro area: 3,128

10. San Antonio, Texas, metro area: 2,998

11. Portland–Vancouver–Beaverton, Oregon–Washington, metro area: 2,427

12. Las Vegas–Paradise, Nevada, metro area: 2,292

13. Sacramento–Arden–Arcade–Roseville, California, metro area: 1,869

14. Dallas–Fort Worth–Arlington, Texas, metro area: 1,820

15. Miami–Fort Lauderdale–Pompano Beach, Florida, metro area: 1,411

16. Raleigh–Cary, North Carolina, metro area: 1,393

17. Indianapolis–Carmel, Indiana, metro area: 1,340

18. Houston–Sugar Land–Baytown, Texas, metro area: 1,154

19. Nashville–Davidson–Murfreesboro–Franklin, Tennessee, metro area: 910

20. New Orleans–Metairie–Kenner, Louisiana, metro area: 694

identified, in order of importance, were North and South Carolina, Florida, Tennessee, Virginia, Arizona, and California.[76] Boomers reported that the factors most influencing their destination choices included (from highest to lowest percentages) places with a lower cost of living, access to preferred healthcare programs, more favorable climate, presence of cultural and recreational amenities, community and networking opportunities, and being close to children or grandchildren.

TYPOLOGY OF OLDER MOVERS: RESIDENTIAL COMFORT AND RESIDENTIAL MASTERY SEEKERS

We can identify nine groups of older movers, each with a distinctive set of motives for changing their addresses. The first six groups include older people who move predominantly because they are out of their residential comfort zones. Other researchers collectively refer to these groups as *amenity driven* or *lifestyle driven* movers. The remaining three groups include older adults who relocate predominantly because they are out of their residential mastery zones, classified as *assistance and nursing home* movers.[77] Assigning older movers to these nine different groups may still oversimplify their relocation decisions because they may be out of both their residential comfort and mastery zones and have multiple motivations for moving.

MOVERS SEEKING THEIR RESIDENTIAL COMFORT ZONE

SIMPLIFYING, DISCRIMINATING, DOWNSIZING SEEKERS

One of the largest groups of movers seek to simplify and downsize, and they come from all demographic backgrounds. Their residential settings often have not changed for the worse in any dramatic way, but they strive to refocus their residential priorities. They may seek places to live where they can conduct their lives and activities in a simpler and less-demanding fashion. For example, they opt for places that have more of a rural than an urban pace of living. Similarly, homeowners seek easier-to-maintain rental accommodations or newer and smaller owned dwellings,[78] sometimes condominiums or townhomes where they have minimal exterior and interior upkeep.[79] Older people in this category may have very specific physical design preferences:

> A wife . . . described being done and past the era for formal entertaining and, therefore, no longer wanted dining room furnishings and fine china. She was not even sure she still needed a home that had a dining room.[80]

Other older people find that their current residential arrangements are inconsistent with their preferred retirement lifestyles. For example, a recently widowed woman is able to move to a high-rise apartment closer to the downtown, a move vetoed by her past husband. After the death of her mother, an older daughter who was her caregiver now is free to pursue her own way of living.

STRESS-AVERSIVE SEEKERS

The people in this category may be healthy and active but feel stressed because of some perceived unfavorable changes to their residential arrangements. Unlike those who are seeking to simplify and downsize, they move not because of new residential or lifestyle preferences but because they are confronting intolerable new housing hassles.

Feeling less energetic in their old-old years, they may have tired of dealing with cold and snowy winters. Alternatively, they may be confronting increasing needs for repairs or maintenance for their older house. They may feel that the new occupants in the apartment across the hall are too noisy, or they are troubled by the ethnic, racial, or age composition changes of their neighborhood. In the extreme, natural calamities may have struck their communities. Hurricanes in Florida and New Orleans, fires in California, floods in Mississippi, and tornados in Arkansas can make life very stressful for even the sturdiest retirees in these locations.

HEDONISTIC SEEKERS

These older movers' conception of the good life involves pursuing an array of fun leisure and recreational activities that they cannot find in their current locales. For example, a recently retired man no longer judges his residential setting by how close it is to his workplace but rather how far it is from where he hunts and fishes. The divorced older woman is pulled to a university or college town because of its plethora of cultural and intellectual events. Another older person is attracted to an active adult community with its extensive regimen of planned recreational activities (Chapter 10). Others relocate to a gentrified neighborhood where they patronize its art galleries, antique stores, and jazz clubs.

VARIATION SEEKERS

These movers seek out places that can offer them new and different experiences. These "can do anything" people enjoy the prospects of planning their own destinies[81] and view old age as a period in life when they can experiment with new styles of living. Researchers have aptly characterized these people as the "adventurous aged"[82] because they are more likely to have stimulus-, sensation-, or variation-seeking personalities and thrive on change, exploration, or novelty. They enjoy being challenged and trying new things, living in unfamiliar places, and forming new personal relationships.[83] They have self-confidence in their abilities to cope with the uncertainties, ambiguities, and risks that accompany a move to a new place.[84] For these older people, *"Moving represents freedom . . . the ability to take off."*[85] These people are also likely to be more optimistic about their lives generally and expect good things to happen to them as they progress through their later years.[86]

Such older people include the "rambling retirees" who roam the United States in recreational vehicles (hotels on wheels),[87] whom one expert described as travelers or explorers with weak residential place attachments.[88] Another group is those retiring outside the United States; about 350,000 American retirees receive Social Security benefits in foreign countries.[89]

CIVIC-MINDED AND PRODUCTIVITY SEEKERS

These older people, often retired, seek out communities where they feel more productive and can help or teach others or contribute in some meaningful way to their communities. They seek *"camaraderie, intellectual stimulation, and the satisfaction of achieving a goal."*[90] They want to serve as volunteers, teachers, counselors, or advocates and feel better about themselves when they actively participate in planning, political, charitable, religious, or philanthropic endeavors or activities; that is, they are civically engaged.[91] The movers in this category typically are better educated, have higher incomes, are in better health, are more socially adept, and have stronger religious affiliations.[92] They look for positions as childcare or elder care providers, home maintainers (e.g., doing housework), transportation providers, or political organizers. Others seek part-time or even full-time employment, sometimes even another career in a very different occupation than in their earlier lives.[93] High on these older people's lists are places that offer them flexible opportunities (i.e., ones that accommodate their time and energy constraints) to perform their civic and education responsibilities and where they feel welcome to contribute their knowledge and compassionate assistance to others.[94] These places must exhibit a "community capacity" and include leaders who *demonstrate a sense of shared responsibility for the general welfare of the community and its individual members.*[95]

SOCIAL NETWORK SEEKERS

The older members of this group are attracted to communities, neighborhoods, or household arrangements that offer them enjoyable and stimulating friendships, companions, and confidants. We can distinguish two subgroups of older people motivated for different sets of reasons.

For one group of older people, the number of their close friends or neighbors may have dwindled in their current locations. Others may just want to add more friends in their retirement years. Whatever their motives, they look to communities *"where they can make friends and connections quickly."*[96] These movers are attracted to places populated by like-minded residents and organizations (e.g., clubs, churches, or fraternal groups) that share their ethnic, racial, religious, or political beliefs. They may specifically seek out places that are sympathetic to their sexual preferences (lesbian, homosexual, or transsexual). They often prefer gated subdivisions, condominiums, or co-op high-rises because they want assurances that a homogeneous group of compatible people will occupy their buildings or neighborhoods. As is true for our hedonistic movers, active adult communities may be high on their list because of their seniors-only policies. Senior cohousing communities will sometimes be attractive because of their more intimate social network (Chapter 10).

A second group of older people, sometimes characterized as chain migrants, desire to live near at least one of their adult children or siblings, or near earlier friends from their former lives.[97] More than 50% of a national sample of people age 60 and older reported that when they thought about their housing needs, *"being close to friends and family are most important."*[98] In particular, they seek this proximity (at least initially) not because they themselves need help. Rather, they may be an older married couple who wants to enjoy their new role as grandparents and help their married children take care of their younger children.[99]

In what is sometimes called the Golden Girls arrangement, a recently widowed older person will move to share a household with another single woman with whom she has long had an emotionally close but physically distant friendship. Along with their social support advantages, these cohabiting households also benefit by sharing their dwelling and household expenses.[100]

Several other moving examples are also worth noting. Historians report that older African-Americans who have lived much of their adult lives in northern states sometimes return to the South after their retirement to be closer to family members and their historical roots.[101] Similarly motivated moves are made by older people who now live in northeastern and midwestern states who seek to be near their grown children who earlier migrated to the fast-growing states of the West and the South.[102] A smaller subgroup have very different motivations for moving. After being single for some period, they marry or remarry and relocate to a location that is closer to their new spouse's family.[103] Some older people take extreme measures to avoid feeling alone, exemplified by former Korean immigrants to the United States who later return to their home country to be close to family.[104]

MOVERS SEEKING THEIR RESIDENTIAL MASTERY ZONE

RESIDENTIAL FINANCIAL RELIEF SEEKERS

This category includes movers who want to feel more in control of their finances. They become overburdened by their dwelling costs and seek less-expensive residential settings to own or rent. It may include those who seek out shared-household arrangements as a way to decrease their living expenses. Other older people reduce their outlays by renting less-expensive apartments or purchasing scaled-down homes in more-affordable housing markets with less-burdensome taxes.[105] A small share seek out government-subsidized rental accommodations that substantially reduce their monthly dwelling costs (Chapter 9). Another residual group is attracted to foreign countries where they can benefit from less-expensive caregiving help and lower medical or long-term care bills.

This group of movers also includes those without financial problems, who seek residential alternatives that will strengthen their future economic worth. Sometimes historical periods offer these older people very attractive moving opportunities. During the 1990s and early 2000s, house prices were at all-time highs, especially in markets such as California, Nevada, and Florida. The retirees in these places had strong financial incentives to move because they had the opportunity to cash out their home's equity and relocate to places with more-affordable housing markets and an overall lower cost of living. Federal tax law offered these house-rich older homeowners an additional incentive to sell their homes because single people do not have to pay taxes on their capital gains of less than $250,000 (on the cost basis of their dwelling), and married people are spared of taxes on gains up to $500,000.

LIGHT HELP, SECURITY, AND PREVENTIVE HEALTH SEEKERS

These moves are precipitated by worsening health, difficulties with instrumental ADLs (IADLs), a drop in household income that has changed the affordability of care, or the death, incapacitation, or institutionalization of a spouse.[106] Family members have much more influence on the decision making of these movers,[107] as do professionals such as physicians, social workers, caseworkers, and senior-housing providers.[108]

These people might have made modifications (e.g., handrails and grab bars) in their dwellings but now feel that these fixes are insufficient to accommodate their aging bodies.[109] Consequently, they relocate to buildings that have design features that are not barriers to their living independently. For example, some renters move because their current multifamily buildings lack an elevator.[110] These movers are also attracted to well-secured residential accommodations (e.g., highrise buildings, guarded communities), where they do not have to feel threatened by unwanted visitors or solicitors and feel secure even though they are living alone. They will also find appealing communities where it is easier or unnecessary for them to perform nondiscretionary activities, such as shopping, preparing meals, or getting to a doctor.[111]

Some hope to feel more secure and competent by moving geographically closer to a friend or family member or possibly sharing the dwellings of these significant others.[112] This is the motive for many older people who relocate from states such as Florida back to northeastern and midwestern destinations. These "return" movers have often suffered a decline in their health or ability to live independently, so they relocate to their original home states to benefit from the nearby assistance of sons, daughters, or siblings.[113] These movers tend to be much older (in their early 80s and older), are less educated, and have lower incomes, which prevented them from earlier hiring professional help. Because of their profiles, demographers sometimes refer to these older people as "negatively selected" migrants. Despite Florida's reputation as a haven for younger retirees, for example, typically more people age 85 and older leave than enter the state.[114]

Other movers in this category seek to distance themselves from their family members because they value their self-reliance and do not want to be a burden. The following is a common refrain: *"I don't want to be a burden on my married daughter and her husband. They have their own problems and responsibilities. Why should they shoulder my problems as well?"* In a national opinion poll of older people, 53% reported that what they most feared about having a long-term illness was being a burden on their family.[115]

To take control of their caregiving needs, these people relocate to residential arrangements such as independent living communities, where they regularly receive prepared meals, door-to-door transportation, and health checkups and can get help quickly in the event of an emergency. Alternatively, they seek out continuing care retirement communities, which offer multiple levels of care (Chapter 12).[116]

This category predominantly includes older people relocating to seek more assistance or care, but this is not always the case. A small share of older people who entered nursing homes to benefit from rehabilitative care or skilled nursing services later no longer need its heavier care. This allows them to relocate to independent living communities or to assisted living developments or to return to dwellings in their communities where they can receive in-home care. Discharge data reveal that 30% of older people admitted to U.S. nursing homes later recuperated and went back to live in the community.[117]

HEAVY HELP SEEKERS

These movers tend to be in their 80s and older and have several chronic health problems and multiple IADL and ADL limitations that necessitate ongoing assistance and supportive services that are not available in their current homes or apartments.[118] To cope with their vulnerabilities, some move into the homes of family members; alternatively, others relocate to an assisted living residence or a nursing home that may specifically accommodate older people who need dementia care. They may be attracted to facilities that are located near family members (often at their urging), who want to visit and serve as their advocates.

Most in this category are transitioning to residential care settings from their ordinary homes and apartments. But largely hidden from the public view are the thousands of moves annually that involve especially vulnerable older people relocating from one long-term care setting to another in order to obtain heavier care.[119]

Some will move from independent living communities to assisted living developments or nursing homes, sometimes located on the same campus of a continuing care retirement community. These moves may be just as traumatic as relocations from ordinary houses and apartments because older people must still sever strong attachments with their accommodations, other occupants, and familiar staff members.

Other frail seniors must move from one nursing home bed to another because a private-pay bed has become unaffordable and there are no beds funded under the Medicaid program. Other moves occur because a family member is dissatisfied with a place's quality of care.

ASSIMILATIVE STRATEGIES: WHY SOME OLDER PEOPLE COPE BETTER

Some older people deal better with their adverse living conditions, are more proactive, and find more optimum residential or care solutions. This book theorizes that older people who are able to initiate adaptive behaviors to achieve their residential normalcy will have more *enriched coping repertoires*.[120] They judge that they have more *available* coping solutions that will be *efficacious* (that is, lead to successful solutions), and *viable* (that is, doable or implementable). Earlier, psychologists Lazarus and Folkman referred to these perceptual and cognitive assessments as a person's *secondary appraisal* process (that is, an estimation of *"what might and can be done"*[121]).

SECONDARY APPRAISAL PROCESS

Older people who feel out of their residential comfort or mastery zones must first identify the range of possible assimilative coping strategies that are available to them. They must scan their current or an alternative residential environment for information to determine which options are feasible and can address their new needs or goals. Using more formal terminology, older people must subjectively appraise the adaptive capacities or *resiliency* of these places to find ways to rectify or manage their incongruent residential or care settings.

Recognizing that this is a subjective assessment is important. Older people occupying the very same incongruent residential settings often differ substantially in their appraisals of how they can remedy their problems. Moreover, their idiosyncratic views of their alternative assimilative coping strategies may not necessarily coincide with the assessments of their families or professionals.

Older people must next evaluate which of these alternative coping solutions are most efficacious—that is, will best resolve the incongruent aspects of their residential environments. These appraisals depend on the number, magnitude, and complexity of their problems. Some solutions may be suitable for fixing only minor difficulties; others will target only particular problems even as the older person needs multifaceted solutions (e.g., a caregiver helps her only with performing IADLs, even though she also needs assistance with her ADLs).

Older people must also assess the immediacy of possible solutions (i.e., how quickly they must act). They must also judge whether in the absence of adaptive strategies, the unfavorable outcomes will occur quickly or slowly, or plateau for a substantive period and then worsen abruptly, and whether the solutions will offer them only short-term relief.[122] For example, a particular residential and care arrangement for someone in the early stages of Alzheimer's disease might be very effective for less than a year, but then a longer-term and more-protected environment will become necessary.

Older people must also assess whether their possible coping solutions are viable. Their adaptive strategies must be not just available and efficacious but also appropriate given their physical, social, psychological, and financial abilities. I already have emphasized that when older people initiate assimilative coping actions such as moving, they can incur substantial *collateral* damages, because such transitions can be psychologically and physically exhausting and financially expensive. For example, hiring an African-American caregiver may be an effective strategy for a homebound white man, but the psychological costs may be too high if he is prejudiced against minorities. Other older people may rule out solutions that involve changes that are simply too radical given their life experiences or set of beliefs.[123]

ENRICHED COPING REPERTOIRES

Three sets of individual and environmental factors influence how older people appraise the availability, efficaciousness, and viability of their assimilative coping strategies (Figure 5.3):

- How resilient they are as individuals
- How resilient their current or alternative environments are, based on objective indicators
- Whether they are making decisions of their own volition or have given decision-making authority to others

RESILIENT INDIVIDUALS

It is easy to categorize our friends and family members according to how well they deal with stress. A good friend returned to his half-million-dollar house one evening to find that it had burned to the ground, apparently because of a malfunctioning electric pool pump. Nearly all of his possessions were lost, one of his dogs died, and he

Figure 5.3. Factors influencing secondary appraisals of coping repertoires by older adults

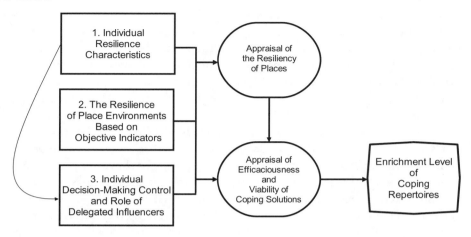

was homeless. He could afford a hotel room, and insurance covered his expenses in the short term, but that hardly compensated for his tragic material and emotional losses. Yet despite this adversity, he bounced back vigorously and gracefully, rebuilt a new and bigger house on the same lot, and successfully moved on with his life. I would not have coped so well.

My friend's responses are characteristic of resilient people who, when confronted with misfortunes and setbacks, have the motivation, confidence, physical capabilities, mental stamina, and flexibility to find appropriate solutions and ways around their environmental difficulties or obstacles. As one study summarized, *"They seemed to have a 'fighting spirit' and refused to resign themselves to their situation."*[124] Their distinctive demographics, life histories, personalities, and physical and mental health statuses help explain their resiliency.

Demographically, they are better educated, culturally literate in American ways, and have more complete and accurate information about how things work. They deliberate more thoughtfully, achieving more constructive solutions that can capitalize on opportunities and overcome barriers. They have the financial means to translate their preferences into actions and to tolerate the collateral costs of their coping strategies. Because of their ethnic and cultural backgrounds—and their can-do attitudes or spirits—they may have greater confidence and strength to implement their solutions.[125]

Resilient older people also have more favorable developmental antecedents or life histories. They draw on lessons learned from earlier stressful experiences and the skills they acquired when they coped with earlier traumas.[126] They often have had more positive life experiences and successful past coping efforts, resulting in their current greater self-esteem (they believe in themselves), self-understanding (are aware of their strengths and limitations), and confidence in their problem-solving abilities.[127]

These older people have more resilient personalities and more inner strength.[128] They are extroverted, outgoing, and curious people who feel comfortable searching for solutions and opportunities and soliciting help or advice. They are more open to change and willing to try innovative solutions. They are more hopeful, confident, and optimistic about the efficacy of their coping solutions. Their affiliative dispositions make them more trustworthy and open to the overtures, recommendations, relationships, and supports of others. They are more able to tolerate *"a reasonable degree of dependence"* because they feel confident that even their weakened personal resources are adequate for them to achieve their preferences.[129] An acceptance of their vulnerability also enables them to allocate the responsibilities for their care to others and to feel they are still taking charge of their lives.[130] They have a stronger perceived internal locus of control, or higher levels of self-efficacy, and do not feel overpowered by their environment. Consequently, they believe that they can exert control over their lives and surroundings and do not believe their fates lie primarily in the decisions or actions of others, most notably "in the hands of God."[131]

Lastly, these older people feel less hampered by poor physical health, physical limitations, or psychological disorders, such as depression or anxiety. Consequently, they have the physical and mental energy to find and implement solutions to their problems, even when confronted with significant collateral costs.

RESILIENT PLACES

Individual resilience does not guarantee enriched coping repertoires. Successful coping efforts also depend on whether older people's current or alternative places of residence offer actual solutions (based on objective indicators). Their aforementioned functional environments (Chapter 1) must have appropriate resources, opportunities, or choices that enable them to resolve the current inadequacies of their housing and care situations (Chapter 1, Figure 1.2).[132] The most motivated and capable older adults have fewer assimilative coping strategies in economically declining and isolated rural settings or in physically unsafe and service-deficient inner cities.

The most *resilient* places are able to adapt to the realities of their aging constituencies by anticipating and reacting to their changing lifestyles, declining capabilities, and nonconforming residential environments.[133] They continually change their infrastructure, products, services, and social networks to conform to their occupants' evolving needs and preferences.

These resource-rich places may better address the needs of older people seeking their residential comfort zones as opposed to their residential mastery zones. Some respond better to older people seeking rewarding new lifestyles by offering them more attractive apartment buildings and interesting leisure opportunities, such as stimulating university lectures or new friendships.[134] Other places might better enable older people to cope more effectively with their chronic health problems and mobility limitations; family members may live nearby, and pharmacies are open 24 hours a day or offer home delivery. In these places, older people can qualify for public programs that offer affordable long-term care solutions (e.g., supportive and affordable housing, transportation, healthcare, and personal assistance), thereby reducing their feelings of vulnerability and dependence. Their churches, mosques, and synagogues offer not only spiritual nourishment and short-term emergency assistance but also hands-on assistance to help them deal with their physical limitations.

ACTING ON THEIR OWN VOLITION

Older people with more enriched coping repertoires make their own decisions.[135] Consequently, they feel more competent and in control after they make changes in their lives and environments. Studies show that when older people are actively involved in their moving decisions, have time to prepare, and visit their new quarters in advance of their moves, they report higher satisfaction with their new arrangements, feel in better physical and mental health, and enjoy an overall higher quality of life.[136]

In contrast, when older people are forced to relinquish control of their residential decision making to others (however well intended), they are less likely to find solutions that are tailored to their needs and wants. Typically, these older people are transitioning on short notice from their own private residence to an adult child's home or a planned residential care facility, such as an assisted living residence or nursing home.

A substantial literature reports on the negative outcomes felt by such movers, including a decline in physical health, less happiness, anxiety, depression, loneliness, a strong sense of loss,[137] lower life satisfaction, and even higher mortality rates. These older people are distressed because other people have decided their fate, and they had little or no decision-making influence. They feel that their moves were coerced, involuntary, and out of their control.[138] They feel rushed, *as though they are being punished or dumped,"*[139] and have little time to make physical preparations (e.g., deciding what possessions to give up) or adjust psychologically to this major transition (e.g., fully evaluating or reconciling the implications of their moves).[140]

These older people should be distinguished from those who maintain a modicum of control over their residential or care decisions or who willingly delegate this authority to another person, known as *"proxy control."*[141] Along with the possibility of receiving good counsel, these older people feel emotional relief when they surrender their decision making to others, referred to as *influencers*, because they do not have to make the hard decisions on their own. Moreover, they feel more competent because they have actively participated in the transfer of decision-making control to family members, friends, or professionals they trust and who they feel are more knowledgeable than themselves. These influencers inevitably shape the subjective appraisals of their coping actions and their outcomes.[142]

SUCCESSFUL COPING AND THE NEW NORMAL

Ideally, the assimilative coping actions of older people yield successful outcomes. But not all older people find solutions to their adverse circumstances. Some still occupy incongruent environments and feel out of their residential comfort or mastery zones (Figure 5.4).[143]

Even those who achieve residential normalcy may not do so quickly—it can take months or even years. Older people are continuously assessing and reassessing how they can best eliminate or counteract their incongruent environments.[144] In their efforts to occupy places of residence or care settings that fit their needs and goals, they may have to try multiple coping behaviors until they find efficacious and viable solutions—and when they are still unsuccessful, they must try again.[145]

Figure 5.4. Theoretical model of residential normalcy

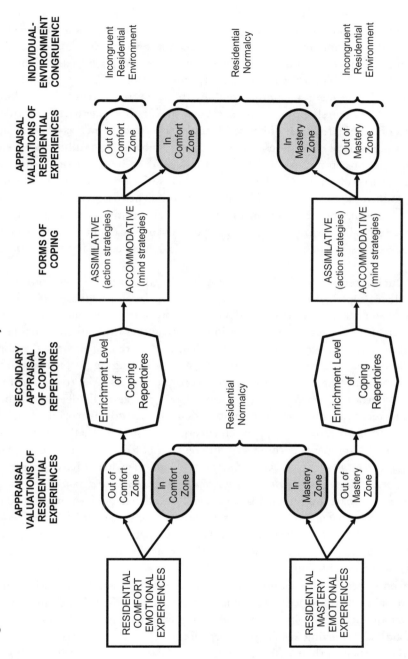

Moreover, even people who find successful solutions to their original problems may perversely find that their coping behaviors have resulted in new adverse outcomes. Consider the example of Teresa, who lives in a place where she thoroughly enjoys all the home-like qualities of her current dwelling, has many good friends in her community, and gets much pleasure from regularly volunteering in her church. She is unquestionably in her residential comfort zone. At the same time, because she no longer can drive, she cannot go shopping on her own, and she has to ask her friends for rides to the doctor's office. She feels out of her residential mastery zone, increasingly incompetent and lacking control. In response, Teresa copes by moving to a full-service continuing care retirement community (CCRC)—its independent living section—where she no longer has to worry about performing her IADLs (Chapter 12). She now feels (back) in her residential mastery zone. But she badly misses her friends and church activities, has not made any new acquaintances, and finds her accommodations unattractive and sterile. Even as her assimilative coping action solved one set of problems, it resulted in an unexpected set of new problems, and she feels (newly) out of her residential comfort zone.

Our conception of residential normalcy also allows for the possibility that even when older people have successfully coped with the incongruent aspects of where they live and feel once again in their residential comfort or mastery zones, they may be pursuing very different activities and relationships than they did in their earlier residential environments. This perspective contrasts sharply with that of Rowe and Kahn's New Gerontology paradigm, which dictates that successfully aging people maintain the activities and experiences of their past lives; continuity is essential to their formulation.

In contrast, this book's interpretation of aging successfully does not require older adults to return to some status quo or to bounce back to their original equilibrium positions.[146] Rather, older people often experience a "new normal" in which their new congruent environments encompass a different set of features or activities. Older people engage in a *"process of continual adjustment,"*[147] and they do not have to return to their *"previous state (like a rubber ball) but can actually adapt, learn, and change."*[148] The renewal strategies of urban and regional planners and developers offer an instructive parallel. They recognize that after communities or regions cope successfully with adverse events such as natural disasters, they emerge as very viable settlements even though they look and function differently than before the calamitous events. New settlement equilibriums or new normals result.[149]

Consequently, older adults may still be aging successfully even when they must depend on assistive devices and home aides. Similarly, they do not necessarily have a poorer quality of life if they pursue less physically active behaviors and become homebodies. Achieving residential normalcy may mean conducting different types of activities than in their pasts and in different places and with different frequencies. This is exemplified by the following "new normal" set of outcomes experienced by one older adult:

> Consider the coping solutions of the recently widowed woman who was feeling alone, bored, and financially stressed paying off her mortgage. She joins a book club, volunteers at a nearby church, and rents out her basement to a

boarder. This does not bring back her husband, his companionship, his financial resources, or their previous lifestyle. The widow's residential normalcy now has some obviously different underpinnings even as she now feels more useful, socially connected, and financially independent.[150]

CONCLUSION

This chapter offers a hopeful message. It emphasizes that older people can counteract the negative outcomes they experience in their residential or care settings by initiating effective coping strategies. How they adapt varies greatly, and there is rarely one right course of action. Nor can older people expect that the experts will always endorse their problem-solving or emotion-based adaptation efforts. They can expect pushback when they rely on mind strategies to get back into their residential comfort or mastery zones, which many stakeholders view as tantamount to doing nothing at all.

Although relocation is the most studied coping strategy, older people often initiate many different *in situ* adaptive responses and view relocating from their residences as an exceptional rather than customary response. Because they must meet the aforementioned four conditions before they initiate this assimilative coping strategy, they often have difficulty overcoming the forces underlying their residential inertia.

When they do move, our typology of older movers emphasizes that they change their residential arrangements for many different reasons. We cannot simply generalize about the individual or environmental circumstances that translate into the "good life" or independent living. This chapter particularly rejects the idea that aging successfully depends on maintaining the status quo. Whether they age in place or move, older people must continually find new ways to establish the congruent qualities of their places of residence. Even when their quest to achieve residential normalcy is successful, the look and feel of their new environs and ways of life may be very different from their pasts. They will often experience many "new normals."

Some older people deal with adversity better. They have more enriched coping repertoires. These more resilient people have demographics, past histories, personalities, and health conditions that motivate and empower them to find good solutions. They typically make their own decisions about how to cope with their incongruent environments or at least have voluntarily assigned this authority to others they trust. But as others have emphasized, *"Resilience is not simply a matter of individual characteristics"*[151] or decision-making autonomy. Resilient places must be part of the equation.

The next chapters describe the strengths and weaknesses of a complex inventory of environmental opportunities and resources available to America's older population seeking their new normals.

NOTES

1. From the movie The Best Exotic Marigold Hotel.
2. (Rosowsky, 2009, p. 100)
3. (Rosowsky, 2009, p. 100)
4. (Baltes & Baltes, 1990)
5. (Pearlin, 2010, p. 211)
6. (Baltes & Baltes, 1990)
7. (Holahan, 1978)
8. (Wild, Wiles, & Allen, 2013; Schulz & Heckhausen, 1996).
9. (Brandtstadter & Greve, 1994)
10. (Brandtstadter & Greve, 1994, p. 74)
11. (Lazarus & Lazarus, 2006)
12. (Heckhausen, 1997)
13. (Lazarus, 1966)
14. (Fried, 2000)
15. (Pinquart & Burmedi, 2003)
16. (Brandtstadter & Greve, 1994)
17. (Lazarus & Lazarus, 2006)
18. (Lazarus & Lazarus, 2006)
19. (Brandtstadter & Greve, 1994)
20. (Fried, 2000)
21. (Lazarus & Lazarus, 2006, p. 59)
22. (Schulz & Heckhausen, 1998)
23. (Seligman, 1991)
24. (Kastenbaum, 1984)
25. (Brandtstadter & Greve, 1994, p. 66)
26. (Brandtstadter & Greve, 1994, p. 72)
27. (Brandtstadter & Greve, 1994, p, 63)
28. (Lazarus & Lazarus, 2006)
29. (Baltes & Baltes, 1990)
30. (Heckhausen, 1997)
31. (Leipold & Greve, 2009)
32. (Rosenbloom, 2007)
33. (Lawton, 1985)
34. (Webber, Porter, & Menec, 2010)
35. (Schulz & Heckhausen, 1996)
36. (Brandtstadter & Greve, 1994, p. 74)
37. (Brandtstadter & Greve, 1994, p. 72)
38. (Brandtstadter & Greve, 1994, p. 66)
39. (Lazarus, 1966)
40. (Carstensen, Gross, & Fung, 1998)
41. (Lazarus, 1966)
42. (Dychtwald & Baxter, 2011, p. 4)
43. (Painter & Lee, 2009; Sabia, 2008; Walters, 2002)
44. (Gobillon & Wolff, 2011)
45. (Janssen, Abma, & Van Regenmortel, 2012)
46. (Chen & Wilmoth, 2004; Kahana & Kahana, 1983; Oswald, Schilling, Wahl, & Gang, 2002)
47. (Cuba, 1991; Johnson, 2006)
48. (Lieberman, 1991; Sergeant, Ekerdt, & Chapin, 2010)
49. (Ekerdt & Sergeant, 2006; Luborsky, Lysack, & Van Nuil, 2011)
50. (National Investment Center for the Seniors Housing & Care Industry, 2007)
51. (Longino, 2002)

52. (Hughes, 2011)
53. (Luborsky et al., 2011, p. 248)
54. (Halpert, 2011)
55. (Halpert, 2011)
56. (Hughes, 2011)
57. U.S. Census Bureau, Current Population Survey, 2012 Annual Social and Economic Supplement. Release Date: December 2012.
58. 3.4% of people age 65 and older moved in the period 2011 to 2012.
59. (Banerjee, 2012)
60. U.S. Census Bureau, Current Population Survey, 2012 Annual Social and Economic Supplement.
61. (Joint Center for Housing Studies of Harvard University, 2013a)
62. Just under 2% of older movers originally lived outside the United States.
63. U.S. Census Bureau, Current Population Survey, 2012 Annual Social and Economic Supplement
64. (He & Schachter, 2003); U.S. Census Bureau, Current Population Survey, 2012 Annual Social and Economic Supplement
65. (Litwak & Longino, 1987; Lovegreen, Kahana, & Kahana, 2010)
66. (Longino, 1998)
67. (Walters, 2002)
68. (Frey, 2013)
69. (Cromartie & Nelson, 2009)
70. (Johnson & Beale, 2002)
71. (Cromartie & Nelson, 2009)
72. (Johnson, 2006, p. 20)
73. (Cromartie & Nelson, 2009, pp. 16–17)
74. 2009 American Housing Survey
75. (MetLife Mature Market Institute, 2011a)
76. (Del Webb, 2010)
77. (Longino, Bradley, Stoller, & Haas, 2008)
78. (Wylde, 2008a)
79. (Ball, 2012)
80. (Luborsky et al., 2011, p. 248)
81. (Diehl & Willis, 2003; Ickes, Snyder, & Garcia, 1997)
82. (Kahana & Kahana, 1983)
83. (Fiske & Maddi, 1961)
84. (Longino et al., 2008)
85. (Hughes, 2011)
86. (O'Connor & Cassidy, 2007)
87. Lou Carlozo, "At 68, Barbara Miller Elegbede is living proof that flower children need not grow up," Reuters, Friday, October 5, 2012.
88. (Gubrium, 1993)
89. "What's Driving Americans to Retire Abroad? Money—or Lack of It." Published July 18, 2012, in Knowledge@Wharton.
90. (Freeman, 2006–2007, p. 41)
91. (Burr, Mutchler, & Caro, 2007)
92. (Morrow-Howell, 2010)
93. (Burr et al., 2007)
94. (Morrow-Howell, 2010)
95. (Henkin & Zapf, 2006–2007, p. 71)
96. (Greene, 2006, p. R1)
97. (Sharma, 2013; Wylde, 2008a)
98. (UnitedHealthcare, 2013, p. 31)
99. (National Investment Center for the Seniors Housing & Care Industry, 2007)
100. (Seltzer & Yahirun, 2013)

101. (Walters, 2002)
102. (Longino et al., 2008)
103. (De Jong, Wilmoth, Angel, & Cornwell, 1995)
104. Jongwon Lee, New America Media, July 9, 2012. http://newamericamedia.org/2012/07/as-korean-elders-lone-deaths-rise-in-us-some-reverse-immigrate-home.php#
105. (Bakija & Slemrod, 2004; Duncombe, Robbins, & Wolf, 2003)
106. (Banerjee, 2012)
107. (Sergeant & Ekerdt, 2008)
108. (Castle, 2001)
109. (Luborsky et al., 2011)
110. (Safron-Norton, 2010)
111. (National Investment Center for the Seniors Housing & Care Industry, 2007)
112. (Sabia, 2008)
113. (Stoller & Perzynski, 2003)
114. (He & Schachter, 2003)
115. (Genworth Financial, 2010)
116. (Krout, Holmes, Erickson, & Wolle, 2003)
117. (American Health Care Association, 2001)
118. (Strohschein, 2011)
119. (Castle, 2001)
120. (Golant, 2014b)
121. (Lazarus & Folkman, 1984, p. 35; Heckhausen, Wrosch, & Schulz, 2010)
122. (Golant, 2003a)
123. (Löfqvist et al., 2013)
124. (Hammarström & Torres, 2012, p. 197)
125. (Aldwin & Igarashi, 2012)
126. (Aldwin & Igarashi, 2012; Perkins, Ball, Whittington, & Hollingsworth, 2012)
127. (Kobasa, 1979)
128. (Windle, Markland, & Woods, 2008)
129. (Rosowsky, 2009, p. 102)
130. (Janssen et al., 2012)
131. (Janssen et al., 2012)
132. (Golant, 2006; Wild, Wiles, & Allen, 2013)
133. (Davoudi, 2012; Denhardt & Denhardt, 2010)
134. (Hall & Zautra, 2010)
135. (Wiseman, 1980)
136. (Bekhet, Zauszniewski, & Nakhla, 2009; Tobin & Lieberman, 1976)
137. (Luborsky et al., 2011)
138. (Bekhet et al., 2009; Schulz & Brenner, 1977)
139. (Bekhet et al., 2009, p. 464)
140. (Lieberman & Tobin, 1983)
141. (Morgan & Brazda, 2013, p. 655)
142. (Gubrium, Rittman, Williams, Young, & Boylstein, 2003)
143. (Coleman & O'Hanlon, 2004; Lazarus & Lazarus, 2006)
144. (Golant, 1998a)
145. (Lazarus, 1966)
146. (Miller, 1978)
147. (Pendall, Foster, & Cowell, 2010, p. 76)
148. (Denhardt & Denhardt, 2010, p. 335)
149. (Pendall et al., 2010)
150. (Golant, 2014b)
151. (Aldwin & Igarashi, 2012, p. 118)

6

PHYSICALLY MANIPULATING THE DWELLING FOR INDEPENDENT LIVING

For many people age 65 and older who are slowing down or developing limitations, smart homes are their ticket to staying independent.[1]

If I know about the World Cup soccer tournament in real time, why can't I know whether my mother took her medications?[2]

Experts fear surveillance by smart home technologies will lead to the "objectification" of older persons whereby they are treated "as if they were a lump of dead matter: to be pushed, lifted, pumped or drained, without proper reference to the fact that they are sentient beings."[3]

PHYSICALLY CHANGING THE DWELLING

A cadre of professionals including environmental psychologists, occupational therapists, and interior designers believe that they have a straightforward physical fix for older people dealing with health declines and mobility limitations while aging in place. They must modify the physical infrastructure, interior design, and contents of their dwellings and use assistive devices, such as walkers, wheelchairs, and motorized chairs or scooters. By adopting these low-tech solutions, they can make their residences more enjoyable to occupy and easier and safer to use and access. Residential normalcy is easily within their reach.

127

Other experts offer a more ambitious solution and believe that "smart home" technologies hold the greatest promise. These are devices and instruments that monitor, communicate, and respond to information about the residents' activities, physical and mental health status, physiological functioning, and the equipment, physical conditions, and operation of their dwellings. The more sophisticated technologies not only diagnose and detect problems but also offer constructive and innovative responses.

ASSISTIVE DEVICES

The unending advertisements on TV for motorized chairs and scooters emphasize that the federal Medicare program covers their costs and that they are indispensable for an older person's quality of life. They appear to have less stigma than wheelchairs. The talented actors hustling these products emphasize how their senior users will increase their mobility and enjoy old age more. Scooters are one option in a category typically known as assistive devices, which include walkers, canes, crutches, wheelchairs, prosthetics, communication aids, and specialized medical equipment. This category also encompasses stand-alone equipment installed or added to the dwelling to make it more accessible or safer to use, such as tub or shower seats and raised toilet seats.[4]

Most assistive devices are designed to address lower-body limitations that make climbing, walking, standing, or transferring (getting up from a seated position) impossible or strenuous. Research shows that assistive devices reduce these difficulties, make homes more accessible, and help older people feel safer and more independent. They may also help older people increase their social activities:

> Mrs. T., an 82-year-old woman suffering from degenerative muscular disease . . . could barely swallow, walk, or get in and out of a chair, and she fell several times a day. Despite all of this, she insisted on taking part in the informal social gathering each afternoon in the courtyard of her building. In the past year, it was only after acquiring a walker that she could even attempt this activity.[5]

Between 14% and 18% of people age 65 and older in the United States, and nearly two-thirds of those who have difficulty performing their activities of daily living (ADLs), rely on one or more of these assistive devices.[6] This percentage has greatly increased over the past couple of decades,[7] but experts stress that even more older people could benefit from these devices.

People age 75 and older are more likely to adopt them, particularly obese people.[8] African-Americans, followed by Hispanics and Whites, have the highest rate of use, especially canes.[9] One notably underserved group consists of older people who are depressed.[10] Studies also show that older people who adopt these devices want more control over their lives and want to rely less on other people to perform their everyday activities. This is consistent with other research showing that older users of assistive devices rely less on the assistance of caregivers, especially hands-on care. This is especially true of those with less-severe disabilities, who use canes and crutches, as opposed to those with more debilitating limitations, who use walkers and wheelchairs.[11]

Assistive devices are not perfect solutions, however. Users of assistive devices report that performing their tasks is more tiring and time consuming than if they had relied on caregivers for the same assistance.[12]

UNIVERSAL DESIGN: DWELLINGS FOR ALL AGES

Many experts contend that the interior and exterior design of America's housing should be accessible, usable, barrier-free, and safe for all. Homes should not target or be restricted to particular user groups or be adapted as an afterthought but rather should be universally designed for the general population. This requires *"abandoning the notion of the 'average' user entirely and adopting an inclusive and pluralistic model in which design for differences is a key strategy."*[13] One environmental gerontologist explains,

> Consider the lever door handle, which could be considered the poster child for universal design. Because the lever door handle can open a door with a minimum amount of pressure, a wide range of users and abilities (ranging from mothers carrying a child to people with reduced strength to anyone carrying groceries) benefit daily from its simple, yet powerful design.[14]

Proponents also stress that the costs of implementing universal design features are not prohibitive when architects include them in their original drawings. The extra construction costs—both materials and labor—are minimal compared with the very large costs of later incorporating them into already built dwellings.[15] Moreover, dwellings with age or disability neutral designs will be marketable to a wider group of consumers.[16] Architects and designers at the Center for Universal Design identify seven specific principles that would fulfill this universal design mission:[17]

1. *Equitable use:* The design is useful and marketable to people with diverse abilities.

2. *Flexibility in use:* The design accommodates a wide range of individual preferences and abilities.

3. *Simple and intuitive use:* Use of the design is easy to understand, regardless of the user's experience, knowledge, language skills, or concentration level.

4. *Perceptible information:* The design communicates necessary information effectively to the user, regardless of ambient conditions or of the user's sensory abilities.

5. *Tolerance of error:* The design minimizes hazards and adverse consequences of accidental or unintended actions.

6. *Low physical effort:* The design can be used efficiently and comfortably and with minimal fatigue.

7. *Size and space for approach and use:* Appropriate size and space are provided for approach, reach, manipulation, and use regardless of user's size, posture, or mobility.

Fair Housing Act

Despite their merits, there has been no widespread implementation of these universal design principles. Nonetheless, federal laws now require that certain categories of housing meet minimum architectural guidelines to address the needs of disabled people, particularly in wheelchairs. A landmark piece of federal legislation, the Fair Housing Amendments Act of 1988 (FHAA), imposed such accessibility requirements,[18] although these standards could be enforced only in "covered multifamily dwellings" constructed for first occupancy after March 1991.[19] These included all dwelling units in owned or rented elevator-equipped residential buildings with four or more units[20] and all ground-floor dwelling units in buildings with four or more units without an elevator.[21] Disability status was broadly defined and included people with any physical or mental impairment that substantially limited one or more major life activities. These included such debilitating conditions as heart disease, arthritis, blindness, Alzheimer's disease, learning disabilities, and nonambulatory status, in addition to clinically recognized mental and addictive conditions such as depression and alcoholism.

The Act included seven broad technical requirements:[22]

1. There must be an accessible route to a building entrance.
2. Public and common use portions of a building must be readily accessible and usable by people who are physical disabled.
3. Doorways must be wide enough so that they can be accessed by someone in a wheelchair.
4. The route into and through the dwelling unit must be wheelchair accessible.
5. Light switches, electrical outlets, thermostats, and other environmental controls must be in accessible locations.
6. Bathroom walls must be reinforced (e.g., wood studs behind the drywall) to allow the installation of grab bars.
7. Kitchens and bathrooms must be wheelchair accessible.

Owners of all existing residential properties (whenever built and however designed) had two additional obligations under the law. First, they had to allow occupants with disabilities to make reasonable modifications to their apartments so they could fully enjoy their premises; these changes might include installing grab bars, replacing doorknobs with lever handles, widening doorways for wheelchair access, and installing a ramp at the entrance to a building. Importantly, this was at the occupant's expense. Along with requiring that professionals do the work and comply with building codes, the landlord could ask the resident to restore the unit to its original condition before vacating.[23]

Second, the law required that housing landlords had to make "reasonable accommodations" in their building rules, policies, practices, or services. A few examples: Landlords would have to waive a no-pets rule for a tenant who is emotionally dependent on a pet or relied on it for accessibility purposes, change parking rules to provide a resident with a parking slot closer to the building or garage entrance, and provide large-print notices to their vision-impaired tenants.

Despite the good intentions of the Fair Housing Act, like all laws, it did not guarantee enforcement. Victims of discrimination often do not complain or seek redress. As one expert observes, *"Lawsuits are expensive and time-consuming,"*[24] and older people often do not have the knowledge, financial resources, motivation, or energy to enforce their legal rights.

Ironically, the accessibility requirements of the federal law also did not cover the types of housing usually occupied by older people, namely buildings with three or fewer units, particularly single-family homes. Moreover, the dwellings not subject to these national standards were often the very ones that had steps at one or more of their entrances, had narrow doorways or hallways, or lacked an accessible bathroom on the main floor. The earliest built of these dwellings were especially likely to be physically inaccessible.[25]

Those advocating for a more comprehensive law argue that we could eliminate this legislative gap by integrating *"a few core accessibility features as a routine construction practice into newly built single-family housing."*[26] These *visitability* home design principles include:

- One zero-step entrance at the front, back, or side of the house, depending on site conditions
- Doorways that provide 32 inches of clear passage space
- At least a half-bath on the main floor with adequate maneuvering room

At least 39 municipalities require their newly constructed residential buildings to meet these broader specifications, and some offer tax credits as incentives to builders and homeowners.[27] Although the visitability movement has been gaining ground, most states or local governments do not view them as essential design requirements, and few housing developers have adopted them.[28]

TAILOR-MADE HOME MODIFICATIONS

Absent these universal requirements, it is up to professionals to make the case that older people should tailor the infrastructure, design, and contents of their dwellings to compensate for their diminished mobility, agility, and sensory functions. A concise but comprehensive set of five intervention categories is offered by Ann Quyen Do Nguyen of the Fall Prevention Center of Excellence in Los Angeles:[29]

> *Minimizing trip hazards:* Remove items from walking surfaces to create clear areas by minimizing clutter; relocate phone wires, extension cords, and cables; or rearrange awkwardly placed furniture.
>
> *Maximizing slip resistance:* Areas with slick surfaces (e.g., tiles or a glossy floor) combined with water or other liquids (e.g., bathroom, kitchen, or pool patio) can increase an individual's risk of falling. Providing additional traction, such as by adding inexpensive adhesive nonslip strips or removing the item or liquid, can help reduce falls.
>
> *Minimizing overreaching:* Relocate commonly used items to easily accessible areas. For example, in the kitchen, pullout drawers can be installed in lower cabinets to decrease bending and reaching.

Maximizing visual support: Aside from key lighting in task areas such as the kitchen, easy access to light switches and standing lamps are a plus for all ages and abilities. Backlit switches and night-lights can be an inexpensive but significant aid when waking up in the middle of the night to go to the bathroom.

Maximizing physical support: Physical support can come in many forms, depending on the room, from grab bars in the bathroom to hand rails on interior or exterior stairs, to specialized chair lifts that elevate patients from a seated to a standing position.

The Research Center of the National Association of Home Builders has created an Aging in Place Smart Ideas Checklist that translates these broad categories of design interventions into a more detailed and implementable set of recommendations (http://www.nahb.org/generic.aspx?sectionID=717&genericContentID=89801). They also helped create the Certified Aging in Place Specialist program, which since 1961 has trained and certified professionals to assess and improve the accessibility and safety of older people's dwellings. The American Institute of Architects also publishes guidelines to improve the built environment of older people.[30]

Experts are at no loss to explain why older people should make these home modifications. About 50% of all falls by older people occur in or near their dwellings, a percentage that increases with age.[31] Experts argue that older people have fewer falling accidents and feel less constrained by their functional limitations and sensory losses when they live in dwellings with fewer accessibility or usability barriers or hazards. Furthermore, they save time and energy as they go about their everyday activities. They also depend less on their family members or paid workers for assistance. These experts passionately believe that *"environments, not people, are 'disabled,' and independence-promoting environments improve the level of functional ability."*[32] They emphasize that the dwelling's physical environment is what prevents people from aging in place successfully.[33]

It is hard to reject these uncomplicated and often inexpensive fixes for changing physically deficient dwellings. As my wife reminds me when something breaks down in the house, it is far simpler to fix or modify inanimate objects than to repair or treat our bodies. And almost any of these physical solutions are far less expensive than the costs incurred after even a short stay in the hospital.

HOME MODIFICATIONS OFTEN ELICIT INDIFFERENT RESPONSES

Unfortunately, the experts' enthusiasm for introducing home modifications is often met with indifference from older people. A 2014 survey of U.S. residents age 60 or older found that only 28% planned to make any home modifications to help them as they age.[34] In a 1-year period, another study reported that only 36% of respondents added at least one home modification.[35] Also consider that the mere presence of a modification does not mean that the older occupant uses it. Indeed, only 40% reported that they used at least one of their modifications in the past 30 days.[36] Most modifications consist of new railings at the home entrance, grab bars in the shower or tub, and a seat for the shower or tub.[37] Those making these changes are usually older than age 70, African-American, less educated, lower income, and on Medicaid. Older renters often have good excuses for avoiding these changes because their landlords make the dwelling improvement decisions. They may also be reluctant to make changes at their own expense when they reside in someone else's property. However, older homeowners cannot use these rationalizations. Indeed, their aging dwellings should be strong motivators of their adaptive behaviors, but this is infrequently so. Newman reported that older dwellings actually contained fewer home modifications (e.g., grab bars, widened doors or hallways, ramps, specially equipped bathrooms, extra lighting).[38]

These home modifications are simply not in the coping repertoires of most older people. They find it structurally unrealistic to modify bathrooms that are physically inaccessible because of stairs.[39] Moreover, they are not swayed by experts who claim that their physical surroundings might affect their moods, restrict their activities, or increase their risk of accidents, even after they have experienced falls and other home accidents. In their words, *"Falling? I don't worry about it. I just go on and do the best I can."*[40] *"Perhaps I'm used to this and never gave it any thought, what it ought to be."*[41]

My own sister, an artist, lives in a modern but very cramped high-rise condominium apartment in Toronto. After she fell and broke an elbow, I tried to share my so-called expertise with her by recommending she de-clutter her living space to prevent future falls. However, despite my advice, she did little to modify her apartment arrangement.

In addition to a resistance to making modifications, and to the chagrin of the experts, older people worry that making changes will be more disruptive than doing nothing; they equate residential normalcy with keeping the status quo. Consistent with the youth-dominated tenets of the New Gerontology paradigm, older people view such modifications as demeaning intrusions because they *"do not wish to be viewed as old and disabled."*[42] Why take actions to admit that they are aging badly or communicate their dependence to others?[43] Consider the following situation:

> One gentleman clearly recognized that the footstool next to his very high antique bed was a problem. His physical therapist and several family members had suggested that he change this arrangement, but he thoroughly enjoyed the daily challenge of climbing into bed. . . . Being able to perform this daily task was clearly important to him, as if his identity as an independent person was at stake.[44]

A wife who participated in one study reported that even though her husband had fallen several times in the bathroom, she refused to install grab bars. She felt it would ruin the home's aesthetic appearance[45] and give it a clinical or institutional look. Another older person proclaimed, *"I don't want my house to end up like a nursing home."*[46] Still, grab bars now come in all kinds of pleasing colors and designs to avoid the institutional feel.

Several other factors also influence older people's openness to these home modifications. Some older people may be unwilling to get rid of a throw rug or high bed because of their sentimental value.[47] Occupants who have lived longer in their current dwellings are less likely to make changes, a troubling indicator given the propensity of older people to stay put. Rather, modifications typically occur within the first 2 years of occupying a dwelling and is more likely when older people sell their units to younger people.[48] Physical prowess matters because older people usually have less energy to do repairs or feel more hampered by their physical limitations than do younger people. Also, many older women have relied on their spouses to perform household maintenance tasks, and they are unprepared to handle these responsibilities after their husbands die or become impaired.[49] It is also not easy for older people to find capable workers who are both affordable and trustworthy.[50]

Money is an obvious impediment, especially if other household expenditures are already burdensome. A national study showed that those who added home modifications in a previous year paid for most of them out of their own pockets, which is often unrealistic for lower-income people.[51]

Only very small percentages (6%) have their home modification costs covered by their insurance or by the government. The costs can be funded through Older Americans Act programs, the U.S. Department of Agriculture (Rural Development Home Repair Loan and Grant Programs), state and local government programs, Medicaid waivers, and PACE programs (Chapter 8). Funding availability, however, depends primarily on location and in many communities affordable repair programs are simply not available.[52] Alternatively, these programs may only cover low-cost repairs but not substantial home improvements (e.g., major design changes or upgrades). Moreover, older people often find these programs confusing to apply for, or they do not meet the eligibility requirements.[53] Other older people may simply be unaware of their alternatives.

Distance-to-death considerations may also be crucial. People may reason that they are not going to live that much longer and will not have enough time to recoup these home improvement expenditures when they sell their dwellings, especially if they are pessimistic about their home values appreciating. This future-time orientation may make them especially reluctant to upgrade or replace their appliances, heating and air conditioning systems, or insulation to make their dwellings more energy efficient. Even if they are convinced that these changes would reduce their monthly bills, they argue that it will take many years of such cost savings to justify the investment. This would be especially unwise financially if they plan to move within the next few years. Finally, they are less likely to take out loans for these physical alterations and consume their housing wealth to pay for what they believe are low-priority home modifications. Rather, as emphasized in Chapter 3, they usually seek to conserve their equity to cover future, perhaps imminent, long-term care and healthcare expenditures.[54]

DO HOME MODIFICATIONS REALLY MAKE A DIFFERENCE?

Professionals often are critical of older people's cynical responses to their home modification recommendations. Yet they themselves are guilty of overzealous causality claims. The unfortunate truth is that there is little scientific support for expecting that home modifications *by themselves* will prevent falls or reduce the risk of fall injuries.[55] A very well-designed dwelling space did not prevent former President Ronald Reagan, who had advanced Alzheimer's disease, from falling and breaking a hip in early 2001.[56] Physical determinism has its limits.

The dilemma for home modification advocates is that there are many competing individual-focused determinants that better predict whether older people will have accidents and become seriously injured in their homes. Those especially at risk are older people who have disorders of the musculoskeletal system (e.g., muscle weaknesses, gait and balance disorders, and weakness of lower extremities) and sensory–nervous system (influencing their postural stability). Diseases of the eye can reduce depth perception and peripheral vision, cause blurriness, and reduce light. The multiple medications older people take (e.g., psychotropic medications, antidepressants, anti-arrhythmic heart medications, and digoxin) and their interactions can result in changes in blood pressure, dizziness, and decreased cognitive ability, all which increase the risk of falls.[57] Taking these drugs with alcohol presents an additional problem.

The personalities and activity patterns of older people also matter. Contrary to the expectations of the New Gerontology paradigm, older people who fall because of environmental hazards are sometimes those who are more vigorous and, therefore, more likely to engage in dwelling-related maintenance tasks such as housework, gardening, and home repairs.[58] By the same logic, falls are also more likely for people with more risk-taking or impulsive personalities.[59] Indeed, one study concluded that environmental hazards pose the greatest risk for people with fair as opposed to poor balance: *"Those with poor balance are less exposed to hazards, and those with good mobility are more able to withstand them."*[60]

The multifaceted etiology of falls helps explain why home intervention strategies designed to reduce fall-related outcomes typically have mixed results. As one expert concluded,

> The existence of home hazards alone is insufficient to cause falls. Rather, the interaction between an older person's physical abilities and their exposure to environmental stressors appears to be more important.[61]

Home modification strategies by professionals appear to be most effective when their interventions target people who are more at risk of falling.[62] Interventions that are environment-specific (e.g., that zero in on bathroom hazards or barriers) also yield better outcomes. Interventions are also more successful when targeting older people with a greater internal locus of control. These people believe that they have more control over their behaviors and environments and that their actions matter.[63]

Because there are many determinants of falls, the consensus is that we cannot prevent falls-related accidents by simply manipulating the physical environments of older people's dwellings. Multipronged (or multifactorial) intervention approaches are necessary, and there is no "one size suits all intervention strategy."[64] Thus, fall risk assessments must include comprehensive medical and functional mobility evaluations of older people (to diagnose and target individuals especially at risk) and intervention strategies, such as exercise programs (strengthening, balance and gait training, endurance training), medication management, activity recommendations, individual counseling, and, of course, home-hazard assessments and environmental modifications.[65] It is also critical that well-qualified professionals perform the intervention strategies and that this group ideally include a multidisciplinary team of geriatric physicians, geriatric nurses, occupational therapists, physical therapists, and exercise therapists.[66]

Successful interventions have also emphasized the effectiveness of decreasing older people's fear of falling and increasing their feelings of self-efficacy—that is, helping them to *"adopt the mindset that falls are preventable."*[67] And, in all instances, follow-up assessments and treatments are crucial given that the health and mobility status of older people can change quickly. In the United States, Gitlin conducted such a multi-faceted occupational and physical therapy intervention, called Advancing Better Living for Elders,[68] that not only reduced the mobility difficulties of older occupants but also increased their feelings of self-efficacy and reduced their fear of falling. Moreover, the intervention strategies reduced the mortality rate of vulnerable participants.[69]

Experts also believe that there should be greater public awareness of the dangers of falls in the home and the benefits of prevention strategies. Educational efforts should target not just older people and their family caregivers but also the professional providers who evaluate and treat them for medical and mobility problems. What is needed is a *"social marketing campaign similar to those that have raised awareness about drunk driving and smoking."*[70]

The preponderance of scientific evidence questioning the linkages between falling and environmental hazards and home intervention strategies relies on objective indicators. Nonetheless, studies do find that after older people make these modifications, they feel more empowered to conduct their *"habitual personal routines or rituals"* in their hazard-free residential environments—even if their modification behaviors do not immediately translate into fewer falls.[71] Once again, we witness the importance of focusing on subjective indicators of well-being.

Not just older people benefit. Family caregivers may enjoy greater peace of mind because they believe that their loved ones are less likely to fall. In particular, researchers find that *"home modifications for patients with dementia are associated with improved caregiver effectiveness and less caregiver upset."*[72]

HIGH-TECH SOLUTIONS: TOWARD A BRAVE NEW WORLD

Older people with mobility limitations must often fend for themselves if they live alone, their spouses are themselves chronically ill or dependent, or they cannot always count on their friends or other family for assistance. Despite these challenges, they still want to be fully engaged in life, live independently, feel safe, and not to feel helpless. They want the means to handle on their own a home repair emergency or a power outage. They want to continue to conduct their physical and social activities and not worry about falling without anyone knowing. They want to be able to cope with an unexplained physical health symptom, a sudden need for medical attention, or a prescription that runs out. Above all, they want to avert serious medical or care crises,[73] *"unnecessary and costly emergency room visits,"*[74] and hospital admissions.

SMART HOMES AND RELATED TECHNOLOGIES

Many experts believe that smart home technologies are the answer (Figure 6.1). These futuristic devices, many still in design and testing stages, are also known as assistive robotic products, intelligent assistive technologies, gerontechnology, ubiquitous or

Figure 6.1. Overview of smart home and related technologies (Bharucha et al., 2009; Center for Technology and Aging, 2013; Demiris & Hensel, 2008, 2009; Johnson, Davenport, et al., 2007; Kutzik et al., 2008; Vierck, 2013)

- Telehealth or telemonitoring technologies (Takahashi et al., 2012), also known as e-care or electronic care, rely on remote physiological monitoring devices implanted on or ingested by older persons so professionals can rely on several modalities to assess the resident's functioning. Results tracked from a central station, such as in a hospital or clinic, continuously monitor and evaluate a person's health status at home, including pulse, respiration, temperature, galvanic skin response, blood pressure, blood sugar, bladder and bowel output, medication intake/adherence, and even mood or depression. Interactive information technologies allow medical or care staff in different physical locations to communicate in real time about an older person's vital signs and health behaviors and offer immediate results and solutions including personalized care protocols. Older people and their family members also view results on their computers, smartphones, iPads, or wearable tech devices.

- Home settings incorporate more user-friendly high-tech medical devices and equipment once available only in hospital settings. Older people and their family members can provide intravenous antibiotic therapy, parenteral or tube feeding, dialysis, and oxygen therapy with less training and supervision and thus find themselves manipulating all the tubing, supplies, pumps, and measuring equipment that go along with these treatments.

- Real-time instruction technologies (cognitive assistants or coaches) inform occupants how to accomplish particular tasks, such as using an appliance or medical device or performing diagnostic procedures (e.g., blood sugar testing).

- Resident tracking systems monitor people with dementias such as Alzheimer's disease and send out alarms when they detect dangerous behaviors. Some systems automatically lock designated doors in a dwelling.

- Behaviors and movements (e.g., upper- and lower-body actions, ADLs, motion, gait, balance, and sleep movements) are detected remotely in real time via radio frequency identification transponders with vibration sensors and other devices attached to residents (wristbands, badges, pendants) or embedded in the ceilings, floors, and walls. Some tracking devices are especially unobtrusive, such as sensor-laden clothing, sheets, or mattresses. Other technologies rely on microchips implanted in the person's upper arm or on ultrafrequency sound waves or configuration lasers to detect deviations in gait and body positioning.

- Passively actuated call systems (i.e., without actions initiated by an older person) alert a central monitoring station of abnormal measurement readings or movements or activities that deviate from individual behaviors or histories and trigger requests for emergency assistance. For example, an episode of urinary incontinence would be detected by ammonia sensors inserted in the resident's bed sheets that can sense the presence of urine and trigger an alarm, setting appropriate responses in motion.

Figure continued next page

Figure 6.1. *Continued*

- Memory-prompting and other cognitive aids remind an occupant when to eat, take medicines, or initiate scheduled tasks or can help the resident find lost items.

- Sensory-monitoring assistance compensates for occupants' deficits in sight, hearing, and touch (e.g., communicating whether water temperature in the shower is too hot).

- Equipment-monitoring and home-automation systems turn lights on or off (e.g., for getting out of bed at night); adjust thermostats; turn on or off air conditioning, heating, and stovetops; monitor refrigerator contents; notify the occupant of some event (e.g., when mail is delivered, when to wash hands, when to buy food); open and close window blinds to control ambient light and privacy; detect water leaks; and operate home security with visual monitoring of the dwelling doorway and remote operation (e.g., opening entrance door of dwelling).

- Safety-monitoring systems enable the detection of home environmental hazards such as fires, gas leaks, neurotoxins, and carbon monoxide poisoning.

- Social-interaction monitoring records the number and types of communications with friends, relatives, and other visitors and support video communications with these significant others.

- Socialization, exploration, and exercise technologies (e.g., computer-based Internet, e-mail, and video teleconferencing) enable older people to communicate with family and friends, participate in online communities, access intellectual and entertainment media, shop, and play interactive games for entertainment. They also provide virtual exercise programs, individually tailored to match the resident's abilities (Kutzik et al., 2008).

- Human-like robots replicate the functions of many of the above devices, and can also physically assist older people with the performance of their IADLs and ADLs.

pervasive healthcare technologies, and domotics.[75] These new technologies offer older people the prospects of living more enjoyable, healthier, and more autonomous lives. They monitor their health, activities, and dwelling environments; diagnose or screen them for physical or psychological problems; alert them or their family members or paid caregivers; get them help faster; and assist them in recovering more effectively from environmental deficits, dysfunctional behaviors, illnesses, accidents, or surgeries by quickly intervening (e.g., through counseling, treatments, and remedies).

Smart house technology relies heavily on wireless devices such as motion detectors, radio frequency sensors, video cameras, webcams, and physiological sensors. These are inserted in the walls, floors, and ceilings of a dwelling or integrated into some feature of the living space (e.g., kitchen appliances and beds). They are placed in various wearable technologies, including clothing ("smart garments"), wristbands, chains, patches, or eyeglasses, as well as those incorporated into basic handheld devices, including smartphones. They also include devices that are implanted in older people's bodies or ingested by them.[76]

In combination with sophisticated software programs, these devices record, measure, and respond to all physiological parameters and sensory modalities (e.g., video, audio, light, motion, acceleration, temperature, moisture, sound, odor, vibration, kinematic, and piezoelectric). In more advanced systems, these monitoring, communication, and response capabilities are integrated at some central control unit. A nurse's office, or even the home of a concerned daughter or son living in another state, could have these monitoring stations. Particularly notable are the claims by their designers that these technologies do not *"require training of or operation by the resident."*[77] Thus, their end users do not have to master instructions for their use.

MONITORING PEOPLE AND THEIR RESIDENCES

Proponents argue that technologically monitoring older people and their dwellings and communicating the findings to trained professionals make it easier and more efficient to identify health and mobility problems and environmental hazards before they become crises.[78] Consequently, healthcare professionals will not have to rely on subjective self-reports to assess potential problems because they will have access to a wealth of objective information. They will also not be restricted by the timetables of other professionals; they will not have to wait until a home care worker or occupational therapist does her weekly assessment to get key results.

Older people will connect in real time with geographically distant doctors, healthcare providers, and long-term care workers who will continuously monitor and evaluate their health and long-term support and service needs. Because they track the older person's behavior and physiological indicators over an extended period, these personnel (or rather their computers) will learn a person's usual or baseline patterns and thus detect when they deviate from established patterns, thereby indicating the onset of illnesses, injuries, and physical and cognitive declines.[79] Spending more than the usual 30 minutes in the shower would trigger an alarm, as would not eating breakfast, not going to the bathroom, or not opening the refrigerator over an extended period. Family members will find it easier to practice caregiving from a distance, confident that they will be alerted to unusual individual behaviors or conditions and dwelling problems that require their physical presence.

Some of these devices are more sophisticated than others. The simplest include personal emergency response systems or electronic call systems[80] that allow older people to communicate their need for assistance through devices placed on their bodies or installed in their dwellings. In contrast, the newest devices trigger alarms even when older people themselves are unaware of or cannot communicate their problems.

More advanced instruments monitor and interpret the bodily functions of older people, such as detecting blood pressure, blood sugar, and respiration. They monitor the gait and walking speed of older people; track their behaviors, activities, movements, and traffic flows in their dwellings; and detect whether they are sleeping, have fallen out of their beds, have taken their prescribed medicines, or are eating properly. Consider the brave new world opened up by the iPill, *"a diagnostic tool that is swallowed by the patient and contains a small camera to monitor the digestive tract,"*[81] and digital pills with sensors that track and monitor the intake of medications by older people.

These technologies can monitor the status, operation, and quality of the equipment found in their dwellings, such as appliances (e.g., refrigerator, stove, and water temperature), lighting, heating, and cooling systems, and security systems. They can detect whether the dwelling's temperature and humidity are acceptable and whether the occupants are exposed to any environmental hazards (e.g., toxins, carbon monoxide). And they are capable of automating most dwelling and household functions (e.g., checking for unlocked windows, locking doors, turning on lights or music, lowering blinds, adjusting temperature thermostats, and turning off appliances).[82]

TAKING ACTION

Once these devices receive information about older occupants and their dwellings, they can be used to analyze the data, make decisions, and take actions if they identify problems or discrepancies.[83] They allow professionals to deliver timely and tailor-made remedies either remotely (by voice, data transfer, videoconferencing, or the Internet) or by physically visiting the homes of older people. They could offer reminders for eating meals, drinking water to avoid dehydration, taking medications, and getting exercise. They could answer questions, ask for additional information about an unmet need (e.g., mail is not picked up, water is running, or stove is left on), make household arrangements (e.g., schedule repair visits, prepare grocery lists, send food orders to a grocery store and arrange for delivery), and initiate dwelling actions, such as locking doors or resetting a burglar alarm system.[84] They could initiate immediate corrective actions if, for example, the older person has unexpectedly fallen asleep, is not breathing properly, is under psychological duress, or has lost an unexplained amount of weight.

AFFECTING THE SOCIAL LIFE OF OLDER PEOPLE

These technologies purport even to help older people, particularly the lonely, become more socially engaged and to enjoy new recreational and leisure activities without leaving their sofas. Some of these efforts involve training older adults to use computers and the Internet or establishing secure social digital networks whereby they can reliably communicate with family or friends. More innovatively, these social interactions will be accomplished by a *"Virtual Senior Center, through which homebound older adults attend events at the local senior center even as they enjoy the comfort of being in their own homes."*[85] It works this way:

> Video cameras, microphones, and monitors enable the homebound seniors to see, hear, and interact with classmates and instructors at the center, and to take part in activities such as armchair yoga, art classes, discussion groups, and tai chi.[86]

Their designers expect that such social health technologies will achieve four goals:[87]

1. Detect changes or declines in social health as an early warning of more serious problems, such as depression or dementia

2. Provide memory assistance and confidence to those who are challenged to even use their phone or answer their front door

3. Connect those who are disenfranchised in the community with those who have the ability, time, and desire to "give back"

4. Offer new online forums for sharing one's story, learning new things, or just virtually hanging out with friends or strangers

ROBOT CAREGIVERS

Experts define a robot as *"a very powerful computer with equally powerful software housed in a mobile body and able to act rationally on its perception of the world around it."*[88] Today, there is a heightened interest in the potential of robots to serve as caregivers. Although they often perform the same functions as the technology described earlier, robots deserve separate attention because throughout history futurists and inventors have proposed that robots are capable of performing a broad range of tasks typically performed by people. Moreover, their designers distinguish these machines not only by what they do but by how they look and act: high tech versus low tech and degree of humanness, size, gender, and personality.[89] Sharkey explains why: *"Humans in general are all too ready to anthropomorphize machines, and other objects, and to imagine that they are capable of more than is actually the case."*[90]

Their duties seem unlimited: helping older people perform their daily tasks (e.g., eating, washing and rinsing, transferring from a bed to a wheelchair, and opening up doors and drawers), monitoring and supervising their health, motivating them to exercise and lose weight, reminding them what self-maintenance tasks to perform and medicines to take, helping with their rehabilitation therapy, identifying safety risks, and providing companionship, either through virtual visits of family or friends or by *"giving them an interesting gadget to talk to other people about."*[91]

BIG BROTHER IS WATCHING

How receptive older Americans (and their family members) are to these new technologies will depend on various factors. Many will enthusiastically embrace them as another strategy enabling them to age in place longer and to feel more comfortable and empowered in their abodes.[92] Others will accept them reluctantly, fearing that if they turn their backs on these technologies they will risk having to deal with a personal crisis alone and not receiving timely care or assistance. Others will accept them to avoid family or friends accusing them of being old fashioned and technologically ignorant.

Some will be late adopters or reject them entirely, viewing these sophisticated technological innovations as unnecessary or unaffordable assaults on their autonomy and worrying about their usability, reliability, and infringements on their privacy by an all-knowing big brother, whether government or corporation.[93] They will have many questions to ponder:

- Is it wise for them to introduce into their dwelling such new devices and technologies when they do not fully understand how they work, how to operate them, or how others will interpret the results? Do older people feel comfortable with the idea of digital devices and databanks being operated remotely by strangers, including perhaps those living in another country?

- In a world where credit card fraud and identity theft are rampant, is there a real danger that personal information will be stolen or the integrity of the system compromised?

- Do they forever want to be dressed in *"wearable computing and wireless applications"*[94] so that they are always on display no matter what they do and where they go because they cannot turn off these devices? Do they really want to give out so much information about how they first look in the morning or when they go to the bathroom? Do they want everything about their medical conditions and the most intimate aspects of their bodies and activities monitored?[95] What are the consequences of such obtrusiveness?[96]

- Do they really want continual reminders of their vulnerability because they have not taken their medicine, have failed to exercise or shower, or have mismanaged some aspect of their care regimen?[97] Do these devices and equipment institutionalize the home environment and thus constantly remind them that they are frail and sick?[98] Will these devices and equipment convey a stigmatizing and demeaning message of vulnerability to their family and friends and cause them to lose the respect of others—and, in turn, their own self-dignity?[99]

- Will these technologies radically change the roles played by their family members as caregivers? Will they see themselves more as trained technicians operating this equipment and less as emotionally connected spouses or children?[100] Will the result be less human contact—fewer hugs? Will they become less attentive, visiting or phoning less, because of their overreliance on this technology's automated operation and its outside monitoring sources?[101]

- These new technologies bridge geographic distances, but does the quality of care or assistance for older people suffer because virtual interactions replace the human contacts of paid workers and professionals? Without face-to-face interactions, will professional caregivers forget they are dealing with real people? What are the consequences of not having on-site diagnostic efforts by caring, sensitive, and compassionate people who show interest and involvement in their well-being?

- Because family members or professionals can scrutinize every aspect of their physical and mental health, will they be more at risk of having to move into a more supportive assisted living residence or a family member's home?[102]

Consequently, will these technologies have the unintended consequence of threatening their ability to age in place?

- Whatever their benefits, will they be worth the costs for new equipment and the monthly fees for monitoring and feedback?

Older people and their families must also confront the dangers inherent in any new technology. Their monitoring and measurement complexities will result in inevitable equipment breakdowns and unanticipated design flaws. There will be temporary interruptions during serious weather-related events (e.g., tornados, hurricanes, and floods).[103] These glitches may have especially dire consequences for older people who are depending heavily on these technologies. As is true for any diagnostic procedure, there will be the danger of overmonitoring and overtesting. Inevitably, there will be false positives (when a signal incorrectly identifies a problem) that result in unnecessary interventions.[104]

Another crucial issue will be whether older people will be required to give informed consent to allow the introduction of these potentially intrusive devices into their homes. This will sometimes pose a dilemma because the need for these technologies will often occur when the decision-making capacity of older people is questionable. At this point, they will be far more likely to depend on family members—or some appointed guardian—to make decisions on their behalf. We usually request that older people assign these powers to trusted people when they are still healthy. Yet it is hard to imagine how older people will be able to foresee how these rapidly changing technologies will look and operate in the future and potentially infringe on their way of life or autonomy. It will be hard for them to judge their utility.[105] Experts suggest that at the minimum, we should offer older people the following four safeguards:[106]

1. *Informed consent to the initiation of monitoring:* Let older people choose.
2. *Continuing consent to monitoring:* Give older people the option to temporarily or permanently stop monitoring.
3. *Control over who has access to the monitoring data:* Informed consent should stipulate who has access to data.
4. *Regular access to the monitoring data generated:* Older people should have access to all of the data collected through these technologies.

FUTURE DEMAND

These technologies unquestionably have the potential to benefit the health and well-being of older people.[107] Many small studies and much anecdotal information report that older people are positively disposed to introducing them into their homes.[108] This is especially true when they feel that these tech solutions will not prevent them from going about their lives in their familiar ways.[109] They are also more receptive when they understand that these technologies will help their family members carry out their caregiving responsibilities.[110] Moreover, critics may be exaggerating older people's worries about having their privacy violated. One study concluded that *"older adults have little to no concern about sharing information about personal health, daily activities, and social engagements with family and health care professionals.*"[111] Other surveys suggest a more qualified acceptance, where older people would consider adopting these solutions for preventive health purposes but only after they experience some threatening or bad outcome.[112] Another study conducted in an independent retirement community reported favorable views regarding video-recorded images but only if the captured views were reduced to silhouette images to preserve anonymity.

Other studies find that older adults' receptiveness to assistance depended on the specific home task.[113] For example, older people preferred robot assistance for house-keeping tasks but generally preferred human assistance with ADLs:

> Older adults were generally accepting of a robot housekeeper-cum-nurse-cum-companion, and preferred a robot's help to a human's for "instrumental activity of daily living"—changing light bulbs, cleaning the house, washing the dishes, making the bed, taking out the trash, keeping pests at bay and nagging them to take their medication.
>
> [They] didn't trust a robot's cooking skills, nor were they thrilled about having a robot shop for groceries [and] were resistant to a robot's help with more personal, intimate care, such as bathing, walking, shaving, getting dressed, eating, and brushing teeth.[114]

Crucial questions about future consumer demand and the efficacy of these technologies remain unanswered. Carefully executed intervention studies that assess whether these technologies will deliver on their promises are rare. Thus it is still impossible to identify those places or circumstances in which these new technologies will diagnose and respond to a problem faster, more accurately, and with better outcomes than might on-site staff. For example, in a large randomized, controlled trial study of older adults with multiple illnesses, there was no difference in the hospitalizations and emergency department visits between patients receiving telemonitoring and those receiving conventional care. Other studies offer more promising findings, but experts agree on the need for more confirmatory research.[115]

Introducing these technologies will be cost-prohibitive for many. Consequently, the adoption patterns of these new technologies may create a new basis for social inequality. We do not know whether private insurance companies will cover the costs of these solutions or whether federal programs such as Medicare and Medicaid will consider these reimbursable care expenses. Much may depend on whether experts show that these technologies reduce healthcare costs over the long term.[116]

Clearly, widespread consumer adoption of these new technologies is still in the future, and how mainstream older America will react is still up in the air. The earliest adopters will be the owners and operators of assisted living developments and other residential care facilities, who will embrace these technologies as a way to reduce their care costs yet still maintain good resident outcomes.[117] Their experiences may set the stage for overall consumer acceptance. We also do not know whether the government's regulatory environment will impede the progress of these innovations because of their efforts to ensure individual privacy or to avoid liability issues.

Despite the uncertainty about these future products and services, the proponents of these technologies point to various factors that bode well for their future growth:[118]

- The rapid pace of technological advances will improve their functionality and their promised outcomes.

- As production techniques improve and devices become more widely adopted, their prices will steadily drop.

- These products will become more physically attractive, easier to use (e.g., voice-based user interfaces), and require minimal user training.

- Older people and their care providers will view them more favorably as the costs of long-term care increase and they need less-expensive strategies to supplement or replace more costly hands-on paid caregivers or family assistance.

- Technology costs will increasingly be covered by private insurance companies and public programs, if only because they will view them as less-expensive solutions.

- Older people will continue to prefer to age in place in their ordinary homes and neighborhoods, especially as family caregivers become less reliable sources of assistance.

- Upcoming boomer generations will embrace these technologies because they will have had more experience with technologically sophisticated products in their younger lives, from computers to smartphones.

CONCLUSION

There are many good reasons to expect that assistive devices, home modifications, and technologically modified dwellings will make it easier for older people to feel that they are in both their residential comfort and mastery zones. However, the widespread adoption of these solutions may be limited by the absence of universal design requirements, low adoption rates of home modification strategies, a reluctance to accept high-tech solutions, and generally mixed evidence about the effectiveness of these solutions. Some older people will reject these strategies because they judge them as unnecessary, feel stigmatized as old people if they use them, or feel intimidated by the unknown.

We expect, however, that in the future a flood of favorably evaluated new high-tech products will result in increased acceptance and demand among older consumers because they will hold so much promise as solutions to help them age in place in their familiar homes, especially those in remote locations. Consequently, experts may have to reassess their dire predictions of an inadequate future supply of both professionals and direct care workers to meet the future long-term care needs of older people.

But even if we create dwellings with designs, infrastructures, and technological devices that perfectly match the lifestyles and competence levels of their older occupants, many experts believe that the human element will still be essential. Family caregivers—at least right now—are the backbone of our long-term care solutions and the focus of the next chapter.

NOTES

1. (Vierck, 2013)
2. Bianca Bosker, "Elderly Say Bring on the Robots—Just Not as Friends," *Huffington Post,* October 26, 2012.
3. (Sharkey & Sharkey, 2012, p. 30)
4. http://www.leadingage.org/cast.aspx
5. (Forlizzi, DiSalvo, & Gemperle, 2004, p. 50)
6. (Cornman, Freedman, & Agree, 2005)
7. (Freedman, Agree, Martin, & Cornman, 2005)
8. (Pressler & Ferraro, 2010)
9. (Cornman & Freedman, 2008)
10. (Mann et al., 2008)
11. (Agree & Freedman, 2003; Dudgeon et al., 2008; Spillman, 2005)
12. (Agree & Freedman, 2003)
13. (Maisel, Smith, & Steinfeld, 2008, p. 7)
14. (Greenhouse, 2012, p. 91)
15. (Hunter et al., 2011)
16. (Greenhouse, 2012)
17. http://www.design.ncsu.edu/cud/pubs_p/docs/poster.pdf
18. The original legislation was Title VIII of the Civil Rights Act of 1968, commonly known as the Fair Housing Act.
19. (Barrier Free Environments, Inc., 1998)
20. Townhouses are covered because the multiple units separated by common walls are considered part of the same building.
21. Earlier legislation (Rehabilitation Act of 1973, Section 504) required housing constructed with public funds to have accessible dwelling units.
22. (U.S. Department of Housing and Urban Development, 2005)
23. (U.S. Department of Housing and Urban Development, 2005)
24. (Allen, 2012, p. 206)
25. (Joint Center for Housing Studies of Harvard University, 2014)
26. (Maisel et al., 2008, p. vii)
27. (Pynoos, Bressett, & McCleskey, 2012; Joint Center for Housing Studies of Harvard University, 2014)
28. (Greenhouse, 2012; Hunter et al., 2011; Unwin et al., 2009)
29. Jon Pynoos, Ph.D., is co-director of the Fall Prevention Center of Excellence in Los Angeles and professor of gerontology and policy, planning, and development at the University of Southern California Andrus Gerontology Center (Valenza, 2007, pp. 2–3).
30. http://www.aia.org/groups/aia/documents/pdf/aiab087283.pdf
31. (Kruse et al., 2010)
32. (Lanspery, Callahan, Miller, & Hyde, 1997, p. 3)
33. (Hiatt, 2004)
34. (UnitedHealthcare, 2014; see also Kruse et al., 2010)
35. (Joint Center for Housing Studies of Harvard University, 2000)
36. (Freedman & Agree, 2008)
37. (Freedman & Agree, 2008)
38. (Newman, 2003)
39. (Hawthorne, 2013)
40. (Kruse et al., 2010, p. 117)
41. (Kruse et al., 2010, p. 118)
42. (Kruse et al., 2010, p. 124)
43. (Bell & Menec, 2013; Forlizzi et al., 2004)
44. (Kruse et al., 2010, p. 122)

45. (Forlizzi et al., 2004)
46. (Kruse et al., 2010, p. 121)
47. (Bezaitis, 2008)
48. (Joint Center for Housing Studies of Harvard University, 2001, p. 2)
49. (Joint Center for Housing Studies of Harvard University, 2003)
50. (Davidoff, 2004)
51. (Fagan, 2007)
52. (Pynoos & Nishita, 2003)
53. (Pynoos & Nishita, 2003)
54. (Guerrero, 2003)
55. (Lord, Menz, & Sherrington, 2006; Pynoos et al., 2006; Wahl, Fange, Oswald, Gitlin, & Iwarsson, 2009)
56. (Smith, 2001)
57. (Pynoos et al., 2006; Wahl et al., 2009)
58. (Steinman, Pynoos, & Nguyen, 2009)
59. (Chan et al., 2007; Lord et al., 2006)
60. (Lord et al., 2006, p. ii58)
61. (Lord et al., 2006, p. ii58)
62. (Clemson, Mackenzie, Ballinger, Close, & Cumming, 2008; Costello & Edelstein, 2008; Freedman & Agree, 2008; Lord et al., 2006; Salminen et al., 2009; Wahl & Oswald, 2009)
63. (Oswald, Wahl, Schilling, & Iwarsson, 2007)
64. (Rose, 2008, p. 1161)
65. (Costello & Edelstein, 2008; Pynoos et al., 2006)
66. (Costello & Edelstein, 2008)
67. (Smith et al., 2012, p. 6)
68. (Gitlin, Hauck, Winter, Dennis, & Schulz, 2006)
69. (Gitlin et al., 2009)
70. (Bezaitis, 2008, p. 29)
71. (Tanner, Tilse, & de Jonge, 2008)
72. (Unwin et al., 2009, p. 965)
73. (Kutzik, Glascock, Lundberg, & York, 2008)
74. (Dishman, 2012, p, 104)
75. (Bharucha et al., 2009; Demiris & Hensel, 2008; Forlizzi et al., 2004; Kutzik et al., 2008; Mann & Milton, 2005)
76. (Bharucha et al., 2009; Mann & Milton, 2005; Matthews, 2006)
77. (Demiris & Hensel, 2009, p. 107)
78. (Dishman, 2012)
79. (Cantor, 2006)
80. (Magan, 2011)
81. Daniel Kraft, "Exploring the future of health & medicine in senior living." Connecting Today for Growth Tomorrow, Executive Summary, ALFA 2012 Senior Living Leadership Forum, October 3–4, 2012, p. 4.
82. (Bharucha et al., 2009)
83. (Bharucha et al., 2009)
84. (Demiris & Hensel, 2008; Mann & Milton, 2005)
85. (Magan, 2011, p. 4)
86. Accessed at http://www.microsoft.com/en-us/news/features/2010/mar10/03-10virtualseniorcenter.aspx
87. (Dishman, 2012, p. 103)
88. (Ikebe et al., 2001, p. 9)
89. (Broadbent, Stafford, & MacDonald, 2009)
90. (Sharkey & Sharkey, 2012)
91. (Sharkey & Sharkey, 2012, p. 36)

92. Paradoxically, many of these tech solutions evolved out of applications originally targeting younger people, but members of the older generation are now the beneficiaries.
93. (Bowman, Hooker, Steggell, & Brandt, 2013)
94. (Demiris & Hensel, 2008, p. 39)
95. (Courtney, 2008)
96. (Zwijsen, Niemeijer, & Hertogh, 2011)
97. (Cantor, 2006)
98. (Demiris & Hensel, 2009)
99. (Forlizzi et al., 2004)
100. (Demiris & Hensel, 2009, p. 111)
101. (Demiris & Hensel, 2008)
102. (Cantor, 2006)
103. (Bowman et al., 2013)
104. (Zwijsen et al., 2011)
105. (Demiris & Hensel, 2009)
106. (Cantor, 2006, p. 52)
107. (Kutzik et al., 2008).
108. (Barrett, 2008; Demiris, Hensel, Skubic, & Rantz, 2008; Demiris, Oliver, Dickey, Skubic, & Rantz, 2008)
109. (Johnson, Davenport, & Mann, 2007; Lorenzen-Huber, Boutain, Camp, Shankar, & Connelly, 2011)
110. (Lorenzen-Huber et al., 2011)
111. (Lorenzen-Huber et al., 2011, pp. 234–235)
112. (Demiris, Oliver, Giger, Skubic, & Rantz, 2009)
113. (Smarr et al., 2012)
114. Bianca Bosker, "Elderly Say Bring on the Robots—Just Not as Friends," *Huffington Post*, October 26, 2012
115. (Ekeland, Bowes, & Flottorp, 2010; Topo, 2009; Takahashi et al., 2012)
116. (Demiris & Hensel, 2008)
117. (Kutzik et al., 2008)
118. (Center for Technology and Aging, 2013; Demiris & Hensel, 2008)

7

THE MULTIFACETED FAMILY
CAREGIVING SOLUTION

The Family Caregiver's World

Spouses face hurdles when caring for themselves, ill loved ones.[1]

Dividing the caregiving duties, it's daughters vs. sons.[2]

Living with in-laws linked to heart risks in Japanese women.[3]

Family caregivers need help, too.[4]

Elder care, an issue for workers.[5]

ACHIEVING NORMALCY: WHO HELPS AND WHO CARES

When older people seeking to age in place have difficulty living independent lives, their first inclination is not to hire paid help but to call on the assistance of their spouses or adult children. Love, sentimentality, self-interest, knowledge gaps, and financial constraints are all possible motives for this response. But whatever the reasons, it is indisputable that this *informal care*—caregiving by their families or cohabitating partners, friends, or neighbors—is the single most important reason why community-residing older people with physical and cognitive limitations are able to age in place and stay out of assisted living or nursing homes.[6]

Excluding the quarter of the community-residing older population with chronic disabilities who manage without help from anyone,[7] about 90% of people age 65 and older with at least some difficulties performing their activities of daily living (ADLs) or instrumental ADLs (IADLs) rely on this informal care.[8] Only 18% of frail older adults rely on paid help or *formal care,* 12% in a primary role and 6% in a secondary role.[9] Even among older people with more severe ADL limitations, 88% rely on informal care, with 29% also depending on paid care, 19% in a primary role and 9% in a secondary role.[10]

Consequently, although paid workers obviously play a key role, their long-term care assistance pales in comparison to the contributions of family caregivers. As one expert argues,

> No evidence accumulated in more than 3 decades of research suggests that formal agency services supplant care provided by family and friends. Whereas informal caregivers provide most care to those in need, formal care acts as a supplement, rather than as substitute, to the unpaid sector.[11]

In the United States, researchers estimated that about 44 million people (age 18 or older) were unpaid caregivers to an adult family member or friend (age 50 years or older).[12] Seventy percent of these caregivers are women. Daughters and wives (or partners) are the most important helpers, although other family members—husbands, daughters-in-law, sons, and grandchildren—can play significant roles. About 9 out of 10 married frail older adults receive help from a spouse, and more than 50% of unmarried frail older adults receive help from their daughters.[13] The average U.S. caregiver is a White, married, and employed woman in her 50s or early 60s who has provided 19 hours of care weekly to one relative for an average of 4 years.[14] The caregiving experiences of women are often repeated throughout their lifetimes, as they care for a parent, then their older husbands, and then themselves (Figure 7.1).

Gender also influences the types of responsibilities assumed by caregivers. Women are more likely to help with ADLs as opposed to IADLs and generally spend more hours doing a wider range of tasks. Men, on the other hand, play an important niche role by assisting with the care recipient's financial affairs, home or yard maintenance, and automobile repairs. Experts portray men as inherently disadvantaged as caregivers because, unlike their wives, they must assume duties that are often very new to them. Relaying her own caregiving experiences, well-known columnist Jane Gross observes,

> Yes, there are daughters who ignore or abandon their aged parents, and there are sons, more of them every day, who prove to be devoted caregivers. But that is not the norm. And even when the division of labor is closer to 50/50 than 90/10, the chores that fall to daughters and sons tend to be different. I have nothing but admiration and gratitude for my brother's labors filling out the Medicaid application and choosing the perfect motorized wheelchair for my mother. But I did all the yucky stuff. . . . It is what it is, and this arduous interval is a dumb time for a feminist hissy fit. Far wiser to bow to the stereotypes

and delegate every male-suitable task you can think of to your brother(s). Then leave them alone; don't micro-manage or tell them what they're doing wrong. It doesn't matter if they do it the way you would, or even if they do it as well, as long as they do it.[15]

Unfortunately, some older people, predominantly the unmarried (i.e., divorced, separated, widowed, or single) or those married without living children, are less able to depend on this informal care. Other older people lack family assistance because their children or siblings live too far away, are too busy with their own children or jobs, or do not have good relationships with their parents.[16] Not surprisingly, people in their late 70s and older will depend more on paid help because they need heavier care and because their spouses—themselves frail—play a declining role.[17] Married women in particular are likely to survive their spouses, and formal care is often their only option.

Also influential are the ethnic or racial backgrounds of older people.[18] About 20% of people age 65 and older are members of minority groups (particularly African-Americans, Asians, and Hispanics).[19] Among non-Hispanic White older adults, only about 4% of men and 13% of women will co-reside with family members, typically their adult children. In contrast, such co-residency is much more common among older people who identify themselves as minorities. Hispanic older adults are especially likely to rely on their families, and they generally receive more hours of informal care. Just over 17% of Hispanic men age 65 and older and 36% of women co-reside with a family member (Chapter 4, Table 4.1). Hispanic caregivers in particular are less likely to place a family member in a nursing home.[20] Perhaps this can be explained by their lower incomes, which make paying for formal care prohibitive; alternatively, older people with these cultural backgrounds often see taking care of older relatives as a family responsibility and may be distrustful or feel guilty about putting the care of their loved ones in the hands of paid help or government bureaucracies.[21]

CAREGIVING IS NOT FOR THE FAINT OF HEART

Labeling the assistance provided by family members as long-term care is particularly apt because it rarely involves short-term responsibilities. Over the course of years rather than months, families are helping their loved ones cope with the debilitating outcomes of chronic illnesses, cognitive declines, depression, and losses of physical mobility. They become front-line witnesses to all of the physical, psychological, and social changes that accompany aging.

Initially, caregiving may be as undemanding as transporting a loved one to a doctor's appointment and spending time talking about their concerns and fears. Over time, caregiving inevitably becomes far more stressful and demanding, requiring caregivers to change diapers because of fecal incontinence, help with eating and bathing, give injections, keep loved ones from wandering outside, and manage the challenging behaviors of a person with Alzheimer's disease or other dementias. The more serious a loved one's chronic health problems and disabilities are, the more time these family caregivers must spend providing care and assistance. A study of caregivers helping

Figure 7.1. The gender raw deal: the life cycle of female caregivers (This is an enlarged version of material that appeared in [Golant, 2009c].)

Scenario 1

The caregiving burden falls heavily on the backs of women in their 40s, 50s, and 60s. Often, they must deal with an older mother or father who needs assistance, or even a mother- or father-in-law who needs support. Daughters feel great pressure to care for an aging parent as long as necessary (Eckroth-Bucher, 2008). They must decide whether to invite their mothers or fathers into their own homes, arrange assistance to allow them to age in place, or encourage them to occupy an independent (congregate) living apartment, assisted living arrangement, or nursing home.

Compared with their mothers, these caring women are more likely to have either full-time or part-time jobs (more than 6 out of 10 will be in the labor force) that are competing with their caregiving responsibilities (Genworth Financial, 2006). Giving up their jobs is often very difficult, not only because of immediate income losses but also because of long-term implications. Future salary levels will be reduced, savings will be drained, and they will experience a lower lifetime earnings record, thereby reducing their Social Security payments (about 20% lower than men) when they reach their own old age. It is estimated that because of their caregiving responsibilities, women are in the paid workforce 12 fewer years than men (Wald, 2013).

As members of the sandwich generation, these women are doubly burdened by both their adult parents and their children, who may still reside in their homes (Johnson & Wiener, 2006; Pierret, 2006). These multiple responsibilities are now more likely with marriage and childbearing occurring at later ages and with older people living longer (Fuller-Thomson & Minkler, 2001), and they *"take a strong personal toll"* (Genworth Financial, 2006, p. 6).

Scenario 2

When women are in their 70s and 80s, they must assist their typically older husbands with managing their chronic health problems or physical or cognitive limitations. With an average age of just over 73, they are assisting at the very time they are coping with their own health problems and physical limitations (Johnson & Wiener, 2006). These new caregiving demands are especially stressful because these women must simultaneously function as wives and personal aides. As one woman responded, *"Instead of just cooking dinner, she might now cut it into pieces that her husband could more easily eat"* (Calasanti, 2006, p. 262).

These caregiver responsibilities do not end if their husbands occupy an assisted living development or nursing home. They must still function as proactive "watchdogs" of their husband's care, especially if he has Alzheimer's disease. They are continually responsible for *"providing comfort and reassurance, and participating in decisions about coming home or moving to a long-stay unit"* (Levine et al., 2010, p. 118).

Women might be able to cope more cheerfully with their heavy responsibilities except for the fact that American society often devalues their contribution. As one expert observes,

Figure continued next page

Figure 7.1. *Continued*

The lack of attention to and support for their social and economic contribution as caregivers ultimately leads many women to feel isolated and unvalued, and, in some cases, to defer or abandon social opportunities and their own aspirations—clear threats to their dignity and the principle of social justice. (Eckenwiler, 2007, p. 12)

Scenario 3

As early as their mid-70s, women experience their own physical and mental declines. They may look in vain for the support that they provided their parents or husbands. (If they were "fortunate" enough to have lived alone much of their lives, they may have been spared their spousal caregiving obligations.) Because of the life expectancy and marriage age differences of older men and women, their husbands have often passed away, and they must depend on their own resources to maintain independent households. Even when their husbands are still alive, they are typically older and can offer little assistance because they have their own chronic health problems and physical limitations. The caregiving responsibilities of the older woman may be especially challenging when she needs different long-term services and supports than her husband. For example, the wife may need only light care—help with her IADLs—whereas her husband needs much heavier hands-on care because he has Alzheimer's disease.

Although these women assumed financial responsibility for the medication and care needs of their aging parents and spouses (Eckenwiler, 2007), their own long-term care and medical expenditures often rest solely on their shoulders. If they are still homeowners, they must also assume all of the costs to maintain their homes. Adding to their plight is the dwindling amount they can count on from their husband's earlier income streams (e.g., pensions and Social Security). Consequently, women consistently worry more than men about outliving their savings.

In the best of worlds, the life cycle will come full circle. A child—most likely a daughter but perhaps also a son or sibling—will step up to assume caregiving responsibilities, maintain their dwellings, and provide financial relief; however, these older women have no guarantees.

family members in the last years of their life estimated that these households had an average of 1.8 family caregivers who spent almost 66 hours a week caregiving.[22]

With the persistent patterns of aging in place and longer life expectancy of their Fourth Age loved ones, family members are assuming an ever-more complex array of caregiving responsibilities.[23] Their job descriptions require them to perform the housekeeping tasks of a maid, the duties of an on-call chauffeur, the assignments of a building janitor, the responsibilities of a nurse's assistant in the office of a primary care physician, the hands-on tasks of multiple personal care and assistance staff at a well-run assisted living community or nursing home, and the medically related duties of nurses. In fact, today's unpaid caregivers must perform as many as 15 different and often painfully challenging types of duties. The demands on their time and energies will be especially great when they care for older people with Alzheimer's disease.[24]

APPRAISAL

Above all, caregivers must understand the reasons for the health or mobility challenges of their spouses or parents and their inability to live independently. They must establish what needs must be addressed, how quickly, and for how long, as well as what types of solutions are likely to be the most effective in the short- and long-term. Caregivers must vigilantly monitor the older person's inability to perform one or more ADLs or IADLs, take medications, or manage health complications.[25] The more complicated the appraisal, the greater the need to seek the expertise of doctors or geriatric care managers (Chapter 8).

INFORMATION GATHERING: PERSONNEL AND SERVICES

"Information is a big deal."[26] Caregivers quickly discover that they need new services or products, but they often know little about where to find this assistance. Even Robert Kane, a geriatric authority on the health and long-term care of older persons, struggled with these caregiving frustrations: *"It was not a matter of paying for her care; the challenge was finding the right kind of care we wanted to pay for."*[27]

Family members must suddenly find providers for services such as door-to-door transportation, food delivery, housekeeping, adult day centers, senior care centers, home care workers, and respite care services that allow caregivers to take a break for a few hours during the day (Chapter 8).[28]

LANGUAGE TRANSLATOR: ETHNIC AND RACIAL CULTURAL MEDIATOR

In my family, we have hired round-the-clock live-in aides from foreign countries as caregivers, and they have proven excellent workers. But language barriers can be a problem, especially when the caregiver must accurately communicate information to professionals in order for the older person to receive appropriate medical services or care. It obviously helps if the older person or the family member can at least minimally speak the language of the caregiver.

Even when they speak English, however, we cannot assume that caregivers from other racial or cultural backgrounds are acceptable to White aging adults. These older people may display intolerant or hostile behaviors toward their hired minority caregivers. More liberal adult children may cringe when their older parents exhibit such behavior, but their condemnation does not make the problem go away. They must hire people who not only address their loved ones' health problems or functional limitations but who are also compatible with their values and personalities.

COORDINATOR OF NONMEDICAL (LONG-TERM) CARE

Often only a fragmented array of providers (individuals, agencies, and businesses) offers the products or services an older person needs. Consequently, family members must act like a general contractor charged with building a house who hires multiple subcontractors. For example, different providers are necessary for an older person recovering from a stroke: help with dressing and transferring, meal preparation, housecleaning, medication counseling, door-to-door transportation, and home modifications.

When affordability is an issue, family members must piece together the services and benefits administered by multiple government-sponsored programs with very different eligibility requirements and terms of service (Chapter 8) that often seem incongruent or unresponsive to the needs of their loved one. As one expert expressed it, *"Informal caregivers face a confusing assortment of badly coordinated providers and care settings that have no incentive to interact due to separate sources of funding, inconsistent care practices, and poor communication."*[29]

COORDINATOR OF TRANSITIONAL CARE

Hospitals are discharging older people faster, resulting in more patients who have not completely healed and need recuperative and rehabilitative care.[30] Regaining lost mobility and stamina takes time; caregivers must plan for a lengthy recovery period during which they must coordinate a host of postoperative needs, such as physical, occupational, or speech therapy and *"more demanding and complex kinds of care that last longer periods—sometimes for decades."*[31]

Yet caregivers must integrate information and obtain assistance from acute and long-term care providers who often act as if they are in different universes. Hospitals are busy ringing up their charges after discharge, and they are less concerned about how well the patient recovers at home or adjusts to everyday living. Consequently, family caregivers do not receive much support from healthcare professionals during the discharge process.[32] As Eric Coleman, an expert in geriatric and chronic disease care, testified to the U.S. Senate Aging Committee,

> By default, patients and their family caregivers have become the silent care coordinators, performing a significant amount of their own care coordination with no specific preparation, tools, or support.[33]

Family members must motivate their older loved ones to comply with their often numerous disease management tasks and ensure that they follow their physician treatments, diets, and exercise regimens as well as obtain future tests and procedures. Risks abound, including

> medication errors, duplicative tests, lack of coordination, poor communication among professionals across settings, problems in the timeliness of care, and lack of access to vital home- and community-based services.[34]

SPOKESPERSON, TROUBLESHOOTER, AND ADVOCATE

In a perfect world, credit card companies, doctors, hospitals, banks, home repair people, and the myriad other services and businesses would always act responsively, responsibly, and compassionately. In the real world, people and businesses make mistakes and seem not to care. Inevitably, family members must be troubleshooters because disputes and screw-ups happen and take inordinate amounts of time to resolve. When a scheduled transportation van does not show up, the caregiver must find a substitute. Pharmacies must refill incorrect prescriptions or fix faulty insurance information. Even in the best-run assisted living developments (Chapter 11), older residents need spokespersons to look out for their interests.

Family advocates are especially needed when the care recipient has Alzheimer's disease.[35] When my father-in-law, who had dementia, was staying in our house, I continually fielded phone calls from all manner of businesses asking to speak directly to their "client." And many wanted to know on what authority I spoke for my father-in-law.

Taking my father-in-law to an emergency room to assess heart attack symptoms presented yet another frustrating scenario. Even after I informed emergency room staff about his reduced cognitive abilities, the well-meaning medical resident insisted that he should communicate his medical history and past symptoms, even though expecting such recall was unrealistic. These examples show the need for the caregiver to have the authority to speak on behalf of an older person; a power of attorney is especially useful.

HANDS-ON CARE WITH ADLS

Some of the most physically demanding responsibilities involve providing assistance with an older person's ADLs. Helping loved ones with their most intimate and personal tasks also takes an emotional toll. It is common for family members to feel uncomfortable bathing or feeding a parent or spouse and to feel frustrated by the downhill trajectory of their abilities.

HANDS-ON CARE WITH IADLS

Older people typically need assistance to perform their IADLs. Food must be purchased, meals prepared, the dwelling kept clean, laundry done, appointments kept, and recreational and social activities planned. Family members must ensure that the older person can live safely and securely in his or her dwelling and that someone (maid service, building superintendent) is taking care of the usual maintenance tasks.

HANDS-ON MEDICAL AND NURSING TASKS

The caregiving responsibilities of family members have traditionally included assistance with ADLs and IADLs. Caregivers increasingly must assist their spouses and parents who are aging in place with a range of medical and nursing services that once only registered nurses delivered.[36] One estimate is that 46% of family caregivers performed nursing tasks,[37] such as wound care and the changing of sterile dressings, insulin injections, intravenous therapy, catheter care, operating specialized medical equipment (e.g., mechanical ventilators, tube-feeding equipment), operating durable medical equipment (e.g., lifts to get people out of bed, and hospital beds), preparing food for special diets, and managing incontinence.[38]

Often the instructions received from professional nursing staff are brief and hurried.[39] Remarkably, these professionals rarely assess the abilities of family members to provide post-hospital care or detect any worsening of the older person's illness or disability.[40] One study reported that African-American and Hispanic caregivers particularly *"felt invisible in the hospital, ignored by hospital staff, and unprepared to manage complex care at home."*[41] As one expert put it, *"Some patients come from the hospital with feeding tubes and even mechanical ventilators {and} family caregivers who are home alone with their loved one report feeling terrified and overwhelmed."*[42]

Even something as straightforward as medication management can be stressful. Family members must make sure older people correctly fill and refill their multiple prescriptions, often five or more medications daily, with different doses and dispensing regimens, as well as purchase the appropriate over-the-counter medicine.[43] These tasks are especially complicated for less-educated and foreign-born families with English-language difficulties.[44]

Caregivers know a simple mistake can mean rehospitalization. Consider these potentially scary sources of error reported by one physician:

> In the home are multiple medication bottles of varied ages bearing several physicians' names from before the hospitalization and new discharge medications with new physician names, often with no refills. There may be redundancy, therapeutic duplication, and dose discrepancies. Some prescribed medications are absent because of miscommunication, noncompliance, lack of finances, or formulary mismatches.[45]

FINANCIAL MANAGEMENT AND ASSISTANCE

We typically treat managing financial affairs as just another IADL, but assisting with this activity requires a distinct set of caregiving responsibilities. Water and electric bills, repair and upkeep costs, mortgage payments, property taxes, and insurance bills do not conveniently stop when older people cannot take care of their usual financial transactions. Bank and brokerage accounts must still be managed. Family members must assume these duties and may have to pay out of their own funds to cover needed expenditures.

In the early stages of his dementia, my father-in-law lived alone in his Florida condo. A disgruntled electric utility, an impatient condominium association, two retailers, and several credit card companies soon made us aware of his trail of unpaid bills. Reluctantly, he began allowing us to pay his debts.

FOREVER HOTEL

Adult children may find it necessary to accommodate older parents in their own dwellings because they cannot safely live on their own and care for themselves, they live too far away to make caregiving feasible, or they lack financial resources for formal care. These co-residence arrangements (Chapter 4, Table 4.1) eliminate geographic separation problems, but inevitably result in lifestyle conflicts. Adult children quickly realize that they can no longer take for granted either their privacy or their favorite activities and now have front row seats to view the travails of their loved one. Older people for their part do not enjoy their dependent status and feel they have become burdens. Living together also exacerbates any pre-existing intergenerational conflicts. The design of the dwelling arrangements may mitigate some of these conflicts, and there are various pros and cons to alternatives, such as a spare bedroom, an accessory apartment, or an elder cottage housing opportunity (ECHO) unit (Figure 7.2).

Figure 7.2. Alternative dwelling arrangements for family caregivers or their hired workers

Spare Bedrooms

Family members, especially homeowners, can use unoccupied bedrooms, attics, or basements in their dwellings to accommodate an older parent. (Alternatively, an older person will have such spaces in her own dwelling to accommodate a caregiver.) This co-residence arrangement facilitates monitoring and caring for the older person. Creating such a spare bedroom requires the least physical effort and financial outlay. However, the care provider may have to renovate a nearby bathroom to make it safer or more accessible. The care provider must also negotiate and limit what possessions the older person is allowed to move into the care provider's house.

Lost privacy for the older care recipient or the caregiver may be a downside. When family members are eating, are entertaining guests, or want to be alone, they must decide whether the older person is allowed or welcome outside her private space. (If the older person lives in her own house and accommodates a live-in boarder to help her, a similar issue arises. Is the boarder or hired live-in welcome in the kitchen or living room?)

Accessory Apartments or In-Law Suites

The creation of this space requires homeowners to renovate areas such as attics, garages, or basements so that the older person has a private entrance, separate from the main entrance, as well as his or her own kitchen, bathroom, bedroom, and living areas. This co-residence arrangement has some obvious advantages over the spare bedroom arrangement because the older person has a more clearly demarcated living space and can come and go without infringing on the privacy of the caregiver.

There are two possible downsides to the accessory apartment option. First, some construction is necessary to create this self-enclosed living area with its own separate entrance and physical infrastructure, and the costs could be prohibitive, especially if there is a need for new plumbing or electrical work. Second, some municipalities or neighborhood associations have zoning ordinances or covenants that prohibit this dwelling arrangement, because it violates their single-family zoning restrictions and their fears of allowing unrelated people as occupants. Families may have to request land use zoning changes to allow higher-density dwelling arrangements and multifamily households (Liebig, Koenig, & Pynoos, 2006).

ECHO Unit (Granny Flat, Carriage House, Accessory Cottage)

This more ambitious and expensive alternative involves installing a small, self-contained, and usually prefabricated or factory-built structure on the side or the rear of the lot of an adult child's single-family home. The most recent versions of this product are equipped with health monitoring and safety features that resemble a hospital room more than a residence. (The latest and most sophisticated commercial version of this cottage is the MedCottage.) It typically is the size of a two-car garage and includes kitchen, bathroom, utility, and living room areas. Adult children would

Figure continued next page

Figure 7.2. *Continued*

opt for this dwelling arrangement if they want their older mother or father close by but in very separate quarters. This living arrangement offers the most privacy to the older person, but the family must establish clear-cut rules regarding when the older person can enter the main house.

Several obstacles restrict its use. First, despite its proximity, the family member must still move from one dwelling to another to perform caregiving tasks, which may involve going outside in inclement weather. Second, many single-family lots are simply too small to accommodate these units. Third, neighbors may oppose the installation or building of a separate unit on a single-family lot, and exclusionary zoning ordinances may simply disallow such separate structures in single-family zoned residential districts. Fourth, this is obviously the most costly of the three alternatives and will be the most expensive to maintain. And fifth, zoning ordinances that initially allow these structures may require the homeowner to remove them after the caregiving relationship ends (Liebig et al., 2006).

FAMILY PEACEKEEPER AND DIPLOMAT

Despite the burdens placed on the only child who is helping a widowed mother, there is an important plus: no other family member to answer to. Family dynamics are more complex when multiple adult children or siblings attempt to be caregivers. Questions continually arise: Who should take responsibility, and how could you make such a stupid decision? Inevitably, the lead family member (and this self-appointed label is itself controversial) must acquire the skills of a U.N. peacekeeper to calm the hurt feelings that often arise when family members disagree.

SOURCE OF EMOTIONAL SUPPORT

Dependency and illness often accelerate the shrinking social network of older people and produce anxieties and fears. The family member increasingly functions as confidant, companion, morale booster, and counselor. The responsibilities are many: someone to talk to, someone who will listen, someone who affirms that everything is going to be okay, and someone who explains what is happening and is able to calm the inevitable age-related anxieties.

MONITORING, REASSESSING, AND PROVIDING NEW SOLUTIONS

Dealing with change is itself a legitimate category of responsibility. Caregiving is rarely a static enterprise; the unexpected always happens, and earlier remedies no longer work. Mobility declines, chronic illnesses arise, and memories get worse. The family member needs additional information and instructions to cope with new symptoms and limitations. Hired service providers may fail to recognize the changing condition of the older person. Unfortunately, it is the last error that counts the most and can negate hundreds of past thoughtful and correct decisions.

END-OF-LIFE DECISIONS

A Florida survey reported that nearly 6 out of 10 AARP members choose to die at home.[46] Most caregivers are on very unfamiliar and shaky territory when they must deal with a dying spouse or parent. A dying person requires the family member to make extraordinarily difficult and emotional decisions about when to intervene with aggressive medical or surgical treatments and when to let death occur calmly and painlessly. An advance directive demanding no heroic actions to keep someone alive takes on a different light when it is no longer just an impersonal and hypothetical paper document.

These decisions are ever more complicated because modern medicine offers so many solutions for prolonging life. It is not easy to decide when not to risk the downsides of inserting a pacemaker for a heart ailment (infection is a serious side effect) or when to withhold radiation therapy (with multiple and debilitating side effects) from someone who has a malignant skin mole. For a younger and healthier person, a hip replacement is usually an easy choice. For a 90-year-old with advanced Alzheimer's disease who cannot cope with the demanding rehabilitation process, it may be disastrous.

Fortunately, hospice services can make the dying experience—for both older people and their family—less traumatic and more predictable. But dealing with a dying old person will always be the most painful caregiving task.

FAMILY CAREGIVING: MANY REWARDS BUT HIGH COSTS

THE POSITIVES

Spouses and adult children often speak of their caregiver responsibilities as a labor of love. Husbands and wives assisting each other particularly feel that they have developed stronger emotional connections and that they are *"sharing a common fate."*[47] In their words, *"I need my spouse as much as he/she needs me."*[48] Many adult children also find caregiving a fulfilling "giving back" emotional experience that enables them to reciprocate the time and energy that their parent spent on raising them.[49] More pragmatically, they feel gratified that they can enable their family members to live longer in their "normal" residential arrangements. They also feel that their efforts set a good example to their own children. Adult children may also believe that their caregiving experiences provide them with on-the-job training that will help prepare them for their own future frailties.[50] Unquestionably, when spouses or adult children view their caregiving responsibilities positively, their older care recipients feel better about accepting their assistance.

THE NEGATIVES

PHYSICAL AND EMOTIONAL STRESS

The positives come with costs. It bears repeating that caregiving is tough work, both physically and emotionally.[51] It is easy for family caregivers to become overwhelmed with the sheer number of responsibilities, especially when they lack emotional support or the financial resources, insurance coverage, or government assistance to get help from professionals.[52] A good deal of caregiving involves physically exhausting and strenuous hands-on care. When compared with noncaregivers with the same demographics, caregivers consistently score lower on a variety of physical health indicators.[53] They are more likely to incur physical injuries (e.g., muscle and ligament strains), have higher blood pressure, use more medications, show symptoms of poorer eating habits, be more sleep deprived, and exercise less frequently. Men caring for their wives have a higher stroke risk, particularly African-Americans.[54]

Caregivers fear that they will miss seeing danger signs of their loved one's decline or will be absent when an emergency happens (e.g., a fall or onset of a stroke). Especially when they are providing more complex health-related services, they are on call several times a day, and because of their inexperience and lack of training they are always afraid of making mistakes and harming their loved ones.[55]

Caregivers generally rate their own health as poor and report feeling burned out,[56] emotionally drained,[57] and with little free time for themselves. They are more likely to report these symptoms the longer they provide care, particularly when they assist older people with dementia.[58] They have higher emergency room and hospital utilization rates and see doctors more frequently.[59] As one commentator put it, *"A family caregiver may ultimately become sicker than the person they are caring for."*[60] One study even found that caregivers have elevated mortality rates.[61]

Adult children get worn down for another reason. Because less than 15% live with their impaired parents,[62] they must travel significant distances to reach their dwellings.[63] This is especially true for caregivers helping loved ones in rural areas.[64] They initially believe, somewhat naively, that they can make these visits at regular times that fit their schedules. They quickly learn that they cannot neatly compartmentalize their caring duties into one time slot of the day or certain days of the week.[65]

A *Dear Abby* letter says it all:

> Dear Abby: My beautiful, loving mother is now in the middle stages of Alzheimer's disease. This cruel disease has robbed her of her memories as well as the ability to reason and function. She held my hand through every trial and triumph in my life, and I want to support her the way she has always supported me. But caring for Mama is becoming more and more difficult as she drifts further and further away. Not only am I caring for my mother, I also have a career and three children. I have so little time to myself. From the financial considerations to the behavioral challenges to safety concerns, I can't keep my head above water. Please tell me what to do.
>
> —Overwhelmed in Cincinnati[66]

FEELING UNAPPRECIATED AND IGNORED

Caregivers report getting irritable and angry about *"having to do this all by myself, with a feeling that there's no relief and there's no one out there that understands."*[67] Even the term *informal care* is dismissive, implying *"casual, unstructured, unofficial care—pleasant but not essential."*[68] One caregiver–journalist accurately sums it up:

> When we became caregivers, my family unwillingly joined one of the least exclusive clubs in America. It is a silent society—one whose members rarely

know one another and almost never discuss their struggles. They don't even see themselves as caregivers. They are just . . . helping.[69]

Adding insult to injury, they feel not only unappreciated but also subject to unfair professional evaluations:

> Families are sometimes perceived as troublesome, interfering with proper care, fighting among themselves, challenging physicians' or nurses' authority, and generally behaving badly.[70]

Consequently, despite all of their efforts, they often have feelings of self-inefficacy, a lack of confidence in their ability to get things done. They feel painfully powerless when watching a loved one go downhill and blame themselves.[71] Because of these pressures, many caregivers feel unhappy, depressed, or hopeless.[72] Their psychological malaise can also contribute to their poorer physical health, because they have less motivation to take care of themselves.[73] Feelings of abjection are especially common among caregivers who assist older people who need larger amounts of care and continual supervision and who exhibit memory or behavior problems. Experts attribute the greater prevalence of depressive symptoms among Hispanic and Asian-American caregivers to their providing more care than their White, non-Hispanic peers. Another study explains that these minority caregivers are often daughters-in-law who have a poor relationship with their care recipients and have little enthusiasm for assuming their responsibilities. On the other hand, perhaps because of their stronger intergenerational ties, African-American caregivers feel less burdened and depressed than White caregivers.[74]

Caregivers also feel more oppressed if they work at full- or part-time jobs and must juggle employment and family demands. Significant shares feel that their caregiving responsibilities negatively impact their employment status because of missed professional opportunities and financial losses.[75] Many employers are not supportive, although some do offer more flexible hours, paid time off, counseling, and emergency day care.[76] Fortunately, under the Family and Medical Leave Act of 1993, some caregivers—at least those working for larger businesses—are entitled to up to 12 weeks of unpaid leave each year.[77] However, this law does not cover all workers, and for many eligible employees, taking unpaid leave is not financially feasible.[78]

Some studies point to interventions that can reduce the stress of caregiving, such as personalized counseling from outside professionals or participation in caregiving support groups. Studies also point to the benefits of respite care, which brings temporary relief to family members from their caregiving burden, consisting of services offered by in-home paid professionals as well as by staff in adult day centers or nursing homes (Chapter 8).[79]

FINANCIAL COSTS

Caregiving is expensive. Average annual out-of-pocket costs are between $5,500 and $12,300 to cover outlays for medical visits and procedures, clothing, travel, home maintenance, home modifications, equipment, supplies, and services.[80] Polls report

25% of caregivers feel financially stressed, cut back on other spending, or worry that their caregiving costs will exhaust their savings.[81] Family members often work additional hours or take on an additional job in order to afford paid help.[82] Alternatively, because of caregiving demands, they cut back on their hours or take temporary leaves of absence from their jobs. Along with lost wages, they risk jeopardizing their job security, career mobility, and employment benefits.[83]

The real costs of family care are unquestionably much larger. Historically, experts assumed that the time family members spent taking care of their loved ones was a free service. They are now measuring what it would cost to assist older people with paid workers if informal care were unavailable. Consider the findings of one national study:

> In 2009, about 42.1 million family caregivers in the United States provided care to an adult with limitations in daily activities at any given point in time, and about 61.6 million provided care at some time during the year. The estimated economic value of their unpaid contributions was approximately $450 billion in 2009, up from an estimated $375 billion in 2007.[84]

The financial impact is even higher when we acknowledge that caregiving is not just a family affair. Lost worker productivity from caregiver absences results in employers losing as much as $33 billion annually because of absenteeism, workplace disruptions, and the replacement and training of new employees.[85]

QUALITY OF CARE AND QUALITY OF LIFE PROVIDED BY FAMILY CAREGIVERS

REASONS FOR OPTIMISM AND CONCERN

Families make it possible for older people to maintain their independent living arrangements without leaving their familiar homes and entering a nursing home. They function as unofficial monitors of the long-term care delivered by professionals. Altogether, their caregiving assistance unquestionably contributes to older people remaining in their residential mastery zones.

Family caregivers also lower the healthcare costs incurred by older Americans:

> When patients follow doctors' orders for their medication and treatment, it can greatly reduce total healthcare costs. The annual costs of patients in the U.S. who don't follow their medication prescriptions approaches an estimated $290 billion, according to the New England Healthcare Institute. But those who do follow their doctor's directions for medications can save the healthcare system as much as $7,800 per patient. With more than 40 million seniors currently enrolled in Medicare, says Caring.com, there's "potential for caregivers' active role in medication management to save the government as much as $100 billion annually."[86]

Yet despite all of these positives, there are reasons for concern. Experts report growing evidence of families providing inadequate and incompetent care.[87] As one expert succinctly puts it, *"It is very difficult to monitor quality in-home–based care."*[88] Ironically, although our society is especially vigilant about ensuring quality of care in places such as assisted living developments and nursing homes, help delivered in the private household is typically unregulated, unsupervised, and exempt from third-party oversight. This is troubling because when older people receive improper care, they are at greater risk of having home accidents, police and fire emergencies, emergency room visits, hospitalizations, and rehospitalizations.[89]

Most care lapses are unintentional, as when caregivers lack necessary skills and training, do not fully understand their treatment or assistance options, do not make the best use of the services in their communities, and make decisions without timely information.[90] Some caregivers are less equipped to meet their loved one's needs. A wife cannot adequately assist her ailing husband if she has her own physical limitations and health problems. Families with competing demands on their time may not allocate enough hours to carry out their responsibilities. Compared with nonemployed caregivers, those who work are less likely to provide large amounts of assistance, even as they provide the same types of care.[91] According to another study, older adults with employed caregivers were *"more vulnerable to service problems and unmet needs of additional assistance."*[92]

ABUSE OF OLDER ADULTS AGING IN PLACE

ETIOLOGY OF ABUSE

Distressingly, a growing problem is older people aging in place who are sometimes physically or psychologically assaulted by their caregivers.[93] We hear most about the abuse that takes place in nursing homes and board and care facilities, but the problem is pervasive in ordinary homes and often goes undetected. Moreover, a family member or someone known to the older person is usually responsible for these abusive acts, not strangers or paid professionals and workers. Note the following conclusion by the American Psychological Association:

> The idea that what happens at home is "private" can be a major factor in keeping an older person locked in an abusive situation. Those outside the family who observe or suspect abuse or neglect may fail to intervene because they believe "it's a family problem and none of my business" or because they are afraid they are misinterpreting a private quarrel. Shame and embarrassment often make it difficult for older persons to reveal abuse. They don't want others to know that such events occur in their families.[94]

Older people most at risk of being abused tend to be the old-old, more impaired, and in poorer health, as well as have lower incomes and fewer social supports (e.g., family members, friends, or social workers). These vulnerable older persons have no one to turn to and cannot easily defend themselves.[95]

Abuse can occur in the most socially intact families. Caregivers experience intense frustration, anger, and fatigue when they are barraged day after day with stressful and time-demanding situations. These conflicts are magnified when family members have poor people skills, feel trapped by their responsibilities, are helping older people with abrasive personalities, and feel alone and unsupported.[96] Some family members are simply not cut out to be caregivers because of their skill sets or personalities. Consider also that some appointed caregivers never wanted their responsibilities or had poor relationships with their parents. The abuse may be a manifestation of a long-standing conflict. The most abusive family caregivers are themselves troubled and socially isolated. They typically have higher rates of unemployment, substance abuse, and mental health problems.[97]

TYPES OF ABUSE

What may first come to mind is physical abuse (e.g., hitting, shaking, kicking, slapping, and bumping) that results in bodily injury, pain, bruises, or impairment. In the United States, it is estimated that annually about 1.6% of people age 60 and older experience physical abuse.[98] Sexual abuse affects about 0.6% of the older population annually. However, the most prevalent type of abuse, experienced annually by 5.1% of the old, is physical neglect (i.e., when they are not getting enough of their essential needs, such as food and sleep).

Sizable percentages of the population age 60 and older—about 4.6% annually—are also emotionally or psychologically mistreated (sometimes called verbal mistreatment). Psychological abuse of older people, such as name-calling, scolding, insulting, threatening, humiliating, giving the "silent treatment," or depriving of social stimulation, has especially insidious effects, exacerbating older people's depressive symptoms and their feelings of low self-esteem.[99]

Not all caregivers psychologically abuse their older loved ones on purpose. Some do not intend harm and immediately feel guilty about their behaviors. Consider a daughter assisting her father who has Alzheimer's disease. In her efforts to "control" his well-being (e.g., by deciding when he should be bathed, groomed, or dressed or receive medical treatment), she risks treating him in an angry, child-like, and depersonalized fashion that threatens his dignity and self-esteem.[100]

A frequently cited national study estimates that 11% of older people (about 5 million as of 2010) are abused annually in at least one of these ways. However, we should cautiously view these estimates. Experts agree that abuse incidents are vastly underreported.[101]

The same national study separately estimated that annually about 5% of older people are abused or exploited financially. Experts have characterized financial elder abuse as *"the crime of the 21st Century."*[102] The National Center on Elder Abuse defines it as

> The illegal taking, misuse, or concealment of funds, property, or assets of a vulnerable elder at risk for harm by another due to changes in physical functioning, mental functioning, or both.[103]

It encompasses such conduct as

> Fraud, scams, undue influence by family members and trusted others, and illegal viatical settlements; abuse of powers of attorney and guardianship; identity theft; Internet phishing; failure to fulfill contracted healthcare services; and Medicare and Medicaid fraud.[104]

This definition does not include the more subtle forms of financial abuse, such as family caregivers who are motivated to provide care only because it increases their chances of acquiring an inheritance. Moreover, it does not fully capture Internet scams, which are on the rise. Financial abuse is also a catalyst for other types of elder abuse, including physically violent acts and neglect.[105]

Elders in the United States lose billions of dollars each year because they are victims of financially fraudulent schemes, even as most abuse goes unreported. One 2010 study put this annual financial loss at $2 billion dollars. For this category of abuse, family members are among the culpable, but most perpetrators are strangers, and the majority are male.[106]

The typical victim is between 70 and 89, White, female, physically or cognitively impaired, or clinically depressed.[107] Women are especially vulnerable, especially when they are in their 80s, unmarried, living alone, and without social supports. They are members of a generation who were not typically responsible for their household's financial affairs; they left these tasks to their spouses. However, older men also are victimized by all types of business, investment, and insurance scams. They are particularly susceptible to the "Sweetheart Scam," where a younger woman becomes intimate with an older man, usually lonely or physically or cognitively impaired, to intentionally manipulate him into giving her expensive gifts, paying off debt, and even signing over his wills or trusts in exchange for her affection.[108]

Aging in Place and the Institutionalization of the Conventional Home

The actions of family caregivers may be hurtful for a very different and not entirely obvious reason. Paradoxically, their well-intended interior design and equipment modifications and hands-on physical assistance to make their older care recipients feel protected, safe, independent, and secure result in their loved ones feeling subservient and powerless in the very dwellings they call home.[109] They unwittingly transform those abodes, where these older adults felt a modicum of control over their lives and environments, into mini–nursing homes with their institutional- and medical-like qualities.[110] Older people inevitably feel out of their residential mastery zones. Such "damaging" responses by family caregivers include the following:

- They introduce medical and technological devices and equipment into the home, such as a hospital bed, oxygen supplies, and procedures (e.g., antibiotic intravenous therapy, peritoneal dialysis, and oxygen therapy).[111]

- They provide too much support and protection, whether equipment or services. They prescribe a hospital bed or scooter chair when the older person can do without or order a harness to facilitate walking when a strong arm would suffice.

- They establish highly structured medical and therapeutic regimens detailing when the older person must eat, drink, sleep, nap, and exercise. They make unannounced or spontaneous visits to the homes of older people. In so doing, they reinforce their feelings of dependence and infringe on their privacy.

- In their quest to minimize undesirable events or actions, they take all decision-making authority and control away from their older loved ones. They fail to inform older people of all of their possible alternatives or courses of action. They adopt a very paternalistic attitude toward their care recipient by *"overruling a person's autonomy for that person's own good."*[112] They ignore the older care recipient while communicating with professional staff. They conclude that their loved ones are incompetent merely because they judge a situation differently than the professional.[113] Caregivers become so preoccupied with their demanding roles that they no longer function as loving and emotionally close daughters, sons, or spouses, but merely as impersonal "staff persons" giving orders to their "patients" and executing care plans.

STRENGTHENING THE ROLE OF FAMILY CAREGIVERS

There are many recommendations as to how to make the family caregiving experience less physically, emotionally, and financially stressful and how to improve the quality of life and care of older people. The following is a summary of some key proposals[114]:

- Promote workplace policies that make it more feasible for adult children to take part-time and full-time absences to perform their caregiving responsibilities without jeopardizing their salaries, benefits, or career trajectories.
- Better educate healthcare providers about how their discharge planning, chronic care coordination, and hospital-to-home care transition programs can be better integrated or linked with the caregiving activities and responsibilities of family members.
- Recommend that long-term care and health providers offer informal caregivers better training courses and education materials that allow them to perform more effectively.
- Encourage primary care providers to routinely assess and monitor the healthcare needs and risks of family members who are performing caregiving duties.
- Better educate the public and increase awareness of what caregiving encompasses, and better direct them to the programs and services of nonprofit charitable (faith-based) organizations and government programs that might alleviate their care burdens.
- Create more user-friendly Internet forums and blogs that communicate to family members that they are not alone in their responsibilities and tribulations and allow them to share their caregiving experiences, problems, and successes.
- Strengthen public policies that make it more feasible for lower-income families to apply for government-sponsored service programs that give them caregiving relief (Figure 7.3).

Figure 7.3. Public policy recommendations to improve the caregiving experiences of low-income families

- Make improvements to the Family and Medical Leave Act, including *"expanding its scope to cover all primary caregivers, regardless of family relationship. Provide paid leave to permit working caregivers to care for an ill child, spouse, or parent. In addition, employers should be required to provide employees with a reasonable number of paid sick days to care for themselves or a loved one."* (Fienberg et al., 2011, p. 16)

- Expand funding for the National Family Caregiver Support Program. The Older Americans Act (OAA) established this program in 2000 (Chapter 8). It mandated that local Area Agencies on Aging design and implement programs to support family caregivers, thus broadening the population served under this federal program. Services include information about community-based services, assistance accessing services, counseling and support groups, caregiving training, and respite services (Wagner, 2006). Current funding is very modest, with some states not participating in this program. Because OAA programs target only low-income older people, this program is not benefiting millions of employed family caregivers (Wagner, 2006).

- Provide more funding for respite programs, including the Lifespan Respite Care Act. *"Lifespan respite programs assist caregivers in gaining access to needed respite services, train and recruit respite workers and volunteers, and enhance coordinated systems of community-based respite services."* (Fienberg et al., 2011, p. 156)

- *"Promote the expansion of consumer-directed models in publicly funded home- and community-based programs that permit payment of family caregivers. Such models allow consumers and their families to choose and direct the types of services and supports that best meet their needs."* (Fienberg et al., 2011, p. 15) (Chapter 8)

- Increase funding of programs supported by the Elder Justice Act and related initiatives that are designed to improve the understanding of, reporting of, and responses to elder abuse (MetLife Mature Market Institute, 2011b).

WHAT THE FUTURE HOLDS

Because of demographic trends and changing societal values, many experts are pessimistic about the future ability of older people to count on informal care. The projected growth of the older population, increases in their life expectancy, and their preferences to age in place despite their chronic health problems and multiple physical and cognitive limitations will guarantee an increased demand for informal care (Chapter 13).[115] But most experts also predict that the numbers of future family caregivers (particularly spouses and adult children) will not keep pace with this demand for care assistance.[116] Moreover, the next generation of family caregivers will be less willing or able to assume caregiving responsibilities of their older relatives.[117] Some of the reasons include the following:

- Over the period 2010 to 2030, the baby boomers, now constituting the main supply of family caregivers (in 2014, age 50–68) will age out of their caregiving responsibilities and increasingly become the care recipients.[118] Beginning in 2026, for example, the oldest baby boomers will start turning 80 and will be at high risk of needing caregiving assistance themselves.

- Higher shares of tomorrow's older population will enter old age unmarried (divorced, separated, or single), childless, or with fewer children and siblings able to assist.

- Because the adult children of older people are marrying and having children later, their own parenting responsibilities will consume a greater share of their time.

- Migration behaviors of families in their younger years will result in greater geographic separations of older and younger generations.

- Adult daughters and older spouses are more likely to be in the labor force and have difficulty assuming even part-time caregiving responsibilities.

- The daughters or daughters-in-law of older people have become comfortable leaving their young children with paid workers and will be less reluctant to turn over their caregiving responsibilities to formal care providers.

- Families will be dealing with loved ones who are older, sicker, and more impaired. Consequently, caregiving responsibilities will become too demanding.

- Government funding of respite programs that target the emotional and physical support needs of older caregivers will wane as the public loses its appetite for supporting the assistance of older people—except for the very impoverished (Chapter 13).

CONCLUSION

Family members have made it possible for older people with functional limitations and chronic health problems to age in place longer.[119] Without their efforts, there would unquestionably be higher hospitalization and emergency room rates and millions more older people who occupy assisted living properties and nursing homes. Only recently have we acknowledged how our healthcare and long-term care costs would skyrocket were it not for the extraordinary efforts of these dedicated people.

Nevertheless, this informal care is often not enough. Family members are recognizing that they alone cannot adequately respond to the long-term care needs of their older relatives. Despite good intentions, they fail to address many of the unmet needs of their care recipients, they make mistakes, and sometimes they are even guilty of abusive behaviors. Furthermore, they may act more like professional caregivers than emotionally close spouses or daughters and turn a loved one's familiar dwelling into an institution-like nursing home. Consequently, older people often find themselves out of their residential comfort and mastery zones, even as they are aging in place in their familiar dwellings with a supportive care environment.

When their informal care falls short, older people's coping repertoires must include other adaptive strategies to ensure that they live independently and can manage their health problems. The next chapter focuses on the role played by community-based paid providers.

NOTES

1. Paula Span, *Kaiser Health News,* May 25, 2010
2. Jane Gross, *New York Times,* September 29, 2008
3. Roni Caryn Rabin, *The New York Times,* December 16, 2008
4. Gary Barg, *MinnPost,* April 28, 2011
5. Laura Raines, *The Atlanta Journal Constitution,* February 15, 2009
6. (Kaye et al., 2010)
7. (Spillman & Black, 2005)
8. (Kaye et al., 2010)
9. The percentages do not add up to 100 because a small share of family members rely on both informal and formal care.
10. (Kaye et al., 2010)
11. (Miller, Allen, & Mor, 2009, p. 7)
12. (National Alliance for Caregiving, 2009)
13. (Johnson & Wiener, 2006)
14. (National Alliance for Caregiving, 2009)
15. (Gross, September 25, 2008). The unmarried includes widowed, divorced, or separated persons.
16. (Hays, 2002)
17. (Johnson & Wiener, 2006; Spillman & Black, 2005)
18. (Scharlach, Giunta, Chow, & Lehning, 2008)
19. (Seltzer & Yahirun, 2013)
20. (Evercare & National Alliance for Caregiving, 2008)
21. (Pinquart & Sorensen, 2005; White-Means & Rubin, 2008)
22. (Rhee, Degenholtz, Lo Sasso, & Emanuel, 2009).
23. (Wolff & Kasper, 2006)
24. (Alzheimer's Association, 2013)
25. (Piette, Rosland, Silveira, Kabeto, & Langa, 2010)
26. (Clemmitt, 2006, p. 850)
27. (Reinhard, Feinberg, & Choula, 2011, p. 11)
28. (Washington, Meadows, Elliott, & Koopman, 2011)
29. (Miller et al., 2009, p. 8)
30. (Gibson, Kelly, & Kaplan, 2012)
31. (Levine, Halper, Peist, & Gould, 2010, p. 117)
32. (Gibson et al., 2012)
33. Cited in Gibson et al. (2012, p. 10)
34. (Gibson et al., 2012, p. 6)
35. (Alzheimer's Association, 2013)
36. (Reinhard, Levine, & Samis, 2012)
37. (Reinhard et al., 2012)
38. (Reinhard et al., 2012)
39. (Gerace, 2012; Gibson et al., 2012)
40. (Eckenwiler, 2007)
41. (Gibson et al., 2012, p. 19)
42. (Levine et al., 2010, p. 118)
43. (Reinhard et al., 2012)
44. (Gibson et al., 2012)
45. (Boling, 2009, p. 136)
46. (Guengerich, 2009)
47. (Poulin et al., 2010, p. 113)
48. (Poulin et al., 2010, p. 110)
49. (Quinn, Clare, & Woods, 2010)
50. (National Alliance for Caregiving, 2011)

51. (Haley, Roth, Howard, & Safford, 2010)
52. (Reinhard et al., 2012)
53. (Clemmitt, 2006; Evercare, 2007; Pinquart & Sorensen, 2003)
54. (Haley et al., 2010)
55. (Reinhard, Levine, & Samis, 2013)
56. (Evercare, 2007)
57. (Genworth Financial, 2006; Spillman & Long, 2007)
58. (Adams, 2008); Dr. Moira Fordyce, president, California Geriatrics Society
59. (National Alliance for Caregiving, Schulz, & Cook, 2011)
60. (Working Mother Research Institute, 2012, p. 13)
61. (Fredman et al., 2008)
62. (Johnson & Wiener, 2006)
63. (Piette et al., 2010)
64. (National Alliance for Caregiving, 2006)
65. (Fienberg, Reinhard, Houser, & Choula, 2011)
66. UExpress: November 10, 2008. Accessed from http://www.uexpress.com/dearabby/?uc_full_date=20081110
67. (Dunham & Cannon, 2008, p. 52)
68. (Levine et al., 2010, p. 119)
69. (Gleckman, 2009, p. 18)
70. (Levine et al., 2010, p. 119)
71. (Dunham & Cannon, 2008)
72. (Genworth Financial, 2006; Reinhard et al., 2012)
73. (O'Rourke, Cappeliez, & Neufeld, 2007)
74. (Pinquart & Sorensen, 2005)
75. (Reinhard et al., 2013)
76. (Eckenwiler, 2007)
77. If employer has 50 or more employees.
78. (Fienberg, 2013)
79. (Ritchie, Roth, & Allman, 2011)
80. (Evercare, 2007)
81. (Fienberg et al., 2011)
82. (Fienberg et al., 2011)
83. (Fienberg et al., 2011)
84. (Fienberg et al., 2011, p. 1) At the state level, the economic value was calculated as (number of caregivers at any given time) × (hours of care per caregiver per week) × (52 weeks/year) × (economic value of 1 hour of family care).
85. (MetLife Mature Market Institute, 2010b)
86. (Gerace, 2012)
87. (Johnson & Wiener, 2006)
88. (Clemmitt, 2006, p. 843)
89. (Clemmitt, 2006)
90. (National Alliance for Caregiving, 2009; Washington et al., 2011)
91. (Scharlach, Gustavson, & Dal Santo, 2007)
92. (Scharlach et al., 2007, p. 760)
93. (Beach et al., 2005)
94. (American Psychological Association, 2010)
95. (Acierno et al., 2010)
96. (Eckroth-Bucher, 2008)
97. (Acierno et al., 2010)
98. (Acierno et al., 2010)
99. (American Psychological Association, 2010; Eckroth-Bucher, 2008)
100. (Dunham & Cannon, 2008)

101. (Acierno et al., 2010)
102. (MetLife Mature Market Institute, 2009b)
103. (MetLife Mature Market Institute, 2009b, p. 7)
104. (MetLife Mature Market Institute, 2009b, p. 8).
105. (MetLife Mature Market Institute, 2011b)
106. (MetLife Mature Market Institute, 2011b)
107. (MetLife Mature Market Institute, 2009b, 2011b)
108. (MetLife Mature Market Institute, 2009b, p. 11)
109. (Dunham & Cannon, 2008; Newsom, 1999)
110. (Gubrium & Sankar, 1990)
111. (Demiris & Hensel, 2009).
112. (Kane, 1988, p. 28)
113. (Kane, 1988)
114. These recommendations are drawn heavily from (Fienberg et al., 2011; Reinhard, Feinberg, et al., 2011)
115. (Freedman et al., 2013)
116. (Redfoot, Feinberg, & Houser, 2013)
117. (Stone, 2011; Wolff & Kasper, 2006)
118. (Redfoot et al., 2013)
119. (Gerace, 2012)

Part IV

COPING TO ACHIEVE
RESIDENTIAL NORMALCY

Looking to Communities

8

AGING IN PLACE WITH THE ASSISTANCE OF PAID HELP

When you ask so-called elderly experts for advice you never get straight or
understandable answers. . . . The laws, regulations, and qualifications regarding
home healthcare entitlements are confusing, contradictory, arcane, vague, and
sometimes arbitrary and capricious. By the time I actually learned what my mother
might have been entitled to, I was almost broke. It was too late.[1]

Agencies are sending to the homes of vulnerable elderly patients workers with little
or no experience or knowledge, no training, and inadequate background checks.[2]

STAYING IN THE COMMUNITY

When caregiving from family or friends is not enough, older people must look to paid
services offered by the private or public sectors to manage their health problems, mobility limitations, and cognitive declines. Whether they can maintain their independent households and age in place depends on their coping repertoires. Critical will be
the resilience of these older adults—their motivation, confidence, and capabilities—to
secure the necessary help. Although their personalities, educational levels, financial
means, and ability to make autonomous decisions will matter greatly (Chapter 5),
their choices will ultimately depend on where they live and how successfully they can
cobble together an appropriate package of long-term services and supports.

Most older people look for assistance in their current communities. About 93%
of people age 65 and older and 78% of those age 85 and older were located in traditional communities as opposed to special-purpose senior housing group options.[3] Only

an estimated 4% of older people occupy alternatives, such as independent living communities, assisted living (including board and care), and continuing care retirement communities.[4]

Nursing homes are especially unpopular; in 2011, about 3% of people age 65 and older and about 15% of people age 85 and older occupied these institutional alternatives.[5] These rates contrast sharply with the 1980s, when the respective percentages were 5.5% and 22.0%.[6] Moreover, current nursing home occupancy rates are inflated by a significant share of older people who need only short-term stays in conjunction with physical rehabilitation after a hospital stay. As assisted living alternatives and care delivered to the homes of older people have become more attractive choices, nursing homes have steadily fallen out of favor.[7]

Consequently, they are now primarily a last-ditch long-term care alternative for the oldest and most impaired aging population, especially those with late-stage Alzheimer's disease, who need full-time skilled nursing assistance. Nearly three-quarters of their occupants are women, often widowed.[8] Very poor older adults (typically Medicaid eligible) are also overrepresented because they cannot afford private senior housing options. Although the majority of nursing home residents are non-Hispanic Whites,[9] recent trends show a decline in the numbers and percentage share of White residents and comparable increases in Hispanic, Asian, and African-American nursing home occupants.[10]

SEEKING TO AGE IN PLACE: INFORMATION IS KEY

Older people seeking to age in place may not have an easy time securing appropriate assistance. They must learn a new vocabulary of job descriptions and understand what types of services and supports they can expect from home-care agencies, senior centers, adult day centers, and PACE centers (Program of All-Inclusive Care for the Elderly). They must discern whether their churches, synagogues, temples, and mosques offer more than just spiritual comfort. This process will take time and energy, but they still have no assurances that these community-based alternatives will be a good match for their aging-in-place needs.

Even the most resilient older people typically do not know whom to call or how to articulate their needs. Unless they earlier served as caregivers to a family member, they often know little about who provides care, how much it costs, or how to judge the backgrounds and qualifications of potential providers or workers. The less educated, more introverted, and more isolated people, especially those lacking good English skills, have the most difficulties. However, even savvy academic gerontologists faced with their own caregiving needs soon recognize their lack of practical expertise.[11]

The family members of these older people are equally in the dark and will empathize with this frustrated daughter confronting her mother's diagnosis of Alzheimer's disease:

> I had never given it a thought that my mom one day could need long-term care. . . . I'm a professional business woman and yet I did not know where to begin. It was completely overwhelming.[12]

This search for answers is especially challenging for those who must rely on government programs to secure their care. Public programs for older Americans differ in their eligibility requirements, the types of services they cover, their minimum qualifying income and assets, the priority they give to specific subgroups, the types, severity, and duration of their covered physical ailments and disabilities, the proportion of the service cost they subsidize, the length of the subsidy, and their quality.[13]

Securing care is further complicated because older people and their families rarely need only one type of assistance or provider. Their list of long-term services and supports often includes assistive devices, transportation, housekeeping assistance, affordable healthcare assistance, home care, medication management, and home modifications. Older consumers transitioning from a hospital stay to their residences may additionally need both recuperative and rehabilitative care. Unfortunately, these different providers rarely coordinate their services and *"have no incentive to interact due to separate sources of funding, inconsistent care practices, and poor communication."*[14]

Older people and their families usually get their information from low-tech sources, such as radio and television advertisements and local community newspapers, and the notices or bulletins found where they conduct their everyday activities, such as doctor's offices, libraries, and churches.[15] They trust the word-of-mouth information from people they already know, such as their physicians or clergy. Even as increasingly larger shares of older people find information via Internet and computer searches, the majority still rely mostly on traditional sources. For them, in-person assistance and counseling are still crucial.[16]

Older people are more likely to use Internet searches in communities where computers are found in public settings (e.g., libraries) and where they have access to interactive electronic databases or websites that help them navigate local long-term care providers and services. Some charitable and nonprofit organizations and state or local governments offer electronic databases of long-term care workers and their qualifications that allow consumers to match their needs with the skills and experience of potential workers.[17] Some states specifically have websites that locate affordable housing accommodations by city, county, or municipality.

Some media outlets are less effective because they provide information that is dominated by jargon, acronyms, and technical labels, intelligible only to the most educated older consumers. Communications using very small type or confusing page layouts are also turnoffs.[18] Automated telephone systems may offer a wealth of information, but only for those who have the ability and patience to navigate their usual maze of options.

Then there is the ultimate barrier, information that is broadcast only in English when the potential older users speak a foreign language. Listen to this older Chinese woman[19]:

> I'm blind because I cannot read documents written in English. I'm deaf because people speak to me in English and I don't understand. And I'm mute because I cannot communicate with anyone who does not know my language.

GETTING SPECIFIC: WHO ARE THE FORMAL CARE PROVIDERS?

The quality of a community's offerings of long-term services and supports ultimately depends on a stable, well-trained, experienced, compassionate, and happy workforce. These workers must be able not only to perform the more highly skilled jobs, such as medically oriented nursing care or therapeutic or rehabilitative care, but also to assist older people with their activities of daily living (ADLs) and instrumental ADLs (IADLs), including the most mundane housekeeping tasks.[20] Two categories of workers (Figures 8.1 and 8.2) provide this assistance: licensed or certified professionals (20% of providers) and direct care workers (80%).

PROFESSIONAL CARE WORKERS

When older people are recovering from an illness, injury, or disease complications, which may or may not have required a hospital stay, they often need short-term recuperative or rehabilitative care. The majority of this care now takes place in their homes. Physicians (infrequently trained as geriatricians) design and oversee their care plans, often with the assistance of nurse practitioners or registered nurses, who instruct older people on how to follow their post-hospital care regimens and monitor the course of their diseases or injuries. Licensed practical or vocational nurses provide direct patient care that can include taking vital signs and administering medications. Under the supervision of registered nurses, they may carry out medically related procedures that might include intravenous or respiratory therapy and wound care. Dietitians offer advice on good nutritional practices. Occupational therapists, speech pathologists, and physical therapists offer rehabilitative care within their specialties (Figure 8.1).

These medical and therapeutic responses are often followed by the preparation of a personalized care plan by professionals known as geriatric care managers, case managers, elder care managers, or service coordinators, who first conduct an extensive evaluation of the older person's long-term and supportive service needs. They focus on three critical care management tasks:

- Assessing the person's capabilities to live independently (e.g., performance of their ADLs and IADLs; evaluation of medical management needs; and dwelling accessibility deficits)
- Arranging for services, delivered by both licensed or certified professionals and direct care workers
- Monitoring and changing care as needed

AVAILABILITY OF PROFESSIONAL CARE WORKERS

We have an insufficient supply of physicians, nurses, social workers, and other healthcare professionals trained to serve older people in community-based settings. In 2010, for example, there was an average of only 3.7 geriatricians per 10,000 adults age 75 and older.[21] There is a particularly acute shortage of professionals trained in psychiatry, psychology, and nursing who can provide mental health services.[22] The current demand–supply gap will only worsen in the future because most experts project an even greater demand for these long-term care professionals.

Figure 8.1. Licensed or certified professionals providing long-term care (Harahan, 2010–2011)

Physicians: Work in nursing homes, assisted living residences, and home health agencies. Assess and oversee medical care of patients and make recommendations regarding long-term care decisions. They will often sign off on residents' care plans recommended by nursing homes and home healthcare agencies. A minority will have special training in geriatric care.

Registered nurses: In charge of the clinical care delivered in long-term care settings, such as nursing homes, assisted living residences, and home healthcare settings. May function as geriatric care or case managers (often after hospital discharge). When employed in home health agencies, they evaluate older person's long-term care needs, provide skilled nursing services and instruct older person and family on self-care procedures, and supervise direct care workers. Nurse practitioners are registered nurses with more advanced medical training who may conduct physical exams, make urgent care visits, prescribe medications, and provide preventive care.

Licensed practical/vocational nurses: Provide direct patient care, including skilled nursing services, when supervised, including monitoring vital signs and administering medications. Assume supervisory roles of lesser-qualified direct care workers. May function as geriatric care or case managers.

Licensed social workers: May function as geriatric care or case managers. Address emotional, legal, and ethical concerns of older persons (and their families) who are coping with chronic, acute, or terminal illnesses and end-of-life issues. May mediate conflicts between older persons and other long-term care workers.

Consultant pharmacists: Offer information and recommendations regarding the prescription and desirability of particular medications.

Physical therapists: Help restore physical functioning and mobility capabilities, often after an accident (e.g., hip break) or acute illness (e.g., stroke). Respond to needs of older people experiencing chronic physical declines or cognitive impairment.

Occupational therapists: Improve ability of older people to perform activities of daily living, recommend dwelling interior design home modifications, and help older persons more effectively and safely negotiate their home environments.

Speech therapists: Assist older persons who are experiencing communication disorders that are often a result of a dementia diagnoses, such as Alzheimer's disease, cardio-vascular accident or stroke, or a traumatic brain injury, such as due to a fall. Assist older people with dysphasia deficits (i.e., difficulty swallowing because of disease onset.

There are many explanations for this problem.[23] Many otherwise qualified professionals do not receive specialized training to work in this country's highly regulated long-term care settings and do not have the people skills to deal on a one-on-one basis with older clients. Furthermore, they have not received the necessary training to help older people transition from a hospital to a home setting and often lack the management skills to supervise direct care workers, the majority of whom are racial or ethnic minorities. Many experts trace the problem to the failure of medical schools to train doctors about the distinct medical and care needs of a geriatric population. Few medical schools require that their students participate in a geriatric rotation, and most medical school graduates do not feel qualified to address the needs of chronically ill and disabled aging patients. Similarly, the majority of social workers complete their bachelor's degree without a course on aging.

Experts also attribute the shortage to the unwillingness of physicians, nurses, and other professionals to tolerate the low salaries offered in the long-term care sector as compared with other medical and care specialties. More generally, long-term care workers do not command as much respect and have as many advancement opportunities, at least partly explaining their high workplace turnover rates.[24]

Recommendations abound on how to recruit and retain a larger and more stable supply of long-term care professionals. Improved salaries, better work benefits, more-favorable working hours and schedules, and better and more-uniform training and certification standards often top the list. Experts recommend that various public policy strategies could make advanced educational training programs more attractive, through grant programs, scholarships, federal traineeships, loan forgiveness, and residency programs.[25] Some proactive states and communities have increased their training and educational opportunities and wage and benefit incentives. They target community colleges, high schools, and other professional schools as a means to encourage the training of future workers and to strengthen certification standards to improve their professionalism.[26]

DIRECT CARE WORKERS

These frontline workers are the *"hands, voice, and face of long-term care,"*[27] assisting older people with their ADLs, IADLs, and medical management. We typically group them into three categories: nursing assistants or aides, home health aides, and personal and home care aides (Figure 8.2).[28] Together, they constitute one of the largest and fastest-growing occupations in the United States and are projected to grow by 50% between 2012 and 2022.[29] They are the indispensable cogs in a large home care and personal assistance industry that had revenues of more than $84 billion in 2009.[30]

Unlike the typically short-term work assignments of professional care workers, these "in the trenches" workers provide assistance over extended periods. They are responsible for performing the most labor-intensive tasks, which involve hands-on lifting, carrying, and assisting clients with their most intimate nonmedical self-care acts.[31] They also offer paramedical assistance, such as blood pressure measurements, wound care, bowel and ostomy hygiene, range-of-motion exercises, and catheter hygiene.[32]

These workers also have distinct demographic profiles. They usually are women between the ages of 25 and 55, typically poor, and less educated, with about 58% having a high school diploma or less.[33] Minorities are overrepresented: 32% are African-American, and 24% were foreign born, predominantly Hispanics.[34]

Figure 8.2. Main categories of direct care workers providing long-term care (These descriptions borrowed from Paraprofessional Healthcare Institute [2012, p. 5].)

Nursing assistants or nursing aides: Generally work in nursing homes, although some work in assisted living residences, other community-based settings, or hospitals. Assist residents with activities of daily living (ADLs), such as eating, dressing, bathing, and toileting. Perform clinical tasks, such as range-of-motion exercises and blood pressure readings.

Home health aides: Provide essentially the same care and services as nursing assistants, but also assist people in their homes or in community settings under the supervision of a nurse or therapist. May perform paramedical or healthcare tasks, such as ostomy hygiene, catheter hygiene, bowel hygiene, changing aseptic dressings, and administering non-injectable medications (Seavey & Marquand, 2011). May also perform light housekeeping tasks, such as preparing food or changing linens.

Personal care aides: Work in either private or group homes. Have many titles, including personal care attendant, home care worker, personal assistant, and direct support professional (the latter work with people with intellectual and developmental disabilities). Provide assistance with ADLs and also often help with housekeeping chores, meal preparation, and medication management. Assist individuals in going to work and remaining engaged in their communities. Consumers employ and directly supervise a growing number of these workers.

In 2012, there were more than 4 million of these workers.[35] Historically, nursing homes and hospitals mainly employed these direct care workers—joined more recently by assisted living residences. Now a growing majority work in home- and community-based settings,[36] such as private home healthcare and personal care agencies, and in other aging organizations, such as senior centers and adult day centers. Public programs that offer personal care services employ an additional 800,000 independent providers.

Many older people and their families shy away from home care workers supplied by private agencies and hire them directly. The size of this vast *"grey market"*[37] of self-employed workers is unknown, although it is believed to be in the hundreds of thousands.[38] Whereas agency-employed workers typically assist older people for only a specified number of hours so many times a week, self-employed workers sometimes hire themselves out as round-the-clock live-ins. A significant share are foreign born, and their immigrant status or language difficulties make it difficult for them to find employment in proprietary home care agencies. They often are willing to work for lower wages without benefits (Social Security, unemployment compensation, health insurance, and workers' compensation[39]) in return for free room and board and a comfortable and secure place to live.

Availability of Direct Care Workers

We lack an adequate supply of well-trained direct care workers to meet the current needs of the older population in the United States. Experts expect this gap to worsen as more older adults attempt to stay in their current homes.

Recruiting and retaining these workers is difficult. Their wages are low, salary increases fail to keep up with higher costs of living, and their employers often deny them overtime pay. Furthermore, they *"have trouble amassing full-time hours on a regular basis, {and} a large share work on a part-time basis."*[40] Consequently, they often are not eligible for healthcare insurance coverage or pension benefits. Despite their low remuneration and poor benefits, they must tolerate very high workloads and injury rates.[41] These workers recognize that their job assignments command little respect and they are in dead-end occupations; their high employment turnover rates are hardly surprising.[42]

Given that these direct care workers are often foreign born, some communities are more disadvantaged, such as those in states that are not home to many immigrants, places that are perceived as hostile to foreign-born workers (e.g., Arizona), more remote rural communities, and those with poor economies, where it is generally difficult to attract long-term care professionals or direct care workers because of inadequate wages or unsatisfactory working conditions.[43]

In contrast, some communities and businesses more aggressively recruit immigrant populations from abroad and tailor training programs to accommodate their language and cultural differences.[44] They believe these minorities have qualities that make them preferable to White U.S. workers, including dedication, patience, a stronger work ethic, a greater willingness to take shift work, and lower turnover rates.[45]

The role of immigrants as direct care workers helps explain why long-term care experts are so concerned about the future immigration policies of the United States. If we make it harder for foreign immigrants to work in the United States, than we are de facto ensuring an inadequate direct care workforce to meet the long-term and supportive service needs of our future older population.

Quality of Care Provided by Direct Care Workers

One might hope that these paid caregivers would offer consistently better care than family members, but there is evidence to the contrary.[46] Studies reveal that high shares of these workers make errors administering medications to their older clients.[47] Additionally, as many as one-third have inadequate health literacy, which refers to their *"ability to read, understand, and use healthcare information to make effective healthcare decisions and follow instructions for treatment."*[48]

Older people recount a litany of other complaints: workers not coming on time, last-minute cancellations of assignments, the inability to perform requested tasks, communication conflicts between the worker and older client or family members, poor worker attitudes, poor quality care, theft and abusive behaviors, and workers arriving drunk or on drugs.[49] Older people particularly resent workers talking down to them and failing to listen to their ideas.[50]

This helps explain why older people report

less physical and psychological safety, less security, less comfort with the care provider, more provider shortcomings, and lower overall satisfaction with care than do those whose care provider is a family member.[51]

When they are dissatisfied with their direct care providers, older people often feel powerless to act. Some fear that disgruntled workers will retaliate or that their complaints will get the worker fired, and so they shy away from such stressful confrontations.[52] Family members may feel pressure not to complain too much because of the shortage of paid workers and the difficulty of securing a new and unfamiliar substitute.

Other discouraging findings came from a study of home care agencies in five states. Inadequate criminal background checks, inadequate worker qualifications, and poor supervision led to the conclusion that *"using an agency to hire paid caregivers may give older adults and their families a false sense of security regarding the background and skill set of the caregivers."*[53]

Older people and their families are also frustrated when direct care workers are available or affordable to hire but only for a limited number of hours a day or days per week. They complain of not having assistance when they need it the most: early in the mornings or in the evenings.[54] Hiring these workers as full-time, sometimes live-in employees solves many of these problems but may create others (Figure 8.3).

Still, we must be careful about making blanket generalizations about the quality and reliability of care provided by these workers. Many older people and their families are satisfied with their performance and feel they are responsive to their needs. They characterize them as *"optimistic, honest, kind, and gentle."* In the words of one older person, *"she treats us like family and we treat her like family."*[55]

Experts argue that the quality of care provided by these direct care workers depends not just on their remuneration and benefits, but also on how much oversight they receive from their home care agencies, how well they are supervised (e.g., by a registered nurse), their experience as individual contractors, and the extent to which they are subject to uniform government oversight.[56]

Inconsistent training requirements for direct care workers also account for variability in care quality. Home health aides and nursing home assistants who work for Medicare- and Medicaid-certified agencies must participate in at least 75 hours of annual training to meet federal health and safety requirements. However, certification or licensing requirements of direct care workers hired by noncertified agencies depend very much on the specific policies set by state governments. Some states require criminal background checks for the employees of home care agencies and include minimum education and training requirements. Others impose licensing requirements on independent providers. On the other hand, in 2010, 19 states did not require licensure requirements for home care agencies performing nonmedical and custodial services.[57] Still, there may be cause for optimism: The Patient Protection and Affordable Care Act of 2010 introduced some new and improved federal initiatives to train home care and personal assistance workers.[58]

Such scattered degrees of oversight and variations in care quality make it very difficult for older consumers or their families to make hiring decisions. To improve care experiences, they make the following insightful recommendations[59]:

- Require caseworker assessment of direct care workers (not only to help with problems, but to give support and credit to the workers who are doing their jobs well)
- Set standards for and oversee home health agencies
- Conduct surveys of the care provided
- Ensure contractors are fulfilling their obligations
- Better inform consumers and workers of their rights
- Be more inclusive of consumers, families, and workers on government committees and in decision-making processes
- License home care workers
- Provide additional services in the home, such as podiatry and dental care
- Require training and certification of workers
- Provide dispute-resolution services
- Enforce existing regulations
- Obtain more funding
- Provide better screening of workers, such as criminal background checks

INCOME INEQUALITY AND PAYING FOR FORMAL CARE

Older people (or their families) often confront sticker shock when they must obtain formal care. The average national hourly private pay rate for most direct care workers in 2012 was more than $20.[60] These rates are higher for people with greater care needs and in certain high-cost locations. The services of these care workers are especially expensive if older people lack long-term care insurance or are ineligible for government assistance. Consequently, even when paid help is needed just to supplement family care, the out-of-pocket costs can quickly escalate and can be especially catastrophic for those with very demanding chronic health conditions and physical or cognitive limitations.[61]

Most older Americans have not taken out long-term care insurance to pay for these costs; in 2008, only 12% of people age 65 and older and about 9% of people age 55 and older had done so.[62] A surprisingly large number also mistakenly believe that the federal government will automatically cover their long-term care costs through public programs. This, of course, is patently false.

The only publicly financed program that older people are universally eligible for health benefits under is the Medicare program. However, Medicare does not cover long-term care for any extended period, although it does partially cover skilled nursing facility services for the first 100 days after at least a 3-day inpatient hospital stay. Medicare also covers postacute care or therapeutic care (e.g., physical, speech, and

Figure 8.3. Micromanaging in-home care: three approaches

The Temporary Paid Worker Household Arrangement

To supplement the assistance provided by family members, older people may schedule visits from a *temporary paid worker*, often hired from a home care agency and who assists with the same tasks at regular weekly times. Older people may positively view the predictability of these visits as a reliable strategy to help them maintain their independence. They may especially welcome workers with whom they have a cordial or pleasant relationship. The downside of such scheduled visits is the unrealistic assumption that these workers can effectively deliver and complete all of the needed tasks in specific time slots. Unfortunately, home care workers are often not around at the very time that older people find themselves in need of help and feel insecure, incompetent, and out of control. The reality of high worker turnover also plagues this arrangement. Often, as soon as older people feel comfortable with their assigned workers and have a good relationship, they may either quit or be reassigned.

The Permanent Paid Worker Live-in Household Arrangement

Older people may hire a live-in caregiver to assist them around the clock. The success of this *employer–employee* relationship depends not just on work performance but also on whether the personalities of caregiver and care recipient mesh and whether they can reach consensus on expected duties and responsibilities. These job descriptions are usually a work in progress because the caregiving needs of the older person are often in flux, and thus the ability of the caregiver to adapt to changing responsibilities may be crucial. Anecdotal reports find that some older people develop a very emotionally close, family-like relationship with this person. However, as is true with any shared household arrangement, the care recipient's privacy needs remain paramount. Many older people view the presence of a stranger in their home as irrefutable evidence that they have lost their ability to live independently and have lost control over their lives (Golant, 1992).

The Boarder Household Arrangement

In this arrangement older people rent out space in their dwellings to a person—usually younger—who agrees to carry out specifically defined chores. Additionally, the rent received may help relieve burdensome dwelling costs. Alternatively, the boarder may offer caregiving tasks at a discounted financial rate in return for free or discounted room and board. Often this person's duties are restricted to satisfying unmet IADL needs—housework, transportation, and grocery shopping—but they may agree to offer assistance with some personal care for an additional monthly stipend. This is essentially a *tenant–landlord relationship*, but these boarders sometimes end up as friends or social companions.

Home-sharing programs administered by nonprofit charitable organizations or municipal governments sometimes facilitate these arrangements. They match prospective housemates with older homeowners or renters who have extra rooms or

Figure continued next page

Figure 8.3. *Continued*

> have created accessory apartments in their dwellings (Chapter 7). An advantage of these programs is that they screen applicants to ensure that roommates are both safe and compatible. They may also counsel older people about the potential problems of home sharing, provide referrals for social services, and mediate disagreements between housemates and older people. Less frequently, nonprofit organizations often funded by Community Development Block Grant programs have purchased houses that will accommodate home-sharing older adults (Vikki Ortiz Healy, "Home sharing an option for seniors," *Chicago Tribune*, October 11, 2013).
>
> Older people often are reluctant to participate in these arrangements because of legitimate worries about having a stranger in their house. For example, they worry about the boarder bringing unwanted visitors into their house or making too much noise. A further challenge presented by these home-sharing relationships is that likely boarders are often themselves in unstable or transitory periods in their lives (e.g., unemployed, divorced, part-time students, recent immigrants) (Golant, 1992). They seek sources of income and affordable accommodations to help get them through these difficult transitory periods. Once they get back on their feet, they leave. The older person faces the prospect of having a succession of such housemates or live-ins (Jaffe & Howe, 1988).

occupational therapy) that may be provided in either home settings or nursing homes, but, again, only on a short-term basis. The program also covers hospice care for terminally ill aged people.[63]

CHOICES OF THE WEALTHY

Money matters when it comes to older people weighing their long-term care alternatives, but not in a clear-cut way. At one extreme, those with higher incomes and savings are able to afford private sector products and services. These older consumers and their families are largely indifferent to the care offerings of public programs. Unless they live in remote rural locations, they can typically find private-pay geriatric care managers who can offer them comprehensive caregiving assessments and solutions. They can afford a full-time live-in and can be more selective about their worker choices.

Higher income older people are also better educated and benefit from their circle of more informed and trusted friends, neighbors, and family members. This grapevine of contacts is crucial because it allows access to better information about their long-term care options.[64]

CHOICES OF THE POOR

At the other extreme, the poorest old have to depend on formal care offered by federal and state government programs. To qualify for some programs, older people typically must have incomes below the federal poverty threshold (Table 8.1) and in some states

Table 8.1. Poverty rates of U.S. population age 65 and older by age, marital status, race, and gender, 2012 (Social Security Administration, 2014)

Population group	% of men in poverty	% of women in poverty	Total % in poverty
All age 65 and older	6.6	11.0	9.1
Age 65–69	6.7	8.9	7.8
Age 70–74	6.5	9.4	8.1
Age 75–79	5.4	12.4	9.4
Age 80 and older	7.7	13.9	11.4
Marital status			
Married	4.5	4.3	4.4
Widowed	10.1	14.5	13.6
Divorced	12.2	17.1	15.2
Never married	15.7	23.2	19.8
Race			
White	5.6	9.6	7.8
Black	14.0	21.2	18.2
Asian	12.3	12.2	12.3
Hispanic	19.1	21.8	20.6

In 2012: 1-person poverty level threshold = $11,011; 2-person poverty threshold = $13,878 (U.S. Census Bureau, 2012).

below the lower Supplemental Security Income (SSI) level (Figure 8.4); but in others, the income threshold is significantly higher (e.g., 300% of SSI).

By historical standards, poverty rates of older people are not high. Currently, about 9% of people age 65 and older have incomes below the 100% poverty threshold. This lower rate largely results from older people who benefit from a steady stream of Social Security income that adjusts upward when the U.S. cost of living rises. As Table 8.1 shows, however, certain subgroups of older adults are especially disadvantaged: the oldest, the unmarried, and racial and ethnic minorities. Unmarried women— widowed, divorced, separated, or never married—have the highest poverty rates. Other research shows that older people living in our core cities have the highest poverty rates, followed by older adults living in rural and small town areas, and then by suburbanites.[65] Moreover, many experts believe that we badly understate the size of the impoverished older population. They argue that using the minimal poverty threshold of 100% grossly understates those having difficulties paying for their housing and long-term care costs, and they recommend including those with incomes up to the 200% poverty threshold or those also in "near poverty."[66] In 2012, this included about 34% of the population age 65 and older.[67] An alternative method for computing poverty rates offered by the U.S. Census Bureau results in even higher numbers, because it defines as poor those with especially large healthcare and long-term care costs.[68] Rates aside, the large size of the aging baby boomer population will result in record *numbers* of low-income older people.

Figure 8.4. Medicaid eligibility

Eligible adults age 65 and older must be American citizens or lawfully residing immigrants who have both very low incomes and limited financial assets. However, income and asset criteria vary by state and by Medicaid programs within any given state. Most states make eligibility automatic for "categorically needy" older people who have qualified to receive income benefits under the federal SSI program. In 2014, SSI-eligible individual recipients received as much as $721 per month and couples up to $1,082 per month (http://www.ssa.gov/oact/cola/SSI.html). However, 11 states have lower SSI income threshold requirements; others cover older people with incomes up to 100% of the federal poverty level; and some state waiver programs cover older participants with incomes up to 300% of the SSI threshold level (Mollica, 2007; O'Keefe, 2010).

"Medically needy" older people can also qualify for coverage in 35 states even if their incomes or savings are initially too high. This occurs if they have high medical or nursing home expenses that reduce (spend down) their "excess" incomes to below their state's "Medicaid needy income eligibility limit" (typically below the SSI needy income limit).

An older person's liquid assets must usually be below $2,000 ($3,000 for couples). Allowable assets differ when only one spouse is applying for Medicaid (for nursing home or community waiver services). This amount varies by state but the noninstitutionalized spouse is allowed to retain up to $117,240 (in 2014).

Medicaid will deny eligibility if the applicant earlier transferred assets in order to qualify; states look back 5 years. Home value is generally exempt from the asset wealth criterion as long as it does not exceed (as of 2014) $543,000 (or, at state discretion, $814,000). There is no equity limit if the Medicaid applicant's spouse (or child under age 21, or disabled child) continues to live there. Legal counsel is often needed to interpret the complex rules regarding asset eligibility, transfers, and estate recovery (e.g., owned dwellings) practices (Moses, 2004; U.S. Government Accountability Office, 2007).

Despite their eligibility for public programs, very poor older people must confront the harsh reality that the growth in funding of government programs offering affordable long-term care is unlikely to keep pace with their demand.[69] Consequently, they face a future in which they will find themselves on waiting lists, even for programs for which they are income-qualified.

Some low-income people may find other ways to get relief. They occupy communities with affordable and comprehensive home- and community-based care that is made available by nonprofit charitable organizations that specifically target older populations of different religions and ethnic persuasions.[70] Examples include social service organizations, such as Catholic Social Services, Family Services Association, Volunteers of America, or Jewish Family and Children Services. Through donations by individuals, foundations, and corporations, they offer lower-income older people personal care and homemaking services, transportation options, and opportunities for companionship.[71]

CHOICES OF THE MIDDLE CLASS

Perhaps surprisingly, a third group of older people in the middle income brackets face a more difficult time paying for their long-term care. These "Tweeners,"[72] or members of the "Gap Income Group,"[73] have higher incomes than the poorest old but are far from wealthy. They often have incomes or assets that are too large to qualify for most public- or government-assistance programs but too small to afford the pricey long-term care options offered by the private sector.

Consequently, even though these older people do not have the lowest incomes, many are at risk of not getting appropriate long-term care. One frustrated middle-class Chicago police officer caring for his mother communicates the dilemma:

> If you are poor or wealthy, one-way or the other, your needs will be taken care of. If you are middle class you face the very real possibility of financial ruin if you or your loved one wants to remain at home and needs constant care for years.[74]

GOVERNMENT PROGRAMS LEVELING THE PLAYING FIELD

Two government programs, Medicare and Medicaid, account for most of the $357 billion of long-term care expenditures in the United States.[75] In 2011, the post-acute home care services funded under the Medicare program represented 21%, and the skilled nursing homes and home- and community-based care covered under the Medicaid program represented 40% of long-term care spending. A very small share of older beneficiaries, the sickest and the poorest, account for a disproportionate share of this spending.[76] These older people (almost 6 million in 2010[77]) are often receiving both Medicare and Medicaid coverage and are referred to as dual eligible beneficiaries.[78]

Private long-term care insurance and other insurance sources (e.g., employer sponsored policies) paid for 7% of the costs; other public programs (including the Older Americans Act) and private funding sources covered 18% of total long-term care expenditures.[79] Finally, direct out-of-pocket costs of older people covered a substantial 15% of total long-term care expenditures.[80] However, this last percentage underestimates the share of costs assumed by older consumers because much of their (and their family's) out-of-pocket costs go unrecorded.[81]

We examine the three most important of these programs in the sections that follows: Medicare Home Health, Medicaid, and the Older Americans Act.

MEDICARE HOME HEALTH

Although the home health services benefit offered under Medicare (Part A) typically offers temporary assistance, older people often progress to needing long-term assistance after receiving the benefits under this program. To be eligible, older people must be under the care of a physician who will design and oversee their care plans, often with the assistance of nurse practitioners or registered nurses. This program does not require out-of-pocket costs as long as a physician recertifies the home care visits as a medical necessity every 60 days.[82] Medicare-certified home health agencies typically provide these home health services, and most are freestanding (i.e., not affiliated with a hospital or nursing facility).[83]

Eligible older people must need part-time or intermittent skilled nursing care (e.g., intravenous or respiratory therapy and wound care) or physical, speech, or occupational therapies (Figure 8.1) and be able to leave their homes only with considerable and taxing effort.[84] Older people who need these services over the long haul must turn to assistance from the Medicaid program or pay the out-of-pocket costs charged by private vendors.

THE MEDICAID PROGRAM

The Medicaid program is funded jointly by the federal and state governments. Although this very large and complex program is subject to federal oversight by the Centers for Medicare & Medicaid Services (CMS) within the U.S. Department of Health and Human Services (HHS), state governments manage and fund this means-tested entitlement program differently.

Medicaid is the most important government-funded source of long-term care for low-income people age 65 and older with limited assets or high medical costs (Figure 8.4). Although these older beneficiaries are usually poor even before they begin paying for their long-term care, significant numbers of older people fall back on this program because they exhaust their savings and assets with ongoing out-of-pocket medical and nursing home costs.[85] They are disproportionately African-American, Hispanic, and unmarried.[86] In response to criticisms that wealthier older people are able to circumvent these minimum income and asset criteria, Medicaid has introduced increasingly more stringent and comprehensive financial tests.[87]

When it began in 1965, the Medicaid program was the safety net for very impaired and very poor older people who needed affordable nursing home care.[88] This is still true today. The Medicaid program—as the primary payer—covers the occupancy and care costs of nearly two-thirds of older nursing home residents.[89] However, the Medicaid program has substantially increased its share of spending on home- and community-based services to allow more older people to deal with their limitations in their homes. In 1995, Medicaid spent only 17% of its long-term care expenditures on home- and community-based services targeting older people and others with physical disabilities; by 2012 the rate had risen to 39%.[90]

This new emphasis resulted from a series of changes in the Medicaid program, the most important of which occurred in 1981. Under section 1915(c) of the Social Security Act, Congress allowed states to fund home- and community-based waiver programs. Older people could receive a comprehensive array of personal assistance and care services (but not room and board) delivered to their homes as long as they needed the level of skilled care that they would receive if they were admitted into their states' nursing homes (Figure 8.5).[91] Waiver program services now account for about two-thirds of Medicaid home- and community-based spending.[92]

Although state governments had offered personal care services to older beneficiaries in their own homes who needed assistance with their ADLs and IADLs under their Medicaid state plans (Figure 8.5), they were very receptive to this new waiver

Figure 8.5. Role of Medicaid in the provision of community-based long-term care

Medicaid expenditures on home- and community-based services (HCBS) occur in three major ways (O'Keefe, 2010): the mandatory Home Health care program (11%); the Optional State Plan Personal Care benefit (23%); and 1915(c) HCBS waiver programs (66%) (Howard et al., 2011).

Home Health Care Program

All states and the District of Columbia offer this mandatory state plan benefit to low-income or medically needy older people. Eligibility does not depend on their need for skilled nursing home (institutional) care. Services include medically necessary nursing services, assistance from home health aides, and medical equipment and supplies suitable for use in the home. States have the option of including physical, occupational, and speech therapies. Services must be ordered by a physician's written care plan and offered on a part-time or intermittent basis by a Medicare-certified home health agency (O'Keefe, 2010).

Medicaid State Plan: Personal Care Benefit

A state Medicaid plan defines how it will operate its Medicaid program, who is covered, and by what services. Since the mid-1970s, personal care services, which are an optional state benefit, could be offered to older people who needed assistance with their ADLs and IADLs. Nursing services and other medical care are not included (The Lewin Group, 2007).

Services are generally provided by Medicare-certified home health agencies, but in some states consumers can hire their own service providers (except spouses) through consumer-directed programs. The amount, duration, or scope of covered services varies across states. Older people do not have to be eligible for their state's skilled nursing homes to qualify, but applicants usually must be SSI eligible, deemed medically needy, or have incomes not higher than the 100% federal poverty level. Because this program must be offered to all age and population groups who meet the state need criteria, states cannot have a waiting list.

A variation of this plan, the Optional State Plan HCBS Benefit, began in 2007 after passage of the 2005 Deficit Reduction Act. Eligibility criteria are more flexible than those of the state plan, with eligible applicant incomes up to 150% of the poverty level. They can also offer a broader range of services (that is, as offered under HCBS waivers). States can limit the number of older people they serve and maintain waiting lists. Eligible people do not necessarily need an institutional level of care; states must establish less-stringent functional health criteria than they use for waivers. Very few states are using this program.

Effective in 2011, the Patient Protection and Affordable Care Act added a new Medicaid state plan option to finance home- and community-based care. Under the Community First Choice Option, states can offer assistance with ADLs and IADLs and other health-related tasks. Older people may choose to receive these services through a consumer-directed plan. The program expressly covers the initial housing costs of older people transitioning from nursing homes to community settings, including 1 month of rent, utilities, and basic kitchen supplies. Services not covered

Figure continued next page

Figure 8.5. *Continued*

include medical supplies and assistive technology devices, room and board, and vocational rehabilitation. Eligibility for the program requires *"(a) being eligible for Medical assistance under the state plan and (b) having income that (1) is equal to or less than 150% of the Federal Poverty Level, or (2) income over 150% of the Federal Poverty Level and meets the state's eligibility criteria for institutional services (in a hospital, nursing facility, intermediate care facility for the mentally challenged, or an institution for mental diseases), or (3) qualifies for Medicaid under the state's special HCBS waiver criteria and is receiving at least one HCBS waiver service per month"* (Harrington et al., 2012, p. 173). States do not have to show budget neutrality. That is, their spending can exceed the costs spent on institutional care. Unlike in their waiver programs, however, states are required to offer the program to all who meet the eligibility requirements, and they cannot set statewide ceilings or geographic restrictions on the number of people who can receive benefits (Harrington et al., 2012; Ng et al., 2010; O'Keefe, 2010). States adopting this program receive a higher federal match (an increase of 6%) for their attendant services and supports.

Medicaid HCBS Waivers

Since 1981 (under section 1915[c] of the Social Security Act), states can apply for waivers to provide services that would otherwise not be covered under their State Optional Personal Care Plans. Unlike their state plans, Medicaid waiver beneficiaries must have a level of skilled care needs that would qualify them for their state's Medicaid-funded nursing home beds (Mollica, 2009). However, states differ significantly as to how physically and cognitively limited older people must be to qualify for a Medicaid-funded bed (The Lewin Group, 2007). States must also demonstrate that their waivers are budget neutral; that is, waiver-funding costs must not exceed what it would cost them to provide the same services in a nursing home. This cost neutrality is not required when they provide services under their state plan.

The overall intent of waivers was to enable very frail older people to remain in their community settings rather than enter nursing homes. Thus, waivers cover a broad range of medical and nonmedical long-term care services that prevent institutionalization and that are not usually covered by state personal care plans. States often favor their Medicaid waiver approach over their state personal care plans because they can offer more services, including case management, homemaker services, home health aide services, personal care, adult day health, habilitation, respite care, rehabilitation, day treatment or other partial hospitalization services, psychosocial rehabilitation services, clinic services for people with chronic illness, and any other services necessary to avoid institutionalization (Stone, 2010; U.S. Department of Health and Human Services Office of Inspector General, 2012).

Along with more flexible service delivery, states have other incentives to apply for these waivers. They are able to serve higher-income older people with incomes up to 300% of the maximum SSI benefit. States can also limit the number of their waiver slots, restrict coverage to certain geographic areas, and target certain population groups (e.g., older people, younger disabled people, or people with intellectual and developmental disabilities). Consequently, during state budget cutbacks, Medicaid waiver funding is especially vulnerable.

option because it gave them *"greater control over the number of participants and spending than the personal care programs allow{ed}."*[93] They could limit the number of older people who used waiver services—and could establish waiting lists—and they could limit the amount of money they paid for these services.[94] The program's greater administrative flexibility also allowed them to offer a broader range of supportive and long-term care services that addressed most of the independent living challenges faced by older people who had difficulties managing their homemaking tasks, performing their ADLs and IADLs, and managing their chronic health problems (Figure 8.5).

The Medicaid program has used two strategies to shift spending from nursing home or institutional care to home- and community-based care, a set of policies known as *rebalancing*. The first, more-significant strategy involves upstream or nursing home diversion programs that provide home- and community-based services to physically disabled and Medicaid-eligible older people to avoid or delay their nursing home admittance. The second strategy includes downstream transition programs that enable older people in nursing homes to relocate to qualified residential arrangements in their communities.[95]

Three factors have contributed to this important shift in Medicaid spending.[96] First, the lobbying and legal challenges of advocates for younger disabled people successfully pressed for more community-based alternatives for their constituencies. Their efforts contributed to the enactment of Title II of the Americans with Disabilities Act in 1990, which requires states to provide services to disabled people (of all ages) in the least-restrictive and most-integrated setting—that is, in home and community settings as opposed to institutions, such as nursing homes. Subsequent court rulings upheld the rights of the disabled, most notably the Supreme Court decision *Olmstead v. L.C.* in June 1999, which found that states were *"obligated to make reasonable modifications in policies, practices, or procedures to avoid discrimination on the basis of disability."*[97]

Second, most state governments believed that keeping older people in their homes would achieve overall savings in Medicaid expenditures, compared with their costs for nursing homes. Third, these policy shifts reflected the strong preferences of older people, who wanted to be cared for in their ordinary residential settings.[98]

Policies initiated in the 2000s have offered states further financial and administrative incentives to qualify older people as Medicaid beneficiaries of home- and community-based services or to transition them out of nursing homes into community residential settings.[99] Medicaid-managed care programs (Managed Long Term Services and Supports [MLTSS]), which are designed to obviate the fragmented fee-for-service delivery networks of states, offered them a new and hopefully more cost-effective and coordinated strategy for addressing the needs of their vulnerable older adults. These state programs pay set monthly fees per enrollee (capitation payments) to an administrative entity (managed care organization [MCO]) to ensure the delivery of all required long-term services and supports to their Medicaid consumers that meet specified quality standards.

The Deficit Reduction Act of 2005 and the Patient Protection and Affordable Care Act of 2010[100] also resulted in regulatory changes, new demonstration programs, and new federal funding commitments for Medicaid options, such as the Money Follows the Person, the Community First Choice Option, amendments to the Home and Community-Based Services state plan benefit, and the State Balancing Incentive Program.[101] Some state governments also are relying more on their own general revenues to fund their home- and community-based programs.[102]

One of the larger recent Medicaid programs, Money Follows the Person, enables older occupants who have resided in nursing homes for more than 90 consecutive days to transition into community settings where they will receive the necessary health-related and supportive services. As of 2013, 46 states and the District of Columbia received grants from this program.[103] From its inception in 2008 through 2013, it has enabled roughly more than 15,000 older people nationwide to transition out of nursing homes (or are in the progress of transitioning), but states receiving these funds differ substantially in their participation. Only a few states (Texas, Washington, Pennsylvania, Maryland, Michigan, Ohio, Connecticut, and Indiana) account for more than two-thirds of the nursing home transitions.[104] States have confronted three major barriers implementing this program: *"a shortage of affordable housing, a poor economic climate, and a weak community-based services and supports infrastructure."*[105] For example, in rural areas it is often difficult to recruit direct service workers.[106]

UNEQUAL AVAILABILITY OF MEDICAID-FUNDED LONG-TERM CARE

Medicaid is often characterized as 50 (plus the District of Columbia) distinct programs because state governments have broad authority to define who is eligible, what benefits and services they receive, and how much to pay. In essence this means *"some individuals may qualify for services in one state and not in a second state."*[107] This helps explain why some states have especially long waiting lists for their Medicaid waiver slots that fund community-based care. As several experts note:

> When that [Medicaid] infrastructure is not in place, people have no choice but to enter an institution because they cannot wait weeks or months for services to be approved and delivered.[108]

The inequality is also explained by some states spending a higher share of their Medicaid dollars to pay for home- and community-based services than for nursing home care.[109] For example, in 2012 Minnesota spent 65% of its Medicaid budget on home- and community-based care serving older people and others with physical disabilities, but Florida spent 23%.[110] Consequently, in some states we are still far away from eliminating the nursing home funding bias.[111]

Some of the reasons for this variation are less controllable. States with colder and snowier climates or with sparsely populated rural populations and inadequate workforces (e.g., personal and home health aides) will have more difficulties offering home- and community-based care.[112] However, far more important will be the funding levels, eligibility rules, and benefits of a state's program (e.g., state personal plan vs. waiver coverage and services), which variously make the provision of home- and community-based care more feasible[113] and nursing home occupancy less likely.[114]

States, for example, differ in their efforts to contain the costs of their Medicaid waiver programs. Some waiver programs have more stringent income eligibility criteria or more demanding asset or wealth tests for potential older participants. Some states also establish stricter waiver eligibility criteria than they use for their nursing home admission. For example, they require people to have difficulties performing three or more ADLs in order to receive home- and community-based services, whereas they require limitations of only two ADLs for their nursing home admission.[115] States also differ in which rebalancing incentives they make available, such as consumer-directed services for older people (or their families) to arrange home care, affordable and supportive renter accommodations, and SSI supplements to help older people pay for their housing costs.[116]

HOME- AND COMMUNITY-BASED CARE PROGRAM COSTS CONTRASTED WITH NURSING HOME CARE

After four decades of research, we still do not know for sure whether it is less costly for Medicaid programs to fund the home- and community-based care of frail older people or to pay for their nursing home stays.[117] Nor is it always clear that these programs have delayed their nursing home admission.[118] However, one analysis did show that living in a state that spent more on home- and community-based care lowered the risk of nursing home admission for older people without children but not for those with living children.[119]

Although we can maintain an individual with physical and cognitive impairments in a conventional setting with supportive services at a lower cost than in a Medicaid-funded nursing home, programs designed to delay or prevent institutionalization must be directed to a *population* of potential beneficiaries who are especially at risk of being admitted to a nursing home (Chapter 4).[120] Many states fear that if they fund these home- and community-based services, their overall Medicaid long-term care costs will actually increase. This is because large shares of their lower-income residents rely on family members to care for them in their dwellings and so do not fall under the purview of the Medicaid program. However, if states expand their Medicaid community-based offerings, their administrators worry about a "woodwork" or moral hazard effect. That is, *"people not currently receiving services will come out of the woodwork in droves to demand services offered at home or in other community settings."*[121] State governments thereby end up *"spending on people who would not have {anyway} entered a nursing home in the absence of these services."*[122] This results in an overall higher growth rate of expenditures on long-term services and supports.[123] Consequently, state governments do not enjoy any absolute cost savings by their funding shift toward home- and community-based programs.[124]

Other experts counter that states investing in these community-based programs have slowed their Medicaid spending growth and have realized cost savings but only in the long run.[125] A study that analyzed 15 years of Medicaid program spending concluded,

> Rebalancing in favor of home- and community-based services can greatly reduce overall spending on long-term services and supports, when done at a deliberate pace. According to the model, a steady, gradual shift of monies toward

waiver programs, personal care services, and home health programs is the best strategy for optimizing the bottom line.[126]

Still other experts argue that cost savings should not be the only criterion to justify serving aging-in-place, lower-income older people. Rather, state governments should emphasize home- and community-based care over nursing homes because older people receive comparable or better care and enjoy an overall improvement in the quality of their lives.[127]

One criticism of Medicaid waiver programs reminds us of how housing and care issues are intermingled. Medicaid does not cover the costs that lower-income older people incur for their housing, board, and utilities. Consequently, it is often not feasible for them to receive home-based care offered under the Medicaid waiver program or to transition out of nursing homes if they cannot find suitable, affordable rental housing (Chapter 9). As emphasized earlier, some but not all states try to alleviate these barriers by offering supplementary SSI funding to help their low-income seniors afford housing costs.[128]

There is agreement that substantially increased government expenditures will be required in order to fund the long-term care needed by our economically deprived older population. Some critics are unhappy about such a scenario, raising questions regarding the appropriate role of government in long-term care and pointing out that Medicaid produces a disincentive for older adults to plan or save for their future long-term care needs by depleting their savings before qualifying for any coverage.[129]

OLDER AMERICANS ACT PROGRAMS

Initiated in 1965, the Older Americans Act (OAA) was one of the first federal programs to fund health and social services to help older people age in place. It has a broad mission:

> To help older people maintain maximum independence in their homes and communities and to promote a continuum of care for the vulnerable elderly.[130]

All people age 60 and older are eligible to receive services, and there is no income means testing. However, the law requires OAA programs to target older people with the greatest social and economic needs, typically populations at or below the poverty level, along with minority or ethnic groups with limited English proficiency, rural residents, and the disabled at risk of institutional care.[131]

A federal agency, the Administration on Aging, now subsumed under the U.S. Department of Health and Human Services Administration for Community Living,[132] drafts regulations and funds OAA programs. State departments or agencies (State Units on Aging) divide their states into planning and service areas (629 throughout the country in 2014) administered by Area Agencies on Aging (AAAs).[133] These local agencies are often nonprofits but also organizational units of county or city governments and the Council of Governments.[134] They plan, develop, and coordinate an array of home- and community-based services—what is called the "aging services network"—targeting the unmet needs of older people living in their geographic planning areas. AAAs, however, are very diverse with very different annual budgets and program and service emphases.[135]

AAAs may provide some services directly, but they also contract with more than 30,000 community providers to deliver the services.[136] For example, AAAs usually directly provide services such as information and referral, outreach, and support to caregivers, whereas they contract out to providers, often nonprofits, services such as home-delivered and congregate meals, legal assistance, and transportation. About 56% of AAAs serve older people who variously live in city, suburban, and rural areas, but 44% serve clients who primarily live in rural areas.[137]

KEY SOURCES OF INFORMATION

AAAs often serve as key starting points for older people and their families seeking information about home- and community-based services.[138] A nationwide service, the National Eldercare Locator Service (under Title II of OAA) was created to connect older Americans and their caregivers (by telephone or Internet) to AAAs and community-based organizations in their specific localities that provide assistance.

Older people and their families prefer to find all of their information in one easy-to-access place.[139] To help achieve this goal, in 2006 the Administration on Aging joined with the Centers for Medicare & Medicaid Services to award funds to states to develop Aging and Disability Resource Centers (ADRCs).[140] In most states, ADRCs are organizationally located within AAAs.[141] These consumer-friendly, one-stop agencies have staffs who provide personal counseling to people of all ages, disabilities, and income levels about how to access and qualify for all of a community's long-term services and supports, especially those funded under Medicaid and the OAA. Higher percentages of AAAs are now serving clients who are younger than age 60 and who are disabled, impaired, or have chronic illnesses.[142]

Along with face-to-face personal assistance, many older consumers access information by telephone or through Web-based systems of ADRCs. Although they are now operating in most states, ADRCs may not offer coverage in all counties or have all adopted a single point of entry.[143] Beginning in 2010, the Patient Protection and Affordable Care Act provided additional funding to develop these comprehensive information and assistance centers.[144] However, it is too early to judge their effectiveness.[145]

TYPES OF HOME- AND COMMUNITY-BASED CARE

The OAA authorizes the delivery of service programs under seven titles, but most long-term services and supports are administered under its Title III programs, which account for just more than 70% of OAA funding ($1.9 billion in 2014).[146] However, limiting one's focus only to OAA funding undoubtedly understates the impact of these programs. State and area agencies also use these federal funds to leverage a substantial amount of non-OAA funds from other federal programs, state and local governments, private philanthropy, and voluntary older client cost-sharing contributions.[147] Medicaid funding in particular has become a more important funding source *"as AAAs have become more aligned with providing health-related services in addition to their historical social programs.*"[148] The majority of AAAs now help administer Medicaid HCBS waivers and hospital care transition programs, and they are increasingly planning or implementing MLTSS, engaging in supportive service activities that MCOs, which are more accustomed to dealing with acute healthcare providers, have limited experience with.

The largest category of Title III program spending (43% of the 70%) is the Nutrition Services Program, which aims to prevent poor nutritional health, hunger, and related adverse health conditions. It funds the delivery of meals to the homes of older people and, to a lesser extent, to congregate settings, such as senior centers.

The second largest category of funding (19% of 70%) is for the Supportive Services Program, which offers services that promote independent living. These predominantly include information, assistance, and case management services to help older people evaluate their care needs and access services in their communities. It also funds transportation services, escort services (i.e., a companion who accompanies older people to businesses and services), and, to a much smaller extent, home care services and legal assistance.

The third and smallest of the Title III programs (1% of 70%), Disease Prevention and Health Promotion Activities, includes *"physical fitness and diabetes control classes and arthritis and nutrition education, as well as more individualized services, such as medical and dental screening, nutrition counseling, medication management consultation, and immunizations.*"[149] These events are also found at senior centers and congregate nutrition sites.

A fourth category of Title III services, the aforementioned National Family Caregiver Support Program (8% of 70%), includes services to assist family caregivers (Chapter 7).

EFFECTIVENESS OF SERVICES

The funding for OAA programs is obviously much smaller than for the Medicaid program. However, experts argue that these services help keep vulnerable older people in their community settings because they provide *"a safety net for people who might otherwise not qualify for Medicaid-financed long-term care support.*"[150]

In fiscal year 2010, about 3 million people in the United States, about 5% of people age 60 and older, regularly received Title III services, such as home-delivered meals, home care, and case management. About 8 million people, about 14% of people age 60 and older, also received other services on an occasional basis, including transportation, information and assistance, and congregate meals.[151]

Supporters argue that these service delivery percentages would be higher if they were expressed as a share of vulnerable older people: those with difficulties performing their ADLs, with serious chronic health problems, and at higher risk of nursing home placement.[152] They also argue that these national indicators are misleading because of the wide variability in the provision of services and number of older people helped in different states and communities.

Some studies find that as states increase these home- and community-based services, they slow their spending rate on their Medicaid programs.[153] Specifically, when they spend more on home-delivered meals, it resulted in a decreased prevalence of older people in their nursing homes with low-care needs (i.e., those who did not need 24-hour skilled nursing care).[154] Supporters also argue that older people enjoy less obvious benefits:

> Drivers [delivering meals] are often the eyes and ears who serve as a "safety check" and report changing health or needs of home-bound older adults. In addition, any unanswered delivery is reported and investigated. Oftentimes, those who deliver food also provide companionship to people who otherwise might be alone all day.[155]

Older users themselves report high levels of satisfaction. For example, more than 70% of older people using transportation services were "always" satisfied, and another 20% reported that their needs were usually met. The participants also report that these transportation services made it easier for them to age in place, because they could reach medical appointments or attend congregate meal programs more easily.[156]

Funding for OAA programs has not kept pace with inflation or a growing older population.[157] Consequently, despite the assistance received by millions of older people, a 2011 Government Accountability Report[158] concluded that there are many older people with unmet needs—most notably, meal services and home-based care—and long waiting lists are common. Experts fear the situation will worsen given future growth projections of the older population[159] and the inadequacy of future federal government funding.[160] To compensate, AAAs are attempting to find new sources of government revenue, investing in new and more-efficient database and software technologies, partnering more with Medicaid-managed care networks, streamlining their operations (e.g., increasing caseloads, cutting business travel, reducing staff benefits, cutting or eliminating staff training, instituting waiting lists for some services, and eliminating services), and cutting budgets.[161]

Researchers have not carefully studied the consequences of these service gaps and responses, and there is *"limited and inconsistent state knowledge about need and unmet need."*[162] Surveys often focus on those already receiving services, rather than on older adults *"who need services, but do not request them."*[163] Many state administrators argue that they simply do not have the funds to conduct such assessments. Consequently, they must rely on anecdotal evidence from state and local government staff familiar with their service delivery areas.

SPECIFIC COMMUNITY-BASED RESOURCES

CHURCHES[164]

The multiple functions played by the church—from places of worship to social centers—allow it to engage large numbers of older Americans. People in their late 50s and 60s have the highest attendance records of any age group. People in their 70s attend less, but still more frequently than other age groups. Attendance is also high among ethnic and racial minorities (e.g., African-Americans, Hispanics, and Asians), which are the fastest-growing segments of today's older population.

Scholars and religious leaders agree that the church could be a more valuable community resource for older people who need assistance with long-term care. But they disagree on how. Should churches provide only information and spiritual supports? Or should they provide more actual hands-on assistance responding to their congregants' care and supportive service needs?

Churches now predominantly offer psychosocial supports and spiritual comfort and healing. When they do offer material supports, these are very narrowly defined and include social gatherings, emergency financial assistance, food distribution, transportation assistance, telephone reassurance, religious activities (e.g., Bible study, prayer groups), and visitation to those in hospitals or nursing homes.

Depressed older people may benefit from spiritual comfort and prayer. However, at issue is whether they would gain more from seeing a mental health therapist arranged by a church. Similarly, the wife of a husband with Alzheimer's disease does not just need emotional support, but also help in the home, help caring for her husband and help securing services ranging from electronic monitoring devices to nursing. Emotional comfort only goes so far when dealing with the repair problems of an older house, for example. Similarly, stressed out caregivers will benefit from sympathetic church ministries, but they would gain more from respite care.

Some churches have broader missions, and although they are in the minority, they offer their members an enriched array of resources for coping with growing old. For example, some assist congregants with their health-related as opposed to long-term care problems. Parish nurses (registered nurses) provide their members with health education and information about healthy lifestyles and disease prevention and help them psychologically cope with short-term illness or hospitalization through counseling and prayer. A very few have launched especially complex programs (e.g., building a low-rent housing property for the vulnerable members of their congregation) that are expensive to develop and operate and require the cooperation of multiple religious and community-based organizations.

Many religious leaders believe that churches are missing an important opportunity to function as a long-term care resource to their congregations, and they say the church has *"abandoned its historical role of community care for its {older} members."*[165] Research articles often refer to churches as underused resources that do not assign a high priority to assisting their older congregants—and most certainly their family caregivers. Here is how they describe their long-term care offerings:

- They are reactive as opposed to proactive.
- Poorly organized, short-lived programs are initiated without a comprehensive plan or clearly stated mission.
- Programs are small in scale and informal in organization.
- Programs do not exclusively target older adults.
- Programs disproportionately target the poor and destitute.
- There is little or no practical assistance to family caregivers, who themselves may be older.

Of course, church leaders do not welcome these criticisms and claim that filling the long-term care gaps left by the private or public sectors is not part of their mission.

They especially do not appreciate the implied devaluation of their spiritual and psychosocial roles.

These shortcomings are notable because church congregations often expect much more from their places of worship—and for unsurprising reasons:

- The needs of older people and their caregivers are community specific, and they look first at what is available locally to meet their needs.
- Churches typically know their communities well: which assisted living developments are best, where there is moderately priced housing, and which members of the community might be available to be hired as caregivers or volunteer their time.
- It is difficult to name a less-controversial social institution that could serve as a liaison between congregation members and the businesses and agencies found in the private or public sectors.
- Many congregation members would feel less stigma about asking help from their church than from government agencies or private vendors.

CONSUMER-DIRECTED CARE

Assessments of the Medicaid program's community-based service focus found that older people and their families wanted greater choice and control over securing their needed assistance, what is referred to as *consumer- or participant-directed care;* that is, they did not want their state governments dictating what home care agencies will provide their care. The Medicaid program offers two alternative strategies to address these concerns for some of its beneficiaries.

In the employer authority model, rather than relying on home care agencies to arrange the services of direct care workers, older people themselves could *"hire, fire, schedule, and supervise aides of their choosing (including hiring their own family members as caregivers)."*[166] In the budget authority model, the Medicaid program gave older people or family members a monetary allowance that they could use not only to employ aides, but also to purchase related services and goods (e.g., transportation services, rehabilitation services, assistive technologies, and installation ramps and home modifications).[167]

A number of "Cash and Counseling Demonstration" evaluations conducted from the late 1990s to the early 2000s[168] showed that giving older consumers decision-making authority over who delivered their care increased their satisfaction with their services, gave them greater feelings of empowerment, and generally improved the quality of their lives.[169] Most crucially, there was no evidence that using this approach degraded the quality of their care. Consider the following personal testimony lauding this person-centered approach to hiring caregivers[170]:

Mrs. Smith, a 74-year-old widow, has diabetes, glaucoma, and significant personal care needs. For 5 years she used an agency that contracted with Medicaid to supply aides. Then her daughter read about Independent Choices (the Arkansas Cash and Counseling Demonstration) and became the representative decision maker for her mother under this program. The daughter says "There's just something about having family look after her. She doesn't get nearly as many allergic reactions or bed sores now, and I think that's because when it's your own you're looking after, you pay more attention." Mother and daughter appreciate the flexibility of the cash allowance. They have used it to pay a granddaughter to come for 2 hours daily and a grandson to do chores around the house and yard. And by careful use of the allowance, they were able to pay for new dentures for Mrs. Smith.[171]

Although these programs are funded primarily by Medicaid—both by its optional state plan services and waivers—they also receive a small share of support from the general revenues of state governments and the U.S. Department of Veteran's Affairs (VA). Every state and the District of Columbia now have at least one participant-directed program, and well over 800,000 people were enrolled as of 2013.[172]

Because they elicit positive reviews and reduce waiting lists for direct care workers, many state governments favor these consumer-directed care programs.[173] They also believe that in the long run they are less expensive to administer than traditional agency provider approaches.

States face challenges implementing these programs, however. Critics argue that they actually cost more to operate, and their implementation requires new program and financial management systems. Consumers need counseling about their new hiring powers. These programs also face opposition from case managers because they are accustomed to a professionally managed service delivery model and are suspicious about the ability and motives of family members substituting as paid aides. Not surprisingly, home care agencies are often opposed to this service delivery approach, fearing competition.[174]

On the other hand, some agency providers acknowledge the shortcomings of their traditional approaches:

> [They] recognize that they cannot recruit enough workers to meet demand and cannot afford to serve people living in rural or frontier areas. Some also recognize that their services might not be culturally attractive to some minority participants. Also, it can be to traditional providers' advantage to refer so-called problem clients, who complain about and often ask to change workers, to consumer-directed services.[175]

SENIOR CENTERS

According to Stuart Spector, senior vice president of the National Council on Aging,

> Senior centers serve as the front door for millions of older Americans who are looking for ways to stay healthy, independent, and engaged in their communities and senior centers empower and support older adults.[176]

These 11,400 community centers are found in U.S. cities, suburbs, and rural areas and daily offer more than 1 million older adults a broad spectrum of services.[177] Most patronize these centers for their meals and nutritional services, their social, recreational, and educational activities, volunteer opportunities, and new friendships, as well as for health, fitness or exercise, and wellness programs (e.g., health screenings, immunizations, diabetes counseling).

We must be careful about generalizing, however. Although some senior centers are operated by professional staff and function as community focal points and sources of service information,[178] others are sparsely staffed, often by volunteers, have narrower missions, and only offer meals—perhaps in response to their smaller constituencies.[179] In a sample of senior centers in Florida, the number of full- or part-time staff numbered from 1 to 54, average daily attendance varied from 6 to 4,000, and the annual operating budget ranged from $6,500 to $1.8 million.

The 1965 Older Americans Act (Title III) was a major catalyst for the growth of senior centers.[180] These community centers also rely on funding from county and municipal governments, nonprofit charitable organizations (e.g., YMCA, United Way, and Catholic Charities), and membership or participant dues.[181] Many senior centers are operated as a division of their city or county governments.

More than for probably any other government-funded program, the older people patronizing senior centers come from all walks of life: the healthy and the frail as well as those from all incomes, educational levels, and ethnic and racial backgrounds. Still, occupants tend to be primarily women and people living alone, with lower incomes, and with minimal physical disabilities.[182] Unlike adult day center attendees, those who use senior centers usually participate in activities without the assistance of staff.[183]

An absence of up-to-date, evidence-based research makes it difficult to assess how these senior centers affect the lives of older Americans.[184] Still, past findings reveal that these places contribute to the positive mental and physical health of their users, improve their nutrition, and reduce their social isolation. However, it is unclear whether these programs improve the chances of older people aging in place. Perhaps because of this lack of compelling evidence, experts worry about the availability of future funding.[185]

ADULT DAY SERVICES

Although professional and direct care workers often meet with their older clients in their own homes, they may also assist them in adult day service centers (also known as adult day healthcare, adult day care, medical adult day care). There were over 5,600 adult day centers throughout the United States in 2014.[186] They are over-represented in less-populated rural areas.[187] These community-based centers offer a structured array of healthcare and long-term supports during the 9-to-5 work week, with about 15% of centers operating during evening or weekend hours.[188] More than half of the centers provide transportation to and from the older person's home.

Most adult day centers are located in either freestanding buildings or buildings that include a senior center, social service agency, religious organization, hospital, or nursing home. Nonprofit charitable providers, many with religious or ethnic affiliations, sponsor most of these adult day centers (55%); a very small share are government sponsored (5%); and for-profit providers operate the remainder (40.0%), but they are a growing share.[189]

USERS OF ADULT CARE CENTERS

It is estimated that more than 260,000 Americans attend adult care centers on a daily basis.[190] Sixty-four percent are age 65 and older,[191] but an important subgroup are younger, often with intellectual or developmental disabilities.[192] Whereas only 20% of the overall population age 65 and older are minorities (African-American, Hispanic, and Asian), these subgroups constituted 53% of adult day care users.[193] Centers typically serve an average of 34 people a day, with an average capacity of about 51, but a minority (5%) daily serve more than 100 people.[194] Some attend for only a short time, others for years. They may leave because of a serious health decline or death, or they may enter a nursing home.

Older people patronize adult care centers because they need monitoring, management, and care for their chronic health problems or help with their ADLs. Substantial numbers are diagnosed with Alzheimer's disease or other dementias (32%) or with depression (24%).[195] Participants are most likely to be women in their mid-70s and older. The current users are more vulnerable than in the past and have significant medical needs and several ADL limitations. Their motives for using these centers include the following[196]:

- They need full-time assistance that cannot be offered in their homes.
- Their family caregivers need temporary relief from their caregiving responsibilities.
- Their family caregivers find their care needs or behavioral problems too demanding.

MAJOR SUBCATEGORIES OF ADULT DAY CARE

Adult day care centers fall within one of three categories depending on their clients, the types and levels of their services, and their licensure status. Some are not much more than adult equivalents of child day care, whereas others offer the care found in a nursing home.

Adult day centers with a *social model of care* offer predominantly nonmedical services that include a secure daytime environment, personal care (help with ADL limitations such as toileting, grooming, eating), medication management, preventive health services, meals, snacks, and planned social and recreational activities. A second category of centers with a *medical or health model of care* provide various rehabilitation services, such as physical, occupational, speech, and hearing therapies as well as skilled nursing services.

The majority of adult day care centers (close to two-thirds) offer both a social and a medical model of care. Almost 80% of these centers have a registered nurse or licensed practical nurse on staff, and almost half employ social workers who can counsel family members. Almost all have direct care workers on staff.[197]

A third category of adult care centers, often subsumed under the medical model, targets their services to specific categories of care recipients, such as those with diagnosed dementias, such as Alzheimer's disease. Conservative estimates are that one out of five centers is dedicated to these cognitively impaired populations.

A small share of centers accept very low-income Medicaid recipients. State governments have a special interest in funding adult day care centers to the extent that they delay or postpone the nursing home occupancy of Medicaid-eligible older people.[198] These typically operate under the medical model, because under the waiver program older recipients must be impaired enough to be admitted into a Medicaid-funded nursing home.

MAJOR BENEFITS OF ADULT DAY CARE

The wide array of health and long-term supports and services provided by an interdisciplinary group of professionals at a single location makes adult day services an attractive option for physically and cognitively frail older people.[199] They hold particular promise for those discharged from hospitals who might otherwise need nursing home care. Older people enjoy the following benefits from this option:

- They can remain in their current homes even if they have difficulty managing their physical and cognitive impairments.[200]
- They receive assistance managing their health and physical activities. Their health problems are treated before they worsen and require emergency room or hospital admittance.
- Those with dementia benefit from therapeutic activities, such as art and music therapy, games, group activities, and exercise.[201]
- Through various planned activities and social opportunities, older people receive sensory and social stimulation that they may not get at home. Older adults report being satisfied and enjoying their time in these settings.[202]
- Family members can avoid quitting their jobs or relocating their loved ones to an assisted living residence or nursing home.[203] Adult day care provides an alternative to hiring direct care workers[204] and ensures that the older person will have needed assistance or emergency help during the workday.
- Family members get respite from their physically and emotionally draining responsibilities for at least some periods during a typical week.[205] They have time to refuel, preventing burnout and allowing them to perform their caregiving duties more vigorously and longer.[206] These family caregivers also experience less depression and an overall increase in well-being,[207] especially those caring for a loved one with Alzheimer's disease, who regularly confront challenging behaviors such as verbal aggressiveness, agitation, or incontinence.[208]
- Adult day care familiarizes family caregivers with the supportive and health services options available for when their loved one is not at the day care center.[209]

COSTS AND FUNDING

In 2014, the national median daily rate for adult day care was $65 (or $16,900 annually),[210] but annual median costs varied widely across the country (e.g., from $6,500 in Alabama to $35,100 in Vermont).[211] Predictably, when their rates are more affordable, older people are more likely to use them.

Funding for these centers comes from a variety of sources, with more than 55% from public sources, state Medicaid waiver programs, OAA, the VA, and the Social

Services Block Grant; 26% from private-pay participants; and 17% from charitable contributions, grants, or a parent organization, such as a nursing home, hospital, or nonprofit social service agency. Only 2% comes from private insurance sources.[212]

AN IMPERFECT ALTERNATIVE

Unfortunately, adult day care centers are not available everywhere, and some states and communities are especially underserved. Nearly 30% of adult centers have a waiting list.[213] Older people living in some rural locations often have to travel long distances to reach their day care sites.[214]

Even when adult care centers are available, they may not provide the same set of services or accommodate the same levels of impairment. Consequently, whether the needs of older people match up to the services offered by a given center depends more on where they live.[215] For example, a center may not cater to those with more severe physical or cognitive impairments or those who need multiple workers to assist them with their ADLs or to calm their disruptive behavior problems. Nursing home admission may be the only alternative for older people who require such services.[216] Adult day centers generally do not delay such placements.[217]

Much of this variation is a result of adult day centers being regulated or certified by state governments rather than the federal government. States also vary greatly in their rules regarding what services adult day centers provide, their hours, and whom they serve, and only some centers serve older people with dementia.[218] The centers also have different mandatory and optional service requirements when accepting new older participants (e.g., must need ADL assistance or specific nursing services) and different requirements for staff-to-participant ratios, staff training, and monitoring procedures. Only some have staff who can communicate with foreign-born clients, and only some states require that their adult day care centers provide transportation.[219]

Finding funding is a continual problem. Most adult centers are not well funded or financially secure.[220] Because they rely so much on public support, they are susceptible to federal budget-tightening efforts.

PROGRAM OF ALL-INCLUSIVE CARE FOR THE ELDERLY (PACE)

Experts argue that older people who receive both postacute Medicare-funded services and Medicaid-funded long-term care services are served by two sets of providers who operate in different administrative silos, creating an inefficient and overly costly care environment. Consequently, professionals and direct care workers operating within these two programs often fail to communicate what services they offer, coordinate care directives, or consult on client outcomes.[221] As one group of experts expresses,

> Medicare focuses on limiting hospital and postacute use and costs, resulting in shifts in care to the Medicaid long-term care program. That program, in turn, has little incentive to reduce Medicare hospital and emergency room use.[222]

Consider the older person who leaves the hospital and requires home care and medication management. If long-term care providers (funded under Medicaid) do not carefully manage her personal assistance and prescribed medications, the latter ordered by a hospital physician (covered under Medicare), the risk is greater that the older person will end up in an emergency room or back into a hospital bed.

The PACE care model attempts to eliminate these types of problems by offering its older participants—typically dually eligible for both the Medicare and Medicaid programs—one-stop shopping for all of their needed healthcare and long-term care services, even as they remain in their own homes or apartments.[223] Although its mission is to keep older people in community settings, about 7% of PACE participants reside in a nursing home. The PACE program covers these costs and continues to coordinate enrollees' care.[224]

PACE users are typically very poor and eligible for admission in their state's Medicaid-subsidized nursing home beds. They tend to be women older than 80, with multiple acute and chronic medical problems (e.g., heart disease, respiratory disease, and diabetes) and more than three ADL limitations (e.g., walking, bathing, dressing, and toileting).[225]

Many PACE programs specifically serve the low-income occupants of affordable rental housing apartments funded with government assistance (Chapter 9), and nearly a third of their adult day care centers are located on or near these buildings.[226] This linkage is not by chance: Program organizers determined that *"finding supported housing was often a barrier to living in the community."*[227]

A Very Comprehensive Healthcare and Long-Term Care Model

Older people enrolled in PACE programs enjoy the benefits of a comprehensive array of primary, specialty, and acute medical and hospitalization care, pharmaceuticals, rehabilitative services, and coordinated medical oversight, as well as all of the homemaking and self-care assistance they need to make independent living possible.[228] They receive in-home visits and attend the day care center during the week (on average 3 days).[229]

An interdisciplinary team of geriatric physicians, nurse practitioners, registered nurses, social workers, therapists, nutritionists, personal care assistants, and transportation workers provide these services. When they enroll, older participants receive a comprehensive in-home assessment of their medical and care needs and an individualized treatment plan that includes a medical care regimen and long-term care plan. The team of professionals continually monitors and responds to any changes in their status.

A typical PACE participant receives instructions from day care nursing staff on how to live a healthier lifestyle, on-site center care from her geriatric physician for diabetes, on-site therapeutic services (including physical, occupational, or speech), a follow-up home visit for a vascular disease problem, help with insulin injections from a nurse who regularly visits her home, help installing grab bars in her dwelling, and regular in-home personal care assistance to help with her ADL limitations.

A Managed Care Financial Model

PACE is also distinctive because it is a managed care program that relies on a capitated financing approach. This is a national trend: Managed care now accounts for an increasingly higher share of long-term services and support expenditures (6.6% in 2012).[230] PACE operators receive a monthly payment per older participant that combines a lump sum from Medicare with a state-negotiated Medicaid payment. This funding approach assumes that the PACE program can cover the entire range of necessary care and services for its participants, based on this average per client cost-of-care remuneration. As is true for most managed care approaches, because the PACE operators assume full risk for covering all of the medical and care needs of these very vulnerable people, they are motivated to avoid costly hospitalizations and nursing home admissions, which are still their financial responsibility.

EFFECTIVENESS OF *PACE*

Most studies offer very positive evaluations of the PACE program, reporting low dropout rates and improvements in the health and care of its frail older participants, including[231]

> greater adult day healthcare use, lower skilled home health visits, fewer hospitalizations, fewer nursing home admissions, higher contact with primary care, longer survival rates, an increased number of days in the community, better health, better quality of life, greater satisfaction with overall care arrangements, and better functional status.

Studies in 2012 and 2014 show that the managed care approach of PACE is cost effective and produces better outcomes than fee-for-service models, although for some states the Medicaid capitated costs are higher.[232]

Nonetheless, PACE is a small program. As of 2013, it served only about 23,000 enrollees annually at some 98 sites in 31 states. To the disappointment of its advocates, its growth has been slow.[233] Participants in the programs must give up their primary care physicians, which is often an unappealing option. The enrollment process takes months.[234] It has limited appeal to older people who are not Medicaid-eligible because they are typically responsible for high out-of-pocket costs.

Large startup capital expenditures (e.g., buildings and equipment) are a major disincentive for prospective developers of this option. Considerable expertise and knowledge are needed to operate and maintain its complex care and administrative infrastructure.[235] It is also difficult to get a program started because of challenging federal and state bureaucratic requirements.[236] Medicaid programs are administered and financed differently in every state, making uniform development and operational procedures far more difficult. Expansion is also hampered by the absence of qualified staff and highly trained multidisciplinary staff and geriatricians, especially in rural America.

CONCLUSION

Older people must sometimes rely on formal care if they want to age in place successfully. Their ability to secure appropriate assistance often depends on their ability to afford private-sector options or to become eligible for public programs. In either case, they must quickly learn to negotiate an incredibly complex array of programs, providers, and funding sources to piece together an appropriate package of services. Some older people have an easier time because they occupy states and communities with easier-to-access and more comprehensive home- and community-based options. Income levels are critical, and paradoxically, middle-income older people sometimes have the greatest difficulties securing affordable care and assistance. The quality of their care also depends on a host of factors, many outside of their control. However, even the best care offered by professionals and direct care workers does not fully substitute for the assistance provided by family members.

The next chapter offers various community-based strategies designed to improve the odds of older adults finding formal care that is best tailored to their current unmet needs. We will scrutinize yet another layer of community resources designed to make it more feasible for older people to age in place.

NOTES

1. (Bella, 2011)
2. ElderLaw Answers, accessed March 27, 2013: http://www.elderlawanswers.com/home-care-agencies-hiring-unqualified-caregivers-study-finds-9966.
3. (Federal Interagency Forum on Aging-Related Statistics, 2012)
4. (Commission on Affordable Housing and Health Facility Needs for Seniors in the 21st Century, 2002; Lipman et al., 2010)
5. (Feng, Fennell, Tyler, Clark, & Mor, 2011; Kaiser Commission, 2013b). In 2011, there were 1,366,390 occupied Medicaid- or Medicare-certified nursing home beds, and about 85%, or about 1,161,431, were occupied by people age 65 and older. There were about 40.3 million people age 65 and older in the United States.
6. (AARP, 2009)
7. (Alecxih, 2006)
8. (U.S. Congressional Budget Office, 2013)
9. (U.S. Congressional Budget Office, 2013)
10. (Feng et al., 2011, p. 1360)
11. (Miller et al., 2009)
12. (Dugas 2013)
13. (Ng, Harrington, & Kitchener, 2010)
14. (Miller et al., 2009, p. 8)
15. (Finkelstein, Garcia, Netherland, & Walker, 2008)
16. (Summer & Howard, 2011)
17. (Institute for the Future of Aging Services, 2007)
18. (Finkelstein et al., 2008)
19. (Finkelstein et al., 2008, p. 22)
20. (Stone, 2011)
21. (Bragg & Hansen, 2011)
22. (Hanarhan, 2010–2011)
23. (Stone & Harahan, 2010)
24. (Hanarhan, 2010–2011)
25. (Stone, 2011)
26. (Institute for the Future of Aging Services, 2007; Leutz, 2011; Long Term Care Coordinating Council Human Services Agency of San Francisco, 2009)
27. (Stone, 2011, p. 65)
28. The 2010 Affordable Care Act adds a fourth category: psychiatric aides (Seavey, 2011).

29. (Paraprofessional Healthcare Institute, 2014)
30. (Seavey & Marquand, 2011)
31. (Seavey, 2011)
32. (Seavey & Marquand, 2011)
33. (Paraprofessional Healthcare Institute, 2014)
34. (Paraprofessional Healthcare Institute, 2014)
35. (Paraprofessional Healthcare Institute, 2013)
36. (Seavey & Marquand, 2011)
37. (Seavey & Marquand, 2011, p. 18)
38. (Paraprofessional Healthcare Institute, 2014)
39. (Seavey & Marquand, 2011)
40. (Seavey, 2011, p. 30)
41. (Harrington et al., 2009)
42. (Paraprofessional Healthcare Institute, 2013)
43. (Golant, 2003d)
44. (Leutz, 2011)
45. (Leutz, 2011)
46. (Harrington et al., 2009)
47. (Lindquist et al., 2012)
48. (Lindquist, Jain, Tam, Martin, & Baker, 2011, p. 474)
49. (Grossman, Kitchener, Mullan, & Harrington, 2007)
50. (National Consumer Voice for Quality Long-Term Care, 2012)
51. (Scharlach et al., 2007, p. 760)
52. (National Consumer Voice for Quality Long-Term Care, 2012)
53. (Lindquist et al., 2012, pp. 1256–1257)
54. (Grossman et al., 2007)
55. (National Consumer Voice for Quality Long-Term Care, 2012, p. 9)
56. (Stone, 2004)
57. (Seavey & Marquand, 2011)
58. (Seavey & Marquand, 2011)
59. (National Consumer Voice for Quality Long-Term Care, 2012, pp. 17–18)
60. (O'Shaughnessy, 2013)
61. (Johnson, Toohey, & Wiener, 2007)
62. (U.S. Department of Health and Human Services, 2012)
63. (Lind, 2012)
64. (World Health Organization, 2007)
65. (Housing Assistance Council, 2012)
66. (Issa & Zedlewski, 2011)
67. (Social Security Administration, 2014)
68. (Short, 2013)
69. (Issa & Zedlewski, 2011)
70. (Golant, 2006)
71. (National Consumer Voice for Quality Long-Term Care, 2011)
72. (Knickman, Hunt, Snell, Alecxih, & Kennell, 2003)
73. (Moore, 2009)
74. (Bella, 2011)
75. (Kaiser Commission on Medicaid and the Uninsured, 2013)
76. (The Lewin Group, 2010b)
77. (Kaiser Commission, 2013a)
78. (Howard, Ng, & Harrington, 2011)
79. Other private spending includes money for nursing homes and home health services. Other public spending includes Department of Veterans Affairs, state and local programs, and general assistance spending for nursing homes and home health services.

80. (Kaiser Commission on Medicaid and the Uninsured, 2013)
81. Other tabulations leave out Medicare expenditures because they are not strictly paying for long-term care. In 2011 Medicaid paid for 62.3%, out-of-pocket costs 21.6%, other public programs 4.6%, and private insurance 11.6% of long-term care expenditures (O'Shaughnessy, 2013).
82. (U.S. Department of Health and Human Services, 2012)
83. (Talega, 2013)
84. Or leaving home is not medically recommended because of older person's condition, and leaving home is not possible without help (such as using a wheelchair or walker, needing special transportation, or getting help from another person).
85. (The Lewin Group, 2010b)
86. (Wiener, Anderson, Khatutsky, Kaganova, & O'Keeffe, 2013)
87. (Moses, 2004)
88. The following summary of the Medicaid program is necessarily brief and inevitably oversimplifies the workings of one of the most complex public programs in the United States. For more detailed overviews, see the following: (Howard et al., 2011; Shirk, 2006; Stone, 2010, 2011)
89. (Fox-Grage & Redfoot, 2011)
90. (Eiken et al., 2014)
91. (Stone, 2011)
92. (O'Shaughnessy, 2013)
93. (Ng et al., 2010, p. 24)
94. (Eiken, Burwell, & Sredl, 2013)
95. (Stone, 2011)
96. (Kaye, 2012; Ng et al., 2010)
97. (Shirk, 2006, p. 7)
98. (Konetzka, Karon, & Potter, 2012)
99. (Stone, 2011)
100. The Patient Protection and Affordable Care Act, P.L. 111-148, enacted March 23, 2010 (Justice, 2010).
101. (Harrington, Ng, Laplante, & Kaye, 2012)
102. (Stone, 2011)
103. (Watts, Musumeci, & Reaves, 2013)
104. (Morris et al, 2013)105. (Watts, 2011, p. 3)
106. (Watts, 2011)
107. (Stone, 2010, p. 5)
108. (Reinhard, Kassner, Houser, Ujvari, Mollica, & Hendrickson, 2014, p. 9)
109. (Reinhard, Kassner, Houser, Ujvari, Mollica, & Hendrickson, 2014)
110. (Eiken et al., 2014, Table AL)
111. (Howard et al., 2011)
112. (Wenzlow, Borck, Miller, Doty, & Drabek, 2013).
113. (Ng et al., 2010)
114. (Stone, 2011)
115. (Howard et al., 2011; Ng et al., 2010)
116. (Wenzlow, Borck, Miller, Doty, & Drabek, 2013)
117. (Eiken et al., 2013; Kane et al., 2013; Weissert & Frederick, 2013)
118. (Grabowski, 2006; Huss, Stuck, Rubenstein, Egger, & Clough-Gorr, 2008; Muramatsu et al., 2007; Wiener & Brown, 2004)
119. (Muramatsu et al., 2007)
120. (Weissert & Frederick, 2013)
121. (Kaye, 2012, 1196)
122. (Stone, 2011, p. 92)
123. (Eiken et al., 2013)
124. (Fox-Grage & Walls, 2013, p. 1)
125. (Mollica, Kassner, Walker, & Houser, 2009)

126. (Kaye, 2012, pp. 1200–1201)
127. (Ng et al., 2010)
128. (Shirk, 2006)
129. (Lehning & Austin, 2010, p. 47)
130. (O'Shaughnessy, 2011, p. 1)
131. (O'Shaughnessy, 2008)
132. In 2012, the Administration for Community Living brought together the Administration on Aging, the Office on Disability, and the Administration on Developmental Disabilities into a single agency.
133. (National Association of Area Agencies on Aging, 2013)
134. (National Association of Area Agencies on Aging and Scripps Gerontology Center, 2011)
135. (Kunkel, Reece, & Straker, 2014). Altogether, the aging services network currently includes 56 state agencies on aging, 629 area agencies on aging, 244 tribal and Native American organizations, 2 organizations serving Native Hawaiians, and 30,000 local service provider organizations. See (Scan Foundation, 2011). The aging services network not only administers the Older Americans Act but also is responsible for the day-to-day management of other federal programs, including Medicaid waiver services programs, the Social Services Block Grant, and the State Health Insurance Program (SHIP). Some state agencies on aging also administer services provided by their adult protective services agencies to protect against abuse, neglect, and exploitation.
136. (National Association of Area Agencies on Aging, 2013; O'Shaughnessy, 2008)
137. (National Association of Area Agencies on Aging and Scripps Gerontology Center, 2011; Kunkel, Reece, & Straker, 2014)
138. (O'Shaughnessy, 2008)
139. (World Health Organization, 2007)
140. Funded under Title II and Title IV of the Older Americans Act.
141. (O'Shaughnessy, 2010)
142. (O'Shaughnessy, 2010; Kunkle, Reece, & Straker, 2013).
143. (O'Shaughnessy, 2010)
144. (Summer & Howard, 2011)
145. (O'Shaughnessy, 2010)
146. (O'Shaughnessy, 2011; Fox-Grage & Ujvari, 2014)
147. (Fox-Grage & Ujvari, 2014)
148. Kunkle, Reece, & Straker, 2014, p. 31
149. (O'Shaughnessy, 2008, p. 18)
150. (Thomas & Mor, 2013, p. 1216)
151. (O'Shaughnessy, 2014)
152. (Altshuler & Schimmel, 2010)
153. (National Association of Area Agencies on Aging, 2013)
154. (Altshuler & Schimmel, 2010; Thomas & Mor, 2013)
155. (Altshuler & Schimmel, 2010, p. 7)
156. (Robinson, Lucado, & Schur, 2012)
157. (Benson & Aldrich, 2013)
158. (U.S. Government Accountability Office, 2011b)
159. (U.S. Government Accountability Office, 2011b)
160. (National Association of Area Agencies on Aging, 2013)
161. (National Association of Area Agencies on Aging and Scripps Gerontology Center, 2011)
162. (U.S. Government Accountability Office, 2011b, p. 34)
163. (U.S. Government Accountability Office, 2011b, p. 33)
164. *Churches* generically refers to churches, synagogues, mosques, and temples patronized by all religions and denominations.
165. (Tirrito, 2000, p. 59; see also Cnaan, Boddie, & Kang, 2005)
166. (Doty, Mahoney, & Sciegaj, 2010, p. 49)
167. (Doty et al., 2010, p. 49)

168. Cash and Counseling Demonstration Grants.
169. (Stone, 2011)
170. (Squillace & Firman, 2002, p. 9)
171. A pseudonym.
172. (National Resource Center for Participant-Directed Services, 2014). A small share of enrollees are nonelderly and intellectually and developmentally disabled adults.
173. (Doty et al., 2010)
174. (Doty et al., 2010)
175. (Doty et al., 2010, p. 54)
176. September 1, 2011: http://www.worldnews.se/news/21467/hear-jazz-legends-in-historic-bohemian-caverns-in-washington-dc/
177. http://www.ncoa.org/national-institute-of-senior-centers/
178. (Pardasani & Thompson, 2012)
179. (Pardasani & Thompson, 2012)
180. (Dal Santo, 2009)
181. (Dal Santo, 2009)
182. (Dal Santo, 2009; Turner, 2004)
183. (Florida Department of Elder Affairs, 2004)
184. (Krout, Oggins, & Holmes, 2000)
185. (Pardasani & Thompson, 2012)
186. http://nadsa.org/learn-more/about-adult-day-services/
187. (Harris-Kojetin, Sengupta, Park-Lee, & Valverde, 2013)
188. (MetLife Mature Market Institute, 2010a)
189. (Harris-Kojetin et al., 2013)
190. (Anderson, Dabelko-Schoeny, & Johnson, 2013)
191. (Harris-Kojetin et al., 2013)
192. (Anderson et al., 2013)
193. (Harris-Kojetin et al., 2013; MetLife Mature Market Institute, 2010a)
194. (Anderson et al., 2013)
195. (Anderson et al., 2013)
196. (MetLife Mature Market Institute, 2010a)
197. (MetLife Mature Market Institute, 2010a)
198. (O'Keefe & Sibenaler, 2006)
199. (Anderson et al., 2013)
200. (O'Keefe & Sibenaler, 2006)
201. (Aaronson et al., 1995; Creech, Hallam, McQueen, & Varvarigou, 2013)
202. (Aaronson et al., 1995)
203. (O'Keefe & Sibenaler, 2006)
204. (Skarupski et al., 2008)
205. (Fields, Anderson, & Dabelko-Schoeny, 2014)
206. (MetLife Mature Market Institute, 2010a)
207. (Gaugler, Zarit, Townsend, Stephens, & Greene, 2003; Gitlin, Reever, Dennis, Mathieu, & Hauck, 2006)
208. (Gaugler, Jarrott, et al., 2003; Gaugler, Zarit, et al., 2003; Gitlin, Reever, Dennis, Mathieu, & Hauck, 2006; Zarit, et al., 2014)
209. (Skarupski et al., 2008)
210. (Genworth Financial, 2014)
211. (Genworth Financial, 2012)
212. (MetLife Mature Market Institute, 2010a)
213. (MetLife Mature Market Institute, 2010a)
214. (Silverstein, Wong, & Brueck, 2008)
215. (MetLife Mature Market Institute, 2010a)
216. (O'Keefe & Sibenaler, 2006)

217. (Fields et al., 2014)
218. (Siebenaler, O'Keeffe, O'Keeffe, Brown, & Koetse, 2005)
219. (Silverstein et al., 2008)
220. (Anderson et al., 2013)
221. (Ng et al., 2010)
222. (Ng et al., 2010, p. 27)
223. (Hirth, Baskins, & Dever-Bumba, 2009)
224. National PACE Association: http://www.npaonline.org/website/article.asp?id=12
225. (Hirth et al., 2009)
226. (National PACE Association, 2003)
227. (Hansen & Hewitt, 2012, p. 39)
228. (Hansen & Hewitt, 2012)
229. (Greenwood, 2001)
230. (Eiken et al., 2014)
231. (Hirth et al., 2009, p. 158)
232. (Ghosh, Schmitz, & Brown, 2014; Hansen & Hewitt, 2012)
233. National Pace Association: http://www.npaonline.org/
234. (Hansen & Hewitt, 2012)
235. (Hansen & Hewitt, 2012; Hirth et al., 2009)
236. (Stone, 2011)

9

COMMUNITY, NEIGHBORHOOD, AND CLUSTERED HOUSING SOLUTIONS

No person is an island—by our human nature, we need one another. Like other primates, we do best in small groups such as villages or neighborhoods, even when located in urban settings. By acknowledging this human condition, we can better design and build homes and neighborhoods to maximize human interaction and interdependence, particularly in later life. By sharing common space, pooling and sharing resources, and fostering reciprocity and mutual support, we give up some privacy and the illusion of "independence" in exchange for deeper human connections and potentially a more meaningful quality of life.[1]

THE COMMUNITY SOLUTION

A growing number of state, county, and municipal governments, regional planning agencies, philanthropic groups, and grassroots organizations are attempting to make their communities more *age-friendly*, that is compatible with the lifestyles and ca-pabilities of their older occupants.[2] In these resilient places *"older people are actively involved, valued, and supported with infrastructure and services that effectively accommodate their needs."*[3]

In the United States, the Advantage Initiative, developed by the Visiting Nurse Service of New York,[4] offers a representative set of goals for these places to achieve:

- Optimize physical and mental health and well-being (e.g., access to preventive health services and medical, social, and palliative services)

215

- Maximize independence (e.g., accessible transportation, support from family and other caregivers)
- Address basic population needs (e.g., affordable housing, safety, service information)
- Promote social and civic engagement (e.g., involvement in community life, opportunities for meaningful paid and voluntary work)
- Make aging issues a community-wide priority

A research initiative by Stanford Center on Longevity and MetLife Mature Market Institute adds safe neighborhoods, emergency preparedness, and healthful food to its list of "livable community" goals.[5] And the initiatives promoted by age-friendly communities are also not easily distinguishable from the Healthy Community initiative of the U.S. Environmental Protection Agency, which focuses on "smart growth" or sustainable community planning efforts (see "Rearranging Land Uses and Changing Zoning Regulations" later in this chapter).[6]

A catalyst for these age-friendly initiatives was the World Health Organization (WHO), Global Age-Friendly Cities project, which was started in 2006. It initially involved some 33 cities in 22 countries where leaders analyzed their communities and neighborhoods for their capacity to support what the WHO called its Active Ageing Framework[7]:

> Active ageing is the process of optimizing opportunities for health, participation and security in order to enhance quality of life as people age.

WHO's network now includes more than 200 cities and communities in 26 countries, but hundreds more urban and rural communities not formally linked to WHO also embrace its conception of active aging.[8]

These healthy or age-friendly community initiatives are driven by two fundamental principles. The first is a reiteration of the position of Rowe and Kahn and their New Gerontology paradigm (Chapter 1) that successful aging is also active aging. That is, getting old by itself is no justification for becoming disengaged and failing to make contributions to the places we live.[9]

The second principle, not addressed by Rowe and Kahn, is that the material and social opportunities or resources found in the buildings, neighborhoods, and communities occupied by older people are partly responsible for whether they keep active, engaged, and independent.[10] Accordingly, if older people experience activity declines or disrupted lifestyles that threaten their ability to age in place, it is partly because of the poor quality of life offered by their places of residence and their absent age-friendly living environments.[11]

This chapter examines how so-called age-friendly communities are influencing the physical health of older people, their connections with the world outside their dwellings, their access to long-term services and supports that allow them to age in place, and, when they seek to move, their ability to find affordable rental dwellings, sometimes offering supportive services (housing-care solutions).

PROMOTING GOOD PHYSICAL HEALTH AND DISEASE PREVENTION

Proponents of the New Gerontology paradigm stress that older people must be proactive about maintaining good health and preventing disease and illness. Age-friendly community advocates take this argument one step further by emphasizing that the communities or neighborhoods occupied by older people should have the facilities or resources to help them achieve these goals. Many studies show that when early interventions target vulnerable community-residing older people, they have lower hospitalization and nursing home admission rates, and even lower mortality rates. These community efforts can make possible three categories of prevention activities.[12]

Primary prevention activities encourage older people to practice healthy lifestyles. Older people must get enough exercise (e.g., stamina building, tai chi, agility, muscle strength, walking programs), eat well, practice good dental hygiene, get enough sleep, not smoke, wear seat belts, get needed vaccinations (e.g., annual flu shot or one-time pneumonia and shingles shot), practice responsible sexual behaviors, and take their prescribed medications.

Secondary prevention activities focus on detecting health and functioning problems before signs or symptoms of a disease are evident or when they are at an early stage. This category broadly includes comprehensive wellness screening and diagnostic checks for health problems such as heart disease, hypertension, diabetes, osteoporosis, obesity, vision or hearing loss, problem drinking, and breast, colorectal, and prostate cancers. It also includes assessments of the older person's ability to perform activities of daily living (ADLs) and instrumental ADLs (IADLs) as well as evaluations for mental health problems, including depressive symptoms and cognitive declines due to dementias, such as Alzheimer's disease.

Tertiary prevention activities prevent the worsening of some disease or functional limitation, to avoid further complications and to prevent or stave off death. This category includes monitoring and treating the high glucose levels of the diabetic or the high cholesterol of a stroke patient or assessing the side effects of a surgical or pharmaceutical solution. These efforts also focus on better educating older people about their disease progression, warning signs of a deteriorated condition, and self-care after a surgical procedure.

Some communities have attempted to establish less-conventional sites where professionals can conduct these preventive assessments. Although medical professionals traditionally work in ambulatory (outpatient) care centers (e.g., clinician offices, urgent care centers, hospital outpatient clinics, mobile wellness clinics), more innovative communities place medical personnel at adult care centers, libraries, educational institutions, recreational facilities, pharmacies, and health fairs.[13] Forward-looking communities can also convert a vacant strip mall into a "medical mall" that offers older people most of their medical services at one destination.[14] Target, CVS, Walmart, grocery stores, and shopping malls are now the sites of retail-based health clinics. Older people are more likely to attend these places because they are more conspicuous and accessible. Their geographic availability especially benefits older people who are otherwise fearful of patronizing health providers or who live in less population-dense suburban and rural areas.

Although home care to provide rehabilitation or skilled nursing care is now very common, we are also witnessing an increase in the number of physicians who are available to make house calls, a throwback to the 1950s, when such practices were more common.[15] Another group of professionals, known as homecare clinicians, also provides more individualized care treatments in older people's homes. They *"coordinate the work of various providers (e.g., clinics, emergency rooms, hospitals, nursing homes, and primary care and specialist physicians) and facilitate communication among them"* in addition to being directly engaged in care.[16] Another effort, the Care Transitions Intervention Program, brings a social worker or nurse to the homes of older persons after a hospital discharge to ensure they are correctly following care instructions for their recuperation.[17]

In older people's homes, it is often easier for healthcare professionals to identify health and functional limitations that may jeopardize coping strategies and to tailor interventions to improve health, safety, and independence.[18] More cost-effective and reliable portable medical equipment and telemedicine technologies are increasingly making such diagnostic testing and in-home care more feasible.

These preventive efforts—which most experts agree are still inadequate—have lowered hospital readmission rates, increased medication compliance, improved the performance of activities, and reduced nursing home admission rates.[19] In recognition of the importance of improving the coordination of healthcare responses, the 2010 Patient Protection and Affordable Care Act included several provisions designed to allow more comprehensive care of Medicare beneficiaries.[20]

Communities can also reduce the health threats created by extreme hazardous events, such as hurricanes, tornadoes, floods, and fires.[21] Older people are especially vulnerable when disasters strike, and they have higher injury and mortality rates.[22] The inadequate postdisaster recovery efforts in New Orleans after Hurricane Katrina in 2005 dramatically illustrated the folly of poor community preparation. For example, nursing homes with medically frail older occupants had no guarantee of help from federal, state, or local emergency responders.[23] Nor were they considered priority places to have their power restored or their generators refilled with diesel fuel.

Although experts now believe that state and local emergency management organizations can reduce injuries and deaths by using carefully planned escape routes and rescue plans to evacuate people who cannot leave independently, these are not always the correct solutions to cope with extreme environmental events.[24] Older people living in assisted living residences, board and care, or nursing homes are often very frail, have health problems, or experience serious cognitive impairments. Consequently, evacuation and placement in poor-quality short-term shelter environments can lead to increases in hospitalization and death rates.[25] Evacuate-all plans must carefully consider not just the usual hazardous effects and the vulnerability of buildings housing older people but also the increased morbidity and mortality risks associated with moving and accommodating a vulnerable older population. Consequently, there will be disaster situations where it may be more advisable to keep the *"residents safe in the facility— called sheltering in place."*[26]

CONNECTIVITY

Older people must be able to reach local businesses, services, and amenities. Communities and neighborhoods have initiated two planning responses to make these resources more accessible:

- Make it easier and safer for older people to use all modes of transportation, including walking.
- Change land use patterns and zoning regulations to increase the probabilities that the preferred destinations of older people are within walking or public transit range.

EASIER AND SAFER MODES OF TRANSPORTATION

DRIVING

Both experts and younger motorists question whether older people should drive at all. In contrast, forward-looking communities are initiating driver education programs designed to help older drivers compensate for their declines in vision, cognition, and psychomotor and physical functioning or at least to make them more aware of their limitations (Chapter 4, Figure 4.5). When these efforts fail, they strive to find them more feasible transportation alternatives.[27]

State vehicle agencies that regulate driving practices vary widely in their licensing standards. Consequently, older drivers experiencing physical or cognitive limitations have much more difficulty renewing their driver's licenses in some states.[28] Many states, concerned for the safety of older people, require them to pass more stringent driving examinations at particular chronological ages when they renew their vehicle licenses. Others restrict their driving to daylight hours or within so many miles from their homes. Most have established medical advisory boards that establish clinical standards for fit older drivers or adjudicate driver disputes after their rulings.[29] They also may encourage or require medical professionals to report older patients who are medically impaired.[30]

Many transportation experts believe that better road design and travel conditions are the answer. They recommend the following traffic engineering and road design changes to help older drivers compensate for their physical or cognitive impairments[31]:

Slow Down: Reduce vehicle travel speeds in areas where drivers and pedestrians interact and where older drivers and pedestrians need more time to make decisions. Reengineer roadways for slower speeds by changing curb radii and perceived or real lane widths, or by replacing typical intersections with roundabouts.

Make It Easy: Make the physical layout of the transportation network easy to navigate for older drivers and pedestrians. To remove some of the complexity of intersections, provide travelers a connected network of streets with lower-speed routes and intersections that are easier to maneuver.

Enjoy the View: Make it easy for drivers and pedestrians to notice, read, understand, and respond to visual cues and information. Make the roadway more intuitive by reducing the visual clutter of signs, creating better access management, and improving landscaping, signage, and lighting.

However, other experts believe there is *"no magic policy that will make the roads safe."*[32] More positively, time and the promise of technological innovations may be on the side of the older driver. Every year brings new car technologies that make driving easier and safer. Engineers are designing cars to help drivers compensate for their loss of driver skills (Chapter 4), reduce crashes, and make surviving a crash without injury more likely.[33] Cars now can warn drivers when they are backing up unsafely, following too close to another vehicle, drifting into another lane, or approaching center dividers. The ultimate technological solution may be closer than we think, in the form of driverless cars that remove driver skills as a risk factor because ubiquitous vehicle and road sensors are operating the vehicles.[34]

Public Transit

Experts propose three categories of community responses to eliminate barriers that restrict transit use by older people (Figure 9.1). The first two sets of potential improvements target older people who are limited in their use of public transportation because of physical or financial limitations. A third set targets those who currently lack adequate information about their transit alternatives.

Many experts emphasize the benefits of increasing the availability of demand-responsive or paratransit alternatives (also known as door-to-door, shared-ride, and supplemental transportation programs), which use paid or volunteer drivers to pick up older people at their homes (usually using vans or minibuses but sometimes cars) and take them right to their specific destinations.[35] This category also includes subcontracting a community's existing taxi fleet of cars to charge reduced fares to lower-income older passengers.

These services may be funded or administered by various public entities: Area Agencies on Aging or Aging and Disability Resource Centers under the Older Americans Act, Centers for Medicare & Medicaid Services (Medicaid waiver programs), the Federal Transit Administration, Department of Veterans Affairs, and state governments. Support from nonprofit organizations may include senior centers, churches, hospitals, adult day centers, health and social service providers, and volunteer groups.[36]

Typically, the use of these paratransit alternatives requires an older person to call in advance to reserve round-trip pickups on a certain day and time. Some programs recruit volunteers to drive seniors in their ordinary vehicles, although liability and insurance concerns discourage this practice. One specific category of paratransit services fulfills the legal requirements of the Americans with Disabilities Act (ADA) of 1990, which requires public transit agencies to provide additional transportation to passengers with disabilities (including older adults) who cannot access existing public bus modes or safely get to transit stops within three-quarters of a mile from their homes.[37]

One of the largest U.S. nonprofit paratransit providers, Independent Transportation Network (ITN), boasts that it operates in more than 20 urban and suburban areas and has provided older people with more than 600,000 rides. Trips for medical purposes were the most common, followed by trips for various consumer uses (e.g., hair

Figure 9.1. Making it easier for older people to use public transportation (Burkhardt, McGavock, Nelson, & Mitchell [2002])

Challenges	Potential improvements
Physical limitations	
Difficulties in boarding transit vehicles	Purchase low-floor vehicles; deploy ramps for boarding; construct raised platforms at major passenger boarding locations; have drivers assist in boarding/alighting as needed
Difficulties in traveling several blocks to access transit vehicles	Provide or contract for door-to-door service (priced at a fare consistent with recovering the full cost of service); make infrastructure improvements to walking environment (sidewalks, curb cuts); offer escort services; feeder service via paratransit, service routes, and contract service providers, including volunteers and taxicabs; more extensive service coverage
Problems traveling from a building to the curb to board a vehicle	Provide passenger assistance from the doors of buildings to vehicles
Inability to wait for extended periods outside	Provide shelters and benches at transit stops; improve schedule reliability; increase service frequency; institute automated vehicle arrival and departure technologies; establish short waiting times for transfers
Difficulties in identifying destinations	Audio and visual announcements of stops within the vehicle; augmented signage at stops
Inability to ride comfortably in certain vehicles	Provide reserved seating for older persons; ensure that seats are of appropriate materials and condition
Financial limitations	
Difficulties in affording the cost of travel	Reduce fares for needy older persons; seek subsidies for certain older riders or all older riders from local and state governments, merchants, professionals (smart card technologies assist in implementing these subsidies); contract for services with agencies employing volunteers as drivers and other staff to reduce the costs of individual trips
Overall public transportation subsidies make it difficult to target cost reductions to those most in need	Look to human service agencies to identify and provide financial support for those specific individuals in need of assistance through tokens or vouchers

Figure continued next page

Figure 9.1. *Continued*

Transit knowledge of older persons	
Lack of knowledge about and understanding of transit services by older persons	Expand outreach and education programs; look for models of transit services by older persons in other markets; develop affinity relationships; develop peer-to-peer training programs; create special incentives, such as free fares for using fixed-route instead of paratransit service
Ineffective customer education	Reach outside the transit industry for advice, counsel, and professional services in developing better programs for reaching customers
Failure to communicate with potential customers to encourage trial use of transit	Develop special customer training programs targeted to the particular needs, concerns, and interests of older persons

appointments, grocery shopping, pharmacies, and banks). Less important were trips for social and recreational purposes. Among the findings of their customer satisfaction surveys,[38]

- 94% of customers are "very satisfied" with the service they receive, with the people at ITN, and would recommend ITN to a friend.
- A majority of customers feel the cost of riding with ITN is either inexpensive or a fair price for the service they receive. Only 2% think it's too expensive.

An evaluation funded by Atlantic Philanthropies similarly showed that ITN customers reported *"a decrease in transportation difficulty"* and *"an increase in confidence in arranging personal transportation for daily needs."*

However, these demand-responsive transportation options have their downsides. Some older people attach a negative stigma to traveling in these vehicles. Others find these services unsuitable because they must plan their trips at least 24 hours in advance or cannot reach certain destinations because of their limited geographic coverage, especially at night and on weekends. Some services may be available only for certain categories of trips, such as visits to a doctor or medical facility. Because of their diverse and uncoordinated funding sources, they have different fare structures and eligibility requirements that may also confuse and turn off older consumers.[39]

Some services are further restricted to those with more serious disabilities even though more minor medical or cognition problems (e.g., *"the inability to quickly turn one's neck, or correctly judge the speed of an oncoming car"*) can limit driving abilities.[40] In other communities, the sponsoring agencies make these services available to only those with very low incomes.

Uneven state and local funding and philanthropic support for these affordable transportation services result in their availability varying widely, and in some communities demand outstrips supply. Overall, these paratransit services are expensive to operate and serve only a very small proportion of older people. Consequently, many experts believe that they *"will likely not be a viable strategy for addressing the community mobility needs of older individuals."*[41]

WALKING

Experts point to a variety of design solutions that can increase the availability and safety of walking opportunities for older Americans[42]:

- Sidewalks or other walking paths with even surfaces that do not end abruptly
- Sidewalks cleared of obstructions, debris, weeds, and weather-related hazards (e.g., snow and ice)
- Sidewalks repaired to eliminate broken pavement
- Sidewalks or other walking paths designed to avoid pedestrian–bicycle conflicts
- Safe street crossings, without abrupt changes in grade
- User-activated and audible signal crossing devices, allowing sufficient time to transverse
- More medians and traffic islands to create a safe refuge for pedestrians waiting to complete a crossing
- Traffic-calming devices (narrowed streets, lower speed limits)
- Curb extensions that extend the sidewalk into the parking lane and reduce effective street width
- Legible signage
- Well-lighted pathways to accommodate evening walks
- Benches and resting places, especially at transit stops
- Security from crime (e.g., more police patrols, surveillance cameras)
- Streetscape amenities with visual appeal
- Increased availability of parks and other recreational areas with physically attractive pathways, safe from crime

Older people benefit in three ways from the introduction of such improvements, especially near their dwellings.[43] First, walking is a form of exercise and thus a pathway to better physical health. This translates into a reduced risk of various diseases, especially coronary heart disease and obesity; more favorable cholesterol and glucose levels; increased cardiovascular fitness; fewer depressive symptoms; and even longer life.[44] Second, these walking improvements increase access to a variety of desired destinations, such as grocery stores, pharmacies, doctors, restaurants, and churches. Third, when transit stops or stations are reachable by safe and easy-to-negotiate walking paths, public transportation becomes a viable alternative.

Realistically, however, walking as a mode of transportation is of value only to certain segments of the older population. For average pedestrians, walking is feasible for distances up to a quarter of a mile. However, older people cannot tolerate such distances if they have physical limitations, rely on a cane or a walker, or are carrying packages.[45]

REARRANGING LAND USES AND CHANGING ZONING REGULATIONS

Advocates of "healthy" or "smart growth" communities often denigrate the conventional suburban developments occupied by older people because of their sprawling and residentially segregated land use patterns, restrictive single-family zoning regulations,[46] large open spaces, vacant lots, large parking expanses, and unconnected cul-de-sac streets, all of which make them inaccessible except by automobiles. Consequently, nondriving older suburban dwellers can be as isolated as occupants of rural counties.

It wasn't always this way. The occupants of our earliest cities and suburbs were able to reach most of their destinations by walking or public transit. These modes of access changed dramatically, however, as Americans demonstrated their preferences for automobile transportation and automobile-oriented residential subdivisions and as federal and state governments funded predominantly road expansion and improvements at the expense of public transit.

THE PROMISE OF NEW URBANISM COMMUNITIES

To reincarnate this past, planners and developers since the early 1980s have attempted to replicate the land use arrangements found in these traditional urban locales. Developers of these New Urbanism or smart growth communities aim to create settlement antidotes to our conventional suburban developments. They envision community development plans that would place common destinations within close walking distance via walking paths that are safe from crime, visually attractive, and responsive to pedestrians trying to avoid the dangers of high-speed vehicle traffic. A later variant of New Urbanism communities, *transit-oriented community developments,* were specifically designed to have public transit alternatives within walking distance, a historical throwback to America's streetcar and railroad suburbs of the late 19th and early 20th centuries.

To be clear, New Urbanism communities were not specifically designed with older people's mobility needs in mind, but their design features are well suited for people in late life. Everything in these communities is closer together because they are more compact and densely settled, and their dwellings, often with porches, are smaller and set close to sidewalks and streets. Unlike the dead-end cul-de-sac routes of today's traditional suburbs, New Urbanism communities have gridded street patterns where the blocks are shorter, intersections are more regularly spaced, and the roadways are not closed to through traffic.[47] This results in walking and street paths that are more convenient for pedestrian use, easier to navigate, and more accessible to other neighborhoods and nonresidential activities. This connectivity yields other benefits; for example, the response times of emergency vehicles are shorter because the availability of alternative routes reduces the likelihood of traffic jams.

The developers of these communities strive to include a variety of owned and rented dwellings of different sizes and prices—single-family detached houses, attached row houses, and multifamily apartments or condos—clustered together and catering to socioeconomically diverse households. They believe that this physical closeness will also help *"recapture the hometown feeling of yesteryear,"*[48] when the residents enjoyed more spontaneous social connections and felt a stronger sense of community.

Residential and nonresidential land uses are not spatially segregated but rather are mixed together so that dwellings are close to commercial or public land uses encompassing all manner of stores, services (e.g., grocery stores, doctors, accountants, home care providers), and businesses. People can live in apartments built above stores and businesses. At the bare minimum, their developers proposed that *"every residential neighborhood must include a corner store to provide its residents with their daily needs, from milk to aspirin."*[49]

But a true mix of uses would also include a neighborhood-scale shopping center (around 20,000 square feet) within walking distance that would include groceries, dry cleaner, and other daily needs. Here would also be the site for civic buildings, such as city halls, libraries, churches, and neighborhood recreation centers.[50] Public schools could share their unused space to accommodate a senior center, health clinic, or meal center.[51]

CRITICS OF NEW URBANISM COMMUNITIES

Not everyone is enthusiastic. Critics claim that only a small share of Americans find New Urbanism communities appealing, and they will always be nothing more than niche urban environments in a predominantly sprawling suburban America.[52] They argue that most Americans will reject these dwelling arrangements because they offer less separation from neighbors and street activity and thus less privacy. Moreover, when scrutinizing the existing examples of New Urbanism communities, they argue that their population or land use densities are still not high enough to support a network of public transit routes.[53]

Critics also point to many examples whereby these communities do not have the social inclusiveness of small town life. They consider them elitist, because in practice they appeal to upwardly mobile professionals seeking more urban places to live, and they are primarily car owners, not pedestrians or transit users.[54] Their houses are also expensive and out of reach of all but higher-income residents. Moreover, when New Urbanism communities evolve from gentrified neighborhoods once in decline, their higher rents, property taxes, and insurance costs force the original, lower-income homeowners and renters to move.[55]

Creating such neighborhoods or communities is also not easy. Private sector developers must be convinced of their economic and political viability. Their participation is needed to create compact housing developments, small stores, and nearby public parks while in the process demolishing vacant buildings and transforming commercial strips once dominated by parking lots.[56] However, developers face opposition when they attempt to replace "modern" single-use zoning to allow residential–nonresidential mixed use.[57] The introduction of these higher-density land use arrangements requires aggressive public advocacy efforts to change a locality's zoning policies, justify the allocation of government dollars, and convince community leaders of the benefits to their constituencies.[58]

If New Urbanism communities are to be true to their goals, public funding must be secured to ensure that some housing units, particularly apartments, will be affordable to low- and moderate-income older families.[59] But not all existing or prospective residents endorse inclusionary zoning requirements that promote affordable rental developments in their communities or encourage a socially diverse resident mix of owners and renters with both high and low incomes. Experts warn that modifying the status quo zoning code now benefiting existing (particularly large) landowners can cause them to leverage their strong political connections to stop any changes or even sue. Recent court cases have often been decided in their favor.[60]

Government funding sources must also be available to ensure the pedestrian-friendly design of sidewalks and roads, new street lighting, the creation of parks and other public spaces, and the installation of bus shelters and benches. And citizen participation—particularly the voices of older people and their advocates—is crucial.[61]

CLUSTERED HOUSING COMPLEXES: NORC-SSPS AND ELDER VILLAGES

Chapter 3 discusses the increased presence of neighborhood and building concentrations of older adults in the older suburbs (but also towns and cities) of U.S. metropolitan areas, called naturally occurring retirement communities (NORCs).[62,63] These residential enclaves are distinctive because they are not the deliberate products of developers or planners but rather a consequence of aging-in-place demographics.[64]

NORCs assume various physical forms—high-rise rentals, co-ops, and condominium multi-unit buildings, as well as clusters of such buildings, but also neighborhood clusters of single-family–owned homes and manufactured home park subdivisions. Most consist of privately-owned rental apartments or owned dwellings, but they also include affordable rent-subsidized apartment buildings funded by various government programs. Although NORCs are predominantly occupied by older people, they will also have small shares of younger residents.

We can divide NORCs into three groups[65]:

- *Housing-based NORCs:* Also called classic, closed, or vertical NORCs, these are located in a single apartment building, a housing complex with multiple buildings under common management, or an area where a number of apartment buildings are clustered together.
- *Neighborhood-based NORCs:* Also known as open or horizontal NORCs, these consist primarily of single-family homes or duplexes.
- *Community-based NORCs:* These are similar to neighborhood-based NORCs, but their catchment areas are larger, encompassing a town, city, county, or multiple such locales.

THREATS TO INDEPENDENT LIVING AND OPPORTUNITIES FOR CHANGE

NORCs present both problems and opportunities.[66] Because of their older age profiles, their occupants are likely to have many of the difficulties associated with aging in place (Chapter 4). However, there is a positive side to these population concentrations with their unmet needs. These clusters of more vulnerable seniors can be ready markets for a wide array of long-term and supportive services. Occupied by those at the same stage in life, they also offer many opportunities for social networking. They have given rise to two service delivery models, known as naturally occurring retirement community supportive service programs (NORC-SSPs) and Elder Villages, that share some important commonalties, even as they differ in significant ways.

In both NORC models, the delivery of services and assistance departs from past approaches. The organizational focus of both NORC-SSPs and Elder Villages is a *place's* aging-in-place older population and its need for a supportive physical or social environment. The targets are geographically defined *residential enclaves of older people* rather than *at-risk individuals*. And the services are not necessarily program specific, such as those funded primarily by Medicaid waivers or programs under the Older Americans Act. In fact, the services may be delivered not by any government programs but by volunteers and vendors in the private sector. As one expert on NORCs elaborates,

> The relatively dense population in NORCs has made it possible to rethink conventional service delivery paradigms. Historically, aging, health, and long-term care services have been delivered to individuals in silos, disconnected from the community where an older adult lives. . . . NORCs have given policymakers and service providers the opportunity to shift their efforts from delivering specific services to specific individuals to focusing on the health and well-being of subpopulations of seniors within communities.[67]

Advocates argue that the demographics of these residential enclaves enable housing managers, service providers, and vendors—whether in the private or public sectors—to offer a more comprehensive array of services more efficiently—organizationally and financially.[68] This is because they can target large clusters—critical masses—of occupants with similar health-related or independence-supporting services and thus enjoy economies of scale. Rather than spending the time and fuel needed to travel to 20 geographically dispersed locations in a metropolitan or rural area to serve 20 clients, a service provider can make a single trip to a building site or neighborhood enclave.[69] Targeting one destination with multiple consumers or clients not only saves time but also allows for more flexible time use. She can provide more services at lower (per unit) costs and better allocate her time because many clients may not need 1- or 2-hour blocks of assistance but simply 15 minutes to confirm a prescription or doctor's order or to adjust an assistive device.

These community-level service delivery models are also distinctive because they do not necessarily target impaired and chronically sick older people (Chapter 8). Rather, the occupants in these settings are given access to services irrespective of their age, health status, limitations, or income level. Some are more active and healthy and benefit from transportation services, social activities, volunteer opportunities, and preventive healthcare; others are older, poorer, sicker, and frail and benefit from assistance performing their ADLs and managing their prescribed medications.[70]

Additionally, rather than just being consumers of services, these older people join with professionals and direct care workers in designing, developing, and coordinating the delivery of their services.[71] As one expert comments, the older residents in these enclaves are far more likely to *"sit on governing bodies, make decisions about the services they want and how and when they want them, and, in some cases, even offer the services themselves."*[72]

NORC-SSPs

NORC-SSPs have been succinctly defined as: *"A formal service agency's efforts to provide a network of supportive services to help older adults age in place within communities that have been identified as NORCs."*[73]

NORC-SSPs typically target adults age 60 and older, although the average age of participants is typically between 75 and 85.[74] These residents often have very diverse religious and ethnic backgrounds. NORC-SSPs may serve a single apartment building or a high-rise complex.[76] For example, in Los Angeles, Jewish Family Services in 2003 helped develop the service support network for a 162-acre private apartment complex of eighteen 13-story towers with approximately 1,500 older residents. Other NORC-SSPs may serve an entire county.

These are often middle-income residential areas. As one expert observes, these programs generally respond to *"middle-class people who are not sick enough for Medicare, who have too much income for Medicaid services, and who are not rich enough for private individual care."*[75] However, some NORC-SSPs operate in lower-income neighborhoods and government-subsidized rental projects.

The earliest NORC-SSPs date from the mid-1980s. Today there are about 100 NORC-SSPs in operation throughout the United States, more than half in New York state.[77] The first, PennSouth Program for Seniors in New York City (where there are now close to 60 such programs), was pioneered in 1986 by the organizational, funding, and marketing efforts of UJA–Federation of Jewish Philanthropies of New York.[78] This was a mega-block 2,800-unit co-op building (10 high-rise apartment buildings) in the densely urban Chelsea area of Midtown Manhattan, in which about 75% of the 6,200 moderate-income occupants (many with union labor organization backgrounds) were older than age 60 and variously confronting challenges aging in place.[79]

A NORC-SSP may be initiated by a building's management or resident association (e.g., condo or co-op association of a multi-unit building).[80] In other buildings, an outside community-based nonprofit charitable service organization, with religious or ethnic affiliations, becomes alerted to residents' needs and initiates a service delivery program. Other programs begin in affordable rental complexes operated by public housing authorities where managers are having difficulty addressing the needs of their frail residents.

In a typical NORC-SSP model, a lead service agency, typically a community-based nonprofit social service provider (often part of the network of Area Agencies on Aging service providers) is responsible for the planning, financial management, implementation, and overall coordination of the program.[81] Often, this service provider carries out an initial need assessment or outreach campaign to ascertain the major problems of the tenants. Full- or part-time staff located at the NORC sites (e.g., resource coordinators, social workers, nurses) often administer the program.

The lead agency provides some services directly but typically contracts and partners with a variety of health and social service organizations, including home health agencies, local hospitals, local businesses, places of worship, higher education programs, government agencies, local police and fire departments, other public safety agencies, and philanthropic organizations to participate as service providers in the NORC program. The NORC-SSP model is fundamentally a collaborative-partnership process between private and public entities whereby *"older adults, building owners and managers, local service providers, funders, and other community partners and institutions come together to cultivate supportive communities."*[82]

The lead agency connects older residents on an as-needed basis to supportive services found in their community.[83] Although they vary by program and location, the core services usually include those provided under the Older Americans Act (Chapter 8), including information and referral, case management, preventive healthcare, chronic care management, home care, congregate meals and meal delivery, transportation, escort services, home modifications, *"recreational activities (e.g., book clubs), and productive activities (e.g., assistance finding volunteer and paid work)."*[84]

Sometimes, with the help of its partners, it can negotiate lower prices for goods and services needed by residents (e.g., lower-cost public transit). In the PennSouth NORC-SSP, a partnership was established with the Visiting Nurse Service of New York that offered free nursing services in return for accessing a large group of potential clients.[85]

Importantly, participation by the residents in NORC-SSPs is voluntary. Those residents who want more involvement have advisory roles in planning their delivered services or serve as volunteers to assist other residents who need service information, provider referrals, escorts to accompany them on their errands, care monitoring, transportation, and other nonlicensed services. Residents also run some programs themselves, such as recreational and educational activities.[86]

The Jewish Federations of North America have been especially effective advocates for expanding these programs, with the assistance of federal funding.[87] Between 2002 and 2010, the Administration on Aging (under Title IV of the Older Americans Act) funded the first 3 years of more than 50 NORC-SSP demonstration projects in 26 states. To sustain these programs, advocates must also secure funding from state and local governments out of their general revenues, state agencies that operate service programs, and state-administered Medicaid programs. They also depend on private sources that include grants from nonprofit charitable organizations and private philanthropic contributions.[88] Obtaining new and continuing funding is one of the challenges confronting NORC-SSPs. They often subsequently receive less funding and must scale down their operations.[89] Residents typically pay only a small part of the costs of these services.

An absence of rigorous research makes it difficult to unequivocally conclude that NORC-SSPs improve the quality of life of older people and make it easier for them to live independently. Nonetheless, the evidence shows that NORC-SSP residents are more aware of the community services to help them, access them more easily, are more involved in their apartment projects' activities, are less likely to feel alone, isolated, or depressed, feel as healthy as or healthier than they did in the past, feel safer because of their home modifications, and express more confidence in their ability to live independently and remain in their communities.[90] They especially feel more equipped to cope with personal or service emergencies. Residents in these NORC-SSP programs also reported that they made more friends and interacted more frequently with their neighbors.[91] On the other hand, other studies emphasize that NORC-SSP communities take time to reach their goals because the older residents distrust outside assistance, particularly from government programs, and lack the organizational skills to assume volunteering efforts.[92]

ELDER VILLAGES: THE BEACON HILL PROTOTYPE

Beacon Hill Elder Village is a primary exemplar of the second category of NORC models. A group of older residents living in the upscale, historic downtown Boston district established a nonprofit corporation, Beacon Hill Village, in 2001 as a means to make it easier for residents aging in place to access the products and services available in their community.

Some 460 residents became members of the original Beacon Hill Village, and they ranged in age from 52 to 99. Demographically, village members primarily include the Tweener middle-income older population that is ineligible for most public programs (Chapter 8).[93] One study characterized them as mainly white, non-Hispanic, and homeowners. They tend to be somewhat younger, less impaired, and have fewer needs than NORC-SSP participants.[94]

Whereas outside stakeholders (from nonprofit agencies and the public sector) typically play a central role in the initiation and operation of NORC-SSPs, "intentional communities" such as Beacon Hill are resident-driven, membership-based, and self-governing neighborhood-based grassroots organizations.[95] As freestanding entities, they typically develop their service model without collaborating with social service or healthcare providers, especially if they have government affiliations.[96] Consistent with their consumer-driven philosophy, their members have stronger leadership roles and assume greater responsibility for the organization, governance, and direction of their service delivery programs.

Consequently, most Elder Villages do not want to rely on state or federal government assistance or surrender control over their long-term care decisions to others.[97] They often appoint their own boards of directors, made up of community members, and establish various committees to work on programming activities, fundraising, marketing, and communication. They rely more heavily on volunteers and have authority to hire their own staff, approve budgets, and serve as spokespersons in the community.[98]

Consistent with their operating model, Elder Villages depend more on annual membership dues than on government funds, grants, or fees for individual services, as do NORC-SSPs.[99] Members pay an annual membership charge, averaging $430 to $600, set by the village's board of directors[100] (in Beacon Hill, $600 for singles and $850 for couples). Families of older members sometimes pay these dues, and some villages charge their poorest members lower rates. Resident dues and gifts pay for about half of the Elder Village's budget; the other half is covered by grants or funding from foundations and nonprofit groups.

The umbrella nonprofit organization sees itself as a consolidator and coordinator of existing community services (in the Beacon Hill case, the greater Boston area).

Consequently, it offers resident members information about a wide range of private and public services and tries to make it easier and more affordable for them to access assistance. To facilitate these connections, Elder Villages often collaborate with other organizations and agencies that work with older adults.

The Elder Village board hires professional staff (e.g., social workers, nurses) to administer the organization, provide case management services, and talk residents through their problems. The original Beacon Hill Village hired an executive director (a geriatric social worker) to help perform these tasks.[101] It coordinates a pool of volunteers to help residents with their grocery shopping, to deliver meals, to visit members who are homebound, and to provide residents with rides, typically using private vehicles, to help them reach their destinations.[102] Volunteers and staff also help older residents purchase services at discounted prices that are offered by independent providers that have been prescreened for their honesty, reliability, and quality. These include taxicabs, food providers, cleaning and cooking services, geriatric care management, handyman services, home inspections and modifications, and home healthcare services. Some Elder Villages use "time dollars," whereby resident volunteers give so many hours of their own time so that when they need assistance they can draw on this bank of hours.

Elder Villages also help organize social, cultural, educational, and recreational events (e.g., lunch groups, trips to concerts, exercise activities, and classes or lectures). These events may be particularly instrumental in connecting members and improving their social relationships.

Elder Villages are oriented toward preventive health, as reflected in their exercise classes, wellness seminars, discounts at health clubs, flu shots, and information on medical issues, and they make access to doctors and home healthcare easier.[103] In the Beacon Hill Elder Village, the Massachusetts General Hospital made its clinical and educational resources available to village members.

The Elder Village model has impressed NORCs throughout the country, and it has been widely replicated, though operated somewhat differently. To promote its model, Beacon Hill Village offers an organizational manual for other prospective Elder Villages and was instrumental in establishing a Village to Village Network as a means to communicate with its members. As of 2014, about 120 Elder Villages were in operation nationwide, and more than 100 more were in the planning stages.[104] Nationally, they had a median of 105 members but ranged in size from 8 to 476 members.[105] Elder Villages are also now found in Australia, Canada, and the Netherlands.

Although Elder Villages seem to have many obvious benefits, research is not available to evaluate whether they are accomplishing their goals. Consequently,

> We do not understand the impact of Village services on long-term care outcomes such as premature institutionalization, quality of life, overall health or cost effectiveness . . . and we do not know the impact of villages at the community level, including the ability to build a sense of community, increase civic engagement, enhance personal and interpersonal empowerment, increase social capital, and engage the leadership of older adults.[106]

The Elder Village model appears to work best when there is a critical mass of residents with similar needs, which allows volume purchasing and service discounts, and when the residents are better educated, can afford membership fees, are somewhat younger, and are able to function as leaders and volunteers.

Stepping Back and Going Forward

For many reasons, only a small number of NORCs in the United States have adopted these types of community organizations. Their demographics may not be top-heavy with old and vulnerable residents, or the residents do not view themselves as needy. Others believe that if they become service delivery nodes, others will stigmatize their buildings or neighborhoods as "nursing homes" or as places populated by "charity cases." Most simply, they are not convinced that the benefits of these service delivery models are worth their efforts.

Other NORCs, such as enclaves in low-density suburbs or rural counties, may not adopt this service delivery model because their residents are spread over too large a geographic area or they lack a centralized administrative unit (e.g., a resident manager, condo association, or homeowners' association) or any physical focal point (e.g., an office or building). These circumstances make it more difficult to organize this service delivery model. Still, other NORCs are in communities that lack public agencies, charitable groups, or volunteers with sufficient experience or motivation to mount such a program.

Not Just a Service Delivery Approach

The desirability of these NORCs—whether SSPs or Elder Villages—also depends on their housing and neighborhood features.[107] In the first NORC-SSP (Penn South), the residents had excellent transit and good access to various retail stores as well as medical and personal services.[108] Likewise, the residents of the Beacon Hill neighborhood had good public transportation and enjoyed the proximity of numerous businesses that could satisfy their nondiscretionary needs (e.g., grocery shopping, hardware stores, medical facilities) and discretionary needs (e.g., art galleries, museums, antique stores, and theaters).

Yet, all is not perfect. Even the prototypical Beacon Hill community has its downsides. Its housing is expensive for those on fixed or limited incomes; many of its historic buildings are not accessible to those relying on canes, walkers, wheelchairs, and other assistive devices; and it has few parks.[109] Its cobblestone-paved and sometimes steep-graded sidewalks are not the best surfaces for those with an unsteady gait. Navigating this community in harsh winter weather is also not easy.

Communities within Communities

Whether NORCs can successfully transform themselves into NORC-SSPs or villages and enable their residents to lead more independent and enriched lives also depends on their ability to function as social communities. The residents of these geographically defined enclaves must hold shared visions, values, and beliefs about their residential setting's service model.[110] They must feel some collective responsibility for the well-being of other residents. Contrary to the "rugged individualism" values espoused by many Americans, they must see themselves as willing and cooperative stakeholders who have the talent, skills, and desire to assist other residents or who have confidence that their appointed leaders or social agencies have such abilities. Residents must also be willing to accept the help of their peers and to solicit assistance from outsiders— professionals and organizations—if they are to connect successfully with the resources appropriate for their needs.[111] In the case of NORC-SSPs, older residents must be willing to trust their government.

Although both the NORC-SSP and Elder Village community-level responses are highly promising approaches to help older people remain in their residential comfort and mastery zones, many unanswered questions and insufficient evidence limit our ability to characterize them as success stories. Their advocates must confront some important questions and issues:

- Will only a very small proportion of NORCs always participate—will these always be niche service delivery models? Can they successfully reach out to moderate-income older people who do not view themselves as "welfare cases"?

- Is it always realistic to expect that older people want to make decisions about their self-care? Do some older people simply want others to decide?

- Are these programs being implemented in the neediest NORC residential enclaves or simply those with effective leadership and residents willing to adopt this particular service model?[112]

- Are these programs being implemented in communities with urban land uses and designs that are compatible with the needs of their less-mobile older residents?

- Because participation is voluntary, are these programs reaching the very frail occupants of these residential enclaves?

- Are programs vigilant about conducting ongoing needs assessments to ensure that their services match the changing vulnerability profiles of their residents?

- Long-term sustainability is a challenge. Some NORC-SSP programs have scaled back or ceased operations. This is critical because older people want assurances that they can depend on solutions over the long-term.

- Funding for NORC-SSPs especially depends on government sources, and future funding commitments are plagued with uncertainty. Can this model succeed when members need heavier and more expensive care?[113]

- Funding for Elder Villages especially depends on resident dues. Does the affordability of these dues restrict the adoption of this community model?

- Although the viability of Elder Villages depends more on member dues, the sustainability of this model is also very much dependent on the fundraising abilities of their organizers. If their leaderships cannot secure stable sources of support, the future of this service delivery model is uncertain.[114]

- Is the dependence of the Elder Village model on volunteers feasible for serving residents who need heavier care to address their more demanding physical or cognitive declines?[115]

- Are the neighborhood or community (i.e., horizontal) NORCs that are implementing these models spreading their resources too thin in their efforts to cover the needs of older people dispersed over an extensive geographic area?

Is it a serious problem when there is no on-site central management (e.g., sited at a building's headquarters) or common community space or when staff or volunteers cannot deliver their services (e.g., security, emergency services, meals, wellness services) to a central location? Because residents are less likely to live in proximity to each other, are their fewer opportunities for social networking and communal activities, and are word-of-mouth communications less effective?[116]

- Have these programs surmounted language and cultural barriers that would prevent the participation of older people with ethnic backgrounds (e.g., Russians, Hispanics, and Asians)?

AFFORDABLE RENTAL PROPERTIES AND HOUSING–CARE SOLUTIONS

SEEKING AFFORDABLE DWELLINGS

Financially stressed older people who feel burdened by their monthly housing costs have seven possible coping strategies:

- If homeowners, obtain a reverse mortgage or home equity loan to increase their incomes or take advantage of public programs that reduce their outlays for property taxes or energy bills.[117]
- If homeowners, sell their dwellings and purchase another that has lower mortgage and upkeep costs.
- Move into the residence of a family member.
- Find a friend or acquaintance to live with and share the dwelling costs.
- Rent a spare room to a boarder.
- Find affordable rental accommodations in the private market.
- Look to various federal or state affordable rental housing programs for relief.[118]

We now focus on the promise of the last strategy.

AVAILABILITY OF AFFORDABLE RENTAL HOUSING PROGRAMS IN THE UNITED STATES

Giving older people the opportunity to live in decent apartment units that charge affordable rents is an effective pathway for communities to help financially burdened older people achieve residential normalcy. They enjoy a more comfortable place to live, and they do not have to worry about how to pay their monthly housing bills.

Affordable rent-subsidized accommodations are offered through federal programs funded and administered by the U.S. Department of Housing and Urban Development (HUD) and to a lesser extent by the U.S. Department of Agriculture (USDA). In 2012, these programs accommodated about 1.5 million older people (defined as age 62 and older), who constituted just over 30%[119] of all rent-assisted occupants in the United States (Table 9.1).[120] These rental housing government programs offer

Table 9.1. Federal rental housing programs accommodating low-income older households, 2012 (Center on Budget and Policy Priorities, 2012)

Federal housing program	Share of units occupied by older households	Number of units occupied by older households
Section 8 project-based assistance	47%	593,772
Housing choice vouchers	19%	408,047
Public housing	31%	346,566
Supportive Housing for Elderly and People with Disabilities Section 202/811	81%	121,009*
Other HUD programs	25%	9,329
USDA Section 521 rental assistance	59%	160,243
Total	31%	1,546,039

* Haley & Grey (2008) estimate there are 263,000 Section 202 units.

for-profit and nonprofit housing developers and local housing authorities financial incentives, such as favorable development financing terms, rental subsidies, operating subsidies, tax breaks, or mortgage insurance guarantees, enabling them to construct, rehabilitate, or operate their properties less expensively. This enables them to charge more affordable rents to their occupants. Apartments are usually considered affordable when their occupants do not have to pay more than 30% of their incomes on rent.

Along with these federal and state funding sources, one of the largest programs producing new affordable multifamily apartment units is the Low Income Housing Tax Credit (LIHTC) program, which was established as part of the Tax Reform Act of 1986 (Section 42 of the Internal Revenue Code) and administered by state housing finance agencies. As of 2012, this program was helping to finance more than 2.4 million apartments and was adding 70,000 to 100,000 units annually.[121] Over its history, it has supported about 321,000 units for older renters.[122] This program offers private housing developers an incentive to produce affordable rental housing by awarding them tax credits to fund the development costs they need to construct, rehabilitate, or acquire rental apartment projects occupied by lower-income tenants. Housing developers also rely on two other federal programs. Since 1974, Community Development Block Grants have provided loans or grants to help developers rehabilitate housing properties for people with low and moderate incomes that include the old.[123] Another federal block grant program, available since 1990 to nonprofit housing sponsors to meet their financing gaps, is the HOME Investment Partnerships program, also administered by HUD.[124]

In practice, any given rental property may be financed or subsidized by multiple federal rental housing programs to make their rents affordable.[125] Many state governments also have introduced their own rent-subsidy programs.

Whereas these HUD and USDA rental assistance programs typically fund or finance the new construction or rehabilitation of low-income rental buildings (referred to as project-based programs), the Housing Choice Voucher program (also called Section 8 tenant-based assistance) administered by local public housing authorities makes existing rental housing units in the private market more affordable (referred to as tenant-based programs). It is HUD's largest rental assistance program and accommodates a substantial number of low-income older people. Qualified landlords receive rental subsidy vouchers reimbursing them for the difference between what a household can afford (usually 30% or less of their monthly incomes) and the actual market rent of the unit (a dollar range established by HUD's fair market rent standards).

These housing vouchers are tied to the tenants rather than to the housing unit, so if they move, they can use the voucher in other rental housing markets.[126] A public housing authority can also use up to 20% of its voucher program funding allocation to subsidize the rents of buildings created by other affordable rental programs (labeled the Section 8 Project-Based Voucher program), such as the HOME, Low Income Tax Credit, Section 221, Section 202, and Section 515 programs. However, these subsidies are tied to the building's rental units, not to the tenants.[127] Voucher programs have been especially instrumental in making LIHTC properties affordable to extremely low-income older people.

Although these rental housing programs have many similarities, they differ in some fundamental ways. Some subsidize rental units that are located in the older and more run-down core areas of larger cities and older suburbs, whereas others are in newer suburban locales and rural counties. Some target the lowest-income older people, others mainly the moderate income old. For example, the LIHTC program is typically occupied by a significant share of households that still pay more than 30% of their incomes—and some even more than 50%—on their monthly rents, even after benefiting from voucher assistance.[128] Some rental buildings are designed exclusively for older people, and specifically those who are more physically impaired, whereas others are occupied by people of all ages, and older people are only a very small share of the tenants.[129]

IMPORTANT PROJECT-BASED RENTAL PROGRAMS FOR OLDER PEOPLE

HUD's Public Housing Program established in 1937 is our oldest and probably best-known federal affordable housing program. A network of 3,100 local public housing authorities located in municipalities and counties own and operate rental units constructed or rehabilitated by this program and help subsidize its operating costs. Beginning with the Housing Act of 1956, public housing projects were allowed to rent to single older people, an important advance because HUD's original definition of "elderly families" (husband–wife couples) had excluded them.[130]

In 1960, the program created the first elderly-only public housing development.[131] However, from 1961 through the early 1990s, younger people with physical and mental disabilities were included in the definition of "elderly families," so the two populations often lived together in the same building. The concerns expressed by older people for their safety and security[132] in these integrated buildings resulted in 1992 legislation that allowed public housing authorities to designate buildings as elderly only, disabled only, or elderly and disabled only.[133] Nonetheless, this legislation did not prevent people age 62 and older from occupying a significant share of today's predominantly family-oriented public housing developments, which they often found more comfortable because of their larger size.[134] With the exception of units to replace those lost from demolished projects, few new apartments have been built under the Public Housing Program since the 1980s, and now they are available to older people primarily through tenant vacancies.

For-profit and nonprofit private sponsors have developed the majority of this country's publicly financed multifamily rental properties. Many originated in the 1960s and 1970s, such as the Section 221(d)(3) Below Market Interest Program and its replacement, the Section 236 program. Both programs could designate apartments for occupancy by elderly households.[135] This was also true for the Section 8 New Construction and Substantial Rehabilitation program, which in 1974 replaced the Section 236 program.[136] Although new rental units have not been constructed under this program since 1983, it now accommodates the largest group of older households (Table 9.1).

The National Housing Act of 1959 created the Section 202 program, and for the first time nonprofit sponsors could develop and design rental housing specifically for older people and, initially, nonelderly people with disabilities. This program is the darling of elder advocates because beyond the appeal of their affordable units, they have often incorporated accessible design features and common areas (e.g., central dining room, community rooms, office space, or libraries) where older occupants can enjoy recreational and dining activities and receive preventive care services. Their sponsors are also more likely to provide on-site meals and make housekeeping, transportation, and personal care assistance available to them.[137] In particular, their managers may hire staff known as service coordinators to help them access various health-related and independence-supporting services in their communities.[138] However, annual housing construction of Section 202 units has continually declined despite the program's record of sound management and benefits for less-independent elder tenants. In the 2012 budget, funding for new apartment construction ended, although existing units continue to be supported.

Since 1962, the USDA Rural Housing Service's Section 515 and 521 programs have developed rental units for older people outside urban areas. The former program offers favorable financing, enabling its developers to construct more affordable rental units, and the latter offers tenant-based financial assistance to help their occupants make up the difference between the market rent and what they can afford. Since the late 1970s, a rural Congregate Housing subprogram has funded the development of congregate care buildings that require property owners to make supportive services—meals, transportation, housekeeping, and recreational activities—available to their older residents, equip their apartments with handrails and emergency call buttons, and make some units wheelchair accessible.[139]

DEMAND AND SUPPLY

Unlike programs such as Social Security or Medicare, these publicly assisted low-rent programs are not entitlements, and older applicants, even when income-qualified, have no guarantees of occupancy.[140] In fact, they often have difficulty finding vacant affordable rental units. Since 1995, spending by the U.S. government on low-income housing has represented a declining share of its nondefense discretionary program spending and a declining share of its gross domestic budget.[141] This trend shows no signs of abating as pressures mount on Congress to further tighten funding of federal social programs. Advocates cynically point out that the U.S. government's spending on low-income rental housing assistance pales when compared with the amount of subsidies it gives to homeowners—mostly with higher incomes—through their tax breaks for their home mortgage interest deductions, property tax deductions, and the capital gains tax exclusion when they sell their dwellings.[142]

However, the problem goes beyond providing enough new affordable rental units. There have been significant losses of rental apartments from the overall inventory of publicly subsidized units. Moreover, these units were often located near public transit, so important to older renters without cars.[143] Annually, public housing authorities lose 10,000 units because they have sold properties that are too costly to maintain or have demolished their largest high-rise properties even as they replaced them with fewer, albeit better, designed buildings. Older occupants of these properties have been among those displaced by these programs.[144] Compared with older occupants of nonsubsidized community housing, they are less mobile and in poorer health, coping with conditions such as hypertension, diabetes, arthritis, and asthma. For them, moving is an especially stressful experience. They often have to sever ties with friends or neighbors, and they have difficulties finding new affordable rental accommodations.[145]

Thousands of privately developed Section 8 Project-Rental Assistance rental apartments have also been lost annually because their owners have paid off their mortgages (ending their participation in the program) or have chosen not to renew their expiring rental assistance contracts.[146] The stock of affordable Section 515 rural rental units has also been dwindling because owners are prepaying their mortgages or because of their physical deterioration.[147] It is also estimated that rental subsidy agreements on about a quarter of the rental units under the key HUD Section 202 program will expire by 2023.[148]

In summary, inadequate development of new affordable rental units and inventory losses of existing units have resulted in an insufficient number of rental units available to meet the current demand by older people.[149] Experts also doubt that the future supply of these rental units will be able to meet the large projected increases in the numbers of lower-income older people in the next few decades.[150]

THE POTENTIAL OF AFFORDABLE CLUSTERED HOUSING–CARE (HOUSING WITH SERVICES)

THE NEED

Government-assisted rental properties have successfully enabled thousands of low-income older adults to afford housing. But the older people occupying these properties often struggle to maintain their independence. Estimates vary, but studies have reported that at least half of these older renters have difficulty performing one or more of their ADLs or IADLs.[151] Older occupants most at risk are women living alone who cannot count on family members to assist them, even for temporary periods when they become sick or disabled.[152] They are also more likely to be African-American or Hispanic and to be eligible for Medicaid assistance.[153]

That these needs exist is not surprising. First, even as many low-income people have entered these properties at younger ages, they remain as occupants for 25 years or more; they have truly aged in place.[154] Second, older people themselves are entering these properties at increasingly higher ages, in their mid-70s or older, because they have delayed moving from their previous residences for so long. Once they become occupants, residential inertia is the norm. Older people are satisfied with these accommodations and the limited affordable housing options in their communities make them even less likely to move.[155] Consequently, in publicly assisted properties predominantly occupied by older people, such as Section 202 properties, the median tenant age was 74, and in LIHTC properties it was 71.[156] The average age of older people leaving these rent-assisted properties is 78, but more than a quarter remain into their 80s.[157]

THE OPPORTUNITY

Only a small share of publicly subsidized rental properties have responded to the aging-in-place needs of these older tenants. Called affordable clustered housing–care ("housing–care") or housing with services properties,[158] they offer significant numbers of older renters not just affordable accommodations but also more accessible units and assistance with chronic health problems and physical or cognitive limitations.[159]

As was true for NORCs, advocates argue that these affordable housing–care properties enjoy economies of scale when they serve large clusters—critical masses—of older residents with similar supportive service and health needs.[160] They can more easily justify expenses such as physically retrofitting the dwellings and common areas of their buildings, hiring a service coordinator or case manager, offering on-site meals, or introducing a health clinic on the building's premises. By allocating to others the responsibility of dealing with their tenants' needs for health and supportive care, building managers can better focus on their traditional management functions.[161]

MORE ACCESSIBLE WITH COMMON AREAS AND SERVICES

The owners or managers of the publicly assisted rental properties offer their more vulnerable older tenants as many as three categories of assistance. First, to make it easier or safer for them to occupy their accommodations, they make physical design changes or modifications (Chapter 6). They introduce grab bars in at least one bathroom, lever door handles, barrier-free wheelchair-accessible entry doors, easy-to-use appliances, emergency call systems, entrance security, grab rails in all public hallways, and elevator access to every floor.[162] Second, they provide common areas, such as commercial kitchens, dining areas, recreational rooms, and office areas, to allow hired or visiting staff to perform health assessments, provide therapeutic activities, prepare hot meals, and offer recreational activities.[163] Third, to help older people remain as healthy as possible and to help them cope with their limitations, they introduce health-related and independence-supporting services (Figure 9.2).

SERVICE DELIVERY STRATEGIES

Housing–care building administrators provide these services by relying on different delivery strategies.[164] They hire their own in-house staff but also contract or partner with home care and healthcare agencies, businesses, health professional schools, or

Figure 9.2. Health-related and independence-supporting services in rent-assisted housing (This figure draws from an excellent overview in "Institute for the Future of Aging Services" [2009, pp. 3–4].)

Health-Related Services

- Information about available community health and preventive services and referral to providers in the community

- Health screening programs and other prevention initiatives (e.g., vision, hearing, and dental exams; blood pressure and blood sugar measurements; weight management programs; flu shots)

- Health promotion and wellness activities (e.g., health education on smoking cessation, alcohol and substance use, diet and nutrition recommendations, and diabetes management; exercise and fitness classes; healthy cooking classes)

- Self-care education and management of chronic conditions such as diabetes, hypertension, asthma, arthritis, and cancer

- Comprehensive health assessments covering health status and physical and cognitive functioning

- Care planning and care management in collaboration with a resident's primary care physician

- Coordination of resident transitions between the housing property, hospital, and assisted living or nursing home facility

- Medication assistance, monitoring, and review

- Mental health and dementia screening, counseling, interventions, and referrals

- Home health services, physical therapy, occupational therapy

- Adult day health

- Hospice

- Primary care (through on-site physician office or medical house calls program)

- Comprehensive package of health and wellness services

Independence-Supporting Services

- Information, counseling, and referral

- Assistance with laundry and heavy or light housekeeping

- Social and recreational activities

- Transportation assistance (Cotrell & Carder, 2010)

- Group meals

- Assistance with self-care activities (ADL limitations)

- Assistance in everyday management of a household (addressing IADL limitations)

- Assistance or reminders to take medications

- Part- or full-time skilled nursing services (Kochera, 2006) hospitals in their community.[165] Most attempt to deliver these services using a social model or person-centered approach (Chapter 11) that respects the autonomy of older renters and gives them as many choices as possible.[166]

To cope with the needs of their more dependent older occupants, building managements often hire *service coordinators*. These staff identify the unmet service needs of their residents, match them with appropriate community services, and continuously monitor and evaluate their effectiveness.[167]

Housing providers rely on various specific strategies to bring supportive services to older residents[168]:

- Use of resident volunteers and other lay people trained by health educators to assist residents with the management of chronic illnesses
- Direct employment of health providers, such as nurses or nurse practitioners, by the housing sponsor to serve residents in one or more properties
- Offering on-site health clinics operated at regularly scheduled times by community health providers, such as nurses, nurse practitioners, or geriatricians
- Formal collaborations with community health providers, such as hospitals, managed care companies, physicians, public health clinics, and pharmacies
- Collaboration with academic health centers to provide clinical learning experiences for medical, nursing, or other health professional students
- Operation of a licensed home health agency, owned and managed by the housing provider on behalf of residents and the broader community
- Partnering with a local home health agency to bring personal care services to residents at a more affordable rate

Housing providers may also arrange for their tenants to use the supportive and health-related services offered by a co-located or nearby center under the Program of All-Inclusive Care for the Elderly (PACE) (Chapter 8).[169]

Some rent-assisted housing–care programs are exemplary, such as those undertaken by state governments and housing providers in Connecticut, Massachusetts, and Vermont, and that successfully integrate multiple service approaches.[170]

OBSTACLES TO CREATING HOUSING–CARE SETTINGS

Publicly assisted rental properties have many difficulties morphing into housing–care settings:

- The sponsors, owners, and management companies of these affordable rental properties do not believe that assisting frail older tenants is in their job description. This response is symptomatic of the bricks-and-mortar orientation of a federal agency, such as HUD, and its belief that other federal agencies (e.g., the Department of Health and Human Services) should be mainly responsible for providing supportive services. More recently, there have been increased collaborative efforts between the Department of Health and Human Services and HUD (e.g., facilitating nursing home–community transitions).[171]

- Providers fear that if they offer supportive services to their older tenants, their properties will look like a nursing home, and healthier tenants will complain that their accommodations look like *"homes for the aged."*[172]

- Their properties do not have common areas to accommodate the co-location of service providers, often essential for the delivery of on-site assistance.

- There may be too few older tenants in a building to economically justify the regular delivery of these services or to make design changes.[173] This is a downside of older residents occupying rental units in the private market subsidized through the voucher program. Studies show that these people tend to move from their affordable rental accommodations at an earlier age because they lack needed support services.[174]

- The managers do not have the administrative capabilities and knowledge about appropriate service options to accommodate frail older tenants. They fail to partner with appropriate social service and healthcare providers. Alternatively, they worry that accommodating frail older tenants will increase the risk of accidents and in turn result in higher insurance premiums.

- The rental buildings are located in communities (e.g., rural communities, outlying suburban areas, or economically depressed locales) with an inadequate supply of affordable home- and community-based services.[175]

- Bureaucratic barriers make it difficult to integrate services into the rental building. Housing and service providers must rely on social programs with very different income or health eligibility and regulatory criteria.[176] For example, older tenants may have low enough incomes to quality for rental occupancy in these properties (based on HUD's regulations) but not to qualify for the home- and community-based programs funded by Medicaid or other state-administered social service programs. Housing providers seeking to put together a package of services often confront an organizational puzzle where the pieces do not match up[177] because *"an older person eligible for Medicare, Medicaid, Older Americans Act programs, and subsidized housing is treated by the government as four different entities."*[178]

- Although rent-assisted programs make their dwellings affordable, very few HUD-sponsored programs fund their supportive and long-term services (Figure 9.3).[179] Obtaining financial support is time-consuming and difficult. Owners or sponsors of multifamily rental properties and public housing projects must solicit assistance from multiple government, philanthropic, and faith-based organizations or rely on resident contributions. One study of Section 202 and elderly-occupied LIHTC properties reported that 30% to 38% of these properties relied solely on funds from residents to pay for their supportive services.[180] Moreover, even if these programs save state governments money (e.g., by lowering Medicaid nursing home bed admission rates), these benefits do not accrue to the rent-assisted provider. Consequently, *"service-enriched programs often have difficulties showing a return on investment."*[181]

- Managers may reject the services funded by some government programs because they come with too many restrictive rules and regulations. As one exam-

Figure 9.3. HUD-funded supportive service programs

Congregate Housing Services Program

Beginning in 1978, this program offered privately owned HUD-subsidized rental projects funding of up to 40% of the costs of securing nonmedical supportive services, such as transportation, personal assistance, housekeeping, meals, and the support of a service coordinator. To be eligible, the older residents had to have difficulty performing at least three ADLs. Since the mid-1990s, it has no longer accepted new applicants, but privately owned HUD-subsidized rental projects currently operate 60 earlier-awarded programs (Perl, 2010).

Service Coordinators

Since the 1992 Housing and Community Development Act, the hiring of service coordinators has been an eligible expense for all HUD multifamily assisted developments designed or designated for low-income older adults (U.S. Department of Housing and Urban Development, 1996). Public housing projects also receive service coordinator funding through the Resident Opportunities and Self-Sufficiency grant program.

Assisted Living Conversion Program

Since 2001, this HUD program has funded the costs of physically renovating and retrofitting the apartment units and common spaces of rent-assisted federal properties so that they could be licensed by their state as assisted living properties (or equivalents). However, these grant funds cannot be used to pay for the supportive services offered by the property. After passage of the Section 202 Supportive Housing for the Elderly Act of 2010, properties could also qualify if they offered Service-Enriched Housing that accommodated older residents requiring ADL assistance or healthcare related services. However, properties do not have to be licensed as assisted living properties, but rather can offer supportive services that are delivered by a licensed or certified third-party service provider (Spillman, Biess, & MacDonald, 2012). At least two states, Minnesota and New Jersey, now administer these latter programs (Stone et al., 2008).

ple, if housing–care settings rely on Medicaid waivers to fund their services, they can help only older applicants with extremely low incomes and limited assets, who must need the heavy care offered to residents admitted to their state's nursing homes (Chapter 8).[182]

The Consumer Dilemma: Not Enough Supply

We lack clear documentation as to what share of rent-assisted properties offer health-related and independence-supporting services to their older tenants. Consequently, older people often have difficulty identifying such housing–care properties when they seek this information from their Area Agency on Aging offices or Aging and Disability Resource Centers.[183]

What experts do agree on is that these housing–care affordable rental properties are in short supply, and waiting lists are often long. Section 202 properties report that there are 10 applicants for every available unit, with an average waiting time of 13.4 months.[184] LIHTC properties occupied predominantly by older people have comparable wait lists. Consequently, housing experts recommend that HUD *"encourage owners of public and assisted housing developments and administrators of the Housing Choice Voucher program to prefer applicants who need supportive housing for admission to appropriate units."*[185] Similarly, they recommend that states give preference to developing LIHTC projects that provide supportive services.[186] Some states also encourage administrators of their Medicaid program to specifically target benefits to older people who live in these rent-assisted properties.[187]

THE CONSUMER DILEMMA: SERVICE VARIABILITY

Even when older consumers can find available housing–care properties, their service offerings differ tremendously. They range from properties that offer only basic service information to those that more resemble assisted living properties because they offer their tenants 24-hour on-site supervision, housekeeping services, and help with ADLs. Consider that even the celebrated HUD Section 202 properties, which serve vulnerable older people, do not uniformly incorporate age-sensitive design features, offer common areas for congregate dining, or offer supportive services.[188]

The unequal availability of service coordinators, considered by most experts as an essential staff resource, is an example. Only 46% of Section 202 properties have HUD-funded service coordination, and 8% have non–HUD-funded service coordination.[189] In rural areas and in the South, Section 202 properties are much less likely to have this staff person, partly because of their smaller buildings and tenant populations.[190] Service coordinators are especially unlikely to be found in other publicly assisted housing properties, such as those financed by the LIHTC program.[191]

Even when a rent-assisted property has a service coordinator on staff, the older tenants cannot be certain about her responsibilities. Some coordinators offer information only in response to queries by their tenants and then refer them to appropriate providers. Others act more proactively on any signs of tenant difficulties or unmet needs, evaluate their functional limitations and health status, refer them to appropriate services, and then monitor the effectiveness of their care and assistance.[192] Along with differences in their job descriptions, the ability of the coordinators to carry out their responsibilities varies widely because some work 40-hour weeks, whereas others work for 20 hours a week or less.[193]

Older residents in some properties do not feel they can confide in their service coordinators.[194] This occurs when they view the service coordinator as simply a representative of the building's management, which makes them *"less inclined to share personal problems with her"*[195] for fear she will tell the management. This is troublesome because managers are more inclined to evict than to help a troubled resident, and the service coordinator is more inclined to act as a tenant advocate.

DO HOUSING–CARE SETTINGS GET RESULTS?

Private and public sector stakeholders that fund or operate these supportive housing–care settings must have evidence that they work. Housing providers must be convinced that they can administer their properties more effectively and that their residents enjoy greater independence and are more satisfied. Policymakers seeking to justify their expenditures want evidence that these housing–care arrangements can positively influence the health and well-being of their lower-income older occupants.[196] State governments are looking for less-costly and more-efficient ways to deliver their home- and community-based services.[197]

There is no shortage of anecdotal, case study, and descriptive empirical studies pointing to the benefits of these housing–care settings.[198] These generally show that when older tenants in affordable rental buildings have better access to supportive and health-related services, they are more likely to avoid serious medical problems and unnecessary emergency room visits as well as spend fewer days in a hospital, thus reducing Medicare and Medicaid expenditures. Altogether, these outcomes increase their chances of successfully aging in place. As one HUD-sponsored study concluded,

> Housing occupied by the elderly seems to be having relatively greater success retaining residents until more advanced ages, compared to primarily non-elderly occupancy housing, even in high poverty neighborhoods.[199]

Owners or managers of these publicly assisted housing–care properties emphasize that they can now better manage their buildings. They particularly laud the role played by service coordinators because they assume responsibility for their residents' assistance and health needs. They report the following favorable outcomes[200]:

- Lower apartment turnover and vacancy rates
- Fewer housekeeping and repair crises
- Decreases in legal fees, evictions, and time in court
- Greater marketability of units
- Fewer unscheduled visits from human service professionals
- Fewer events such as fires and accidents
- Fewer off-hour emergency calls to management and local paramedics
- Fewer failed unit inspections
- Reduced time pressures on administrators
- Better tenant–housing management relations[201]

Federal agencies such as HUD and state government agencies often judge the effectiveness of these housing with services arrangements differently—that is, by whether they delay or prevent their tenants from occupying nursing homes and thus yield lower Medicaid-reimbursed nursing home costs.[202] Although generally positive, these studies have reported mixed results. The long-term services and supports offered as part of HUD's Congregate Housing Services Program (Figure 9.3) did not consistently lower nursing home use, hospital admission rates, costs, or mortality rates or produce gains in individual physical functioning.[203] On the other hand, those receiving the services generally experienced better mental health (anxiety, depression, behavioral and emotional control and psychological well-being), social functioning (quantity and quality of social activities), vitality (energy level and fatigue), and social well-being.[204] Thus, the authors concluded that these services improved *"quality of life and care rather than changing such overt outcomes as institutionalization or otherwise having to leave one's home due to frailty."*[205]

Judging the success of these services by overall cost savings from reduced nursing home use may be shortsighted. In contrast, studies that measure the success of these housing–care settings based on quality of care and health outcomes show that older tenants experience the following beneficial outcomes[206]:

- Increased knowledge of healthy living habits and answers to health-related questions
- Early detection of health problems and problems with medications
- Increased knowledge of and skills to manage chronic health conditions
- Better communication and trusting relationships with healthcare professionals
- Assistance with coordinating healthcare appointments and services
- Increased level of exercise and fitness activities
- Easier access to care, particularly for those with mobility and transportation difficulties

Other studies show that service coordinators increase the service and care awareness of older tenants,[207] giving them a greater *"sense of security and emotional support."*[208] A similar conclusion was reached by a study focused on the Massachusetts Supportive Housing Program (developed in 1999) and designed to create *"an assisted living like environment in state funded, public elderly housing."*[209] It offered *"service coordination and case management, 24-hour personal care, on-call response, homemaker services, laundry, medication reminders, social activities, and at least one meal a day."*[210] Among the findings: Tenant needs were recognized earlier, tenants and family members felt safer and more secure, and services helped prevent tenant crises.

Another group of researchers studied the effects of an intervention designed to improve the nutrition of older and younger people with disabilities living in the Seattle Housing Authority's Low Income Public Housing program.[211] Here the residents reported fewer chronic health problems.

The operation of a clinic through which student nurses provided health screenings, education, outreach, and referral services 2 days a week in the community rooms of several public housing properties also reported favorable resident results: better access to needed care, better identification and management of hypertension, improved diabetes disease outcomes, and better preparation for emergency medical situations.[212] Similarly, a study of the effects of an academic nursing clinic introduced in a high-rise for low-income seniors found a reduction in hospitalizations and emergency room use over a 1-year period.[213]

However, many experts do not consider these past studies to be sufficiently rigorous or scientific because their methods cannot equivocally show that the property's design, infrastructure, and service approaches account for the observed outcomes.[214]

Although we still lack such strong confirmatory research, the cumulative evidence gives us reason to be optimistic about the aging in place role played by these housing–care settings.

CONCLUSION

This chapter raises hope that older people who are out of their residential comfort or mastery zones may find that the worlds outside their dwellings present sufficient opportunities to enrich their coping repertoires and enable their return to residential normalcy. To take advantage of these resources, they must be willing to learn a new vocabulary: age-friendly communities, preventive health, connectivity, supplemental transportation programs, New Urbanism communities, NORC-SSPs, Elder Villages, and clustered housing–care (or housing with services).

Although it is easy to be enthusiastic about the initiatives described in this chapter, there are reasons to reserve judgment. First, although many communities are willing to assess their need for such programmatic responses and have formulated action plans, they have implemented few actual age-friendly initiatives or have achieved only modest results.[215] Other programs have been short lived because funding stopped. Second, there is no evidence that the neighborhoods or communities participating in the healthy community movement are the best candidates for these initiatives; that is, their older occupants have more demanding dwelling and neighborhood problems or unmet service needs than other places. Rather, the catalysts for these community-based programs seem to have more to do with the efforts of innovative, knowledgeable, and aggressive grassroots organizers (i.e., effective leaders) who recognize the potential advantages of helping their elder constituencies with innovative policies and programs.

Third, whether we focus on affordable housing, affordable clustered housing–care initiatives, or the various service-enhanced NORC communities, it is abundantly clear that the supply of these opportunities is not keeping pace with the growth of America's older population.

Fourth, although advocates for these programs emphasize how they improve the quality of life and care of older people, rigorous scientific assessments are often lacking. We sometimes do not know how older users of these programs differ from other community-dwelling elders, how competently these programs are operated, and whether they achieve their intended outcomes. There is a dearth of careful evaluative studies—relying on quasi-experimental research designs—that show conclusively that without these programs, older people would have been worse off.[216]

And, fifth, however successful the experts might judge these programs to be, some older people do not feel that these community-based initiatives are viable ways for them to achieve residential normalcy. These people must take more extreme coping actions, such as moving to housing and care options specifically designed with their lifestyles and impairments in mind—the focus of the remaining chapters of this book.

NOTES

1. (Stambolian & Blanchard, 2013, p. 241)
2. If the neighborhoods and communities occupied by older people are made more livable or healthier, many other population groups—children, younger adults, and the families of older people—will also benefit throughout their lifetimes.
3. (Alley, Liebig, Pynoos, Banerjee, & Choi, 2007, p. 4)
4. (Feldman & Oberlink, 2003)
5. (Stanford Center on Longevity & MetLife Mature Market Institute, 2013)
6. (Sykes, 2014)
7. (World Health Organization, 2007, p. 5)
8. John Feather, "What Does Age-Friendly Look Like?" *Huffington Post*, June 5, 2014, accessed at http://www.huffingtonpost.com/john-feather-phd/what-does-age-friendly-look-like_b_5453548.html
9. (Feldman, Oberlink, Simantov, & Gursen, 2004, p. xviii)
10. (World Health Organization, 2007)
11. (Farber & Shinkle, 2011)
12. (Ferrini & Ferrini, 2008)
13. (MetLife Foundation, 2005)
14. (Dunham-Jones & Williamson, 2011)
15. (Bayne & Boling, 2009)
16. (Castle et al., 2009, p. 45)
17. (Coleman et al., 2006)
18. (Naik et al., 2010)
19. (Castle et al., 2009)
20. (Katz & Frank, 2011)
21. (Greenberg, 2014)
22. (Kamo, Henderson, & Roberto, 2011)
23. (Hyer, Brown, Polivka-West, & Berman, 2010)
24. (Hyer et al., 2010)
25. (Brown et al., 2012; Dosa et al., 2012; Hyer et al., 2010)
26. (Hyer et al., 2010, p. 1963)
27. (Marottoli & Coughlin, 2011)
28. (Wahl, Oswald, & Zimprich, 1999)
29. (Dugan, Barton, Coyle, & Lee, 2013)
30. (McKnight, 2003; Vanderbur & Silverstein, 2011)
31. (Lynott et al., 2009)
32. (Dugan et al., 2013, p. 347)
33. (Rosenbloom, 2009)
34. http://www.slashgear.com/google-driverless-cars-safety-bill-passes-in-california-22229354/
35. (Lynott, Fox-Grage, & Guzman, 2013)
36. (Lynott et al., 2013; Robinson et al., 2012)
37. (Ball, 2012)
38. Testimony of Katherine Freund, founder and president of ITNAmerica, before the Senate Special Committee on Aging hearing on "Transportation: A Challenge to Independence for Seniors," November 6, 2013.
39. (Farber & Shinkle, 2011)
40. (Rosenbloom, 2013, p. 1)
41. (Vanderbur & Silverstein, 2011, p. 28)
42. (Koffman, Weiner, Pfeiffer, & Chapman, 2010; Rosenbloom, 2009)
43. (Kerr et al., 2012)
44. (Kerr et al., 2012)
45. (Dumbaugh, 2008)
46. Thereby discouraging accessory dwelling units (see Chapter 8).

47. (Farber & Shinkle, 2011)
48. (Grant, 2007, p. 495)
49. (Duany, Plater-Zyberk, & Speck, 2000)
50. (Duany et al., 2000)
51. (Farber & Shinkle, 2011)
52. (Marshall, 2000)
53. (Meredith, 2003)
54. (Pollack, Bluestone, & Billingham, 2010)
55. (Netherland et al., 2011)
56. (Atlanta Regional Commission, 2009)
57. (Atlanta Regional Commission, 2009)
58. (Hunter et al., 2011)
59. (Harrell, Brooks, & Nedwick, 2009)
60. (Duany et al., 2000)
61. (Duany et al., 2000)
62. Some define NORCs as places where at least 40% of the residents are age 60 and over.
63. (Hunt & Gunter-Hunt, 1985)
64. (Vladeck, 2008)
65. (Craig, 2008; Greenfield, Scharlach, Lehning, Davitt, & Graham, 2013; United Hospital Fund, 2010)
66. (Lawler, 2001; Ormond et al., 2004)
67. (Vladeck, Segel, Oberlink, Gursen, & Rudin, 2010, p. 69)
68. (Golant, 1999, 2008a)
69. (Evashwick & Holt, 2000; Medicare Payment Advisory Commission, 2001)
70. (Colello, 2007; Engquist, Johnson, & Johnson, 2010)
71. (Engquist et al., 2010)
72. (Bedney, Goldberg, & Josephson, 2010, p. 316)
73. (Greenfield, 2011, p. 2)
74. (Greenfield, 2011)
75. (Moody, 2008, p. 8)
76. (Greenfield, 2011)
77. (Greenfield, 2013)
78. It is the largest federation of the Jewish Federations of North America.
79. (Ball, 2012; Ormond et al., 2004; Vladeck, 2008)
80. (Bedney et al., 2010)
81. (Enguidanos, Pynoos, Siciliano, Diepenbrock, & Alexman, 2010)
82. (Bedney et al., 2010, p. 308)
83. (Enguidanos et al., 2010)
84. (Greenfield, 2011, p. 2)
85. (Ball, 2012)
86. (Craig, 2008)
87. (Bedney et al., 2010). These NORC SSPs were led by Jewish Federations of North America's National NORCs Aging in Place Initiative and administered by the Administration on Aging (Greenfield, 2013).
88. (Ormond et al., 2004)
89. (Greenfield, 2011)
90. (Craig, 2008)
91. (Anetzberger, 2010)
92. (Enguidanos et al., 2010)
93. (Scharlach, Graham, & Lehning, 2012)
94. (Greenfield et al., 2013)
95. In about a quarter of Elder Village models, however, the residents have joined with a not-for-profit service organization to run their programs rather than establish and control the organization themselves (Greenfield, Scharlach, Graham, Davitt, & Lehning, 2012).

96. (McDonough & Davitt, 2011; Scharlach et al., 2012)
97. (Greenfield, Scharlach, Graham, et al., 2012)
98. Bruce Craig, aging program specialist, U.S. Administration on Aging, personal communication, 2010.
99. (Greenfield et al., 2013)
100. (Greenfield, Scharlach, Graham, et al., 2012)
101. (McWinney-Morse, 2009)
102. (Greenfield, Scharlach, Lehning, & Davitt, 2012)
103. (McWinney-Morse, 2009)
104. See http://www.vtvnetwork.org/.
105. (Scharlach et al., 2012)
106. (McDonough & Davitt, 2011, p. 539)
107. (Ball, 2012)
108. (Ball, 2012)
109. (Ball, 2012)
110. (McDonough & Davitt, 2011)
111. (Bronstein, Gellis, & Kenaley, 2011)
112. (Golant, 2014a)
113. (Greenfield et al., 2013)
114. (Scharlach et al., 2012)
115. (Greenfield et al., 2013)
116. (Bronstein & Kenaley, 2011; Enguidanos et al., 2010)
117. The selling value of the dwelling minus the current mortgage obligation and any selling transaction costs.
118. The number of older people who occupy rental units subsidized by state and local government programs is unknown.
119. (Joint Center for Housing Studies of Harvard University, 2013b)
120. Perhaps surprisingly, accurate statistical overviews of the availability of affordable rental housing assistance are difficult to obtain. This difficulty reflects the variety of rental assistance programs in operation often funding the same rental project, making unduplicated counts difficult, and the poor documentation of the presence of elderly occupants.
121. National Council of State Housing Agencies, Q & A on the Housing Credit Program, 2012
122. (Joint Center for Housing Studies of Harvard University, 2014)
123. (National Low Income Housing Coalition, 2012)
124. (National Low Income Housing Coalition, 2012)
125. For example, a property might be financed under the Section 202 program and receive Section 8 project-based rental assistance.
126. (National Low Income Housing Coalition, 2012)
127. (U.S. Government Accountability Office, 2005)
128. (Williamson, 2011)
129. (Enterprise Community Partners, 2011)
130. (Perl, 2010)
131. (Perl, 2010)
132. (Enterprise Community Partners, 2011)
133. (Perl, 2010)
134. (Smith & Ferryman, 2006)
135. (U.S. Government Accountability Office, 2005)
136. (Perl, 2010)
137. (Haley & Gray, 2008)
138. The Section 202 program now targets older adults only, but some of its units may also be occupied by nonelderly tenants because until 1992, the program also produced housing (Section 811) for the disabled (U.S. Government Accountability Office, 2005).
139. (U.S. Government Accountability Office, 2005)
140. (Olsen, 2003)

141. (Rice & Sard, 2009)
142. (Rice & Sard, 2009)
143. Harrell, Brooks, & Nedwick, 2009)
144. (National Low Income Housing Coalition, Public Housing Fact Sheet, June 2012 & Smith & Ferryman, 2006)
145. (Smith & Ferryman, 2006)
146. (Rice & Sard, 2009)
147. (National Low Income Housing Coalition, 2012)
148. (Joint Center for Housing Studies of Harvard University, 2013a)
149. (National Low Income Housing Coalition, 2012)
150. (Joint Center for Housing Studies of Harvard University, 2013a)
151. (Commission on Affordable Housing and Health Facility Needs for Seniors in the 21st Century, 2002; Redfoot & Kochera, 2004)
152. (Golant, 1999)
153. (Redfoot & Kochera, 2004)
154. (Smith & Ferryman, 2006)
155. (Kochera, 2006)
156. (Kochera, 2006)
157. (Locke, Lam, Henry, & Brown, 2011)
158. (Golant, 2008a)
159. (Golant, 2008a; Golant, Parsons, & Boling, 2010; Stone, Harahan, & Sanders, 2008)
160. (Golant, 1999, 2008a)
161. (Stone et al., 2008)
162. (Kochera, 2006; Joint Center for Housing Studies of Harvard University, 2014)
163. (Haley & Gray, 2008)
164. (Sheehan & Oakes, 2006)
165. (Golant et al., 2010, p. 13)
166. (Golant, 2008a)
167. (Levine & Johns, 2008, p. 2)
168. The following service delivery examples are drawn from "Institute for the Future of Aging Services" (2009, pp. 4–5)
169. (National PACE Association, 2003)
170. (American Association of Homes and Services for the Aging, 2010)
171. U.S. HUD, Notice PIH-2012-31 (HA).
172. (Golant, 2003c)
173. (Kochera, 2006)
174. (Locke et al., 2011)
175. (Golant, 2003c, 2006)
176. (Golant et al., 2010, p. 7; Stone et al., 2008)
177. (Golant, 2003c)
178. (Elderly Housing Coalition, 2000, p. 7)
179. (Cohen, 2010)
180. (Kochera, 2006)
181. (Castle & Resnick, 2014, p. 116; and see also, Golant, 2003c)
182. (Jenkens, Carder, & Maher, 2004)
183. (Khadduri & Locke, 2012)
184. (Kochera, 2006)
185. (Khadduri & Locke, 2012, p. 6)
186. (Khadduri & Locke, 2012)
187. (Khadduri & Locke, 2012)
188. (Haley & Gray, 2008)
189. (Levine & Johns, 2008)
190. (Haley & Gray, 2008; Levine & Johns, 2008)
191. (Redfoot & Kochera, 2004)

192. (Sheehan & Guzzardo, 2008; Stone et al., 2008)
193. (Levine & Johns, 2008; Sheehan & Guzzardo, 2008; Stone et al., 2008)
194. (Sheehan & Guzzardo, 2008, p. 242)
195. (Sheehan & Guzzardo, 2008, p. 240)
196. (Golant et al., 2010)
197. (Stone et al., 2008)
198. (Castle & Resnick, 2014; "Institute for the Future of Aging Services," 2009; Pynoos, Liebig, Alley, & Nishita, 2004; Wilden & Redfoot, 2002)
199. (Locke et al., 2011, p. 18)
200. (Commission on Affordable Housing and Health Facility Needs for Seniors in the 21st Century, 2002; Golant, 2003c; Levine & Johns, 2008; Stone et al., 2008)
201. (Golant et al., 2010)
202. (Black, Rabins, & German, 1999; Weinberger et al., 1986)
203. (Ficke & Berkowitz, 2000; Monk & Kaye, 1991)
204. (Ficke & Berkowitz, 2000)
205. (Ficke & Berkowitz, 2000, p. 3)
206. This draws heavily on "Institute for the Future of Aging Services" (2009, p. 3).
207. (Levine & Johns, 2008; Sheehan & Guzzardo, 2008)
208. (Sheehan & Guzzardo, 2008, p. 263)
209. (Mollica & Morris, 2005, p. i)
210. (Mollica & Morris, 2005, p. 2)
211. (Siu, 2009)
212. (Ellenbecker, Byrne, O'Brien, & Rogosta, 2002)
213. (Badger & McArthur, 2003)
214. (Stone, 2009; but see Castle & Resnick, 2014)
215. (Golant, 2014a)
216. (Golant, 2014a)

Part V

Coping to Achieve Residential Normalcy

Tailor-Made Housing and Care

10

MOVING TO FULLY ENGAGE IN LIFE

Active Adult Communities and Senior Cohousing Developments

When Sun City, the first 55-plus retirement community, opened {in 1960}, average life expectancy for Americans was 69.7. It seemed like the perfect spot to live out the last 10 or 15 years of your life. They'd be golden years, indeed, colored by sunny days and the carefree lifestyle of age-segregated developments: no traffic, no kids, no nonsense. Just heated pools and exercise classes and nights full of Mah Jong and bridge. Amid cookie cutter homes, retirement communities promised companionship.[1]

STRIVING TO BE FULLY ENGAGED IN LIFE

A small proportion of older people feel more fully engaged in life when they occupy residential alternatives known as active adult communities and senior cohousing communities. These are purposively planned housing options produced by the private sector that target moderate- and higher-income older adults. These consumers are not urgently seeking solutions to address their inability to live independently, to manage their health ailments, or to remedy unmanageable or intolerable housing problems. Rather, these typically active, healthy, and financially independent Third Age populations are leaving their current abodes in the hopes of spending their remaining, mostly retirement years, in places that offer them a more enjoyable, stimulating, and comfortable way of life. Older people are moving to these alternatives to feel more squarely in their residential comfort zones.

However, these housing options also enable older adults to feel more secure and in control of their environs. An early researcher of these communities recognized that

255

they appealed to older adults not just for their material and social comforts but also because they helped them feel more self-reliant, autonomous, and independent.[2] Here these older occupants feel out of harm's way,[3] have confidence in the future appearance and valuations of their dwellings and neighborhoods, and have considerable say in how they spend their days and with whom they interact. Because they feel more competent and in control at their new addresses, they are also squarely in their residential mastery zones.

ACTIVE ADULT COMMUNITIES

We often think of active adult communities as a homogeneous category, but in reality, they include a diverse array of housing products. Although some of the most popular communities consist of single-family, detached, and owned dwellings sited on well-manicured lawns in well-planned subdivisions, others consist of attached dwellings, duplexes, and townhomes and still others of low-rise, mid-rise, or high-rise condominiums or apartment complexes. Although homeownership dominates, the occupants of some mobile (manufactured) home parks own their dwellings but only lease or rent their lots or pods. Many active adult communities (about 35%) also fall into the category of gated communities because fences and walls physically separate them from other residential areas and security personnel patrol their grounds.[4]

The population size, physical space, and scope of leisure amenities of these communities vary dramatically.[5] At one end of the continuum are some of the largest and often earliest developed communities, built in California and Arizona in the 1960s by such famous developers as Del Webb and Ross W. Cortese. They include places such as Sun City, Leisure World, and Rossmoor Leisure World. Tens of thousands of seniors occupy these communities that often spread over thousands of acres.

These communities offer a full complement of indoor and outdoor recreation and leisure activities, some with more extravagant amenities than others, including swimming pools, shuffleboards, fitness centers, spas, aerobics studios, billiard rooms, bistros, beauty salons, arts and crafts centers, movie theaters, libraries, computer and investment clubs, educational classes, jogging and bicycle trails, water aerobics classes, softball leagues, cross-country skiing, ice skating, bocce courts, and game rooms. Some contain commercial districts that mimic those found in towns and small cities and include retail stores, banks, restaurants, hair stylists, brokerage houses, and small hospitals. In some of these communities, the residents access their neighborhoods and commercial centers not with cars but with golf carts, whereas in others they get around by a minibus.

The largest single-site retirement community in the world, The Villages in central Florida, is occupied by more than 70,000 occupants on 25,000 acres and contains 91 recreational centers, 69 pools, 1,000 clubs, and 47 golf courses. It contains multiple neighborhoods (about 50) bordered by lakes and recreation centers, all with access to three downtowns with extensive retail and entertainment establishments. Suburban strip mall shopping centers are aligned along the development's periphery, and passing through The Villages complex is a highway corridor that contains a large complex of health-related services and businesses.[6]

At the other end of the continuum, the smallest active adult communities consist of fewer than 25 units located on less than 10 acres.[7] These communities are best called residential subdivisions or building complexes. In Massachusetts, for example, 80% of existing active adult developments have fewer than 100 units.[8] Other residential enclaves, such as high-rise condominium projects, may be concentrated on but a square mile of land.[9] These residential enclaves blend into their suburban surroundings, typically lack commercial establishments, and often include only the amenities of a clubhouse, along with swimming pools, tennis courts, and golf courses.

In between these two extremes are retirement villages, which include medium-sized and smaller communities (with a median size of 566 dwelling units and median area of 282 acres).[10] They may offer a full complement of recreation and leisure activities but typically are not self-contained communities, and their residents must rely on outside commercial establishments for their everyday shopping and services. These may be accessible only by auto transportation.[11]

Traditionally, active adult communities were built in year-round warm and sunny places, such as Florida, Arizona, and California. As developers recognized that older people were attracted to these places not just because of their climates, they increasingly developed them in locations outside the Sunbelt, in states such as Connecticut, Illinois, New York, Massachusetts, New Jersey, North and South Carolina, and Virginia.[12] Older occupants were clearly willing to give up good weather in return for the benefits of remaining in their familiar states and communities, close to family, friends, services, and their religious congregations.

Developers also found that local governments throughout the country welcomed these residential enclaves. Not only did they bring the usual economic benefits (e.g., more jobs, local tax revenues, and consumer spending), but they also did not add any fiscal burden to the local school system (see also Chapter 3), and active adults imposed less of a burden on most public services than people in other types of residential developments.[13]

ONLY FOR THE OLD?

The developers of these communities must initially decide whether older people will be their exclusive occupants. *Age-qualified or age-restricted communities* restrict their occupancy to older people—usually defined as age 55 and older—who they believe favor age-homogeneous enclaves.[14] In contrast, other developers of *age-targeted active adult communities* seek to reach a larger and more diverse group of consumers, focusing on older people in their marketing efforts but remaining open to younger people as residents. They do not have explicit age restrictions and cannot legally prohibit children or teenagers from living in their developments.[15]

As of 2009, just over 1 million households, or about 3% of households headed by those age 55 and older, occupied age-qualified or age-restricted active adult communities.[16] If we include age-targeted owner-occupied communities (mostly occupied by older households), we add an additional 8.2 million households, or 21% of households headed by those age 55 and older.[17] National polls of people in their mid-50s and early

60s indicate that the demand for these communities is likely to remain strong, if only because of the size of the baby boomer population.[18]

THE GOVERNMENT DECIDES WHO IS OLD

The 55-and-older age cutoff to define who is "old" in these communities did not happen by chance. It was a product of federal legislation and illustrates how government policies can influence a housing option created by the private sector.[19] Originally, Title VIII of the Civil Rights Act of 1968 or the Fair Housing Act protected several classes of population (based on their race, color, religion, national origin, and sex) from being discriminated against in the housing market. Twenty years later, in 1988, Congress passed the Fair Housing Amendments Act, which added another protected group, families with children (and it also added "handicapped" people). This was in response to much evidence that apartment managers were refusing to rent (or charging higher rents) to families with babies and children.

But to placate advocates for older population groups, Congress recognized the virtues of housing exclusively for older people because of their special needs and preferences. Consequently, they exempted an age-distinct category, "housing for older persons," from having to meet the nondiscriminatory familial requirements of the Fair Housing Amendments Act. Simply put, senior housing developers could exclude families with children as residents. The final rule issued as part of the Housing for Older Persons Act of 1995[20] exempted housing intended and operated for occupancy by people 55 years of age and older as long as it met the following three requirements:

- At least 80% of the units in the housing facility are occupied (not owned) by at least one person age 55 or older.
- The owner or manager of the housing facility or community must publish and adhere to policies and procedures that show the owner's intent to provide housing for people age 55 or older (e.g., in its marketing materials).
- The community must comply with HUD rules for verification of occupancy (e.g., conducting resident surveys on an ongoing basis inquiring about the age of the residents).[21]

OCCUPANTS OF ACTIVE ADULT COMMUNITIES

We usually associate active adult communities with healthy, empty nest couples in their late 50s and 60s. However, statistical profiles reveal a more complex mosaic of resident demographics. For example, one occupant analysis revealed that about 35% were older than age 75. A significant share was also not married but lived alone (43%). Among these one-person households, 11% were men, and 32% were women.[22] Other studies had different results. Among residents sampled in Del Webb–developed communities (mostly in western states), 83% were married or living with a partner.[23] More generally, the age, sex, and marital status composition of these places depend on how long ago they were developed and whether their earlier residents have aged in place.

Most occupants of these communities have higher incomes and are better edu-cated. The average income of movers to these communities is just under $81,000, and only about 20% have a high school (or less) education.[24] However, smaller numbers of lower-income older people also occupy these communities, and about 21% reported annual incomes under $21,000.[25] These people often occupy the more affordable slices of these communities, such as manufactured home parks or low-rise condominium complexes.[26]

Most occupants make these communities their year-round residence, although a small share reside there only in the winter.[27] A significant percentage of the occupants of these communities, particularly the youngest, are still working full or part time, and this is an increasing trend. This accounts for why, after the mid-1960s, developers dropped "retirement" from their active adult retirement community labeling.[28]

Minorities, particularly African-Americans and Hispanics, are underrepresented in these communities, and this is true for some religious groups, such as Jewish peo-ple,[29] although we can find examples with substantial shares of this religious group.[30] According to data from a 2009 American Housing Survey, 12% of recent movers to active adult communities were minorities, a percentage that is likely to increase in the future.[31]

CONSUMER PREFERENCES AND THE ATTRACTIONS OF THIS ALTERNATIVE

More than 90% of older people who purchased homes in age-qualified active adult communities believe they are now occupying better or comparable units than the ones they moved from, and 100% believe their new neighborhoods are comparable or better in quality. Many but not all are living in smaller dwellings than before they moved.[32] About 86% of the residents in these communities report paying the same or a higher price for their new homes. Moreover, although most paid cash for their dwellings, compared with earlier occupants of these communities, they were also more likely to take out a mortgage.[33]

Attractive dwelling designs and high-quality amenities are often a key market-ing pitch of developers. Along with single-level housing with an accessible layout that is easy to maintain inside and out, today's older boomers want dwellings with home offices, cathedral ceilings, spacious kitchens, walk-in closets, sufficient storage, two-car garages, an extra bedroom for visiting grandchildren, Jacuzzis, and high-speed Internet. An increasing number of active adult communities (e.g., Stonebridge in Lake Bluff, Illinois, and Saddleback in Tucson, Arizona) now also offer extra-wide hallways and walk-in showers in anticipation of occupants who will welcome such design ele-ments when they become physically limited.[34]

They also want their dwellings to be near a shopping center and hospital or doc-tor's office.[35] Herein lies the appeal of the New Urbanism–like design of many of these active communities. In the very large Villages active adult community, the majority of the residents get around using their golf carts.

As would be expected, the newest occupants of active adult communities, namely the older baby boomers (in 2015, ages 51 to 69), have consumer preferences that dis-tinguish them from the earlier Silent Generation (born 1923–1945). One experienced consultant with extensive knowledge of the active adult industry identifies the following trends[36]:

- Boomers are much more savvy retirement housing consumers and have typically purchased between 3–9 homes in their lifetime. These buyers know what they want and are reluctant to compromise.

- Recreation preferences continue to change. Unlike the late 80s, where virtually all active adult communities relied on golf as the primary amenity, golf now ranks much lower than such activities as walking facilities, fishing, bocce, tennis, and pickleball.

- Retirees prefer one-story single-family homes with no steps between parking and front door. The size of individual dwellings can be smaller but still well constructed and featuring no reduction in amenities. Large multi-use spaces are replacing specialty rooms (e.g., family rooms, living rooms, dining rooms). They are more likely to demand design and construction techniques that conserve water, electricity, and natural gas.

- They seek somewhat smaller dwelling unit sizes, on average about 2,363 square feet.

- Newly developed communities are smaller than in the past, ranging from 10,000 to 2,500 units located in more intimate communities. This trend reflects the difficulties of financing these developments.

- The majority of boomers are attracted to communities that are in places with colleges or established higher education programs because they desire to continue their education. Communities not in proximity to higher learning institutions have brought in private education, on-line, and community educational entities.

- "Resort-style active adult communities" appeal to only 7% of the age- and income-qualified boomer market. Boomers are increasingly seeking to spend their retirement in small towns and rural locations.

- Many factors attract retirees, including affordability, healthcare, transportation, established social fabric, significant retention of visual history, and moderate climate. Increasingly, however, boomers are attracted by their proximity to family, especially grandchildren. High on the list is also a community that guarantees safety and security. Developers are having difficulty achieving these goals because of a growing reluctance by municipalities to allow private roads and secure entry gates as a facet of the community's security program. The New Urbanism requirement for street connectivity is also making this difficult.

- Contrary to some predictions, boomers are not relocating from either the suburbs or rural communities to multi-family dwellings in urban cores.

Developers are also acutely aware that no single housing product will appeal to all older boomers, and success will depend on knowing local consumer preferences and values. As senior housing expert Andrew Carle emphasizes, *"Retirees want more choices. . . . They have a lot of expectations with retirement."*[37] In the language of the New Gerontology paradigm, older adults are looking to active adult communities as a means to be fully engaged in life, but they may differ substantially as to what they mean by "fully engaged." Some of the newer communities offer recreational or leisure activities that particularly appeal to aspiring artists, astronomy lovers, former letter carriers, art and music lovers, and equestrians. More communities now make healthy lifestyles their major focus by offering sporting activities (e.g., tennis, volleyball, workouts, water aerobics), professionally equipped fitness centers, healthful eating (e.g., organic gardens), marathon running, extensive biking trails, and tai chi.[38] To appeal to older adults with strong intellectual interests, especially university alumni, college-affiliated retirement communities offer their residents access to higher education classes and events.[39]

In recognition of the diversity of this older consumer market, we can identify a complex array of motives that most influence their decisions.

AGE, PEOPLE, RELATIONSHIPS, AND ENGAGING IN LIFE: SHARPLY DIVIDED OPINIONS

ADVANTAGES OF AN AGE HOMOGENEOUS OR RESTRICTED POPULATION

Although they may not cite the similar ages of their neighbors as a prime reason for their selecting these communities, most occupants view age homogeneity as a positive feature.[40] This should not surprise us given that these older people are well aware of the demographic distinctiveness of these places when they make their moving decisions. In one poll, a sample of residents now living in Del Webb retirement communities were asked if they moved again, would they prefer another community that was also age restricted. Almost three-quarters answered in the positive, 20% had no preference, and only 6% responded that they preferred to live in a community with people of all ages.[41]

Studies of these communities have consistently reported that their occupants were comfortable with the demographics of their neighbors. The earliest research by sociologists found that the residents of age-segregated communities were more likely to have higher morale, greater residential satisfaction, and higher levels of social interaction.[42]

The occupants of today's age-restricted communities simply do not feel that ongoing intergenerational relationships are important. Some may even feel that including a younger population in their community would reduce safety and increase *"drug busts, wild parties, loud stereos, and auto accidents."*[43] Occasional visits with children are one thing; continually confronting the playing and screaming of their neighbors' insensitive and uncaring children is quite another.

Their occupants also emphasize that their communities enable them to avoid ageist attitudes and behaviors that continually assault their self-worth. One Sun City resident sadly recalls his experiences in a prior residence:

I mean, it was as though people were being pushed away because they were retired, and the assumption was they had nothing to contribute.[44]

These views give credibility to a conclusion I have held for three decades in examining these places; namely, living in an age-segregated setting gives older people the option of reducing their involvement with a society that seems overly preoccupied with the desirability of youth, the rewards of employment, and the joys of child-raising.[45]

In contrast, the older people living in these communities respect and appreciate others of their own age.[46] Being around people who are more understanding and accepting makes it easier for them to embark on new activities and lifestyles and to try out never-before-contemplated recreational and leisure activities. They can forge social connections based less on what they have done in the past and more on what they will be doing during retirement.[47]

Many volunteer their time, such as helping with landscaping, serving as ambulance drivers, organizing recreational activities, and functioning as first responders in medical emergencies. In the Sun City (Arizona) active adult community, residents volunteer to become members of the Posse neighborhood watch group, who ride in police cars and supplement the regular county law enforcement.[48]

In a homogenous social setting, they also feel freer to voice their opinions.[49] Often the older people in these communities hold similar political views. Because they are more likely to vote as a "single-minded" electorate, they can get their candidates into office and achieve more favorable outcomes on local and state voting referendums.[50]

Occupants of these communities also share common individual histories as members of the same generation. They were influenced by the same social events and trends, benefited from the same life-saving vaccinations against major diseases, engaged in the same wars, experienced the same economic downturns and boom periods, benefited from the same advances in computer technology, and together witnessed how attitudes changed toward racial and ethnic minorities. Consequently, when the occupants of these communities talk about their lives, they can understand and relate to each other.

The rapid pace of social and technological change also contributes to the social attractions of these age homogeneous residential enclaves—but in different ways. On the one hand, their physical distance from friends and family is no longer a barrier to communication. E-mail, text messages, and Skype have made it easier to maintain social ties with loved ones, even when separated by thousands of miles. Thus, older people can easily keep in close touch with adult children and former friends living elsewhere; intimacy at a distance is now feasible.

On the other hand, older people still have a fundamental human need for authentic face-to-face relationships. In a society where interpersonal relationships are increasingly sustained by artificial conduits such as Facebook, older people feel an even greater urgency to have trusting and sympathetic friends close by to share their feelings. Older people in active adult communities can enjoy this closeness with their age and generation peers. Listen to an older resident of a town-like retirement community on Vancouver Island in Canada:

It means knowing there are people close by that care about you, that keep in touch with you, that when you walk down into town you're going to meet people you know . . . being recognized in stores and banks and other places where you do business. Having people be glad to visit and come to your home.[51]

Altogether, such community responses have led me also to conclude that there is nothing intrinsically evil, malicious, or immoral about advocating that large numbers of older people live near each other. Neither geographic nor social isolation is a necessary result.[52]

DISADVANTAGES OF AN AGE HOMOGENEOUS OR RESTRICTED POPULATION

We must remind ourselves that the positive views about age-segregated living are typically expressed by a self-selected group of active adult community residents. Many older people who do not live in these communities and many expert commentators do not share these enthusiastic assessments. For these critics, such communities are examples of blatant exclusionary and discriminatory population practices that prevent younger and older populations from together enjoying the same built environments, social opportunities, and activities. They view these enclaves as *"sterile, isolated, and artificial"*[53] and *"cold and depressing"*[54] because they prevent old and young from living together, communicating, and sharing a common way of life. As two experts explain: *"Spatial separation reflects and engenders ageism and reverse ageism. Propinquity and social contact are important in facilitating intergenerational relations and understanding."*[55]

These criticisms are timeless. In the 1950s, great urban historian Lewis Mumford claimed that planned age-segregated residential enclaves *"regard the aged as a segregated group"* that should be removed from *"their families, their neighbors, and their friends, from their familiar quarters and their familiar neighborhoods."*[56]

Not surprisingly, given the period in which he was writing, Mumford saw age-segregated communities as geriatric ghettos that put older people, seen as vulnerable, dependent, and largely inactive, at a distinctive interpersonal disadvantage because they were separated from the love and respect of friends, family, and neighbors and were deprived of communications and stimulation from the outside world. Such physical separation contradicted what he viewed as normal aging, which is to remain with known social networks in long-occupied housing arrangements.[57]

Other early authorities held similar views and even tried to discourage the first developers of these communities. When the Del Webb developers were deciding whether to build Sun City (Arizona), they sought the opinion of the University of Chicago's Dr. Robert Havighurst, an authority on work and retirement patterns of older people. A staunch believer in intergenerational relationships, Havighurst nixed the idea. When they asked the advice of top developers at the Urban Land Institute, they, too, argued that older people wanted to be with their families and would shun living together in an isolated community.[58] Mumford's legacy seemed intact. The experts were all wrong, of course, and Sun City turned out to be a major success story, attracting 100,000 visitors (10,000 were expected) on the opening weekend and creating one of the largest traffic jams in Arizona's history.[59]

Some contemporary commentators, such as popular writer Andrew Blechman, are upset for a different reason. He views these exclusive residential enclaves as made up of selfish, self-indulgent, and overly self-righteous older people. He seriously questions why we *"should want to promote communities where birth certificates are scrutinized at points of entry"*[60] and help their older occupants practice their fraudulent pleasure-oriented lifestyles?

Others argue that age-segregated communities have made older people too politically powerful.[61] For these critics, *"The emergence and proliferation of active adult communities says a lot about the growing affluence, health, and social values of a certain percentage of broadly defined, middle-class retirees in the United States and their impact on social, cultural, and political issues."*[62] They resent that the older residents in these communities have the ability to vote against government bond issues that would support the development of new public schools or funding for future road networks.[63] This criticism is also not new. In the mid-1990s, a noted economist, Lester C. Thurow, characterized segregated elderly communities as a calculated consumer strategy by which seniors seek political power and tax breaks.[64] Similarly, it galls Blechman that younger generations are paying for the government programs that fund the Social Security, Medicare, Medicaid, and pensions received by these secluded and privileged old. He asks why should we expect American taxpayers *"to foot the bill for millions of hedonistic young seniors living in gated geritopias?"*[65] *"Why are we providing these 'seniors' with a legally codified right to keep the rest of society at bay?"*[66]

The negative views of these detractors once again illustrate how the subjective experiences of older people can diverge tremendously from the assessments by others—especially experts and pundits—who do not live in these communities and are in much earlier stages of their own lives.

Moreover, for unexplained reasons we do not criticize the age-segregated residential enclaves of younger populations. Most Americans over the course of their (younger) lives occupy age-homogeneous buildings or communities (e.g., summer camp, college dormitories, singles high-rise buildings, neighborhoods of mainly younger married couples). These age-homogeneous locales seldom elicit the same visceral reactions as age-segregated communities of older adults. We rarely debate the pros and cons of what these younger population enclaves communicate about ways of life, self-worth, or power. Somehow, we avoid discussing whether intergenerational relationships are strengthened or weakened when younger age groups live together.

ACTIVELY ENGAGED IN LIFE OR PRACTICING AN UNPRODUCTIVE AND WASTEFUL LIFESTYLE

The leisure- and recreational-oriented lifestyles offered by these communities are unquestionably a key attraction for many older occupants. Yet many experts condemn the way of life promoted by age-homogenous communities. They argue that the "lifestyle products" marketed by these communities are inconsistent with how older people should be actively engaged in life (Chapter 1).

For celebrated feminist Betty Friedan, *"the activities in active adult communities were quite empty"*[67] and had no meaning or purpose. For her, these communities were *"adult playpens"* that failed to offer their older residents—particularly their women—mentally challenging jobs, causes, or projects. Marc Freedman, who was described by *The New York Times* as *"the voice of aging baby boomers who are eschewing retirement for . . . meaningful and sustaining work later in life,"*[68] similarly argues, *"Activity for activity's sake can be vapid, self-indulgent, and ultimately boring."*[69]

These commentators seek to fine-tune the successful aging prescriptions of the New Gerontology paradigm by arguing that only certain types of activity are acceptable. Thus, they would take issue with The Villages active adult community in central Florida marketing itself as a *"vacation that never ends,"*[70] a *"Disneyworld of retirement,"* and a place where *"retirees' dreams come true."*[71] They cringe at the idea that a Third Age lifestyle might help older people recall the fantasies of childhood or remind them of the small town America they once knew.[72] In their minds, older people enjoying these make-believe worlds cannot be aging successfully.

These interpretations are at odds with a late-2009 survey sponsored by the Del Webb corporation[73] that actually paints the older residents in these active adult communities as advocates of the New Gerontology paradigm. They hold decidedly upbeat self-images even as they are getting old and feel they are living life to the fullest. The majority see themselves as seniors, but only because they get senior discounts. In fact, 80% report that they feel younger than their age. Only 37% of the Del Webbers felt they were less active than 15 years earlier; rather, most felt healthier than their parents. They particularly attributed their upbeat dispositions to their ability to practice their hobbies, enjoy continued education opportunities, and participate in volunteer activities.

As one scholar concluded after studying the large Villages community of central Florida,

> The Villages may be seen as a built embodiment of the logic upon which the Third Age is based—that is, the denial of the existence of the last period of life, the Fourth Age of decrepitude, dependence, and death.[74]

Other experts, even those not particularly enamored of these planned communities, have reached similar conclusions.[75] Geographer Kevin McHugh admits, *"Active adult communities arose as an antidote to negative stereotypes of older age as a period of decline in physical and social competencies."*[76] Similarly, gerontologist Robert Kastenbaum interprets these communities as an antidote to the *"erosion of change."*[77]

BORING AND CONTROLLING VERSUS PREDICTABLE AND SECURE

Critics often lambaste active adult communities for their boring sameness, but their older occupants see them differently. They like their predictable, unchanging, and controlled residential surroundings. They are not turned off by dwellings, lawns, and neighborhoods that all look plastic and artificial; rather, they like *"lawns that are perfectly edged"* and *"driveways so clean they look scrubbed."*[78] Older occupants of active adult communities generally view their simple, low-maintenance dwellings as attractive. These contrasting views remind us of how critics decried the Long Island, New York, suburban Levittown homes that were mass-produced after World War II as artificial and suffering from a cookie-cutter uniformity, even as they sold like hotcakes.

Rather, the residents of active adult communities seem happy to live in their boring and predictable urban environments. They do not miss having to confront undesirable changes in the composition of their neighbors, the quality of their public services, the level of their safety, or the physical appearance of nearby dwellings. Unless they make outrageously bad decisions, they do not object if developers or neighborhood associations impose rigid management rules and regulations, such as prohibiting *"hedges over four feet high"* or *"the keeping of more than two pets"* or forbidding visiting children to stay for any time limit *"exceeding a thirty-day duration."*[79] Although the critics might interpret such policies as infringing on the ability of older people to influence their community's affairs—and thus an assault on their autonomy—most residents are willing to let management make these policies.[80]

As prominent gerontologist Gordon Streib concluded after studying 36 communities in four states, their occupants look favorably on these rules because of their long-term benefits:

> Most residents of retirement communities are seeking stability—a continuation of the conditions they thought were present when they moved in. Autonomy means maintaining the status quo.[81]

And as I have noted,

> A critical latent function provided by the retirement community—far more effectively than by the natural community setting—is the predictability of its future status. The retirement village gives considerable assurance to the occupants that the social environment and the facilities that presently exist will not significantly change in the near future. It represents, therefore, an example, of a stable, planned community whose future is predictable.[82]

Many older adults value this certainty and predictability, because they are anxious enough worrying that their aging bodies will change in unexpected and unfavorable ways. Just as they want to freeze the aging process and its unfavorable declines, they want to keep their communities as is.[83] In preventing the unexpected, they feel more competent and in control—they have heightened feelings of residential mastery.

Older people are also attracted to active adult communities because of their perceived guarantees of privacy and security. Fostering what one expert calls, somewhat disparagingly, a *"fortress mentality,"*[84] these communities offer their residents assurances that they will keep out the undesirable. This obviously includes criminals but also door-to-door salespeople, pollsters, and other vendors pitching their products and services or charities. Older residents in these communities seek to avoid situations where they feel intruded upon, put upon, and threatened.

Geographer McHugh relates a pertinent observation by Madeline,[85] a former editor of the *Daily Sun,* a Sun City (active adult community) newspaper. She speaks of the insider–outsider mentality of its residents and both the real and symbolic importance of the white walls that surround the community. In her words,

It keeps out crime and it keeps out people they don't want. It keeps out young people and it keeps out children, and it keeps out all the things that were attendant on their lives when they lived in other places. And so there is a concerted feeling of splendid isolation.[86]

These responses help explain why older people find gated communities particularly attractive. Many appreciate that this enforced physical separation helps to ensure that "outsiders" do not use their recreational facilities (e.g., golf courses or swimming pools). They like living in fenced in communities patrolled by crime watch groups.[87] They feel safer walking in their neighborhoods, and when they travel away from their communities, they feel more protected from home burglaries. Some older people also prefer gated communities because they associate these enclosures with social exclusivity and status.[88] They feel their enclaves and the people living in them are something special and different—that is, more privileged or higher status—than other communities.

NOT FOR EVERYONE

Active adult communities elicit more love–hate emotional reactions than perhaps any other older adult housing option. Seven categories of individual differences explain the disparate views of older people (and the experts) toward age-segregated living.

THE AGE IDENTIFICATION FACTOR

Older people hold different attitudes about the desirability of aging and consequently about surrounding themselves with other old people. To elucidate these differences, we turn to the work of Irving Rosow, who identified three patterns of age identification: dissociation, integration, and deviance.[89]

Dissociation Patterns of Age Identification

Older people in this category vigorously deny their oldness and are devout followers of the New Gerontology paradigm. Consequently, these people avoid residential complexes such as active adult communities, which would stereotype them as older people. Similarly, they take great pains to exempt themselves from membership in anything that smacks of a senior citizen group.[90] Despite the financial benefits, these people avoid cashing in on store or movie coupons that give them reduced rates because they are old.

Rather, they try to deny and disguise their aging to prevent others from perceiving them as old and devaluing their worth. They consider being old as tantamount to admitting they are inferior, unattractive, or unwanted members of society or, more recently, as overly self-righteous, greedy, and powerful because they are unfairly receiving government benefits. They look with suspicion on the use of age as an indicator of anything because "you're only as old as you feel and act."

These Third Age older adults also make a special effort to dissociate themselves from members of the Fourth Age, who they consider as abhorrent reminders of aging. Even if they were inclined to associate with other Third Age people in an active adult community, they would diligently avoid residents older than themselves. A study of a long-standing active adult community named Woodhaven, in which most occupants were in their 70s and 80s, dramatically illustrates this avoidance. The management had renovated its facilities, including its clubhouse, to attract young-old occupants. However, the new residents, who were in their 50s and 60s, wanted little to do with its much older occupants. They made this very clear by starting their own exclusive "boomer club," which excluded the majority of older residents.[91]

The conflict between the Third and Fourth Agers was vividly illustrated when a Fourth Ager attempted to formally welcome the younger boomers:

> "Would you mind if I just speak a few minutes to invite people to come and join [in the activities here]?" . . . She was met with a silent and cold reception. There was not a smile in the crowd. [Finally,] . . . this woman raised her hand and she said, "I just wanted to say, we're not really interested in joining the old people. You can just save your breath. We didn't come here to hang out with people old enough to be our parents."[92]

The authors' conclusions make clear the practical implications of people holding a dissociation pattern of age identification:

> At Woodhaven, although both boomers and established residents shared their decisions to live in an age-restricted setting, there . . . was little mutuality between the two and, for some boomers, an abhorrence of common identity. . . . In the end, it is ageism, more precisely fear of age-related illness and decline, that runs throughout this exploration.[93]

Integration Patterns of Age Identification

Older people who display integration patterns of aging strongly identify with their age peers. Consequently, they are more favorably disposed toward living in age-segregated residential settings. They appreciate the many important similarities between themselves and other older people—in their appearance, behaviors, lifestyles, and common historical circumstances (e.g., veterans of World War II or Vietnam or survivors of the Holocaust). They look to these age peers to legitimize how they look and behave in their old age and share information about how to age well. They like people surrounding them who understand their needs, outlooks, and activities and who can celebrate their joys and commiserate with their failings as aging adults.[94]

They also share a common perception of themselves as outsiders in a youth-oriented society. Thus, their association with other older people enables *"a defensive alliance against a shared fate {and} the insulation which peers provide against an indifferent and hostile world."*[95] Through such associations, they reduce potential conflicts or insults that would result from their interactions with younger people.

Deviance Patterns of Age Identification

A third older population group displays deviance patterns of age identification. Whether they identify themselves as being old depends on how they compare themselves with younger people. They hold more negative self-images—and are more likely to identify themselves as old—when they perceive greater age differences between themselves and the young. That is, if they are surrounded by younger people, these older people become painfully more aware of their unproductive lifestyles, old-fashioned values, technological ineptness, and greater physical limitations. Consequently, this subgroup of older people will be favorably disposed toward living in residential settings with other older people but for very different reasons than the "integration" group. In such age-segregated settings, an older person *does not stand out so markedly from his {youthful} neighbors, so it is easier for him to deny his age and flatter himself.*[96] By similar reasoning, these people also think better of themselves when they surround themselves with people older than themselves, because they then perceive *themselves* as being closer to the youth standard than their neighbors.

THE SOCIABILITY FACTOR

Even if older people feel comfortable living side by side with others their age, not all enjoy the amount or intensity of social contacts, neighborly relationships, or friendships found in these communities. Some people, the more introverted, may be happier without such a heightened social environment. Alternatively, other older people already have very satisfactory friendships and family and have little desire to add to their interpersonal relationships. Consistent with Laura Carstensen's socioemotional selectivity theory of aging, some older people want to maintain their level of social involvement but with a smaller set of family and friends than in the past.[97] In contrast, older people who have lost friends because they died or moved away may be anxious to replenish their supportive social relationships. The following typology (also constructed by Rosow) distinguishes five groups of older people with different needs for social contacts and interpersonal relationships[98]:

- *The cosmopolitan:* They have the least contact with neighbors and are oriented to "outside groups," such as children, distant friendships, and organizations outside their neighborhoods. No single type of residential setting is appropriate for them because wherever they live, their social sphere will be outside their neighborhood. *Prediction:* They will have indifferent or negative reactions to living in active adult communities.

- *The phlegmatic:* They do not want any friends or organizational involvement. They interact mainly with spouses, grown children, grandchildren, or siblings. They are candidates for low-density neighborhoods with low friendship opportunities because they are not interested in friends or in seeking support from neighbors. *Prediction:* They will have negative reactions to living in active adult communities.

- *The isolated:* They have low contact with neighbors or friends but seek more social contacts and friends; however, for whatever reasons, they have few or limited social opportunities. *Prediction:* They will have very positive reactions to living in active adult communities.

- *The sociable:* They have moderate or high contact with neighbors and do not want or need more friends. They already lead an active social life with children, friends, and organizational involvements. *Prediction:* Because they already have their social needs fulfilled, they will have negative reactions to living in active adult communities.

- *The insatiable:* They have high contact with neighbors and friends and have an active social life. Nonetheless, these people always want more friends and are looking for opportunities to increase their social interactions. *Prediction:* They will have very positive reactions to living in active adult communities.

THE POLITICAL ORIENTATION AND MINORITY GROUP FACTORS

Researchers question whether groups with certain political orientations will feel comfortable or accepted in these active adult communities. For example, we know that in many active adult communities (e.g., The Villages), the residents have Republican political leanings. Consequently, these places risk turning off older people with more liberal views. Other communities that are primarily Democratic (e.g., Century Village communities of southeast Florida) may turn off Republicans.[99] We expect that the political affiliations of an active adult community will be especially important for older people with stronger political beliefs.

Older people with strong ethnic or religious identities (e.g., Muslims, Jews, African-Americans, Hispanics, and Asians) may similarly feel uncomfortable in these communities because in most they are underrepresented. However, sufficient numbers of minority residents in some of the larger communities will allow them to form their own clubs or chapters. The trend line is favorable. Active adult communities are becoming more racially and ethnically diverse, both because of the disproportionately growing number of minority older baby boomers and because of the efforts of their developers to broaden their market. Still, prospective occupants who identify strongly with their minority status may feel less welcome or comfortable in some of these communities. As Judith Trolander observes, *"These communities in general have a long way to go before their racial diversity mirrors that of the United States."*[100]

THE GENDER AND MARITAL STATUS FACTOR

Historically, developers of these active adult communities targeted married couples and geared their leisure and recreational activities to them. As the populations of these communities have become older—especially in the earliest developed communities—and as the appeal of these communities has widened, an increasing share of the residents are now unmarried (widowed, single, and divorced) women and men.

At issue is whether these unmarried residents feel excluded, lonely, out of place, or continually reminded of their single status. Do they feel comfortable participating in leisure and recreational activities when they are in the minority?[101] Research on these questions is limited, but the few studies suggest that what matters most to unmarried adults is to enjoy the emotional closeness of a few salient friendships. If this is possible, they feel comfortable even when outnumbered by married couples.[102] Still, other studies suggest that loneliness is common among unmarried women, because they outnumber the single men in these communities.[103] However, in the largest retirement community in the United States, The Villages, there are apparently enough widows and relevant activities to create a satisfactory social environment. Many communities also have active singles clubs, and others are targeting single women in their marketing efforts.[104] Consequently, many unmarried women express positive views:

> This is an excellent place for singles. I don't care if I never go back north again. There's an excellent support system for single women here.[105]

One resident further lauds its safer environment:

> As a single woman, I feel safe and secure here. I don't feel threatened like I did back in Boston. Back home, I'd be stuck in the house, scared. Here I can go down to the square by myself, listen to the music, see people dancing, go home, and I feel like I did something.[106]

The gender imbalance is also a two-way street, and many older single men are happy with their social situations.

THE SEXUAL ORIENTATION FACTOR

Recent generations of older people have become more open about their sexual orientations and are admitting to their gay, lesbian, bisexual, or transgender (LGBT) status. Increasing numbers of these older people now seek to live in places that not only tolerate them but also embrace their distinctive social and emotional needs.[107]

Although studies have not focused specifically on active adult communities, polls and marketing sites reveal that LGBT older adults still believe that if they occupy most senior housing developments, other residents or staff will discriminate against them,[108] and, consequently, they must hide their sexual orientation.[109] These responses unquestionably have generational origins. Historically, members of today's older populations were less tolerant and more critical of LGBT people and still feel uncomfortable when they witness public signs of affection and emotional closeness. Thus, LGBT older adults often feel unwelcome in many senior housing communities and could live in them only if they went back into the closet.

THE PERSONALITY FACTOR

The personality makeup of older people, particularly their openness to change, is likely to influence how favorably disposed they are to relocating to active adult communities. Many aspects of these alternatives—their design, management, planned activities, and social composition—differ substantially from where they live now. Occupying these communities means not just pulling up stakes and leaving the status quo but also adjusting to a new style of residential living. Consequently, we might expect that people moving to these communities would have more flexible patterns of behavior, be more open to different lifestyles, and have more self-confident personalities and a positive future orientation.[110]

To initiate and manage their relationships with a very new group of neighbors, we might also expect these older people to have more affiliative personalities and be more willing and able to get along with others.[111]

Older people who have a greater need for order also favor these communities. They feel more secure in situations that present well-defined and scheduled events or activities; conversely, they feel more anxious when they find themselves in ambiguous or unstructured surroundings.

THE LIFESTYLE ORIENTATION FACTOR

To market their retirement communities, owners or managers often highlight their hedonistic lifestyles and their kaleidoscope of recreation-focused activities—from golf to computer clubs—and their exclusion of children and younger adults. However, not all older people feel comfortable with this way of life, including

- Those who enjoy more home-centered or passive activities (e.g., playing cards, watching TV, reading, self-reflection), either alone or in the company of only a few close friends
- Those who dislike more regimented, goal-directed (as opposed to spontaneous, less planned) leisure activities
- Those who do not want to feel pressured to participate in organized activities
- Those who feel that these organized activities will not satisfy their intellectual or continuing learning needs
- Those who already enjoy a busy schedule of planned recreational activities in their current communities
- Those who have difficulty severing their part-time work connections or their participation in their religious congregations
- Those who enjoy regularly interacting with younger people
- Those who want frequent and regular contacts with their married children and grandchildren

Consider this comment by an occupant of The Villages in central Florida, one of the most recreation-rich communities in the country:

> My heart is still in Boston. . . . Everything is the same here. There's nowhere to go. We're in the middle of nowhere. Where's the art museum? Where's the library in Copley Square? Where's the Boston Pops? I miss the mix. I miss not seeing any children around. But what I really miss is my family. I miss them terribly.[112]

THE BLACK BOX OF ACTIVE ADULT COMMUNITIES

Older people relocating to active adult communities expect to spend the rest of their lives in their new destinations. Thus, even as young-old populations are initially occupants, over time, significant proportions will reach their 80th and 90th birthdays and must cope with the usual physical and social declines of aging adults. If they seek to age in place in these communities, developers or managements confront a dilemma: How can they maintain their "active adult" image with the presence of these much older pockets of Fourth Age occupants, and, in particular, how can they market their communities to a young-old population?

We have few data on these issues,[113] but communities have adapted their residential settings in multiple ways to accommodate their aging occupants[114]:

- They have introduced design features such as grab bars and ramps into the dwellings, often in the apartments of high-rise condo structures.
- They have remodeled clubhouses to accommodate wheelchairs.
- They have installed lifts or elevators in low-rise building structures.
- They have located a service center just outside of the community that provides affordable home care, crisis counseling services, medical services, hospice care, an emergency response system, and transportation services.
- They have introduced supportive housing facilities, such as independent living properties, assisted living developments, and nursing homes.

It comes as no surprise that the younger or healthier occupants of active adult communities often do not welcome such changes because they are reminders of what is ahead of them. We have many examples of residents in these communities trying to block the introduction of supportive housing or long-term care services, particularly independent living and assisted living developments. Often, managers compromise by locating these options just outside the boundaries of their communities.[115]

WHAT ACTUALLY IS BEING EVALUATED?

As remarkable as it may sound, both the supporters and detractors of these communities are perhaps unwittingly evaluating not the active adult communities but rather the people aging within these communities. They are viewing these very visible enclaves of older adults as microcosms of an aging America. Consequently, their commentaries—whether positive or negative—are less about active adult communities than they are about what it means to age successfully in American society.

Their observations of Fourth Age people aging in place have generated especially dismal portrayals. After viewing the documentary by Emmy-nominated film editor Sari Gilman about the Delray Beach, Florida, Kings Point active adult condominium community, home to her very old grandparents and their like neighbors, one journalist characterized these places as *"the tragedy of modern retirement communities."*[116] Listen to the words of Sari Gilman:

> Once able to fully participate in community life, my grandmother and her neighbors began to slow down. Friends, spouses, and activity partners died. Visits to the clubhouse or the mall were replaced by appointments at the doctor's office. The sound of ambulances heading to the newly built medical center just down the road became more frequent. Social interaction, once based on the various ways everyone "kept busy," shifted to common complaints of body aches, limited mobility, and serious disease.

Loneliness became endemic. With women far outnumbering men the competition was brutal, and residents had plenty of time to gossip ("I hear she's got a boyfriend! The wife is barely in the ground.")

I began to notice that what was at first an opportunity—living among your peers in a community of "active retirees"—was becoming, for many residents, an unsustainable way of life.

If you had your health, you were popular. If not, people stopped coming by. At the pool, I heard the whispers: "Oh, Ida . . . yeah, she's going down."[117]

In the end, Gilman moved her grandmother to an assisted living residence close to her parents. But she reluctantly concedes,

Although she was thrilled to see her family on a more regular basis, she missed the home where she had spent the last third of her life.

Therein lies the dilemma confronting those who evaluate active adult communities. Commentators fail to ask the "what if" question: Would the older adults now residing in these retirement communities have fared better elsewhere? Would they have aged more successfully in another place? Gilman fails to ask whether it would have been different—better or worse—if her aging grandparents were living in a single-family home in a cul-de-sac suburb. Would they have enjoyed a different—better—set of outcomes?

At least one journalist offered an honest appraisal of Gilman's documentary:

Retirement communities all have the same unhappy ending: death. They are battling aging and all the bad things that go with it—physical problems, emotional problems, loneliness. There is an underlying sadness to the film, made sadder by a forced gaiety.

None of this is unique to Kings Point, it's just *more in your face there* [emphasis, Golant] since everyone is going through it at the same time.

One of the toughest things for my mother as she aged was watching her friends and relatives die off. That was a matter of life, not geography.[118]

SENIOR COHOUSING COMMUNITIES

Older people attracted to senior cohousing communities interpret what it means to be fully engaged in life very differently than the occupants of active adult communities. They are a highly self-selected group of people who enjoy the prospects of living in a very physically compact and socially close-knit residential setting with only a few older neighbors, without recreational amenities such as tennis courts, golf courses, hobby-intense clubhouses, and formally organized leisure pursuits.

Like our active retirement community occupants, they enjoy interacting with people their own age in a variety of everyday activities (e.g., eating meals, sharing afternoon drinks, engaging in hobbies, gardening, and participating in social gatherings).[119] However, these are far more intimate and informal gatherings than the organized events found in active adult communities, and they are initiated by the cohousing residents rather than some impersonal management.

A strong sense of social community is the hallmark of these intentionally designed, neighborhood-based residential enclaves. They attract older people seeking a strong network of more intimate interpersonal relationships. As one developer emphasizes,

> Cohousing helps individuals and families to find and maintain the elements of traditional neighborhoods—family, community, a sense of belonging. [It] reestablishes many of the advantages of traditional villages within the context of twenty-first century life.[120]

However, it is not just the presence of friendly, warm, and trusting neighbors that distinguishes these residential arrangements. Their occupants also enjoy the prospects of regularly helping each other with a variety of household- and neighborhood-based tasks or activities (e.g., providing transportation, preparing group meals, maintaining outside common areas, hosting communal parties, and assisting the sick). These mutually beneficial relationships enable their occupants to feel more competent and empowered than those in unplanned residential settings.

Senior cohousing communities strive to achieve what at first glance might appear as two contradictory goals. On the one hand, like any residential development, they hope to create a friendly neighborhood of conventional single-family accommodations or rental units occupied by people conducting their usual home-centered activities in the privacy of their own dwellings. On the other hand, they seek a communal way of living that encourages and enables various types of shared group activities and, inevitably, some sacrifice of individual privacy.

ORIGINS AND CATALYSTS

There are two major types of cohousing communities: an intergenerational model that attracts people of all age groups, ranging from young married families raising very young children to childless older people living alone, and a senior cohousing model, occupied by those older than age 55.

The first American cohousing projects, like their earlier Danish prototypes, were intergenerational and date from 1991. There are now more than 120 of these communities in 37 states, with more than 100 more in the construction or planning stages.[121] Senior cohousing developments are a much more recent phenomenon and are very few in number. The first senior development in the United States (Glacier Circle), in Davis, California, was built in 2005 and was followed in 2006 by ElderSpirit in Abingdon, Virginia, and then in 2007 by Silver Sage in Boulder, Colorado.[122] A fourth was started in 2009 in New Mexico, and two have recently opened in California and in Oklahoma.[123] They are now predominantly occupied by young-old and old-old women.[124]

Cohousing communities distinguish themselves from other planned neighborhoods because of their development origins and physical designs as well as by how they are operated and managed. Most cohousing communities grow out of a partnership between a developer or architect and a group of potential residents who work together to create a mutually agreed-upon housing and neighborhood product.[125] Residents are strongly involved in all aspects of the development and design of their communities, and they will have a major hand in managing and organizing their activities and events. They try to tailor cohousing communities to fit their housing and lifestyle preferences.

There may be many catalysts for these communities. They may be initiated by a group of common friends who seek a strong and reliable social network, people who share common interests, members of a common organization or with common work ties, and people with shared views on sustainable environments or with similarly strong spiritual or religious convictions. Typically, they seek out a developer in the private sector to help them plan and implement their community vision.[126] Advertised public gatherings initiated by a developer that discuss the cohousing option may also attract people with common lifestyle or aging preferences.

For potential occupants, securing an architect or developer and a group of interested participants are only the first steps. They will then typically spend 2 or 3 years in multiple planning sessions, over which time they decide on where to locate and how to design and operate their community.[127] Consequently, unlike in other residential enclaves, the occupants of cohousing communities often know each other very well even before move-in day.

DESIGNS AND OPERATING PRINCIPLES

Although a small share of cohousing occupants rent their dwellings, most are homeowners. Condominiums are typical, whereby the residents jointly own and administer the common facilities and form a resident association for management purposes. These geographically compact developments typically consist of 15 to 35 one- or two-story attached single-family dwellings tightly arranged along a pedestrian street or clustered around a courtyard in a very residential-like setting. Although developers now believe that 20 to 50 dwellings is the optimal size, some developments have as few as 8 units. Whereas intergenerational cohousing dwelling units average 1,250 square feet in size, units in senior cohousing communities tend to be smaller. Houses often have front porches, and a central path connects all dwellings. There is often an outside plaza or other spaces (e.g., communal garden) in the center of the community where residents can gather and easily spot and interact with each other. Parking spaces for the residents are typically at the edge of the community and accessible by well-defined pedestrian pathways. Senior cohousing developments usually follow the principles of universal design (Chapter 6) to ensure that their buildings and site features are physically accessible to those with mobility limitations.

Everything about the architectural design of the cohousing development, including its buildings and surroundings, is intended to encourage resident interactions. Integral to this mission is the presence of a "common house" in all cohousing developments that is considered *"an extension of each private residence"* because it is *"an essential part of daily community life."*[128] This single-family structure is always open and functions as the hub of communal activities; cohousers regularly meet here to manage their community and participate in group meals, afternoon drinks, crafts, workshop and hobby activities, laundry and drying chores, and all types of social gatherings. The common house may also contain large guest rooms or apartments designed to accommodate temporary visits by the residents' family members or their hired caregivers.

Unlike active adult communities, cohousing communities are resident managed. They are also different from traditional communes because they avoid a hierarchical decision-making structure whereby the views of one or two people dominate and those in the leadership positions assign mandatory tasks to their members. Rather, all cohousing residents have equal opportunities to express their ideas and feel empowered to make their residential arrangement whatever they want it to be.[129] They collectively debate operational or management issues and reach final decisions by consensus. These deliberations include who should be responsible for preparing communal meals and what their frequency should be as well as how often they should hold educational and cultural events, exercise classes, and other recreational activities.[130] Although there are inevitable disagreements, major conflicts are minimal because the occupants share a set of common values or beliefs about what constitutes a desirable way of life.[131] In the first senior cohousing community, Glacier Circle, the residents begin all of their meetings by reading their authored covenant (Figure 10.1).[132]

They must also deal with the difficult question of exactly how much assistance they should expect from each other. Some debates are more mundane, such as what tools and appliances (from lawn mowers to freezers) they will share. Other issues are more complex because residents must decide how much of their own time and energy they are willing to sacrifice for others. These deliberations focus on the extent to which an occupant should help the other residents with their household chores, assist with home maintenance, provide transportation, and help with everyday activities such as shopping. Other issues are even more controversial, such as whether occupants should expect their neighbors to assist them when they have difficulty performing their ADLs and IADLs or share the costs of hired caregivers. Deliberating on these cooperative behaviors, or what experts call a "collaborative lifestyle," is unquestionably unique to cohousing communities.[133] As one developer sums up, *This division of labor is based on what each person feels he or she can fairly contribute . . . and no one person should become excessively taxed by the process.*[134]

Figure 10.1. Covenant of Glacier Circle Senior Cohousing Community

We, the members of Glacier Circle Covenant, agree:

- To listen deeply and thoughtfully in our dialogues, mindful that our relationships are sacred.

- To be patient with each other, appreciating our differing gifts and welcoming creative ideas. When necessary, we will confront courageously with love.

- We agree to assume appropriate leadership roles and to participate fully in the group process.

- While we value our time together, we also respect our members' need for privacy.

- We will remember to assume the good intent of others and to strive to treat other members as well as ourselves with loving kindness.

LIFESTYLE NOT FOR EVERYONE

The paucity of carefully conducted studies makes it difficult to judge how successfully these communities are meeting the needs of their occupants. The literature is particularly silent on whether older people who reside in intergenerational as opposed to senior cohousing developments feel better about their communities.

The studies that do exist emphasize that residents of senior cohousing are very satisfied and happy in these community settings and enjoy their close-knit social networks.[135] As one overview concludes,

> Cohousing makes life more fun and easier, while preserving the privacy of each individual adult and child. The magic is that nothing is rigid in such a place: it all depends on what the community can afford and wants to create.[136]

Their occupants not only derive pleasure from these places but also feel they are practicing especially autonomous lifestyles, thus increasing their feelings of residential mastery. As one study reports

> Cohousers felt they were valued members of their communities, involved in decision-making processes and delivery, which increased their feelings of empowerment and well-being.[137]

Yet despite their overall positive ratings, some older occupants will not feel that these are wonderful places to live. They will not get along because their personalities or lifestyles clash, or they disagree on the desirability of some "cooperatively shared" behaviors or practices. Even as they entered these communities with the best of intentions, some residents may have difficulty surrendering their individual self-interests; they will continually object to the decisions made by the majority, and they will resist compromising even for the so-called collective good of the community. There is that danger that once ostracized from others because of their belligerent behaviors, these cohousing residents will feel left out and isolated.

OUT OF FINANCIAL REACH

These communities are not affordable to all, especially prospective homeowners. Their higher dwelling prices limit their occupancy to the more affluent.[138] Unlike in traditional communes, the residents must be financially independent, and the community does not generate income for its residents.[139] Consequently, they are typically not options for poor older people, although at least one cohousing community offers a few federally subsidized rental units.[140] Given the current (2015) partisan political climate in the United States, the prospects appear slim that developers will have access to predevelopment loan programs or that low-income older people will be able to count on rental subsidies. In their defense, developers counter that they price their houses competitively with other U.S. middle-class housing developments, and they point to examples where their dwellings are more affordable than comparable units in nearby neighborhoods.

Developers also emphasize that they are creating sustainable communities that are less expensive to occupy because of their small lot footprints and the energy-efficient infrastructure and technologies of their dwellings. Some cohousing communities are especially ecologically conscious and have adopted cost-saving solar and wind energy technologies, practice recycling, and grow organic community gardens. Consequently, their residents spend less on utilities and maintenance.

They also point out that cohousing occupants have lower living expenses because they share equipment and appliances as well as the costs of hiring maintenance workers and outside caregivers. Cohousers also have overall lower transportation costs because they share rides and conduct most of their social and recreational activities in their communities.[141] These practices may help mitigate the downsides of cohousing communities that are not located within walking or public transit distance of everyday destinations.

HELPFUL NEIGHBORS

Not all older adults look favorably on having to depend on their neighbors. Nonetheless, for those choosing these communities, the availability of people who can look out for them and help—whether with everyday needs or emergencies—is very likely to contribute to their feeling safer and more secure. These cooperative helping arrangements bode well for older people who need help living independently, especially with IADLs such as meal preparation, housekeeping, shopping, and laundry. Concerned neighbors are also more likely to detect early evidence of their declining health or mobility.

However, not all cooperative helping arrangements are straightforward. Cohousing residents with more severe physical limitations or cognitive declines may have difficulty bundling together the necessary heavy care from their neighbors to avoid relocating to an assisted living development or nursing home. Much depends on the willingness and ability of the residents to offer needed assistance. As one developer notes,

> What sort of agreements should a resident group make about allowing a disabled senior into the community early on, and when does someone become too sick to remain? Where does the group draw the line? It may not sound politically correct, but it can never be assumed that it is OK for a community member not to do his or her share. . . . How does the community make sure that there are enough caregivers? Answers to these questions all depend on the group and their individual and collective sensibilities.[142]

It is also unclear how well this model works when the majority of the cohousing residents enters their late chronological ages and collectively are so impaired that they cannot assume their communal responsibilities.

Another unknown is what happens when the original cohousing occupants sell their dwellings to newer buyers. A key question is whether these new owners will be as committed to the ideals of the cohousing community and conform to its style of living and obligations.

However, there are reasons for optimism. Like occupants of conventional neighborhoods, senior cohousing residents can solicit help from their families or hire their own caregivers to assist with even their high-acuity needs (Chapters 7 and 8). And they will benefit from their community's common house because it can accommodate their caregivers, and when this assistance is unavailable, other cohousing residents can fill in and offer respite care.

SUMMARY

Despite their many positive attributes, very few older adults in the United States occupy senior cohousing developments. There are many reasons for this small census and its limited appeal. The majority of older Americans rejects the communal lifestyle practices, more intimate social networks, and shared responsibilities of this alternative. The idea that individuals should take responsibilities for others is not likely to resonate with many older Americans, with their values of rugged individualism. Critics will be dismayed that even as cohousing residents are happily engaged in the activities of their community, they spend little of their time outside their residential enclaves. This is the same criticism leveled at occupants of active adult communities who express little interest in engaging in social or civic engagement activities in their larger urban or rural locales.

The process of finding and occupying a desirable cohousing community also takes a great deal of energy and time. Practically speaking, unless we witness some broad-based public education campaign, older Americans will generally remain unaware of this alternative.[143] Moreover, discovering this option is only the beginning, and potential occupants must find a group of like-minded people to be their neighbors. They must find a developer or architect who is willing to guide them through a challenging and bureaucratic building process while faithfully attending to their preferences. In particular, they must find a sufficiently affordable land site in a community with flexible enough zoning regulations to accommodate this model. Only the most dedicated fans of this alternative will be brave enough to tolerate these home building steps. However, those motivated and able to survive this exercise will unquestionably feel more squarely in their residential comfort and mastery zones.

CONCLUSION

Active adult and senior cohousing communities are planned residential options that showcase the eclectic ways that older Americans achieve their residential normalcy. Their occupants have distinctive preferences for how they want to be fully engaged in life or live in their residential comfort zones. But even as these housing options are praised or criticized for their lifestyle implications, their occupants benefit from a more secure and predictable way of life that nurtures their feelings of autonomy and enables them to feel squarely in their residential mastery zones.

When we question older people, these options typically elicit extreme emotional reactions—ranging from very positive to very negative. Their responses offer many insights about why residential normalcy is such a subjective experience. Moreover, we gain further understanding into the complex linkages between aging successfully and place of residence when we examine the wide array of reasons why older people (and the experts) are attracted to or repelled by these alternatives.

The next two chapters focus on Fourth Agers who also move from their typically long-occupied dwellings and neighborhoods. But these older persons relocate because of their inability to cope with an unending stream of stressful life events, inadequate care, and uncontrolled changes in their residential settings that altogether jeopardize their abilities to maintain independent households. These people have acknowledged—although not necessarily on their own—that aging in place is no longer feasible, and they must move if they are to regain control of their lives and environments. Yet they are still hopeful that they can find in their new addresses a modicum of the pleasurable and enjoyable features they have left behind.

NOTES

1. (Davis, 2012)
2. (Streib, 1990)
3. (Suchman, 2001)
4. (MetLife Mature Market Institute, 2011a)5. (Suchman, 2001)
6. (Blechman, 2008; Simpson, 2010; Trolander, 2011b)
7. (Suchman, 2001)
8. (Citizens' Housing and Planning Association, 2005)
9. (Suchman, 2001)
10. (Suchman, 2001)
11. (Suchman, 2001)
12. (Citizens' Housing and Planning Association, 2005; Trolander, 2011b)
13. (Ball, 2012; Suchman, 2001)
14. (Suchman, 2001)
15. (Suchman, 2001)
16. (MetLife Mature Market Institute, 2011a)
17. (MetLife Mature Market Institute, 2011a). An additional 1.6 million households occupy age-restricted rentals, but because of their demographics (top heavy with women and men living alone), it is unclear whether these are appropriately classified as active adult communities or rather as senior apartments, independent living communities, and affordable HUD senior-occupied apartment buildings.
18. (MetLife Mature Market Institute, 2011a)
19. The developers of these communities also must often seek modifications in their municipality's or county zoning laws to build these active adult complexes. They rely on such approaches as overlay zoning, whereby the ownership of properties is limited to older people; deed restrictions or covenants specifying age restrictions on property ownership; or the designation of senior housing districts and clustered or planned unit developments restricted to older residents (Citizens' Housing and Planning Association, 2005).
20. Section 807(b)(2)(C) of the Fair Housing Act (42 U.S.C. 3607(b)(2)(C))
21. HUD is the federal agency that enforces the Fair Housing Act, and any person who feels discriminated against files a complaint with this agency.
22. (MetLife Mature Market Institute, 2011a)
23. (Del Webb, 2010)
24. (MetLife Mature Market Institute, 2011a)
25. (MetLife Mature Market Institute, 2011a)
26. (Suchman, 2001)

27. (Trolander, 2011b)
28. (Trolander, 2011b)
29. (Trolander, 2011b)
30. (Trolander, 2011b)
31. (MetLife Mature Market Institute, 2011a)
32. (MetLife Mature Market Institute, 2009a)
33. (MetLife Mature Market Institute, 2011a)
34. (Mitchell, 2009)
35. (MetLife Mature Market Institute, 2009a)
36. (Verdoorn, 2011). This is a summary of his predictions.
37. (Bortz, 2012)
38. (Smith, 2012)
39. (Hill, 2011)
40. (Golant, 1985)
41. (Del Webb, 2010)
42. (Bultena & Wood, 1969)
43. (Blechman, 2008, p. 171)
44. (McHugh & Larson-Keagy, 2005, p. 246)
45. (Golant, 1985, p. 24)
46. (Golant, 1985)
47. (Simpson, 2010)
48. (Trolander, 2011b)
49. (Trolander, 2011b)
50. (Golant, 1985)
51. (Cloutier-Fisher & Harvey, 2009, p. 250)
52. (Golant, 1985)
53. (Frolik, 2008, p. 19)
54. (Frolik, 2008, p. 19)
55. (McHugh & Larson-Keagy, 2005, p. 253)
56. (Mumford, 1956, p. 192)
57. (Frolik, 2008, p. 19)
58. (Trolander, 2011b)
59. (Trolander, 2011b)
60. (Blechman, 2008, p. 221)
61. (Trolander, 2011b)
62. (Trolander, 2011b, p. 10)
63. (McHugh & Larson-Keagy, 2005)
64. (Thurow, 1996)
65. (Blechman, 2008, p. 225)
66. (Blechman, 2008, 221)
67. (Trolander, 2011b, p. 243)
68. Reported in his biography at http://www.encore.org/book/marc.
69. (Trolander, 2011a, p. 244)
70. (Simpson, 2010, p. 68)
71. (Simpson, 2010, p. 79)
72. (Simpson, 2010)
73. (Del Webb, 2010)
74. (Simpson, 2010, p. 116)
75. (McHugh, 2000)
76. (McHugh & Larson-Keagy, 2005, p. 252)
77. (Kastenbaum, 1993, p. 181)
78. (Blechman, 2008, p. 15)
79. (Blechman, 2008, p. 56)

80. (Streib, Folts, & La Greca, 1985)
81. (Streib et al., 1985, p. 409)
82. (Golant, 1975)
83. (Streib et al., 1985)
84. (Kastenbaum, 1993)
85. A pseudonym.
86. (McHugh, 2007, p. 296)
87. (Streib, Folts, & La Greca, 1984)
88. (Trolander, 2011b)
89. (Rosow, 1967)
90. (Golant, 1985, p.26)
91. (Roth et al., 2012, p. 194)
92. (Roth et al., 2012, p. 190)
93. (Roth et al., 2012, pp. 197–198)
94. (Rosow, 1967)
95. (Rosow, 1967, p. 261)
96. (Rosow, 1967, p. 265)
97. (Carstensen, 2006)
98. (Rosow, 1967, pp. 108–118)
99. (Trolander, 2011b)
100. (Trolander, 2011b, p. 226)
101. (Sun, Waldron, Gitelson, & Ho, 2012)
102. (Sun et al., 2012)
103. (Trolander, 2011b)
104. (Trolander, 2011b)
105. (Blechman, 2008, p. 169)
106. (Blechman, 2008, p. 170)
107. (MetLife Mature Market Institute, 2010c)
108. http://www.topretirements.com/blog/lgbt/retiring-in-lgbt-friendly-cities-what-to-look-for-what-to-watch-out-for.html/
109. (Addis, Davies, Greene, MacBride-Stewart, & Shepherd, 2009)
110. (Kahana & Kahana, 1983)
111. (Tobin & Lieberman, 1976)
112. (Blechman, 2008, p. 168)
113. (Trolander, 2011b)
114. (Trolander, 2011b)
115. (Trolander, 2011b)
116. (Davis, 2012)
117. Sari Gilman, "Kings Point: Aging out of retirement." Special to CNN, Wednesday, August 1, 2012: http://www.cnn.com/2012/08/01/living/retirement-community-living.
118. Michael Winerip, "Kings Point, a magic kingdom for the retirement set," *New York Times,* March 9, 2013: http://www.nytimes.com/2013/03/10/booming/kings-point-a-magic-kingdom-for-the-retirement-set.html?_r=0.
119. (Glass & Vander Plaats, 2013)
120. (Durrett, 2011, p. 2)
121. (Williams, 2008); http://www.cohousing.org/directory
122. (Durrett, 2009)
123. (Glass, 2014)
124. (Glass, 2014)
125. (Durrett, 2009)
126. (Williams, 2008)
127. (Durrett, 2009)128. (Durrett, 2011, p. 28)
129. (Lietaert, 2010)

130. (Williams, 2008)
131. (Lietaert, 2010; Williams, 2008)
132. (Durrett, 2009, p. 204)
133. (Williams, 2008, p. 271)
134. (Durrett, 2009, p. 27)
135. (Choi, 2004; Williams, 2008)
136. (Lietaert, 2010, p. 577)
137. (Williams, 2008, p. 272)
138. (Williams, 2008)
139. (Durrett, 2011)
140. (Glass, 2014)
141. (Durrett, 2009)
142. (Durrett, 2009, p. 199)
143. (Wardrip, 2010)

11

MOVING TO INDEPENDENT LIVING AND ASSISTED LIVING DEVELOPMENTS

Question: *After two weeks in the assisted living facility my mom is intensely unhappy. How much time should we let pass by if she continues to feel so uncomfortable?*

Answer: *Since she has lived in California so long and has family members nearby, it seems you should give her more time to adjust. . . . Two weeks isn't very long and change is hard for anyone, let alone someone her age. There's no set time, but if the center is a good one, they should be able to get her to start engaging. She could turn out to love it.*[1]

My family had one excellent assisted living experience and one dreadful one, which left us feeling misled and then abandoned when my mother's needs exceeded what the facility was willing or able to provide.[2]

ALTERNATIVES TO NURSING HOMES

Like active adult and senior cohousing communities, independent living and assisted living developments are also age-restricted housing options, but they attract a very different demographic. Their older occupants are mainly women in their late 70s and older, not in the labor force, and living alone or with an impaired spouse. They move after reluctantly acknowledging that aging in place is no longer viable. They feel well out of their residential mastery zones because their aging bodies make it difficult for them to easily or safely perform their activities of daily living (ADLs) or instrumental

285

ADLs (IADLs), manage their chronic health problems, and negotiate their environments, even with the help of their family members or community-based providers. They worry about having unanticipated accidents or care needs with no one to help. They are still marginally in their residential comfort zones because of the very positive attractions of their current dwellings, but they can no longer tolerate the everyday hassles of maintaining their households. Their transitions to a more supportive housing and care arrangement are need-driven.[3]

They are also living during a time in history when it is easier than ever to make these moving decisions. The presence of independent living communities and assisted living residences means that today's older adults—at least those with higher incomes—usually do not have to choose between aging in place and occupying a nursing home. Although not all older Americans have gotten the message, several factors have made these alternatives more viable[4]:

- They have grown in number and are more physically visible in their communities.
- They show up more frequently in commercials and movies; the media no longer focuses solely on nursing homes to dramatize the long-term care needs of older adults.
- They do not have the same unfavorable institutional connotations as nursing homes.
- Older people are more likely to have visited someone (a friend or relative) in these properties.

INDEPENDENT LIVING UNIT PROPERTIES

A typical advertisement for these options:

> Our independent living communities offer a range of lifestyle options for the way you want to live. Even very active seniors value the confidence that choice, personalized services and tailored amenities can bring. Sunrise Independent Living offers all the benefits of being in your own home, but removes the worry of maintenance, chores, and even cooking. Our senior communities offer a wealth of lifestyle choices, including a selection of senior-friendly floor plans, a variety of meal plans and menus, and service options to meet residents' wellness needs.[5]

Developed primarily by the private sector (98% of communities), these age-restricted properties, once known as congregate senior housing, usually consist of efficiency to two-bedroom apartments in low- or high-rise multifamily apartment buildings. These units may be found in standalone or freestanding structures, but they are also on separate floors or wings of a building that offers assisted living units. Alternatively, they may be sited on a campus and may include either apartment buildings or small, single-family rental dwellings and townhomes.

Freestanding independent living unit properties have a median number of 128 rental apartments, but about a quarter have more than 200 units.[6] These properties typically resemble ordinary apartment complexes or single-family dwellings, but their units are smaller, and they have scaled-down kitchens, living rooms, and bedrooms. Nationally, the median size of units is 614 square feet, but among newer properties, the median size is more than 900 square feet. In 2014, there were 1,500 independent living communities in the United States with 179,000 units.[7]

Older people typically furnish their own apartments, and they have some design features to help them compensate for their limitations. However, these may be limited to accessible bathrooms with grab bars and some type of hard-wired emergency alert system (e.g., wall switches, pull cords).

These properties offer their residents hotel-like or hospitality services such as housekeeping, linen service, and transportation and one or more daily meals, typically eaten in a central dining room. They also offer their occupants various recreational and leisure activities and organized social events.

These housing alternatives are also distinguishable by what they do not provide. Because residents are expected to live on their own, they do not have hired staff who help them perform their ADLs, such as bathing, dressing, and toileting, and they do not offer medication supervision and certainly not skilled nursing care.

Independent living communities should not be confused with two other options. *Senior apartments* also consist of multifamily, age-restricted rental unit properties (at least 80% of residents age 55 and older) that offer some indoor recreational amenities but do not offer any congregate services, especially meals served in a common dining room.[8] They also should not be confused with *clustered-care apartment complexes* that government programs have made affordable to lower-income older people (Chapter 10).

WHO MOVES HERE AND WHY?

Older people relocating to independent living communities are typically much older than occupants of active adult communities, and they enter at higher chronological ages than previous waves of occupants. Nationally, new residents (moved in over the past 6 months) have an average age of almost 84, and 72% are women. Only 29% are married, whereas 63% are widowed, and the remaining 8% are single (divorced, separated, or never married). Most owned their previous residences.[9] When a married couple occupies these accommodations, often a healthier spouse has chosen to live with the more dependent one. Compared with other older people in the United States, they are more likely to have a college education and less likely to identify themselves as a member of a minority group (e.g., African-Americans, foreign born).

These older people rarely are enthusiastic about relocating to independent living alternatives. Some worry about being able to afford these accommodations, and others fear losing their independence and freedom, leaving familiar homes, possessions, and friends, and adjusting to a new life and making new friends (Chapter 3).[10] Minority and lesbian, gay, bisexual, and transgender people worry about how they will relate to the other residents.[11] At some point, however, these concerns are outweighed by the challenges confronting those living independently in their current residences, in combination with the benefits offered by independent living communities.

Compared with assisted living consumers, prospective independent living occupants do not have the same urgency when they make their residential transitions.[12] They typically are still ambulatory (although many depend on some assistive device) and able to function without significant hands-on assistance, but they may be struggling to perform their ADLs and have started to worry about being on their own. Among new residents, typically about 12% to 15% have difficulty bathing or showering and 12% with dressing. Larger percentages have difficulty performing their IADLs, with about 27% reporting moderate or significant difficulty shopping for groceries and 33% having problems preparing a hot meal.[13] They are also more likely to encounter difficulties performing what were once routine actions. About 78% have at least some difficulty lifting or carrying something over 10 pounds; about 87% have difficulty stooping, kneeling, or crouching; about 71% have difficulty climbing one flight of stairs without resting; and about 57% have trouble walking one block.[14]

They have started to worry about their physical health or the onset of a debilitating illness.[15] One national survey reported that about 27% of the new residents in these properties assessed their health as fair or poor. Moreover, over the past two years, about 53% of them were hospitalized, about 25% were overnight patients in a nursing home or rehabilitation center, and about 20% reported receiving home health services before their moves.[16]

Although most make their own decisions about moving to these places, they are often influenced by their adult children.[17] Indeed, a desire to be geographically close to family or friends may narrow their independent living community choices.[18] Along with location, a good reputation and the recommendations of others guide their decisions.[19]

Whether these properties are freestanding or attached to an assisted living residence may also matter. Some older people want easy access to a higher level of care when they experience health or mobility declines and have to move. Proximate assisted living accommodations reduce the time and energy needed to search for a new place on very short notice. Yet, given a median length of stay of 30.5 months in freestanding independent living properties, many older people (or their families) may not worry about such a future decision. Furthermore, some older people may find that living near occupants who are far more physically or cognitively frail than they is an unpleasant reminder of what's to come. However, one study of a combined independent living community and assisted living property found that fewer than 3% of the respondents reported that the *"advanced levels of care had a negative influence on their decision to move to the community."*[20]

STILL SEEKING TO BE FULLY ENGAGED IN LIFE

Although older adults do not seek out independent living communities primarily because of their physical amenities or their recreational opportunities, these aspects may influence how they evaluate the merits of any given property. Some are more architecturally attractive, *"with more creative use of light, sound, water, and greenery to enhance socialization areas."*[21] Their common areas are architecturally spacious, well appointed, and resort-like, rather than bland, small, and boxy. Others offer higher-quality hospitality services, are staffed by better-trained and friendlier personnel, and serve better food offered in alternative venues (e.g., bistros, cafés, and sports bars). Higher-end independent living communities may offer swimming pools or spas, exercise or fitness centers, gardening areas, libraries and reading rooms, on-site chapel services, and beautician or barber services. Other properties distinguish themselves because they offer on-site wellness programs and health clinics where medical professionals or nursing staff hold part-time office hours. These offerings contribute greatly to the preventive health practices of their occupants (Chapter 9).[22]

Some properties offer a richer array of recreational and cultural events (e.g., lectures from invited speakers, baking classes, bingo, wine tastings) and more frequently transport their residents in property-owned vans to community outings (e.g., plays, movies, concerts, and lectures). They are located in safer and more physically attractive neighborhoods, where residents can easily walk to nearby shopping and personal services.

The resident profiles of some properties are more attractive because potential occupants view their religious, ethnic, racial, sexual orientation, or even age composition favorably. On the other hand, complexes with higher shares of old-old people may be a turn-off for healthier and more active older people.

CONTRACTUAL OBLIGATIONS, COSTS, AND OCCUPANTS' FINANCES

Older occupants typically rent their accommodations and sign monthly leases. At the end of 2012, the median base monthly fee for freestanding communities (i.e., unconnected with assisted living accommodations) was $2,216, but the lowest quartile of properties charged $1,652, and the highest quartile $3,085. For a second occupant in an apartment (e.g., a spouse), communities usually charge an additional base median monthly fee of about $900 (but as low as $342, and as high as $1,006).[23] This base fee covers a standard service package, including housekeeping, scheduled transportation, a specified number of meals per day, an activity program, and security. Depending on the property, some services are not considered standard (e.g., beauty shop or preventive care checkups, or all three daily meals) but are available for additional fees.[24]

Independent living unit occupants pay out of their own pockets for these living spaces and services, because government programs rarely fund their development or operation. However, the financial wherewithal of the occupants varies substantially.[25] One national survey found that about a third had incomes of less than $30,000 and about 36% had incomes greater than $50,000. About 27% had a net worth of more than $500,000, but 11% had a net worth of less than $50,000. Those with lower incomes sometimes afford these accommodations only by receiving financial assistance from family members or drawing down on their own assets, often from the sale of their dwellings.[26]

LONG-TERM SERVICES AND SUPPORTS

Although these properties do not provide staff to assist older occupants with their ADLs, many allow older occupants to hire their own caregivers or home health aides to assist them with their health problems, medication management, or personal care.

Thus, it is very common to see multiple workers from home care agencies in these buildings. The community's management may facilitate these supports by providing a list of qualified private pay direct care workers or by renting space in their building to accommodate the offices of a home health agency, which they own or have organizational affiliations.

The availability of these outside services makes it more difficult to generalize about where we position independent living communities on the long-term care continuum. Because their residents rely more extensively on à la carte or unbundled home- and community-based services provided by outside vendors, they are less likely to move because of physical or health declines, and they more resemble the frail occupants found in assisted living properties, which we focus on next in this chapter.[27]

RESIDENTIAL SATISFACTION OF OLDER PEOPLE

Proprietary studies consistently report that the residents of independent living properties are very satisfied,[28] with numbers as high as 87% either satisfied or very satisfied with their accommodations.[29] Particularly revealing were the reasons they gave for recommending these communities to their friends.[30] Such endorsements are crucial to managers, because after properties are open for more than 2 years, most (7 out of 10) new residents learn about them from a family member, friend, or employee, not from advertising or direct mail marketing.[31]

According to one study, it was not the physical ambience of these properties that was most important to older consumers but rather their activities, services, staff, sociability, and flexible programs[32]:

- Community activities that contribute to the quality of their daily lives: cultural, musical, arts and crafts, entertainment, and social opportunities
- Dining flexibility and quality: tasty and interesting types of food, a variety of menu items, and multiple times available for dining
- Quality of staff: *"employees who are capable of creating an environment that is open, supportive, and stimulating and builds a sense of belonging and being part of a family-like environment"*[33]
- Availability of privacy, predictability of community support, and safety and security
- A comfortable and home-like place where it is easy to make friends and feel one belongs

Clearly, the best independent living properties offer older occupants a living environment in which they feel squarely in both their residential comfort and mastery zones. A better-educated and informed generation of older adults expects to live in a place that is comfortable enough to call home; where they are entertained and stimulated; where they enjoy interesting and well-prepared food[34]; where they can relate easily with staff; and where they feel they have friends, and belong. At the same time, they want to feel autonomous, in control of their living environments, free to eat and sit with whomever they want, able to trust the community's personnel, treated like customers and not clients, and that their belongings are secure.[35]

ASSISTED LIVING RESIDENCES

> States use many different terms for residential [care] settings: boarding homes, rest homes, adult care homes, domiciliary care homes, personal care homes, community based residential facilities, assisted living, and adult foster care (AFC). Until the mid-1990s, the most frequently used term was *board and care*. Today all types of group residential care are commonly referred to as assisted living.[36]

In the past, when older people experienced significant declines in their physical or cognitive functioning and were unable to maintain their private residences, they often had little choice but to enter a nursing home.[37] This was not a happy decision. They dreaded the prospect of living and receiving assistance in these more hospital-like alternatives. Since the mid-1980s, older adults with the financial means have found a more desirable alternative in a category of group residential care properties now known as assisted living. When polled, older people *"would prefer to be cared for in an assisted living facility over a nursing home if they needed twenty-four hour care, by a margin of six to one."*[38]

WHAT IS ASSISTED LIVING?

People are surprised to learn that experts or providers cannot agree on exactly what assisted living is. Usually these stakeholders define this alternative by how it differs from other long-term care settings, particularly independent living communities and nursing homes.

Like independent living communities, they offer their older residents hospitality or concierge services (e.g., housekeeping, meals, transportation, and recreational activities) to address their unmet IADL needs. But they also make available staff, some on a 24-hour basis, to assist residents with both their scheduled and unscheduled needs for assistance with ADLs. Many properties also provide some nursing-related services to help their older residents cope with chronic illnesses.[39] In most states, terminally ill residents already residing in assisted living properties can receive hospice services from an outside agency, typically funded by Medicare. An increasing share now also contain separate wings or floors—referred to as *special care units* (SCUs)—dedicated to serving residents with Alzheimer's disease or other forms of dementia.

Some assisted living properties provide respite care and temporarily accommodate older people to give their family caregivers some relief. Others admit older people just discharged from a hospital, who live in these settings until they have sufficiently recuperated and are able to return to their own homes or independent living communities.[40]

Unlike nursing homes, assisted living residences do not accommodate those with unstable chronic illnesses who need a 24-hour skilled level of nursing care, as opposed to intermittent or discrete skilled nursing services. They also typically do not tolerate residents whose dementia symptoms include violent, destructive, or physically abusive behaviors.[41] Overall, the occupants of today's nursing homes still have a higher prevalence of chronic health conditions and are more physically or cognitively impaired.[42]

However, these distinctions are less clear-cut than in the past because assisted living properties have been accommodating increasingly frail older occupants.

Assisted living properties also distinguish themselves from nursing homes because they try to emulate a *social* rather than a *medical* model of care. When successful, these long-term care alternatives have a more residential-like and less institutional-like architectural and interior design appearance, and they eschew the rigid operational regulations of nursing homes. Their staff also tries to accommodate the idiosyncratic eating, sleeping, and care preferences of their residents and respect as much as possible their individual choices, privacy, and personal autonomy.[43]

AVAILABILITY OF ASSISTED LIVING IN THE UNITED STATES

In 2010, there were 51,367 state-licensed or regulated assisted living properties in the United States, with 1,233,690 beds or dwelling units.[44] However, this is a very liberal estimate because it includes very small properties with as few as two beds or dwelling units. If we restrict assisted living properties to those with four or more units or beds (that is, exclude adult foster care and many board and care facilities), there were 31,100 properties with 971,000 beds or units.[45] Even in this universe, however, 50% of properties have only 4 to 10 units or beds and another 16% have only 11–25 units or beds. So-called large properties ranging from 26 to 100 beds or units represented only 28% of all properties, and extra large facilities with more than 100 beds represented another 7%. Despite this high share of small assisted living residences, more than 80% of the residents lived in the larger properties.[46] In particular, the very small facilities (4–10 beds or units and more than 50% of the total properties) served only 10% of the assisted living population.

Even though assisted living properties are the fastest-growing category of senior housing, they are not equally available in all parts of the country. Most units or beds (more than 60%) are found in only 11 states.[47] A better measure of their availability, their penetration rates—the number of properties available for every 1,000 people age 65 and older—also differ greatly. At the top end with measures of more than 29 are California, Indiana, Iowa, Maine, Minnesota, Nebraska, North Carolina, Oregon, Pennsylvania, Virginia, and Washington. At the low end with measures of less than 15 are Alabama, Arkansas, Connecticut, Hawaii, Illinois, Louisiana, Massachusetts, Michigan, Mississippi, Nevada, and West Virginia.[48]

Even within states, their availability is unequal. Typically, counties with the highest older adult penetration rates are in urban areas; have populations with higher median incomes (between $42,000 and $43,000), smaller shares of Medicaid beneficiaries, higher educational attainment, and smaller percentages of minorities (5%–6%); and have homes with higher median values ($96,000–$98,000).[49]

WHO ARE ASSISTED LIVING RESIDENTS?

Assisted living residents have demographically distinct profiles. Their average age is at an historical high, about 87 years old,[50] with the majority (54%) older than 85 or in the 75–84 age group (27%).[51] Only 9% are members of the young-old (age 65–74), and about 11% are younger than age 65. The occupants are predominantly female, typically widowed, and to a lesser extent divorced or separated; only a very small share are married or men. Minority groups are grossly underrepresented compared with nursing homes, although they are more likely to occupy the less expensive, older, and smaller-sized board and care and adult foster care properties.[52]

Before they relocated, the majority of assisted living residents lived less than 25 miles away, most (70%) in their conventional dwellings, with a smaller share in the dwellings of family members (7%). The remainder previously occupied independent living communities or other assisted living properties where they could not secure enough care or were unhappy with their accommodations.[53]

On average, older people remain in their new assisted living homes for about 2 years, whereupon they die or move to a nursing home for more extensive care. Overall, 33% have lived in these settings for less than a year, 36% for 1–3 years, and 31% for longer.[54]

CATALYSTS FOR ASSISTED LIVING MOVES

When older people seek out assisted living accommodations, they usually are confronting significant physical and cognitive declines and health management challenges. They are having trouble living independently because they need too much help managing their health conditions, cannot secure enough assistance to perform their IADLs and ADLs, or are simply tired of relying on others for help.[55] The death of a spouse and the vacuum created by this loss may precede these moves. Other catalysts include falls, hospital stays, embarrassing moments of helplessness, and an excruciating fear of being alone.

Moves by older people to assisted living developments often mark the first time that others have made their relocation decisions for them (Chapter 5). In one small study examining these deliberations, the authors found that only 21% assumed proactive roles in their relocations.[56] The decisions of the others were under the control of family members, social workers, or friends.[57]

More than three quarters of older assisted living residents have at least two of the most common chronic health conditions: high blood pressure, heart disease, depression, arthritis, osteoporosis, and diabetes.[58] Particularly high shares of residents have arthritis (29%) and diabetes (16%). Most need help with more than four of their IADLs, with 87% needing help taking their medications.[59] More than three quarters need help with at least one of their ADLs, with almost 40% needing help with three to five ADLs. Specifically, about 75% need help with bathing, 54% with dressing, 37% with toileting, and 22% with eating. About 14% need assistance with transferring (i.e., getting in or out of a bed or chair).[60] A significant share experiences depression (26%).[61]

Substantial and growing shares of assisted living residents also have dementia, usually Alzheimer's disease, although prevalence varies greatly from one development to another. One national assessment reports that 46% of residents age 65 and older have some type of dementia, and 67% have some type of cognitive impairment. About 36% displayed difficulties in managing behavioral problems. Another national analysis found that 23% of assisted living residents (including those younger than age 65) were cognitively moderately impaired and 19% severely impaired.[62] Sadly, even as many of these residents have the physical ability to perform most of their ADLs, they need much cueing and hands-on assistance because of severe memory losses and disoriented and challenging behaviors. Often, they also must be housed in a physically secure section of a building to keep them from wandering. However, most residents with moderate or severe dementia (70%) are not in such separate quarters.[63]

MANY VARIETIES OF ASSISTED LIVING

The diversity of these options is linked partly to their being private sector developments. Providers have different conceptions of how assisted living properties should look and operate. The most important reason for their differences, however, is that there are no federal or national standards dictating what this product should look like, what it should be called, what care it offers, and whom it should serve. Consequently, we now have documents of 250 plus pages summarizing how more than 40 state governments and the District of Columbia regulate the design and operation of their assisted living residences differently.[64] Adding to the complexity, many state governments have several assisted living licensing categories, each with a different set of requirements specifying the extent to which properties can accommodate residents with higher-acuity care needs. Assisted living is also a moving target because states are continually modifying their requirements as they attempt to accommodate an ever-more physically and cognitively vulnerable group of older consumers.

PHYSICAL APPEARANCE AND CONGREGATE SERVICES

Because of these open-ended definitions, assisted living properties often look very different from each other. Consider this overview:

> Their buildings variously encompass Victorian mansions, boxy multiunit apartment style structures, luxurious Trump-like high-rise apartment structures, and resort-like two- or three-story buildings. Their interior architectural designs sometimes resemble the décor of luxurious hotels, but (sadly) at times are more similar to the medical-like interiors of nursing homes. Most have predominantly one-bedroom and studio apartments, but some assisted living properties have a wider mixture of one-, two-, and even three-bedroom apartments. Some features, however, are more widespread among new model assisted living properties. Most [of these] living units have their own self-contained kitchens, full bathroom facilities, doors that lock, and individual temperature controls, and their residents can fill them with their own furnishings. Most occupants (90 percent) do not share their apartments or rooms.[65]

Property size is a key factor influencing their physical design and operation. Some states license or certify residences that have fewer than five beds as assisted living properties, although they may refer to them as adult foster or family care, personal care homes, or board and care. Other states regulate these smaller properties under separate programs. The smallest properties typically consist of physically more-modest buildings that look more like single-family homes. The common areas in these smaller and often older buildings do not resemble the attractively appointed spaces found in higher-end hotels or resorts but instead look like ordinary living rooms. The residents do not eat in large, formally appointed dining rooms but rather in regular kitchens. Because they often have tight operating budgets, one typically finds fewer *"safety enhancing architectural design features"*[66] in these properties and fewer new care-related technologies.

Typically, a small handful of employees, as opposed to professionally trained staff, operate these smaller board and care facilities. They infrequently have dedicated staff, such as activity directors, and they consequently offer few organized social and recreational activities and scheduled religious services or opportunities to take their residents to outside entertainment events in their communities.[67] An exception to this generalization are the few board and care properties that cater to a higher-end clientele and offer more physically upscale quarters and better-quality amenities.[68]

The larger properties are usually owned by for-profit or publicly held corporations (about 78%), as opposed to not-for-profit sponsors, and are now often part of large corporate chains.[69] Whereas about 37% of assisted living properties are free-standing properties, about 28% are in buildings that also have SCUs. About 25% of assisted living properties are found in buildings or on campuses that also offer independent living unit accommodations or nursing home services. Finally, another 10% are part of continuing care retirement communities that contain various combinations of independent living units, assisted living, and nursing homes (Chapter 12).[70]

On average, these assisted living developments consist of about 120 units, bedrooms, or apartments.[71] These more modern buildings are more likely to include apartment-like units with their own kitchen areas, personal heating and cooling controls, and self-contained bathrooms. Attractively designed common areas come in all different sizes and shapes to accommodate a wide range of leisure and recreational activities. Still, this is a diverse category, and some of the larger but older properties retain the look and feel of more institutional settings.

State regulations do produce some uniformity. For example, most states impose some minimum building and safety requirements, such as handrails, smoke alarms, emergency alert technologies, multiple exits, and the use of fire-retardant materials.[72] Still, states differ in this regard. In Minnesota, for example, assisted living means a category or package of *licensed services* rather than a *licensed setting* having minimum architectural features.[73] Here, establishments must comply primarily with state and local building codes; however, their service regulations may specify what types of buildings and living spaces qualify as assisted living.

Typically, if a property offers an SCU (by one estimate, only 17% of assisted living residences[74]), state regulations have more specific physical plant requirements. Resident accommodations in these dementia "neighborhoods" often consist of only studio or one-bedroom units, and semiprivate units are more common. SCUs are also found on floors or wings that have extra security features (e.g., locks, alarms, and passcode systems) to prevent their older occupants from wandering outside their living areas.[75]

However, state regulations still leave assisted living property owners with much flexibility as to how they design their dwelling units and common areas. The larger properties, in particular, hire consultants who influence their architectural designs, paint colors, floor materials (e.g., carpets vs. tile), lighting levels and systems, and types and quality of upholstered furniture. These decisions not only influence the aesthetics of a property—both its physical ambience and its stimulating qualities—but also determine how easily and safely their residents can move around their living spaces because they are aided by color-coded walls, easy visual access, and shortened corridors, and they affect the availability of attractive physical spaces where residents can interact.[76]

LEVEL OF CARE ENVIRONMENTS AND STATE REGULATIONS

Nearly all properties help their older occupants perform their IADLs and most of their ADLs. The larger ones also offer basic health monitoring (e.g., blood pressure), special diets, and access to case management services and social service counseling.

However, the resident acuity levels that assisted living properties accommodate vary substantially. Consider that only 40% of assisted living residents live in properties that provide (intermittent) skilled nursing care,[77] and just over 50% live in places with occupational and physical therapy.[78] The licensing policies of their state governments are key. They specify minimum admitting and discharge criteria to regulate whether more seriously impaired older people with chronic illnesses can age in place in these properties or must move elsewhere—usually nursing homes—to receive heavier care. States also typically give assisted living providers the discretion to accommodate less frail older people than their regulations allow.[79]

Most assisted living properties put a cap on just how frail older people can be. For example,

> No states allow persons who need a skilled level of nursing home care to be served in residential care settings (e.g., individuals who require 24-hour-a-day skilled nursing oversight or daily skilled nursing services).[80]

The regulations in other states may not permit the retention of residents who need two staff people to help them transfer to and from their beds or chairs.[81] Some state regulations also emphasize that

> Assisted living is not appropriate for people who are incapable of responding to their environment, expressing volition, interacting, or demonstrating independent activity.[82]

Still, some states, such as New Jersey and California, allow assisted living properties to push these boundaries and provide a very high level of care. For example, New Jersey has few entry requirements or restrictions, although residents must be discharged if they need severe behavior management or specialized long-term care, such as respirators or ventilators. Properties in California can admit older people if they need such procedures as administration of oxygen, catheter care, colostomy or ileostomy care, injections, stage I and II dermal ulcer care, and wound care.[83]

Assisted living regulations also specify the qualifications of staff who must be available during awake and sleeping hours.[84] Other rules specify whether only certain staff can perform certain nursing procedures, such as catheterization, ostomy care, care of skin wounds, oxygen therapy, and pain management. They may also specify whether licensed health personnel, such as registered nurses, can delegate these procedures to less-trained or unlicensed staff, such as nurses' aides or certified nurse assistants. Rules also specify which services can be provided by the assisted living establishment's hired staff as opposed to being contracted out to an outside home care agency.[85] Some states waive retention and discharge criteria if a home health agency contracted by the older person provides the extra (usually heavier) personal care or rehabilitation services not offered by the assisted living property.[86]

All of this means that older people and their family members must be vigilant consumers. Consider, for example, that Rhode Island will not allow its assisted living employees to apply bandages to their residents. In Louisiana, state laws prevent some assisted living providers from administering medication to their residents, who instead must contract with third-party home care providers to obtain this very basic service. Assisted living residents in Massachusetts cannot receive skilled nursing services at their communities unless they are provided by third-party home care agencies.[87]

When state regulations allow properties to accommodate older people with behavioral problems—ranging from wandering to aggressive, defiant, destructive, or eccentric behaviors—they often impose another layer of requirements. These may call for better-trained staff, more-rigorous medication management practices, and assurances that the property can safely evacuate residents in the event of a fire or other emergency.[88] For example, Virginia requires that administrators and direct care staff working in properties that care for older people with dementia who cannot recognize danger or protect their own safety and welfare must *"complete four hours of training in cognitive impairments within two months of employment,"* and *"at least two direct care staff members must be in the special care unit at all times."*[89]

Beyond the requirements of their state regulations, however, some properties offer more and better assistance than others. Here we find[90]

- Greater staffing, particularly more registered nurses or licensed practical nurses, on site during both the day and nighttime hours, especially in SCUs
- In-house training programs for direct care staff
- More-sophisticated management programs to ensure that residents take their medicines correctly
- More individualized care
- More-vigilant management of the dietary needs and restrictions of residents
- Dedicated space and equipment to support various rehabilitation activities
- Dedicated SCUs
- Space allocated for nurses or doctors to offer periodic preventive or wellness care
- Presence of on-site clinics where residents can have their primary care needs met

- More-advanced technology to detect resident falls or major changes in resident activity levels
- Greater use of wireless emergency call systems that include pendants or wristwatches worn by residents

In contrast, small board and care facilities typically offer much more pared-down care, with the proprietors providing most of the assistance.[91] These providers are also less qualified, and although many have previously held jobs as human service professionals (e.g., nurses, physician assistants), others have acquired their skills only from caring for their own family members.[92]

LEASES, COST OF OCCUPANCY, AND RESIDENT INCOMES

The occupants of assisted living residences typically sign monthly leases and pay a monthly fee. This practice allows property owners to ask residents to leave on short notice when their care needs become too demanding, and it also gives residents unhappy with the quality of care an easy exit strategy.

Corporate-owned assisted living properties tend to charge higher monthly fees than the smaller board and care variety, which are more likely to accommodate lower-income occupants. When deliberating on assisted living alternatives, older consumers and their families may find it difficult to compare costs. Some corporate-managed properties quote a lower occupancy price, but it covers a limited assistance package. Experts stress that consumers should differentiate occupancy costs of assisted living properties according to what is included in both their basic and more extensive service packages.

In 2014, the U.S. median monthly rate for a one-bedroom single-occupancy unit (an average of all of their service packages) was $3,500, or $42,000 annually.[93] Older people who occupy an SCU will pay, on average, another $1,000 or more per month.[94] Consumers must still interpret these national estimates cautiously because assisted living costs differ dramatically by geographic area. In 2014, for example, the median annual cost was $65,160 in New Jersey but only $30,000 in Missouri.[95] By comparison, the national median annual cost of a private room in a nursing home was just short of $77,380.[96]

Older residents usually pay for their assisted living accommodations out of their own pockets. Medicare offers no coverage, and the majority of occupants do not have long-term care insurance. Two studies offer different estimates of the financial means of residents entering assisted living. A 2009 analysis estimated residents had a median income of only $19,000, but a later 2011 study estimated a median income of just over $35,000. It is also clear that a significant share of occupants will afford this option by drawing down on their savings and the equity realized from a prior house sale (sometimes with the purchase of annuities).[97] Between 80% and 84% are the primary payers, and financially less able residents rely on funds from their families.[98]

Residents living longer in assisted living developments run the risk of exhausting their income sources. When they are unable to pay their monthly fees, they generally must move because only a small percentage of these options accept Medicaid beneficiaries. Some assisted living properties try to prevent such scenarios by financially prequalifying prospective residents before they admit them. Others, often owned by larger nonprofit charitable groups, have endowment funds to assist financially stressed residents.[99]

BOARD AND CARE AND ASSISTED LIVING FOR MEDICAID AND SUPPLEMENTAL SECURITY INCOME BENEFICIARIES

Very low-income older people, disproportionately from racial and ethnic minorities, typically cannot afford the monthly fees charged by the corporate-operated assisted living alternative. However, some properties, especially the smaller board and care variety, admit Medicaid beneficiaries.[100]

States are not required to accommodate Medicaid-eligible older adults in their assisted living properties as they do for their nursing homes, but 45 states now make at least some Medicaid coverage available.[101] Overall, however, most state enrollments are low, and about half of the Medicaid recipients in assisted living residences are found in only three states: North Carolina, Florida, and Michigan.[102]

The majority of states (37) cover assisted living services through their Medicaid waivers (Chapter 8), and only a small number use their Medicaid state plans (13).[103] Qualified older beneficiaries under the waiver program must meet the earlier identified requirements of this program, such as being *"eligible for Medicaid payments in a nursing home if they applied for admission."*[104]

To be eligible for Medicaid waiver funding, assisted living facilities must also operate as "community-based settings" (that is, maintain "a home and community character").[105] However, some advocates argue that current "community-based" standards are not stringent enough and that many eligible facilities are still too institutional.[106] Consider the problem reported by the following resident:

> Ms. Clark lives in an assisted living facility. Her care is funded by Medicaid through a Home and Community-Based Services (HCBS) waiver. HCBS funding is meant to provide alternatives to nursing home care for persons with significant care needs. As the name suggests, Home and Community-Based Services should be provided in a non-institutional environment. For Ms. Clark, however, her assisted living care has many institutional characteristics. Her living unit has one bedroom and one bathroom, each of which Ms. Clark shares with another resident. Facility staff members routinely go in and out of the living unit without knocking or otherwise asking permission. Ms. Clark has little privacy, and the care that she receives does not feel to her to be "community-based."[107]

This is unlikely to be an isolated incident. A national study of Medicaid facilities confirmed that their living quarters offered less privacy, and the occupants were more likely to live in multiperson rooms.[108] Some states allow their operators to accommodate two or more people in the same bedroom and allow 8 to 10 residents to share a bathroom.[109]

As of 2010, nearly 20% of all assisted living residents were receiving Medicaid benefits. Compared with non-Medicaid residents, they tended to be younger: 56% of assisted living residents younger than age 65, 39% of those age 65–74, 16% of those age 75–84, and 10% of those age 85 and older were Medicaid beneficiaries.[110] They were also likely to be male, never married, less educated, and ethnic or racial minorities.[111] Medicaid residents were also more likely to have diabetes, to have more serious mental illness, to be intellectually challenged, and to exhibit problem behaviors (e.g., wandering and being physically abusive).[112]

States are motivated to offer Medicaid coverage to assisted living providers to reduce their more costly demand for Medicaid-reimbursed nursing home beds.[113] Because per-resident care costs are lower in assisted living than nursing homes, they hope to cover more lower-acuity Medicaid recipients. However, states again worry about the woodwork effect (Chapter 8)—that is, low-income older people who would otherwise not enter a nursing home deciding to enter an assisted living property to benefit from this coverage, inflating the number of Medicaid beneficiaries and overall state long-term care expenditures.

For their part, assisted living providers are reluctant to accept Medicaid beneficiaries. Most consider this program's reimbursement policies too low to cover their service delivery costs, as compared with private pay rates. This is especially troublesome when they accommodate older occupants who need heavier and more expensive care.[114] Providers also argue that these reimbursements do not keep pace with their rising expenses and that state governments can unpredictably and unfavorably change their coverage.

The Medicaid program also does not cover the room and board expenses of assisted living providers, and states may limit the amount properties can charge. This is why providers often argue that they must pack multiple low-income residents in the same room to make their properties financially viable. Additionally, to help Medicaid beneficiaries pay for their room and board, about 28 states use their State Supplement Programs to augment the federal Supplemental Security Income payments received by these low-income older people (Chapter 8), but the amounts of these supplements vary widely.[115] Alternatively, many states allow older people to use the federal food stamp program—thereby reducing their property's food costs—and also allow family members to contribute income to older relatives who are living in these properties. However, many providers still do not consider even these additional financial sources adequate to cover their room and board and service delivery costs.

Many operators are reluctant to participate because they do not want to spend the time or incur the expenses of dealing with the increased state regulatory oversight that comes with accepting Medicaid occupants. This is especially true for smaller board and care properties with tighter operating budgets. These properties must meet more stringent physical plant requirements, more rigorous training standards, and higher staff–resident ratios as well as accommodate more physically or cognitively frail older people.

On the flipside, assisted living providers who worry about their low or unstable occupancy rates are motivated to accept Medicaid beneficiaries. They *must decide which is worse: letting a bed remain empty for a month or more or accepting a very poor resident who may remain for a long time.*[116]

Medicaid-certified assisted living properties find ways to restrict the number of qualified beneficiaries. Some properties deny admission to applicants because their care needs are too great. Other assisted living providers evict their current Medicaid occupants when they are temporarily hospitalized because they are unable to obtain Medicaid reimbursement to cover their absent days.[117] And when private-pay residents run out of money and qualify as Medicaid beneficiaries, they often have no guarantees that their properties will allow them to remain as occupants. Providers may simply assert that they have no Medicaid-certified beds available,[118] when in fact they are saving their accommodations for higher-income, private-pay residents.[119]

Some of the more tragic situations arise when a property completely withdraws from the Medicaid program and residents face mass evictions, often on short notice.[120] This occurred in 2007 when Assisted Living Concepts, which was founded with the express purpose of serving low- and moderate-income residents, including those eligible for Medicaid, involuntarily discharged residents from their eight New Jersey facilities after the company had depleted its financial resources.[121]

QUALITY OF SERVICES AND CARE IN ASSISTED LIVING RESIDENCES

When we rate the quality of services offered by assisted living properties, we should ideally separate out the different categories of their operation: concierge or hospitality services (including building management), personal care, and nursing services. For example, in the case of the hospitality or concierge services in the assisted living property occupied by my father-in-law, staff did not keep his room clean or regularly change the sheets on his bed. Pieces of his clothing sent to the wash disappeared, and the food quality went from mediocre to bad. The staff person charged with organizing the social and recreational activities quit because of conflicts with her new director.

Some assisted living properties do a poor job in all three of these categories. The Assisted Living Federation of America (ALFA) contacted state regulatory agencies and compiled a list of the 10 most common problems in their assisted living developments (Figure 11.1).[122]

Other reports indicate that assisted living staff allow their residents to fall frequently.[123] Another study specifically focused on the poor quality of care offered by assisted living properties occupied by Medicaid (waiver) beneficiaries. In the seven states with the highest number of beneficiaries, reported deficiencies included *"failing to furnish services outlined in residents' plans of care," "failing to dispense or administer medication as prescribed by a physician,"* and *"failing to ensure that staff had the required education and training prior to furnishing services to residents."*[124] More serious are reports of staff abusing their residents. One small study of the experiences of former nursing aide employees reported significant evidence of verbal, physical, psychological, and caregiving abuse committed by assisted living employees. A larger study, however, found resident abuse by staff to be relatively uncommon.[125]

Often it is the media that communicates such horror stories.[126] Consider the following headline report about a property operated by a well-known and industry-respected assisted living corporate chain:

Figure 11.1. Most common assisted living deficiencies according to state reports (ALFA, 2012, pp. 2–3)

1. *Medication administration:* Deficiencies relating to all aspects of medication administration, including failure to properly document pre-pours, secure a physician's order, or discard expired medication.

2. *Resident admission requirements:* Deficiencies including initial TB tests, evaluation, and documentation required upon move in.

3. *Ongoing resident assessment:* Deficiencies due to not reevaluating residents' conditions and updating various aspects of their care plan as required.

4. *Maintenance and building code:* Violations of regulations pertaining to the construction and maintenance of various parts of the physical building. This includes cleanliness and the placement of furniture.

5. *Staff training:* Deficiencies attributed to improper training and orientation of new hires as well as training lapses for other employees.

6. *Resident care:* Citations due to all other aspects of resident care.

7. *Emergency preparedness:* Deficiencies for communities that have not created and conducted drills of an adequate disaster plan.

8. *Food service:* Deficiencies relating to the safe handling, storage, and delivery of meals.

9. *Staff health:* Deficiencies related to testing and recording aspects of employee health, such as tuberculosis tests.

10. *Administrative record keeping:* Deficiencies that are clearly paper-oriented, which do not fall into any other category.

Sunrise Cited for Neglect After Assisted Living Facility Fails to Provide Timely Treatment for an Injured Resident
—Officials at the Minnesota Department of Health have cited a Sunrise Senior Living facility in Rochester, MN, for improper care after the facility failed to provide medical attention to a patient who was visibly injured in an altercation with another patient. . . . Despite visible bruising and swelling on his head, staff at the Sunrise facility failed to summon any medical attention for more than 24 hours after the condition was originally noticed. The man died due to a traumatic brain injury approximately two weeks following the incident.[127]

Sometimes, a state's overall assisted living program receives bad marks. On April 20, 2011, the *Miami Herald* published a three-part series titled "Neglected to Death," which reported on abuses that had recently occurred in Florida assisted living properties.[128] Among the more egregious examples:

- A 74-year-old woman was bound for more than 6 hours, the restraints pulled so tightly that they ripped into her skin and killed her.

- A 71-year-old man with mental illness died from burns after he was left in a bathtub filled with scalding water.

- A 75-year-old Alzheimer's man was torn apart by an alligator after he wandered from his assisted living facility for the fourth time.

- A 74-year-old with diabetes and depression died after going 13 days without crucial antibiotics and several days without food or water.

- A caregiver strapped down a 74-year-old woman for at least 6 hours, so tightly that she lost circulation in her legs. As a result, a blood clot formed that killed her.

Evidence of human error abounds when it comes to medication management.[129] Examples include improperly prescribed medications, inaccurately administered dosages, and ignorance of side effects, especially from combining medications.[130] The extent of these problems may be greater, however, because older residents often cannot easily communicate or recognize such errors.[131]

Of course, these errors also occur at pharmacies in our communities and most definitely in home environments, but consumers might expect better results in professionally administered assisted living properties. In defense of assisted living providers, we must remember that their staff must daily respond to the medication needs of many residents with complex administration regimens (e.g., dosage, time of day, side effects). Consider that nearly 81% of assisted living occupants receive help from staff with the self-administration of their medications or have staff administer their prescribed medications, an average of 4.6 medications per month.[132] Thirty-seven percent of residents are on four to seven prescription medications, and 11% take eight or more.[133]

WHY DOES INADEQUATE PERSONAL ASSISTANCE AND CARE HAPPEN?

Various factors help explain why assisted living occupants sometimes receive inferior assistance or care. First, they are more functionally impaired than residents of the past because they have opted to age in place longer in their conventional homes. When they finally occupy an assisted living alternative, they have multiple difficulties performing most of their IADLs and several of their ADLs. Whereas in the past these residents would have occupied nursing homes, they presently reside in assisted living residences.[134] Now their providers are asked to deliver assistance to a high-risk group of occupants—a recipe for errors.[135]

Second, because these residents are typically in their late 80s and 90s, they are sicker; they are managing several chronic health problems and are more likely to be experiencing depression and dementia.[136] They need a broad range of medical services, both primary and specialty care.[137] Even so, assisted living providers are reticent about becoming too involved as healthcare providers because they fear being liable for medical errors. Furthermore, even as residents are responsible for securing primary care physicians, assisted living providers sometimes do not have standardized procedures to ensure their participation.

Consequently, many providers do not offer an organized program of preventive care, a critical component of good medicine. They do not routinely assess for symptoms such as shortness of breath, lack of appetite, or the presence of gum disease. They do not proactively respond to diseases and illnesses at their earlier stages, which would prevent emergency room use and hospitalization.[138] As one critic lamented, *"Assisted living doesn't provide much healthcare, so residents risk becoming 'frequent fliers'—they're going in and out of hospitals for conditions that could perhaps be treated in a nursing home."*[139] Similarly, a well-known academic geriatrician complains that *"Residents are rushed off in ambulances for minor ailments and accidents because the staff is not medically qualified . . . Each hospitalization {for my mother} made things worse, forcing her eventual transfer to a nursing home."*[140] In 2010, 35% of assisted living residents had at least one hospital emergency room visit, and almost 25% had at least one overnight hospital stay.[141]

Assisted living providers also fail to consult or communicate adequately with medical providers after the discharge of their residents from a hospital stay to ensure that they receive the appropriate disease management and recuperative measures. Decisions often are made quickly, but physicians working with the assisted living property or hired by the resident may have insufficient information or unclear responsibilities. Consequently, appropriate care follow-ups do not take place.[142]

Third, many studies conclude—as did the Florida Senate investigation of the problems found in the state's assisted living residences—that their staff are not adequately trained to deal with impaired or sick residents. A 2010 analysis found that in 21% of assisted living residences medication was administered by staff members who were *"neither licensed nurses nor trained in medication administration."*[143] This problem is more apparent in some places because staffing requirements and qualifications vary so much from state to state.[144] For example, in Florida there is no requirement that staff receive training to deal with the wandering behaviors of older people with Alzheimer's disease.[145] In fact, only a handful of states have established minimum staffing requirements for their licensed assisted living properties, even as the evidence shows that better-trained and more-motivated staff produce better quality-of-care outcomes and more-satisfied older residents.[146]

Assisted living properties resist increasing their staff resources for a simple reason: operating costs. To achieve greater financial returns, they rely heavily on direct care workers rather than licensed nurses to manage the medication regimens of their residents and to detect and respond to their health problems. As emphasized in Chapter 8, these workers are willing to accept low wages, few health and retirement benefits, and limited career advancement. Thus, by default, they attract less-educated, more poorly trained, and less-motivated personnel who have lower levels of organizational commitment and higher levels of burnout and are at greater risk of providing inferior care.[147] Not surprisingly, they also have a high level of staff turnover, estimated at about 33% in 2013.[148]

Fourth, properties deliver poor-quality care because state governments lack effective agency oversight. Not surprisingly, this results in calls for the federal government to assume a greater role regulating the assisted living industry.[149] In Florida, for example, multiple state agencies or entities oversee or regulate a large number of assisted living providers that operate under multiple licensing categories. This results in difficulties determining *"which agency has final authority to carry out administrative penalties, and confused residents, family members, or staff"* who are unsure *"which entity is best to contact should a certain concern arise."*[150] Of course, state regulatory agencies also do not respond because they do not have adequate staff to monitor and correct rule violations. On the other hand, one nationally renowned legal expert argues that states have self-serving motives:

> State regulations tend to be soft because if a board-and-care home were to be shut down, there might be no alternative for the low-income residents. States are well aware that these homes are not optimal environments, but nevertheless, they fill a vital role in providing housing and service to a great many old.[151]

EQUATING ASSISTED LIVING WITH A SOCIAL MODEL OF CARE

Even as assisted living properties are very different from the conventional homes of their older occupants, advocates argue that they can still offer them a residential and care environment where they can achieve residential normalcy. However, these properties must subscribe to a social model of care and implement a set of *person-centered*[152] principles offering guidelines for both their physical design and operating environments (Figure 11.2).

A national study that assessed whether the residents of assisted living were satisfied with their accommodations at least partially supports these claims. It found that 45% of the occupants rated their places as excellent and 46% as good.[153] Ratings were particularly high for *"respectfulness of staff," "safety of facility,"* and *"courteousness of dining staff."* On the other hand, respondents gave much lower scores for the appeal of the food, *"grow as a person opportunities,"* and *"adequacy of storage space."*[154]

One nationally renowned consultant, Margaret Wylde (CEO of Promatura), argues that the assisted living alternative sometimes falls short for another reason. She argues that older occupants want to be treated not just as *residents* but also as *customers,* which they usually are not:

> When you move to an assisted living residence, you are no longer an individual; you become "one of our residents." Indeed, despite the fact that you pay for your apartment, services, and dining room fare you are not even one of our "customers," you are simply one of the residents to whom we provide high-quality care. There is a huge difference between being a customer with preferences and purchasing power and being a resident.[155]

IN THEIR RESIDENTIAL MASTERY ZONES: RESIDENTS IN CONTROL OF THEIR CARE AND DAILY LIFE

Advocates of a social model of care believe that if assisted living residents are to maintain their dignity and autonomous lives, they must be able to influence their care

Figure 11.2. Ideal person-centered principles of assisted living residences (reprinted with permission from Calkins & Keane, 2008, pp. 114–115)

Individual Experiences and Activities

- *Daily routines* focus on the choices and preferences of residents, remembering they had pasts with idiosyncratic styles of living.

- *Individualized activities* reflect the interests, past life-styles, and life histories of residents.

- *Resident involvement* is encouraged in the design and operation of the home.

- *Maximal functional independence* is supported as much as possible within the constraints of regulatory requirements.

- *Choices* exist, such as where residents can spend their time and enjoy different experiences, when they can eat their meals, and when and how often they are bathed.

- *Personal possessions* of residents are placed everywhere.

- *Alternative, therapeutic experiences* are centered around holistic well-being, spirituality, physical exercise, the enjoyment of animals, continued learning, and opportunities to develop.

- *Productive contributions* are encouraged and facilitated as much as possible to reinforce residents' self-esteem.

- *Dining experiences* resemble those that occur in conventional homes (such as in conventional kitchens), go beyond nutrition requirements, and become an event to anticipate every day.

- *Aromas* of foods or flowers that are found in conventional residences are present.

- *Fun experiences* are encouraged, such as having pets and visits by children.

- *Privacy* is maximized as much as possible in both shared or common areas and personal spaces of the building, such as bedrooms.

Design of the Physical and Proximate Natural Settings

- *Carefully designed spaces* reflect public, semi-private, and private needs. A major illustration is the breaking down of large 40–60-bed units into smaller clusters—usually called "households" or "neighborhoods"—with kitchens, dining rooms, and living rooms instead of the ubiquitous multi-purpose day room.

- *Buildings and spaces* are smaller scaled and thus accommodate fewer residents, but in more intimate and friendly settings.

- *Richly-textured interior spaces* with different characters and styles counter one of the hallmarks of an "institutional" environment—namely, the sameness of

Figure continued next page

Figure 11.2. *Continued*

everything, chairs, color palette, only soft and muted colors. This helps people feel they have a choice of where to spend time.

- *Orientation in space* is achieved. This means more than a few signs directing residents to the dining room. Rather, layering as many cues as possible to distinguish different sides of a building. For instance, two parallel corridors are visibly different—color, art, theme, and what is visible at the ends.

- *Non-glare and indirect lighting* should be incorporated throughout the setting.

- *Institutional-like paraphernalia* is eliminated or minimized, everything from the large nursing station to carts in the hallways. Medications do not have to come from a huge cart rolled down the hall by nurses, which sits in the dining room during all meals. There are systems where medications are kept in the residents' rooms, or where the cart is more like a piece of furniture and is restocked by the night shift.

- *Natural outdoor environments* that are accessible to both residents and staff and have a variety of uses.

Staffing Environment

- *Staff teams* include the elder and family in decision making and planning. Staff is well-trained, consistently assigned to promote relationships, and have career ladder opportunities for growth.

- *Staff teams* respect residents' individualized needs, especially for autonomy.

- *Direct care workers*, usually referred to as CNAs (certified nursing assistants) or STNAs (state tested nursing assistants) and traditionally looked down on as the least knowledgeable and capable people, receive more training and assume more responsibility for supporting residents' decisions about daily routine and care.

- *Electronic charting* exists, which eliminates the need for a large central nursing station that usually separates staff from residents.

- *Performance is evaluated* on not only how much care is delivered but also the extent to which staff supports person-centered care principles.

Connections with Family and Community

- *Family and community connectedness* is nurtured, such as family participation in the daily life of the home. Family members participate in joint activities with other residents and families. Residents are still considered active members of the community and are encouraged to participate in community-based events.

- *End-of-Life care* is dignified and inclusive of all members of the community, celebrating life and honoring the experience of grief.

regimens. They want to feel in control over what services they receive, when they happen, and who provides them. They want to feel that property managers are responsive, give them choices, and respect their preferences.[156] They want to receive good-quality assistance and care yet still feel as competent as their aging bodies allow; and they do not want managers to treat them like helpless patients. In the parlance of our emotion-based model, older assisted living residents want to feel in their *residential mastery zones* despite their obvious declines and limitations. As assisted living provider and scholar Joan Hyde emphasizes,

> All staff members who interact with residents affect the resident's sense of autonomy and ability to live with dignity and respect. Direct care workers play a critical role in the lives of the most impaired assisted living residents because they provide the greatest amount of care. Each interaction they have with residents can either positively or negatively impact their quality of life.[157]

But older people want more than just control over the care they receive. They want to live in a place that mimics the activities and way of life that they conducted in the less restrictive environments of their earlier homes. They want to have their own locked living areas, get up and go to bed when they want, and talk only to people with whom they give and receive affection.[158] In board and care settings, they are turned off when the owners try to exert control over residents by establishing curfews and having *"a set time for bathing and lights out."*[159]

IN THEIR COMFORT ZONES: IT'S MY HOME

Older people want also to feel in their *residential comfort zones* (Chapter 2). They seek to *"satisfactorily bridge the divide between their lives before and now within the facility."*[160] The property's size, architecture, furnishings, and overall physical ambience are all important. Older people want to occupy settings that are reminiscent of their past home-like environments.[161] They do not want to confront architectural designs and paraphernalia that resemble institutional settings, such as nurses' stations, long hallways, double-loaded corridors, institutional tile floors, furniture with vinyl upholstery, and boxy hospital-like rooms. They want to have their own private accommodations furnished with their favorite possessions. They want attractively designed common areas and outdoor spaces (e.g., libraries, seating areas, lobbies, porches, and gardens) that encourage them to engage in activities and cultivate friendships.[162] They do not want managers who frown on their romantic relationships or prevent them from having a glass of wine with dinner.[163]

As our consultant maven Wylde argues, what creates happy older occupants is not just the quality of their care but also the quality of their daily living[164]:

> The fact that she is bathed, her meals and snacks are prepared, her bed is made, and her apartment is cleaned is not the focus of her existence. Those things are appreciated because they are needed, but they play minimally into her assessment of the quality of her life.[165]

She does not want to settle for *"lukewarm processed dinners served in the middle of the after-noon, and spirited discussion of someone's latest trip to the podiatrist."*[166]

The solution, she emphasizes, is for assisted living properties to help their older customers feel more at home and, in turn, more alive. Her research indicated that older residents were most influenced by the following[167]:

1. Opportunities to pursue individual interests (variety and number of educational programs and the quality of social activities)
2. Friendliness and courteousness of staff
3. Quality, variety, and frequency of fitness programs
4. Quality and variety of food and the overall dining experience
5. Quality and timeliness of maintenance services
6. Sense of safety and security[168]
7. Quality, variety, and frequency of day trips
8. Quality and timeliness of housekeeping services
9. Extent to which friendships have been formed with other residents and staff
10. Friendliness and courteousness of the executive director
11. Friendliness and courteousness of the dining room servers
12. Opportunity to volunteer outside of the assisted living residence
13. Quality and timeliness of personal care services

A CONGENIAL SOCIAL ENVIRONMENT

Residential normalcy also means that assisted living residents experience enjoyable and supportive social relationships of their own choosing.[169] They especially seek to maintain strong connections with their families,[170] as evidenced by a proprietary study that reported that 77% of older assisted living residents received family visits at least weekly.[171] Even with his diagnosis of dementia, my father-in-law enjoyed his weekly excursions out of his assisted living accommodations to spend time with his daughter and granddaughter when they took him out for lunch or a haircut.

Older people also want to keep in contact with prior friends.[172] One study concluded that *"residents lacking meaningful ties to people from their past often had the most difficult time maintaining a sense of continuity and adapting to inevitable changes in facility culture."*[173] This warns against the older person relocating to an assisted living property that is geographically distant from family members and friends.

Supportive staff–resident social exchanges are also key. Older occupants appreciate staff who pay special attention to their needs and show true interest in their well-being.[174] Predictably, they are reluctant to confide in workers who use their social exchanges against them.[175] Better-trained and experienced staff with more congenial personalities are instrumental in encouraging social activities, contacts, conversations, and friendships.[176] Consequently, problems arise when staff and residents cannot easily communicate because of language, racial and ethnic, or sexual orientation barriers.[177]

By far, however, the most important social contacts are the other residents in the assisted living property, if only because they must spend so much time together, whether as acquaintances to engage in pleasant conversations or as confidants to share more intimate thoughts.[178] In the best social worlds, older residents find themselves among people who share the same educational, ethnic, racial, religious, political, sexual orientation, and work backgrounds or come from similar city, suburban, or rural settings.[179] In worst-case scenarios, older people confront residents with whom they have little in common,[180] and they are subjected to *"bullying, name-calling intolerance, gossiping, shunning, harassing, disagreements, and physical confrontation."*[181] Residents with these less satisfactory social relationships are more likely to be depressed.[182] That is why living in the close quarters of small board and care properties may be a double-edged sword. Older people may find it easier to make friendships but difficult to escape from undesirable relationships.

Older occupants of assisted living properties have no guarantees of a congenial social environment, and in some places the other residents are offensively territorial. Columnist Paula Span reported on the work of researchers Marsha Frankel and Robin Bonifas, who described such power grabs by assisted living residents:

> **Attempts to turn public spaces into private fiefdoms.** "There's a TV lounge meant to be used by everyone, but one person tries to monopolize it—what show is on, whether the blinds are open or shut, who can sit where."
>
> **Exclusion.** "Dining room issues are ubiquitous." When there's no assigned seating, a resident may loudly announce that she's saving a seat, even if no one else is expected, to avoid someone she dislikes. In an exercise class, "one resident told another, in a condescending way, that she was doing it all wrong and shouldn't be allowed to take the class."[183]

What constitutes a compatible social environment may depend on whether the older residents themselves have ageist attitudes. Some react very negatively to residents with more serious impairments and try to distance *"themselves from others perceived as socially unacceptable to avoid being stigmatized by association."*[184] They may be particularly averse to sharing common spaces or engaging with less cognitively alert people with Alzheimer's disease[185] because they get upset with their public sexuality displays, disruptive dining behavior, conversation difficulties, and abusive or violent outbursts.[186]

These reactions are predictable. Much social and psychological theory questions the advisability of mixing residents with different competence levels.[187] The frail older occupants may shy away from organized leisure and recreational activities geared to more active residents because they continually find themselves in uncomfortable situations.[188] By the same token, those with intact sensory skills have difficulty communicating with residents with hearing or comprehension difficulties. And similarly, the more functionally able older occupants are less motivated to participate in activities with residents who are more sedentary than they are and become depressed when they must interact with other frail residents.[189]

Consider again the views of our prominent national marketing consultant Wylde:

> Becoming older does not increase one's desire to live among those who are frail. Prospective customers of assisted living will size up future neighbors and

determine whether these are the people they want to see everyday. The reality is that they will open the doors of assisted living residences and see people who are frailer and less able than themselves, whereupon they will close the door and go home and hang on for as long as they can in their homes where they are not constantly reminded of human limitations.[190]

Older people experience another downside when they have social relationships with vulnerable residents. As one assisted living resident poignantly put it,

> Yeah, I don't want [friends] anymore. I don't want to see the friend die. Or, eat supper and be dead by breakfast time. And they come in and they go out to nursing homes.[191]

COMFORT FOOD WHEN THEY WANT IT

Whether older people are in their residential comfort and mastery zones may depend on the quality of their eating experiences.[192] It matters whether there are upscale dining rooms with tasty food and friendly staff as opposed to bare-bones rooms, mundane cafeteria fare, and curt servers. It matters whom they eat with. Some managers are more responsive and creative than others. They offer flexible dining times and different types of dining areas—both formal and less formal—and relaxed rules about where the residents sit, what they eat or drink, and whether they are allowed to take food back to their rooms. These practices contrast with those of managers who dictate the tables and times at which older people must eat, which stifle spontaneity and the residents' ability to make friends.[193]

Still, dining may fall short of the home experience:

> Even though many residents, mostly women, expressed gratitude that they no longer had to cook meals each day, some missed their favorite foods and the ability to prepare it in familiar ways. Food, as well as mealtime memories, intrinsically links individuals to memories of home.[194]

As part of a proprietary survey, assisted living residents gave disturbingly low scores to the food offered by their residence, and 28% of the time they judged the food as only fair or poor.[195]

THREATS TO RESIDENTIAL NORMALCY: STABILITY NOT GUARANTEED

The feelings underlying the residential normalcy of older people will not always be stable over the course of their time in an assisted living community. They may find themselves unexpectedly out of their residential comfort and mastery zones. Reassuring family visits may abruptly end if a daughter must move out of state for a new employment opportunity. Once-reliable friends living outside the assisted living community may lose interest. A stroke may incapacitate the helpful neighbor across the hall.

During their stays, the organizational environment of their property may change.[196] Staff changes may result in the loss of trusting relationships or a decline in the quality of services. Changing admission and discharge policies may result in an overall more-impaired resident population, creating an undesirable social situation. For example, one study reported that an assisted living property began admitting younger mentally ill male residents to fill its beds.[197] Because of a corporate merger, new managers may be less sympathetic to a social model of care and impose more stringent rules and regulations. In response to competitive pressures, managers may radically change the culture of their properties without concern for the feelings of their current residents. In one instance, managers of an upscale African-American property began to admit White residents.[198]

DOWNSIDES OF A SOCIAL MODEL OF CARE

There is much to like about the social model of care and its person-centered principles. Nevertheless, even its proponents worry about the dangers of assisted living properties offering less competent care if they adopt this model. Their reasoning:

> Respecting and supporting resident autonomy also entails allowing a resident to take risks in order to maintain acceptable quality of life. For example, a resi-dent with diabetes may choose a less-restrictive diet than has been prescribed for her in order to increase her dining pleasure . . . even though she risks shortening her life, or a physically impaired resident may choose to preserve her privacy and dignity by showering alone despite her risk of falling. At the same time, however, assisted living providers have a responsibility to safeguard residents' well-being.[199]

And therein lies the conundrum.[200] Critics question whether assisted living residences operating under a social model of care can accommodate older occupants when their health problems and limitations begin to resemble those of nursing home occupants. They argue that we must impose strict building codes, micromanage all aspects of the assisted living operation setting, and set *"eligibility standards, monitoring everything from medical equipment and personal care to safety, cleanliness, and other physical aspects of the care setting."*[201] Absent the regulatory vigilance of a medical model of care, the older occupants will be at risk of receiving incompetent care, having accidents, and needing more demanding and expensive medical assistance and care down the road.

In a nutshell, critics of a social model of care argue that there is a resident vulner-ability threshold above which the physical plant, staffing patterns, operating proce-dures, and heavily regulated environment of the nursing home become necessary. They remind us that the quality of care in nursing homes improved only after state govern-ments tightened their regulations. They point to research showing that when assisted living residences have well-trained and licensed full-time nurses, the occupants enjoy better care outcomes and are hospitalized less frequently, especially when they have dementia.[202] But these studies also acknowledge that when nurses work in assisted liv-ing, a hospital-like environment is more likely.

Their message is clear. If dependent older residents want the best care, they must inevitably sacrifice some rights and individual freedoms.[203] These critics continue to lobby state legislatures for a more regulated assisted living environment that threatens its "social" model and, because of compliance costs, may drive up consumer prices.

Assisted living advocates retort that in return for a more normalized housing-like environment and a more autonomous and dignified way of life, residents and their family members must assume greater responsibilities and risks as well as be prepared to be monitored less intensively than residents in a nursing home. However, this position creates an ethical dilemma for providers whose background and experiences have often been in the healthcare professions. As one expert observes,

> In a health care system that has traditionally made safety a hierarchy among values, how can providers recognize risk taking as a normal element in adult life, an inalienable part of being autonomous, even when one is elderly and frail? What boundaries or better, what tolerances should long-term care develop for the "behavioral outliers," for individuals who are sharply singular or eccentric, who persistently breach social decorum and convention? How should providers balance the right of elderly individuals to take risks with their own obligations to protect these individuals from harm—and from harming others?[204]

Not all experts believe it is productive to frame these issues in this way. They argue that it presumes a false dichotomy between quality of life and quality of care, and it is impossible to achieve one without the other. In the words of two experts,

> If the quality of healthcare—either preventive, diagnostic, or therapeutic—is substandard, the effect on the client's overall well-being—that is quality of life—can be profound. Adequate healthcare leading to expected outcomes is a necessary aspect of quality of life. Too often, a salutary emphasis on psychological and social well-being is paired with a harmful de-emphasis on the importance of healthcare.[205]

Many assisted living providers and state regulatory agencies have staked out a middle ground. There is growing consensus that properly trained nonnursing staff can perform the same procedures as nursing professionals, less expensively and less obtrusively. For example, most states now allow delegated nurse supervision for the administering of oral medications and injections.[206] How well this organizational strategy works varies across assisted living properties and depends on the usual supervisory and training factors. One study reported that nonnurses trained as medication aides had similar medication administration error rates as licensed practical nurses, but nonnurses without special training committed more errors.[207]

Some providers look for other ways to offer their residents greater autonomy but at the same time reduce costly lawsuits. They ask residents to sign *negotiated risk agreements*. In so doing, residents acknowledge and accept responsibility for the potentially negative consequences of their specified "risky" behaviors.[208] Thus, the resident who wants to eat eggs on the weekend, even though she is mildly allergic to eggs, can practice this risky behavior if she agrees to release the provider of any liability.

Detractors argue that these negotiated risk agreements are legally vague and potentially unenforceable instruments that allow providers to *"avoid liability for a lack of medical services and expertise, or for a relatively low level of supervision."*[209] According to these skeptics, assisted living residents *"already have the right to act autonomously and there is, therefore, no necessity to negotiate about it."*[210] Others fear that providers will use these instruments to force residents to accept substandard care.[211] Studies have not revealed the pervasiveness of these agreements.

CONCLUSION

Perhaps because they must be concerned with profits and fill-up rates, private providers are especially aware of the diverse needs of aging American consumers. The availability of options such as independent living and assisted living developments that respond to older adults' significantly different service and assistance needs testifies to the success of their segmentation efforts. Older Americans now have real choices if they cannot age in place comfortably and competently in their homes.

The physical appearances and operating environments of independent living developments differ less dramatically from those of their past homes. Consequently, older adults need less specialized knowledge when they evaluate the pros and cons of these properties. Still, the architectural ambience, hospitality services, dining experiences, and recreation opportunities offered in these places can vary substantially; some properties even offer wellness and preventive health services. Others are more accommodating of vulnerable residents seeking to hire their own caregivers, enabling them to prolong their residential stay. And in properties connected to an assisted living option, the transition to a higher level of care is certainly easier.

Selecting an assisted living property as a long-term care option is more challenging, and older consumers and their families face two difficult tasks. The first is to establish the severity of physical and mental impairments and chronic illnesses that the property will accommodate—not just in the present but also in the future. If it is only a temporary way station from which they will soon have to relocate, older people must decide whether occupying even the most attractive assisted living residence can justify the energy and stress if they must soon move again. This may be an especially tough decision for those who currently have only minor dementia symptoms that will worsen over time. Such considerations might influence whether they would say no to stand-alone assisted living properties because they are not physically connected to dementia care units or nursing homes.

Their second and equally difficult task is to find high-quality care and accommodations where residents are likely to feel in both their residential comfort and mastery zones. There are both very good and very bad assisted living properties. They differ substantially with regard to their physical amenities, hospitality services, food quality, and overall atmosphere. They do not all offer the same quality of assistance and care or hire staff with the same expertise, training, and congeniality. And some managements will be better able to adapt to the idiosyncratic social and care needs of their residents.

Although assessments of these properties are difficult to make, word-of-mouth endorsements or critiques by other families or friends may be the best way to evaluate alternatives. Prospective residents and their families should make several visits to the property to observe operations firsthand. As superficial as it may sound, the best candidates may be properties where the residents look involved, happy, and content and where staff members are calmly carrying out their duties in an upbeat fashion. Last, when making their determination, families should give higher marks to properties that are closer by. Their caregiving responsibilities are unlikely to end just because their loved ones are no longer ensconced in their homes.

State governments will continue to regulate assisted living properties in the future and will generally support their social model of care and person-centered principles. However, as consumers become more demanding of better-quality care and as reports of incompetent care continue, it would not be surprising to see greater federal oversight over this industry and regulatory changes that advocates would interpret as the imposition of a medical model of care.[212]

NOTES

1. Answer by author, columnist, and speaker Carol Bradley Bursack to query of reader: http://www.agingcare.com/Questions/time-pass-if-elder-hates-assisted-living-facility-138827.htms
2. (Gross, 2008); http://newoldage.blogs.nytimes.com/2008/11/03/commended-not-condemned-a-reader-on-assisted-living/
3. (Brecht, 2002)
4. (Mullen, 2011)
5. Sunrise Senior Living advertisement.
6. (American Seniors Housing Association, 2013)
7. (American Seniors Housing Association, 2013); Ziegler Investment Banking/Senior Living Z-News. 2014. Accessed at http://www.ziegler.com/investment-banking/senior-living/.
8. (American Seniors Housing Association, 2011)
9. (American Seniors Housing Association, 2009)
10. (American Seniors Housing Association, 2009)
11. (Ball, Perkins, Hollingsworth, Whittington, & King, 2009)
12. (National Research Corporation, 2013)
13. (American Seniors Housing Association, 2009)
14. (American Seniors Housing Association, 2009)
15. (American Seniors Housing Association, 2011)
16. (American Seniors Housing Association, 2009). All the percentages quoted in the above sections are likely to be higher in 2015 as this option accommodates a more vulnerable older population.
17. (Mullen, 2011)
18. (American Seniors Housing Association, 2009)
19. (National Research Corporation, 2013)
20. (American Seniors Housing Association, 2009, p. 87)
21. (Setar & Son, 2013, p. 3)
22. (Antonucci, 2013)
23. (American Seniors Housing Association, 2013)
24. (Brecht, 2002)
25. Based on findings from a survey of independent living providers (American Seniors Housing Association, 2009).
26. (Coe & Boyle, 2009)
27. (Yedinak, 2012)
28. (National Research Corporation, 2013)
29. (American Seniors Housing Association, 2009; Mullen, 2011)

30. (Wylde, Smith, Schless, & Berstecker, 2009)
31. (Wylde et al., 2009)
32. (Wylde et al., 2009)
33. (Wylde et al., 2009, p. 12)
34. Operators of independent living communities often cite the food and beverage amenities as a key determinant of resident satisfaction. *Senior Housing News,* March 2, 2011, http://seniorhousingnews. com/2011/03/02/op-ed-the-future-of-food-service-in-senior-living/
35. (National Research Corporation, 2013; Wylde et al., 2009)
36. (Mollica, Houser, & Ujvari, 2012, p. 1)
37. (New Jersey, 2009)
38. (Stevenson & Grabowski, 2010, p. 35)
39. (Hyde, Perez, & Forester, 2007)
40. (Frolik, 2008)
41. (Mollica, Sims-Kastelein, & O'Keeffe, 2007)
42. (Khatutsky, Wiener, Greene, Johnson, & O'Keeffe, 2013)
43. (Mollica et al., 2012)
44. (Mollica et al., 2012) This total does not include an unknown number of unregulated or unlicensed group homes occupied by older people.
45. (Park-Lee et al., 2011)
46. (Park-Lee et al., 2011)
47. These are California, Florida, Minnesota, New York, North Carolina, Ohio, Pennsylvania, Texas, Virginia, Wisconsin, and Washington (Stevenson & Grabowski, 2010).
48. (Stevenson & Grabowski, 2010)
49. (Stevenson & Grabowski, 2010)
50. (American Association of Homes and Services for the Aging, 2009)
51. (Caffrey et al., 2012)
52. (Ball et al., 2009)
53. (American Association of Homes and Services for the Aging, 2009)
54. (Mollica et al., 2012)
55. (Chen et al., 2008)
56. (Ball et al., 2009)
57. (Ball et al., 2009)
58. (Caffrey et al., 2012)
59. (Khatutsky et al., 2013)
60. (Caffrey et al., 2012)
61. (Khatutsky et al., 2013)
62. (Khatutsky et al., 2013; Zimmerman, Sloane, & Reed, 2014)
63. (Golant & Hyde, 2015; Zimmerman, Sloane, & Reed, 2014)
64. (Polzer, 2012)
65. (Golant & Hyde, 2014)
66. (Hernandez & Newcomer, 2007, p. 113)
67. (Hedrick, Sullivan, Sales, & Gray, 2009)
68. (Golant & Hyde, 2008)
69. (American Seniors Housing Association, 2011); Investment Banking/Senior Living Z-News. 2014). Accessed at http://www.ziegler.com/investment-banking/senior-living/.
70. (Assisted Living Federation of America, 2009)
71. (Park-Lee, Sengupta, & Harris-Kojetin, 2013)
72. (Sloane, Zimmerman, & Walsh, 2001)
73. (Mollica et al., 2007; National Center for Assisted Living, 2012a)
74. (Zimmerman, Sloane, & Reed, 2014)
75. (Hyde et al., 2007)
76. (Regnier, 2002)

77. Skilled nursing services must be performed (or delegated) by a registered nurse or licensed practical nurse.
78. (Khatutsky et al., 2013)
79. (Mollica et al., 2007)
80. (Mollica et al., 2007)
81. (Mitty & Flores, 2008)
82. (Polzer, 2012, p. 136)
83. (Polzer, 2013)
84. (Mollica et al., 2007)
85. (Mollica et al., 2007)
86. (Mitty & Flores, 2008)
87. (Gerace, 2013a)
88. (Hyde et al., 2007)
89. (Polzer, 2012, p. 219)
90. (Khatutsky et al., 2013; Zimmerman, Sloane, & Reed, 2014)
91. (Assisted Living Federation of America, 2009; Hedrick et al., 2009)
92. (Mollica et al., 2012)
93. (Genworth Financial, 2014). These are the prices charged by mainly the larger developments.
94. (American Seniors Housing Association, 2011)
95. (Genworth Financial, 2014)
96. (Genworth Financial, 2014)
97. (Assisted Living Federation of America, 2009; Coe & Wu, 2014)
98. (Assisted Living Federation of America, 2009; Coe & Wu, 2014)
99. Jim Antonucci, personal communication, 2014.
100. (Greene, Wiener, Khatutsky, Johnson, & O'Keeffe, 2013)
101. (National Senior Citizens Law Center, 2010)
102. (Carlson, Coffey, Fecondo, & Newcomer, 2010)
103. (U.S. Department of Health and Human Services, Office of Inspector General, 2012). State totals as of 2009.
104. (Mollica, 2009, p. 4)
105. (Mollica, 2009, p. 4; National Senior Citizens Law Center, 2011a).
106. A final rule in 2014 from the Centers for Medicare & Medicaid Services (CMS 2249-F/2296-F) establishes new requirements for the qualities of settings that are eligible for reimbursement under the Medicaid home- and community-based services provided under 1915(c) of the Medicaid statute. These new standards may make it more difficult for assisted living facilities with such institutional qualities to qualify for this program.
107. (National Senior Citizens Law Center, 2011b, p. 1)
108. (Greene et al., 2013)
109. (Carlson, 2007)
110. (Caffrey et al., 2012)
111. (Greene et al., 2013)
112. (Kyllo & Polzer, 2013)
113. (Mollica et al., 2007)
114. (National Senior Citizens Law Center, 2011c)
115. (National Senior Citizens Law Center, 2011c)
116. (Carder, Morgan, & Eckert, 2008, p. 160)
117. (National Senior Citizens Law Center, 2011b)
118. (National Senior Citizens Law Center, 2010)
119. (National Senior Citizens Law Center, 2011b)
120. (National Senior Citizens Law Center, 2010)
121. (New Jersey, 2009)
122. (ALFA, 2012)

123. (Kyllo & Polzer, 2013)
124. (U.S. Department of Health and Human Services, Office of Inspector General, 2012, p. 14)
125. (Castle & Beach, 2011; Castle, 2013)
126. *Frontline,* "Life and Death in Assisted Living" (http://www.pbs.org/wgbh/pages/frontline/life-and-death-in-assisted-living/); U.S. General Accounting Office (1999)
127. (Rosenfeld, 2010)
128. (The Florida Senate, 2011, p. 20)
129. (Kane & Mach, 2007; Mollica et al., 2007; Zimmerman et al., 2011)
130. (Castle & Beach, 2011)
131. (Mollica et al., 2007)
132. (Kemp, Luo, & Ball, 2012)
133. (Mollica et al., 2007)
134. (Grabowski, Stevenson, & Cornell, 2012)
135. (Grabowski et al., 2012)
136. (Hyde, Perez, & Reed, 2008)
137. (Kane & Mach, 2007)
138. (Kane & Mach, 2007)
139. (Span, 2011a)
140. (Gross, 2005)
141. (Khatutsky et al., 2013)
142. (Kane, 2010)
143. (Zimmerman, Sloane, & Reed, 2014, p. 661)
144. (The Florida Senate, 2011)
145. (The Florida Senate, 2011)
146. (Hyde et al., 2008; Stearns et al., 2007; Zimmerman, Sloane, & Reed, 2014)
147. (Hyde et al., 2007)
148. 2013–2014 Assisted Living Salary and Benefits report produced by Hospital & Healthcare Compensation Service. See also Hyde et al. (2008); National Center for Assisted Living (2012b).
149. (Kyllo & Polzer, 2013)
150. (The Florida Senate, 2011, p. 30)
151. (Frolik, 2008, pp. 217–218)
152. (Calkins & Keane, 2008)
153. (National Research Corporation, 2012)
154. (National Research Corporation, 2012)
155. (Wylde, 2008b, p. 172)
156. (National Research Corporation, 2012)
157. (Hyde et al., 2008, p. 73)
158. (Fienberg, 2012; Polivka & Salmon, 2008)
159. (Hedrick et al., 2009, p. 47)
160. (Yamasaki & Shari, 2011, p. 13)
161. (Regnier, 2002)
162. (Kemp, Ball, Hollingsworth, & Perkins, 2012)
163. (Park, Zimmerman, Sloane, Gruber-Baldini, & Eckert, 2006)
164. (Wylde, 2008b, p. 173)
165. (Wylde, 2008b, p. 173)
166. (Wylde, 2008b, pp. 171–172)
167. (Wylde, 2008b, p. 190)
168. Safety and security are a source of residential mastery.
169. (Perkins et al., 2012, p. 220)
170. (Hyde et al., 2007; Perkins, Ball, Kemp, & Hollingsworth, 2013)
171. (National Research Corporation, 2013)
172. (Yamasaki & Shari, 2011)
173. (Perkins et al., 2012, p. 220)

174. (Park et al., 2006)
175. (Eckert et al., 2009)
176. (Park, Zimmerman, Kinslow, Shin, & Roff, 2012)
177. (Hyde et al., 2007)
178. (Perkins et al., 2013)
179. (Park et al., 2006; Perkins et al., 2012)
180. (Kemp, Ball, et al., 2012, p. 495)
181. (Kemp, Ball, et al., 2012, p. 495)
182. (Perkins et al., 2013)
183. (Span, 2011b)
184. (Perkins et al., 2012, p. 221)
185. (Park et al., 2006; Street, Burge, Quadagno, & Barrett, 2007)
186. (Regnier, Hamilton, & Yatabe, 1995)
187. (Golant, 1998b; Zimmerman et al., 2014)
188. (Gubrium, 1973)
189. (Golant, 1998b)
190. (Wylde, 2008b, p. 187)
191. (Park et al., 2006, p. 223)
192. (Kemp, Ball, et al., 2012)
193. (Park et al., 2006)
194. (Eckert et al., 2009, p. 155)
195. (National Research Corporation, 2013)
196. (Morgan et al., 2014; Perkins et al., 2012)
197. (Perkins et al., 2012)
198. (Perkins et al., 2012)
199. (Polivka & Salmon, 2008, p. 491)
200. I earlier raised these issues in Golant (1998b)
201. (Collopy, 1995, p. 65)
202. (Chou, Boldy, & Lee, 2003; Stearns et al., 2007)
203. (Parmelee & Lawton, 1990)
204. (Collopy, 1995, p. 61)
205. (Kane & Kane, 1989, p. 67)
206. (Polivka & Salmon, 2008)
207. (Zimmerman et al., 2011)
208. (Jenkens, O'Keefe, Carder, & Wilson, 2006)
209. (Carlson, 2007, p. 295)
210. (Mitty & Flores, 2008, p. 98)
211. (Jenkens et al., 2006)
212. (Golant, 2008c)

12

MOVING TO CONTINUING CARE RETIREMENT COMMUNITIES

Many people choose CCRCs because of a vibrant campus lifestyle that offers opportunities for learning and to engage in activities with far more mental stimulation and social engagement than staying in one's current home.[1]

Our investigation has found many CCRC ownership structures to be very complex and that financial troubles at any level can have real consequences for individual residents. Evaluating such a transaction can be quite challenging for the average consumer without professional assistance.[2]

Inspect the CCRC facilities you may utilize in the future. Inquire about standards for admission, the transition from one level of care to another, and your obligation to pay for additional costs.[3]

WHAT IS DISTINCTIVE ABOUT CCRCS?

When I first began studying senior housing options, one of my most vivid memories resulted from a visit to a continuing care retirement community (CCRC). As I observed each of its distinctive levels of care, I felt that I was watching the aging process unfold in real time. The heterogeneity of the population older than age 65 and the rationale for distinguishing the young-old from the old-old was never clearer.

The ability of a single housing option to accommodate the changing leisure, health, and long-term care needs of both Third Age and Fourth Age older people is the claim to fame of CCRCs. Few other social institutions can boast providing a continuum of care delivery model that ranges from independent living to skilled nursing services. The owners and managers of these properties envisage that healthy and active older people in their 70s will initially occupy their independent living communities and benefit from their hospitality, hotel-like services as well as planned social and recreational activities. Some years later, when these older people begin to have difficulty performing their activities of daily living (ADLs) and instrumental ADLs (IADLs), they will enter the assisted living quarters of the CCRC and sometimes its memory care unit. When they confront more serious physical and cognitive health and functional declines, they will occupy the CCRC's skilled nursing facility. However, some residents stay only a short time in the nursing home to receive rehabilitative care while they recover from an accident injury or a short-term acute illness, whereupon they return to their prior accommodations.

This alternative also stands out because its occupants make a unique financial and contractual commitment to guarantee that they will receive as-needed long-term care for the rest of their lives and will never have to move again (at least outside their CCRC home). It is the ultimate aging-in-place experience, but it requires older people to trust that a private organization will have a physical infrastructure, management and financial skills, staff resources, and integrity to keep its continuum of care promises. In return for their residential and care guarantees, most CCRC residents contractually agree to occupancy rules and a payment structure that have a striking resemblance to a long-term care insurance contract. Most pay a one-time entrance fee and an agreed-upon schedule of monthly fees to guarantee a predetermined package of residential accommodations and long-term services and supports.[5]

The physical layout of a CCRC usually includes a collection of purposely designed buildings—a mixture of single-family homes, cottages, townhouses, and mid- and high-rise buildings—sited on a campus setting (typically more than 35 acres but ranging from less than 2 to more than 40 acres).[4] These variously house the independent living and assisted living options (Chapter 11) and the skilled nursing facility. A memory care, or special care unit (SCU) may occupy a stand-alone building or be located in a physically secured wing of a building connected to an assisted living section or a nursing home.

Architecturally and operationally, these residential and care components often differ little from their stand-alone counterparts (Chapter 11). However, CCRCs employ overall larger staffs and the occupants of their independent living communities typically enjoy a more extensive array of social, leisure, recreational, and wellness activities.

CCRCS IN THE UNITED STATES

In 2014, there were 1,926 CCRCs in operation in the United States with 676,000 units.[6] CCRCs have been around since the late 19th century. Initially they were known as life-care communities and were operated by churches and charitable organizations, which promised to provide food, shelter, and healthcare to their older, often widowed members for the rest of their lives. In return for this perpetual care, the residents would turn over all of their savings and assets.[7]

Some of the oldest CCRCs in the U.S. were initially nursing homes that gradually added independent living units to their complex, but they did not offer assisted living.[8] Another very small share of today's CCRCs built in the 1980s and 1990s offer only assisted living and nursing home care. However, most communities built since the 1960s, when the modern CCRC terminology originated, typically have a mix of accommodations that include three levels of shelter and care.[9] In these large "purpose-built" CCRCs,[10] independent living units dominate, with only about 20% of the accommodations dedicated to assisted living and nursing home units.[11]

Most CCRCs are owned by not-for-profit entities (81%) and are mainly faith-based, with Catholic, Jewish, and Protestant affiliations and much fewer with fraternal group sponsors, such as the Masons or Odd Fellows.[12] The not-for-profit identities of CCRCs may be misleading, however. For-profit companies manage about 15% of these CCRCs[13] and make the operating decisions.[14] It is also typical for multiple CCRCs to be owned by a large healthcare organization or CCRC corporate chain.[15] For example, Seattle-based Emeritus operates 505 communities in 43 states totaling more than 50,000 units, and the Greystone Corporation, formed in 1982, operates some 53 CCRCs but has been responsible for the development, redevelopment, or expansion of some 100 communities.[16]

Today, the median size of a CCRC is 250 total units (with all levels of care), but greater than a third have more than 300 units and about 8% have less than 100 units. Some are very large: 1 in 10 has between 500 and 1,000 units; and 18 CCRCs have more than 1,000 units.[17] CCRCs are found in all states and the District of Columbia, except in Alaska and Wyoming. The states with the largest numbers include (from high to low) Pennsylvania, Ohio, California, Illinois, Florida, Texas, Kansas, Indiana, Iowa, and North Carolina.[18] Small urban places or rural counties are the locales of only about 1 in 10 CCRCs. The majority of properties (89%) are found in Metropolitan Statistical Areas (MSAs), usually their suburbs, with 10 MSAs accounting for 22% of the total. They include Philadelphia–Camden–Wilmington, Chicago–Naperville–Joliet, Cincinnati–Middleton, Los Angeles–Long Beach–Sana Ana, New York–northern New Jersey–Long Island, Minneapolis–St. Paul–Bloomington, Washington–Arlington–Alexandria, St. Louis, Cleveland–Elyria–Mentor, and Phoenix–Mesa–Scottsdale.[19]

Developers usually locate their CCRCs in communities top heavy with older and higher-income residents, consistent with the demographics of their targeted consumer markets. Most of their occupants (about 69%) have moved from single-family homes and apartments located less than 10 miles away.[20] Developers additionally favor states with friendlier regulatory and financial environments.[21]

Despite their large numbers and diverse geographic locations, CCRCs have poor name recognition. For some reason, perhaps related to poor marketing or the complexity of this alternative, older consumers and their families are less familiar with CCRCs than with freestanding independent living communities or assisted living properties. According to one national study, a *"full 60 percent of 50 to 70 year olds do not know anyone who has been a resident of a CCRC, with 11 percent having never heard of CCRCs."*[22]

LIFETIME SERVICE AGREEMENTS AND FINANCIAL OBLIGATIONS

Whereas older consumers who occupy assisted living properties sign monthly contracts and can easily leave—at worst losing their security deposit and last month's rent—residents of CCRCs typically must sign lengthy, complex, and confusing contractual agreements that penalize them heavily if they try to terminate them and move elsewhere.

The CCRC industry offers as many as five different contract options that specify what residential accommodations and types of services older people can expect to receive, the conditions under which they must transition to higher levels of care, and what these alternative shelter and care options will cost them, in both the short and the long term. In practice, some CCRCs offer fewer contract alternatives and blended versions of these major types.[23]

TYPE A: LIFE-CARE OR EXTENSIVE CONTRACTS

Available since the 1960s, the Type A contract was one of the earliest to be offered by CCRCs, and it replaced the "giving up all assets" arrangements offered by the original life-care communities. It is also the most expensive. Residents agree to pay an upfront entrance fee plus regular monthly fees to occupy the independent living units of the property and receive its various hospitality, wellness, and social and recreational services. The CCRC management guarantees that they will transfer these older occupants to as-needed higher levels of care, and they will incur little or no increase in their independent living unit monthly fees (except for inflation adjustments). If these were occupied as stand-alone facilities, the monthly fees would be much more expensive. More important, the entrance fee payment does not confer ownership status, rather, only the right to remain in the community and receive the care promised by the contract. CCRCs use the entrance fees to help pay off their construction debts, build financial reserves, finance future infrastructure initiatives, fund their healthcare services, and sometimes establish endowment funds.

This contract most resembles a long-term care insurance policy because CCRCs assume the risk of receiving monthly fees lower than the market rate from residents when they use their more expensive assisted living and nursing home facilities.[24] In turn, older people are insured against ever incurring the catastrophic costs of long-term care.[25] This arrangement is advantageous to older consumers who take advantage of the higher levels of care but still pay very low monthly fee rates. On the other hand, if they die early or live active and healthy lives right up to their deaths, then they never benefit from the expensive long-term care implicitly covered by their high entrance fees.

TYPE B: MODIFIED CONTRACTS

Type B contracts also require an upfront fee and monthly fees, but the entrance fee is typically lower than charged for Type A contracts. CCRCs also agree to transfer older people to higher levels of care when they experience health or functional declines.

However, unlike in Type A contracts, CCRCs charge lower monthly rates for assisted living or nursing home accommodations but only for a pre-determined, often shorter period. After this covered period ends, older residents must pay the much higher per-diem rate for their assisted living and nursing home occupancy that would be charged to older people admitted from outside the CCRC. From an insurance perspective, older people assume more financial risk paying for their long-term care, and the CCRC assumes less financial risk. However, this contract category makes the CCRC option more affordable to older people—at least on the front end.

TYPE C: FEE-FOR-SERVICE CONTRACTS

Under Type C contracts, older consumers also pay an upfront entrance fee and monthly fees to occupy the CCRC's independent living community. They still receive priority or guaranteed admission to the CCRC's higher levels of care, but they must then pay market (or just below) per diem rates, as someone from outside the CCRC would.[26] In the short term, the typically lower entrance fee makes Type C contracts the most affordable way to occupy a CCRC. Moreover, the management often refunds the entrance fee when the older person leaves the community or dies.[27] Older consumers still have the peace of mind of knowing that they can receive heavier care in the future, but they must be willing and able to pay the much higher (market rate) monthly fees for this assistance.

TYPE D: RENTAL AGREEMENT CONTRACTS

Unlike the other contract types, older consumers pay only monthly fees to cover their specified package of services under Type D contracts. CCRCs sometimes admit older people directly into their independent living communities, assisted living, or nursing home sections as if they were stand-alone properties and charge them the per diem market rates.[28] However, they are generally not guaranteed access to more than one level of care. CCRCs commonly offer the Type D contract in the first years of their operation when their (entrance fee) independent living occupants have yet to transfer to higher levels of care, and many of their assisted living and nursing home units are vacant. They also rely on this option during economic downturns when occupancy rates are overall lower as a way to broaden their consumer base. This is the least expensive way older people can *initially* occupy a CCRC, but it may be a very costly choice over the long run, if they need extensive long-term care assistance.

TYPE E: EQUITY AGREEMENT CONTRACTS

Equity agreement contracts are unique in that older people receive ownership rights to their independent living units, based on current market values. This transaction is comparable to purchasing a condominium or buying shares in a cooperative and paying fees for the common services.[29] Owners must pay property taxes and other ownership fees. The older occupants (or their heirs) must resell their units only to age- and income-qualified buyers and may benefit from the appreciated value of their units.[30]

A dwelling unit's association or board operates the CCRC, and it contracts with a management firm to run the community and provide its services. Often older people sell their condominiums if they permanently move into the CCRC's assisted living or nursing home quarters. Then, they purchase healthcare and long-term care services for additional and substantially higher monthly market rate fees.

CONTRACTS, ENTRY FEES, AND MONTHLY PAYMENTS

From 65% to 75% of CCRCs currently offer entrance fee contracts, with the remainder relying mostly on rental contracts. Currently, Type A and Type B contracts are the most popular, followed by Type C contracts, with Type D and E contracts being the least available. Whereas Type A contracts have become less favored than in the past, Type B contracts and to a lesser extent Type C contracts are now used more frequently.[31]

Whether or not older CCRC occupants can expect to have their entrance fees refunded when they leave their communities or die varies greatly. Some CCRCs offer larger refunds for shorter stays, but others offer no refunds after a specified period. Some repayments are contingent on the CCRC finding another occupant for the vacated unit. In all instances, residents incur a substantial opportunity cost because they do not receive any financial return on their entrance fees. In effect, they make an interest-free loan to the CCRC.

In 2010, entrance fees of CCRCs averaged $248,000, but they ranged from less than $100,000 to more than $1,000,000 depending on the luxuriousness and size of properties and dwelling accommodations, the extensiveness of their long-term care and healthcare offerings, and whether they were in higher-cost housing markets.[32] CCRCs also charged higher entrance fees for residents with Type A or extensive contracts and for those with more generous refund terms. Occupants of independent living communities with entry fee contracts typically pay higher monthly fees (average $4,000) than rental CCRC occupants (average $2,700).[33]

Most CCRCs request detailed information about the income, assets, and past taxes of prospective residents to confirm that they have the financial means for long-time occupancy. In the event that older consumers run out of money to pay for their accommodations and care, some, but certainly not all CCRCs, will offer them "benevolence care."[34] They draw on endowment funds to assist needy residents with their monthly fees.[35]

RESIDENT DEMOGRAPHICS AND ENTRANCE REQUIREMENTS

According to a small CCRC survey conducted in 2011, the *"typical CCRC resident is an 85-year old female who moved to her community from a private residence."*[36] Generally, there are twice as many female residents as males, but couples made up 35% of CCRC residents.[37] Older people have an average age of 81 when they first occupy the independent living units of CCRCs,[38] but the residents in assisted living quarters and nursing homes are on average older (88 years).[39]

There are, however, significant differences in the occupant profiles of entrance fee and rental CCRCs. Younger, healthier, and less-impaired older people initially occupy independent living communities of entrance fee CCRCs—a reflection of their health screening practices, whereby they exclude people with serious medical problems who need assistance. Entrance fee CCRC residents are also more likely to be married (43% vs. 27% rental CCRC) than widowed (46% vs. 61% rental CCRC), although in both types of CCRCs, the unmarried occupants are predominantly women.

Occupants in independent living units stay for about 8 or 9 years before transitioning to other levels of care, whereas assisted living residents stay an average of 2.5 years.[40]

The occupants of entrance-level CCRCs on average have higher annual incomes and higher net worth (close to $1 million) than those of rental CCRCs.[41] The reliance on the equity of their homes to pay for their CCRC occupancy helps explain the historically low occupancy rates during the Great Recession and housing meltdown of 2007–2010, when older people were reluctant to sell their homes and buyers were in short supply (Chapter 3). By 2013, CCRC occupancy rates hovered higher, close to 90%.[42]

WHY OLDER PEOPLE ARE ATTRACTED TO CCRCS

Older people are typically not in a crisis mode when they are deciding on whether to move to CCRCs, unless they are seeking to move directly into their assisting living or nursing home accommodations. Family or friends are very influential in the CCRC selection process, making them a key target audience for those marketing this option.[43]

The CCRC option enables older people to remove the uncertainty and stress of securing and paying for their future long-term care.[44] When later in their lives they experience declines or losses that make it difficult for them to live independently, they do not have to worry about who will evaluate and assist them. Unlike the majority of Americans, this very self-selected group anticipates potential threats to their health and well-being and plans for their future long-term care.[45]

They typically are better educated, have higher incomes, are in better health, and believe they can control their own fates. They sometimes have no families or friends to look out for them, or they do not want (or expect) them to assume the burdensome role of caregivers.[46] These are the feelings of one married CCRC couple:

> My wife and I looked after our parents, and we kind of realized that the thing to do would be to get in a continuing-care community. We didn't want the neighbors and friends to be responsible for us, and we had no close kin in the area.[47]

The CCRC is particularly appealing to married couples who are concerned that one spouse will need a more supportive care environment than the other. Both spouses can live close to each other (e.g., one in the independent living community and the other in the nursing home), as described in the following scenario:

> Bonnie and George move into an independent living unit of a CCRC. Although both are in fairly good health, George suffered a heart attack a few years ago and fears that his health might decline. In fact, George does suffer a second heart attack and moves into the nursing home in the CCRC. However, Bonnie's

apartment in the independent living section is only one building away, so she can visit George whenever she wants to. She is free from the necessity of driving, and George feels comfortable knowing that Bonnie is in a secure, safe environment with supportive services. The cost of George's nursing home care is also substantially less than it would be if George had to pay market rate.[48]

A national study of 3,700 family members of residents living in 221 CCRCs in the United States confirmed that the major draws are their assisted living and nursing home care. Respondents also pointed to the following CCRC features as important: cost and value of the community, reputation of the owner, availability of onsite healthcare, community location, grounds and building maintenance services, transportation services, housekeeping services, and choices in dining venues. The respondents also emphasized the importance of having wellness services and fitness activities and the ability to pursue hobbies. Most important CCRC dwelling features included a two-bedroom home, an emergency call system, Wi-Fi connectivity, a patio or balcony, and garages or covered parking. Nearly 6 out of 10 preferred a CCRC residence in a suburban location in their current region.[49] Echoing the ideals of the New Gerontology paradigm, a high share of these family members also believed that, compared with single-family dwelling living, CCRC occupancy afforded greater opportunities for staying fit, eating well, lifelong learning, keeping active, and enjoying an overall better quality of life.[50]

A proprietary study of 521 residents who recently occupied the independent living units of CCRCs also identified the following attributes as influencing their decisions[51]:

- security
- appearance and upkeep of the facility
- a warm and friendly atmosphere
- a sense of pride in their living space
- availability of wellness programs
- access to quality medical care
- sense of well-being
- food quality

HOW OLDER PEOPLE AND THEIR FAMILIES FEEL ABOUT LIVING IN CCRCS

OVERALL ASSESSMENTS

Perhaps surprisingly, few comprehensive scientific studies report on how older people or their families currently feel about their CCRC experiences. The aforementioned survey of 3,700 family members found that 90% were pleased overall with the services and care received by their loved ones and would recommend the communities to others.[52]

Another proprietary study of residents occupying their CCRCs' independent living communities reported that 79% were very satisfied and 17% were satisfied with their accommodations. About 88% would be very likely to choose their communities if they had to do it again, and 88% would be very likely to recommend their communities to a friend.

A particularly revealing finding emerged when residents responded to this query: "How would you describe the change in your quality of life since moving into this community?"[53] Only 26% reported that it was much better, and 33% reported it was somewhat better. On the other hand, 38% reported it was neither better nor worse, and 3% that it was somewhat worse. Although these are far from harsh assessments, they do suggest that a substantial share of older CCRC occupants feel that their moves to a CCRC did not improve the quality of life they had in their earlier residences.

THE SOCIAL LIFE AND ACTIVITIES OF CCRCs' INDEPENDENT LIVING COMMUNITY RESIDENTS

A few studies draw attention to the less-than-perfect social lives of CCRC occupants.[54] They show that interpersonal relationships in their independent living communities were not as strong, intimate, and emotionally close as in their past communities. The reasons are straightforward. Long-standing friendships of older people are hard to replicate, and they find it difficult to establish comparable relationships. As one resident relates, *"Everyone speaks to you here and there, but I don't have any real friends. I still can't say, 'This is my friend.'"*[55]

Nonetheless, although not ideal, the CCRC may still offer a far better social scene than what older people experienced in their prior communities with the result that they now feel *more* squarely in their residential comfort zones. As one study concluded,

> Even though this resident did not report satisfaction with her current social network because she was still missing intimacy in her relationships, she referred to the availability of social interactions at the CCRC as an advantage when compared to the isolation she had experienced in the community.[56]

> Given the subjective feelings of loneliness and the objective isolation that characterized some older people's lives in the community, the CCRC often served as a good alternative to the lack of social connection. This was primarily attributed to the social activities and social interactions that it provided, rather than to true social intimacy, which many reported as lacking in the CCRC.[57]

At least part of the explanation for the better—if far from perfect—social environment found in the CCRC is that the older residents feel more competent and in control of their surroundings. They are not afraid to relate to others:

> The sense of safety and protection associated with the CCRC allowed residents to live their lives in a more peaceful manner and to engage in social activities within the CCRC with fewer fears about their own personal safety.[58]

These residents simply find it easier and less stressful to be more active and fully engaged:

> People from outside cannot get in. I can wake up in the morning, put my robe on and go downstairs to the pool, and then go back without driving and without looking for parking.[59]

> You always read in the newspapers that someone attacked an older adult somewhere, [or] they came to a house and robbed it. We had an alarm, but every sound used to scare us and [my husband] used to sleep with a big stick next to him and a gun under his pillow. It is certainly much more quiet and relaxed here.[60]

An adult daughter of one of the residents echoes these feelings:

> I think that the good thing about this place is that everything is there, all the social activities, culture, sports. As time goes by, you have less energy, less motivation, you open your door and it's there—that's an advantage.[61]

Still, other residents are less satisfied with their social scene because they have less privacy than they enjoyed in their previous residential settings. In many respects, the CCRC resembles the small town environment where everyone lives together and knows each other, and it becomes difficult for them to maintain their private lives.[62] Consequently, if the older person decides to spend more time in her private quarters, it becomes everyone's concern: *"How come she participates in this and not in that?"*[63] Yet some residents cope better with these perceived infringements:

> My husband and I were looking ahead to how we would cope with being with so many people, day in, day out, whether it was residents in our villa, or in the dining room. We cherished our privacy very much. But we found that you can sit back. You don't have to join everything, and you can find time to be just the couple you would like to be.[64]

CCRC RESIDENTS REPORT HIGHER SELF-RATED HEALTH

Proponents argue that because CCRCs offer a comprehensive array of social services, healthcare services, and rehabilitation care, older people receive higher-quality long-term care. Consequently, they will *feel* in better physical health and have fewer ADL limitations and overall lower dependency than their community counterparts. One study of 131 residents occupying independent living apartments in an Ithaca, New York, CCRC complex confirmed these expectations, even though they were significantly older, had a higher number of chronic health conditions, and were more likely to live alone than the community residents.[65]

Another study specifically investigated whether CCRCs offering Type A contracts (all-inclusive care covered by entry fee and monthly fees) as opposed to Type C, fee-for-service CCRCs (residents must pay out of pocket for their assistance on an as-needed basis) offered a better care experience. Both CCRCs offered similar services and facilities, but after other confounding influences were controlled for, the residents in the all-inclusive care CCRCs had better ADL and IADL functioning, although both groups positively perceived the quality of their lives.[66]

AVOIDING THE FRAIL — AGAIN

The aversion that younger, healthier residents in active adult communities displayed toward their older and frailer neighbors is also evident in CCRCs. Even without formal rules governing their physical separation, a study found that *"it was rare for assisted living or nursing level residents to come to the independent living dining room for dinner, the most social time of the day."*[67] The independent living residents reported that they perceived the assisted living residents as being more disengaged, less active, and less likely to interact with others. In the words of one resident, *"They spend way too much time {in their apartments} watching TV and sitting in their rooms."*[68]

This avoidance is explained by the importance independent living community residents place on being active and occupying places that are *"vibrant, engaged, and full of able, autonomous agents, especially in contrast to other levels of care."*[69] Their participation in activities of the independent living community allows them to feel *"part of this place."*[70] They also want to maintain *"the feeling of a healthy, young, fun group,"*[71] which would be dampened by the presence of the more-dependent assisted living residents who rely on assistive devices. Moreover, those independent living community residents who might be more receptive to socializing with assisted living residents feel informal pressures not to.[72]

These attitudes also influence the extent to which independent living community residents help others in their section with health and functional declines. Although willing to assist their neighbors with tasks such as transportation, they are reluctant to help them cope with their chronic health conditions or functional declines. Consequently, they would not help a woman with a cancer diagnosis with her ADLs (e.g., getting out of bed). This signals her lack of independence and an impending move to the CCRC's assisted living or nursing home. Studies have long noted this willingness of CCRC residents to help with minor tasks but not with heavier care or psychological problems.[73]

These attitudes do not bode well for independent living community residents when their own health declines and functional limitations start to restrict their social participation. They become disadvantaged not only because of their more limited ability to participate (e.g., poor eyesight, speech impairments, and mobility limitations), but because they do not want to embarrass themselves or confront the other residents' negative reactions and because they fear being stigmatized.[74] In one independent living community, the residents became annoyed and frustrated when some occupants could not fully participate in some activity because it was a clear sign that they needed more care and would slow everyone else down. Any association with these more impaired or less healthy people threatened their *"pleasant interaction"*[75] and home-like environment.[76]

The reluctance of young-old and old-old groups of residents to mingle is troublesome not just for its implications for resident well-being. It is also a hot button issue for managers of CCRCs. They must decide on the permeability of the boundaries between their different levels of care and the consequences of removing any physical separation between their property's independent living community and assisted living sections. These social interaction patterns are also worrisome because of the age-creep problem of senior housing demographics. Increasingly, managers are allowing their independent living community's residents to age in place by allowing them to secure needed in-home health services. However, they worry that such policies will turn off prospective younger residents.[77] The greater presence of those who are older and more frail works against their marketing efforts to dispel the idea of sick and dying people dominating their occupants and to describe living at CCRCs as *"a new chapter in life."*[78]

CONSUMER PROTECTION ISSUES[79]

ENTRANCE AND MONTHLY FEES AND CONSUMER CONTRACTUAL OBLIGATIONS

Older people contemplating occupying a CCRC must evaluate whether its physical design, hospitality, recreation and care services, staffing, rules and regulations, and potential as a social environment are consistent with their preferences and expectations. However, the decision to select a CCRC demands yet another layer of evaluation because of the contractually controlled long-term commitments and lack of flexibility for *"buyer's remorse."*[80] When disgruntled residents leave a stand-alone assisted living property, they do not suffer financially, but disenchanted CCRC residents stand to lose a substantial part of their entrance fee.

Despite their affluence and education, many consumers do not fully understand the contracts they have signed, their rights and responsibilities, or the obligations of the CCRC.[81] For example, older people should determine whether there is a "cooling off" period, during which they have a right to cancel a signed contract without financial penalty. They must also ascertain what percentage of their entrance fee (if any) the CCRC will return to them if they depart after a certain time period. Some CCRCs offer a declining-scale feature, whereby the longer the stay, the smaller the refund. For others, refunds do not depend on the length of stay, and residents receive a refund of 50% or less.[82]

Older people who fail to ask the right questions may also face surprises about what their monthly fees entitle them to (Figure 12.1).[83] They must be clear on what amenities and services are included, both in their current independent living communities and in their prospective assisted living or nursing care quarters.[84] As Steve Maag, director of continuing care and assisted living at LeadingAge, an industry group, emphasizes, *"You want to understand what you are actually buying for your monthly fee."*[85]

Consumers must also anticipate increases in their monthly fees to cover new or higher costs for their services or care that could make CCRC living unaffordable for those who are less affluent.[86] For example, management may decide that their once free transportation or podiatry services are now added costs.

Potential residents should also ask what happens if their money runs out and they cannot afford to pay their monthly fees. Will the CCRC offer any "benevolence

Figure 12.1. Questions to ask about CCRC fee structures (Taken from CARF International [2013, pp. 15–16])

1. Are there financial deposits for which I am responsible? If so, what is the refund policy if I decide not to move to the community?

2. What types of service contracts or agreements are available in this community?

3. How much is the current entrance fee? Are there plans to increase the amount of this fee in the future?

4. Is there a structure for refund or rebate of entrance fees? If so, what is the time period in which the refund/rebate can be granted, and when and under what conditions will the refund/rebate be paid?

5. What services are included in the monthly fee?

6. What are the costs for additional services?

7. How does the organization determine how often and by how much fees will be raised?

8. Over the last 5 years, what has been the history of monthly fee increases? How frequently have fees been raised and by what percent each time? Why were the fees increased?

9. How will I be notified of changes in the fee structure?

10. If I require more services or move to a different level of care, how will that affect my monthly fee?

11. What happens if I encounter financial difficulty?

care"? Married couples must also inquire to what extent they will incur extra monthly fees if their spouse needs a higher level of care and must occupy a different unit.

Failing to ask the right questions and misinterpreting or ignoring contract provisions have obvious material consequences. Such lapses also result in older occupants feeling anxious, less secure, and in less control of their lives, contrary to the very feelings of residential mastery that they hoped for as CCRC residents in the first place.

Unquestionably, one of their most formidable tasks is to assess the financial health of CCRC options. These properties risk financial insolvency when their independent living unit occupancy rates are lower than expected (e.g., during initial fill-up stages or in economic downturns, such as the Great Recession of 2007–2010) or if they have set their entrance and monthly fees too low to cover the future costs of providing long-term care.[87]

The financial well-being of CCRCs also depends on accurate actuarial assumptions about apartment turnover and resident care transition rates. They must also have financial reserves to cover the contingency of unplanned operating costs and infrastructure and equipment upgrades. Such upgrades are key to their ability to attract new (and younger) residents, an issue especially faced by older and outdated CCRCs.

Societal economic downturns can also be devastating to CCRCs because they have difficulty raising capital or borrowing funds at affordable rates, with the result that they are forced into bankruptcy.[88] Fortunately, most CCRCs in the United States today are financially sound.[89] However, experts warn that when older people enter a new CCRC, they run the risk that management has made incorrect actuarial assumptions about its fill-up (occupancy) rates and future health services costs. As advisors also continually stress, past financial viability does not guarantee future performance.

Accreditations from the Continuing Care Accreditation Commission[90] may reassure some consumers that a CCRC has met rigorous financial and business practice standards, but there is little evidence that such recognition significantly predicts the financial solvency or quality of care of CCRCs.

Nonetheless, older consumers can take heart in the conclusion of a 2010 report:

> Financial failures have been relatively rare, and even in cases of bankruptcy, a new provider usually takes over the CCRC's operations, ensuring that residents can remain in their apartments. In past CCRC insolvencies, the lenders and investors were most likely to suffer financial loss and not the individual residents. Because many CCRCs are financed with long-term debt, lenders and investors have a long-term interest in the health of the CCRC and often establish covenants (financial requirements) in order to ensure its long-term financial health.[91]

THE PROMISE OF HEAVIER CARE

One of the major benefits of the CCRC option is that older people feel confident that they can quickly access higher levels of care when they confront health or functional declines. However, moving from one level of care to another can be just as stressful as any conventional residential move (Chapter 5). Older people are forced to admit that they can no longer take care of themselves and need help. They must cope with an entirely different social scene and a new activity regimen, and they must sacrifice privacy if they share their new rooms with a stranger. These moves signify that they are reaching the end of their lives and must adopt a *"dying role."*[92]

Therein lies the paradox of CCRC occupancy. Even as contractual promises of access to long-term care attract older people to CCRCs in the first place, they often resent management informing them that they must now move to a higher level of care.[93] When they first enter a CCRC, this moving decision appears hypothetical and far off, and it is difficult for them to anticipate the health and limitation scenarios whereby they will be required to relocate. They may not feel that they are ready and complain that the CCRC's care transition rules *"were unclear and ambiguous."*[94] This has prompted residents to file discrimination suits (usually unsuccessfully) that challenge whether group residence providers can force them to make these residential care moves.[95]

Because these transitions have such financial, physical, and emotional significance, prospective older occupants must pay attention to the management's aging in place and relocation policies, which will dictate—perhaps involuntarily—when they will be required to relocate from their independent living community units to receive heavier care offered by the CCRC's assisted living section and nursing home facility. They must also inquire as to the ability of the CCRC's higher levels of care to accommodate older adults who become violent or abusive toward others.[96] They must be especially clear on who will make their care transition decisions: their families, the CCRC's medical director, or the resident's personal physician. Above all, they must be satisfied with the types and quality of services and support they will subsequently receive in the CCRC's long-term care offerings.

REGULATIONS AND CONSUMER RECOURSE

Like any large and complex service organization, CCRCs sometimes fall short of consumer expectations. Staff misinterprets the rules, fails to perform promised services, or worse, provides incompetent care. How CCRCs handle these problems varies greatly. Some CCRCs have policy procedures in place whereby the residents can complain about staff's actions with the expectation that management will respond courteously and constructively to their concerns. A small CCRC survey in 2011 revealed that 61% of CCRCs had residents serving on their governing boards and gave them the ability to review their performance and management decisions.[97]

Older consumers looking for assistance from regulatory agencies to resolve their problems will receive mixed results. State governments are primarily responsible for regulating the development and operation of CCRCs, whereas only the nursing homes of CCRCs typically fall under the federal Medicare program's quality standards.[98] Some 38 states oversee their CCRCs in departments charged with administering insurance, financial services, banking, and, to a lesser extent, in agencies responsible for social services, aging services, or community affairs. Twelve states do not have such CCRC-specific regulations, although their agencies may oversee their different levels of care (e.g., assisted living properties) as stand-alone facilities.[99]

Public regulation of CCRCs by state governments increased substantially beginning in the 1980s,[100] sometimes in response to earlier bankruptcies. Many of the new licensing standards focused on the legal and financial rights of the residents, their ability to form associations, entrance fee refund policies, how long the entrance fees and deposits are escrowed to ensure the stability of the CCRC, penalties for misleading or fraudulent business practices, disclosures pertaining to the financial health of the CCRC and its history of fee increases, and resident rights in case of insolvency.

After CCRCs are licensed, many states also require annual information to judge their ongoing financial health. Additionally, if the CCRC development obtained financing by debt instruments such as bonds, the lenders and bondholders may also impose financial requirements (such as the size of a CCRC's financial reserves) that are often more stringent than state regulations.

Even with these regulatory protections, a 2010 study by the Government Accountability Office concluded that corrective actions depend on informed CCRC older consumers willing to initiate complaints or actions against noncompliant CCRC providers. Disappointingly, it found no assessments of the effectiveness of state regulations in protecting consumers at either the national level or the state level, and state officials, resident advocates, and experts expressed a wide range of opinions on the adequacy of state law to protect consumers.[101]

However, it also found no correlation with the level of state protections and the incidence of bankruptcy or failures.[102]

CONTINUING CARE AT HOME PROGRAMS (CCRC WITHOUT WALLS)

Potentially large numbers of community-residing older people would benefit from the amenities and services offered by CCRCs. However, the majority would be loath to step inside these places, whereas others would be unable to afford their costs. To reach out to both these market segments, many CCRCs (about 72% of the largest corporate owners) provide homemaker assistance, personal care, and healthcare in residents' homes on a fee-for-service basis.[103]

A very small number of CCRCs do much more. Since the 1990s, some properties have transplanted the CCRC model into the residences of older people aging in place. These residents sign up for Type A contracts to receive the same care opportunities and future long-term care guarantees as the residents of CCRCs. They are also able to use the dining, social, and fitness amenities of the campus-based CCRC.[104]

In return for an entrance fee and monthly fees, these continuing care at home (CCaH) programs, like traditional CCRCs, provide them with a comprehensive package of in-home services and assistance to accommodate their care needs when they become physically and cognitively frail (Figure 12.2). One commentator sums up the model in this way: *"Let us bring what you need to you—or find a way to make it easy for you to get it."*[105]

For example, a CCRC would arrange for residents to receive a 24-hour live-in—to help them perform their ADLs—and the delivery of rehabilitation services after an accident or hospital stay.[106] Sometimes, a CCRC will manage these services (e.g., with their own licensed home care agency), or, alternatively, they will subcontract with a variety of community-based service providers. If at some point it becomes infeasible for older people to remain in their current homes, they can occupy the campus-based assisted living or nursing home accommodations of a CCRC.

Despite the similarities between the CCaH program and conventional CCRC property models, there are some significant differences. First of all, it is a very small program. At the end of 2014, there were only about 20 CCRCs offering these in-home contracts, mainly along the east coast and in the Midwest; 25 are projected to exist by the end of 2015.[107] Current participants now number in the low thousands.

Second, whereas traditional CCRCs carefully screen their independent living occupants to ensure that they are healthy and functionally able, the CCaH program typically imposes even stiffer requirements. Along with the usual financial screening, only aging adults without any current need for services or without a diagnosis of Alzheimer's disease (or other dementias) and Parkinson's disease are accepted into

Figure 12.2. CCaH services

- Home inspections

- Referrals for home maintenance, housekeeping, lawn care, and so forth

- Social and educational opportunities

- Access to campus amenities and services

- Annual physical and other wellness programs

- Transportation

- Care coordination

- Emergency response system

- Homemaker and personal care services

- Home nursing

- Companion or live-in care

- Meals

- Adult day care

- Assisted living care

- Nursing home care

this program.[108] Thus, only healthy, active older people need apply, and they must have healthcare coverage from Medicare and a supplemental private insurance carrier. Consequently, CCaH programs typically have higher rejection rates of new members than traditional CCRCs.

Third, this program is much more affordable than traditional Type A CCRC contracts, with lower entrance and monthly fees. Entrance fees currently range from the low $20,000s to $70,000 and are variously refundable; monthly fees typically range from $250 to $800.[109] Predictably, CCRCs offering more extensive service packages charge higher fees.

Fourth, preventive health programs and the ongoing monitoring of the member's physical well-being are elevated in importance. In one CCaH program, for example, members initially receive

> a thorough fitness assessment, a home assessment to identify changes needed to age in place safely (like grab bars in the bathroom and extra lighting), and a home maintenance assessment to figure out what work needs to be done on a house or an apartment (a new furnace, or to turn up the temperature in the fridge?).[110]

From the start, the program assigns each member a care coordinator, who develops a close relationship with the member and *"will regularly assess a member's health and functional status, recommend needed services, and obtain and manage those services on behalf of the member."*[111] Some CCRC communities assign a physical therapist to work with residents to improve their strength and balance and reduce their risk of falling.[112] These programs also try to help older people receive the necessary home care after a hospital stay. Care coordinators have better information about their residents' medical histories and consequently

> can develop a more effective discharge plan based on our understanding of their support systems, level of independence prior to their hospitalization, family involvement, and home situation.[113]

According to one respondent who came home after foot surgery, *"Someone was there 24/7 for seven days; it was all arranged."*[114] Because of their efforts, care coordinators claim that their older clients experience very low hospitalization readmission rates.[115]

Unfortunately, in the absence of carefully designed comprehensive assessments of this program, we must rely on anecdotal evidence. The database is also limited, because only the earliest established CCaH programs (where the once-healthy participants have experienced health and functional declines) offer reliable actuarial evidence. Based on one of the oldest CCaH programs (22 years in operation) in the country, for example, only about 2% of the members had relocated to their campus-based CCRCs' assisted living or nursing home properties.[116] According to industry spokespersons, however, this finding would be typical for most of their earlier-established programs.[117]

As with traditional CCRCs, older consumers must scrutinize the details of their contracted long-term care plans and financial obligations. As one analyst points out, *"There is no common model structure for a CCRC without walls."*[118] For example, some CCaHs allow consumers to access their assisted living or nursing care in their CCRCs at the same monthly fee rate as they were paying at home; others provide only discounted services and for more limited periods. Still others offer service packages for which residents are responsible for copays, especially if they need assisted living or nursing care.

Interested older people will have a hard time finding CCaH programs because of their scarcity. CCRC operators are not convinced that it is a financially viable business model, and for many it would be a radical departure from their campus model. Consequently, despite the large potential market for this option, the CCRC industry has expressed little interest in developing this alternative.

FUTURE TRENDS

CCRCs are changing in four discernible ways in their efforts to respond to older consumers who expect to be squarely in their residential comfort and mastery zones but are reluctant to trade off one set of emotional needs to achieve the other.[119]

First, they are catering to more demanding and discerning older adults who want more control over their CCRC experience.[120] They seek shelter and care accommodations that provide them with individually customized wellness, eating, leisure, and recreational experiences. They want their residential quarters to resemble their prior dwelling arrangements and their campus settings to contain the goods, services, and amenities that resemble their earlier neighborhoods and communities, including stores, restaurants, personal services, health clubs, and healthcare.

They also want a greater say in the CCRC decisions that influence their financial situations, everyday activities (from meals to recreation), and long-term care. In their quest to stay as long as possible in their independent living communities despite their declines, they increasingly resist management's decisions to move them to higher levels of care, where they fear losing not just their autonomy but also their comfortable accommodations and congenial social network.

Second, CCRC managers are developing stronger connections with their surrounding communities. They are partnering more with colleges and universities, fitness or health clubs, healthcare organizations, religious organizations, and property and service management companies. Their advisory boards are also more likely to include prominent community leaders. These linkages allow older CCRC residents to remain active participants in their surrounding communities and to benefit from relationships with outside healthcare and other groups of professionals.

Third, in response to the persistent aging-in-place behaviors of community-residing older residents, CCRCs will increasingly make their on-campus amenities and services accessible to non-occupants. They will offer these nonresidents everything from home maintenance and renovations to home healthcare by relying on outsourced or subcontracted outside providers.[121] Some CCRCs target the older and aging-in-place occupants of active adult communities. They will offer these residents services delivered to their home, as well as short-term stays in their assisted living and nursing home accommodations. All of these efforts will not only immediately increase revenues, but over long term will also help market the CCRCs.

Fourth, to achieve better care delivery efficiencies and outcomes when serving the older occupants throughout their communities, and to achieve significant cost savings in their operations, CCRCs like other senior housing options are likely to be the first adopters of the newer smart home technologies (Chapter 6). The introduction of these technologies will enable their managements to detect and respond more quickly to the healthcare and long-term care needs of their residents and will be consistent with their efforts to develop stronger linkages with their surrounding communities.

In Figure 12.3, Susan Brecht, a prominent senior housing consultant, shows how these broad changes translate into a very specific set of predictions and trends.[122]

Figure 12.3. Major trends in CCRCs (Trends based on Web survey of senior living organizations conducted by Mather LifeWays Institute on Aging and Brecht Associates, Inc., and distilled from Brecht et al. [2009].)

Physical Plant or Buildings

- More amenities in the individual's dwelling (especially baths and kitchens), larger bedroom sizes, more storage space, remodeling of physical plant to create higher-end finishes

- Dining areas that are no longer restricted to a traditional formal dining room, including bistros, cafes, casual dining rooms, sports bars, food-to-go shops, and chain restaurants

- State-of-the-art health and wellness facilities that include *"swimming pools, Jacuzzis, well-equipped exercise rooms with personal trainers, massage therapy tables, and locker rooms"* (Brecht et al., 2009, p. 50)

- More diverse recreational opportunities that widely cater to individual desires and expectations (e.g., indoor aquatic centers, putting greens, performing arts theaters, dance ballrooms, art galleries, and club-like entertainment rooms with TVs, computer terminals, billiards, other table games, etc.) (LCS, 2012)

- Family-centered facilities that accommodate visiting grandchildren

- More *"open, free-flowing floor plans . . . [so that] when residents return to the community, instead of walking through a staid, formal living room, they will be energized as they pass through areas of interaction and activity"* (LCS, 2012, p. 3)

- Inclusion of office or business spaces to accommodate older people still pursuing work or business activities

- More eco-friendly and environmentally sensitive designs that satisfy requirements of Leadership in Energy & Environmental Design (LEED) certified communities

Healthcare Design

- Shift from traditionally designed institutional or hospital-like nursing homes, with *"double-loaded corridors and large, fixed nursing stations and the associated assembly-line operating philosophy"* (Brecht et al., 2009, p. 52), to smaller-scaled care environments that implement many person-centered principles (Chapter 11) and try to mimic upscale bed and breakfast establishments (e.g., The Green House® model or small house model [Figure 12.4])

- More diverse and flexible nursing home programs that include rehabilitation, dementia care, hospice, or palliative care and serve short-stay residents seeking *"private rooms, attractive décor, restaurant-style dining, and a more spa-like environment"* (Brecht et al., 2009, p. 53)

Figure continued next page

Figure 12.3. *Continued*

- A smaller share of CCRC units dedicated to nursing home beds, in recognition of residents seeking to age in place longer in independent living and assisted living units

Programs and Services

- More flexible dining experiences that mimic restaurant dining, including cooked-to-order selections, take-out entrees, food court options, and individualized meal plans that give residents more choice over what meals they take and at what times of the day

- Shift from sedentary to active and resident-initiated activities that include life-long learning programs (e.g., partnerships with colleges and universities), overnight trips, Web-based education, computer training, more-flexible transportation options, and volunteer opportunities

- Stronger decision-making roles for residents on the boards or committees of CCRCs regarding the operation of their properties

- More relocation assistance for community-residing older adults transitioning from homes to CCRCs

- More diverse wellness programs, including state-of-the-art fitness, exercise, and healing gardens, with dedicated staff

- More services that enable older occupants to age in place longer in independent living units, including home healthcare services, adult day care services, geriatric assessment services, and smart home technologies (Chapter 6) (LCS, 2012)

- Unbundled services that allow residents to tailor their long-term care offerings and pay for only what they need

- Expanded service programs for nonresidents in the community (see earlier section on Continuing Care at Home program [CCaH])

- More flexible financial options regarding size of upfront fee, refundability provisions, and long-term care and healthcare costs, in recognition that future residents want more control over their assets and will reject large entry fees in favor of a rental CCRC model

Figure 12.4. The Green House model®

The Green House® model is a skilled nursing facility and an exemplar of the culture change movement that grew out of the deinstitutionalized care missions of The Eden Alternative® and the Pioneer Network (Calkins & Keane, 2008). The culture change movement represents *"a fundamental shift in thinking about nursing homes. Facilities are viewed not as healthcare institutions, but as person-centered homes offering long-term care services. Culture-change principles and practices have been shaped by shared concerns among consumers, policy makers, and providers regarding the value and quality of care offered in traditional nursing homes. . . . Policy makers can encourage culture change and capitalize on its transformational power through regulation, reimbursement, public reporting, and other mechanisms"* (Koren, 2010, p. 1).

Dr. William Thomas originally articulated The Green House® model. In 2002, the first version was established in Tupelo, Mississippi. As of May 2014, there were 153 open homes in 32 states, with 160 homes in development (http://thegreen-houseproject.org/doc/27/about-evaluation.pdf).

Architecturally similar to conventional single-family homes, small apartments, or duplexes, a Green House is designed to accommodate about 6 to 12 older people in need of skilled nursing care (Cohen & Zimmerman, 2010). Consequently, a traditional 100-bed nursing home would be divided into about ten Green House homes, each with 10 beds and each averaging about 6,800 square feet.

These are typically sited on a campus-like setting that also includes a traditional nursing home. Each of the residents has his or her own bedroom and private bathroom, with separate heating and cooling controls and its own locked medication cabinet. These accommodations open up to a great room area that consists of a living room, dining areas, and kitchen. There is easy access to an outdoor patio and garden area.

Operationally, Green House homes attempt to emulate the person-centered care approach of assisted living residences (Chapter 11), which support the *"dignity, autonomy, comfort, choice, privacy, and security of residents"* (Loe & Moore, 2011, p. 756). maximize their functional abilities, offer them meaningful activities, and foster their emotional well-being. A consistent and self-managed team of specially trained certified nursing assistants (direct care workers) called *Shabazim* provide nearly all care, including preparing meals, housekeeping, laundry, assisting with ADLs, and leading social activities. These empowered workers *"set their own schedules, find replacements for absent staff, determine resident assignments, and decide how the work will be shared"* (Bowers, 2011, p. 110). A clinical care team (nurses, therapists, dietitians, and other professionals) is located nearby, typically elsewhere on the campus, but is not based in the Green House home. However, nurses visit the home daily to administer medications and treatments and monitor resident conditions (Bowers, 2011), and other clinical professionals will provide as-needed assistance.

Overall, the expert assessments of The Green House® model of care have been very positive. Proponents contend that it delivers significant improvements in care, with greater resident, family, and staff satisfaction. Operating costs of The Green House® model are comparable to those of traditional nursing homes (Jenkens, Sult, Lessell, Hammer, & Ortigara, 2011). However, these positive findings must be tempered for three reasons. First, the evaluations to date have methodological limitations; second, studies have not shown consistently positive outcomes; and, third, it is not always clear what particular environmental or operational aspects of this model actually contribute to the reported positive outcomes (Shier, Khodyakov, Cohen, Zimmerman, & Saliba, 2014).

CONCLUSION

As a strategy by which older people can achieve residential normalcy, CCRCs are somewhat of a paradox. On the one hand, they appeal to wealthier older Americans who want to take control of their future long-term care before they experience physical and cognitive health declines. On the other hand, and consistent with the earlier-identified profiles of resilient individuals (Chapter 5), they are willing to relinquish control of their long-term care to an impersonal organization they often know little about.

They must have confidence that their new independent living communities will allow them to be fully engaged in their lives, they must trust their CCRC managers to decide when they will need heavier care and must relocate to the assisted living or nursing home levels, and they must then feel certain that they are receiving high-quality long-term services and supports—with no cost surprises.

CCRCs are a success story for most of their older residents. But as some studies point out, they must make difficult tradeoffs. Although they have rich friendship circles, an abundance of leisure activities, and a physically secure place to live and receive care, older residents lack the intimate and close friendships that they enjoyed in their earlier lives, and they may feel they have less privacy because of the small-town atmosphere of the CCRC. They also must sometimes interact with frail neighbors who remind them of their own vulnerable futures. Furthermore, they may not always agree with the residential care transition decisions of their CCRC managers and may have difficulty coping with the radical changes in their environs. Older residents must also worry that they have misjudged the financial viability, management capabilities, and goodwill of their CCRC. Finally, although the CCaH program offers an alternative for aging in place, currently very few community-residing older people can enjoy the benefits of the CCRC model and still remain occupants in their comfortable homes.

NOTES

1. (AgingOptions, 2013, p. 2)
2. (U.S. Senate, Special Committee on Aging, 2010a, p. 2)
3. (Connecticut Continuing Care Residents Association, n.d.)
4. (LeadingAge, 2012)
5. (Zarem, 2010)
6. Ziegler Investment Banking/Senior Living Z-News. 2014 (Accessed at http://www.ziegler.com/ investment-banking/senior-living/)
7. (Liebig, Kennedy, & Cory, 2003)
8. (LeadingAge, 2012)
9. (LeadingAge, 2012)
10. (LeadingAge, 2012)
11. (Ziegler Capital Markets, 2009)
12. Ziegler Investment Banking/Senior Living Z-News. 2014 (Accessed at http://www.ziegler.com/ investment-banking/senior-living/)
13. (Ziegler Capital Markets, 2009)
14. (Ziegler Capital Markets, 2009)
15. (Ziegler Capital Markets, 2009)
16. (Ziegler Capital Markets, 2009)
17. (Ziegler Capital Markets, 2009). The average size of a CCRC in the U.S. in 2014 was 350 units (Ziegler Investment Banking/Senior Living Z-News. 2014; accessed at http://www.ziegler.com/ investment-banking/senior-living/)
18. (Ziegler Capital Markets, 2009)
19. (Ziegler Capital Markets, 2009)
20. (LeadingAge, 2012)
21. (Ziegler Capital Markets, 2009)
22. (Aramac Senior Living Services, 2012, p. 1)
23. (CARF International, 2013; Zarem, 2010)
24. (Nelms, Mayes, & Doll, 2012)
25. (Young, 2009)
26. (Frolik, 2008)
27. (AgingOptions, 2013)
28. (U.S. Government Accountability Office, 2010)
29. (Frolik, 2008)
30. (CARF International, 2013)
31. Ziegler Capital Markets/Senior Living Finance, *Z-News,* 2008.
32. (LeadingAge, 2012)
33. (American Seniors Housing Association, 2009)
34. (Zarem, 2010)
35. (CARF International, 2013)
36. (LeadingAge, 2012, p. 39)
37. (American Seniors Housing Association, 2009; LeadingAge, 2012)
38. (American Seniors Housing Association, 2009)
39. (LeadingAge, 2012)
40. (American Seniors Housing Association, 2009; LeadingAge, 2012)
41. (LeadingAge, 2012)
42. (Gerace, 2013b)
43. (Ruffenach, 2006)
44. (Golant, 2011b)
45. (Wethington, 2003)
46. (Krout, Moen, Holmes, Oggins, & Bowen, 2002)

47. (Ruffenach, 2006)
48. (Frolik, 2008, p. 169)
49. (Mather Lifeways Institute on Aging, Ziegler & Brecht Associates, 2011)
50. (Mather Lifeways Institute on Aging, Ziegler & Brecht Associates, 2011)
51. (Aramac Senior Living Services, 2012, p. 5)
52. (Mather Lifeways Institute on Aging, Ziegler & Brecht Associates, 2011)
53. (Aramac Senior Living Services, 2012, p. 2)
54. (Golant, 2003a)
55. (Ayalon & Green, 2012, p. 400)
56. (Ayalon & Green, 2012, p. 400)
57. (Ayalon & Green, 2012, p. 400)
58. (Ayalon & Green, 2012, p. 401)
59. (Ayalon & Green, 2012, p. 401)
60. (Ayalon & Green, 2012, p. 401)
61. (Ayalon & Green, 2012, p. 401)
62. (Ayalon & Green, 2012)
63. (Ayalon & Green, 2012, p. 402)
64. (Ruffenach, 2006)
65. (Young, Spokane, Shaw, Macera, & Krout, 2009)
66. (Young, Inamdar, & Hannan, 2010)
67. (Shippee, 2012, p. 6)
68. (Shippee, 2012, p. 6)
69. (Shippee, 2012, p. 5)
70. (Shippee, 2012, p. 8)
71. (Shippee, 2012, p. 10)
72. (Shippee, 2012)
73. (Gubrium, 1975; Stacey-Konnert & Pynoos, 1992)
74. (Shippee, 2012, p. 10; Zimmerman et al., 2014)
75. (Shippee, 2012, p. 11)
76. (Shippee, 2012)
77. (LCS, 2012)
78. (Dychtwald & Baxter, 2011, p. 14)
79. This section draws from various sources (CARF International, 2013; Connecticut Continuing Care Residents Association, n.d.; U.S. Government Accountability Office, 2010; U.S. Senate, Special Committee on Aging, 2010b; Zarem, 2010).
80. (U.S. Government Accountability Office, 2010, p. 22)
81. (U.S. Government Accountability Office, 2010)
82. (Zarem, 2010)
83. (Zarem, 2010)
84. (LeadingAge, 2012)
85. (Larson, 2007)
86. (U.S. Government Accountability Office, 2010)
87. (U.S. Government Accountability Office, 2010)
88. (U.S. Senate Special Committee on Aging, 2010b)
89. Between 2007 (the start of the Great Recession) and January 2012, Stephen Maag of LeadingAge reported that there were only 12 CCRC bankruptcies in the United States. He emphasizes that the CCRCs remained open in all cases, and the residents were not forced to relocate.
90. Part of the Commission on Accreditation of Rehabilitation Facilities (CARF).
91. (Zarem, 2010, p. 3)
92. (Shippee, 2009, p. 423)
93. (Shippee, 2009; Zimmerman et al., 2014)
94. (Shippee, 2009, p. 422)

95. Palo Alto Online, Sue Dremann, "Settlement in Landmark Channing House Case," May 12, 2010.
96. (Frolik, 2008)
97. (LeadingAge, 2012)
98. Few if any CCRCs participate in the Medicaid program.
99. (U.S. Government Accountability Office, 2010)
100. (Pearson, 2010)
101. (U.S. Government Accountability Office, 2010, p. 32)
102. (U.S. Government Accountability Office, 2010)
103. Dan Hermann, head of investment banking, Ziegler. Quoted in *Z-News,* August 24, 2014
104. (Spellman & Townsley, 2012)
105. (Graham, 2012)
106. (Graham, 2012; Larkin, 2012)
107. (LeadingAge & Ziegler Capital Markets, 2013; Reinstra & Yee, 2013)
108. (Spellman & Townsley, 2012)
109. (Maag, 2012)
110. (Graham, 2012)
111. (Spellman & Townsley, 2012, p. 2)
112. (Larkin, 2012)
113. (Spellman & Townsley, 2012, p. 6)
114. (Graham, 2012)
115. (Spellman & Townsley, 2012)
116. (Spellman & Townsley, 2012)
117. (Spellman & Townsley, 2012)
118. (Maag, 2012, p. 6)
119. (Brecht, Fein, & Hollinger-Smith, 2009)
120. (Golant, 2011a)
121. (LCS, 2012)
122. (Brecht et al., 2009)

Part VI

CONCLUSION

13

PUTTING IT ALL TOGETHER

Aging Successfully in the
Best Possible Places

Residential Normalcy

Places where older people experience overall pleasurable, hassle free, and memorable feelings that have relevance to them; and where they feel both competent and in control—that is, they do not have to behave in personally objectionable ways or to unduly surrender mastery of their lives or environments to others.[1]

THE DIVERSITY OF AMERICA'S AGING POPULATION

The diversity of older Americans makes it difficult to generalize about the quality of their lives and warns us about making one-size-fits-all prescriptions for their aging successfully (Chapter 1). Their demographic differences alone alert us to the fallacy of such pronouncements. Although population watchers remind us that between 2010 and 2040, the population age 65 and older in the United States will double from roughly 40 to 80 million and rise from 13% to 21% of the population (Figures 13.1 and 13.2),[2] they fail to scrutinize the sharp divide between its Third Age and Fourth Age adults. The majority of the young-old population will be retired, married, physically active, largely disability-free, and healthy. In contrast, the old-old population—especially those who have reached their 80s and 90s—will be top heavy with unmarried women living alone or in multigenerational households, who are more likely to

Figure 13.1. Projected size of the older population (in millions) (*Source:* Projections of the Population by Age and Sex for the United States: 2015 to 2060 (NP2012-T12). U.S. Census Bureau, Population Division. Release date: December 2012)

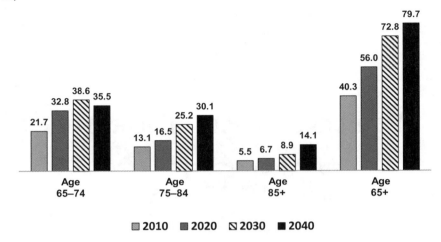

Figure 13.2. Projected percentage growth of older population (*Source:* Projections of the Population by Age and Sex for the United States: 2015 to 2060 (NP2012-T12). U.S. Census Bureau, Population Division. Release date: December 2012.

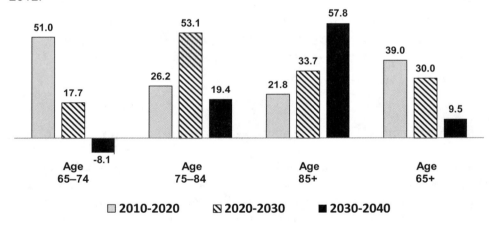

suffer from chronic health problems and functional impairments that restrict their lifestyles and make independent living difficult.

Initially in the 2010–2020 decade, the fast-growing baby boomer generation (born from 1946 to 1964) will make up our young-old (age 65–74), and they will coexist with a much smaller group of old-old people in their mid-70s and older, members of our Silent Generation (born 1945 and earlier). A decade later, in 2030, our baby boomers will inflate the old-old population and will share their neighborhoods and retirement communities with the later born baby boomers who will only have reached their mid-60s and early 70s. With this diverse chronological age makeup—38 million young-old and 25 million old-old—making generalizations about the 2030 baby boom population will be more difficult than ever. By 2040, all of our surviving 44 million baby boomers will be in their mid-70s and older, with about 14 million (4% of all Americans) being in their mid-80s and older. They will substantially outnumber the newest crop of young-old elders, Generation Xers (born from 1965 to 1976).[3]

But these demographic realities only begin to capture how the heterogeneity of this country's old will differently influence their conceptions of the good life and their abilities to live independently. The quality of life of these individuals will also depend on their financial situations, educational achievements, life histories, personalities, and ethnic and racial backgrounds. These differences will further explain why some older people will have an easier time pursuing their preferred ways of life, feeling independent, and aging successfully.

ENVIRONMENT MATTERS: MAJOR TAKEAWAYS

However, even our most exhaustive individual typologies cannot fully convey the dissimilar aging experiences of Americans because they occupy places with very different residential and care environments (Chapter 1). The New Gerontology's focus on individual indicators—such as physical health, functional abilities, and cognitive functioning—ignored a simple axiom: Where people grow old influences their ability to age successfully. Because they live in very different regions, states, communities, neighborhoods, buildings, and dwellings, they will occupy built, natural, social, economic, retail, service, recreational, organizational, and political environments that make it both easier and harder for them to lead active, enjoyable, and comfortable lifestyles, fend off disease and disability, and feel autonomous, competent, and in control of their lives (Chapter 2).

Demonstrating that environment matters is a challenging scientific exercise. Most studies establishing these linkages are observational research inquiries (such as survey or household research analyses) or are based on small, unrepresentative convenience samples. Rigorous experimental design studies are rare that can separate out how individual indicators and environmental factors influence whether older people age successfully. While acknowledging these limitations, this book should leave readers with the following 10 takeaways.

THE QUALITY OF PLACES: THE VIEWS OF EXPERTS AND OLDER PEOPLE ARE BOTH ESSENTIAL

We must be open to alternative ways to conceptualize and measure the qualities of older people's residential and care environments. Both expert appraisals and older people's self-reported feelings or emotions offer valuable insights, even as they sometimes offer contradictory quality-of-life conclusions. We must listen to the professionals and experts to avoid misdiagnosing problems and misdirecting solutions for older people. Yet, to avoid the pitfalls of successful aging theorists, with their singular formula for aging well, we must also listen to the voices of older people and how they differently experience aging and their housing and care worlds. Consequently, in our search for solutions to improve the quality of their living environments, we should not dismiss either set of appraisals but rather allow for the possibility of alternative remedial actions.

RESIDENTIAL AND CARE ENVIRONMENTS OFTEN COEXIST

Where older adults live can no longer be characterized as just residential arrangements or just care environments, whether they live in ordinary dwellings in regular communities or in purposively built group care arrangements, such as assisted living residences or continuing care retirement communities (CCRCs). Determined to age in place, older adults now can physically redesign and modify their current dwellings to cope with their physical, sensory, and cognitive declines and demanding health problems (Chapter 6). They can also draw on family caregivers and paid workers to provide all manner of healthcare and assistance and can introduce assistive devices, medical equipment, and smart home technologies into their homes that once were only found in laboratories and hospital rooms (Chapters 7, 8, and 9). Consequently, their conventional residential arrangements sometimes resemble and operate like assisted living residences or even nursing homes.

At the same time, when older people consider moving to group care facilities, they no longer base their judgments on just the quality of their assistance and care. Rather, they evaluate whether these places subscribe to person-centered principles, with the home-like qualities, activities, and caregiving experiences that were present in their prior dwellings and neighborhoods, including their dining activities, social relationships, recreational opportunities, and staff–vendor relationships (Chapter 11).

ENVIRONMENTS MATTER DIFFERENTLY BECAUSE OLDER PEOPLE ARE DIVERSE

Residential and care settings influence how older adults conduct and experience their lives but in ways that depend on their demographics, personalities, mental well-being, personal histories, lifestyles, and functional abilities. We can point to many examples. Older people living in cluttered and poorly designed dwellings will have a greater risk of falling if they also suffer from gait disorders. Older people living in low-density cul-de-sac suburbs or rural counties will have difficulty accessing their basic shopping needs if they have also suffered declines in their driver skills. Those living alone will benefit from the social activities found in their nearby senior center, but not if they feel depressed when they surround themselves with other older people who are more frail than themselves. Despite the attractive physical design of dining rooms and higher-quality food found in assisted living residences, older residents may feel their eating experiences are lonely, stressful, and unbearable because they are ignored by others at their table who are turned off by their physical or cognitive impairments.

COPING WITH INCONGRUENT ENVIRONMENTS: KEY TO AGING SUCCESSFULLY

If they are to age successfully, older adults occupying incompatible places must not passively resign themselves to their unfortunate circumstances. Rather, they initiate coping actions that enable them to occupy or conduct their activities in places that are more congruent with their personal needs and goals. The most successful will have enriched coping repertoires. These more resilient older individuals make their own assimilative (action) coping decisions and are able to solve their problems because they benefit from the resources and opportunities found in their current neighborhoods or communities or in newly occupied places (Chapter 5).

Consequently, if their current communities offer inadequate recreational opportunities, they relocate to an active adult community or to a university town to enjoy a more enriched and stimulating lifestyle. When they feel lonely after a spouse's death, they participate in the activities of their church or join a book club. To reduce their likelihood of falling, they install grab bars or raised toilet seats in their bathrooms. When they can no longer perform their self-care tasks (e.g., bathing or grooming), they hire a home aide, move closer to a family member, or relocate to an assisted living development. Many older people must initiate multiple coping solutions to address their unmet needs and goals.

These efforts may take time, be plagued by setbacks, and result in older people pursuing ways of life in their residential and care settings that are very different from their pasts. To feel once again that they are occupying a comfortable place where they feel competent and in control—thereby achieving residential normalcy—older people do not have to maintain their status quo lifestyles, activities, or environments. They may still enjoy their lives when they practice sedentary and home-centered lifestyles— so very different from their pasts. Continuity may be neither an attainable nor an essential outcome. Moreover, coping with the adversities of where they live will often be an ongoing process, and they may experience many "new normals."

RESIDENTIAL AND CARE CONTEXTS ENABLE VULNERABLE OLDER PEOPLE TO AGE SUCCESSFULLY

Older adults can still age successfully when they have chronic health problems, disabilities, or cognitive deficits. This is a crucial conclusion because although older people are living longer, they are also unlikely to be disability-free and healthy during the last years of their lives. Unlike the New Gerontology paradigm, the theory of residential normalcy does not preclude vulnerable groups of older people from feeling autonomous and engaged and from achieving the good life.[4] By offering these older individuals residential and care opportunities that strengthen their coping repertoires, we enable them to achieve their evolving needs and goals. We can make available leisure and recreational activities that are congruent with their interests and abilities; encourage their friends and families to visit them more frequently; counsel and train their family members to provide assistance that is timely and appropriate; modify the physical designs of their dwellings to help them compensate for their functional limitations; ensure they can receive services and assistance to fully address their self-care and medication management needs; and give them the means to access both their discretionary and nondiscretionary goods and services.

Moving Not Necessary to Cope with Incongruent Places

When younger adults occupy inappropriate residential environments, they typically cope by moving, but this is not the case for older adults (Chapter 5). For a host of social, economic, psychological, and societal and public policy reasons, residential inertia or aging in place is the norm. This is often true even after their spouses die, they retire, their health or functional abilities decline, their dwellings fall into disrepair, or their neighborhoods become unsafe or unpleasant places to live. Moreover, even when they do move, their new addresses are usually not far away. Even older occupants of CCRCs resist moving to a higher level of care within their campus settings, even though being able to make this transition was an important reason for why they were attracted to this option in the first place (Chapter 12).

Historical (or period) effects may especially influence the residential relocation decisions of older people. Housing price bubbles, recessions, tight housing markets, mortgage financing practices, and changing levels of public support of home- and community-based care options are just a few of the many societal conditions that make moving more or less likely (Chapter 3).

Older people would probably move even less if their relocation decisions were always their own. However, their moves are often dictated by influencers such as family members or professionals, especially at older ages. Unfortunately, when their moving decisions are made by others and outside of their control, older people are more likely to experience bad outcomes in their new settings.

A major challenge for researchers and professionals is to distinguish older people who stay put or age in place despite their incongruent living situations (Chapter 4) because they believe—accurately or not—that efficacious and viable residential or care alternatives are not in their coping repertoires (Chapter 5). That is, they do not have any good relocation options. These older people would especially benefit from private or public sector solutions that offered them alternative housing and care arrangements catering to their idiosyncratic needs and capabilities (Chapters 8–12).

Even the Most Lauded Housing and Care Options Have Downsides

We must not over-romanticize the solutions available to older people to achieve residential normalcy. Despite the strong psychological, social, and economic attractions of their abodes and their "groupthink" endorsements, staying put is sometimes a failed strategy. Older people aging in place are often afflicted with problems that include burdensome housing costs, physically inaccessible dwellings in disrepair, unmet needs for long-term services and supports, inadequate care for chronic health conditions, social isolation and loneliness, unsafe or inhospitable neighborhoods and communities, and unavailable or unsafe transportation options (Chapter 4).

The solutions prescribed by the experts—whether to age in place or to move elsewhere—may be ineffective because they clash with the values or beliefs of older people, they are poorly implemented, or they do not respond to the totality of their unmet needs. So, for example, even the best home care services may be rejected by older people if they do not get along with their direct care workers (home health or personal aides). And although no one questions the crucial roles played by family caregivers, not all perform their duties competently, and their errors can result in costly remedial health and long-term care responses. Even worse, some family members abuse those in their care.

The potential of smart home technologies to detect the unhealthy and dysfunctional behaviors of older people and offer effective remedies seems indisputable, but there will always be some older people who view these solutions as intrusive assaults on their autonomy. Dwellings may be made physically accessible and safe, but these may be inadequate solutions if their occupants are socially isolated. Age-friendly community initiatives, such as demand-responsive transportation vans, obviously have merit, but not when they are unavailable at the times and days when people need them the most (Chapter 9). And the thoughtfully designed housing opportunities available in New Urbanism communities, with their easy-to-reach businesses and services, may be out of the price range of lower-income older people who would most benefit from them. Similarly, despite their plentiful leisure and recreational offerings, older people may be bored in their active adult communities because they miss the theater, music, and restaurants found in their previous urban centers or they miss seeing their children (Chapter 10). And older people who occupy assisted living residences may still view them as nothing less than institutions even though they incorporate person-centered design principles (Chapter 11).

ACHIEVING RESIDENTIAL NORMALCY: A DIFFICULT BALANCING ACT

Despite their best coping efforts, older Americans must often settle for the least imperfect places to live, with a balance of both desirable and undesirable qualities. The places in which they live and receive care often have split personalities. Consequently, older adults aging in place may feel squarely in their residential comfort zones, receiving pleasure and enjoyment from their physically attractive neighborhoods, memorable personal possessions, and activities with their good friends, but at the same time may be out of their residential mastery zones, overwhelmed by the financial and maintenance demands of homeownership. Here they may be struggling to perform their most basic self-care tasks because family members are unavailable or they cannot afford to pay for help. Not able to drive and located in low-density suburbs, they feel prisoners in their own homes.

Alternatively, they may occupy assisted living residences where they receive good quality care that makes them feel more independent and autonomous, and they no longer are anxious about getting their groceries or getting to their doctors. But to realize these benefits, they must give up their earlier-occupied, more-comfortable dwellings that were associated with home cooked meals and lifelong memories (Chapter 2). Similarly, even as healthy older occupants feel fully engaged in life as occupants of active adult communities, they may also have difficulty coping with the regimented lifestyles of these places and resent others dictating how they should spend their time (Chapter 10).

RUGGED INDIVIDUALISM VERSUS IT TAKES A VILLAGE

We can discern two very different strategies available to older people seeking to make where they live more congruent with their lifestyles and capabilities. Consistent with the rugged individualism of some older Americans, they take personal responsibility to address their changing lifestyles and new long-term care needs. They rely on their own resources to find new leisure-related activities for their retirement years or to secure caregivers to help them cope with their mobility limitations. In contrast, others are willing to give up some of their self-determination to find solutions to their aging challenges. Adopting a perspective of "it takes a village" (Chapter 9), they seek communally organized residential and care settings that offer them help to feel more actively engaged in life or to maintain their independent households despite declines and losses. They give up some control over their lifestyle and care decisions to a trusted group of neighbors, administrators, or professionals, in return for the collective benefits of some organization, management team, or social collectivity taking at least partial responsibility for their physical or mental well-being. The newest examples are Elder Villages, clustered housing-care, and cohousing communities, which join such earlier standbys as active adult communities, independent living communities, assisted living developments, CCRCs, NORC-SSPs, and PACE centers (Chapters 8–12).

ACHIEVING RESIDENTIAL NORMALCY: NOT JUST THE CONCERN OF OLDER PEOPLE

A broad group of stakeholders—not just older people themselves—are invested in the residential or care decisions of older adults:

- Family members of all ages—whether spouses, grandchildren, adult children, or siblings—whose lives are disrupted by the demanding problems of their aging relatives
- Family members—particularly spouses, daughters, and sons—who are investing their physical and mental energies as caregivers
- Builders, sponsors, professionals, managers, providers, and administrators in the private, charitable, and public sectors who are variously responsible for elder housing accommodations and long-term care products, benefits, and services
- Retailers offering a host of products
- Segments of the labor force whose livelihoods depend on serving the growing population of frail older adults
- Younger people whose home-buying opportunities often depend on whether older homeowners age in place or move

- Neighbors of older homeowners, whose house values depend on whether their nearby aging in place occupants maintain or upgrade their dwellings

- Community and state governments whose economic fortunes are influenced by older consumers' spending and savings activities, job creation, charitable and volunteering activities, and tax revenues as well as by the costs (and benefits) of providing them housing and care

- All taxpayers who bear the costs of public programs that provide for the housing and care needs of older adults, particularly our most economically deprived and sickest individuals.

BOTTOM LINE

The diversity of older Americans and the eclectic ways they appraise and cope with the inadequacies of their residential and care environments make it possible for them to achieve residential normalcy in many different types of places. Moreover, older people who cope successfully with the assaults on their well-being will sometimes end up occupying and conducting their lives in residential and care settings that are very different than in their pasts. Consequently, unlike the authors of the New Gerontology paradigm, this book argues that there are many pathways to aging successfully; environmental continuity is not a prerequisite, and it cannot simply prescribe one set of "best" places for older people to live or receive care. As a national AARP survey of older adults emphasized, there are many different types of places that are livable.[5] Unfortunately, it is also true that older persons will not always be successful in their quest for residential normalcy. They will fail to find places to live and receive care where they feel comfortable, competent, and in control.

GOING FORWARD: ACHIEVING RESIDENTIAL NORMALCY

Will it become easier or harder for future older Americans to feel in their residential comfort and mastery zones? Making this call is difficult.

PESSIMISTICALLY SPEAKING

On the negative side, experts predict that baby boomers will have higher rates of chronic health problems and functional limitations linked with their higher prevalence of obesity, diabetes, high blood pressure, and musculoskeletal problems, factors that will increase their risk for hospitalizations, emergency room visits, and long-term care, altogether complicating their ability to successfully age in place. An alarming share of older adults are retiring with insufficient pensions, savings, and assets, thereby increasing their risk of requiring public assistance to afford good quality housing and care (Chapter 4).[6] Younger boomers entering old age are also less likely to be homeowners and thus will be unable to rely on their home equity as a means to pay for their future long-term care. Some subgroups will be especially at risk: the less educated, the poor, unmarried women, and some ethnic and racial minorities.[7]

Those older boomers who own their homes will confront various unmet needs and problems as they seek to age in place. They will occupy overly large and older dwellings that need ongoing and expensive maintenance and repairs, and they will lack the physical design and home modification features that would help them compensate for their mobility limitations. They will have more burdensome mortgage and credit card debt than any previous generation. As occupants of cul-de-sac suburbs or sparsely populated rural areas, they will risk their safety by continuing to drive as long as possible despite a decline in their abilities. When they can no longer depend on their automobiles, they will curtail their everyday activities, reluctantly depend on others for getting around, and more likely find themselves isolated and alone.

Over the next three decades, today's baby boomers, who themselves are now family caregivers, will age out of their caregiving responsibilities and increasingly become the care recipients. They are members of a generation with high divorce and low fertility rates and often with no living children.[8] Consequently, they will be able to draw on a historically low number of potential family caregivers when they themselves confront difficulties performing their activities of daily living or just need comfort and reassurance. Unmarried low-income older women are especially at risk. Attitudes toward taking care of our older family members will also change. Tomorrow's adult children—and potential caregivers—will be busy with their own careers and family rearing and more predisposed to allowing professionals to take care of their loved ones, as they did with their own young children. They will be less willing to endure the physical and psychological demands of caregiving. The inadequate funding of programs supporting the needs of these caregivers and the prevalence of unsympathetic employers will only exacerbate this trend. Making matters worse will be the predicted shortage of professionals (e.g., geriatric specialists) and adequately trained direct care workers that older people can draw on to provide them with long-term care, especially if the United States tightens its immigration policies (Chapter 8). Moreover, absent improvements in the remunerations and benefits received by our professional and direct care workforce, older people will receive below standard long-term care. Although smart home technologies hold much promise as a strategy to reduce the demand for both informal and formal care providers, the willingness of older consumers to use these new technologies and their overall effectiveness are still not certain.

Certainly older people with higher incomes will benefit from the increased availability of residential care options, such as independent living communities, assisted living, and CCRCs and their increasing propensity to offer person-centered living and care environments. But the quality of these options varies dramatically and older consumers must be especially vigilant to ensure that they make sound selections. To be in both their residential comfort and residential mastery zones, they must not only be able to enjoy a physically and socially attractive home-like environment and feel fully engaged in life, but also feel protected, secure, well cared for, and not overly burdened financially.

Sadly, multiple surveys report that most older Americans have not seriously planned for their long-term care needs and how to pay for them. Advocates for lower-income Americans should be especially pessimistic, especially when they consider the plight of renters with no home equity safety net or homeowners with highly mort-gaged or low-valued dwellings. Even as we expect a much greater future demand by lower income older people for affordable rental housing (some of which offers support-ive services) and home- and community-based care, most experts predict that federal and state governments will probably cut back on program funding for older adults, thereby exacerbating their unmet needs for these services and benefits[9] (Chapters 8 and 9).

Yet it is not only the poorest older Americans who are at risk. Moderate-income older adults will also confront financial challenges even as they have few stakeholders speaking on their behalf. Their economic resources, however limited, will be too large for them to qualify for the current safety net of government-funded social, long-term care, and housing programs, yet they will fall well short of affording the costly housing and care options developed by the private sector, especially if they are living in areas with a high cost of living.[10] Their coping repertoires will contain far more limited solutions that enable them to age in place comfortably and securely or to find desirable places to move, severely reducing the quality of their aging lives.

Some observers are especially worried about what they see as a larger trend in American society. Since the 1980s, stakeholders, such as professionals, the business community, the media, and legislators, are no longer portraying aging adults as needy and vulnerable, but rather as healthy, happy, economically sound consumers capable of thriving in their own homes. In many respects, these characterizations echo the mes-sages of the New Gerontology paradigm—namely, that old age need not constitute a period of decline and contraction. Consequently, American society no longer compas-sionately views their older residents as deserving of public benefits based on their age.[11] Rather, the media are far more likely to portray older people as selfish and indulgent recipients of government handouts, as exemplified by newspaper and magazine stories leading with captions such as "Meet the Greedy Grandparents: Why America's Elderly Are So Spoiled."[12] Symptomatic of these positions are experts who advocate that vener-able age-based entitlement programs such as Social Security and Medicare should be available only to low-income, means-tested seniors. They argue that absent such policy shifts, we will underfund the health and social benefits of our future younger popula-tions and load them with unbearable debt.[13] The tragic irony is that if we ignore our traditional age boundaries and eliminate program guarantees, we will reverse all of the historically achieved health, social, and economic gains of older people.

OPTIMISTICALLY SPEAKING

These undesirable outcomes may be offset by some notable countertrends, making residential normalcy and successful aging more achievable. Many older people will ease their financial difficulties by delaying retirement or at least maintaining part-time employment. They may also enjoy larger disposable incomes drawn from their savings accounts and certificates of deposit as bank deposit and money market interest rates rise. As home values moderately increase—and assuming borrowing rates are not excessively high—older residents will be better positioned to obtain home eq-uity loans or reverse mortgages or to sell their current dwellings in order to downsize to smaller, better-designed quarters—both owned and rented—in more compatible neighborhoods.

In recognition of the diverse lifestyles of older Americans, the private sector is offering these consumers a host of idiosyncratic niche retirement housing opportunities tailored to those favoring college educational opportunities, fitness programs, healthful eating, marathon running, cruise ships, tai chi clubs, garden clubs, and so on (Chapter 10). Other older people, particularly unmarried women, will embrace home-sharing and cohousing alternatives.

Tomorrow's old may also be better able to age in place even with their chronic health problems and functional limitations because of continuing advances in individually tailored medical screening, diagnoses, procedures, and pharmacologic solutions. They will also benefit from better home-based preventive and hospital transition care (Chapter 8), thereby reducing their likelihood of experiencing setbacks in their health and functioning that would put them into emergency rooms and hospital beds. Medical advances that could delay the onset of Alzheimer's disease symptoms would dramatically influence the ability of older people to remain in their familiar homes. As states increasingly reallocate their Medicaid budgets to favor the funding of home- and community-based care instead of nursing homes and better target their Older Americans Act programs, the poorest segments of older people will be more able to age in place in their conventional homes and neighborhoods.

Obtaining informal care could also become easier as a larger share of the U.S. labor force increasingly works out of their homes and has more flextime, and employers see the advantages of compensating their workers for days lost when they assist their aging relatives. A greater use of better designed assistive devices may help reduce the help older people require from their caregivers. Smart home technologies—including robotic devices—offer great promise as means to better diagnose and respond to the health and long-term care needs of older Americans. These new technologies promise to reduce the caregiving responsibilities and burdens of family members and direct care workers alike (Chapter 6). They even purport to improve the social lives of more isolated older adults. More technologically savvy aging baby boomers will be more receptive to these innovations, especially as their costs drop and federal and private insurance programs find it economically advantageous to treat them as reimbursable healthcare or long-term care expenditures.

Older people who are now disadvantaged because they cannot drive but live in auto-dependent neighborhoods in outlying metropolitan suburbs and rural counties will increasingly depend on online purchases to obtain even their most fundamental nondiscretionary needs. New automobile technologies will also make operating a car safer for aging adults, allow them to drive longer, and reduce driver errors and accidents attributed to their physical or cognitive declines. Car-dependent residential locations may also become far less of a problem given the potentially revolutionary impact of "driverless" car technology and its ability to increase the mobility of older people otherwise unable to drive (Chapter 9).

A healthier private housing market in the United States will also be cause for optimism. The recovery from the sharp past downturns in housing prices, the foreclosure epidemic, and the frozen credit (home loan) markets experienced during the Great Recession (between 2007 and 2010) will make it far more feasible for older Americans to move as a means to cope with their incongruent residential environments (Chapters 4 and 5). With housing prices rebounding and economic wealth increasing, older homeowners will be able and motivated to sell the dwellings that are now incompatible with their aging bodies or retirement lifestyles. Alternatively, if they choose to age in place, they will have confidence knowing that they will have stronger dwelling equity positions to eventually fund their in situ long-term care or their later moves to options such as independent living communities, assisted living, or continuing care retirement communities (Chapters 11 and 12).

The growing number of localities participating in healthy, lifelong, or age-friendly community efforts will also be a hopeful trend as they increasingly target enclaves of older people with unmet housing and care needs. The more widespread availability of these age-friendly initiatives will result in more leisure and recreational opportunities, better transit access, more usable walking paths, more proximate shopping opportunities, and New Urbanism–inspired land use design and zoning strategies.

We also expect to witness more versions of grassroots communal efforts, such as Elder Villages, that will cater to the aging-in-place preferences of older Americans (Chapter 9). These communities are especially likely to thrive if the next generation of older people surrenders their rugged individualism values and appreciates how these neighborhood- and community-based collectivities can help them cope with their aging challenges.

The purposively designed senior housing options offered by the private sector are also likely to evolve in ways that better respond to a generation of older boomers with more discriminating shelter and care preferences. They will treat older people more like customers than clients and offer them a hotel- or resort-like experience that is responsive to both their idiosyncratic vulnerabilities and lifestyles. In recognition of their preferences to age in place, independent living communities will introduce more health and supportive service options designed to reduce the need for these older people to move to a higher level of care. Similarly, as our future assisted living residences provide heavier care, the vulnerability profiles of their older residents will look remarkably similar to our nursing home occupants.

The barriers that now separate planned senior housing options, such as independent living communities, assisted living developments, and CCRCs, from their surrounding communities of older residents will continue to become more porous. These will be not only residential and care centers for their own occupants but also product and service suppliers for their surrounding community-residing older populations and their family caregivers (Chapter 12).

To greatly increase their market share, expect that tomorrow's private sector providers will also offer older people with modest incomes more stripped down but also less-expensive versions of their current senior housing and care options. These will satisfy the residential and long-term care needs of this less-affluent group, just as how affordable manufactured homes earlier gave them the opportunities for homeownership.

NOTES

1. (Golant, 2011b, p. 193)
2. (Ortman, Velkoff, & Hogan, 2014)
3. (Ortman et al., 2014)
4. (Jeste et al., 2013)
5. (Harrell et al., 2014)
6. (Martin, Freedman, Schoeni, & Andreski, 2010; U.S. Congressional Budget Office, 2013; Wolf, Hunt, & Knickman, 2005).
7. (Seltzer & Yahirun, 2013; Joint Center for Housing Studies of Harvard University, 2014)
8. (Redfoot et al., 2013)
9. (The Lewin Group, 2010b)
10. This argument is more fully developed in Golant (2014a)
11. (Binstock, 2005)
12. (Chapman, 2003)
13. (Binstock, 2005)

BIBLIOGRAPHY

Aaronson, W.E., Zinn, J.S., & Rosko, M.D. (1995). Structure, environment and strategic outcome: A study of Pennsylvania nursing homes. *Health Services Management Research, 8*(1), 23–37.

AARP. (2009). *AARP, across the states*. Washington, DC: AARP.

AARP Public Policy Institute. (2011). *United States: State housing profiles, 2011*. Washington, DC: AARP Public Policy Institute.

Achenbaum, W.A., & Levin, J.S. (1989). What does gerontology mean? *The Gerontologist, 29*(3), 393–400.

Acierno, R., Hernandez, M.A., Amstadter, A.B., Resnick, H.S., Steve, K., Muzzy, W., et al. (2010). Prevalence and correlates of emotional, physical, sexual, and financial abuse and potential neglect in the United States: The national elder mistreatment study. *American Journal of Public Health, 100*(2), 292–297.

Adams, K.B. (2008). Specific effects of caring for a spouse with dementia: Differences in depressive symptoms between caregiver and non-caregiver spouses. *International Psychogeriatric Association, 20*(3), 508–520.

Addis, S., Davies, M., Greene, G., MacBride-Stewart, S., & Shepherd, M. (2009). The health, social care and housing needs of lesbian, gay, bisexual and transgender older people: A review of the literature. *Health & Social Care in the Community, 17*(6), 647–658.

AgingOptions. (2013). *Continuing care retirement communities: Benefits and risks of choosing a CCRC*. Federal Way, WA: AgingOptions.

Agree, E.M., & Freedman, V.A. (2003). A comparison of assistive technology and personal care in alleviating disability and unmet need. *The Gerontologist, 43*(3), 335–344.

Aldwin, C., & Igarashi, H. (2012). An ecological model of resilience in late life. In B. Hayslip & G.C. Smith (Eds.), *Annual review of gerontology and geriatrics* (pp. 115–130). New York: Springer.

Alecxih, L. (2006). *Nursing home use by "oldest old" sharply declines*. Washington, DC: The Lewin Group.

ALFA. (2012). *Top ten deficiencies, 2012: executive summary*. Washington, DC: ALFA.

Allen, M. (2012). Fair Housing Act. In A.T. Carswell (Ed.), *The encyclopedia of housing* (2nd ed., pp. 203–206). Thousand Oaks, CA: Sage.

Alley, D., Liebig, P., Pynoos, J., Banerjee, T., & Choi, I.H. (2007). Creating elder-friendly communities: Preparations for an aging society. *Journal of Gerontological Social Work, 49*, 1–18.

Altman, I. (1975). *The environment and social behavior: Privacy, personal space, territory, and crowding*. Monterey, CA: Brooks/Cole.

Altshuler, N., & Schimmel, J. (2010). *Aging in place: Do Older Americans Act Title III services reach those most likely to enter nursing homes*. Princeton, NJ: Mathematica Policy Research.

Alzheimer's Association. (2012). *Alzheimer's disease facts and figures*. Washington, DC: Alzheimer's Association.

Alzheimer's Association. (2013). *Alzheimer's disease facts and figures*. Washington, DC: Alzheimer's Association.

Alzheimer's Association. (2014). *Alzheimer's disease facts and figures*. Washington, DC: Alzheimer's Association.

American Association of Homes and Services for the Aging. (2009). *2009 overview of assisted living*. Washington, DC: American Association of Homes and Services for the Aging (now LeadingAge).

American Association of Homes and Services for the Aging. (2010). *Moving forward with transitional and integrated services: The long-term services and supports providers' perspective*. Washington, DC: American Association of Homes and Services for the Aging (now LeadingAge).

American Health Care Association. (2001). *Facts and trends: The nursing facility sourcebook*. Washington, DC: American Health Care Association.

American Psychological Association, Office on Aging. (2010). *Elder abuse and neglect: In search of solutions*. Washington, DC: American Psychological Association.

American Seniors Housing Association. (2009). *The independent living report*. Washington, DC: American Seniors Housing Association.

American Seniors Housing Association. (2011). *The state of senior housing 2011*. Washington, DC: American Seniors Housing Association.

American Seniors Housing Association. (2013). *The state of senior housing 2013*. Washington, DC: American Seniors Housing Association.

Anderson, K.A., Dabelko-Schoeny, H., & Johnson, T.D. (2013). The state of adult day services: Findings and implications from the MetLife national study of adult day services. *Journal of Applied Gerontology, 32*(6), 729–748.

Anetzberger, G.J. (2010). Community options of greater Cleveland, Ohio: Preliminary evaluation of a naturally occurring retirement community program. *Clinical Gerontologist, 33*(1), 1–15.

Antonucci, J. (2013). The village's vitality program. *Journal of Active Aging, 12*(7), 50–54.

Aramac Senior Living Services. (2012). *What seniors think about CCRCs*. Philadelphia, PA: Aramac Senior Living Services.

Assisted Living Federation of America. (2009). *2009 overview of assisted living*. Washington, DC: Assisted Living Federation of Ameri.

Atlanta Regional Commission. (2009). *Lifelong communities: A regional guide to growth and longevity*. Atlanta, GA: Atlanta Regional Commission.

Ayalon, L., & Green, V. (2012). Social ties in the context of the continuing care retirement community. *Qualitative Health Research, 23*(3), 396–406.

Badger, T.A., & McArthur, D.B. (2003). Academic nursing clinic: Impact on health and cost outcomes for vulnerable populations. *Applied Nursing Research, 16*(1), 60–64.

Baily, L. (2004). *Aging Americans: Stranded without options*. Washington, DC: Surface Transportation Policy Project.

Bakija, J., & Slemrod, J. (2004). *Do the rich flee from high state taxes? Evidence from federal estate tax returns*. Working paper 10645. Cambridge, MA: National Bureau of Economic Research.

Ball, M.M., Perkins, M.M., Hollingsworth, C., Whittington, F.J., & King, S.V. (2009). Pathways to assisted living: The influence of race and class. *Journal of Applied Gerontology, 28*(1), 81–108.

Ball, M.S. (2012). *Livable communities for aging populations*. Hoboken, NJ: Wiley.

Baltes, P.B., & Baltes, M.M. (1990). Psychological perspectives on successful aging: A model of selective optimization with compensation. In P.B. Baltes & M.M. Baltes (Eds.), *Successful aging: Perspectives from the behavioral sciences* (pp. 1–34). New York: Cambridge University Press.

Banerjee, S. (2012). Own-to-rent transitions and changes in housing equity for older Americans. *EBRIorg Notes, 33*(7), 1–9.

Bankers Life and Casualty Company. (2011). *Best U.S. cities for seniors 2011*. Chicago: Bankers Life and Casualty Company.

Barrett, L.F. (2006). Solving the emotion paradox: Categorization and the experience of emotion. *Personality and Social Psychology Review, 10*(1), 20–46.

Barrett, L.F., Mesquita, B., Ochsner, K.N., & Gross, J.J. (2007). The experience of emotion. *Annual Review of Psychology, 58*, 373–403.

Barrett, L. L. (2008). *Healthy @ home*. Washington, DC: AARP Foundation.

Barrier Free Environments, Inc. (1998). *Fair Housing Act design manual*. Raleigh, NC: U.S. Department of Housing and Urban Development.

Bayne, C.G., & Boling, P.A. (2009). New diagnostic and information technology for mobile medical care. *Clinics in Geriatric Medicine, 25*(1), 93–107, vii.

Beach, S.R., Schulz, R., Williamson, G.M., Miller, L.S., Weiner, M.F., & Lance, C.E. (2005). Risk factors for potentially harmful informal caregiver behavior. *Journal of American Geriatrics Society, 53*(2), 255–261.

Beard, J.R., Blaney, S., Cerda, M., Frye, V., Lovasi, G.S., Ompad, D., et al. (2009). Neighborhood characteristics and disability in older adults. *Journal of Gerontology: Social Sciences, 64B*(2), 252–257.

Beard, J.R., Cerda, M., Blaney, S., Ahern, J., Vlahov, D., & Galea, S. (2009). Neighborhood characteristics and change in depressive symptoms among older residents of New York City. *American Journal of Public Health, 99*(1), 1–7.

Bedney, B.J., Goldberg, R.B., & Josephson, K. (2010). Aging in place in naturally occurring retirement communities: Transforming aging through supportive service programs. *Journal of Housing for the Elderly, 24*, 304–321.

Bekhet, A.K., Zauszniewski, J.A., & Nakhla, W.E. (2009). Reasons for relocation to retirement communities: A qualitative study. *Western Journal of Nursing Research, 31*(4), 462–479.

Bell, S., & Menec, V. (2013, January 6). "You don't want to ask for the help." The imperative of independence: Is it related to social exclusion? *Journal of Applied Gerontology.*

Bella, P. (2011, November 20). The elderly dilemma: Medicare–Medicaid fail middle class families. *The Washington Times.*

Benson, W.F., & Aldrich, N. (2013). The aging middle class and public policy. In J. Blanchard (Ed.), *Aging in community* (pp. 171–182). Chapel Hill, NC: Second Journey Publications.

Berke, E.M., Ackermann, R.T., Lin, E.H., Diehr, P.H., Maciejewski, M.L., Williams, B., et al. (2006). Distance as a barrier to using a fitness-program benefit for managed Medicare enrollees. *Journal of Aging and Physical Activity, 14*(3), 313–324.

Bernard, T.S. (2013, July 12). Rules for reverse mortgages may become more restrictive. *New York Times.*

Berridge, K.C., & Kringelbach, M.L. (2011). Building a neuroscience of pleasure and well-being. *Psychology of Well-Being, 1*(1), 1–3.

Bezaitis, A.G. (2008). Successful strategies for fall prevention. *Aging Well Magazine, 1*(1), 28–31.

Bharucha, A.J., Anand, V., Forlizzi, J., Dew, M.A., Reynolds, C.F. III, Stevens, S., et al. (2009). Intelligent assistive technology applications to dementia care: Current capabilities, limitations, and future challenges. *American Journal of Geriatric Psychiatry, 17*(2), 88–104.

Bierman, A. (2009). Marital status as contingency for the effects of neighborhood disorder on older adults' mental health. *Journal of Gerontology: Social Sciences, 64*(3), 425–434.

Binstock, R.H. (2005). Old-age policies, politics, and ageism. *Generations, 29*(1), 73–78.

Black, B.S., Rabins, P.V., & German, P.S. (1999). Predictors of nursing home placement among elderly public housing residents. *The Gerontologist, 39*(5), 559–568.

Blaikie, A. (1999). *Ageing and popular culture.* Cambridge, England: Cambridge University Press.

Blechman, A. D. (2008). *Leisureville: Adventures in America's retirement.* New York: Grove/Atlantic.

Boling, P.A. (2009). Care transitions and home health care. *Clinics in Geriatric Medicine, 25*(1), 135–148, viii.

Bortz, D. (2012). Boomers flock to niche retirement communities. *U.S. News & World Report* (April 13).

Bowers, B. (2011). Empowering direct care workers: Lessons learned from the green house model. *Seniors Housing & Care Journal, 19*(1), 109–120.

Bowling, A., & Stafford, M. (2007). How do objective and subjective assessments of neighbourhood influence social and physical functioning in older age? Findings from a British survey of ageing. *Social Science & Medicine, 64*(12), 2533–2549.

Bowman, S., Hooker, K., Steggell, C.D., & Brandt, J. (2013). Perceptions of communication and monitoring technologies among older rural women: Problem or panacea? *Journal of Housing for the Elderly, 27*(1–2), 48–60.

Bragg, E., & Hansen, J.C. (2011). A revelation of numbers: Will America's eldercare workforce be ready for to care for an aging America? *Generations, 34*(4), 11–19.

Brandon, E. (2011, October 17). The 10 best places to retire in 2012. *US News & World Report.*

Brandtstadter, J., & Greve, W. (1994). The aging self: Stabilizing and protective processes. *Developmental Review, 14,* 42–80.

Brecht, S.B. (2002). *Analyzing seniors' housing markets.* Washington, DC: Urban Land Institute.

Brecht, S.B., Fein, S., & Hollinger-Smith, L. (2009). Preparing for the future: Trends in continuing care retirement communities. *Seniors Housing & Care Journal, 16*(1), 48–62.

Broadbent, E., Stafford, R., & MacDonald, B. (2009). Acceptance of healthcare robots for the older population: Review and future directions. *International Journal of Social Robotics, 1*(4), 319–330.

Bronstein, L., Gellis, Z.D., & Kenaley, B.L. (2011). A neighborhood naturally occurring retirement community: Views from providers and residents. *Journal of Applied Gerontology, 30*(1), 104–112.

Bronstein, L., & Kenaley, B.L. (2011). Learning from vertical NORCs: Challenges and recommendations for horizontal NORCs. *Journal of Housing for the Elderly, 24*(1), 237–248.

Brown, L.M., Dosa, D.M., Thomas, K., Hyer, K., Feng, Z., & Mor, V. (2012). The effects of evacuation on nursing home residents with dementia. *American Journal of Alzheimer's Disease and Other Dementias, 27*(6), 406–412.

Bultena, G.L., & Wood, V. (1969). American retirement community: Bane or blessing. *Journals of Gerontology, 24*(2), 209–217.

Burkhardt, J.E., McGavock, A.T., Nelson, C.A., & Mitchell, C. G.B. (2002). *Improving public transit options for older persons: TCRP report 82.* Washington, DC: Transportation Research Board.

Burns, V.F., Lavoie, J.P., & Rose, D. (2011, October 13). Revisiting the role of neighbourhood change in social exclusion and inclusion of older people. *Journal of Aging Research.*

Burr, J.A., Mutchler, J.E., & Caro, F.G. (2007). Productive activity clusters among middle-aged and older adults: Intersecting forms and time commitments. *Journal of Gerontology: Social Sciences, 62*(4), S267–275.

Caffrey, C., Sengupta, M., Park-Lee, E., Moss, A., Rosenoff, E., & Harris-Kojetin, L. (2012). Residents living in residential care facilities: United States, 2010. *NCHS Data Brief, 91,* 1–8.

Cagney, K.A., Browning, C.R., & Wen, M. (2005). Racial disparities in self-rated health at older ages: What difference does the neighborhood make? *Journal of Gerontology: Social Sciences, 60*(4), S181–190.

Calasanti, T. (2006). Spousal caregiving and crossing gender boundaries: Maintaining gendered identities. *Journal of Aging Studies, 20,* 253–263.

Calkins, M., & Keane, W. (2008). Tomorrow's assisted living and nursing homes: The converging worlds of residential long-term care. In S.M. Golant & J. Hyde (Eds.), *The assisted living residence: A vision for the future* (pp. 86–118). Baltimore, MD: The John Hopkins University Press.

Campbell, A., Converse, P.G., & Rodgers, W. (1976). *The quality of American life.* New York: Russell Sage.

Cantor, M.D. (2006). No information about me without me: Technology, privacy, and home monitoring. *Generations, 30*(2), 49–53.

Cantor, M.H. (1975). Life space and the social support system of the inner city elderly of New York. *The Gerontologist, 15*(1 Pt 1), 23–27.

Carder, P.C., Morgan, L.A., & Eckert, J.K. (2008). Small board-and-care homes: A fragile future. In S.M. Golant & J. Hyde (Eds.), *The assisted living residence: A vision for the future* (pp. 143–168). Baltimore, MD: The John Hopkins University Press.

CARF International. (2013). *Consumer guide to understanding financial performance and reporting in con- tinuing care retirement communities.* Tucson, AZ: Commission on Accreditation of Rehabilitation Facilities.

Carlson, E.M. (2007). Protecting rights or waiving them? Why "negotiated risk" should be removed from assisted living law. *Journal of Health Care Law & Policy, 10,* 287–337.

Carlson, E., Coffey, G., Fecondo, J., & Newcomer, R. (2010). Medicaid funding for assisted living care: A five-state examination. *Journal of Housing for the Elderly, 24,* 5–27.

Caro, F.G., Caspi, E., Burr, J.A., & Mutchler, J.E. (2009). Global activity motivation and activities of older people. *Activities, Adaptation & Aging, 33*(3), 191–208.

Carstensen, L.L. (2006). The influence of a sense of time on human development. *Science, 312*(5782), 1913–1915.

Carstensen, L.L., Gross, J.J., & Fung, H.H. (1998). The social context of emotional experience. In K.W. Schaie & M.P. Lawton (Eds.), *Annual review of gerontology and geriatrics: Focus on emotion and adult development* (pp. 325–352). New York: Springer.

Carstensen, L.L., Isaacowitz, D.M., & Charles, S.T. (1999). Taking time seriously. A theory of socioemotional selectivity. *American Psychologist, 54*(3), 165–181.

Castle, N.G. (2001). Relocation of the elderly. *Medical Care Research and Review, 58*(3), 291–333.

Castle, N. (2013). *An examination of resident abuse in assisted living facilities, final report.* Washington, DC: Department of Justice.

Castle, N., & Beach, S. (2011). Elder abuse in assisted living. *Journal of Applied Gerontology, 32*(2), 248–267.

Castle, N.G., Ferguson, J., & Schulz, R. (2009). Aging-friendly health and long-term care services. *Generations, 33*(2), 44–50.

Castle, N., & Resnick, N. (2014). Service-enriched housing: The staying at home program. *Journal of Applied Gerontology.* Published online before print July 9, 2014.

Center on Budget and Policy Priorities. (2012). *Federal rental assistance facts.* Washington, DC: Center on Budget and Policy Priorities.

Center for Technology and Aging. (2013). *The new era of connected aging: A framework for understanding technologies that support older adults in aging in place.* Oakland, CA: SCAN Foundation.

Centers for Disease Control and Prevention. (2008). Self-reported falls and fall-related injuries among persons aged > or = 65 years: United States, 2006. *Morbidity and Mortality Weekly Report, 57*(9), 225–229.

Chan, B.K., Marshall, L.M., Winters, K.M., Faulkner, K.A., Schwartz, A.V., & Orwoll, E.S. (2007). Incident fall risk and physical activity and physical performance among older men: The osteoporotic fractures in men study. *American Journal of Epidemiology, 165*(6), 696–703.

Chapman, S. (2003, December 10). Meet the greedy grandparents: Why America's elderly are so spoiled. *Slate.*

Chatterjee, A., & DeVol, R. (2012). *Best cities for successful aging.* Santa Monica, CA: Milken Institute.

Chen, P. C., & Wilmoth, J. M. (2004). The effects of residential mobility on ADL and IADL limitations among the very old living in the community. *Journal of Gerontology: Social Sciences, 59*(3), S164–172.

Chen, S.-L., Brown, J.W., Mefford, L.C., de La Roche, A., McLain, A.M., Haun, M.W., et al. (2008). Elders' decisions to enter assisted living facilities: A grounded theory study. *Journal of Housing for the Elderly, 22*(1), 86–103.

Choi, J.S. (2004). Evaluation of community planning and life of senior cohousing projects in northern European countries. *European Planning Studies, 12*(8), 1189–1216.

Choi, N. G., Wilson, N. L., Sirrianni, L., Marinucci, M. L., & Hegel, M. T. (2014). Acceptance of home-based telehealth problem-solving therapy for depressed, low-income homebound older adults: Qualitative interviews with the participants and aging-service case managers. *The Gerontologist, 54*(4), 704–13.

Chou, S.C., Boldy, D.P., & Lee, A.H. (2003). Factors influencing residents' satisfaction in residential aged care. *The Gerontologist, 43*(4), 459–472.

Christopherson, R.C. (2005). Missing the forest for the trees: The illusory half-policy of senior citizen property tax relief. *Elder Law Journal, 13,* 195–226.

Citizens' Housing and Planning Association. (2005). *Age restricted active adult housing in Massachusetts.* Boston: Citizens' Housing and Planning Association.

Clarke, P., Ailshire, J.A., Bader, M., Morenoff, J.D., & House, J.S. (2008). Mobility disability and the urban built environment. *American Journal of Epidemiology, 168*(5), 506–513.

Clarke, P., & George, L.K. (2005). The role of the built environment in the disablement process. *American Journal of Public Health, 95*(11), 1933–1939.

Clarke, P., Morenoff, J., Debbink, M., Golberstein, E., Elliott, M.R., & Lantz, P.M. (2014). Cumulative exposure to neighborhood context: Consequences for health transitions over the adult life course. *Research on Aging, 36*(1), 115–142.

Clemmitt, M. (2006). Caring for the elderly. *Congressional Quarterly Researcher, 16*(36), 841–864.

Clemson, L., Mackenzie, L., Ballinger, C., Close, J.C., & Cumming, R.G. (2008). Environmental interventions to prevent falls in community-dwelling older people: A meta-analysis of randomized trials. *Journal of Aging Health,* 20(8), 954–971.

Cloutier-Fisher, D., & Harvey, J. (2009). Home beyond the house: Experiences of place in an evolving retirement community. *Journal of Environmental Psychology, 29*(2), 246–255.

Cnaan, R. A., Boddie, S. C., & Kang, J. (2005). Religious congregations as social services providers for older adults. *Journal of Gerontological Social Work, 45*(1–2), 105–130.

Coe, N.B., & Boyle, M.H. (2009). *The asset and income profile of residents in senior care communities.* Boston: Center for Retirement Research at Boston College.

Coe, N. B., & Wu, A. Y. (2014). Who pays for seniors housing and care communities? Evidence from the Residents Financial Survey. *Journal of Housing for the Elderly, 28,* 165–181.

Cohen, L.W., & Zimmerman, S. (2010). Evidence behind the green house and similar models of nursing home care. *Aging Health, 6*(6), 717.

Cohen, R. (2010). *Connecting residents of subsidized housing with mainstream supportive services: Challenges and recommendations.* Washington, DC: Center for Housing Policy.

Colello, K.J. (2007). *Supportive services programs to naturally occurring retirement communities.* Washington, DC: Congressional Research Service.

Coleman, E. A., Parry, C., Chalmers, S., & Min, S. J. (2006). The care transitions intervention: Results of a randomized controlled trial. *Archives of Internal Medicine, 166*(17), 1822–1828.

Coleman, P.G., & O'Hanlon, A. (2004). *Ageing and development.* London: Arnold.

Collins, A.L., Goldman, N., & Rodriguez, G. (2007). *Are life satisfaction and optimism protective of health among older adults?* Princeton, NJ: Princeton University, Office of Population Research.

Collins, A.L., Goldman, N., & Rodriguez, G. (2008). Is positive well-being protective of mobility limitations among older adults? *Journal of Gerontology: Social Sciences, 63*(6), P321–327.

Collopy, B.J. (1995). Home versus nursing home: Getting beyond the differences. In E. Olson, E.R. Chichin, & L.S. Libow (Eds.), *Controversies in ethics in long-term care* (pp. 57–72). New York: Springer.

Commission on Affordable Housing and Health Facility Needs for Seniors in the 21st Century. (2002). *A quiet crisis in America: A report to Congress.* Washington, DC: U.S. Government Printing Office.

Connecticut Continuing Care Residents Association. (n.d.). *Continuing care retirement communities: A guide book for the Connecticut consumer.* Stamford, CT: LeadingAge.

Connell, C.M., Harmon, A., Janevic, M.R., & Kostyniuk, L.P. (2013). Older adults' driving reduction and cessation: Perspectives of adult children. *Journal of Applied Gerontology, 32*(8), 975–996.

Consumer Financial Protection Bureau. (2012). *Reverse mortgages: Report to Congress.* Washington, DC: Consumer Financial Protection Bureau.

Cornman, J.C., & Freedman, V.A. (2008). Racial and ethnic disparities in mobility device use in late life. *Journal of Gerontology: Social Sciences, 63*(1), S34–S41.

Cornman, J.C., Freedman, V.A., & Agree, E.M. (2005). Measurement of assistive device use: Implications for estimates of device use and disability in late life. *The Gerontologist, 45*(3), 347–358.

Cornwell, B., Laumann, E.O., & Schumm, L.P. (2008). The social connectedness of older adults: A national profile. *American Sociological Review, 73*(2), 185–203.

Cornwell, E.Y. (2014). Social resources and disordered living conditions: Evidence from a national sample of community-residing older adults. *Research on Aging, 36*(4), 399–430.

Cornwell, E.Y., & Waite, L.J. (2009). Social disconnectedness, perceived isolation, and health among older adults. *Journal of Health and Social Behavior, 50*(1), 31–48.

Costello, E., & Edelstein, J.E. (2008). Update on falls prevention for community-dwelling older adults: Review of single and multifactorial intervention programs. *Journal of Rehabilitation Research and Development, 45*(8), 1135–1152.

Cotrell, V., & Carder, P.C. (2010). Health-related needs assessment of older residents in subsidized housing. *Cityscape, 12*(2), 47–66.

Courtney, K.L. (2008). Privacy and senior willingness to adopt smart home information technology in residential care facilities. *Methods Informatics Medicine, 47*(1), 76–81.

Craig, B.M. (2008). *Naturally occurring retirement community (NORC) supportive services congressional earmark demonstrations (FY 2002–FY 2005)*. Washington, DC: Administration on Aging, U.S. Department of Health and Human Services (unpublished manuscript).

Creech, A., Hallam, S., McQueen, H., & Varvarigou, M. (2013). The power of music in the lives of older adults. *Research Studies in Music Education, 35*(1), 87–102.

Cromartie, J., & Nelson, P. (2009). *Baby boom migration and its impact on rural America*. Washington, DC: U.S. Department of Agriculture, Economic Research Service.

Csikszentmihalyi, M., & Rochberg-Halton, E. (1981). *The meaning of things: Domestic symbols and the self*. Cambridge, UK: Cambridge University Press.

Cuba, L. (1991). Models of migration decision making reexamined: The destination search of older migrants to Cape Cod. *The Gerontologist, 31*(2), 204–209.

Cumming, E., & Henry, W. (1961). *Growing old: The process of disengagement*. New York: Basic Books.

Cumming, J., & Cumming, E. (1963). *Ego and milieu*. New York: Atherton Press.

Daffner, K.R., Chong, H., Riis, J., Rentz, D.M., Wolk, D.A., Budson, A.E., & Holcomb, P.J. (2007). Cognitive status impacts age-related changes in attention to novel and target events in normal adults. *Neuropsychology, 21*(3), 291–300.

Dal Santo, T.S. (2009). *Senior center literature review*. Sacramento: California Commission on Aging.

Davidoff, T. (2004). *Maintenance and the home equity of the elderly*. Berkeley: University of California, Berkeley, Haas School of Business, Fisher Center for Real Estate and Urban Economics Paper No. 03-288.

Davis, L.S. (2012, October 3). The tragedy of modern retirement communities. *The Atlantic Cities*.

Davoudi, S. (2012). Resilience: A bridging concept or a dead end? *Planning Theory & Practice, 12*(2), 299–333.

De Jong, G.F., Wilmoth, J.M., Angel, J.L., & Cornwell, G.T. (1995). Motive and the geographic mobility of very old Americans. *Journal of Gerontology: Social Sciences, 50*(6), S395–404.

Del Webb. (2010). *2010 Del Webb baby boomer survey*. Bloomfield Hills, MI: PulteGroup.

Demiris, G., & Hensel, B.K. (2008). Technologies for an aging society: A systematic review of "smart home" applications. *IMIA Yearbook of Medical Informatics, 47*(Suppl), 33–40.

Demiris, G., & Hensel, B. (2009). "Smart homes" for patients at the end of life. *Journal of Housing for the Elderly, 23*(1), 106–115.

Demiris, G., Hensel, B.K., Skubic, M., & Rantz, M. (2008). Senior residents' perceived need of and preferences for "smart home" sensor technologies. *International Journal of Technology Assessment in Health Care, 24*(1), 120–124.

Demiris, G., Oliver, D.P., Dickey, G., Skubic, M., & Rantz, M. (2008). Findings from a participatory evaluation of a smart home application for older adults. *Technology and Health Care, 16*(2), 111–118.

Demiris, G., Oliver, D.P., Giger, J., Skubic, M., & Rantz, M. (2009). Older adults' privacy considerations for vision based recognition methods of eldercare applications. *Technology and Health Care, 17*(1), 41–48.

Denhardt, J., & Denhardt, R. (2010). Building organizational resilience and adaptive management. In J.W. Reich, A.J. Zautra & J.S. Hall (Eds.), *Handbook of adult resilience* (pp. 333–349). New York: Guilford Press.

De Nardi, M., French, E., & Jones, J. B. (2014). *Medicaid and the elderly*. Boston: Center for Retirement Research at Boston College.

Diehl, M., & Willis, S.L. (2003). Everyday competence and everyday problem solving in aging adults: The role of physical and social context. In H.-W. Wahl, R.J. Scheidt & P.G. Windley (Eds.), *Annual review of gerontology and geriatrics*, Vol. 23, *Aging in context: Socio-physical environments* (pp. 130–166). New York: Springer.

Diez Roux, A.V. (2002). Invited commentary: Places, people, and health. *American Journal of Epidemiology, 155*(6), 516–519.

Dishman, E. (2012). Technology solutions. In H. Cisneros, M. Dyer-Chamberlain & J. Hickie (Eds.), *Independent for life* (pp. 99–112). Austin: University of Texas Press.

Dosa, D., Hyer, K., Thomas, K., Swaminathan, S., Feng, Z., Brown, L., & Mor, V. (2012). To evacuate or shelter in place: Implications of universal hurricane evacuation policies on nursing home residents. *Journal of the American Medical Directors Association, 13*(2), 190 e1–7.

Doty, P., Mahoney, K.J., & Sciegaj, M. (2010). New state strategies to meet long-term care needs. *Health Affairs, 29*(1), 49–56.

Doxiadēs, K.A. (1968). *Ekistics: An introduction to the science of human settlements.* New York: Oxford University Press.

Duany, A., Plater-Zyberk, E., & Speck, J. (2000). *Suburban nation: The rise of sprawl and the decline of the American dream.* New York: North Point Press.

Dudgeon, B.J., Hoffman, J.M., Ciol, M.A., Shumway-Cook, A., Yorkston, K.M., & Chan, L. (2008). Managing activity difficulties at home: A survey of Medicare beneficiaries. *Archives of Physical Medicine and Rehabilitation, 89*(7), 1256–1261.

Dugan, E., Barton, K.N., Coyle, C., & Lee, C.M. (2013). U.S. Policies to enhance older driver safety: A systematic review of the literature. *Journal of Aging & Social Policy, 25*(4), 335–352.

Dugas, C. (2013). Long-term care: Investigate your options early. *USA Today, May 29.*

Dumbaugh, E. (2008). Designing communities to enhance the safety and mobility of older adults: A universal approach. *Journal of Planning Literature, 23*(1), 17–36.

Duncombe, W., Robbins, M., & Wolf, D.A. (2003). Place characteristics and residential location choice among the retirement-age population. *Journal of Gerontology: Social Sciences, 58*(4), S244–252.

Dunham, C.C., & Cannon, J.H. (2008). "They're still in control enough to be in control": Paradox of power in dementia caregiving. *Journal of Aging Studies, 22*(1), 45–53.

Dunham-Jones, E., & Williamson, J. (2011). *Retrofitting suburbia: Urban design solutions for redesigning suburbs.* Hoboken, NJ: Wiley.

Durazo, E.M., Jones, M.R., Wallace, S.P., Arsdale, J.V., & Aydin, M. (2011). *The health status and unique health challenges of rural older adults in California.* Los Angeles: UCLA Center for Health Policy Research.

Durrett, C. (2009). *The senior cohousing handbook: A community approach to independent living.* Gabriola Island, BC: New Society Publishers.

Durrett, C. (2011). *Creating cohousing: Building sustainable communities.* Gabriola Island, BC: New Society Publishers.

Dychtwald, K., & Baxter, D. (2011). *Five myths & realities of continuing care retirement communities.* Emeryville, CA: Age Wave.

Eckenwiler, L. (2007). *Caring about long-term care: An ethical framework for caregiving.* Washington, DC: Center for American Progress.

Eckert, J.K., Morgan, L.A., Carder, P.C., Frankowski, A.C., & Roth, E.G. (2009). *Inside assisted living.* Baltimore, MD: The John Hopkins University Press.

Eckroth-Bucher, M. (2008). Devious damage: Elder psychological abuse. *Aging Well Magazine, 1*(4), 24–27.

Eiken, S., Burwell, B., & Sredl, K. (2013). An examination of the woodwork effect using national medicaid long-term services and supports data. *Journal of Aging & Social Policy, 25*(2), 134–145.

Eiken, S., Sredl, K., Gold, L., Kasten, J., Burwell, B., & Saucier, P. (2014). *Medicaid expenditures for long-term services and supports in FY 2012* Ann Arbor, MI: Truven Health Analytics.

Ekeland, A. G., Bowes, A., & Flottorp, S. (2010). Effectiveness of telemedicine: A systematic review of reviews. *International Journal of Medical Informatics, 79*(11), 736–771.

Ekerdt, D.J., & Sergeant, J.F. (2006). Family things: Attending the household disbandment of older adults. *Journal of Aging Studies, 20*(3), 193–205.

Ekerdt, D.J., Sergeant, J.F., Dingel, M., & Bowen, M.E. (2004). Household disbandment in later life. *Journal of Gerontology: Social Sciences, 59*(5), S265–273.

Elderly Housing Coalition. (2000). *Providing an affordable continuum of care for low-income residents of senior housing.* Washington, DC: American Association of Homes and Services for the Aging, The Elderly Housing Coalition.

Ellenbecker, C.H., Byrne, K., O'Brien, E., & Rogosta, C. (2002). Nursing clinics in elder housing: Providing access and improving health care outcomes. *Journal of Community Health Nursing, 19*(1), 7–15.

Engelhardt, G.V. (2006). *Housing trends among baby boomers.* Washington, DC: Research Institute for Housing America.

Engelhardt, G.V., Eriksen, M.D., & Greenhalgh-Stanley, N. (2013). *A profile of housing and health among older Americans.* Washington, DC: Research Institute for Housing America.

Engquist, G., Johnson, C., & Johnson, W.C. (2010). *Medicaid-funded long-term supports and services: Snapshots of innovation.* Washington, DC: Center for Health Care Strategies.

Enguidanos, S., Pynoos, J., Siciliano, M., Diepenbrock, L., & Alexman, S. (2010). Integrating community services within a NORC: The Park La Brea experience. *Cityscape, 12*(2), 29–45.

Enterprise Community Partners. (2011, March 10–11). *Summit on aging in place in public housing.* Atlanta, GA: Hosted by Enterprise Community Partners, Inc., LeadingAge.

Evashwick, C., & Holt, T.J. (2000). *Integrating long-term care, acute care, and housing: Building success through a continuum of care*. St. Louis, MO: The Catholic Health Association of the United States.

Evercare. (2007). *Family caregivers: What they spend, what they sacrifice*. Minnetonka, MN: Evercare.

Evercare & National Alliance for Caregiving. (2008). *Hispanic family caregiving in the U.S.* Bethesda, MD: National Alliance for Caregiving.

Fagan, L.A. (2007). Funding sources for home modification services. *Home & Community Health, 14*(3), 1–4.

Farber, N., & Shinkle, D. (2011). *Aging in place: A state survey of livability policies and practices*. Washington, DC: AARP Public Policy Institute.

Fausset, C.B., Kelly, A.J., Rogers, W.A., & Fisk, A.D. (2011). Challenges to aging in place: Understanding home maintenance difficulties. *Journal of Housing for the Elderly, 25*(2), 125–141.

Federal Interagency Forum on Aging-Related Statistics. (2010). *Older Americans 2010: Key indicators of well-being*. Washington, DC: U.S. Government Printing Office.

Federal Interagency Forum on Aging-Related Statistics. (2012). *Older Americans 2012: Key indicators of well-being*. Washington, DC: U.S. Government Printing Office.

Feldman, P.H., & Oberlink, M.R. (2003). The AdvantAge initiative: Developing community indicators to promote the health and well-being of older people. *Family and Community Health, 26*(4), 268–274.

Feldman, P.H., Oberlink, M., Simantov, E., & Gursen, M.D. (2004). *A tale of two older Americas: Community opportunities and challenges: AdvantAge initiative*. New York: Visiting Nurse Service of New York, Center for Home Care Policy and Research.

Feng, Z., Fennell, M.L., Tyler, D.A., Clark, M., & Mor, V. (2011). The care span: Growth of racial and ethnic minorities in U.S. Nursing homes driven by demographics and possible disparities in options. *Health Affairs, 30*(7), 1358–1365.

Fenton. (2011). *Health care's blind side: The overlooked connection between social needs and good health*. Princeton, NJ: Robert Wood Johnson Foundation.

Ferrini, A.F., & Ferrini, R.L. (2008). *Health in the later years*. New York: McGraw Hill.

Ficke, R.C., & Berkowitz, S.G. (2000). *Report to Congress: Evaluation of the HOPE for elderly independence demonstration program and the new congregate housing services program*. Washington, DC: U.S. Department of Housing and Urban Development.

Fields, N.L., Anderson, K.A., & Dabelko-Schoeny, H. (2014). The effectiveness of adult day services for older adults: A review of the literature from 2000 to 2011. *Journal of Applied Gerontology, 33*(2), 130–163.

Fienberg, L. (2012). *Moving toward person- and family-centered care*. Washington, DC: AARP Public Policy.

Fienberg, L. (2013). *Keeping up with the times: Supporting family caregivers with workplace leave policies*. Washington, DC: AARP Public Policy.

Fienberg, L., Reinhard, S.C., Houser, A., & Choula, R. (2011). *Valuing the invaluable: 2011 update—the growing contributions and costs of family caregiving*. Washington, DC: AARP Public Policy Institute.

Filipe, S.-H. (1996). Motivation and emotion. In J.E. Birren & K.W. Schaie (Eds.), *Handbook for psychology and aging* (4th ed., pp. 218–235). San Diego: Academic Press.

Finkelstein, R., Garcia, A., Netherland, J., & Walker, J. (2008). *Toward an age-friendly New York City: A findings report*. New York: The New York Academy of Medicine.

Fisher, J.D., Johnson, D.S., Marchand, J.T., Smeeding, T.M., & Torrey, B.B. (2007). No place like home: Older adults and their housing. *Journal of Gerontology: Social Sciences, 62*(2), S120–128.

Fiske, D.W., & Maddi, S.W. (1961). A conceptual framework. In D. W. Fiske & S. W. Maddi (Eds.), *Functions of varied experience* (pp. 11–56). Homewood, IL: The Dorsey Press.

Florida Department of Elder Affairs. (2004). *Florida's senior centers: Bring the picture into focus*. Tallahassee: Florida Association of Senior Centers.

The Florida Senate. (2011). *Senate interim work plan 2012 session, report 2012-128, review regulatory oversight of assisted living facilities in Florida. Tallahassee,* Florida: Retrieved from http://www.flsenate.gov/UserContent/Session/2012/Publications/Interim Reports/pdf/workplan.pdf

Fogel, B.S. (1992). Psychological aspects of staying at home. *Generations, 16*(2), 15–19.

Foley, D.J., Heimovitz, H.K., Guralnic, J.M., & Brock, D.B. (2002). Driving life expectancy of persons aged 70 and older in the United States. *American Journal of Public Health, 92*(8), 1284–1289.

Forlizzi, J., DiSalvo, C., & Gemperle, F. (2004). Assistive robotics and an ecology of elders living independently in their homes. *Human Computer Interaction, 19,* 25–59.

Fox-Grage, W., & Redfoot, D. (2011). *Medicaid: A program of last resort for people who need long-term services and supports*. Washington, DC: AARP Public Policy Institute.

Fox-Grage, W., & Ujvari, K. (2014). *The Older Americans Act*. Washington, DC: AARP Public Policy Institute.

Fox-Grage, W., & Walls, J. (2013). *State studies find home and community-based services to be cost-effective*. Washington, DC: AARP Public Policy Institute.

Fredman, L., Cauley, J.A., Satterfield, S., Simonsick, E., Spencer, S.M., Ayonayon, H.N., et al. (2008). Caregiving, mortality, and mobility decline: The health, aging, and body composition study. *Archives of Internal Medicine, 168*(19), 2154–2162.

Fredrickson, B.L. (2001). The role of positive emotions in positive psychology. The broaden-and-build theory of positive emotions. *American Psychologist, 56*(3), 218–226.

Freedman, V.A., & Agree, E.M. (2008). *Home modifications: Use, cost, and interactions with functioning among near-elderly and older adults.* Washington: Office of the Assistant Secretary for Planning and Evaluation.

Freedman, V.A., Agree, E.M., Martin, L.G., & Cornman, J.C. (2005). Trends in the use of assistive technology and personal care for late-life disability, 1992–2001. *The Gerontologist, 46*(1), 124–127.

Freedman, V.A., Spillman, B., Andreski, P., Cornman, J., Crimmins, E., Kramarow, E., et al. (2013). Trends in late-life activity limitations in the United States: An update from five national surveys. *Demography, 50*(2), 661–671.

Freeman, M. (2006–2007). The social-purpose encore career: Baby boomers, civic engagement, and the next stage of work. *Generations, 30*(4), 41–46.

Frey, W.H. (2007). *Mapping the growth of older America: Seniors and boomers in the early 21st century.* Washington, DC: The Brookings Institution, Center on Urban and Metropolitan Policy.

Frey, W.H. (2013). *Millennial and senior migrants follow different post-recession paths.* Washington, DC: Brookings Institution.

Fried, M. (2000). Continuities and discontinuities of place. *Journal of Environmental Psychology, 20,* 193–205.

Frolik, L.A. (2008). *Residence options for older and disabled clients.* Chicago: American Bar Association.

Fry, R., Parker, K., Passel, J. S., & Rohal, M. (2014). *In post-recession era, young adults drive continuing rise in multi-generational living.* Washington, DC: Pew Research Center.

Fuller-Thomson, E., & Minkler, M. (2001). American grandparents providing extensive child care to their grandchildren: Prevalence and profile. *The Gerontologist, 41*(2), 201–209.

Gardner, P.J. (2011). Natural neighborhood networks: Important social networks in the lives of older adults aging in place. *Journal of Aging Studies, 25*(3), 263–271.

Gaugler, J.E., Jarrott, S.E., Zarit, S.H., Stephens, M.-A.P., Townsend, A., & Greene, R. (2003). Respite for dementia caregivers: The effects of adult day service use on caregiving hours and care demands. *International Psychogeriatrics, 15*(01), 37–58.

Gaugler, J.E., Zarit, S.H., Townsend, A., Stephens, M.P., & Greene, R. (2003). Evaluating community-based programs for dementia caregivers: The cost implications of adult day services. *Journal of Applied Gerontology, 22*(1), 118–133.

Gecas, V. (1989). The social psychology of self-efficacy. *Annual Review of Sociology, 15,* 291–216.

Genworth Financial. (2006). *The impact of long term care on women.* New York: Genworth Financial.

Genworth Financial. (2010). *Our family, our future.* New York: Genworth Financial.

Genworth Financial. (2012). *Genworth 2012, cost of care survey.* New York: Genworth Financial.

Genworth Financial. (2014). *Genworth 2014, cost of care survey.* New York: Genworth Financial.

George, L.K. (2006). Perceived quality of life. In R. H. Binstock & L. K. George (Eds.), *Handbook of aging and the social sciences* (pp. 320–336). New York: Academic Press.

Gerace, A. (2012, June 27). Boomer caregivers keeping seniors out of long-term care facilities. *Senior Housing News.*

Gerace, A. (2013a, May 21). Old state laws present new problems for senior living. *Senior Housing News.*

Gerace, A. (2013b, April 7). Senior housing occupancy expected to reach 89.7% in 2013. *Senior Housing News.*

Gershon, R., Canton, A., Raveis, V., Silver, A., Chen, C., Qureshi, K., et al. (2008). Household-related hazardous conditions with implications for patient safety in the home health care sector. *Journal of Patient Safety, 4*(4), 227–234.

Ghosh, A., Schmitz, R., & Brown, R. (2014). *Effect of PACE on costs, nursing home admissions, and mortality: 2006–2011.* Washington, DC: Office of Disability, Agoing and Long-Term Care Policy, U.S. Department of Health and Human Services.

Gibson, M.J., Kelly, K.A., & Kaplan, A.K. (2012). *Family caregiving and transitional care: A critical review.* San Francisco, CA: Family Caregiver Alliance.

Ginzler, E. (2012). From home to hospice: The range of housing alternatives. In H. Cisneros, M. Dyer-Chamberlain & J. Hickie (Eds.), *Independent for life* (pp. 53–69). Austin: University of Texas Press.

Gitlin, L.N. (2000). Adjusting "person–environment systems": Helping older people live the "good life" at home. In R.L. Rubinstein, M. Moss, & M.H. Kleban (Eds.), *The many dimensions of aging* (pp. 41–53). New York: Springer.

Gitlin, L.N., Hauck, W.W., Winter, L., Dennis, M.P., & Schulz, R. (2006). Effect of an in-home occupational and physical therapy intervention on reducing mortality in functionally vulnerable older people: Preliminary findings. *Journal of American Geriatrics Society, 54*(6), 950–955.

Gitlin, L.N., Reever, K., Dennis, M.P., Mathieu, E., & Hauck, W.W. (2006). Enhancing quality of life of families who use adult day services: Short- and long-term effects of the adult day services plus program. *The Gerontologist, 46*(5), 630–639.

Gitlin, L.N., Winter, L., Vause Earland, T., Adel Herge, E., Chernett, N.L., Piersol, C.V., et al. (2009). The tailored activity program to reduce behavioral symptoms in individuals with dementia: Feasibility, acceptability, and replication potential. *The Gerontologist, 49*(3), 428–439.

Glass, A.P. (2014). Elder cohousing: The epitome of aging in community, American Society on Aging Ageblog. Retrieved from http://asaging.org/blog/elder-cohousing-epitome-aging-community.

Glass, A.P., & Vander Plaats, R.S. (2013). A conceptual model for aging better together intentionally. *Journal of Aging Studies, 27*(4), 428–442.

Glass, T.A., & Balfour, J.L. (2003). Neighborhoods, aging, and functional limitations. In I. Kawachi & L.F. Berkman (Eds.), *Neighborhoods and health* (pp. 303–334). Oxford, UK: Oxford University Press.

Gleckman, H. (2009). *Caring for our parents: Inspiring stories of families seeking new solutions to America's most urgent health crisis.* New York: St. Martin's Press.

Gober, P., & Zonn, L.E. (1983). Kin and elderly amenity migration. *The Gerontologist, 23*(3), 288–294.

Gobillon, L., & Wolff, F.-C. (2011). Housing and location choices of retiring households: Evidence from France. *Urban Studies, 48*(2), 331–347.

Goda, G.S., Golberstein, E., & Grabowski, D.C. (2011). Income and the utilization of long-term care services: Evidence from the social security benefit notch. *Journal of Health Economics, 30*(4), 719–729.

Golant, S.M. (1975). Residential concentrations of the future elderly. *The Gerontologist, 15*(II), 16–23.

Golant, S.M. (1976). Intraurban transportation needs and problems of the elderly. In M.P. Lawton, R. Newcomer, & T.O. Byerts (Eds.), *Community planning for an aged society* (pp. 282–316). Stroudsburg, PA: Dowden, Hutchinson, and Ross.

Golant, S.M. (1984). *A place to grow old: The meaning of environment in old age.* New York: Columbia University Press.

Golant, S.M. (1985). In defense of age-segregated housing. *Aging, 348,* 22–26.

Golant, S.M. (1986). Subjective housing assessments by the elderly: A critical information source for planning and program evaluation. *The Gerontologist, 26,* 122–127.

Golant, S.M. (1992). *Housing America's elderly: Many possibilities, few choices.* Newbury Park, CA: Sage.

Golant, S.M. (1998a). Changing an older person's shelter and care setting: A model to explain personal and environmental outcomes. In P.G. Windley & R.J. Scheidt (Eds.), *Environment and aging theory: A focus on housing* (pp. 34–60). New York: Greenwood Press.

Golant, S.M. (1998b). The promise of assisted living as a shelter and care alternative for frail American elders: A cautionary essay. In B. Schwarz & R. Brent (Eds.), *Aging, autonomy, and architecture: Advances in assisted living* (pp. 32–59). Baltimore, MD: John Hopkins Press.

Golant, S.M. (1999). *The CASERA project.* Tallahassee, FL: Stephen M. Golant and Margaret Lynn Duggar & Associates, Inc.

Golant, S.M. (2003a). Conceptualizing time and space in environmental gerontology: A pair of old issues deserving new thought. *The Gerontologist, 43*(5), 638–648.

Golant, S.M. (2003b, Fall). Government-assisted rental accommodations: Should they accommodate homeowners with unmet needs? *Maine Policy Review,* pp. 36–57.

Golant, S.M. (2003c). Political and organizational barriers to satisfying low-income U.S. seniors need for affordable rental housing with supportive services. *Journal of Aging and Social Policy, 12*(2), 36–57.

Golant, S.M. (2003d). The urban–rural distinction in gerontology: An update of research. In H.-W. Wahl, R. Scheidt, & P. Windley (Eds.), *Annual review of gerontology and geriatrics* (pp. 280–312). New York: Springer.

Golant, S.M. (2005). Invited commentary: Subjective health and the dangers of absent individual effects and crude contextual proxies of causal mechanisms. *Journal of Gerontology: Social Sciences, 60*(4), S191–192.

Golant, S.M. (2006). Supportive housing for frail, low-income older adults: Identifying need and allocating resources. *Generations, 24*(4), 37–43.

Golant, S.M. (2008a). Affordable clustered housing–care: A category of long-term care options for the elderly poor. *Journal of Housing for the Elderly, 22*(1/2), 3–44.

Golant, S.M. (2008b). Commentary: Irrational exuberance for the aging in place of vulnerable low-income older homeowners. *Journal of Aging and Social Policy, 20*(4), 379–397.

Golant, S.M. (2008c). The future of assisted living residences: A response to uncertainty. In S.M. Golant & J. Hyde (Eds.), *The assisted living residence: A vision for the future* (pp. 3–45). Baltimore, MD: The John Hopkins University Press.

Golant, S.M. (2008d). Low-income elderly homeowners in very old dwellings: The need for public policy debate. *Journal of Aging and Social Policy, 20*(1), 1–28.

Golant, S.M. (2009a). Aging in place solutions for older Americans: Groupthink responses not always in their best interests. *Public Policy & Aging Report, 19*(1), 33–39.

Golant, S.M. (2009b, July/August). Aging in the American suburbs. *Aging Well Magazine.* Retrieved from http://todaysgeriatricmedicine.com/news/ex_06309_01.shtml

Golant, S.M. (2009c). The gender inequalities of eldercare. *Aging Today, 30*(2), 2.

Golant, S.M. (2011a). The changing residential environments of older people. In R.H. Binstock & L.K. George (Eds.), *Handbook of aging and the social sciences* (7th ed., pp. 207–220). New York: Academic Press.

Golant, S.M. (2011b). The quest for residential normalcy by older adults: Relocation but one pathway. *Journal of Aging Studies, 25*(3), 193–205.

Golant, S.M. (2012). Out of their residential comfort and mastery zones: Toward a more relevant environmental gerontology. *Journal of Housing for the Elderly, 26*(1/2), 26–43.

Golant, S.M. (2014a). *Age-friendly communities: Are we expecting too much?* Montreal: Institute for Research on Public Policy.

Golant, S.M. (2014b, May 18). Residential normalcy and the enriched coping repertoires of successfully aging older adults. *The Gerontologist.* Retrieved from http:// gerontologist.oxfordjournals.org/ content/ early/2014/05/18/geront.gnu036.abstract

Golant, S.M., & Hyde, J. (Eds.). (2008). *The assisted living residence: A vision for the future.* Baltimore, MD: The John Hopkins University Press.

Golant, S.M., & Hyde, J. (2015). Assisted living. In G. Rowles & P.B. Teaster (Eds.), *Long-term care in an aging society.* Clinton Park, NY: Delmar Cengage Learning.

Golant, S.M., & Lagreca, A.J. (1994a). Differences in the housing quality of white, black, and Hispanic United States elderly households. *Journal of Applied Gerontology, 13*(4), 413–437.

Golant, S.M., & Lagreca, A.J. (1994b). Housing quality of U.S. elderly households: Does aging in place matter? *The Gerontologist, 34*(6), 803–814.

Golant, S.M., Parsons, P., & Boling, P.A. (2010). Assessing the quality of care found in affordable clustered housing–care arrangements: Key to informing public policy. *Cityscape, 12*(2), 5–28.

Golant, S.M., & Salmon, J.R. (2004). The unequal availability of affordable assisted living units in Florida's counties. *Journal of Applied Gerontology, 23*(4), 349–369.

Golden, J., Conroy, R.M., Bruce, I., Denihan, A., Greene, E., Kirby, M., & Lawlor, B.A. (2009). Loneliness, social support networks, mood and wellbeing in community- dwelling elderly. *International Journal of Geriatric Psychiatry, 24*(7), 694–700.

Grabowski, D.C. (2006). The cost-effectiveness of noninstitutional long-term care services: Review and synthesis of the most recent evidence. *Medical Care Research and Review, 63*(1), 3–28.

Grabowski, D.C., Stevenson, D.G., & Cornell, P.Y. (2012). Assisted living expansion and the market for nursing home care. *Health Services Research,* 1–20.

Grafova, I.B., Freedman, V.A., Kumar, R., & Rogowski, J. (2008). Neighborhoods and obesity in later life. *American Journal of Public Health, 98*(11), 2065–2071.

Graham, J. (2012, September 17). A choice of community care, in your own home. *The New York Times.*

Grant, J.L. (2007). Two sides of a coin? New urbanism and gated communities. *Housing Policy Debate, 18*(3), 481–501.

Greenberg, M.R. (2014). *Protecting seniors against environmental disasters: From hazards and vulnerability to prevention and resilience.* New York: Routledge, Earthscan.

Greene, A.M., Wiener, J.M., Khatutsky, G., Johnson, R., & O'Keeffe, J. (2013). *Medicaid in residential care.* Washington, DC: Office of Disability, Aging and Long-Term Care Policy, U.S. Department of Health and Human Services.

Greene, K. (2006, October 2). Forget golf courses, beaches & mountains. *The Wall Street Journal,* pp. R1, R4.

Greenfield, E.A. (2011). *An overview of naturally occurring retirement community supportive services programs in New Jersey.* New Brunswick, NJ: Rutgers School of Social Work.

Greenfield, E.A. (2013). Community aging initiatives and social capital: Developing theories of change in the context of NORC supportive service programs. *Journal of Applied Gerontology, 33*(2), 227–250.

Greenfield, E.A., & Russell, D. (2011). Identifying living arrangements that heighten risk for loneliness in later life: Evidence from the U.S. national social life, health, and aging project. *Journal of Applied Gerontology, 30*(4), 524–534.

Greenfield, E.A., Scharlach, A., Graham, C.L., Davitt, J. K., & Lehning, A.J. (2012). *A national overview of villages: Results from a 2012 organizational survey.* New Brunswick, NJ: Rutgers School of Social Work.

Greenfield, E.A., Scharlach, A., Lehning, A.J., & Davitt, J.K. (2012). A conceptual framework for examining the promise of the NORC program and Village models to promote aging in place. *Journal of Aging Studies, 26*(3), 273–284.

Greenfield, E.A., Scharlach, A.E., Lehning, A.J., Davitt, J.K., & Graham, C.L. (2013). A tale of two community initiatives for promoting aging in place: Similarities and differences in the national implementation of NORC programs and villages. *The Gerontologist, 53*(6), 928–938.

Greenhouse, E. (2012). The home environment and aging. In H. Cisneros, M. Dyer-Chamberlain & J. Hickie (Eds.), *Independent for life* (pp. 87–97). Austin, TX: University of Texas Press.

Greenwood, R. (2001). *The PACE model*. Washington, DC: Center for Medicare Education.

Gross, J. (2005, November 10). When experts need experts. *The New York Times*.

Gross, J. (2008, November 3). Commended, not condemned: A reader on assisted living. *New York Times*.

Gross, J. (2008, September 25). Dividing the caregiving duties, it's daughters versus sons. *The New York Times*.

Gross, J. (2013, March 1). Why can't I live with people like me? *New York Times*.

Grossman, B.R., Kitchener, M., Mullan, J.T., & Harrington, C. (2007). Paid personal assistance services: An exploratory study of working-age consumers' perspectives. *Journal of Aging and Social Policy, 19*(3), 27–45.

Gubrium, J.F. (1973). *The myth of the golden years*. Springfield, NJ: Charles Thomas.

Gubrium, J.F. (1975). *Living and dying at Murray Manor*. New York: St. Martin's.

Gubrium, J.F. (1993). *Speaking of life: Horizons of meanings for nursing home residents*. New York: Aldine De Gruyter.

Gubrium, J.F., Rittman, M.R., Williams, C., Young, M.E., & Boylstein, C.A. (2003). Benchmarking as everyday functional assessment in stroke recovery. *Journal of Gerontology: Social Sciences, 58*(4), S203–211.

Gubrium, J.F., & Sankar, A. (Eds.). (1990). *The home care experience*. Newbury Park, CA: Sage.

Guengerich, T. (2009). *Caregiving and end-of-life issues: A survey of AARP members in Florida*. Washington, DC: AARP.

Guerrero, A.M. (2003). *Home improvement finance: Evidence from the 2001 consumer practices survey*. Cambridge, MA: Harvard University, Joint Center for Housing Studies.

Gurin, P., & Brim, O.G. (1984). Change in self in adulthood: The example of sense of control. In P.B. Baltes & O.G. Brim (Eds.), *Life-span development and behavior* (Vol. 6, pp. 281–334). New York: Academic Press.

Haley, B.A., & Gray, R.W. (2008). *Section 202 Supportive Housing for the Elderly: Program status and performance measurement*. Washington, DC: U.S. Department of Housing and Urban Development, Office of Policy Development and Research.

Haley, W.E., Roth, D.L., Howard, G., & Safford, M.M. (2010). Caregiving strain and estimated risk for stroke and coronary heart disease among spouse caregivers: Differential effects by race and sex. *Stroke, 41*(2), 331–336.

Hall, J.S., & Zautra, A.J. (2010). Indicators of community resilience: What are they, why bother? In J.W. Reich, A.J. Zautra, & J.S. Hall (Eds.), *Handbook of adult resilience* (pp. 350–371). New York: Guilford Press.

Halpert, J. (2011, April 28). Retirement: How not to kill your spouse. *The Fiscal Times*.

Hammarström, G., & Torres, S. (2012). Variations in subjective well-being when "aging in place": a matter of acceptance, predictability and control. *Journal of Aging Studies, 26*(2), 192–203.

Hansen, J.C., & Hewitt, M. (2012). PACE provides a sense of belonging for elders. *Generations, 36*(1), 37–43.

Harahan, M.F. (2010–2011). A critical look at the looming long-term care workforce crisis. *Generations, 34*(4), 20–26.

Harrell, R., Brooks, A., & Nedwick, T. (2009). *Preserving affordability and access in livable communities: Subsidized housing opportunities near transit and the 50+ population*. Washington, DC: AARP Public Policy Institute.

Harrell, R., Lynott, J., Guzman, S., & Lampkin, C. (2014). *What is livable? Community preferences of older adults*. Washington, DC: AARP Public Policy Institute.

Harrington, C., Ng, T., Kaye, S.H., & Newcomer, R. (2009). *Home and community-based services: Public policies to improve access, costs, and quality*. San Francisco: University of California, San Francisco, Center for Personal Assistance Services.

Harrington, C., Ng, T., Laplante, M., & Kaye, H.S. (2012). Medicaid home- and community-based services: Impact of the Affordable Care Act. *Journal of Aging & Social Policy, 24*(2), 169–187.

Harris-Kojetin, L., Sengupta, M., Park-Lee, E., & Valverde, R. (2013). *Long-term services in the United States*. Hyattsville, MD: National Center for Health Statistics.

Havighurst, R.J., Neugarten, B.L., & Tobin, S.S. (1968). Disengagement and patterns of aging. In B.L. Neugarten (Ed.), *Middle age and aging: A reader in social psychology* (pp. 161–172). Chicago: The University of Chicago Press.

Hawthorne, F. (2013, September 9). Choices give new meaning to home, sweet home. *The New York Times*.

Hays, J.C. (2002). Living arrangements and health status in later life: A review of recent literature. *Public Health Nursing, 19*(2), 136–151.

Hayutin, A.M., Dietz, M., & Mitchell, L. (2010). *New realities of an older America*. Stanford, CA: Stanford Center on Longevity.

He, W., & Schachter, J.P. (2003). *Internal migration of the older population: 1995 to 2000, census 2000 special reports*. Washington, DC: U.S. Census Bureau.

Heckhausen, J. (1997). Developmental regulation across adulthood: Primary and secondary control of age-related challenges. *Developmental Psychology, 33*(1), 176–187.

Heckhausen, J., Wrosch, C., & Schulz, R. (2010). A motivational theory of life-span development. *Psychological Review, 117*(1), 32–60.

Hedrick, S.C., Sullivan, J.H., Sales, A.E., & Gray, S.L. (2009). Mom and pop versus the big boys: Adult family homes as providers of Medicaid-funded residential care. *Journal of Aging and Social Policy, 21*(1), 31–51.

Henkin, N., & Zapf, J. (2006–2007). How communities can promote civic engagement of people age 50-plus. *Generations, 30*(4), 72–77.

Hernandez, M., & Newcomer, R. (2007). Assisted living and special populations: What do we know about differences in use and potential access barriers? *The Gerontologist, 47*(Special Issue III), 110–117.

Hiatt, L.G. (2004). Environmental design in evoking the capacities of older people. In L.M. Tepper & T.M. Cassidy (Eds.), *Multidisciplinary perspectives on aging* (pp. 63–87). New York: Springer.

Hill, C. (2011, June 29). A retirement made for you (and people just like you). *Smartmoney*.

Hirth, V., Baskins, J., & Dever-Bumba, M. (2009). Program of all-inclusive care (PACE): Past, present, and future. *Journal of the American Medical Directors Association, 10*(3), 155–160.

Holahan, C.J. (1978). *Environment and behavior: A dynamic perspective*. New York: Plenum.

Holstein, M.B., & Minkler, M. (2003). Self, society, and the "new gerontology." *The Gerontologist, 43*(6), 787–796.

Hong, S.I., Hasche, L., & Bowland, S. (2009). Structural relationships between social activities and longitudinal trajectories of depression among older adults. *The Gerontologist, 49*(1), 1–11.

Hormuth, S.E. (1990). *The ecology of the self: Relocation and self-concept change*. Cambridge, MA: Cambridge University Press.

Housing Assistance Council. (2003). *Rural seniors & their homes*. Washington, DC: Housing Assistance Council.

Housing Assistance Council. (2012). *Poverty in rural America*. Washington, DC: Housing Assistance Council.

Howard, J., Ng, T., & Harrington, C. (2011). *Medicaid home and community-based services programs: Data update*. Washington, DC: Kaiser Commission on Medicaid and Uninsured.

Hudnut, W.H. (2003). *Halfway to everywhere: A portrait of America's first-tier suburbs*. Washington, DC: Urban Land Institute.

Hughes, C.J. (2007, May 18). Not just any port for migrating snowbirds. *The New York Times*.

Hughes, K.A. (2011, March 21). He says Maine. She says Florida. *The Wall Street Journal Online*.

Hunt, M.E., & Gunter-Hunt, G. (1985). Naturally occurring retirement communities. *Journal of Housing for the Elderly, 3*(3/4), 3–21.

Hunter, R.H., Sykes, K., Lowman, S.G., Duncan, R., Satariano, W.A., & Belza, B. (2011). Environmental and policy change to support healthy aging. *Journal of Aging & Social Policy, 23*(4), 354–371.

Hurd, M.D., Martorell, P., Delavande, A., Mullen, K.J., & Langa, K.M. (2013). Monetary costs of dementia in the United States. *New England Journal of Medicine, 368*(14), 1326–1334.

Huss, A., Stuck, A.E., Rubenstein, L.Z., Egger, M., & Clough-Gorr, K.M. (2008). Multidimensional preventive home visit programs for community-dwelling older adults: A systematic review and meta-analysis of randomized controlled trials. *Journals of Gerontology Series A, Biological Sciences and Medical Sciences, 63*(3), 298–307.

Hyde, J., Perez, R., & Forester, B. (2007). Dementia and assisted living. *The Gerontologist, 47*(Special Issue III), 51–67.

Hyde, J., Perez, R., & Reed, P.S. (2008). The old road is rapidly aging: A social model for cognitively or physically impaired elders in assisted living's future. In S.M. Golant & J. Hyde (Eds.), *The assisted living residence: A vision for the future* (pp. 46–85). Baltimore, MD: The John Hopkins University Press.

Hyer, K., Brown, L.M., Polivka-West, L., & Berman, A. (2010). Helping nursing homes prepare for disasters. *Health Affairs, 29*(10), 1961–1965.

Ickes, W., Snyder, M., & Garcia, S. (1997). Personality influences on the choice of situations. In R. Hogan, J. Johnson & S. Briggs (Eds.), *Handbook of personality psychology* (pp. 165–195). San Diego: Academic Press.

Ikebe, T., Ozawa, H., Lida, M., Shimamoto, T., Handa, K., & Komachi, Y. (2001). Long-term prognosis after stroke: A community-based study in Japan. *Journal of Epidemiology, 11*(1), 8–15.

Institute for the Future of Aging Services. (2007). *The long-term care workplace: Can the crisis be fixed*. Washington, DC: Institute for the Future of Aging Services.

Institute for the Future of Aging Services. (2009). *Affordable senior housing communities and health-related services*. Washington, DC: Institute for the Future of Aging Services.

Insurance Institute for Highway Safety, H. L. D. I. (2011). *Fatality facts 2009, older people*. Arlington, VA: Insurance Institute for Highway Safety.

Issa, P., & Zedlewski, S.R. (2011). *Poverty among older Americans, 2009* (Vol. 1, February, Retirement Security Data Brief). Washington, DC: Urban Institute.

Iwarsson, S., Wahl, H.-W., Nygren, C., Oswald, F., Sixsmith, A., Sixsmith, J., et al. (2007). Importance of the home environment for healthy aging: Conceptual and methodological background of the European Enable-Age Project. *The Gerontologist, 47*(1), 78–84.

Jaffe, D.J., & Howe, E. (1988). Agency-assisted shared housing: The nature of programs and matches. *The Gerontologist, 28,* 318–324.

James, R.N. (2008). Residential satisfaction of elderly tenants in apartment housing. *Social Indicators Research, 89,* 421–437.

James, W. (1902). *The varieties of religious experience: A study of human nature*. New York: Longmans.

Janis, I. (1982). *Groupthink: Psychological studies of policy decisions and fiascos*. Boston: Houghton Mifflin.

Janssen, B.M., Abma, T.A., & Van Regenmortel, T. (2012). Maintaining mastery despite age related losses. The resilience narratives of two older women in need of long-term community care. *Journal of Aging Studies, 26,* 343–354.

Jenkens, R., Carder, P.C., & Maher, L. (2004). The coming home program: Creating a state road map for affordable assisted living policy, programs, and demonstrations. *Journal of Housing for the Elderly, 18*(3/4), 179–201.

Jenkens, R., O'Keefe, J., Carder, P.C., & Wilson, K.B. (2006). *A study of negotiated risk agreements in assisted living: Final report*. Washington, DC: U.S. Department of Health and Human Services, Office of Disability, Aging and Long-Term Care Policy.

Jenkens, R., Sult, T., Lessell, N., Hammer, D., & Ortigara, A. (2011). Financial implications of the green house model. *Seniors Housing & Care Journal, 19*(1), 4–22.

Jeste, D.V., Savla, G.N., Thompson, W.K., Vahia, I.V., Glorioso, D.K., Martin, A.S., et al. (2013). Association between older age and more successful aging: Critical role of resilience and depression. *American Journal of Psychiatry, 170*(2), 188–196.

Johnson, J.L., Davenport, R., & Mann, W.C. (2007). Consumer feedback on smart home applications. *Topics in Geriatric Rehabilitation, 23*(1), 60–72.

Johnson, K.M. (2006). *Demographic trends in rural and small town America*. Durham, NH: Carsey Institute, University of New Hampshire.

Johnson, K.M., & Beale, C.L. (2002). Nonmetro recreation counties: Their identification and rapid growth. *Rural America, 17*(4), 12–19.

Johnson, R.W., Toohey, D., & Wiener, J.M. (2007). *Meeting the long-term care needs of the baby boomers: How changing families will affect paid helpers and institutions*. Washington, DC: Urban Institute.

Johnson, R.W., & Wiener, J.M. (2006). *A profile of frail older Americans and their caregivers*. Washington, DC: Urban Institute.

Joint Center for Housing Studies of Harvard University. (2000). *Housing America's seniors*. Cambridge, MA: Joint Center for Housing Studies of Harvard University.

Joint Center for Housing Studies of Harvard University. (2001). *Remodeling homes for changing households*. Cambridge, MA: Joint Center for Housing Studies of Harvard University.

Joint Center for Housing Studies of Harvard University. (2003). *Measuring the benefits of home remodeling*. Cambridge, MA: Joint Center for Housing Studies of Harvard University.

Joint Center for Housing Studies of Harvard University. (2007). *Foundations for future growth in the remodeling industry*. Cambridge, MA: Joint Center for Housing Studies of Harvard University.

Joint Center for Housing Studies of Harvard University. (2008). *The state of the nation's housing, 2008*. Cambridge, MA: Joint Center for Housing Studies of Harvard University.

Joint Center for Housing Studies of Harvard University. (2013a). *America's rental housing: Evolving markets and needs*. Cambridge, MA: Joint Center for Housing Studies of Harvard University.

Joint Center for Housing Studies of Harvard University. (2013b). *The state of the nation's housing, 2013*. Cambridge, MA: Joint Center for Housing Studies of Harvard University.

Joint Center for Housing Studies of Harvard University. (2013c). *The U.S. housing stock ready for renewal*. Cambridge, MA: Joint Center for Housing Studies of Harvard University.

Joint Center for Housing Studies of Harvard University. (2014). *Housing America's older adults*. Cambridge, MA: Joint Center for Housing Studies of Harvard University.

Jung, C.G. (1969). *The structure and dynamics of the psyche* (2nd ed.). Princeton, NJ: Princeton University Press.

Justice, D. (2010). *Implementing the Affordable Care Act: New options for Medicaid home and community based services*. Washington, DC: National Academy for State Policy.

Kahana, E., & Kahana, B. (1983). Environmental continuity, futurity, and adaptation of the aged. In G. Rowles & R.J. Ohta (Eds.), *Aging and milieu* (pp. 205–228). New York: Academic Press.

Kahana, E., Liang, J., & Felton, B. (1980). Alternative models of person-environment fit: Prediction of morale in three homes for the aged. *Journal of Gerontology, 35,* 584–595.

Kaiser Commission. (2013a). *Medicaid's role for dual eligible beneficiaries.* Washington, DC: Kaiser Commission.

Kaiser Commission. (2013b). *Overview of nursing facility capacity, financing, and ownership in the United States in 2011.* Washington, DC: Kaiser Commission.

Kaiser Commission on Medicaid and the Uninsured. (2013). *Five key facts about the delivery and financing of long-term services and supports.* Washington, DC: Kaiser Commission on Medicaid and the Uninsured.

Kalish, R.A., & Knudtson, F.W. (1976). Attachment versus disengagement: A life-span conceptualization. *Human Development, 19,* 171–181.

Kamo, Y., Henderson, T.L., & Roberto, K.A. (2011). Displaced older adults' reactions to and coping with the aftermath of hurricane Katrina. *Journal of Family Issues, 32*(10), 1346–1370.

Kamptner, N.L. (1989). Personal possessions and their meanings in old age. In S. Spacapan & S. Oskamp (Eds.), *The social psychology of aging* (pp. 165–196). Newbury Park, CA: Sage.

Kane, R.A. (1988). Case management: Ethical pitfalls on the road to high-quality managed care. *Quality Review Bulletin, 14*(5), 161–166.

Kane, R.A., & Kane, R.L. (1989). Reflections on quality control. *Generations, 13,* 63–68.

Kane, R.A., Kane, R.L., & Ladd, R.C. (1998). *The heart of long-term care.* New York: Oxford University Press.

Kane, R.L. (2010). Reimagining nursing homes: The art of the possible. *Journal of Aging & Social Policy, 22*(4), 321–333.

Kane, R.L., Lum, T.Y., Kane, R.A., Homyak, P., Parashuram, S., & Wysocki, A. (2013). Does home- and community-based care affect nursing home use? *Journal of Aging & Social Policy, 25*(2), 146–160.

Kane, R.L., & Mach, J.R., Jr. (2007). Improving health care for assisted living residents. *The Gerontologist, 47*(3), 100–109.

Kanne, A.D., Coyne, J.C., & Schaefer, C. (1981). Comparison of two modes of stress management: Daily hassles and uplifts versus major life events. *Journal of Behavioral Medicine, 4*(1), 1–39.

Kastenbaum, R.J. (1984). When aging begins: A lifespan developmental approach. *Research on Aging, 6,* 105–117.

Kastenbaum, R. (1993). Encrusted elders: Arizona and the political spirit of postmodern aging. In T.R. Cole, W.A. Achenbaum, P.L. Jacobi, & R. Kastenbaum (Eds.), *Voices and visions of aging: Toward a critical gerontology* (pp. 160–183). New York: Springer.

Katz, R.E., & Frank, R.G. (2011). A vision for the future: New care delivery models can play a vital role in building tomorrow's eldercare workforce. *Generations, 34*(4), 82–88.

Katz, S., Branch, L.G., Branson, M.H., Papsidero, J.A., Beck, J.C., & Greer, D.S. (1983). Active life expectancy. *New England Journal of Medicine, 309*(20), 1218–1224.

Kawachi, I., & Berkman, L.F. (2003). *Neighborhoods and health.* New York: Oxford University Press.

Kaye, H.S. (2012). Gradual rebalancing of Medicaid long-term services and supports saves money and serves more people, statistical model shows. *Health Affairs, 31*(6), 1195–1203.

Kaye, H.S., Harrington, C., & LaPlante, M.P. (2010). Long-term care: Who gets it, who provides it, who pays, and how much? *Health Affairs, 29*(1), 11–21.

Kemp, C.L., Ball, M.M., Hollingsworth, C., & Perkins, M.M. (2012). Strangers and friends: Residents' social careers in assisted living. *Journal of Gerontology: Social Sciences, 67*(4), 491–502.

Kemp, C.L., Luo, S.Z., & Ball, M.M. (2012). "Meds are a real tricky area": Examining medication management and regulation in assisted living. *Journal of Applied Gerontology, 31*(1), 126–149.

Kemper, P., Komisar, H.L., & Alecxih, L. (2005). Long-term care over an uncertain future: What can current retirees expect? *Inquiry, 42*(4), 335–350.

Kemper, T.D. (1978). *A social interactional theory of emotions.* New York: Wiley-Interscience.

Kendig, H., Clemson, L., & Mackenzie, L. (2012). Older people: Well-being, housing and neighbourhoods. *International Encyclopedia of Housing and Home, 5,* 150–155.

Kerr, J., Rosenberg, D., & Frank, L. (2012). The role of the built environment in healthy aging. *Journal of Planning Literature, 27*(1), 43–60.

Kerschner, H. (2003). Low-cost, low-maintenance approach: The Pasadena PasRide pilot. *Generations, 27*(3), 63–67.

Khadduri, J., & Locke, G. (2012). *Making subsidized rental housing a platform for improved health for vulnerable populations.* Cambridge, MA: Abt Associates.

Khatutsky, G., Wiener, J.M., Greene, A.M., Johnson, R., & O'Keeffe, J. (2013). *Do services and staffing in residential care vary with resident needs?* Washington, DC: Office of Disability, Aging and Long-Term Care Policy, U.S. Department of Health and Human Services.

King, D. (2008). Neighborhood and individual factors in activity in older adults: Results from the neighborhood and senior health study. *Journal of Aging and Physical Activity, 16*(2), 144–170.

Klapp, O.E. (1986). *Overload and boredom.* Westport, CN: Greenwood Press.

Klumb, P.L., & Maier, H. (2007). Daily activities and survival at older ages. *Journal of Aging Health, 19*(4), 594–611.

Kneale, D., Bamford, S.-M., & Sinclair, D. (2012). *Downsizing in later life and appropriate housing size across our lifetime.* Staines, UK: International Longevity Centre.

Knickman, J.R., Hunt, K.A., Snell, E.K., Alecxih, L.M., & Kennell, D.L. (2003). Wealth patterns among elderly Americans: Implications for health care affordability. *Health Affairs, 22*(3), 168–174.

Kobasa, S.C. (1979). Stressful life events, personality, and health—inquiry into hardiness. *Journal of Personality and Social Psychology, 37*(1), 1–11.

Kochera, A. (2002). *Accessibility and visitability features in single-family homes: A review of state and local activity.* Washington, DC: AARP Public Policy Institute.

Kochera, A. (2006). *Developing appropriate rental housing for low-income older persons: A survey of Section 202 and LIHTC property managers.* Washington, DC: AARP Public Policy Institute.

Koffman, D., Weiner, R., Pfeiffer, A., & Chapman, S. (2010). *Funding the public transportation needs of an aging population.* San Francisco, CA: Nelson/Nygaard Consulting Associates.

Konetzka, R.T., Karon, S.L., & Potter, D.E.B. (2012). Users of Medicaid home and community-based services are especially vulnerable to costly avoidable hospital admissions. *Health Affairs, 31*(6), 1167–1175.

Koren, M. J. (2010). Person-centered care for nursing home residents: The culture-change movement. *Health Affairs, 29*(2), 312–317.

Krause, N. (2003). Neighborhoods, health, and well-being in late life. In H.W. Wahl, R.J. Scheidt, & P.G. Windley (Eds.), *Annual review of gerontology and geriatrics: Focus on aging in context, socio-physical environments* (pp. 223–249). New York: Springer.

Kromer, B., & Howard, D. (2013). *Labor force participation and work status of people 65 years and older.* Washington, DC: U.S. Department of Commerce, U.S. Census Bureau.

Krout, J.A., Holmes, H., Erickson, M.A., & Wolle, S. (2003). Residential relocation. In J.A. Krout & E. Wethington (Eds.), *Residential choices and experiences of older adults* (pp. 27–48). New York: Springer.

Krout, J.A., Moen, P., Holmes, H.H., Oggins, J., & Bowen, N. (2002). Reasons for relocation to a continuing care retirement community. *Journal of Applied Gerontology, 21*(2), 236–256.

Krout, J.A., Oggins, J., & Holmes, H.H. (2000). Patterns of service use in a continuing care retirement community. *The Gerontologist, 40*(6), 698–705.

Kruse, R.L., Moore, C.M., Tofle, R.B., LeMaster, J.W., Aud, M., Hicks, L.L., et al. (2010). Older adults' attitudes toward home modifications for fall prevention. *Journal of Housing for the Elderly, 24*(2), 110–129.

Kunkel, S. R., Reece, H. R., & Straker, J. K. (2014). The evolution, innovation, and future of Area Agencies on Aging. *Generations, 38*(2), 30–39.

Kutzik, D., Glascock, A.P., Lundberg, L., & York, J. (2008). Technological tools of the future: Contributing to appropriate care in assisted living. In S.M. Golant & J. Hyde (Eds.), *The assisted living residence: A vision for the future* (pp. 223–247). Baltimore, MD: The John Hopkins University Press.

Kyllo, D., & Polzer, K. (2013). *Assisted living national update.* Paper presented at the American Health Lawyers Association, February 25, Austin, Texas.

Labouvie-Vief, G., & Medler, M. (2002). Affect optimization and affect complexity: Modes and styles of regulation in adulthood. *Psychology and Aging, 17*(4), 571–588.

Langer, E.J., & Abelson, R.P. (1983). *The psychology of control.* Beverly Hills, CA: Sage.

Lanspery, S. (2002). Aging in place. In D. J. Ekerdt (Ed.), *Encyclopedia of aging.* New York: Macmillan Reference USA. Retrieved August 18, 2014 from Encyclopedia.com: http://www.encyclopedia.com/doc/1G2-3402200026.html

Lanspery, S., Callahan, J.J., Miller, J.R., & Hyde, J. (1997). Introduction: Staying put. In S. Lanspery & J. Hyde (Eds.), *Staying put: Adapting the places instead of the people* (pp. 1–24). Amityville, NY: Baywood Publishing Co.

Larkin, M. (2012, November/December). CCRC without walls. *Journal of Active Aging,* 32–42.

Larson, C. (2007, June 10). As continuing care grows, so do the payment options. *The New York Times.*

Lawler, K. (2001). *Aging in place: Coordinating housing and health care provision for America's growing elderly population.* Cambridge, MA: Harvard Joint Center on Housing Studies.

Lawton, M.P. (1983). Environment and other determinants of well-being in older people. *The Gerontologist, 23*(4), 349–357.

Lawton, M.P. (1985). The elderly in context: Perspectives from environmental psychology and gerontology. *Environment and Behavior, 17,* 501–519.

Lawton, M.P., & Nahemow, L. (1973). Ecology and the aging process. In C. Eisdorfer & M.P. Lawton (Eds.), *The psychology of adult development and aging* (pp. 619–674). Washington, DC: American Psychological Association.

Lazarus, R.S. (1966). *Psychological stress and the coping process.* New York: McGraw-Hill.

Lazarus, R.S. (1991). Progress on a cognitive–motivational–relational theory of emotion. *American Psychologist, 46*(8), 819–834.

Lazarus, R.S., & Folkman, S. (1984). *Stress, appraisal, and coping.* New York: Springer.

Lazarus, R.S., & Lazarus, B.N. (2006). *Coping with aging.* New York: Oxford University Press.

LCS. (2012). *The CCRC consumer of the future.* Des Moines, IA: LCS.

LeadingAge. (2012). *Continuing care retirement communities: 2011 profile.* Washington, DC: LeadingAge.

LeadingAge & Ziegler Capital Markets. (2013). *LeadingAge Ziegler 100. The nation's 100 largest not-for-profit multi-site senior living organizations.* Washington, DC and Chicago: LeadingAge & Ziegler Capital Markets.

Lehning, A.J., & Austin, M.J. (2010). Long-term care in the United States: Policy themes and promising practices. *Journal of Gerontological Social Work, 53*(1), 43–63.

Lehning, A.J., Smith, R.J., & Dunkle, R.E. (2013, April 13). Do age-friendly characteristics influence the expectation to age in place? A comparison of low-income and higher income Detroit elders. *Journal of Applied Gerontology.*

Leinberger, C.B. (2005). *Turning around downtown: Twelve steps to revitalization.* Washington, DC: Brookings Institution.

Leipold, B., & Greve, W. (2009). A conceptual bridge between coping and development. *European Psychologist, 14*(1), 40–50.

Leland, J. (2011, November 25). A community of survivors dwindles. *New York Times.*

Lemke, S., & Moos, R.H. (1980). Assessing the institutional policies of sheltered care settings. *Journal of Gerontology, 35*(1), 96–107.

Leutz, W. (2011). The changing face of long-term care and how a new immigrant workforce will shape its future. *Generations, 34*(4), 89–96.

Levine, C., Halper, D., Peist, A., & Gould, D.A. (2010). Bridging troubled waters: Family caregivers, transitions, and long-term care. *Health Affairs, 29*(1), 116–124.

Levine, C.A., & Johns, A.R. (2008). *Multifamily property managers satisfaction with service coordination.* Washington, DC: U.S. Department of Housing and Urban Development, Policy Development and Research.

Lewin, K. (1936). *Principles of topological psychology.* New York: McGraw Hill.

The Lewin Group. (2007). *Medicaid and assisted living: Opportunities and challenges.* Washington, DC: American Seniors Housing Association.

The Lewin Group. (2010a). *Individuals living in the community with chronic conditions and functional limitations: A closer look.* Washington, DC: The Lewin Group.

The Lewin Group. (2010b). *Medicaid and long-term care: New challenges, new opportunities.* Falls Church, VA: The Lewin Group.

Lewis, M., Haviland-Jones, J., & Barrett, L.F. (Eds.). (2008). *Handbook of emotions* (3rd ed.). New York: Guilford.

Li, F., Fisher, J., & Brownson, R.C. (2005). A multilevel analysis of change in neighborhood walking activity in older adults. *Journal of Aging and Physical Activity, 13*(2), 145–159.

Li, H. (2004). Barriers to and unmet needs for supportive services: Experiences of Asian-American caregivers. *Journal of Cross-Cultural Gerontology, 19*(3), 241–260.

Lieberman, M.A. (1975). Adaptive processes in late life. In N. Datan & L. H. Ginsberg (Eds.), *Life-span developmental psychology.* New York: Academic Press.

Lieberman, M.A. (1991). Relocation of the frail elderly. In J.E. Birrren, J.E. Lubben, J.C. Rowe, & D.E. Deutchman (Eds.), *The concept and measurement of quality of life in the frail elderly* (pp. 120–141). New York: Academic Press.

Lieberman, M.A., & Tobin, S.S. (1983). *The experience of old age: Stress, coping and survival.* New York: Basic Books.

Liebig, P., Kennedy, M.C., & Cory, S. (2003). Continuing care retirement communities. In L. A. Vitt (Ed.), *Encyclopedia of retirement and finance* (Vol. I, pp. 123–130). Westport, CT: Greenwood.

Liebig, P.S., Koenig, T., & Pynoos, J. (2006). Zoning, accessory dwelling units, and family caregiving: Issues, trends, and recommendations. *Journal of Aging and Social Policy, 18*(3–4), 155–172.

Lietaert, M. (2010). Cohousing's relevance to degrowth theories. *Journal of Cleaner Production, 18*(6), 576–580.

Lind, K.D. (2012). *Setting the record straight about Medicare.* Washington, DC: AARP Public Policy Institute.

Lindquist, L.A., Cameron, K.A., Messerges-Bernstein, J., Friesema, E., Zickuhr, L., Baker, D.W., et al. (2012). Hiring and screening practices of agencies supplying paid caregivers to older adults. *Journal of the American Geriatrics Society, 60*(7), 1253–1259.

Lindquist, L.A., Jain, N., Tam, K., Martin, G.J., & Baker, D.W. (2011). Inadequate health literacy among paid caregivers of seniors. *Journal of General Internal Medicine, 26*(5), 474–479.

Lipman, B., Lubbell, J., & Salomon, E. (2010). *Housing an aging population: Are we prepared.* Washington, DC: Center for Housing Policy.

Litwak, E., & Longino, C.F. (1987). Migration patterns among the elderly: A developmental perspective. *The Gerontologist, 27*(3), 266–272.

Locke, G., Lam, K., Henry, M., & Brown, S. (2011). *End of participation in assisted housing: What can we learn about aging in place?* Washington, DC: Abt Associates.

Loe, M., & Moore, C. D. (2012). From nursing home to green house: Changing contexts of elder care in the United States. *Journal of Applied Gerontology, 31*(6), 755–763.

Löfqvist, C., Granbom, M., Himmelsbach, I., Iwarsson, S., Oswald, F., & Haak, M. (2013). Voices on relocation and aging in place in very old age: A complex and ambivalent matter. *The Gerontologist, 53*(6), 919–927.

Long Term Care Coordinating Council Human Services Agency of San Francisco. (2009). *Living with dignity in San Francisco, part one of two, 2009–2013.* San Francisco: City and County of San Francisco.

Longino, C.F. Jr. (1998). Geographical mobility and the baby boom. *Generations, 22*(1), 60–64.

Longino, C.F. Jr. (2002). The geographic mobility of retirees. *Contemporary Gerontology, 9*(1), 2–6.

Longino, C.F. Jr., Bradley, D.E., Stoller, E.P., & Haas, W.H. III. (2008). Predictors of non-local moves among older adults: A prospective study. *Journal of Gerontology: Social Sciences, 63*(1), S7–14.

Lord, S.R., Menz, H.B., & Sherrington, C. (2006). Home environment risk factors for falls in older people and the efficacy of home modifications. *Age and Ageing, 35*(suppl 2), ii55–ii59.

Lorenzen-Huber, L., Boutain, M., Camp, L.J., Shankar, K., & Connelly, K.H. (2011). Privacy, technology, and aging. *Ageing International, 36,* 232–252.

Louie, J., Belsky, E.S., & McArdle, N. (1998). *The housing needs of lower-income homeowners.* Cambridge, MA: Harvard University, Joint Center for Housing Studies.

Lovegreen, L.D., Kahana, E., & Kahana, B. (2010). Residential relocation of amenity migrants to Florida: "Unpacking" post-amenity moves. *Journal of Aging and Health, 22*(7), 1001–1028.

Luborsky, M.R., Lysack, C.L., & Van Nuil, J. (2011). Refashioning one's place in time: Stories of household downsizing in later life. *Journal of Aging Studies, 25*(3), 243–252.

Ludwig, S. (2007, Summer). Losing ground. *Shelteforce Online, 150,* 1–13.

Lynott, J., Haase, J., Nelson, K., Taylor, A., Twaddell, H., Ulmer, J., McCann, B., & Stoloff, E. (2009). *Planning complete streets for an aging America.* Washington, DC: AARP Public Policy Institute.

Lynott, J., & Figueiredo, C. (2011). *How the travel patterns of older adults are changing: Highlights from the 2009 Household Travel Survey.* Washington, DC: AARP Public Policy Institute.

Lynott, J., Fox-Grage, W., & Guzman, S. (2013). *Weaving it together: A tapestry of transportation funding for older adults.* Washington, DC: AARP Public Policy Institute.

Maag, S.J. (2012). *CCRCs without walls: Care models of the future.* Washington, DC: LeadingAge.

Magai, C. (2001). Emotions over the life span. In J.E. Birren & K.W. Schaie (Eds.), *Handbook for psychology and aging* (5th ed., pp. 399–426). San Diego, CA: Academic Press.

Magan, G.G. (2011). *Preparing for the future: Developing technology-enabled long-term services and supports for a new population of older adults.* Washington, DC: LeadingAge CAST.

Magnusson, D. (1981). Wanted: A psychology of situations. In D. Magnusson (Ed.), *Toward a psychology of situations: An interactional perspective* (pp. 3–32). Hillsdale, NJ: Erlbaum.

Magnusson, D. (1985). Implications of an interactional paradigm for research on human development. *International Journal of Behavioral Development, 8*(2), 115–137.

Magnusson, D., & Torestad, B. (1992). The individual as an interactive agent in the environment. In W.B. Walsh, K.H. Craik, & R.H. Price (Eds.), *Person–environment psychology: Models and perspectives* (pp. 89–125). Hillsdale, NJ: Erlbaum.

Maisel, J.L., Smith, E., & Steinfeld, E. (2008). *Increasing home access: Designing for visitability.* Washington, DC: AARP Public Policy Institute.

Mann, W.C., Johnson, J.L., Lynch, L.G., Justiss, M.D., Tomita, M., & Wu, S.S. (2008). Changes in impairment level, functional status, and use of assistive devices by older people with depressive symptoms. *AJOT: American Journal of Occupational Therapy, 62*(1), 9(9).

Mann, W.C., & Milton, B.R. (2005). Home automation and smart homes to support independence. In W.C. Mann (Ed.), *Smart technology for aging, disability, and independence* (pp. 33–66). Hoboken, NJ: Wiley.

Margulis, S.T. (2003). On the status and contribution of Westin's and Altman's theories of privacy. *Journal of Social Issues, 59*(2), 411–429.

Marottoli, R.A., & Coughlin, J.F. (2011). Walking the tightrope: Developing a systems approach to balance safety and mobility for an aging society. *Journal of Aging & Social Policy, 23*(4), 372–383.

Marshall, A. (2000). *How cities work: Suburbs, sprawl, and the roads not taken*. Austin, TX: University of Texas Press.

Martin, L.G., Freedman, V.A., Schoeni, R.F., & Andreski, P.M. (2010). Trends in disability and related chronic conditions among people ages fifty to sixty-four. *Health Affairs, 29*(4), 725–731.

Masnick, G.S., Di, Z.X., & Belsky, E.S. (2006). Emerging cohort trends in housing debt and home equity. *Housing Policy Debate, 17*(3), 491–527.

Masnick, G.S., Will, A., & Baker, K. (2011). *Housing turnover by older owners: Implications for home improvement spending as baby boomers age into retirement*. Cambridge, MA: Joint Center for Housing Studies, Harvard University.

Mather Lifeways Institute on Aging, Ziegler & Brecht Associates. (2011). *National survey of family members of residents living in continuing care retirement communities*. Evanston, IL: Authors.

Matthews, J.T. (2006). Existing and emerging healthcare devices for elders to use at home. *Generations, 30*(1), 13–19.

McAuley, W.J., Spector, W., & Van Nostrand, J. (2009). Formal home care utilization patterns by rural–urban community residence. *Journal of Gerontology: Social Sciences, 64*(2), 258–268.

McDonough, K.E., & Davitt, J.K. (2011). It takes a Village: Community practice, social work, and aging-in-place. *Journal of Gerontological Social Work, 54*(5), 528–541.

McGinty, J.C. (2004, March 2). Growing risk for elderly: Dying at home, and alone. *Newsday*.

McHugh, K.E. (2000). The "ageless self"? Emplacement of identities in sun belt retirement communities. *Journal of Aging Studies, 14*(1), 103–115.

McHugh, K.E. (2007). Generational consciousness and retirement communities. *Population Space and Place, 13*(4), 293–306.

McHugh, K.E., & Larson-Keagy, E.M. (2005). These white walls: The dialectic of retirement communities. *Journal of Aging Studies, 19*, 241–256.

McKnight, A.J. (2003). The freedom of the open road: Driving and older adults. *Generations, 27*(2), 25–31.

McWinney-Morse, S. (2009). Beacon Hill Village. *Generations, 33*(2), 85–86.

Medicare Payment Advisory Commission. (2001). *Report to the Congress: Medicare in rural America*. Washington, DC: Medicare Payment Advisory Commission.

Megbolugbe, I., Sa-Aadu, J., & Shilling, J.D. (1997). Oh, yes, the elderly will reduce housing equity under the right circumstances. *Journal of Housing Research, 8*(1), 53–74.

Mehrabian, A. (1980). *Basic dimensions for a general psychological theory: Implications for personality, social, environmental, and developmental studies*. Cambridge, MA: Oelgeschlager, Gunn & Hain, Publishers.

Melnick, J.A., Ferrer, G., Shanks-McElroy, H., & Dunay, S. (2013). *Home and community-based alternatives to nursing home care*. Harrisburg, PA: The Center for Rural Pennsylvania.

Mendes de Leon, C.F., Cagney, K.A., Bienias, J.L., Barnes, L.L., Skarupski, K.A., Scherr, P.A., et al. (2009). Neighborhood social cohesion and disorder in relation to walking in community-dwelling older adults: A multilevel analysis. *Journal of Aging Health, 21*(1), 155–171.

Meredith, J.R. (2003). Sprawl and the new urbanist solution. *Virginia Law Review, 89*, 447–492.

MetLife Foundation. (2005). *The maturing of America: Getting communities on track for an aging population*. Westport, CT: MetLife Foundation.

MetLife Mature Market Institute. (2009a). *55+ housing: Builders, buyers and beyond—what are builders building? What do buyers want?* Washington, DC: National Association of Home Builders & MetLife Mature Market Institute.

MetLife Mature Market Institute. (2009b). *Broken trust: Elders, family, and finances*. Westport, CT: MetLife Mature Market Institute.

MetLife Mature Market Institute. (2009c). *Tapping home equity in retirement*. Washington, DC: MetLife Mature Market Institute.

MetLife Mature Market Institute. (2010a). *The MetLife national study of adult day services*. Westport, CT: MetLife Mature Market Institute.

MetLife Mature Market Institute. (2010b). *The MetLife study of working caregivers and employer health care costs*. Westport, CT: MetLife Mature Market Institute.

MetLife Mature Market Institute. (2010c). *Still out, still aging*. Westport, CT: MetLife Mature Market Institute.

MetLife Mature Market Institute. (2011a). *Housing trends update for the 55+ market*. Washington, DC: National Association of Home Builders & MetLife Mature Market Institute.

MetLife Mature Market Institute. (2011b). *The MetLife study of elder financial abuse*. Westport, CT: MetLife Mature Market Institute.

MetLife Mature Market Institute. (2012). *Changing attitudes, changing motives*. New York: MetLife Mature Market Institute.

Meyer, M.J. (2004). The hidden benefits of property tax relief for the elderly. *Elder Law Journal, 12,* 417–448.

Mezuk, B., & Rebok, G.W. (2008). Social integration and social support among older adults following driving cessation. *Journal of Gerontology: Social Sciences, 63*(5), S298–303.

Michael, Y.L., Green, M.K., & Farquhar, S.A. (2006). Neighborhood design and active aging. *Health & Place, 12*(4), 734–740.

Miller, E.A., Allen, S.M., & Mor, V. (2009). Commentary: Navigating the labyrinth of long-term care: Shoring up informal caregiving in a home- and community-based world. *Journal of Aging and Social Policy, 21*(1), 1–16.

Mitchell, J. (2009, Spring). Top trends in 50+ housing. *C2, 25,* 14–15.

Mitty, E., & Flores, S. (2008). Aging in place and negotiated risk agreements. *Geriatric Nursing, 29*(2), 94–101.

Molla, M.T., & Madans, J.H. (2010). Life expectancy free of chronic condition- induced activity limitations among white and black Americans, 2000–2006. *Vital Health Statistics, 3*(34), 1–21.

Mollica, R. (2007). *A Medicaid primer for housing officials.* New Brunswick, NJ: Rutgers Center for State Health Policy.

Mollica, R.L. (2009). *State Medicaid reimbursement policies and practices in assisted living.* Washington, DC: National Center for Assisted Living, American Health Care Association.

Mollica, R., Houser, A., & Ujvari, K. (2012). *Assisted living and residential care in the states in 2010.* Washington, DC: AARP Public Policy Institute.

Mollica, R.L., Kassner, E., Walker, L., & Houser, A. (2009). *Taking the long view: Investing in Medicaid home and community-based services is cost effective.* Washington, DC: AARP Public Policy Institute.

Mollica, R., & Morris, M. (2005). *Massachusetts Supportive Housing Program.* New Brunswick, NJ: Rutgers Center for State Health Policy.

Mollica, R.L., Sims-Kastelein, K., & O'Keeffe, J. (2007). *Residential care and assisted living compendium.* Washington, DC: U.S. Department of Health and Human Services, Office of Disability, Aging and Long-Term Care Policy.

Monk, A., & Kaye, L.W. (1991). Congregate housing for the elderly: Its need, function, and perspectives. In L.W. Kaye & A. Monk (Eds.), *Congregate housing for the elderly: Theoretical, policy, and programmatic perspectives* (pp. 5–19). New York: Haworth Press.

Moody, H.R. (2008). *The new aging enterprise.* Washington, DC: AARP, Office of Academic Affairs.

Moore, J. (2009). *Independent living and CCRCs.* Fort Worth, TX: Westridge Publishing.

Moos, R.H., & Lemke, S. (1980). Assessing the physical and architectural features of sheltered care settings. *Journal of Gerontology, 35*(4), 571–583.

Moos, R.H., & Lemke, S. (1996). *Evaluating residential facilities: The multiphasic environment assessment procedure.* Thousand Oaks, CA: Sage Publications.

Morgan, L.A., & Brazda, M.A. (2013). Transferring control to others: Process and meaning for older adults in assisted living. *Journal of Applied Gerontology, 32*(6), 651–668.

Morgan, L.A., Rubinstein, R.L., Frankowski, A.C., Perez, R., Roth, E.G., Peeples, A.D., et al. (2014, March 18). The facade of stability in assisted living. *Journals of Gerontology Series B: Psychological Sciences and Social Sciences, 69(3),* 431–441.

Morris, E. et al. (2014). *Money follows the person demonstration: Overview of state grantee progress, July to December 2013.* Cambridge, MA: Mathematica Policy Research.

Morrow-Howell, N. (2010). Volunteering in later life: Research frontiers. *Journal of Gerontology: Social Sciences, 65*(4), 461–469.

Moses, S.A. (2004). *The realist's guide to Medicaid and long-term care.* Seattle, WA: Center for Long-Term Care Financing.

Mullen, A.J. (2011). The market for independent living: Understanding drivers of demand. *Senior Housing & Care Journal, 19*(1), 131–138.

Mumford, L. (1956, May). For older people: Not segregation but integration. *Architectural Record,* 191–194.

Munnell, A.H. (2014). *The government's redesigned reverse mortgage program.* Boston: Center for Retirement Research of Boston College.

Munnell, A.H., Soto, M., & Aubry, J.-P. (2007). *Do people plan to tap their home equity in retirement?* Boston: Center for Retirement Research at Boston College.

Muramatsu, N., Yin, H., Campbell, R.T., Hoyem, R.L., Jacob, M.A., & Ross, C.O. (2007). Risk of nursing home admission among older Americans: Does states' spending on home- and community-based services matter? *Journal of Gerontology: Social Sciences, 62*(3), S169–178.

Muramatsu, N., Yin, H., & Hedeker, D. (2010). Functional declines, social support, and mental health in the elderly: Does living in a state supportive of home and community-based services make a difference? *Social Science & Medicine, 70*(7), 1050–1058.

Myers, D., & Ryu, S. (2008). Aging baby boomers and the generational housing bubble. *Journal of the American Planning Association, 74*(1), 17–33.

Naik, A.D., Kunik, M.E., Cassidy, K.R., Nair, J., & Coverdale, J. (2010). Assessing safe and independent living in vulnerable older adults: Perspectives of professionals who conduct home assessments. *Journal of the American Board of Family Medicine: JABFM, 23*(5), 614–621.

National Alliance for Caregiving. (2006). *Caregiving in rural America*. Bethesda, MD: National Alliance for Caregiving.

National Alliance for Caregiving. (2009). *Caregiving in the U.S.* Bethesda, MD: AARP & MetLife Foundation.

National Alliance for Caregiving. (2011). *What made you think Mom had Alzheimer's?* Bethesda, MD: National Alliance for Caregiving.

National Alliance for Caregiving, Schulz, R., & Cook, T. (2011). *Caregiving costs*. Bethesda, MD: National Alliance for Caregiving.

National Association of Area Agencies on Aging. (2013). *Squeezing seniors: Aging community fears national crisis as a result of federal budget cuts*. Washington, DC: National Association of Area Agencies on Aging.

National Association of Area Agencies on Aging and Scripps Gerontology Center. (2011). *Area Agencies on Aging: Advancing health and long-term services and supports*. Washington, DC: National Association of Area Agencies on Aging.

National Association of Home Builders (Toolbase.Org). (2001). *Aging-in-place design checklists*. Marlboro, MD: NAHB Research Center.

National Center for Assisted Living. (2012a). *Assisted living state regulatory review 2012*. Washington, DC: National Center for Assisted Living.

National Center for Assisted Living. (2012b). *Findings from the NCAL 2011 assisted living staff vacancy, retention, and turnover survey*. Washington, DC: National Center for Assisted Living.

National Consumer Voice for Quality Long-Term Care. (2011). *Piecing together quality long-term care: A consumer's guide to choices and advocacy*. Washington, DC: National Consumer Voice for Quality Long-Term Care.

National Consumer Voice for Quality Long-Term Care. (2012). *Consumer perspectives on quality home care*. Washington, DC: National Consumer Voice for Quality Long-Term Care.

National Highway Traffic Safety Administration. (2013). *Traffic safety for older people: 5 year plan* (report no. DOT HS 811 837). Washington, DC: National Highway Traffic Safety Administration.

National Investment Center for the Seniors Housing & Care Industry. (2007). *NIC national housing survey of adults age 55+*. Annapolis, MD: National Investment Center for the Seniors Housing & Care Industry.

National Investment Center for the Seniors Housing & Care Industry and American Seniors Housing Association. (2014). *Classifications for seniors housing property types*. Retrieved from http://www.Nic.Org/research/classifications.Pdf

National Low Income Housing Coalition. (2012). *2012 advocates' guide*. Washington, DC: National Low Income Housing Coalition.

National Mortgage Professional Magazine. (2013, March 20). Senior home equity reaches new three-year high. *National Mortgage Professional Magazine*.

National PACE Association. (2003). *PACE and senior housing survey*. Alexandria, Virginia: National PACE Association.

National Research Corporation. (2012). *2011–2012 national survey of customer and employee satisfaction in assisted living communities*. Lincoln, NE: National Research Corporation.

National Research Corporation. (2013). *Empowering customer-centric healthcare for post-acute providers*. Lincoln, NE: National Research Corporation.

National Resource Center for Participant-Directed Services. (2014). *Facts and figures: 2013 national inventory survey on participant direction*. Boston: National Resource Center for Participant-Directed Services.

National Senior Citizens Law Center. (2010). *Medicaid payment for assisted living: Preventing discrimination against Medicaid-eligible residents*. Washington, DC: National Senior Citizens Law Center.

National Senior Citizens Law Center. (2011a). *Medicaid payment for assisted living: Providing a home-like environment*. Washington, DC: National Senior Citizens Law Center.

National Senior Citizens Law Center. (2011b). *Medicaid payment for assisted living: Residents have a right to return after hospitalization*. Washington, DC: National Senior Citizens Law Center.

National Senior Citizens Law Center. (2011c). *Medicaid payment for assisted living: State supplementation for SSI recipients*. Washington, DC: National Senior Citizens Law Center.

Nehrke, M.F., Morganti, J.B., Cohen, S.H., Hulicka, I.A., Whitbourne, S.K., Turner, R.R., et al. (1984). Differences in person–environment congruence between microenvironments. *Canadian Journal on Aging, 3*, 117–132.

Nelms, L.L., Mayes, S.L., & Doll, B. (2012). The interface between continuing-care retirement communities and long-term-care insurance. *Journal of Financial Planning, 25*(5), 54–60.

Nelson, J.A., & Gingerich, B.S. (2010). Rural health: Access to care and services. *Home Health Care Management & Practice, 22*(5), 339–343.

Netherland, J., Finkelstein, R., & Gardner, P. (2011). The age-friendly New York City project: An environmental intervention to increase aging resilience. In B. Resnick, L.P. Gwyther, & K.A. Roberto (Eds.), *Resilience in aging: Concepts, research, and outcomes* (pp. 273–287). New York: Springer.

Neugarten, B. (1974). Age groups in American society and the rise of young-old. *Annals of the American Academy of Political and Social Science, 415,* 187–198.

Neugarten, B., & Hagestad, G. (1976). Age and the life course. In R.H. Binstock & E. Shanas (Eds.), *Handbook of aging and the social sciences* (pp. 35–55). New York: Van Nostrand Reinhold Company.

Neugarten, B.L., Havighurst, R.J., & Tobin, S.S. (1961). The measurement of life satisfaction. *Journal of Gerontology, 16,* 134–143.

New Jersey, Office of the Public Advocate. (2009). *Aging in place: Promises to keep.* Trenton, NJ: Department of the Public Advocate, Division of Elder Advocacy.

Newcomer, R., Kang, T., Laplante, M., & Kaye, S. (2005). Living quarters and unmet need for personal care assistance among adults with disabilities. *Journal of Gerontology: Social Sciences, 60*(4), S205–S213.

Newman, S. (2003). The living conditions of elderly Americans. *The Gerontologist, 43*(1), 99–109.

Newsom, J.T. (1999). Another side to caregiving: Negative reactions to being helped. *Current Directions in Psychological Science, 8*(6), 183–187.

Ng, T., Harrington, C., & Kitchener, M. (2010). Medicare and Medicaid in long-term care. *Health Affairs, 29*(1), 22–28.

Norberg-Schulz, C. (1971). *Existence, space, and architecture.* New York: Praeger.

O'Brien, E., Wu, K.B., & Baer, D. (2010). *Older Americans in poverty: A snapshot.* Washington, DC: AARP.

O'Connor, R.C., & Cassidy, C. (2007). Predicting hopelessness: The interaction between optimism/ pessimism and specific future expectancies. *Cognition and Emotion, 21*(3), 596–613.

O'Keefe, J. (2010). *Understanding Medicaid home and community services: A primer.* Washington, DC: U.S. Department of Health and Human Services.

O'Keefe, J., & Sibenaler, K. (2006). *Adult day service: A key community service for older adults.* Washington, DC: Office of the Assistant Secretary of Planning and Evaluation, U.S. Department of Health and Human Services.

Olsen, E.O. (2003). Housing programs for low-income households. In R.A. Moffitt (Ed.), *Means-tested transfer programs in the United States* (pp. 365–441). Chicago: University of Chicago Press.

Ormond, B.A., Black, K.J., Tilly, J., & Thomas, S. (2004). *Supportive services programs in naturally occurring retirement communities.* Washington, DC: Office of Disability, Aging and Long-Term Care Policy.

O'Rourke, N., Cappeliez, P., & Neufeld, E. (2007). Recurrent depressive symptomatology and physical health: A 10-year study of informal caregivers of persons with dementia. *Canadian Journal of Psychiatry, 52*(7), 434–441.

Orshan, B.E.A. (2013). *Money follows the person demonstration: Overview of state grantee progress, January to June 2013.* Cambridge, MA: Mathematica Policy Research.

Ortman, J.M., Velkoff, V.A., & Hogan, H. (2014). *An aging nation: The older population in the United States.* Washington, DC: U.S. Census Bureau.

Osgood, C.E., Suci, G.J., & Tannenbaum, P.H. (1957). *The measurement of meaning.* Urbana: University of Illinois Press.

O'Shaughnessy, C.V. (2008). *The aging services network: Accomplishments and challenges in serving a growing elderly population.* Washington, DC: National Health Policy Forum, The George Washington University.

O'Shaughnessy, C.V. (2010). *Aging and disability resource centers (ADRCs).* Washington, DC: National Health Policy Forum, The George Washington University.

O'Shaughnessy, C.V. (2011). *Older Americans Act of 1965: Programs and funding.* Washington, DC: National Health Policy Forum, The George Washington University.

O'Shaughnessy, C.V. (2013). *National spending for long-term services and supports, 2011.* Washington, DC: National Health Policy Forum.

O'Shaughnessy, C. V. (2014). *Serving seniors through the Older Americans Act of 1965. Hearing before the Committee on Education & the Workforce, U.S. House of Representatives.* Washington, DC.

Ostir, G.V., Eschbach, K., Markides, K.S., & Goodwin, J.S. (2003). Neighbourhood composition and depressive symptoms among older Mexican Americans. *Journal of Epidemiology & Community Health, 57*(12), 987–992.

Oswald, F., Schilling, O., Wahl, H.-W., & Gang, K. (2002). Trouble in paradise? Reasons to relocate and objective environmental changes among well-off older adults. *Journal of Environmental Psychology, 22,* 273–288.

Oswald, F., Wahl, H.W., Schilling, O., & Iwarsson, S. (2007). Housing-related control beliefs and independence in activities of daily living in very old age. *Scandinavian Journal of Occupational Therapy, 14*(1), 33–43.

Owens, P.L., Russo, C.A., Spector, W., & Mutter, R. (2009). *Emergency department visits for injurious falls among the elderly, statistical brief #80.* Washington, DC: Agency for Healthcare Research and Quality.

Painter, G., & Lee, K. (2009). Housing tenure transitions of older households: Life cycle, demographic, and familial factors. *Regional Science and Urban Economics, 39*(6), 749–760.

Paraprofessional Healthcare Institute. (2012). *America's direct-care workforce.* Bronx, NY: Paraprofessional Healthcare Institute.

Paraprofessional Healthcare Institute. (2013). *America's direct-care workforce.* Bronx, NY: Paraprofessional Healthcare Institute.

Paraprofessional Healthcare Institute. (2014). *America's direct-care workforce.* Bronx, NY: Paraprofessional Healthcare Institute.

Pardasani, M., & Thompson, P. (2012). Senior centers: Innovative and emerging models. *Journal of Applied Gerontology, 31*(1), 52–77.

Park, N.S., Zimmerman, S., Kinslow, K., Shin, H.J., & Roff, L.L. (2012). Social engagement in assisted living and implications for practice. *Journal of Applied Gerontology, 31*(2), 215–238.

Park, N.S., Zimmerman, S., Sloane, P.D., Gruber-Baldini, A.L., & Eckert, J.K. (2006). An empirical typology of residential care/assisted living based on a four-state study. *The Gerontologist, 46*(2), 238–248.

Park-Lee, E., Caffrey, C., Sengupta, M., Moss, A.J., Rosenoff, E., & Harris-Kojetin, L.D. (2011). Residential care facilities: A key sector in the spectrum of long-term care providers in the United States. *NCHS Data Brief* (78), 1–8.

Park-Lee, E., Sengupta, M., & Harris-Kojetin, L.D. (2013). Dementia special care units in residential care communities: United States, 2010. *NCHS Data Brief* (134), 1–8.

Parkes, C.M. (1972). *Bereavement: Studies of grief in adult life.* New York: International University Press.

Parmelee, P.A., & Lawton, M.P. (1990). The design of special environments for the aged. In J.E. Birren & K.W. Schaie (Eds.), *Handbook of the psychology of aging* (3rd ed., pp. 465–488). New York: Academic Press.

Pearlin, L.I. (2010). The life course and the stress process: Some conceptual comparisons. *Journal of Gerontology: Social Sciences, 65B*(2), 207–215.

Pearson, K.C. (2010, July 21). *The importance of resident voices in regulation of continuing care retirement communities* Testimony to the U.S. Senate, Special Committee on Aging Hearing, Continuing Care Retirement Communities: Secure Retirement or Risky Investment? Washington, DC.

Pendall, R., Foster, K.A., & Cowell, M. (2010). Resilience and regions: Building understanding of the metaphor. *Cambridge Journal of Regions, Economy and Society, 3*(1), 71–84.

Perin, C. (1970). *With man in mind: An interdisciplinary prospectus for environmental design.* Cambridge, Mass.: MIT Press.

Perissinotto, C.M., Stijacic Cenzer, I., & Covinsky, K.E. (2012). Loneliness in older persons: A predictor of functional decline and death. *Archives of Internal Medicine, 172*(14), 1078–1083.

Perkins, M.M., Ball, M.M., Kemp, C.L., & Hollingsworth, C. (2013). Social relations and resident health in assisted living: An application of the convoy model. *The Gerontologist, 53*(3), 495–507.

Perkins, M.M., Ball, M.M., Whittington, F.J., & Hollingsworth, C. (2012). Relational autonomy in assisted living: A focus on diverse care settings for older adults. *Journal of Aging Studies, 26*(2), 214–225.

Perl, L. (2010). *Section 202 and other HUD rental housing programs for low-income elderly residents.* Washington, DC: Congressional Research Service.

Pierret, C.R. (2006, September). The "sandwich generation": Women caring for parents and children. *Monthly Labor Review,* 3–9.

Piette, J.D., Rosland, A.M., Silveira, M., Kabeto, M., & Langa, K.M. (2010). The case for involving adult children outside of the household in the self-management support of older adults with chronic illnesses. *Chronic Illness, 6*(1), 34–45.

Pinquart, M., & Burmedi, D. (2003). Correlates of residential satisfaction in adulthood and old age: A meta-analysis. In H.W. Wahl, R.J. Scheidt, & P.G. Windley (Eds.), *Annual review of gerontology and geriatrics: Focus on aging in context, socio-physical environments* (pp. 195–222). New York: Springer.

Pinquart, M., & Sorensen, S. (2003). Differences between caregivers and noncaregivers in psychological health and physical health: A meta-analysis. *Psychology and Aging, 18*(2), 250–267.

Pinquart, M., & Sorensen, S. (2005). Ethnic differences in stressors, resources, and psychological outcomes of family caregiving: A meta-analysis. *The Gerontologist, 45*(1), 90–106.

Pisarski, A.E. (2006). *Commuting in America III.* Washington, DC: Transportation Research Board.

Polivka, L., & Salmon, J.R. (2008). Assisted living: What it should be and why. In S.M. Golant & J. Hyde (Eds.), *The assisted living residence: A vision for the future* (pp. 397–418). Baltimore, MD: The John Hopkins University Press.

Pollack, S., Bluestone, B., & Billingham, C. (2010). *Maintaining diversity in America's transit-rich neighborhoods.* Boston: Dukakis Center for Urban and Regional Policy.

Polzer, K. (2012). *Assisted living state regulatory review, 2012.* Washington, DC: National Center for Assisted Living.

Polzer, K. (2013). *Assisted living state regulatory review, 2013*. Washington, DC: National Center for Assisted Living.

Population Reference Bureau. (2013). *Helping Americans age in place*. Washington, DC: Population Reference Bureau.

Porter, E.J. (2008). Home care as a complex experience: A chronological case study. *Home Health Care Services Quarterly, 27*(3), 167–186.

Pottow, J.A.E. (2011). The rise in elder bankruptcy filings and failure of U.S. bankruptcy law. *Elder Law Journal, 19*(1), 119–158.

Potts, I., Stutts, J., Pfefer, R., Neuman, T.R., Slack, K.L., & Hardy, K.K. (2004). *Guidance for implementation of the ASSHTO strategic highway safety plan: Volume 9, A guide for reducing collision involving older drivers*. NCHRP Report 500. Washington, DC: Transportation Research Board.

Poulin, M.J., Brown, S.L., Ubel, P.A., Smith, D.M., Jankovic, A., & Langa, K.M. (2010). Does a helping hand mean a heavy heart? Helping behavior and well-being among spouse caregivers. *Psychology and Aging, 25*(1), 108–117.

Pressler, K.A., & Ferraro, K.F. (2010). Assistive device use as a dynamic acquisition process in later life. *The Gerontologist, 50*(3), 371–381.

Pressman, S.D., & Cohen, S. (2005). Does positive affect influence health? *Psychological Bulletin, 131*(6), 925–971.

Prisuta, R., Barrett, L.L., & Evans, E.L. (2006). *Aging, migration, and local communities: The views of 60+ residents and community leaders*. Washington, DC: AARP.

Pruchno, R.A., & Rose, M.S. (2002). Time use by frail older people in different care settings. *Journal of Applied Gerontology, 21*(1), 5–23.

Pruchno, R.A., Wilson-Genderson, M., Rose, M., & Cartwright, F. (2010). Successful aging: Early influences and contemporary characteristics. *The Gerontologist, 50*(6), 821–833.

Puentes, R., & Orfield, M. (2002). *Valuing America's first suburbs*. Washington, DC: The Brookings Institution, Center on Urban and Metropolitan Policy.

Puentes, R., & Warren, D. (2006). *One-fifth of America*. Washington, DC: The Brookings Institution.

Pynoos, J., Bressett, M., & McCleskey, S. (2012). Elderly. In A.T. Carswell (Ed.), *The encyclopedia of housing* (pp. 149–154). Thousand Oaks, CA: Sage.

Pynoos, J., Liebig, P., Alley, D., & Nishita, C.M. (2004). Homes of choice: Towards more effective linkages between housing and services. *Journal of Housing and the Elderly, 18*(3/4), 5–49.

Pynoos, J., & Nishita, C.M. (2003). The cost and financing of home modifications in the United States. *Journal of Disability Policy Studies, 14*(2), 68–73.

Pynoos, J., Rose, D., Rubenstein, L., Choi, I.H., & Sabata, D. (2006). Evidence-based interventions in fall prevention. *Home Health Care Services Quarterly, 25*(1–2), 55–73.

Quinn, C., Clare, L., & Woods, R.T. (2010). The impact of motivations and meanings on the wellbeing of caregivers of people with dementia: A systematic review. *International Psychogeriatrics / IPA, 22*(1), 43–55.

Redfoot, D.L., Feinberg, L., & Houser, A. (2013). *The aging of the baby boom and the growing care gap: A look at future declines in the availability of family caregivers*. Washington, DC: AARP Public Policy Institute.

Redfoot, D., & Kochera, A. (2004). Targeting services to those most at risk: Characteristics of residents in federally subsidized housing. *Journal of Housing and the Elderly, 18*(3/4), 137–163.

Regnier, V. (2002). *Design for assisted living: Guidelines for housing the physically and mentally frail*. New York: Wiley.

Regnier, V., Hamilton, J., & Yatabe, S. (1995). *Assisted living for the aged and frail innovations in design, management, and financing*. New York: Columbia University Press.

Reinhard, S.C., Feinberg, L., & Choula, R. (2011). *A call to action: What experts say needs to be done to meet the challenges of family caregiving*. Washington, DC: AARP Public Policy Institute.

Reinhard, S.C., Kassner, E., Houser, A., & Mollica, R. (2011). *Raising expectations: A state scoreboard on long-term services and supports for older adults, people with physical disabilities, and family caregivers*. Washington, DC: AARP.

Reinhard, S. C., Kassner, E., Houser, A., Ujvari, K., Mollica, R., & Hendrickson, L. (2014). *Raising expectations: A state scoreboard on long-term services and supports for older adults, people with physical disabilities, and family caregivers*. Washington, DC: AARP.

Reinhard, S.C., Levine, C., & Samis, S. (2012). *Home alone: Family caregivers providing complex care*. Washington, DC: AARP Public Policy Institute.

Reinhard, S.C., Levine, C., & Samis, S. (2013). *Employed family caregivers providing complex care*. Washington, DC: AARP Public Policy Institute.

Reinstra, D., & Yee, R. (2013). *Continuing care at home: Is it an option for your community?* Paper presented at 2013 National Senior Living CFO Workshop, New Orleans, April 10–12.

Rhee, Y., Degenholtz, H.B., Lo Sasso, A.T., & Emanuel, L.L. (2009). Estimating the quantity and economic value of family caregiving for community-dwelling older persons in the last year of life. *Journal of American Geriatrics Society, 57*(9), 1654–1659.

Rice, D., & Sard, B. (2009). *Decade of neglect has weakened federal low-income housing programs*. Washington, DC: Center on Budget and Policy Priorities.

Ritchie, C.S., Roth, D.L., & Allman, R.M. (2011). Living with an aging parent: "It was a beautiful invitation." *JAMA: Journal of the American Medical Association, 306*(7), 746–753.

Ritter, A.S., Straight, A., & Evans, E. (2002). *Understanding senior transportation: Report and analysis of a survey of consumers age 50+*. Washington, DC: AARP.

Robinson, K., Lucado, J., & Schur, C. (2012). *Use of transportation services among OAA Title III program participants, research brief number 6*. Washington, DC: Administration on Aging.

Rodin, J. (1986, September 19). Aging and health: Effects of the sense of control. *Science, 233,* 1271–1276.

Rose, D.J. (2008). Preventing falls among older adults: No "one size suits all" intervention strategy. *Journal of Rehabilitation Research & Development, 45*(8), 1153–1166.

Rosenbloom, S. (2007). Transportation patterns and problems of people with disabilities. In M.J. Field & A.M. Jette (Eds.), *The future of disability in America*. Washington, DC: The National Academies Press.

Rosenbloom, S. (2009). Meeting transportation needs in an aging-friendly community. *Generations, 33*(2), 33–43.

Rosenbloom, S. (2013). *Roadblocks ahead for seniors who don't drive*. Washington, DC: Urban Institute.

Rosenfeld, J. (2010, April 15). "Sunrise cited for neglect after assisted living facility fails to provide timely treatment for an injured resident." Nursing Homes Abuse blog. Retrieved from http://www.nursinghomes abuseblog.com/

Rosow, I. (1967). *Social integration of the aged*. New York: Free Press.

Rosowsky, E. (2005). Ageism and professional training in aging: Who will be there to help? *Generations, 29*(3), 55–58.

Rosowsky, E. (2009). Challenge and resilience in old age. *Generations, 33*(3), 100–102.

Roth, D.L., Haley, W.E., Wadley, V.G., Clay, O.J., & Howard, G. (2007). Race and gender differences in perceived caregiver availability for community-dwelling middle-aged and older adults. *The Gerontologist, 47*(6), 721–729.

Roth, E.G., Keimig, L., Rubinstein, R.L., Morgan, L., Eckert, J.K., Goldman, S., et al. D. (2012). Baby boomers in an active adult retirement community: Comity interrupted. *The Gerontologist, 52*(2), 189–198.

Rowe, J.W., & Kahn, R.L. (1998). *Successful aging*. New York: Pantheon.

Rowles, G., Oswald, F., & Hunter, E.G. (2004). Interior living environments in old age. In H.W. Wahl, R.J. Scheidt, & P.G. Windley (Eds.), *Annual review of gerontology and geriatrics-focus on aging in context: Socio-physical environments* (pp. 167–194). New York: Springer.

Rowles, G.D., & Ravdal, H. (2002). Aging, place and meaning in the face of changing circumstances. In R.S. Weiss & S.A. Bass (Eds.), *Challenges of the third age: Meaning and purpose in later life* (pp. 81–114). New York: Oxford University Press.

Rubinstein, R.L. (1998). The phenomenology of housing for older people. In P.G. Windley & R.J. Scheidt (Eds.), *Environment and aging theory: A focus on housing* (pp. 89–110). New York: Greenwood Press.

Ruffenach, G. (2006, October 6). Care vs. Constraints: Why people say yes—and no—to living in a continuing-care community. *The Wall Street Journal*, p. R8.

Russell, J.A. (2003). Core affect and the psychological construction of emotion. *Psychological Review, 110*(1), 145–172.

Russell, J.A., & Mehrabian, A. (1976). Some behavioral effects of the physical environment. In S. Wapner, S.B. Cohen, & B. Kaplan (Eds.), *Experiencing the environment* (pp. 5–18). New York: Plenum.

Sabia, J.J. (2008). There's no place like home: A hazard model analysis of aging in place among older home-owners in the PSID. *Research on Aging, 30*(1), 3–35.

Safron-Norton, C.E. (2010). Physical home environment as a determinant of aging in place for different types of elderly households. *Journal of Housing for the Elderly, 24,* 208–231.

Salminen, M., Vahlberg, T., Salonoja, M.T., Piertti, T.T., Aarnio, P., & Kivela, S.L. (2009). Effects of risk-based multifactorial fall prevention program on the incidence of falls. *Journal of the American Geriatrics Society, 57,* 612–619.

Saloman, E. (2010). *Housing policy solutions to support aging in place*. Washington, DC: AARP Public Policy Institute.

Scan Foundation. (2011). *The aging network*. Long Beach, CA: Scan Foundation.

Scharlach, A.E., Giunta, N., Chow, J.C., & Lehning, A. (2008). Racial and ethnic variations in caregiver service use. *Journal of Aging Health, 20*(3), 326–346.

Scharlach, A., Graham, C., & Lehning, A. (2012). The "Village" model: A consumer-driven approach for aging in place. *The Gerontologist, 52*(3), 418–427.

Scharlach, A.E., Gustavson, K., & Dal Santo, T.S. (2007). Assistance received by employed caregivers and their care recipients: Who helps care recipients when caregivers work full time? *The Gerontologist, 47*(6), 752–762.

Scheidt, R.J., Humpherys, D.R., & Yorgason, J.B. (1999). Successful aging: What's not to like? *Journal of Applied Gerontology, 18*(3), 277–282.

Scheidt, R.J., & Schwarz, B. (2009). Environmental gerontology: A sampler of issues and applications. In J. Cavanaugh & C. Cavanaugh (Eds.), *Aging in America: Vol. I: Psychological aspects* (pp. 156–176). Santa Barbara, CA: Praeger Perspectives.

Scheidt, R.J., & Windley, P.G. (2006). Environmental gerontology: Progress in the post-Lawton era. In J. Birren & K.W. Schaie (Eds.), *Handbook of the psychology of aging* (6th ed., pp. 105–125). New York: Academic Press.

Schiller, J.S., Kramarow, E.A., & Dey, A.N. (2007). Fall injury episodes among noninstitutionalized older adults: United States, 2001–2003. *Advance Data from Vital and Health Statistics, 392,* 1–16.

Schulz, R., & Brenner, G. (1977). Relocation of the aged: A review and theoretical analysis. *Journal of Gerontology, 32,* 323–333.

Schulz, R., & Heckhausen, J. (1996). A life span model of successful aging. *American Psychologist, 51*(7), 702–714.

Schulz, R., & Heckhausen, J. (1998). Emotion and control: A life-span perspective. In K.W. Schaie & M.P. Lawton (Eds.), *Annual review of gerontology and geriatrics: Focus on emotion and adult development* (pp. 185–205). New York: Springer.

Scommengna, P. (2013). Elderly immigrants in the United States. *Population Reference Bureau, Today's Research on Aging, 29,* 1–9.

Seavey, D. (2011). Caregivers on the front line: Building a better direct-care workforce. *Generations, 34*(4), 27–35.

Seavey, D., & Marquand, A. (2011). *Caring in America: A comprehensive analysis of the nation's fastest growing jobs: Home health and personal care aides*. Bronx, NY: Paraprofessional Healthcare Institute.

Seligman, M.E.P. (1991). *Helplessness: On depression, development, and death*. New York: W.H. Freeman.

Seltzer, J.A., & Yahirun, J.J. (2013). *Diversity in old age: The elderly in changing economic and family contexts*. Unpublished paper retrieved from http://www.s4browneedu/us2010/data/report/report11062013.pdf

Sergeant, J.F., & Ekerdt, D.J. (2008). Motives for residential mobility in later life: Post-move perspectives of elders and family members. *International Journal of Aging & Human Development, 66*(2), 131–154.

Sergeant, J.F., Ekerdt, D.J., & Chapin, R.K. (2010). Older adults' expectations about move: Do they predict actual community-based or nursing facility moves within 2 years? *Journal of Aging and Health, 22*(7), 1029–1053.

Setar, L., & Son, A. (2013). *Baby boomers: A burgeoning customer market*. Los Angeles, CA: IBISWorld.

Sharkey, A., & Sharkey, N. (2012). Granny and the robots: Ethical issues in robot care for the elderly. *Ethics and Information Technology, 14*(1), 27–40.

Sharma, A. (2013). The chain is only as strong as the weakest link: Older adult migration and the first move. *Research on Aging, 35*(5), 507–532.

Shaw, B.A., Krause, N., Liang, J., & Bennett, J. (2007). Tracking changes in social relations throughout late life. *Journal of Gerontology: Social Sciences, 62*(2), S90–99.

Sheehan, N.W., & Guzzardo, M.T. (2008). Resident service coordinators: Roles and challenges in senior housing. *Journal of Housing for the Elderly, 22*(3), 240–262.

Sheehan, N.W., & Oakes, C.E. (2006). Bringing assisted living services into congregate housing: Housing directors' perspectives. *Journal of Aging and Social Policy, 18*(1), 65–86.

Shelter Partnership. (2008). *Homeless older adults strategic plan*. Los Angeles: Shelter Partnership.

Shenk, D., Kuwahara, K., & Zablotsky, D. (2004). Older women's attachments to their home and possessions. *Journal of Aging Studies, 18,* 147–169.

Shier, V., Khodyakov, D., Cohen, L.W., Zimmerman, S., & Saliba, D. (2014). What does the evidence really say about culture change in nursing homes? *The Gerontologist, 54*(Suppl 1), S6–S16.

Shih, R.A., Ghosh-Dastidar, B., Margolis, K.L., Slaughter, M.E., Jewell, A., Bird, C.E., et al. (2011). Neighborhood socioeconomic status and cognitive function in women. *American Journal of Public Health, 101*(9), 1721–1728.

Shippee, T.P. (2009). "But I am not moving": Residents' perspectives on transitions within a continuing care retirement community. *The Gerontologist, 49*(3), 418–427.

Shippee, T.P. (2012). On the edge: Balancing health, participation, and autonomy to maintain active independent living in two retirement facilities. *Journal of Aging Studies, 26*(1), 1–15.

Shirk, C. (2006). *Rebalancing long-term care: The role of the Medicaid HCBS waiver program*. Washington, DC: National Health Policy Forum, the George Washington University.

Shirk, C. (2007). *Trading places: Real choice systems change grants and the movement to community-based long-term care supports*. Issue brief no. 822. Washington, DC: National Health Policy Forum, the George Washington University.

Short, K. (2013). *Current population reports: The research supplemental poverty measure: 2012*. Washington, DC: U.S. Census Bureau, Department of Commerce.

Siebenaler, K., O'Keeffe, J., O'Keeffe, C., Brown, D., & Koetse, B. (2005). *Regulatory review of adult day services: Final report*. Washington, DC: U.S. Department of Health and Human Services, Office of Disability, Aging and Long-Term Care Policy.

Silverstein, N.M., Wong, C.M., & Brueck, K.E. (2008). *Living with Alzheimer's disease: A study of adult day health services in Massachusetts*. Washington, DC: Alzheimer's Association.

Simpson, D. (2010). *Third age urbanism: Retirement utopias of the young-old*. PhD dissertation. Zurich: Eth Zurich.

Siu, C. (2009). *Impacts of nutrition and human services interventions on the health of elderly and disabled persons in public housing*. Washington, DC: Congressional Hunger Center.

Skarupski, K.A., McCann, J.J., Bienias, J.L., Wolinsky, F.D., Aggarwal, N.T., & Evans, D.A. (2008). Use of home-based formal services by adult day care clients with Alzheimer's disease. *Home Health Care Services Quarterly, 27*(3), 217–239.

Sloane, P.D., Zimmerman, S., & Walsh, J.F. (2001). The physical environment. In P.D. Sloane, S. Zimmerman, & J.K. Eckert (Eds.), *Assisted living needs, practices, and policies in residential care for the elderly* (pp. 173–197). Baltimore, MD: The John Hopkins University Press.

Smarr, C.-A., Prakash, A., Beer, J.M., Mitzner, T.L., Kemp, C.C., & Rogers, W.A. (2012). Older adults' preferences for and acceptance of robot assistance for everyday living tasks. *Proceedings of the Human Factors and Ergonomics Society Annual Meeting, 56*(1), 153–157.

Smith, B.P. (2012, April 21). Baby boomers redefine the terms of retirement. *Herald Tribune*.

Smith, I.K. (2001, January 21). No fall insurance, *Time Magazine*.

Smith, K., & Baughman, R. (2007, September). Caring for America's aging population: A profile of the direct-care workforce. *Monthly Labor Review*, 20–26.

Smith, M.L., Ahn, S.N., Sharkey, J.R., Horel, S., Mier, N., & Ory, M.G. (2012). Successful falls prevention programming for older adults in Texas: Rural–urban variations. *Journal of Applied Gerontology, 31*(1), 3–27.

Smith, R.E., & Ferryman, K. (2006). *Saying good-bye: Relocating senior citizens in the HOPE VI panel study*. Washington, DC: Urban Institute.

Smith, S.K., & House, M. (2006). Snowbirds, sunbirds, and stayers: Seasonal migration of elderly adults in Florida. *Journal of Gerontology: Social Sciences, 61*(5), S232–239.

Social Security Administration. (2013). *Expenditures of the aged chartbook, 2010*. Washington, DC: Social Security Administration.

Social Security Administration. (2014). *Income of the population 55 or older, 2012*. Washington, DC: Social Security Administration.

Span, P. (2011a, June 10). Assisted living or a nursing home. *The New York Times*.

Span, P. (2011b, May 31). Mean girls in assisted living. *The New York Times*.

Spellman, S., & Townsley, S. (2012). *Continuing care at home: Evolution, innovation, and opportunity*. Minneapolis, MN: CliftonLarsonAllen.

Spillman, B.C. (2005). *Assistive device use among the elderly: Trends, characteristics of users, and implications for modeling*. Washington, DC: U.S. Department of Health and Human Services, Office of Disability, Aging, and Long-Term Care Policy.

Spillman, B.C., Biess, J., & MacDonald, G. (2012). *Housing as a platform for improving outcomes for older renters*. Washington, DC: Urban Institute.

Spillman, B.C., & Black, K.J. (2005). *Staying the course: Trends in family caregiving*. Washington, DC: AARP.

Spillman, B.C., & Long, S.K. (2007). *Does high caregiver stress lead to nursing home entry?* Washington, DC: U.S. Department of Health and Human Services, Office of Disability, Aging, and Long-Term Care Policy.

Squillace, M.R., & Firman, J. (2002). *The myths and realities of consumer-directed services for older persons*. Washington, DC: National Council on Aging.

Stacey-Konnert, C., & Pynoos, J. (1992). Friendship and social networks in a continuing care retirement community. *Journal of Applied Gerontology, 11*(3), 298–313.

Stambolian, J., & Blanchard, J. (2013). Back to the garden: Woodstock nation values re-emerge. In J. Blanchard (Ed.), *Aging in community* (pp. 235–244). Chapel Hill, NC: Second Journey Publications.

Stanford Center on Longevity & MetLife Mature Market Institute. (2013). *Livable community indicators for sustainable aging in place*. Westport, CT: MetLife Mature Market Institute.

Stearns, S.C., Park, J., Zimmerman, S., Gruber-Baldini, A.L., Konrad, T.R., & Sloane, P.D. (2007). Determinants and effects of nurse staffing intensity and skill mix in residential care/assisted living settings. *The Gerontologist, 47*(5), 662–671.

Stefanonovic, I.L. (1998). Phenomenological encounters with place: Cavtat to square one. *Journal of Environmental Psychology, 18,* 31–44.

Steinman, B.A., Pynoos, J., & Nguyen, A.Q. (2009). Fall risk in older adults: Roles of self-rated vision, home modifications, and limb function. *Journal of Aging and Health, 21*(5), 655–676.

Stevenson, D.G., & Grabowski, D.C. (2010). Sizing up the market for assisted living. *Health Affairs, 29*(1), 35–43.

Stoller, E.P., & Perzynski, A.T. (2003). The impact of ethnic involvement and migration patterns on long-term care plans among retired Sunbelt migrants: Plans for nursing home placement. *Journal of Gerontology: Social Sciences, 58*(6), S369–376.

Stone, A.A., Schwartz, J.E., Broderick, J.E., & Deaton, A. (2010). A snapshot of the age distribution of psychological well-being in the United States. *Proceedings of the National Academy of Sciences of the United States of America, 107*(22), 9985–9990.

Stone, J. (2010). *Long-term care (LTC): Financing, overview and issues for Congress.* Washington, DC: Congressional Research Service.

Stone, R.I. (2004). The direct care worker: The third rail of home care policy. *Annual Review of Public Health, 25,* 521–537.

Stone, R.I. (2009). *Affordable senior housing plus services: Opportunities for research.* Paper presented at Gerontological Society of America (Pre-Conference), November 18, Atlanta, GA.

Stone, R. (2011). *Long-term care for the elderly.* Washington, DC: The Urban Institute Press.

Stone, R., & Harahan, M.F. (2010). Improving the long-term care workforce serving older adults. *Health Affairs, 29*(1), 109–115.

Stone, R.I., Harahan, M.F., & Sanders, A. (2008). Expanding affordable housing with services for older adults: Challenges and potential. In S.M. Golant & J. Hyde (Eds.), *The assisted living residence: A vision for the future* (pp. 329–350). Baltimore, MD: The Johns Hopkins University Press.

Strawbridge, W.J., Wallhagen, M.I., & Cohen, R.D. (2002). Successful aging and well-being: Self-rated compared with Rowe and Kahn. *The Gerontologist, 42*(6), 727–733.

Street, D., Burge, S., Quadagno, J., & Barrett, A. (2007). The salience of social relationships for resident well-being in assisted living. *Journal of Gerontology: Social Sciences, 62*(2), S129–134.

Streib, G.F. (1990). Retirement communities: Linkages to the locality, state, and nation. *Journal of Applied Gerontology, 9*(4), 405–419.

Streib, G.F., Folts, W.E., & La Greca, A.J. (1984). Entry into retirement communities. Process and related problems. *Research on Aging, 6*(2), 257–270.

Streib, G.F., Folts, W.E., & La Greca, A.J. (1985). Autonomy, power, and decision-making in thirty-six retirement communities. *The Gerontologist, 25*(4), 403–409.

Strohschein, L. (2011). Spousal bereavement as a triggering mechanism for a loss of residential independence among Canadian seniors. *Research on Aging, 33*(5), 576–597.

Strohschein, L. (2012). I want to move, but cannot: Characteristics of involuntary stayers and associations with health among Canadian seniors. *Journal of Aging and Health, 24*(5), 735–751.

Stucki, B. (2013). New directions for policy and research on reverse mortgages. *Public Policy & Aging Report, 23*(1), 9–13.

Suchman, D.R. (2001). *Developing active adult retirement communities.* Washington, DC: Urban Land Institute.

Summer, L., & Howard, J. (2011). *A challenge for states: Assuring timely access to optimal long-term services and supports in the community.* Washington, DC: Kaiser Commission on Medicaid and Uninsured.

Sun, F., Waldron, V., Gitelson, R., & Ho, C.H. (2012). The effects of loss of loved ones on life satisfaction among residents in a southwest retirement community: The mediating roles of social connectedness. *Research on Aging, 34*(2), 222–245.

Sweaney, A.L., Mimura, Y., Vanderford, S.E., & Reeves, J. (2006). Assessing the pride of housing ownership options among older adults in Georgia. *Housing and Society, 33*(2), 33–41.

Sykes, K. (2014). Making the right moves: Promoting smart growth and active aging in communities *Journal of Aging & Social Policy, 26,* 166–180.

Takahashi, P.Y., Pecina, J.L., Upatising, B., Chaudhry, R., Shah, N.D., Van Houten, H., et al. (2012). A randomized controlled trial of telemonitoring in older adults with multiple health issues to prevent hospitalizations and emergency department visits. *Archives of Internal Medicine, 172*(10), 773–779.

Talega, S.R. (2013). *Medicare home health benefit primer.* Washington, DC: Congressional Research Service.

Tang, F., & Lee, Y. (2011). Social support networks and expectations for aging in place and moving. *Research on Aging, 33*(4), 444–464.

Tanner, B., Tilse, C., & de Jonge, D. (2008). Restoring and sustaining home: The impact of home modifications on the meaning of home for older people. *Journal of Housing for the Elderly, 22*(3), 195–215.

Thomas, K.S., & Mor, V. (2013). The relationship between Older Americans Act Title III state expenditures and prevalence of low-care nursing home residents. *Health Services Research, 48*(3), 1215–1226.

Thomas, W.H. (2004). *What are old people for?* Acton, MA: VanderWyk & Burnham.

Thurow, L.C. (1996, May 19). The birth of a revolutionary class. *The New York Times Magazine,* pp. 46–47.

Tirrito, T. (2000). The church and social services. *Social Thought: The Journal of Religion and the Social Services, 19*(3), 59–76.

Tobin, S.S., & Lieberman, M.A. (1976). *Last home for the aged.* San Francisco, CA: Jossey-Bass.

Topo, P. (2009). Technology studies to meet the needs of people with dementia and their caregivers: A literature review. *Journal of Applied Gerontology, 28*(1), 5–37.

Torres-Gil, F., & Hofland, B. (2012). Vulnerable populations. In H. Cisneros, M. Dyer-Chamberlain, & J. Hickie (Eds.), *Independent for life: Homes and neighborhoods for an aging population* (pp. 221–232). Austin, TX: University of Texas Press.

Transportation for America. (2011). *Aging in place, stuck without options.* Washington, DC: Transportation for America.

Trawinski, L.A. (2012). *Nightmare on Main Street: Older Americans and the mortgage market crisis.* Washington, DC: AARP Public Policy Institute.

Trolander, J.A. (2011a). Age 55 or better: Active adult communities and city planning. *Journal of Urban History, 37*(6), 952–974.

Trolander, J.A. (2011b). *From Sun Cities to the Villages: A history of active adult, age restricted communities.* Gainesville, FL: University Press of Florida.

Tuan, Y.-F. (1975). Place: An experiential perspective. *Geographical Review, 65*(2), 151–165.

Tuan, Y.-F. (1980). The significance of the artifact. *Geographical Review, 70*(4), 462–472.

Turner, J.H. (2007). *Human emotions: A sociological theory.* New York: Routledge.

Turner, K.W. (2004). Senior citizens centers: What they offer, who participates and what they gain. *Journal of Gerontological Social Work, 43*(1), 37–47.

United Hospital Fund. (2010). NORC blueprint: A guide to community action. Retrieved from http://www.Norcblueprint.Org/.

UnitedHealthcare. (2013). *The United States of aging survey.* Washington, DC: National Council on Aging.

UnitedHealthcare. (2014). *The United States of aging survey.* Washington, DC: National Council on Aging.

Unwin, B.K., Andrews, C.M., Andrews, P.M., & Hanson, J.L. (2009). Therapeutic home adaptations for older adults with disabilities. *American Family Physician, 80*(9), 963–968.

U.S. Census Bureau. (2009). *American housing survey for the United States: 2009 current housing reports, series H50/09.* Washington, DC: U.S. Government Printing Office.

U.S. Census Bureau. (2012). *Income, poverty, and health insurance coverage in the United States: 2012.* Washington, DC: U.S. Department of Commerce.

U.S. Census Bureau. (2013). *Table 15, geographical mobility: 2012 to 2013.* Retrieved from http://www.Census.Gov/hhes/migration/data/cps/cps2013.Html

U.S. Congressional Budget Office. (2013). *Rising demand for long-term services and supports for elderly people.* Washington, DC: U.S. Congressional Budget Office.

U.S. Department of Health and Human Services. (2012a). *ASPE research brief, background briefing: Long-term care insurance.* Washington, DC: U.S. Department of Health and Human Services.

U.S. Department of Health and Human Services, Administration on Aging. (2012b). *A profile of older Americans, 2012.* Washington, DC: U.S. Department of Health and Human Services.

U.S. Department of Health and Human Services, Office of Inspector General. (2012c). *Home and community-based services in assisted living facilities.* Washington, DC: U.S. Department of Health and Human Services.

U.S. Department of Housing and Urban Development. (1996). *Rental housing assistance at a crossroads.* Washington, DC: HUD, Office of Policy Development and Research.

U.S. Department of Housing and Urban Development. (2005). *Making housing accessible through accommodations and modifications.* Washington, DC: U.S. Department of Housing and Urban Development. Retrieved from http://www.fairhousingfirst.org/documents/AccommodationsAndModifications.pdf

U.S. Department of Housing and Urban Development. (2011). *American Housing Survey for the United States, 2009.* Washington, DC: U.S. Government Printing Office.

U.S. Department of Housing and Urban Development. (2013). *American housing survey for the United States, 2011.* Washington, DC: U.S. Government Printing Office.

U.S. Department of Transportation, National Highway Traffic Safety Administration. (2014). *Traffic safety facts, 2012 data.* Washington, DC: NHTSA National Center for Statistics and Analysis.

U.S. General Accounting Office. (1999). *Assisted living: Quality-of-care and consumer protection issues in four states.* Washington, DC: U.S. General Accounting Office.

U.S. Government Accountability Office. (2005). *Elderly housing: Federal housing programs that offer assistance for the elderly.* Washington, DC: U.S. General Accounting Office.

U.S. Government Accountability Office. (2007). *Medicaid long-term care: Few transferred assets for applying for nursing home coverage.* Washington, DC: U.S. General Accounting Office.

U.S. Government Accountability Office. (2010). *Continuing care retirement communities can provide benefits, but not without some risk.* Washington, DC: U.S. General Accounting Office.

U.S. Government Accountability Office. (2011a). *Nutritional assistance: Additional efficiencies could improve services to older adults.* Washington, DC: U.S. General Accounting Office.

U.S. Government Accountability Office. (2011b). *Older Americans Act: More should be done to measure the extent of unmet need for services.* Washington, DC: U.S. General Accounting Office.

U.S. Senate Special Committee on Aging. (2010a). *Continuing care retirement communities: Risks to seniors.* Washington, DC: U.S. Senate Special Committee on Aging.

U.S. Senate Special Committee on Aging. (2010b). *Hearing. Continuing care retirement communities: Secure retirement or risky investment?* Washington, DC: U.S. Senate Special Committee on Aging.

Valenza, T. (2007, June 1). Home sweet home modification. *Rehabilitation Management.* Retrieved from http://www.rehabpub.com/?s=T+Valenza

Vanderbur, M., & Silverstein, N.M. (2011). *Community mobility and dementia.* Washington, DC: Alzheimer's Association Public Policy Division.

Venti, S.F., & Wise, D.A. (2001). *Aging and housing equity: Another look, working paper 8608.* Cambridge, MA: National Bureau of Economic Research.

Verdoorn, J. (2011, September 20). What boomers are choosing. *Newgeography.* Retrieved from http://www.newgeography.com/content/002451-what-boomers-are-choosing

Vierck, B. (2013, Spring). Smart homes: The future is here. *CSA Journal, 54,* 5–7.

Vladeck, F. (2008, January/February). Naturally occurring retirement communities. *Designer Builder,* pp. 43–47.

Vladeck, F., Segel, R., Oberlink, M., Gursen, M.D., & Rudin, D. (2010). Health indicators: A proactive and systematic approach to healthy aging. *Cityscape, 12*(2), 67–84.

Wachs, T.D. (1999). Celebrating complexity: Conceptualization and assessment of the environment. In S.L. Friedman & T.D. Wachs (Eds.), *Measuring environment across the life span: Emerging methods and concepts* (pp. 357–292). Washington, DC: American Psychological Association.

Wagner, D.L. (2006). Families, work, and an aging population: Developing a formula that works for the workers. *Journal of Aging & Social Policy, 18*(3–4), 115–125.

Wahl, H.-W., Fange, A., Oswald, F., Gitlin, L.N., & Iwarsson, S. (2009). The home environment and disability-related outcomes in aging individuals: What is the empirical evidence? *The Gerontologist, 49*(3), 355–367.

Wahl, H.-W., & Oswald, F. (2009). Environmental perspectives on aging. In D. Dannefer & C. Phillipson (Eds.), *International handbook of social gerontology* (pp. 111–124). Thousand Oaks, CA: Sage.

Wahl, H.W., Oswald, F., & Zimprich, D. (1999). Everyday competence in visually impaired older adults: A case for person–environment perspectives. *The Gerontologist, 39*(2), 140–149.

Wald, M.D. (2013). *An uphill climb: Women face greater obstacles to retirement security.* Washington, DC: AARP Public Policy Institute.

Walker, L. (2004). *Elderly households and housing wealth: Do they use it or lose it?* Working paper WP 2004-070. Ann Arbor: University of Michigan Retirement Research Center.

Walker, R., Smith, P., & Adam, J. (2009). Making partnerships work: Issues of risk, trust and control for managers and service providers. *Health Care Analysis, 17,* 17–67.

Walters, W.H. (2002). Later-life migration in the United States: A review of recent research. *Journal of Planning Literature, 17*(1), 38–66.

Wardrip, K.E. (2010). *Cohousing for older adults.* Washington, DC: AARP Public Policy Institute.

Washington, K.T., Meadows, S.E., Elliott, S.G., & Koopman, R.J. (2011). Information needs of informal caregivers of older adults with chronic health conditions. *Patient Education and Counseling, 83*(1), 37–44.

The Washington Economics Group. (2012). *Best choice for retiring boomers: Head south—an analysis of selected U.S. cities.* Washington, DC: Dawson & Associates.

Watts, M.O.M. (2011). *Money follows the person: A 2011 survey of transitions, services and costs.* Washington, DC: Kaiser Commission on Medicaid and Uninsured.

Watts, M.O.M., Musumeci, M., & Reaves, E. (2013). *How is the Affordable Care Act leading to changes in Medicaid long-term services and supports (LTSS) today? State adoption of six LTSS options.* Washington, DC: Kaiser Commission on Medicaid and Uninsured.

Webber, S.C., Porter, M.M., & Menec, V.H. (2010). Mobility in older adults: A comprehensive framework. *The Gerontologist, 50*(4), 443–450.

Weinberger, M., Darnell, J.C., Tierney, W.M., Martz, B.L., Hiner, S.L., Barker, J., et al. (1986). Self-rated health as a predictor of hospital admission and nursing home placement in elderly public housing tenants. *American Journal of Public Health, 76*(4), 457–459.

Weissert, W.G., & Frederick, L. (2013). The woodwork effect: Estimating it and controlling the damage. *Journal of Aging & Social Policy, 25*(2), 107–133.

Wenzlow, A., Borck, R., Miller, D., Doty, P., & Drabek, J. (2013). *An investigation of interstate variation in Medicaid long-term care use and expenditures across 40 states in 2006.* Washington, DC: Office of Disability, Aging and Long-Term Care Policy, U.S. Dept. HHS.

Wethington, E. (2003). Residential differences in life stress and perceived health. In J. Krout & E. Wethington (Eds.), *Residential choices and experiences of older adults* (pp. 157–176). New York: Springer.

White-Means, S.I., & Rubin, R.M. (2008). Parent caregiving choices of middle- generation Blacks and Whites in the United States. *Journal of Aging Health, 20*(5), 560–582.

Wiener, J., Anderson, W.L., Khatutsky, G., Kaganova, Y., & O'Keeffe, J. (2013). *Medicaid spend down: Implications for long-term services and supports and aging policy.* Long Beach, CA: The Scan Foundation.

Wiener, J.M., & Brown, D. (2004). *Home and community-based services: A synthesis of the literature.* Washington, DC: Administration on Aging.

Wight, R.G., Ko, M.J., & Aneshensel, C.S. (2011). Urban neighborhoods and depressive symptoms in late middle age. *Research on Aging, 33*(1), 28–50.

Wild, K., Wiles, J. L., & Allen, R. E. S. (2013). Resilience: Thoughts on the value of the concept for critical gerontology. *Ageing & Society, 33*, 137–158.

Wilden, R., & Redfoot, D.L. (2002). *Adding assisted living services to subsidized housing serving frail older persons with low incomes.* Washington, DC: AARP, Public Policy Institute.

Williams, J. (2008). Predicting an American future for cohousing. *Futures, 40*(3), 268–286.

Williamson, A.R. (2011). Can they afford the rent? Resident cost burden in low income housing tax credit developments. *Urban Affairs Review, 47*(6), 775–799.

Windle, G., Markland, D.A., & Woods, R.T. (2008). Examination of a theoretical model of psychological resilience in older age. *Aging and Mental Health, 12*(3), 285–292.

Wiseman, R.F. (1980). Why older people move. *Research on Aging, 22,* 242–254.

Wolf, D.A., Hunt, K., & Knickman, J. (2005). Perspectives on the recent decline in disability at older ages. *Milbank Quarterly, 83*(3), 365–395.

Wolf, D.A., & Longino, C.F. Jr. (2005). Our "increasingly mobile society"? The curious persistence of a false belief. *The Gerontologist, 45*(1), 5–11.

Wolf, D., & Wilmoth, J.M. (2010). *Housing consumption in late life: The role of income, health shocks, and marital shocks.* Boston: Boston College Center for Retirement Research Working Paper No. 2010-10.

Wolff, J.L., & Kasper, J.D. (2006). Caregivers of frail elders: Updating a national profile. *The Gerontologist, 46*(3), 344–356.

Wolinsky, F.D., Callahan, C.M., Fitzgerald, J.F., & Johnson, R.J. (1993). Changes in functional status and the risks of subsequent nursing home placement and death. *Journal of Gerontology, 48*(3), S94–101.

Working Mother Research Institute. (2012). *Women and Alzheimer's disease: The caregiver's crisis.* New York: Working Mother Research Institute.

World Health Organization. (2007). *Global age-friendly cities: A guide.* Geneva, Switzerland: World Health Organization.

Wylde, M. (2008a). *Right house right place right time.* Washington, DC: National Association of Home Builders.

Wylde, M.A. (2008b). The future of assisted living: Residents' perspectives. In S.M. Golant & J. Hyde (Eds.), *The assisted living residence: A vision for the future* (pp. 169–197). Baltimore, MD: The John Hopkins University Press.

Wylde, M.A., Smith, E.R., Schless, D., & Berstecker, R. (2009). Satisfied residents won't recommend your community, but very satisfied customers will. *Seniors Housing & Care Journal, 17*(1), 3–13.

Yamasaki, J., & Shari, B.F. (2011). Opting out while fitting in: How residents make sense of assisted living and cope with community life. *Journal of Aging Studies, 25*(1), 13–21.

Yamashita, T., & Kunkel, S.R. (2012). Geographic access to healthy and unhealthy foods for the older population in a U.S. metropolitan area. *Journal of Applied Gerontology, 31*(3), 287–313.

Yao, L., & Robert, S.A. (2008). The contributions of race, individual socioeconomic status, and neighborhood socioeconomic context on the self-rated health trajectories and mortality of older adults. *Research on Aging, 30*(2), 251–273.

Yedinak, G. (2012, January 9). Top 10 trends in senior housing for 2012. *Senior Housing News.* Retrieved from http://seniorhousingnewscom/2012/01/09/top-10-trends-in-senior-housing-for-2012/

Yeom, H.A., Fleury, J., & Keller, C. (2008). Risk factors for mobility limitation in community-dwelling older adults: A social ecological perspective. *Geriatric Nursing, 29*(2), 133–140.

Young, Y.C. (2009). Factors associated with permanent transition from independent living to nursing home in a continuing care retirement community. *Journal of the American Medical Directors Association, 10*(7), 491–497.

Young, Y., Inamdar, S., & Hannan, E.L. (2010). Comparison study on functional outcomes and perceived quality of life between all-inclusive and fee-for-service continuing care retirement communities. *Journal of the American Medical Directors Association, 11*(4), 257–262.

Young, Y., Spokane, L.S., Shaw, B.A., Macera, M.A., & Krout, J.A. (2009). Comparison study: The impact of on-site comprehensive service access on self-reported health and functional status of older adults. *Journal of the American Medical Directors Association, 10*(3), 167–173.

Zarem, J.E. (Ed.). (2010). *Today's continuing care retirement community (CCRC)*. Washington, DC: American Association of Homes and Services for the Aging and American Seniors Housing Association.

Zarit, S. H., Kim, K., Femia, E. E., Almeida, D. M., & Klein, L. C. (2014). The effects of adult day services on family caregivers' daily stress, affect, and health: Outcomes from the daily stress and health (DASH) study. *The Gerontologist, 54*(4), 570–579.

Zautra, A.J., Potter, P.T., & Reich, J.W. (1998). The independence of affects is context-dependent: An integrative model of the relationships between positive and negative affect. In K.W. Schaie & M.P. Lawton (Eds.), *Annual review of gerontology and geriatrics: Focus on emotion and adult development* (pp. 75–103). New York: Springer.

Ziegler Capital Markets. (2009). *Ziegler national CCRC listing and profile*. Chicago: B.C. Ziegler and Company.

Zimmerman, S., Love, K., Sloane, P.D., Cohen, L.W., Reed, D., & Carder, P.C. (2011). Medication administration errors in assisted living: Scope, characteristics, and the importance of staff training. *Journal of the American Geriatrics Society, 59*(6), 1060–1068.

Zimmerman, S., Sloane, P. D., & Reed, D. (2014). Dementia prevalence and care in assisted living. *Health Affairs, 33*(4), 658–666.

Zimmerman, S., Dobbs, D., Roth, E. G., Goldman, S., Peeples, A. D., & Wallace, B. (2014). Promoting and protecting against stigma in assisted living and nursing homes. *The Gerontologist, Advance Access published June 13, 2014.*

Zwijsen, S.A., Niemeijer, A.R., & Hertogh, C.M. (2011). Ethics of using assistive technology in the care for community-dwelling elderly people: An overview of the literature. *Aging and Mental Health, 15*(4), 419–427.

INDEX

Note: *f* indicates figures, *t* indicates tables.